Rave reviews for
Bed & Breakfast U.S.A.
from the press:

"Today *Bed & Breakfast U.S.A.* is a best-selling travel book that is updated every year and contains descriptions of over 600 places to stay, as well as reservation services that can book an additional 10,000 homes."—*Reader's Digest*

"The best source of nationwide information"—*Changing Times*

"The most comprehensive B&B guide"—*Sylvia Porter's Personal Finance*

"The most comprehensive B&B guide"—*Savvy*

"One of the best"—*Akron Beacon Journal*

"Your best bet"—*Philadelphia Inquirer*

"Makes enjoyable reading"—*Country Living*

"Extremely useful, well-organized guide"—*American Library Association Booklist*

"The best source for B&Bs throughout the country"—*Let's Go USA*

"Many a first-time B&B guest vows never again to stay in a motel . . . business travelers—particularly women traveling alone—have found this personal touch just the ticket."—*Karen Cure, TWA Ambassador*

"Bed and breakfast lodging has been sweeping the United States by storm. . . . *Bed & Breakfast USA* is one of the bibles of the business. . . ."—*Chicago Tribune*

"Squeezed budgets get relief at B&Bs. . . . *Bed & Breakfast USA* [is] an extensive list of establishments. . . ."—*United Press International*

"The best overall view . . . Betty Rundback is so enthusiastic that she even gives readers pointers on how to start their own B&Bs."—*Detroit News*

"Fills a need for travelers who are watching their wallets. . . . Especially helpful . . . especially valuable."—*New York Daily News*

"For those who have embraced the B&B way to travel, there is no going back to hotel highrises and motel monotony."—*Time*

"America's newest and hottest accommodations trend is B&B."—*Boston Globe*

Rave reviews from hosts and guests:

Our guests write: "I feel I must write to you to express my complete satisfaction with your book—*Bed & Breakfast U.S.A.*"

"You should be ashamed—keeping me up half the night reading that super book of yours!! It's the stuff dreams are made of!"

"All B&Bs exceeded our expectations and all hosts were very friendly. Thank you for a marvelous guide."

"I feel I must write to express my complete satisfaction with your book."

"Our B&B in New York was an excellent experience. . . . It was our home away from home."

"We were completely satisfied and will never stay any place but a B&B. Can't say enough about our delightful stay."

"The B&B was immaculate, comfortable and inviting. Our hosts were absolutely charming. . . . It felt like a visit with friends."

"It's not just the fact that the accommodations are comfortable, attractive, and reasonable—but it's the pleasant, gracious touch. It's being able to get directions, find out about current attractions. . . ."

"We, being English, have stayed at many B&Bs in Europe and we can truthfully say that we have never experienced such hospitality and kindness anywhere."

"We were complete strangers when we arrived, and departed a few days later as good friends. Absolutely beautiful accommodations and exceptional hospitality."

Our hosts report: "Travelers continue to flock to our house in response to your book. We are also getting many guests for a second, third, and fourth visit."

"We've had the most interesting people in the world come up our driveway clutching *Bed & Breakfast U.S.A.* as though it were a passport to heaven."

"Your book is, without a doubt, the most widely used and the most trusted by our guests."

"Each guest has been a real joy for us and there is a sadness when they leave. We have been so impressed with your book—year after year it has improved and is so attractive. It is evident that you put a great amount of thought and work into the best bed & breakfast book in the U.S.A."

"I have had wonderful responses to my listing. Many people have never been to a B&B and ask me all sorts of questions."

"Thanks once again for writing *Bed & Breakfast U.S.A.* It is definitely the best of the B&B guides."

Bed & Breakfast U.S.A.

A GUIDE TO
Tourist Homes
AND
Guest Houses

*Betty Revits Rundback
and
Nancy Kramer*

Tourist House Association of America

E. P. Dutton • New York

With love to Bob Rundback
because this whole project was his idea,
and to Ann Revits,
ever the proud mother and grandma.

Copyright © 1989 by Betty Revits Rundback and Nancy Kramer

All rights reserved. Printed in the U.S.A.

Front cover photo: Cedarym, Redmond, Washington, by Randy DeMoss.
Back cover photos: porch, The Homeplace, Charlotte, North Carolina, by Peggy and Frank Dearien; living room, Villa Galleria, Fountain Hills, Arizona, by Helmut Fiedler.

No part of this publication may be reproduced or transmitted in any form or by any means, electronic or mechanical, including photocopy, recording or any information storage and retrieval system now known or to be invented, without permission in writing from the publisher, except by a reviewer who wishes to quote brief passages in connection with a review written for inclusion in a magazine, newspaper or broadcast.

Published in the United States by E. P. Dutton, a division of NAL Penguin Inc., 2 Park Avenue, New York, N.Y. 10016

Published simultaneously in Canada by Fitzhenry & Whiteside Limited, Toronto

ISBN: 0-525-48462-0

Editor: Sandra W. Soule

Designer: Stanley S. Drate/Folio Graphics Co. Inc.

10 9 8 7 6 5 4 3 2 1

Contents

	Preface	xxxiii
	Acknowledgments	xxxv
1.	Introduction	1
2.	How to Start Your Own B&B	9
3.	How to Start Your Own B&B Reservation Service Organization	27
4.	B&B Recipes	51
5.	State-by-State Listings	69

ALABAMA
Bed & Breakfast—Birmingham	71
Millbrook—**Montgomery Bed & Breakfast**	72
Mobile—Vincent-Doan Home	72

ALASKA
Accommodations Alaska Style—Stay with a Friend	73
Anchorage—**Alaska Private Lodgings**	74
All the Comforts of Home	74
The Green Bough	75
Bethel—Wilson's Hostel	75
Juneau—**Alaska Bed and Breakfast Association**	76
Kodiak—**Kodiak Bed & Breakfast**	76
Palmer—Russell's Bed & Board	76
Wasilla—Ede Den	77

ARIZONA
Mi Casa-Su Casa Bed & Breakfast	78
Chandler—Cone's Tourist Home	79
Flagstaff—Cedar Bed and Breakfast	79
Dierker House	80
Walking L Ranch	80
Fountain Hills—Villa Galleria	81
Phoenix—Bed 'n' Breakfast in Arizona	81
Prescott—**Bed & Breakfast Scottsdale and the West**	82
Ford's Bed & Breakfast	82

Reservation service organizations appear here in boldface type.

    Scottsdale—La Maison de Mettille   83
        Valley o' the Sun Bed & Breakfast   84
    Tucson—**Old Pueblo Homestays, R.S.O.**   84
        The Bird's Nest   84
        Myers' Blue Corn House   85
        O' Desert Dream   85
        Redbud House Bed & Breakfast   86

ARKANSAS
    Bed & Breakfast of the Arkansas Ozarks   87
    Eureka Springs—Bridgeford Cottage B&B   88
        Crescent Cottage Inn   88
        Harvest House   89
        Sally's Bed and Breakfast   89
        Singleton House Bed & Breakfast   90
    Fayetteville—Eton House   91
    Heber Springs—Oak Tree Inn   91
    Hot Springs—Stillmeadow Farm   92
        Williams House Bed & Breakfast Inn   92

CALIFORNIA
  DESERT AREA   94
    Desert Hot Springs—Travellers Repose   94
    Nipton—Hotel Nipton   95
    Palm Springs—Inn at Palm Valley Ranch   96
  GOLD COUNTRY   96
    Ione—The Heirloom   96
  LOS ANGELES AREA   97
    Bed & Breakfast of Los Angeles   97
    El Camino Real Bed & Breakfast   97
    House Guests U.S.A., Inc.   98
    Burbank—**Beautiful Downtown Burbank B&B Service**   98
        Belair   99
    Los Angeles—Casablanca Villa   99
        Terrace Manor   100
    Malibu—Casa Larronde   100
    Northridge—Hideaway House   101
    Rancho Palos Verdes—The Exley House "By-the-Sea"   101
    Redondo Beach—Sea Breeze Bed & Breakfast   102
    Torrance—Noone Guest House   102
        The Whites' House   102
    West Covina—Hendrick Inn   103
    Whittier—Coleen's California Casa   103

Reservation service organizations appear here in boldface type.

MENDOCINO/WINE COUNTRY/NORTH COAST 104
 Bed & Breakfast Exchange 104
 Angwin—Big Yellow Sunflower Bed & Breakfast 104
 Calistoga—Scarlett's Country Inn 105
 Clearlake—Muktip Manor 106
 Crescent City—Pebble Beach B&B 106
 Eureka—The Carter House 107
 Geyserville—Campbell Ranch Inn 107
 Healdsburg—Camellia Inn 108
   Frampton House 109
 Littleriver—The Victorian Farmhouse 109
 Lower Lake—The Swiss Chalet 110
 St. Helena—Wine Country Cottage 110
 Santa Rosa—Hilltop House B&B 111
 Ukiah—Oak Knoll Bed & Breakfast 111
MONTEREY PENINSULA 112
 Carmel—Happy Landing Inn 112
 Pebble Beach—Unicorn 112
 Santa Cruz—Babbling Brook Inn 113
SACRAMENTO AREA 113
 Grass Valley—Annie Horan's 113
 Orland—The Inn at Shallow Creek Farm 114
 Quincy—The Feather Bed 114
 Sacramento—Bear Flag Inn 115
   The Briggs House 115
SAN DIEGO AND ORANGE COUNTY AREA 116
 American Historic Homes Bed & Breakfast 116
 Hospitality Plus 117
 Del Mar—The Blue Door 117
   Gulls Nest 118
 Orange—Country Comfort Bed and Breakfast 118
 Rancho Cucamonga—Christmas House B&B Inn 119
 San Diego—Betty's Bed & Breakfast 119
   E's Inn 120
   Vera's Cozy Corner 120
 Temecula—Loma Vista Bed & Breakfast 121
 Westminster—Friends-We-Haven't-Met 121
SAN FRANCISCO AREA 122
 American Family Inn 122
 Bed & Breakfast International—San Francisco 122
 Burlingame—Burlingame B&B 123
 Castro Valley—Lore's Haus 123
 Danville—Danville Bed & Breakfast 124
 El Granada—The Village Green Inn 124

viii • CONTENTS

Montara—Montara Bed & Breakfast 125
San Francisco—Casa Arguello 125
               Casita Blanca 126
San Gregorio—Rancho San Gregorio 126
San Jose—Mrs. "K's" Retreat 127
Santa Clara—Madison Street Inn 127
Walnut Creek—Gasthaus zum Bären 128
SAN JOAQUIN VALLEY 128
Orosi—Valley View Citrus Ranch 128
Reedley—Tatum's Bed & Breakfast 129
Taft—Larson's Bed 'n Breakfast 129
SAN LUIS OBISPO AREA 130
Megan's Friends 130
Arroyo Grande—The Village Inn 130
Los Osos—Gerarda's Bed & Breakfast 131
SANTA BARBARA AREA 131
Carpinteria—D & B Schroeder Ranch 131
               George and Jean Harris 132
Santa Barbara—Hidden Valley Home 132
               Long's Seaview Bed & Breakfast 133
               Ocean View House 133
               Primrose Patio Inn 134

COLORADO
Bed and Breakfast of Colorado, Ltd. 135
A "Skier's" Bed & Breakfast 136
Berthoud—Parrish's Country Squire 136
Boulder—Briar Rose Bed & Breakfast 137
Central City—Two Ten Casey 137
Colorado Springs—Griffin's Hospitality House 138
               Holden House—1902 138
               Katie's Korner 139
               Trout City Inn at Buena Vista 139
Crested Butte—The Claim Jumper Inn 140
Denver—Queen Anne Inn 140
Dolores—"Little Southfork" Ranch B&B 141
Durango—Country Sunshine B&B 141
             River House B&B 142
             Scrubby Oaks Bed & Breakfast 142
Estes Park—Cottonwood House 143
             Emerald Manor 144
             Wanek's Lodge at Estes 144
Ft. Collins—Elizabeth Street Guest House 145
Georgetown—Hardy House 145

Reservation service organizations appear here in boldface type.

CONTENTS • ix

Glenwood Springs—Sojourner's Inn	146
Sunnyside Bed & Breakfast	146
Talbott House	147
Golden—The Dove Inn	147
Grand Junction—The Gate House B&B	148
Hotchkiss—Ye Ole Oasis Bed and Breakfast	149
Manitou Springs—Onaledge Bed & Breakfast Inn	149
Minturn—The Eagle River Inn	150
Olathe—Uncompahgre Cabin	151
Ouray—The Main Street House	151
Ouray 1898 House	152
Pagosa Springs—Davidson's Country Inn	152
Echo Manor Inn	153
Pine—Meadow Creek B&B Inn	153
Salida—Sweet Adeline's	154
Silverton—The Alma House	154
Yellow Jacket—Wilson's Pinto Bean Farm	155

CONNECTICUT

Bed & Breakfast, Ltd.	156
Covered Bridge Bed & Breakfast	157
Clinton—Captain Dibbell House	157
Groton Long Point—Shore Inne	158
Mystic—Comolli's House	158
Norfolk—Weaver's House	159
Old Lyme—Janse Bed and Breakfast	159
Somersville—The Old Mill Inn	160
Westbrook—Captain Stannard House	161

DELAWARE

Bethany Beach—The Sand Box & Sea-Vista Villas	162
Dover—Biddles Bed and Breakfast	163
New Castle—William Penn Guest House	163
Rehoboth Beach—Tembo Guest House	164
Wilmington—The Boulevard Bed & Breakfast	164
The Pink Door	165
Small Wonder B&B	165

DISTRICT OF COLUMBIA

The Bed & Breakfast League, Ltd.	167
Bed 'n' Breakfast Ltd. of Washington, D.C.	168
Sweet Dreams & Toast, Inc.	168

FLORIDA

A & A Bed & Breakfast of Florida, Inc.	169
Bed & Breakfast Co.—Tropical Florida	170

CONTENTS

Bed & Breakfast Registry of Volusia County	170
Central Florida B&B Reservations	171
Open House Bed & Breakfast Registry—Gold Coast	171
Big Pine Key—The Barnacle	171
Bed & Breakfast-on-the-Ocean "Casa Grande"	172
Canal Cottage Bed & Breakfast	173
Deer Run	173
Clearwater—Bed & Breakfast of Tampa Bay	174
Crescent City—Sprague House Inn	174
Eastlake Weir—Lakeside Inn Bed and Breakfast	175
Estero—Feller House	176
Ft. Lauderdale—Casa Alhambra B&B Inn	176
Dolan House	176
Fort Myers—Windsong Garden & Art Gallery	177
Gainesville—Country Meadows	177
Indian Shores—Meeks B&B on the Gulf Beaches	178
Lantana—A Sunny Place Guest House	178
Miami—Bette Lane	179
Orlando—Action Center of Orlando	179
Bed & Breakfast of Orlando	180
Esther's B&B	180
Jarman's Friendly Inn	181
Rinaldi House	181
The Rio Pinar House	182
The Spencer Home	182
Pensacola—Sunshine Inn	183
St. Augustine—Carriage Way Bed & Breakfast	183
Casa de la Paz	183
Casa de Solana	184
Kenwood Inn	184
St. Francis Inn	185
Victorian House Bed & Breakfast	186
St. Petersburg—Bayboro House on Old Tampa Bay	186
Sarasota—Crescent House	187
Summerland Key—Knightswood	187
Sunnyside—Cobb's Gulf View Inn	188
Tarpon Springs—Fiorito's Bed & Breakfast	188
Spring Bayou Inn	189
GEORGIA	
Bed & Breakfast—Atlanta	190
Quail Country Bed & Breakfast, Ltd.	191
Blakely—Layside	191

Reservation service organizations appear here in boldface type.

Cleveland—Schlemmer's Bed & Breakfast 192
Dahlonega—The Mountain Top Lodge 192
Helen—Hilltop Haus 193
Marietta—Blue and Grey Bed and Breakfast 193
Newnan—Parrott-Camp-Soucy House 194
R.S.V.P. Savannah—B&B Reservation Service 195
Savannah—Bed & Breakfast Inn 195
Senoia—The Culpepper House 196

HAWAII
Bed & Breakfast—Hawaii 197
Bed & Breakfast Honolulu and Statewide 198
Bed and Breakfast "Maui Style" 198
Anahola, Kauai—Mahina Kai 198
Captain Cook, Big Island—Adrienne's Bed & Breakfast Paradise 199
Haiku, Maui—Haikuleana 200
Haleiwa, Oahu—Bob & Val's Sunset Beach B&B on Oahu 200
Holualoa, Big Island—Holualoa Inn 201
Honolulu, Oahu—Bed & Breakfast Waikiki Beach 201
Bev & Monty's Bed & Breakfast 202
Kailua, Oahu—Papaya Paradise 202
Kapaa, Kauai—Kay Barker's Bed & Breakfast 203
Koloa, Kauai—Poipu Bed and Breakfast Inn 203
Kula, Maui—Kilohana 204
Lawai, Kauai—Victoria Place 205

IDAHO
Bed and Breakfast of Idaho 206
Boise—Idaho Heritage Inn 207
Coeur d'Alene—Greenbriar Bed and Breakfast Inn 207
Inn The First Place 208
The Sleeping Place of the Wheels 208
Salmon—Heritage Inn 209
Shoup—Smith House Bed & Breakfast 209

ILLINOIS
Bed & Breakfast/Chicago, Inc. 211
Arcola—Curly's Corner 212
Cisco—Country House 212
Champaign—The Golds 213
Decatur—Hamilton House 213
Galena—Aldrich Guest House 214
Avery Guest House 215

Lyons—Ahern's Bed & Breakfast — 215
Naperville—Die Blaue Gans (The Blue Goose) — 216
Oak Park—Toad Hall Bed & Breakfast House — 216
Quincy—The Kaufmann House — 217
Rockford—Victoria's B&B — 217
Rock Island—Top o' the Morning — 218
St. Charles—The Stagecoach Inn — 218
Springfield—Mischler House — 219

INDIANA
Indiana Homes Bed & Breakfast, Inc. — 220
Chesterton—Gray Goose Inn — 221
Corydon—The Kintner House Inn — 221
Evansville—Brigadoon Bed & Breakfast Inn — 222
Knightstown—Old Hoosier House — 222
Madison—Old Madison House — 223
Morgantown—The Rock House — 223
Nashville—Allison House — 224
         Sunset House — 224
Paoli—Braxtan House Inn B&B — 225
Rockport—The Rockport Inn — 225
Westfield—Country Roads Guesthouse — 226

IOWA
Bed and Breakfast in Iowa, Ltd. — 227
Ames—B&B on Ash — 228
Calmar—Calmar Guesthouse — 228
Davenport—River Oaks Inn — 229
Elk Horn—Rainbow H Ranch and Campground — 229
Fort Madison—The Morton House — 230
Marengo—Loy's Bed and Breakfast — 230

KANSAS
Bed & Breakfast Kansas City —Missouri & Kansas — 232
Abilene—Balfours' House — 233
Fort Scott—Country Quarters — 233
Melvern—Schoolhouse Inn — 234
Modoc—Krause House — 234
Tonganoxie—Almeda's Inn — 235
Valley Falls—The Barn Bed and Breakfast Inn — 235
WaKeeney—Thistle Hill — 236

KENTUCKY
Bluegrass Bed & Breakfast — 237
Kentucky Homes Bed & Breakfast, Inc. — 238
Bowling Green—Bowling Green Bed & Breakfast — 238

Reservation service organizations appear here in boldface type.

Frankfort—Olde Kantucke Bed and Breakfast	239
Georgetown—Log Cabin Bed and Breakfast	239
Grays Knob—Three Deer Inn	240
Paducah—Ehrhardt's B&B	240

LOUISIANA

Southern Comfort Bed & Breakfast	242
Baton Rouge—Joy's B&B	243
Covington—Plantation Bell Guest House	243
Lafayette—Ti Frere's House	244
New Orleans—**Bed & Breakfast, Inc.—New Orleans**	244
New Orleans Bed & Breakfast	245
Jensen's Bed & Breakfast	245
The Levee View	246
Terrell House	246
St. Francisville—Cottage Plantation	247
The St. Francisville Inn	247
Shreveport—The Columns on Jordan	248
Fairfield Place	249

MAINE

Bed & Breakfast Down East, Ltd.	250
Bath—"Glad II"	251
Belfast—Horatio Johnson House	251
Boothbay—Kenniston Hill Inn	251
Bucksport—L'ermitage	252
Camden—Blue Harbor House	252
Hawthorn Inn	253
Maine Stay Bed and Breakfast	254
Cherryfield—Ricker House	254
Damariscotta—Brannon-Bunker Inn	255
Freeport—Isaac Randall House	255
Kennebunk—Arundel Meadows Inn	256
Kennebunkport—1802 House Bed & Breakfast Inn	256
The Green Heron Inn	257
The Inn at Harbor Head	257
Kittery Point—Harbour Watch	258
Litchfield—Old Tavern Inn	258
Mt. Desert Island—Black Friar Inn	259
Hearthside Inn	259
Holbrook House	260
The Kingsleigh	260
Lindenwood Inn	261
Penury Hall	261
Two Seasons	262

Ogunquit—The Gazebo	262
Morning Dove Bed and Breakfast	263
Waldoboro—Broad Bay Inn & Gallery	263
Tide Watch Inn	264
York—The Wild Rose of York B&B	265

MARYLAND

Baltimore—Betsy's Bed and Breakfast	266
Mulberry House	267
Bethesda—The Winslow Home	267
Burtonsville—The Taylors' B&B	268
Chestertown—Inn at Mitchell House	268
Radcliffe Cross	269
Chevy Chase—Chevy Chase Bed & Breakfast	269
Dameron—**Country Hosting**	270
Elkton—The Garden Cottage at Sinking Springs Herb Farm	270
Ellicott City—Hayland Farm	271
Girdletree—The Stockmans	271
Hagerstown—Lewrene Farm B&B	272
Harwood—Oakwood	272
Havre De Grace—Vandiver Inn	272
Scotland—St. Michael's Manor B&B	273
Sharpsburg—Inn at Antietam	274
Smithsburg—Blue Bear Bed & Breakfast	274
Sykesville—Long Way Hill	275
Vienna—The Tavern House	275
Westminster—Winchester Country Inn	276

MASSACHUSETTTS

Pineapple Hospitality, Inc.	277
Bed & Breakfast Associates—Bay Colony, Ltd.	278
Bed & Breakfast Marblehead & North Shore	278
Bed & Breakfast in Minuteman Country	279
Be Our Guest Bed & Breakfast, Ltd.	279
BOSTON AREA	280
Greater Boston Hospitality	280
Host Homes of Boston	280
Gloucester—Williams Guest House	280
Sudbury—Checkerberry Corner	281
Swampscott—Marshall House	281
Oak Shores	282
CAPE COD/MARTHA'S VINEYARD	283
Bed & Breakfast—Cape Cod	283
House Guests—Cape Cod and the Islands	283

Reservation service organizations appear here in boldface type.

CONTENTS • xv

Orleans Bed & Breakfast Associates	284
Barnstable—Thomas Huckins House	284
Bass River—Old Cape House	285
Brewster—Old Sea Pines Inn	285
Centerville—Copper Beech Inn on Cape Cod	286
Dennis—Isaiah B. Hall House	286
Eastham—The Penny House	287
East Orleans—The Parsonage	287
Edgartown—The Arbor	288
Falmouth—Captain Tom Lawrence House—1861	289
Palmer House Inn	289
Village Green Inn	290
Wyndemere House	290
Harwich Port—The Coach House	291
The Inn on Bank Street	291
Sandwich—Hawthorn Hill	292
Sterling—"Glen Cara"—An Irish Bed & Breakfast	292
Wareham—Little Harbor Guest House	293
Mulberry Bed and Breakfast	293
West Yarmouth—The Manor House	294
CENTRAL/WESTERN/SOUTHERN MASSACHUSETTS	294
Buckland—House of Amacord	294
Peru—Chalet d'Alicia	295
Rehoboth—Perryville Inn	295
Sturbridge—Lakeshore Bed and Breakfast	296
Tyringham—The Golden Goose	296
Ware—The Wildwood Inn	297
NANTUCKET	297
Lynda Watts Bed & Breakfast	297
MICHIGAN	
Allen—The Olde Bricke House	298
Beulah—Windermere Inn	299
Blaney Park—Celibeth House	299
Calumet—The Calumet House	300
Dimondale—Bannicks B&B	300
Douglas—Rosemont Inn	301
Fennville—Hidden Pond Farm	301
Frankenmuth Bed & Breakfast Reservations	302
Harbor Beach—Wellock Inn	302
Hillsdale—Shadowlawn Manor	303
Holland—Dutch Colonial Inn	303
Kalamazoo—Hall House	304
Laingsburg—Seven Oaks Farm	304
Lamont—The Stagecoach Stop	305

Lexington—Governor's Inn — 305
Vickie Van's Bed and Breakfast — 306
Ludington—Bed and Breakfast at Ludington — 306
Mecosta—Blue Lake Lodge — 307
Port Sanilac—Raymond House Inn — 307
Saugatuck—Twin Gables Country Inn — 307
Sebewaing—Rummel's Tree Haven — 308
Union City—The Victorian Villa Guesthouse — 308
Walled Lake—Villa Hammer — 309
Williamston—Williamston Bed and Breakfast — 309

MINNESOTA
Bed & Breakfast Registry Ltd. — 311
Dassel—Gabrielson's B&B — 312
Garvin—Glenview B&B — 312
Lake City—Red Gables Inn — 313
Lanesboro—Carrolton Country Inn & Cottage — 313
Minneapolis—Creekside Bed & Breakfast — 314
Evelo's Bed & Breakfast — 315
North Branch—Red Pine Log B&B — 315
Rochester—Canterbury Inn Bed & Breakfast — 316
St. Paul—Chatsworth Bed and Breakfast — 316
Spring Valley—Chase's Bed & Breakfast — 317
Stacy—Kings Oakdale Park Guest House — 318

MISSISSIPPI
Lincoln, Ltd. Bed & Breakfast—Mississippi Reservation Service — 319
Holly Springs—Hamilton Place — 320
Port Gibson—Oak Square Plantation — 320
Woodville—Square Ten Inn — 321

MISSOURI
Ozark Mountain Country B&B Service — 322
Arrow Rock—Borgman's Bed & Breakfast — 323
Bonne Terre—Mansion Hill Country Inn — 323
Branson—Country Gardens B&B — 324
Camdenton—Lakeside Guest House — 324
Ramblewood Bed and Breakfast — 325
Carthage—Brewer's Maple Lane Farms B&B — 325
Grandview—The Fountains — 326
Gravois Mills—Lingerlong — 326
Hannibal—Garth Woodside Mansion — 327
Hartville—Frisco House — 327
Independence—Woodstock Inn — 328
Kansas City—Pridewell — 328

Reservation service organizations appear here in boldface type.

CONTENTS • xvii

Louisiana—Grey Goose House	329
Macon—Wardell Guest House	329
Parkville—Down-to-Earth Lifestyles	330
Rogersville—Anchor Hill Lodge	330
St. Louis—Lafayette House	331
Stelzer Bed & Breakfast	332
Tower Grove House	332
Washington—The Schwegmann House B&B Inn	333
Weston—Benner House Bed and Breakfast	333

MONTANA

Bigfork—O'Duach'Ain Country Inn	335
Big Sandy—Sky View	336
Bozeman—Voss Inn	336
Kalispell—Ballymurray B&B	337
Kila—Whitetail Lodge	337
St. Ignatius—Mission Mountains B&B	338
Stevensville—Country Caboose	338
Whitefish—Duck Inn	339

NEBRASKA

Bed & Breakfast of the Great Plains	341
Dixon—The Georges	342
Gretna—Bundy's Bed and Breakfast	342
Lincoln—The Rogers House	342
North Platte—Watson Manor Inn	343
Omaha—The Offutt House	344

NEVADA

Carson City—Winters Creek Ranch	345
Lake Tahoe—Haus Bavaria	346
Las Vegas—Las Vegas B&B	346
Reno—B&B—Northern Nevada	347
Virginia City—Edith Palmer's Country Inn	347

NEW HAMPSHIRE

New Hampshire Bed & Breakfast	349
Bethlehem—The Mulburn Inn	350
Campton—Mountain-Fare Inn	350
Easton—Blanche's B&B	351
Franklin—Maria W. Atwood Inn	351
Webster Lake Inn	352
Gilford—Cartway House Inn	352
Gorham—The Gables	353
Hampton Beach—Roy Family Bed & Breakfast	353
Holderness—The Inn on Golden Pond	354
Intervale—The Forest—A Country Inn	354

Jaffrey—The Galway House	355
Jefferson—The Jefferson Inn	356
Laconia—Ferry Point House	356
The Tin Whistle Inn	357
Littleton—The Beal House Inn	357
Marlborough—Peep-Willow Farm	358
Mt. Sunapee—Blue Goose Inn	358
Newport—The Inn at Coit Mountain	359
North Conway—The Foothills Farm	359
Northwood—Meadow Farm	360
Plymouth—Crab Apple Inn	361
Portsmouth—Leighton Inn	361
Rindge—Grassy Pond House	362
The Tokfarm	362
Sugar Hill—The Hilltop Inn	363
Sunapee—Times Ten Inn	363
Suncook—Suncook House	364
Wolfeboro—Isaac Springfield House	364
Tuc' Me Inn	365

NEW JERSEY

Bed & Breakfast of New Jersey, Inc.	367
Bed & Breakfast of Princeton—A Reservation Service	368
Cape May—Albert G. Stevens Inn	368
Barnard-Good House	369
Columns-by-the-Sea	369
The Mainstay Inn	370
Dennisville—The Henry Ludlam Inn	370
Denville—Lakeside B&B	371
Jobstown—Daffodil	371
Lyndhurst—Jeremiah J. Yereance House	372
Milford—Chestnut Hill on-the-Delaware	373
North Wildwood—Candlelight Inn	373
Home Suite Home	374
Spring Lake—Ashling Cottage	374
Stanhope—Whistling Swan Inn	375

NEW MEXICO

Bed & Breakfast Rocky Mountains—New Mexico	376
Albuquerque—The Corner House	377
Cedar Crest—Santa Fe Casita	377
Chimayó—La Posada de Chimayó	378
Mesilla Park—The Elms	378
Pecos—Wilderness Inn	379
Roswell—The Boellner House	379
Santa Fe—**Bed & Breakfast of Santa Fe**	380

Reservation service organizations appear here in boldface type.

Water Street Inn	380
Taos—American Artists Gallery-House	381
Harrison's B&B	381
Ranchos de Taos—Two Pipe Bed & Breakfast	382

NEW YORK
CATSKILLS

CATSKILLS	383
Chichester—Maplewood	383
Roxbury—Scudder Hill House	384
Tannersville—The Eggery Inn	384
Walton—Sunrise Inn	385
CENTRAL NEW YORK/LEATHERSTOCKING AREA	385
Bed & Breakfast—Leatherstocking	385
Afton—Jericho Farm Inn	386
Binghamton—B&B Adagio	386
Cooperstown—Creekside Bed & Breakfast	387
The Inn at Brook Willow Farm	387
The Inn at Mill Pond	387
Litco Farms Bed & Breakfast	388
Whisperin Pines Chalet	388
Richfield Springs—Jonathan House	389
CHAUTAUQUA/ALLEGHENY AREA	390
Rainbow Hospitality—Chautauqua	390
Alfred—Hitchcock House	390
Ashville—Green Acres	391
Falconer—Mansard Inn	391
Little Valley—Napoli Stagecoach Inn	392
Mayville—The Village Inn B&B	392
Rushford—Klartag Farms	393
South Dayton—Town & Country Bed & Breakfast	393
FINGER LAKES/ROCHESTER AREA	394
Bed & Breakfast—Rochester	394
Canaseraga—The Country House	394
Corning—1865 White Birch Bed & Breakfast	395
Rosewood Inn	396
Dundee—Lakeside Terrace	396
Willow Cove	397
Geneseo—American House	397
Geneva—The Cobblestones	398
Ithaca—Buttermilk Falls Bed & Breakfast	398
Glendale Farm	399
Peregrine House	399
Newfield—The Historic Cook House B&B	400
Penfield—Strawberry Castle Bed & Breakfast	400
Penn Yan—The Wagener Estate Bed & Breakfast	401

Rushville—Lake View Farm Bed & Breakfast — 401
Trumansburg—Sage Cottage — 402
HUDSON VALLEY/ALBANY/KINGSTON AREA — 402
   The American Country Collection — 402
   Bed and Breakfast, U.S.A., Ltd. — 403
   Albany—Riell's Bed & Breakfast — 403
   Averill Park—Ananas Hus Bed and Breakfast — 404
              The Gregory House Inn — 404
   Cambridge—Battenkill Bed and Breakfast Barn — 405
   Canaan—The Lace House — 405
   Cold Spring—One Market Street — 406
   Garrison—Golden Eagle Inn — 406
   High Falls—House on the Hill — 407
   Johnson—Elaine's Guest House — 407
   Pearl River—**Bed-N-Breakfast Reservation Services of Greater New York** — 408
   Pine Bush—Sunrise Farm — 408
   Pittstown—Maggie Towne's B&B — 408
   Slate Hill—Ridgebury Inn and Hunt Club — 409
LAKE GEORGE AREA — 410
   Bolton Landing—Hayes's B&B Guest House — 410
              Hilltop Cottage — 410
   Glens Falls—The Crislip's Bed and Breakfast — 411
LAKE PLACID/ADIRONDACKS AREA — 412
   North Country B&B Reservation Service — 412
   Lake Placid—Highland House — 412
LONG ISLAND — 413
   A Reasonable Alternative — 413
   Hampton Bays—Hampton-on-the-Water — 413
   Hempstead—Duvall Bed and Breakfast On-the-Garden City-Line — 414
   Mattituck—Mattituck Bed & Breakfast — 415
   Westhampton Beach—Seafield House — 415
NEW YORK CITY AREA — 416
   Bed & Breakfast (& Books) — 416
   Bed & Breakfast Network of New York — 416
   City Lights B&B, Ltd. — 416
   Hosts & Guests, Inc. — 417
   Judith Mol Agency — 417
   New World Bed & Breakfast — 418
   Urban Ventures — 418
   New York City—A Bit o' the Apple—New York City — 418
NIAGARA/BUFFALO AREA — 419
   Rainbow Hospitality — 419

Reservation service organizations appear here in boldface type.

Buffalo—B&B of Niagara Frontier ... 419
Castile—The Eastwood House ... 420
Eden—The Davidson House ... 420
Gowanda—The Fox's Den ... 421
Lockport—Chestnut Ridge Inn ... 421
THOUSAND ISLANDS AREA ... 422
Fulton—Battle Island Inn ... 422

NORTH CAROLINA
Charlotte Bed and Breakfast ... 424
Asheville—Cedar Crest Victorian Inn ... 425
    Cornerstone Inn ... 425
    Flint Street Inns ... 426
    The Ray House ... 426
Bath—Bath Guest House ... 427
Black Mountain—The Blackberry Inn ... 427
Brevard—The Inn at Brevard ... 428
Burnsville—Hamrick Inn ... 428
Charlotte—The Homeplace ... 429
    The Inn on Providence ... 430
    The Overcarsh House ... 430
Durham—Arrowhead Inn ... 431
Franklin—Buttonwood Inn ... 431
Glenville—Mountain High ... 432
Greensboro—College Hill Bed & Breakfast ... 432
    Greenwood ... 433
Hertford—Gingerbread Inn ... 433
Hickory—The Hickory Bed & Breakfast ... 434
Highlands—Colonial Pines Inn ... 434
Leicester—Greenfield B&B ... 435
Milton—Woodside Inn ... 435
Mt. Airy—Pine Ridge B&B Inn ... 436
New Bern—Harmony House Inn ... 436
    Kings Arms Inn ... 437
    New Berne House Bed & Breakfast Inn ... 437
Raleigh—The Oakwood Inn ... 438
Salisbury—Rowan Oak House ... 438
Smithfield—Eli Olive's ... 439
Sparta—Turby Villa B&B ... 439
Spruce Pine—The Richmond Inn ... 440
Swansboro—Scott's Keep ... 440
Tarboro—Little Warren ... 441
Tryon—Mill Farm Inn ... 441
Valle Crucis—Bluestone Lodge ... 442

Wilmington—Anderson Guest House 443
                Murchison House B&B Inn 443
Wilson—Pilgrims Rest 444

NORTH DAKOTA
Stanley—The Triple T Ranch 445

OHIO
Ohio Valley Bed & Breakfast 446
Akron—Helen's Hospitality House 447
           Portage House 447
Andover—Vickery's Bed & Breakfast 448
Avon—A French Creek House 448
Avon Lake—Williams House 449
Celina—Das Winkeljohn Haus 449
Cincinnati—Berry Hill House 450
Cleveland—**Private Lodgings, Inc.** 450
           The Sarah Frisch House 451
Columbus—**Columbus Bed & Breakfast** 451
Cuyahoga Falls—Studio 12 Bed and Breakfast 451
East Fultonham—Hill View Acres 452
Lakeville—Quiet Country 452
Lewisville—Grandma Betty's 453
Mansfield—Happy Hill 453
Martins Ferry—Mulberry Inn 454
Morrow—Locust Hill 454
North Ridgeville—St. George House 455
Peebles—The Bayberry Inn 456
Pettisville—Tudor Country Inn 456
Poland—Inn at the Green 457
Put-in-Bay—The Vineyard 457
Seville—Colonial Manor 458
Spring Valley—3 B's Bed 'n' Breakfast 458
Warren—Shirlee's Chambers 459
West Milton—Locust Lane Farm 459
Westerville—Priscilla's Bed & Breakfast 460
Wooster—The Howey House 460

OKLAHOMA
Bed & Breakfast—Oklahoma City 461
Claremore—Country Inn 462
Clayton—Clayton Country Inn 462
Tulsa—Robin's Nest Bed & Breakfast 463
           Sunrise Bed and Breakfast 463

OREGON
Northwest Bed and Breakfast Travel Unlimited 464

Reservation service organizations appear here in boldface type.

CONTENTS • xxiii

Ashland—Chanticleer	465
The Coach House Inn	465
Mt. Ashland Inn	465
Neil Creek House	466
Royal Carter House	466
Bend—Cedar Crest Inn	467
Mirror Pond House	467
Brookings—Sea Dreamer Inn	468
Coburg—Wheeler's Bed & Breakfast	468
Coos Bay—Captain's Quarters Bed & Breakfast	469
This Olde House B&B	469
Corvallis—Huntington Manor	470
Elmira—McGillivray's Log Home and Bed and Breakfast	471
Eugene—The House in the Woods	471
Shelley's Guest House	472
Gold Beach—Endicott Gardens	472
Fair Winds Bed and Breakfast	473
Grants Pass—Ahlf House Bed & Breakfast	473
The Handmaiden's Inn	474
Mt. Baldy Bed & Breakfast	474
The Washington Inn Bed & Breakfast	475
Lakeside—Country Lane Bed & Breakfast	475
Leaburg—Marjon Bed and Breakfast Inn	476
Newberg—The Owl's View B&B	476
North Bend—The Highlands Bed and Breakfast	477
Oakland—The Pringle House	478
Portland—Corbett House B&B	478
John Palmer House	479
Port Orford—Home-by-the-Sea B&B Homestay	479
Seaside—The Boarding House Bed & Breakfast	480
Stayton—Horncroft	481
PENNSYLVANIA	
Bed & Breakfast in Pennsylvania	482
ALLEGHENIES AREA	483
Allegheny Bed & Breakfast Association	483
BUCKS COUNTY	483
Gardenville—Maplewood Farm	483
Holicong—Ash Mill Farm	484
New Hope—Pineapple Hill	484
CENTRAL PENNSYLVANIA	485
Rest & Repast Bed & Breakfast Service	485
Boiling Springs—The Garmanhaus	485
Huntingdon—Yoders	486

Tyrone—The White House B&B Inn 486
GETTYSBURG AREA 487
   Bendersville—Historic Paul Sourss Plantation House 487
   East Berlin—The Leas-Bechtel Mansion Inn 487
   Fayetteville—The Herb Cottage 488
   Gardners—Goose Chase 488
   Gettysburg—The Brafferton Inn 489
      Keystone Inn 489
      The Old Appleford Inn 490
      Twin Elms 491
   Gettysburg Battlefield—The Doubleday Inn 491
   Hanover—Beechmont Inn 492
      Country View Acres 493
   Red Lion—Red Lion B&B 493
PENNSYLVANIA DUTCH AREA 494
   Atglen—Umble Rest 494
   Bird-in-Hand—Greystone Manor B&B 494
   Christiana—Winding Glen Farm Tourist Home 494
   East Petersburg—Red Door Studio B&B 495
   Elverson—Rocky-Side Farm 495
   Ephrata—Covered Bridge Inn 496
      Gerhart House B&B 496
   Hershey—**Hershey Bed & Breakfast Reservation Service** 497
      Gibson's Bed & Breakfast 497
   Kinzers—Groff Tourist Farm Home 498
   Kirkwood—White Rock Farm Guest House 498
   Lampeter—Walkabout Inn 499
   Lancaster—The Dingeldein House 499
      Hollinger House 500
      The King's Cottage 500
      Meadowview Guest House 501
      Wheatland Hills B&B 501
   Leesport—The Loom Room 502
      The Sleepy Fir Bed & Breakfast 502
   Lititz—Dot's Bed & Breakfast 503
   Manheim—Herr Farmhouse Inn 503
   Mount Joy—Cedar Hill Farm 504
   Mountville—Carriage House Manor 504
   Paradise—Maple Lane Guest House 505
      The Rose and Crown 505
   Peach Bottom—Lofty Acres 506
   Rehrersburg—Kurr House 506
   York—The Inn at Mundis Mills 507

Reservation service organizations appear here in boldface type.

PHILADELPHIA AREA	507
Bed & Breakfast—The Manor	507
Bed & Breakfast of Chester County	508
Bed & Breakfast of Philadelphia	508
Bed & Breakfast of Valley Forge	508
The Bed & Breakfast Connection	509
Guesthouses	509
Kennett Square—Buttonwood Farm	510
Meadow Spring Farm	510
Mrs. K's Bed & Breakfast	511
Langhorne—The Waln House	511
West Chester—The Barn	512
POCONO MOUNTAINS	512
Beach Lake—Beach Lake Hotel and Country Store	512
Blakeslee—Toby Valley Lodge	513
Canadensis—Nearbrook	514
Cresco—La Anna Guest House	514
Greentown—Hemlock Grove Bed and Breakfast	514
Hawley—Academy Street Bed & Breakfast	515
Jim Thorpe—The Harry Packer Mansion	516
Milford—The Vines	516
Millrift—Bonny Bank	517
Mount Bethel—Elvern Country Lodge	517
White Haven—The Redwood House	518
SCRANTON/NORTH-CENTRAL PENNSYLVANIA	518
Liberty—Hill Top Haven	518
Montoursville—The Carriage House at Stonegate	519
Muncy—The Bodine House	519
SOUTHEASTERN PENNSYLVANIA	520
Allentown—Brennans B&B	520
Mertztown—Longswamp Bed and Breakfast	520
WESTERN PENNSYLVANIA	521
Pittsburgh Bed & Breakfast	521
Cowansville—Garrott's Bed & Breakfast	521
Donegal—Mountain View Bed and Breakfast	522
Erie—Blueberry Acres	522
Hickory—Shady Elms Farm B&B	523
Mercer—Magoffin Guest House	523
The Stranahan House	524
Pittsburgh—Oakwood	524
Schellsburg—Millstone Inn	525
RHODE ISLAND	
Bed & Breakfast of Rhode Island	526
Green Hill—Fairfield-By-The-Sea	527

xxvi • CONTENTS

Kingston—Hedgerow Bed & Breakfast 527
Narragansett—The House of Snee 528
    Ilverthorpe Cottage 529
Newport—Ellery Park House 529
    The Melville House 530
    The Pilgrim House 530
Westerly—Woody Hill Guest House 531

SOUTH CAROLINA
Beaufort—Old Point Inn 532
    The Rhett House Inn 533
Beech Island—The Cedars 533
Camden—The Carriage House 534
Charleston—**Charleston East Bed & Breakfast** 534
    Historic Charleston Bed & Breakfast 535
    Ann Harper's Bed & Breakfast 535
    1837 Bed & Breakfast & Tea Room 535
Dale—Coosaw Plantation 536
Georgetown—Shaw House 536
Hilton Head Island—Ambiance Bed & Breakfast 537
    Marsh Winds 537
Myrtle Beach—Serendipity, an Inn 538
Summerville—Gadsden Manor Inn 538

SOUTH DAKOTA
South Dakota Bed and Breakfast 540
Canova—Skoglund Farm 541
Deadwood—Adams House 541
Lead—Cheyenne Crossing B&B 542
Rapid City—Audrie's Cranbury Corner B&B 542
    Bed and Breakfast Domivara 543
    Willow Springs Cabin 543
Webster—Lakeside Farm 544
Yankton—The Mulberry Inn 544

TENNESSEE
Bed & Breakfast Host Homes of Tennessee 546
Greeneville—Big Spring Inn 546
Knoxville—The Graustein Inn 547
    Mountain Breeze Bed & Breakfast 548
    Windy Hill B&B 548
Limestone—Snapp Inn B&B 549
Loudon—River Road Inn 549
Memphis—Lowenstein-Long House 550
Murfreesboro—Clardy's Guest House 550
Nashville—Miss Anne's Bed & Breakfast 551

Reservation service organizations appear here in boldface type.

CONTENTS • xxvii

Normandy—Parish Patch Farm and Inn	551
Paris—The Oaks	552
Pickwick Dam—The Homestead House Inn	552
Rogersville—Hale Springs Inn	553
Sevierville—Blue Mountain Mist Country Inn	554

TEXAS

The Bed & Breakfast Society of Texas	555
Bed & Breakfast Texas Style	556
Amarillo—Parkview House	556
Austin—The McCallum House	557
Southard House	557
Canyon—Hudspeth House	558
Columbus—Lain's Bed and Breakfast	558
Fredericksburg—**Be My Guest**	559
Georgetown—Lone Star Inn	559
Houston—Sara's Bed & Breakfast Inn	560
Woodlake House	560
Jefferson—McKay House	561
Marshall—Three Oaks	561
New Braunfels—The White House	562
San Antonio—**Bed & Breakfast Hosts of San Antonio**	562
The Belle of Monte Vista	563
Cardinal Cliff	563
International House	564
Tyler—Rosevine Inn	564
Victoria—Bellsen Bed & Breakfast	565

UTAH

Bed 'n' Breakfast Homestay of Utah	566
Bed and Breakfast Rocky Mountains—Utah	567
Bluff—Bluff Bed and Breakfast	567
Logan—Center Street Bed and Breakfast Inn	567
Monroe—Peterson's Bed and Breakfast	568
Provo—The Pullman Bed and Breakfast	568
St. George—Seven Wives Inn	569
Salt Lake City—Anton Boxrud House	570
The National Historic Bed & Breakfast	570
Sandy—Quail Hills Country Guesthouse	571
Springdale—Under the Eaves Guest House	572

VERMONT

Barre—Woodruff House	573
Belmont—The Parmenter House	574
Bethel—Greenhurst Inn	574
Poplar Manor	575

Brookfield—Green Trails Country Inn	575
Chelsea—Shire Inn	576
Chester—Stone Hearth Inn	576
Craftsbury Common—Craftsbury Bed & Breakfast on Wylie Hill	577
Cuttingsville—Buckmaster Inn	577
Danby—The Quail's Nest Bed and Breakfast	578
Dorset—The Little Lodge at Dorset	578
Maplewood Colonial House	579
East Dorset—The Kiln Guest House	579
Gaysville—Cobble House Inn	580
Jericho—Milliken's	580
Manchester Center—Brook 'n' Hearth	581
Middlebury—Brookside Meadows	581
North Hero—Charlie's Northland Lodge	582
North Troy—Rose Apple Acres Farm	582
Plainfield—Yankees' Northview Bed & Breakfast	582
Reading—The Peeping Cow Bed & Breakfast	583
Rutland—Hillcrest Guest House	584
South Strafford—Watercourse Way	584
Stowe—Bittersweet Inn	585
Ski Inn	585
Townshend—Boardman House	586
Warren—South Hollow Farm	586
Waterbury—Inn at Blush Hill House	587
West Charleston—Hunt's Hideaway	587
West Dover—The Weathervane	588

VIRGINIA

Bed & Breakfast of Tidewater Virginia	589
Blue Ridge Bed & Breakfast	590
Shenandoah Valley Bed & Breakfast Reservations	590
Abingdon—Summerfield Inn	590
Bowling Green—The Old Mansion	591
Cape Charles—Nottingham Ridge	592
Picketts Harbor	592
Capron—Sandy Hill Farm B&B	593
Charlottesville—**Guesthouses Reservation Service**	593
Culpeper—Fountain Hall	593
Flint Hill—Caledonia Farm	594
Floyd—Brookfield Inn	595
Fredericksburg—La Vista Plantation	595
The McGrath House	596
Gore—Rainbow's End B&B	596
Lexington—Fassifern Bed & Breakfast	597

Reservation service organizations appear here in boldface type.

Llewellyn Lodge at Lexington	598
Luray—Shenandoah Countryside	598
Mathews—Riverfront House	599
Mollusk—Greenvale Manor	599
Montross—The Inn at Montross	600
Mt. Jackson—The Widow Kip's	600
Newport—The Newport House	601
Norfolk—Erika's Bed & Breakfast	602
Orange—Mayhurst Inn	602
Richmond—**Bensonhouse**	603
Hanover Hosts	603
The Leonine Experience	603
Roanoke—The Mary Bladon House	604
Scottsville—High Meadows—Virginia's Vineyard Inn	605
Smithfield—Isle of Wight Inn	605
Smith Mountain Lake—The Manor at Taylor's Store	606
Staunton—Thornrose House at Gypsy Hill	606
Swoope—Lambsgate Bed and Breakfast	607
Virginia Beach—At-the-Beach	607
The Picket Fence	608
Washington—The Foster-Harris House	608
Waterford—The Pink House	609
Williamsburg—**The Travel Tree**	609
Bluebird Haven	610
For Cant Hill Guest Home	610
Fox Grape of Williamsburg	611
Himmelbed B&B	611
War Hill	611
The Williamsburg Legacy	612
Woodstock—The Country Fare	612
Schlisselsmith	613

WASHINGTON

Pacific Bed & Breakfast Agency	615
Anacortes—Burrow's Bay B&B	616
The Channel House	616
Dutch Treat House	617
Ashford—Mountain Meadows Inn	618
Bellevue—Bellevue Bed and Breakfast	618
Cathlamet—The Gallery Bed & Breakfast	619
Deer Harbor—Palmer's Chart House	619
Eastsound—Turtleback Farm Inn	620
Edmonds—The Harrison House	620
Heather House	621
Hudgens Haven	621

The Maple Tree	621
Ferndale—Anderson House	622
Hill Top Bed and Breakfast	622
Gig Harbor—No Cabbages B&B	623
The Parsonage	623
Langley—Log Castle Bed & Breakfast	624
Lummi Island—West Shore Farm B&B	624
Maple Valley—Maple Valley Bed & Breakfast	625
Olympia—Puget View Guesthouse	626
Sylvester House B&B	626
Orcas—Orcas Hotel	627
Pateros—French House at Lake Pateros	627
Port Orchard—Ogle's Bed and Breakfast	628
Redmond—Cedarym—A Colonial Bed & Breakfast	628
Seabeck—Summer Song B&B	629
Seattle—Beech Tree Manor	629
Chambered Nautilus Bed and Breakfast Inn	630
Galer Place B&B Guest House	630
Hainsworth House	631
Hanson House B&B	631
Marit's Bed and Breakfast	632
Roberta's Bed and Breakfast	632
Salisbury House	633
Seattle Bed & Breakfast	634
William House Bed & Breakfast	634
Spokane—Luckey's Residence	635
Tacoma—Inge's Place	635
Keenan House	636
White Salmon—Llama Ranch Bed & Breakfast	636

WEST VIRGINIA

Gerrardstown—Prospect Hill	637
Marlinton—The Carriage House Inn	638
Mathias—Valley View Farm	638
Moorefield—McMechen House Inn	639
Shepherdstown—Thomas Shepherd Inn	639
Summit Point—Countryside	640
Wheeling—Yesterdays Ltd. Bed and Breakfast	641

WISCONSIN

Bed & Breakfast Guest-Homes	642
Bed & Breakfast Information Service—Wisconsin	643
Appleton—The Parkside	643
Baraboo—The Barrister's House	644
Frantiques Showplace	644

Reservation service organizations appear here in boldface type.

CONTENTS • xxxi

The House of Seven Gables	645
Belleville—Abendruh Bed and Breakfast Swiss Style	645
Burlington—Hillcrest	646
Cedarburg—Stagecoach Inn Bed & Breakfast	647
Delavan—The Allyn House	647
Eau Claire—Westlin Winds	648
Green Bay—La Baye House	648
Janesville—Jackson Street Inn	649
Lac Du Flambeau—Ty Bach B&B	649
La Farge—Trillium	650
Lake Delton—O.J.'s Victorian Village Guest House	650
Madison—Hill House Bed & Breakfast	651
The Plough Inn Bed & Breakfast	651
Milwaukee—**Bed & Breakfast of Milwaukee, Inc.**	652
Ogden House	652
Mineral Point—The Wilson House Inn	653
Newton—Rambling Hills Tree Farm	653
Phelps—The Limberlost Inn	654
Portage—Breese Waye Bed & Breakfast	654
Country Aire	655
Sturgeon Bay—Inn at Cedar Crossing	655
White Lace Inn—A Victorian Guest House	656

WYOMING

Big Horn—Spahn's Big Horn Mountain Bed and Breakfast	657
Bondurant—Fall River Ranch	658
Cody—The Lockhart Inn	658
Evanston—Pine Gables Bed and Breakfast Inn	659
Glenrock—Hotel Higgins	659
Lander—Black Mountain Ranch	660
Riverton—Cottonwood Ranch	660
Wilson—Teton Tree House	661

6. CANADA

ALBERTA	662
Alberta Bed & Breakfast	662
BRITISH COLUMBIA	663
Canada-West Accommodations	663
Chilliwack—Charterre B&B House	663
Fulford Harbour—Weston Lake Inn	664
North Vancouver—Grouse Mountain Bed and Breakfast	665
Laburnum Cottage B&B	665

xxxii • CONTENTS

Vancouver—Kenya Court Guest House At-the-Beach	666
Victoria—Sunnymeade House Inn	666
V.I.P. Bed and Breakfast	667
West Vancouver—Beachside Bed and Breakfast	667
NEW BRUNSWICK	668
New Brunswick—Oakley House	668
NOVA SCOTIA	669
National Bed 'n Breakfast™	669
ONTARIO	670
Bed & Breakfast—Kingston	670
Brockville—The Webster House	670
Elmira—Knechtel's Guest House	671
Lakefield—Windmere Bed & Breakfast	671
Niagara-on-the-Lake—Hiebert's Guest House	672
Ottawa Area Bed & Breakfast	672
Toronto—**Toronto Bed & Breakfast**	673
PRINCE EDWARD ISLAND	674
Kensington—Woodington's Country Inn	674
O'Leary—Smallman's Bed and Breakfast	674
Summerside—Dyment Bed & Breakfast	675
QUEBEC	676
Montreal—**Bed & Breakfast à Montréal**	676
Montrealers at Home	676
Quebec—**Bed & Breakfast Bonjour Quebec**	677
Appendix: United States and Canadian Tourist Offices	678
Reservation Request Form	683
Membership Applications	685
We Want to Hear From You	691
Information Order Form	693

Reservation service organizations appear here in boldface type.

Preface

If you have read earlier editions of *Bed & Breakfast U.S.A.*, you know this book has always been a labor of love. It is personally gratifying to see how it has grown from the first 16-page edition, titled *Guide to Tourist Homes and Guest Houses*, which was published in 1975 and contained 40 individual listings. Fourteen years later, the thirteenth revised edition lists 924 homes and 135 reservation agencies, giving travelers access to over 11,000 host homes. This spectacular success indicates how strongly the revived concept of the guest house has recaptured the fancy of both travelers and proprietors.

On the other hand, what was welcomed as a reasonably priced alternative to the plastic ambience of motel chains has, in some instances, lost its unique qualities. Our mailbox is crammed with letters from grand hotels, condominium rental agencies, campground compounds, and chic inns with nightly tariffs topping the $100 mark. All share a common theme—they all serve breakfast and they all want to be listed in *Bed & Breakfast U.S.A.* Who can blame them? Since 1976, over 500,000 people have read this best-selling guide.

We also receive a substantial amount of mail from our readers, and we have tailored our book to meet their needs. We have given a great deal of thought to what we feel a B&B should be and are again focusing on our original definition: an owner-occupied residence with breakfast included at a fair rate, where the visitor is made to feel more like a welcome guest than a paying customer.

Based on personal experience, and comments from our readers, several key problems are apparent in some B&Bs: Waiting your turn to use a bathroom shared with five other guests is unpleasant, especially when you're paying upward of $40 a night. Nor is it enjoyable to pay $90 and up simply for staying in someone's home, no matter how exquisite the decor. Finally, when paying $35 or $40, no one wants to go out to a restaurant for breakfast—no matter how close it may be, it's just not the same as breakfast "at home."

As a result of these problems, we have regretfully deleted several listings that have been on our roster for years. This does not imply, in any way, that these B&Bs aren't nice; it simply means that, *in our opinion*, they do not fit the traditional B&B experience. We've had a goodly share of irate letters from several "old friends" disputing our opinion and pointing out that rising operating expenses must be reflected in their charges. Newcomers to the business decry our stand and tell us of their high costs that must somehow be recouped. While we sympathize and understand fully their positions, we must, in all fairness, be firm.

This is not a project where listings are compiled just for the sake of putting a book together; bigger isn't necessarily better. *Bed & Breakfast U.S.A.* is a product of a membership organization whose credo is "Comfort, Cleanliness, Cordiality, and fairness of Cost." We solicit and rely on the comments of readers. For this purpose, we include a tear-out form on page 691. If we receive negative reports, that member is dropped from our roster. We genuinely appreciate comments from guests . . . negative if necessary, positive when warranted. *We want to hear from you!*

All of the B&Bs described in this book are members of the Tourist House Association of America. THAA dues are $25 annually. We share ideas and experiences by way of our newsletter, and arrange regional seminars and conferences. To order a list of B&Bs that joined after this edition went to press, use the form at the back of this book.

BETTY R. RUNDBACK
Director, Tourist House Association of America
RD 2, Box 355A Greentown, Pennsylvania 18426

January 1989

Acknowledgments

A special thanks to Michael Frome, who saw promise in the first 16-page "Guide" and verbally applauded our growth with each subsequent edition. And many thanks to all the other travel writers and reporters who have brought us to the attention of their audience.

Many hugs to family and friends who lovingly devoted time to the "office" chores: Mike, Peggy and Justin Ackerman, Harry Revits, Harriet Frank, Karen Zane, Travis Kali, Brian Shepard, Joe Fusco, Donna Sweeney, Sherry Judd, Lesley Fagen, Gail Rubenfeld, Judy Tygard, Burt Kearns, and David Peterkin. We are most grateful to Joyce and James McGhee for their artwork.

Our appreciation goes to our editor, Sandy Soule. She exhausted her supply of blue pencils but never her patience.

EASTERN PM

ATLANTIC PM

807 ONTARIO 705 | **819 QUEBEC 418**

Thunder Bay

NEWFOUNDLAND 709

NEW BRUNSWICK 506

906 Escanaba

Quebec

514 Montreal — Sherbrooke

North Bay

715 Eau Claire

WISCONSIN

608 Madison — Milwaukee

414

Rockford

815 Chicago **312**

319

ILLINOIS

Peoria **309**

217 Springfield

Centralia

Louis **618**

URI **314**

MICH. 616 / 517 Lansing **313** Grand Rapids — Detroit

South Bend **219**

Toledo **419**

Indianapolis **317** **IND. 812**

Evansville

Covington

Louisville

KENTUCKY 502

606

Nashville

901 Memphis

TENN. 615

601 MISS.

205 ALA.

904

504 New Orleans

Ottawa **613**

416 Toronto

519 London

Cleveland **216**

513 Columbus **614**

OHIO

Cincinnati

W. VA. 304

207 MAINE

802 VT.

518

NEW YORK

Syracuse **315** Albany

Buffalo **716**

607 Binghamton

814 PA. 717

Altoona **412** Pittsburgh

N.H. 603

617 Boston

MASS. 413 | 508

CONN. 203

R.I. 401

914

Newark **201** Trenton

215 Phila **N.J. 609**

Harrisburg

MD. 301 302

703

Arlington

VIRGINIA 804 Richmond

Raleigh

704 NORTH CAROLINA 919

Charlotte

SOUTH CAROLINA 803

Atlanta **404**

GEORGIA

Savannah **912**

Jacksonville

FLORIDA

Ft Myers **407** Orlando **813**

305 Miami

516

White Plains

Hempstead

New York City (212 or 718)

DEL.

WASH., D.C. 202

NOVA SCOTIA & PRINCE EDWARD ISLAND 902

809
ANGUILLA, ANTIGUA, BAHAMAS, BARBADOS, BEQUIA, BERMUDA, CAYMAN ISLANDS, DOMINICA, DOMINICAN REPUBLIC, JAMAICA, MONTSERRAT, MUSTIQUE, NEVIS, PALM ISLAND, PUERTO RICO, ST. KITTS, ST. LUCIA, ST. VINCENT, TRINIDAD AND TOBAGO,*
UNION ISLAND, VIRGIN ISLANDS

Bed
&
Breakfast
U.S.A.

1

Introduction

Bed and Breakfast is the popular lodging alternative to hotel high rises and motel monotony. B&Bs are either private residences where the owners rent spare bedrooms to travelers, or small, family-operated inns offering a special kind of warm, personal hospitality. Whether large or small, B&Bs will make you feel more like a welcome guest than a paying customer.

The custom of opening one's home to travelers dates back to the earliest days of Colonial America. Hotels and inns were few and far between, and wayfarers relied on the kindness of strangers to provide a bed for the night. Which is why, perhaps, there is hardly a Colonial-era home in the mid-Atlantic states that does not boast: "George Washington Slept Here!"

During the Depression, the tourist home provided an economic advantage to both the traveler and the host. Travelers always drove through the center of town; there were no superhighways to bypass local traffic. A house with a sign in the front yard reading "Tourists" or "Guests" indicated that a traveler could rent a room for the night and have a cup of coffee before leaving in the morning. The usual cost for this arrangement was $2. The money represented needed income for the proprietor as well as the opportunity to chat with an interesting visitor.

In the 1950s, the country guest house became a popular alternative to the costly hotels in resort areas. The host compensated for the lack of hotel amenities, such as private bathrooms, by providing comfortable bedrooms and bountiful breakfasts at a modest price. The visitors enjoyed the home-away-from-home atmosphere; the hosts were pleased to have paying houseguests.

The incredible growth in international travel that has occurred over the past 30 years has provided yet another stimulus. Millions

2 • INTRODUCTION

of Americans now vacation annually in Europe and travelers have become enchanted with the bed and breakfast concept so popular in Britain, Ireland, and other parts of the Continent. In fact, many well-traveled Americans are delighted to learn that we "finally" have B&Bs here. But, as you now know, they were always here . . . just a rose by another name.

Bed and breakfasts are for:

- **Parents of college kids:** Tuition is costly enough without the added expense of "Parents' Weekends." Look for a B&B near campus.
- **Parents traveling with children:** A family living room, play room, or backyard is preferable to the confines of a motel room.
- **"Parents" of pets:** Many proprietors will allow your well-behaved darling to come too. This can cut down on the expense and trauma of kenneling Fido.
- **Business travelers:** Being "on the road" can be lonely and expensive. It's so nice, after a day's work, to return to a home-away-from-home.
- **Women traveling alone:** Friendship and conversation are the natural ingredients of a guest house.
- **Skiers:** Lift prices are lofty, so it helps to save some money on lodging. Many mountain homes include home-cooked meals in your room rate.
- **Students:** A visit with a family is a pleasant alternative to camping or the local "Y."
- **Visitors from abroad:** Cultural exchanges are often enhanced by a host who can speak your language.
- **Carless travelers:** If you plan to leave the auto at home, it's nice to know that many B&Bs are convenient to public transportation. Hosts will often arrange to meet your bus, plane, or train for a nominal fee.
- **Schoolteachers and retired persons:** Exploring out-of-the-way places is fun and will save you money.
- **History buffs:** Many B&Bs are located in areas important to our country's past. A number have the distinction of being listed on the National Register of Historic Places.
- **Sports fans:** Tickets to championship games are expensive. A stay at a B&B helps to defray the cost of attending out-of-town events.
- **Antique collectors:** Many hosts have lovely personal collec-

tions, and nearby towns are filled with undiscovered antique shops.
- **House hunters:** It's a practical way of trying out a neighborhood.
- **Relocating corporate executives:** It's more comfortable to stay in a real home while you look for a permanent residence. Hosts will often give more practical advice than professional realtors.
- **Relatives of hospitalized patients:** Many B&Bs are located near major hospitals. Hosts will offer tea and sympathy when visiting hours are over.
- **Convention and seminar attendees:** Staying at a nearby B&B is less expensive than checking into a hotel.

And everyone else who has had it up to here with plastic motel monotony!

What It Is Like to Be a Guest in a B&B

The B&B descriptions provided in this book will help you choose the places that have the greatest appeal to you. A firsthand insight into local culture awaits you; imagine the advantage of arriving in New York City or San Francisco and having an insider to help you sidestep the tourist traps and direct you to that special restaurant or discount store. Or explore the countryside, where fresh air and home-cooked meals beckon. Your choice is as wide as the U.S.A.

Each bed and breakfast listed offers personal contact, a real advantage in unfamiliar environments. You may not have a phone in your room or a TV on the dresser. You may even have to pad down the hall in robe and slippers to take a shower, but you'll discover little things count:

- In Williamsburg, Virginia, a visitor from Germany opted to stay at a B&B to help improve her conversational English. When the hostess saw that she was having difficulty understanding directions, she personally escorted her on a tour of Old Williamsburg.
- In Pennsylvania, the guests mistakenly arrived a week prior to their stated reservation date and the B&B was full. The hostess made a call to a neighbor who accommodated the couple. (By the way, the neighbor is now a B&B host!)

- In New York City, the guest was an Emmy Award nominee and arrived with his tuxedo in need of pressing. The hostess pressed it; when he claimed his award over nationwide TV, he looked well groomed!

Expect the unexpected, like a pot of coffee brewed upon your arrival or fresh flowers on the nightstand. At the very least, count on our required standard of cleanliness and comfort. Although we haven't personally visited all the places listed, they have all been highly recommended by Chambers of Commerce or former guests. We have either spoken to or corresponded with all the proprietors; they are a friendly group of people who enjoy having visitors. They will do all in their power to make your stay memorable.

Our goal is to enable the traveler to crisscross the country and stay only at B&Bs along the way. To achieve this, your help is vital. Please take a moment to write us of your experiences; we will follow up on every suggestion. Your comments will serve as the yardstick by which we can measure the quality of our accommodations. For your convenience, an evaluation form is included at the back of this book.

Cost of Accommodations

Bed and Breakfast, in the purest sense, is a private home, often referred to as a "homestay," where the owners rent their spare bedrooms to travelers. These are the backbone of this book.

However, American ingenuity has enhanced this simple idea to include more spectacular homes, mansions, small inns, and intimate hotels. With few exceptions, the proprietor is the host and lives on the premises.

There is a distinction between B&B homestays and B&B inns. Inns are generally defined as a business and depend upon revenue from guests to pay expenses. They usually have six or more guest rooms, and may have a restaurant that is open to the public. The tariff at inns is usually higher than at a homestay because the owners must pay the mortgage, running expenses, and staff, whether or not guests come.

Whether plain or fancy, all B&Bs are based on the concept that people are tired of the plastic monotony of motels and are disappointed that even the so-called budget motels can be quite expensive. Travelers crave the personal touch and they sincerely enjoy "visiting" rather than just "staying."

Prices vary accordingly. There are places in this book where lovely lodging may be had for as low as $10 a person a night and others that feature a gourmet breakfast in a canopied bed for $85. Whatever the price, if you see the sign ✪, it means that the B&B has guaranteed its rates through 1989 to holders of this book, so be sure to mention it when you call or write! (If there is a change in ownership, the guarantee may not apply. Please notify us in writing if any host fails to honor the guaranteed rate.)

Accommodations vary in price depending upon the locale and the season. Peak season usually refers to the availability of skiing in winter and water sports in summer; in the Sunbelt states, the winter months are usually the peak season. Some B&Bs require a two-night weekend minimum during peak periods, and three nights on holiday weekends. Off-season rate schedules are usually reduced. Resorts and major cities are generally more expensive than out-of-the-way places. However, B&Bs are always less expensive than hotels and motels of equivalent caliber in the same area. A weekly rate is usually less expensive than a daily rate. Special reductions are sometimes given to families (occupying two rooms) or senior citizens. Whenever reduced rates are available, you will find this noted in the individual listings.

Meals

Breakfast: "Continental" refers to fruit or juice, rolls, and a hot beverage. Many hosts pride themselves on home-baked breads, homemade preserves, plus imported teas and cakes, so their Continental breakfast may be quite deluxe. Several hosts have regular jobs outside the home, so you may have to adjust your schedule to theirs. A "full" breakfast includes fruit, cereal and/or eggs, breakfast meats, breads, and hot beverage. The table is set family-style and is often the highlight of a B&B's hospitality. Either a Continental breakfast or full breakfast is included in the room rate unless otherwise specified.

Other Meals: If listed as "available," you can be assured that the host takes pride in his or her cooking skills. The prices for lunch or dinner are usually reasonable but are not included in the quoted room rate unless clearly specified as "included."

Making Reservations

- Reservations are a MUST or you may risk missing out on the accommodations of your choice. Reserve *early* and confirm with a deposit equal to one night's stay. If you call to inquire about reservations, please remember the difference in time zones. When dialing outside of your area, remember to dial the digit "1" before the area code.
- Many individual B&Bs now accept charge cards. This information is indicated in the listings by the symbols "MC" for Master Card, "AMEX" for American Express, etc. A few have a surcharge for this service, so inquire as to the policy.
- Cash or traveler's checks are the accepted method of paying for your stay. Be sure to inquire whether or not tax is included in the rates quoted so that you will know exactly how much your lodging will cost.
- Rates are based on single or double occupancy of a room as quoted. Expect that an extra person(s) in the room will be charged a small additional fee. Inquire when making your reservation what the charge will be.
- If a listing indicates that children or pets are welcome, it is expected that they will be well behaved. All of our hosts take pride in their homes and it would be unfair to subject them to circumstances where their possessions might be abused or the other houseguests disturbed by an unruly child or animal.
- Please note that many hosts have their own resident pets. If you are allergic or don't care to be around animals, inquire before making a reservation.
- In homes where smoking is permitted, do check to see if it is restricted in any of the rooms. Most hosts object to cigars.
- Where listings indicate that social drinking is permitted, it usually refers to your bringing your own beverages. Most hosts will provide ice; many will allow you to chill mixers in the refrigerator, and others offer complimentary wine and snacks. A few B&B inns have licenses to sell liquor. Any drinking should not be excessive.
- If "Yes" is indicated in the listings for airport/station pickup, it means that the host will meet your plane, bus, or train for a fee.
- Feel free to request brochures and local maps so you can better plan for your visit.

- Do try to fit in with the host's house rules. You are on vacation; he isn't!
- A reservation form is included at the back of this book for your convenience; just tear it out and sent it in to the B&B of your choice.

Cancellations

Cancellation policies vary from one B&B to another, so be sure to read the fine print on the reservation form. Many require a 15-day notice to refund the entire deposit, after which they will refund only if the room is rebooked. When a refund is due, most keep a "processing fee" and return the balance. A few keep the deposit and apply it to a future stay.

While the above may seem harsh, please keep in mind that B&Bs are not hotels, which commonly overbook and where no-show guests can easily be replaced. Your host may have turned down a prospective guest and may have bought special breakfast food in anticipation of your visit and should not be penalized. If you feel you've been unfairly treated in a cancellation situation, please do let us know.

B&B Reservation Services

There are many host families who prefer not to be individually listed in a book, and would rather have their houseguests referred by a coordinating agency. The organizations listed in this book are all members of the Tourist House Association. They all share our standards regarding the suitability of the host home as to cordiality, cleanliness, and comfort.

The majority do a marvelous job of matching host and guest according to age, interests, language, and any special requirements. To get the best match, it is practical to give them as much time as possible to find the host home best tailored to your needs.

Many have prepared descriptive pamphlets describing the homes on their rosters, the areas in which the homes are located, and information regarding special things to see and do. *Send a self-addressed, stamped, business-size envelope to receive a descriptive directory by return mail along with a reservation form for you to complete.* When returning the form, you will be asked to select the home or homes listed in the brochure that most appeal to you. (The homes are usually given a code number for reference.) The required deposit should accompany your reservation. Upon receipt, the coordinator will make the reservation and advise you of the name, address, telephone number, and travel instructions for your host.

A few agencies prepare a descriptive directory and *include* the host's name, address, and telephone number so that you can contact the host and make your arrangements directly. They charge anywhere from $2 to $5 for the directory.

Several agencies are *membership* organizations, charging guests an annual fee ranging from $5 to $25 per person. Their descriptive directories are free to members and a few of them maintain toll-free telephone numbers for reservations.

Most reservation services have a specific geographic focus. The coordinators are experts in the areas they represent. They can often make arrangements for car rentals, theater tickets, and touring suggestions, and offer information in planning a trip best suited to your interests.

Most work on a commission basis with the host, and that fee is included in the room rates quoted in each listing. Some make a surcharge for a one-night stay; others require a two- or three-night minimum stay for holiday periods or special events. Some will accept a credit card for the reservation but the balance due must be paid to the host in cash or traveler's checks.

All of their host homes offer Continental breakfast and some may include a full breakfast.

Many reservation services in the larger cities have, in addition to the traditional B&Bs, a selection of apartments, condominiums, and houses *without hosts in residence.* This may be appealing to those travelers anticipating an extended stay in a particular area.

The statewide services are listed first in the section for each state. City or regionally based organizations are listed first under the heading for that area. For a complete description of their services, look them up under the city and state where they're based.

NOTE: When calling, do so during normal business hours (for that time zone), unless otherwise stated. Collect calls are not accepted.

2
How to Start Your Own B&B

What It's Like to Be a Host

Hosts are people who like the idea of accommodating travelers and sharing their home and the special features of their area with them. They are people who have houses too large for their personal needs and like the idea of supplementing their income by having people visit. For many, it's a marvelous way of meeting rising utility and maintenance costs. For young families, it is a way of buying and keeping that otherwise-too-large house and furnishing it, since many of the furnishings may be tax deductible. Another advantage is that many state and local governments have recognized the service that some host families perform. In browsing through this book you will note that some homes are listed on the National Historic Register. Some state governments allow owners of landmark and historical houses a special tax advantage if they are used for any business purpose. Check with the Historical Preservation Society in your state for details.

If you have bedrooms to spare . . . if you sincerely like having overnight guests . . . if your home is clean and comfortable . . . this is an opportunity to consider. It is a unique business because *you* set the time of the visit and the length of stay. (Guest houses are not boarding homes.) You invite the guests at *your* convenience, and the extras, such as meals, are entirely up to you. You can provide a cup of coffee, complete meals, or just a room and shared bath. Remember that your income may be erratic and should not be depended upon to pay for monthly bills. However, it can afford you some luxuries.

Although the majority of hosts are women, many couples are

finding pleasure in this joint venture. The general profile of a typical host is a friendly, outgoing, flexible person who is proud of his or her home and hometown. The following information and suggestions represent a guideline to consider in deciding whether becoming a B&B host is really for you.

There are no set rules for the location, type, or style of a B&B. Apartments, condos, farmhouses, town houses, beach houses, vacation cottages, houseboats, mansions, as well as the traditional one-family dwelling are all appropriate. The important thing is for the host to be on the premises. The setting may be urban, rural, or suburban; near public transportation or in the hinterlands. Location is only important if you want to have guests every night. Areas where tourism is popular, such as resort areas or major cities, are often busier than out-of-the-way places. However, if a steady stream of visitors is not that important or even desirable, it doesn't matter where you are. People will contact you if your rates are reasonable and if there is something to see and do in your area, or if it is near a major transportation route.

Setting the Rates

Consider carefully four key factors in setting your rates: location, private vs. shared bath, type of breakfast, and your home itself.

Location: If you reside in a traditional resort or well-touristed area, near a major university or medical center, or in an urban hub or gateway city, your rates should be at least 40% lower than those of the area's major motels or hotels. If you live in an out-of-the-way location, your rates must be extremely reasonable. If your area has a "season"—snow sports in winter, water sports in summer—offer off-season rates when these attractions are not available. Reading through this book will help you to see what is the going rate in a situation similar to yours.

The Bath: You are entitled to charge more for a room with private bath. If the occupants of two rooms share one bath, the rate should be less. If more than five people must share one bathroom, you may have complaints, unless your rates are truly inexpensive.

The Breakfast: Figure the approximate cost of your ingredients, plus something for your time. Allow about $1 to $2 for a Continental breakfast; $2 to $3 for a full American breakfast; then *include* it in the rate.

Your Home: Plan on charging a fair and reasonable rate for a typical B&B home, one that is warm and inviting, clean and comfortable. If your home is exceptionally luxurious, with king-size beds, Jacuzzi baths, tennis courts, or hot tubs, you will find guests who are willing to pay a premium. If your home is over 75 years old, well restored, with lots of antiques, you may also be able to charge a higher rate.

The Three B's—Bed, Breakfast, and Bath

The Bedroom: The ideal situation for a prospective host is the possession of a house too large for current needs. The children may be away at college most of the year or may have left permanently, leaving behind their bedrooms and, in some cases, the extra bath. Refurbishing these rooms does not mean refurnishing; an extraordinary investment need not be contemplated for receiving guests. Take a long, hard look at the room. With a little imagination and a little monetary outlay, could it be changed into a bedroom *you'd* be pleased to spend the night in? Check it out *before* you go any further. Are the beds comfortable? Is the carpet clean? Are the walls attractive? Do the curtains or shades need attention? Are there sturdy hangers in the closet? Would emptying the closet and bureau be an impossible task? Is there a good light to read by? A writing table and comfortable chair? A mirror? Peek under the bed and see if there are dust balls or old magazines tucked away. While relatives and friends would "understand" if things weren't perfect, a paying guest is entitled to cleanliness and comfort.

If the idea of sprucing up the room has you overwhelmed, forget the idea and continue to be a guest rather than a host! If, however, a little "spit and polish," replacement of lumpy mattresses, sagging springs, and freshening the room in general presents no problem . . . continue!

Mattresses should be firm, covered with a mattress pad, attractive linens, and bedspread. Although seconds are OK, good quality linens are a wise investment, since cheap sheets tend to

Jackson Street Inn
Janesville, Wisconsin

pill. Offer a selection of pillows of different firmnesses—a choice of down or fiberfill is the ultimate in consideration! Twin beds are often preferred, since many people do not wish to share a bed. Sofa beds are really not comfortable and should be avoided. Is there a bedside lamp and night table on each side of the bed? Bulbs should be 75 watts for comfortable reading. A luggage rack is convenient for guests and keeps the bedspread clean. Provide a varied assortment of books, current magazines in a rack, a local newspaper, and some information on what's doing in your town along with a map. If yours is a shared-bath accommodation, do provide a well-lit mirror and convenient electric outlet for makeup and shaving purposes. It will take the pressure off the bathroom! A fresh thermos of ice water and drinking glasses placed on an attractive dresser tray is always appreciated. Put it in the room while the guest is out to dinner, right next to the dish of hard candy or fruit. A fancy candlestick is a pretty accessory and a useful object in case of a power failure. Dresser drawers should be clean and lined with fresh paper. A sachet, flashlight, and a pad and pencil are thoughtful touches. For safety's sake, prohibit smoking in the bedroom. Besides, the odor of tobacco clings forever. Always spray the bedroom with air freshener a few minutes before the guest arrives. On warm or humid days, turn on the air-conditioner as well.

From time to time sleep in each guest room yourself. It's the best test.

The Breakfast: Breakfast time can be the most pleasant part of the guest's stay. It is at the breakfast table with you and the other guests that suggestions are made as to what to see and do, and exchanges of experiences are enjoyed. From a guest's point of view, the only expected offering is what is known as Continental breakfast, which usually consists of juice, roll, and coffee or tea.

Breakfast fare is entirely up to you. If you are a morning person who whips out of bed at the crack of dawn with special recipes for muffins dancing in your head, to be drenched with your homemade preserves followed by eggs Benedict, an assortment of imported coffee or exotic tea . . . hop to it! You will play to a most appreciative audience. If, however, morning represents an awful intrusion on sleep and the idea of talking to anyone before noon is difficult, the least you should do is to prepare the breakfast table the night before with the necessary mugs, plates, and silverware. Fill the electric coffee pot and leave instructions that the first one up should plug it in; you can even hook it up to a timer, so that it will brew automatically!

Most of us fall somewhere in between these two extremes. Remember that any breakfast at "home" is preferable to getting dressed, getting into the car, and driving to some coffee shop. Whether you decide upon a Continental breakfast or a full Amer-

The Bayberry Inn
Peebles, Ohio

ican breakfast, consisting of juice or fruit, cereal or eggs, possibly bacon or sausage, toast, rolls, coffee, or tea, is up to you. It is most important that whatever the fare, it be included in your room rate. It is awkward, especially after getting to know and like your guests, to present an additional charge for breakfast.

Some Suggestions

- Don't have a messy kitchen. If you have pets, make sure their food dishes are removed after they've eaten. If you have cats, make sure they don't walk along the counter tops, and be certain that litter boxes are cleaned without fail. Sparkling clean surroundings are far more important than the decor.
- Let guests know when breakfast will be served. Check to see if they have any allergies, diet restrictions, or dislikes. Vary the menu if guests are staying more than one night.
- Do offer one nonsweet bread for breakfast.
- Consider leaving a breakfast order sheet in each room with a request that it be returned before guests retire. It might read:

We serve breakfast between 7 AM and 10 AM. Please check your preference and note the time at which you plan to eat.

☐ Coffee ☐ Tea ☐ Milk ☐ Decaf ☐ Toast ☐ Muffins
☐ Sweet Rolls ☐ Orange Juice ☐ Tomato Juice ☐ Fruit Cup

The Bath: This really is the third "B" in "B&B." If you are blessed with an extra bathroom for the exclusive use of a guest, that's super. If guests will have to share the facilities with others, that really presents no problem. If it's being shared with your family, the family must always be "last in line." Be sure that they are aware of the guest's importance; the guest, paying or otherwise, always comes first. No retainers, or used Band-Aids, or topless toothpaste tubes are to be carelessly left on the sink. The tub, shower, floor, and toilet bowl are to be squeaky clean. The mirrors and chrome should sparkle, and a supply of toilet tissue, fresh soap, and unfrayed towels goes a long way in reflecting a high standard of cleanliness. Make sure that the grout between tiles is free of mildew and that the shower curtain is unstained; add nonskid tape to the tub. Cracked ceilings should be repaired, the paint free of chips, and if your bath is wallpapered, make certain no loose edges mar its beauty.

Although it is your responsibility to check out the bath at least twice a day, most guests realize that in a share-the-bath situation they should leave the room ready for the next person's use. It is a thoughtful reminder for you to leave tub cleanser, a cleaning towel or sponge, and bathroom deodorant handy for this purpose. A wastepaper basket, paper towels, and paper cups should be part of your supplies. Needless to say, your hot water and septic systems should be able to accommodate the number of guests you'll have without being overtaxed. Call the plumber to fix any clogged drains or dripping faucets. Make sure that there are enough towel bars and hooks to accommodate the towels. Extra bathroom touches:

- Use liquid soap dispensers in lieu of bar soap on the sink.
- Provide a place for guests' personal toilet articles; shelves add convenience and eliminate clutter.
- Give different colored towels to each guest.
- Supply each guest room with its own bath soap in a covered soap dish.
- Provide guests with one-size-fits-all terry robes.

The B&B Business

Money Matters: Before embarking upon any business, it's a good idea to discuss it with an accountant and possibly an attorney. Since you'll be using your home for a business enterprise there are things with which they are familiar that are important for you to know. For instance, you may want to incorporate, so find out what the pros and cons are. Ask about depreciation. Deductible business expenses may include refurbishing, furnishings, supplies, printing costs, postage, etc. An accountant will be able to guide you with a simple system of record keeping. Accurate records will help you analyze income and expense, and show if you are breaking even or operating at a profit or a loss.

Taxes: Contact your state department of taxation requesting specific written information regarding tax collection and payment schedules. Get a sales tax number from your county clerk. If you rent rooms less than 15 days a year, you need not report the B&B income on your federal return. Income after the fourteenth day is taxable, and you can take deductions and depreciation allowances against it. If the revenues from running the B&B are insignificant, you can call it "hobby income" and avoid taxes. However, you can't qualify as a business and may lose other tax advantages.

Record Keeping: Open a B&B checking account and use it to pay expenses and to deposit all income, including sales tax. Write checks whenever possible for purchases; get dated receipts when you can. Estimate the cost of serving breakfast and multiply it by the number of guests you feed annually; keep track of extra expenses for household supplies and utilities.

The Case for Credit Cards: Many guests prefer to stay now and pay later; business travelers like the easy record keeping for their expense sheets. Even if you don't wish to accept them on a regular basis, credit cards give you the opportunity to take a deposit over the phone when there isn't time to receive one by mail. The cost is negligible, generally 4%.

If you do accept a last-minute reservation without a credit card number to guarantee it, make certain the caller understands that if they don't show up, and you have held the room for them, you will have lost a night's rent. You may also remind them that if they aren't there by a mutually-agreed-upon-time, you may rent the room to someone else. Needless to say, it is equally important for you to remain at home to receive the guests or to be on hand for a phone call should they get lost en route to your home.

Insurance: It is important to call your insurance broker. Many homeowner policies have a clause covering "an occasional overnight paying guest." See if you will be protected under your existing coverage and, if not, what the additional premium would be. As a member of the THAA, you may participate in our group liability policy under the auspices of Brown, Schuck, Townshend, and Associates.

Every home should be equipped with smoke detectors and fire extinguishers. All fire hazards should be eliminated; stairways and halls should be well lit and kept free of clutter. If you haven't already done so, immediately post prominently the emergency numbers for the fire department, police, and ambulance service.

Regulations: If you have read this far and are still excited about the concept of running a B&B, there are several steps to take at this point. As of this writing, there don't seem to be any specific laws governing B&Bs. Since guests are generally received on an irregular basis, B&Bs do not come under the same laws governing hotels and motels. And since B&Bs aren't inns where emphasis is on food rather than on lodging, no comparison can really be made in that regard either. As the idea grows, laws and regulations will probably be passed. Refer to the back of *Bed & Breakfast U.S.A.* and write to your state's office of tourism for information. The address and phone number are listed for your convenience. You might even call or write to a few B&Bs in your state and ask the host about his or her experience in this regard. Most hosts will be happy to give you the benefit of their experience, but keep in mind that they are busy people and it would be wise to limit your intrusion upon their time.

If you live in a traditional, residential area and you are the first in your neighborhood to consider operating a B&B, it would be prudent to examine closely the character of houses nearby. Do physicians, attorneys, accountants, or psychologists maintain offices in their residences? Do dressmakers, photographers, cosmeticians, or architects receive clients in their homes? These professions are legally accepted in the most prestigious communities as "Customary House Occupations." Bed and breakfast has been tested in many communities where the question was actually brought to court. In towns from La Jolla, California, to Croton-on-Hudson, New York, bed and breakfast has been approved and accepted.

Zoning boards are not always aware of the wide acceptance of the B&B concept. Possibly the best evidence that you could present to them is a copy of *Bed & Breakfast U.S.A.*, which indicates that it is an accepted practice throughout the entire country. It illustrates the caliber of the neighborhoods, the beauty of the homes, and the fact that many professionals are also hosts. Reassure the zoning board that you will accept guests only by advance reservation. You will not display any exterior signs to attract attention to your home. You will keep your home and grounds properly maintained, attractive, and in no way detract from the integrity of your neighborhood. You will direct guests to proper parking facilities and do nothing to intrude upon the privacy of your neighbors.

After all, there is little difference between the visit of a family friend and a B&B guest, because that is the spirit and essence of a B&B. Just as a friend would make prior arrangements to be a houseguest, so will a B&B guest make a reservation in advance of arriving. Neither would just "drop in" for an overnight stay. We are happy to share letters from hosts attesting to the high caliber, honesty, and integrity of B&B guests that come as a result of reading about their accommodations in this book. There are over 12,000 B&Bs extending our kind of hospitality throughout the United States and the number is increasing geometrically every day.

You should also bring along a copy of *Bed & Breakfast U.S.A.* when you go to visit the local Chamber of Commerce. Most of them are enthusiastic, because additional visitors mean extra business for local restaurants, shops, theaters, and businesses. This is a good time to inquire what it would cost to join the Chamber of Commerce.

The Name: The naming of your B&B is most important and will take some time and consideration because this is the moment when dreams become reality. It will be used on your brochures, stationery, and bills. (If you decide to incorporate, the corporation needs a name!) It should somehow be descriptive of the atmosphere you wish to convey.

Brochure: Once you have given a name to your house, design a brochure. The best ones include a reservation form and can be mailed to your prospective guests. The brochure should contain the name of your B&B, address, phone number, best time to call, your name, a brief description of your home, its ambience, a brief history of the house if it is old, the number of guest rooms, whether or not baths are shared, the type of breakfast served, rates, required deposit, minimum stay requirement if any, dates when you'll be closed, and your cancellation policy. Although widely used, the phrase "Rates subject to change without notice" should be avoided. Rather, state the specific dates when the rates will be valid. A deposit of one night's stay is acceptable and the promise of a full refund if cancellation is received at least two weeks prior to arrival is typical. If you have reduced rates for a specific length of stay, families, senior citizens, etc., mention it.

If you can converse in a foreign language, say so, because many visitors from abroad seek out B&Bs; it's a marvelous plus to be able to chat in their native tongue. Include your policy regarding children, pets, or smokers, and whether you offer the convenience of a guest refrigerator or barbecue. It is helpful to include directions from a major route and a simple map for finding your home. It's a good idea to include a line or two about yourself and your interests, and do mention what there is to see and do in the area as well as proximity to any major university. A line drawing of your house is a good investment since the picture can be used not only on the brochure but on your stationery, postcards, and greeting cards as well. If you can't have this taken care of locally, write the Tourist House Association. We have a service that can handle it for you.

Take your ideas to a reliable printer for his professional guidance. Don't forget to keep the receipt for the printing bill since this is a business expense.

Confirmation Letter: Upon receipt of a paid reservation, do send out a letter confirming it. You can design a form letter and have it offset by a printer, since the cost of doing so is usually nominal. Include the dates of the stay, number of people expected, the rate including tax, the cancellation policy, as well as explicit directions by car and, if applicable, by public transportation. A simple map reflecting the exact location of your home in relation to major streets and highways is most useful. It is a good idea to ask your guests to call you if they will be traveling and unavailable by phone for the week prior to their expected arrival. You might even want to include any of the house rules regarding smoking, pets, or whatever.

Successful Hosting

The Advantage of Hosting: The nicest part of being a B&B host is that you aren't required to take guests every day of the year. Should there be times when having guests would not be convenient, you can always say you're full and try to arrange an alternate date. But most important, keep whatever date you reserve. It is an excellent idea at the time reservations are accepted to ask for the name and telephone number of an emergency contact should you have to cancel unexpectedly. However, *never* have a guest come to a locked door. If an emergency arises and you cannot reach your prospective guests in time, do make arrangements for someone to greet them and make alternate arrangements so they can be accommodated.

House Rules: While you're in the "thinking stage," give some thought to the rules you'd like your guests to adhere to. The last thing you want for you or your family is to feel uncomfortable in your own home. Make a list of House Rules concerning arrival and departure during the guests' stay and specify when breakfast is served. If you don't want guests coming home too late, say so. Most hosts like to lock up at a certain hour at night, so arrange for an extra key for night owls. If that makes you uncomfortable, have a curfew on your House Rules list. If smoking disturbs you, confine the area where it's permitted.

Some guests bring a bottle of their favorite beverage and enjoy a drink before going out to dinner. Many hosts enjoy a cocktail hour too, and often provide cheese and crackers to share with the guests. B&Bs cannot sell drinks to guests since this would require licensing. If you'd rather no drinks be consumed in your home, say so.

Many hosts don't mind accommodating a well-behaved pet. If you don't mind or have pets of your own, discuss this with your guests before they pack Fido's suitcase. Your House Rules can even be included in your brochure. That way both the host and the guest are aware of each other's likes and dislikes, and no hard feelings are made.

Entertaining: One of the most appealing features of being a guest at a B&B is the opportunity of being able to visit in the evening with the hosts. After a day of sightseeing or business, it is most relaxing and pleasant to sit around the living room and chat. For many hosts, this is the most enjoyable part of having guests. However, if you are accommodating several people on a daily basis, entertaining can be tiring. Don't feel you'll be offending anyone by excusing yourself to attend to your own family or personal needs. The situation can be easily handled by having a room where you can retreat and offering your guests the living room, den, or other area for games, books, magazines, and perhaps the use of a television or bridge table. Most guests enjoy just talking to each other since this is the main idea of staying at a B&B.

The Telephone: This is a most important link between you and your prospective guests. As soon as possible, have your telephone number included under your B&B name in the White Pages. It is a good idea to be listed in the appropriate section in your telephone directory yellow pages. If your home phone is used for a lot of personal calls, ask the local telephone company about call-waiting service, or think about installing a separate line for your B&B. If you are out a lot, give some thought to using a telephone answering device to explain your absence and time of return, and record the caller's message. There is nothing more frustrating to a prospective guest than to call and get a constant busy signal or no answer at all. Request that the caller leave his name and address, "at the sound of the beep," so you can mail a reservation form. This will help eliminate the necessity of having to return long-distance calls. If the caller wants further information, he will call again at the time you said you'd be home.

B&B guests don't expect a phone in the guest room. However, there are times when they might want to use your phone for a long-distance call. In your House Rules list, suggest that any such calls be charged to their home telephone. Business travelers often have telephone charge cards for this purpose. In either case, you should keep a telephone record book and timer near your instrument. Ask the caller to enter the city called, telephone number, and length of call. Thus, you will have an accurate record should a charge be inadvertently added to your bill. Or, if you wish, you can add telephone charges to the guest bill. The telephone operator will quote the cost of the per-minute charge throughout the country for this purpose.

Maid Service: If you have several guest rooms and bathrooms, you may find yourself being a chambermaid as part of the business. Naturally, each guest gets fresh linens upon arrival. If a guest stays up to three days, it isn't expected that bed linen be changed every day. What is expected is that the room be freshened and the bath be cleaned and towels replaced every day. If you don't employ a full-time maid you may want to investigate the possibility of hiring a high school student on a part-time basis to give you a hand with the housekeeping. Many guests, noticing the absence of help, will voluntarily lend a hand, although they have the right to expect some degree of service, particularly if they are paying a premium rate.

Keys: A great many hosts are not constantly home during the day. Some do "hosting" on a part-time basis, while involved with regular jobs. There are times when even full-time hosts have to be away during the day. If the guests are to have access to the house while you are not on the premises, make extra keys and attach them to an oversize key chain. It is also wise to take a key deposit of $50 simply to assure return of the key. Let me add that in the 11 years of my personal experience, as well as in the opinions of other hosts, B&B guests are the most honest people you can have. No one has ever had even a washcloth stolen, let alone the family treasures. In fact, it isn't unusual for the guest to leave a small gift after a particularly pleasant visit. On the other hand, guests are sometimes forgetful and leave belongings behind. For this reason it is important for you to have their names and addresses so you can return their possessions. They will expect to reimburse you for the postage.

Registering Guests: You should keep a regular registration ledger for the guest to complete before checking in. The information should include the full name of each guest, home address, phone number, business address and telephone, and auto license number. It's a good idea to include the name and phone number of a friend or relative in case of an emergency. This information will serve you well for other contingencies, such as the guest leaving some important article behind, or an unpaid long-distance phone call, or the rare instance of an unpaid bill. You may prefer to have this information on your guest bill, which should be designed as a two-part carbon form. You will then have a record and the guest has a ready receipt. (Receipts are very important to business travelers!)

Settling the Bill: The average stay in a B&B is two nights. Since a deposit equal to one night's lodging is the norm, when to collect the balance is up to you. Most guests pay upon leaving, but if they leave so early that the settling of the bill at that time is inconvenient, you can request the payment the previous night. You might want to consider the convenience of accepting a major credit card, but contact the sponsoring company first to see what percentage of your gross is expected for this service. If you find yourself entertaining more business visitors than vacationers, it might be something you should offer. Most travelers are aware that cash or traveler's checks are the accepted modes of payment. Accepting a personal check is rarely risky, but again, it's up to you. You might include your preference in your brochure.

Other Meals: B&B means that only breakfast is served. If you enjoy cooking and would like to offer other meals for a fee, make sure that you investigate the applicable health laws. If you have to install a commercial kitchen, the idea might be too expensive for current consideration. However, allowing guests to store fixings for a quick snack or to use your barbecue can be a very attractive feature for families traveling with children or for people watching their budget. If you can offer this convenience, be sure to mention it in your brochure. (And be sure to add a line to your House Rules that the guest is expected to clean up.) Some hosts keep an extra guest refrigerator on hand for this purpose.

It's an excellent idea to keep menus from your local restaurants on hand. Try to have a good sampling, ranging from moderately priced to expensive dining spots, and find out if reservations are required. Your guests will always rely heavily upon your advice and suggestions. After all, when it comes to your town, you're the authority! It's also a nice idea to keep informed of local happenings that might be of interest to your visitors. A special concert at the university or a local fair or church supper can add an extra dimension to their visit. If parents are visiting with young children they might want to have dinner out without them; try to have a list of available baby-sitters. A selection of guide books covering your area is also a nice feature.

The Guest Book: These are available in most stationery and department stores, and it is important that you buy one. It should contain designated space for the date, the name of the guest, home address, and a blank area for the guest's comments. They generally sign the guest book before checking out. The guest book is first of all a permanent record of who came and went. It will give you an idea of what times during the year you were busiest and which times were slow. Second, it is an easy way to keep a mailing list for your Christmas cards and future promotional mailings. You will also find that thumbing through it in years to come will recall some very pleasant people who were once strangers but now are friends.

Advertising: Periodically distribute your brochures to the local university, college, and hospital, since out-of-town visitors always need a place to stay. Let your local caterers know of your existence since wedding guests are often from out of town. If you have a major corporation in your area, drop off a brochure at the personnel office. Even visiting or relocating executives and salesmen enjoy B&Bs. Hotels and motels are sometimes overbooked; it wouldn't hurt to leave your brochure with the manager for times when there's no room for their last-minute guests. Local residents sometimes have to put up extra guests, so it's a good idea to take an ad out in your local school or church newspaper. The cost is usually minimal. Repeat this distribution process from time to time, so that you can replenish the supply of brochures.

Check the back of this book for the address of your state tourist office. Write to them, requesting inclusion in any brochures listing B&Bs in the state.

The best advertising is being a member of the Tourist House Association since all member B&Bs are fully described in this book, which is available in bookstores, libraries, and B&Bs throughout the U.S. and Canada. In addition, it is natural for THAA members to recommend each other when guests inquire about similar accommodations in other areas. The most important reason for keeping your B&B clean, comfortable, and cordial is that we are all judged by what a guest experiences in any individual Tourist House Association home. The best publicity will come from your satisfied guests who will recommend your B&B to their friends.

Additional Suggestions

Extra Earnings: You might want to consider a few ideas for earning extra money in connection with being a host. If guests consistently praise your muffins and preserves, you might sell attractively wrapped extras as take-home gifts. If you enjoy touring, you can plan and conduct a special outing, off the beaten tourist track, for a modest fee. In major cities, you can do such things as acquiring tickets for theater, concert, or sports events. A supply of *Bed & Breakfast U.S.A.* for sale to guests is both a source of income and gives every THAA member direct exposure to the B&B market. Think about offering the use of your washer and dryer. You may, if you wish, charge a modest fee to cover the service. Guests who have been traveling are thrilled to do their wash or have it done for them "at home" rather than wasting a couple of hours at the laundromat.

Several hosts tell me that a small gift shop is often a natural offshoot of a B&B. Items for sale could include handmade quilts, pillows, potholders, and knitted items. One host has turned his hobby of woodworking into extra income. He makes lovely picture frames, napkin rings, and footstools that many guests buy as souvenirs to take home. If you plan to do this, check with the Small Business Administration to inquire about such things as a resale license and tax collection; the Chamber of Commerce can advise in this regard.

Transportation: While the majority of B&B guests arrive by car, there are many who rely on public transportation. Some hosts, for a modest fee, are willing to meet arriving guests at airports, train depots, or bus stations. Do be knowledgeable about local transportation schedules in your area and be prepared to give explicit directions for your visitors' comings and goings. Have phone numbers handy for taxi service, as well as information on car rentals.

Thoughtful Touches: Guests often write to tell us of their experiences at B&Bs as a result of learning about them through this book. These are some of the special touches that made their visit special: fresh flowers in the guest room; even a single flower in a bud vase is pretty. One hostess puts a foil-wrapped piece of candy on the pillow before the guest returns from dinner. A small decanter of wine and glasses, or a few pieces of fresh fruit in a pretty bowl on the dresser are lovely surprises. A small sewing kit in the bureau is handy. Offer guests the use of your iron and ironing board, rather than having them attempt to use the bed or dresser. Writing paper and envelopes in the desk invite the guest to send a quick note to the folks at home. If your house sketch is printed on it, it is marvelous free publicity. A pre-bed cup of tea for adults and cookies and milk for children are always appreciated.

By the way, keep a supply of guest-comment cards in the desk, both to attract compliments as well as to bring your attention to the flaws in your B&B that should be corrected.

Join the Tourist House Association: If you are convinced that you want to be a host, and have thoroughly discussed the pros and cons with your family and advisers, complete and return the membership application found at the back of this book. Our dues are $20 annually. The description of your B&B will be part of the next issue of the book *Bed & Breakfast U.S.A.*, as well as in the interim supplement between printings. Paid-up members receive a complimentary copy of *Bed & Breakfast U.S.A.* You will also receive the THAA's newsletter; regional seminars and conferences are held occasionally and you might enjoy attending. And, as an association, we will have clout should the time come when B&B becomes a recognized industry.

Affiliating with a B&B Reservation Agency: Over 145 agencies are listed in *Bed & Breakfast U.S.A.* If you do not care to advertise your house directly to the public, consider joining one in your area. Membership and reservation fees, as well as the degree of professionalism, vary widely from agency to agency, so do check carefully.

Prediction for Success: Success should not be equated with money alone. If you thoroughly enjoy people, are well organized, enjoy sharing your tidy home without exhausting yourself, then the idea of receiving compensation for the use of an otherwise dormant bedroom will be a big plus. Your visitors will seek relaxing, wholesome surroundings and unpretentious hosts who open their hearts as well as their homes. Being a B&B host or guest is an exciting, enriching experience.

3

How to Start Your Own B&B Reservation Service Organization

by Megan Backer

About Megan: In 1980 Megan Backer founded *Megan's Friends*, the first and only private membership B&B/Reservation Service Organization in San Luis Obispo County, California. She devised simple and economical methods to operate the service as an informal part-time home hobby-business. Now, *Megan's Friends* has new owners and Megan is a B&B consultant, speaker, and fiction writer. Our thanks to her for contributing this chapter.

What's an RSO?

A Bed & Breakfast *Reservation Service Organization* (B&B/RSO) represents a group of B&B home owners or renters who have listed their lodgings with an RSO. The RSO owner (or manager or director or coordinator) arranges guest bookings in host homes. The RSO owner is in personal contact by telephone and/or letter with both guest and host. The guest does not arrange his own booking, but selects a home from the RSO's list, either weeks in advance by letter or, more typically, during a telephone consultation with the owner several days to two weeks before his expected arrival.

Note: Read Chapter 2, *How to Start Your Own B&B*, again. You and your hosts need this information.

A Reservation Service Organization is just that. It is different from a B&B directory that is compiled, sold for a fee, and contains listings of B&B homes, owners' names, addresses, telephone numbers, and sometimes prices. If guests use this method of securing B&B reservations, they telephone hosts directly and arrange their own reservations. The homes on such a list may or may not be inspected by the compiler. A true RSO not only arranges bookings for the guests after detailed consultation, but promises dependable quality of accommodations and hospitality of hosts. Some RSOs charge a fee for their directory to help cover expenses; this amount should then be applied as a credit when reservations are made.

A local concentration of homes seems to be the best guarantee of individual, caring B&B service. The ideal number of homes for an RSO varies according to both the owner's and the hosts' available time, and the volume of guests. Generally, 10 to 25 homes usually permit the owner to maintain control of standards and know every host and home.

If the B&B/RSO grows too large, personal attention to each guest's needs may give way to automated efficiency. A small, well-organized RSO may net as much income for the time invested as a vast empire of homes in faraway places, without the grueling hours, paid employees, and competition with motels.

Here is a typical RSO structure. (*Megan's Friends* differs in some respects, which will be noted parenthetically.)

1. Hosts pay a listing fee to their RSO; typically $50 to $75. (*Megan's Friends* had no host listing fee.)
2. The RSO retains 20% commission for each night's guest stay.
3. The RSO often requires a two-night minimum stay (*Megan's Friends* accepted one-night stays.) The desirability of this requirement depends on your location. Is it a "pass-through" area or does it have attractions that detain travelers? An efficiently organized RSO can make money on one-night stays and often gains valuable goodwill and business otherwise lost.
4. The RSO provides hosts with screened guests, publicity, and bookkeeping assistance.
5. The RSO offers guests ease of booking, centralized information, and assurance of inspected homes.

The RSO owner maintains two relationships: one with hosts, and the other with guests. Trust is an integral part of the business. Once lost, it is hard to rebuild. Nothing is more to be prized than the confidence of your hosts and guests.

Is It for You?

Several personal qualities are essential to a successful RSO owner: management and organizational skills, the ability to get along with a diverse group of people, and tact.

You will be the *manager* of a group of hosts and their homes. As such, your responsibilities are different from and greater than those of an individual host.

You advise prospective guests and help them make appropriate selections. Often you do this during a long-distance telephone call lasting five to ten minutes. You are responsible for quality control, complaints, compliments, and everything else you, the hosts, and the guests can think of; you must handle it using all the good taste and tact you can muster.

Do you have organizational ability? Do you have experience in working with people? Do you have, or can you obtain, helpful community contacts that will bring you hosts and guests? (For instance, a Chamber of Commerce membership, participation in your PTA, church, local sports.) Can you develop your own PR, becoming known locally through friendly community contacts, such as schools, banks, supermarkets, other businesses, and nationally, through letters and telephone calls to other B&B and RSO owners?

A useful background for a B&B/RSO owner could include interviewing skills (have you been a receptionist? teacher? survey-taker? counselor?), a friendly, trust-inspiring telephone voice, and good recordkeeping ability (do you balance the family checkbook, make appointments, write letters?) Success will come easily if you are efficient and have friendly good manners and enthusiasm for B&B.

Does It Make Sense in Your Area?

Educate yourself about the local attitudes toward B&Bs generally and about your proposed B&B/RSO specifically. Follow the usual sensible guideline for any beginning small business: be discreet. You do not want possible competitors to become established first; you do not want to instigate a rash of unnecessary restrictive local rulings; you do not want to alarm anyone's neighbors.

If you decide that local attitudes are benign and informed—or at least neutral—proceed to the next step. Does the volume of tourists and other travelers through or to your area warrant a B&B/RSO? Your Chamber of Commerce has these figures. Look at its brochures. What are the area attractions and how many visitors do they have? Are the motel/hotel rooms in your area fully booked? Is your area growing or declining in number of residents and tourists? Are other B&Bs already operating? Busy? Why? Why not? Is there a need for an RSO?

There are no formula numbers to answer these questions. Every location is unique. You must make a decision based on your own judgment and acquired knowledge, or consult an expert. (If you talk with a local business person, bank president, or Chamber of Commerce officer, be sure your discussion is confidential. Everyone is eager to tell a friend about a good new business idea.)

Getting Started

This list of needs is for present and future reference. Some items can wait until you've been in business for a few months. Save money and time until you know that your new B&B/RSO will succeed. Needs depending on your specific situation:

1. Equipment: Telephone with call-waiting and call-forwarding, or two telephone lines. Answering machine (with a friendly, informative message). Two ledgers.
2. Descriptive listing of B&Bs, guest and host applications, maps, and directions to host homes.
3. Business cards.
4. A rubber stamp with your business name, address, telephone.
5. Chamber of Commerce membership. One major, active, tourist-oriented group.
6. Business license. City, county, as applicable. Required.
7. Bank account under business name.
8. Membership in a *few* large B&B organizations for referrals. (First choice is the Tourist Home Association of America,

Box 355A, RD 2, Greentown, Pennsylvania 18426. See page 685 for an application.)
9. Letters of introduction to other B&Bs enclosing your brochure and business card. (For example, write to selected B&B owners from this book.) Mail only to those who are apt to send referrals to you.
10. Fictitious business name statement. Required by the state for any business name that does not include the owner's surname. You must file this statement with your county clerk's office, and publish it for four consecutive weeks in a local newspaper. If your name is Kathy Jones and you decide to call your RSO "Seaside B&B," you'll need to file a statement. If you prefer to call it "Jones B&B," the name is not "fictitious" and no statement is needed.
11. Service mark, logo. Register with state. Optional, for protection of your name and logo.

Start very simply by signing up a few local homes (probably friends of yours) on your host application forms. Make yourself known at the local tourist centers and have a minimum order of business cards made.

Alone or with a Partner: A B&B/RSO is ideally operated by a couple who live on the premises—a mom-&-pop business. There is better telephone coverage and relief time for the partner who is not on duty. However, successful RSOs exist with one owner, or with two partners who do not live together. It can be difficult to find a compatible partner, and you may not want to halve your profits.

Start-up Expenses: Some RSOs have spent $10,000 on initial equipment, office rent, advertising, brochures, and so on. My own RSO started five years ago with $10! A reasonable sum might be $200 if you have the basic equipment already mentioned, and plan to work in your home.

Finances

Try out tax preparers—preferably an accountant—until you find one who is careful, honest, and knowledgeable. An accountant's advice and work for you will more than cover the (deductible) fee. He or she will know all of the tax deductions that apply to your part-time home business and can show you how to keep simple records during the year.

Open a special B&B bank account in your business name. There is usually no charge for this, although the bank may ask to see your fictitious business name statement. It is very convenient to have a rubber stamp made by the bank with your business name and account number on it for use in endorsing your numerous guests' checks for deposit.

Keep your income-expense ledger up-to-date daily to maintain an accurate record of payments and commissions. Sometimes your hosts or guests will challenge you about payments made; you cannot afford to be slipshod. Keep a record of all checks received (name, number, bank, date, amount) and sent as well as cash payments.

Establish a deposit-and-refund policy for guests and stick to it. Always quote your listed prices. Some guests will try to cut the price by requesting bed without breakfast or other options. Unless you have a resort situation in which guests typically stay a week or more, keep the price the same for each night. On request, quote special prices for group reservations, such as wedding parties, which are negotiated individually in advance with the host(s) involved.

Credit card use is optional. It increases your costs 2% to 5% and requires more record keeping. In my area, a famous large inn does not accept credit cards, but many businesses do. You may decide it is worthwhile to accept credit cards as a way of guaranteeing telephone reservations or for payment in full.

Legalities

Insurance coverage is still generally unregulated, and you will need to investigate your own state's rules. It is advisable to consult a lawyer to be sure you have correct wording on your host and guest forms that places liability responsibility on them, as you are only a booking agency. Setting up as a "private membership" organization may give you some legal protection, as you are then not in the business of serving the general public. (You must collect membership fees and retain signed member applications in your files.)

B&B regulations still vary widely, and government officials may not even be familiar with the term *B&B*. If yours is such a community, organize your RSO as simply, carefully, and legally as you can and wait for your local government to become informed. When the time comes, you may need to supply them with helpful information, so start collecting precedents and examples of how B&B is done elsewhere. For example: a large, well-known B&B/RSO successfully won a court case rescinding the collection of bed tax from B&B homes in that state.

Zoning requirements may apply to your B&B homes. You need to check local rules. This still seems to be a "point of view" question. There may be some B&B homes operating in local areas that are prohibited to you, but continue because they are listed with out-of-town RSOs and locations are unknown to local officials.

Check out your health department rules regarding the serving of food and drink. For example, serving liquor may require a special license. Let your hosts know this. It is best to avoid potential problems!

Host Relationships

Your hosts become your friends, since you talk with them often. Take a genuine interest in them. Treasure and appreciate them, for you are exchanging trust, confidence, and loyalty. Value your business relationship, but respect your friendship, too.

Signing Up Hosts: To get your first hosts, if you do not already have eager friends, do some local PR work. *Talk* about B&B and your new RSO *everywhere* to *everybody*. This is "word-of-mouth" awareness. Also, try to be interviewed (phone the newspaper's "new business" editor) for an article favorable to you, B&B, and B&B/RSO. Publicize your RSO by speaking about B&B to local groups who are always looking for new speakers and new topics. Visit the senior citizens' center, libraries, banks, churches, schools, stores, offices—leave your business card and your smile everywhere you go.

Avoid placing newspaper ads for hosts. You will find that you get many replies from unsuitable hosts with substandard homes. This will waste your time and test your tact in saying no gracefully.

Exclusive Listings: Exclusive listings are those homes that accept paying guests only through one RSO. If you opt for exclusive listings (some or all), try to keep them local. It's hard to know whether a less-used host of yours is "filling in the chinks" by accepting outside reservations. List, describe, and price your exclusive listings. List nonexclusives and referrals only by the name of their city.

Exclusive listings are a boon to you, for you have absolute knowledge of availability and can often complete a reservation on the first call. You use your exclusives more often; you know them well and you can count on the hosts' willingness, interest, and hospitality. Guests tend to choose homes that are described and priced, so will favor your exclusives. An RSO without some dependable exclusives obviously incurs more expense and frustration.

Sometimes B&B hosts are unhappy with their RSOs. They have told me that some RSOs are inconsiderate, inefficient, dishonest, send very few guests, require host fees, share no deposit money on cancellations, and so on! These hosts often ask to be added to your listings. Emphasize the need for new hosts to inform their former agencies if they have signed an exclusive agreement with you.

The Ideal Host: The ideal hosts are generally middle-aged or retired, well-educated world travelers. They enjoy having houseguests and consider the money a bonus, not a necessity. They are usually available and flexible, so they naturally earn more money than those who often travel, or have headaches or other reasons for not taking guests. A host's popularity with guests will be enhanced by reasonable prices, fine beds, private baths, excellent breakfasts, and unflagging hospitality.

When you interview a prospective host, be direct and clear about your rules. *This* is the time to test the bed, check the bath and general housekeeping, and be assertive in speaking up about anything that does not meet your standards. Give second chances if there is an outstanding plus in the listing, such as an ocean view, scrumptious food, or charming hosts, but be sure the dirty windows are clean and the spiders are gone on your second visit. Reinspect host homes occasionally, with only a same-day telephone appointment with the host. The host whose room and bath are always ready is a habitual good housekeeper. Encourage it.

Host Instructions: When you enroll a new host, provide a list of requirements and suggestions similar to the following:

Memo to All Host Families

Required: Freshly laundered sheets (change every third day or with each new guest) and towels (change daily). Spotless room and bath. No personal items of yours in sight. Each guest room needs: a nightstand, a lamp to turn on from bed, two pillows and a wastepaper basket. Bed must be standard size (no hideabed, trundle, etc., for primary accommodation), firm, and used less than five years. Please, no used soaps, spiders, or other bugs! No pets are permitted in the guest room.

For breakfast: juice or fruit, protein (perhaps eggs), starch (perhaps a sweet bread), and a beverage. (Examples: pancakes, combining starch and protein, ham and eggs, or simply cold breakfasts. This is your choice.)

Suggested: Make up room same day guest departs; always be prepared for new guest, except for dusting, fresh flowers, and airing.

Stock freezer with staples such as breads, rolls, waffles, juices, instant coffee, ice cubes, etc. Stock a cold cereal and a hot cereal, fresh milk or half and half, tea, etc.

You may put a card with a typed list of your rules in each guest room. (Example: 8–9 AM breakfast, please close shower door when showering.) Some hosts think this is too intimidating and use no list. You need only be available for one hour in the morning to serve and talk with your guests. If you wish, volunteer help-yourself breakfast before or after the hour, or prepare a cold breakfast tray. Don't rattle around in the kitchen or house earlier than one hour prior to arranged breakfast time! Your guest's sleep WILL be disturbed.

Keep a calendar near phone for reservations. Mark unconfirmed reservations with a question. Always treat your guests as you would expect to be treated in a B&B home.

Note: Shy guests will appreciate being told which areas of your home and garden they may use.

Call your RSO when you have a problem, and remember that everyone makes mistakes!

Undesirable Hosts: How can you turn away unwanted hosts tactfully? There is always a telephone conversation prior to home inspection. If you determine over the telephone that this home is not suitable—for example, it has a shared bath or old bed or grumpy host—you can graciously explain why the house does not meet the requirements of your RSO, but, "thank you very much for calling."

On the other hand, if the house sounds desirable, say that although you have no immediate need for another home, the situation may unexpectedly change, so you would like to come to see the home and meet the hosts.

Once there, if you want to list it, do so! Explain your system, especially the seniority preference you give to hosts who have been with you longer, if there are two similar homes available.

If you do not want the home, give praise anyway and repeat that there is no immediate need, but that you will call if the situation changes. (Of course, you never call.)

Rates: How do you arrive at the right price for a B&B rental? One helpful guideline is this: ask the prospective host—and yourself—how much you really would be willing to pay for a similar accommodation in someone's home when traveling. Also, how much are similar B&B homes in the area renting for? How busy are they? (Many overpriced B&B inns are now up for sale.) New hosts need to familiarize themselves with local prices and amenities offered by B&B homes, B&B inns, motels, and hotels. What can the prospective host offer? Color TV in the room? Private bath? King-size bed? Full or Continental breakfast? Children free? Swimming pool? Nearby restaurant?

Negotiating a fair price with your host is a delicate matter. It is up to you to understand human nature, to encourage hosts to comparison-shop fairly (not quote the price of the fanciest motel in town!), and to hold the line on prices. With a few hosts, greed eventually corrupts original intent.

Of course you should be fair to your hosts and list their rooms at the best price possible. With the standard commission, for every dollar your hosts earn, you receive 20 cents. If the price becomes too high, you will have a much harder job of "selling" the room, followed by complaints from your host that you aren't sending as many guests anymore!

RSO/Host Agreement: Sometimes a host will become a problem to you. Perhaps housekeeping or cooking inadequacies develop, or perhaps the host turns out to be either overbearing or indifferent, or perhaps the host inspects the guests' belongings during their absence from the home. Whatever the fatal flaw, you need to be aware of it and decide whether to keep the hosts and educate them or, if the problems—or hosts!—are intractable, to stop sending guests.

An RSO/host agreement clarifies your relationship. Here is one I devised, which is brief enough not to annoy new hosts, yet informative and protective to the RSO.

Host Application

This is a private membership B&B/RSO group. I will not accept paying guests from other sources. I will not refuse guests solely on the basis of color, creed, or marital status. I understand that (RSO name), its agents and employees, do not warrant the suitability of guests or vouch for their conduct. Accordingly, I hereby release and hold harmless (RSO name) from all liability arising out of my participation as a host member. I certify that I have homeowner's or renter's liability insurance covering my paying guests and I am responsible for obtaining and paying for any license, bed tax, etc. required by any government agency. For services, I will pay 20% of my rental fees, due weekly, to (RSO name).

SIGNATURE _____ DATE _____
ADDRESS _____
TELEPHONE _____
Price for one ____ Bed size ____ Price for two ____ Bed size ____
three ____ ____ four ____ ____

Specify your limitations, such as no children under a certain age, nights not available on a regular basis, etc.

List special features such as a wheelchair ramp. Resident dog or cat? Special treat always ready, such as fresh room flowers, new magazines, books, local tourist brochures? Tea?

Describe your home and yourself for listing guideline, mentioning features such as nearby attractions, garden, Jacuzzi, ocean view, beach, room features such as balcony, TV, breakfast specialties, areas of home that your guests may use, your occupation, hobbies, interests (tour guide, cooking, local flora and fauna, history, business, shopping, recreation).

Concise road directions to your home from major highway.

This agreement may be terminated in writing and with good cause with 30 days' notice by host or by (RSO name).

Host Finances

Advise your hosts (verbally and in writing) that it is wise to accept only cash or traveler's checks from the guests. If the host allows guests to write personal checks, they are to be made out to the host, not to the RSO. You do not need to take the (small) risk of a bad check from someone you haven't met. Also, tell your hosts to have change for $50 or $100; some guests do not have small bills. Guests usually pay cash at the host home or send personal checks in advance to the RSO.

If time has not allowed for any advance deposit, and you do not interview the guests at your office before their arrival at your host's home, the host may ask for payment on arrival. (My RSO policy was to ask for an advance deposit of 20% only, the balance being due on arrival. This greatly simplified bookkeeping and saved time.) Payment on arrival rather than at departure ensures a relaxed host. One "skip" and a host becomes sufficiently assertive and creative in getting payment promptly and pleasantly. Unless prepaid, guest payment is the host's responsibility.

Pay your hosts regularly. My RSO checks were sent every Monday and hosts agreed to send commissions due to the RSO every Monday. Most RSOs pay monthly or even bimonthly. Let your hosts know what to expect.

"Delayed payments" were the most frequent complaint I heard from hosts listed with other agencies, followed by resentment of the RSO owners' callous attitude or even neglect to notify the host when a guest cancelled. B&Bs have far fewer "no shows" than commercial travel agencies, but it does happen. If a deposit has been made but the guest does not materialize, it was my policy to split the amount equally with the host, to provide us both some compensation for our preparations. If no deposit had been made, we were both out of luck. So far as I know, sharing a forfeited deposit was unique with my RSO.

A price break I always gave was to forfeit my commission when my own hosts traveled and booked my RSO homes.

These generosities will be appreciated by your hosts. Fairness and concern for them results in their loyalty and best efforts for you. Don't take advantage of their good nature and let them do work that is really your responsibility as RSO owner. If you are consistently open and honest, and frankly admit your mistakes, you will maintain comfortable, cooperative relations with your hosts, guests, and other B&Bs.

Organizing Your Information

Simplicity and uniformity are the keys to good organization. Physically, your work area needs a typewriter, telephone, answering machine, pens and pencils, paper, your ledgers, and a file cabinet with suspended hanging files headed "Guest Applications," "Host Applications," "Brochures," "Maps," "PR," "Correspondence with guests, with RSO, with hosts," etc. (You can start with a cardboard box and manila folders before investing in a file cabinet.)

After using individual host calendars, then recipe card files for two years, I devised a ledger system. At a glance, all the needed information about guests and hosts is available on an opened "double" page. Buy two inexpensive hard-bound simple ledgers (the other is for your expenses). Make your own headings, rule vertical lines as indicated. Here are examples:

LEDGER FOR BOOKINGS—COMMISSIONS

Month	Reserved Date	1st Call	Host Name	Guest Name & Phone	Address	Occupation	Referred By	Advance Deposit
Jan 1								
2								
3								
4								

If you have a small RSO, at bottom of each page list your regular host names and dates not available.

Smith 1, 4
Allen
Jones 1
Brown 2, 4

Donovan
Baker 1, 2, 4
etc.

LEDGER FOR EXPENSES

Date	Item	Paid Out	Travel, Entertainment	Outside Labor	Telephone	Office Supplies, Postage	Advertising
Jan 1							
2							
3							
4							

HOW TO START YOUR OWN B&B RESERVATION SERVICE • 41

Host Nets	RSO Owes Host	RSO Commission	Total Fee	Application	List	Membership	Map	ETA

(ETA = estimated time of arrival. Check off the last four items after mailing them. Or write "H" if the host supplies on arrival.)

Automobile	Legal, Professional Fees	Taxes, Licenses	Equipment, Repairs	Referral Fees Paid Out	Dues, Publications

RSO/Guests Relationships

When guests call an RSO, they expect to be given a choice of suitable homes with detailed information about each so that they can comparison-shop, then make a selection over the telephone. If they are planning an extensive trip and have confidence in you, they will also make reservations for distant homes of yours or for your referral homes. Occasionally, guests will ask *you* to make the lodging selections for them.

Quote the same price for every guest reserving the same lodging. This evidences your reliability and fairness. Do not dicker or haggle, or agree to add on charges when cooperating with another B&B on a reservation. Be honest and friendly, but be firm about your listed prices.

If potential guests call only to "shop," ask if they would like to receive your brochure and application. Many future reservations will result.

Later on, if you can afford it, all the names and addresses you have collected make a fine bulk mailing list for sending out updated brochures.

Brochures and Printed Materials

Contrary to popular belief, I learned that guests in all income brackets trust a "homespun" simple copied listing sheet more than an expensive "commercial" brochure featuring, for example, lithography on parchment paper. Pass the savings on to the guests.

Many B&Bs are failing because they are overpriced. Most travelers look for a guarantee of CLEANLINESS, COMFORT, and CORDIALITY. Stress this in your brochure and forgo the chocolate on the bedpillow or the Victorian wallpaper, unless it is included at a reasonable price.

Your brochure should provide essential information for the guest, such as office hours, location and description of listings (partial or complete), your special rules, payment procedures, and of course, your own telephone and address. Most RSOs absorb mailing and printing costs and send their brochures at no charge. Next to your vocal salesmanship, appealing listings attract customers. Guests will happily mull over their choices. A honeymoon cottage on the ocean? A room and bath in town? Describe the advantages of each listing, including special features. Hire a writer if necessary. Beware of sounding like you're selling real estate. Think of what you, as a traveler, would want to know. Here is an excerpt of *Megan's Friends'* listing sheet:

Inspected Referrals
(not exclusive)

Angwin, Napa area, kitchen
Pebble Beach, kitchen
Orosi, Fresno-Sierras
Incline Village, Lake Tahoe
Santa Barbara, kitchen
Carpenteria
Ojai

Rancho Palos Verdes
Laguna Niguel
Newport Beach
El Cajon, pool
Sausalito, S. F. houseboat
San Diego, kitchen

Suggested Calling Hours

3:30 to 8:30 PM on school days; other hours when available, or messages taken. Weekends OK.

No Smoking Inside

Full breakfasts free at your option. Children, supervised, by permission. Usual check-in after 2, check-out by 10. Otherwise by arrangement. Notify if delayed over an hour. Reservations held 7 days pending receipt of deposit. Unpaid last-minute reservations held until 4 PM.

Payment: Personal check in advance for total amount or for $10 one-time membership plus 20% deposit for each night's stay. The balance is due in cash or traveler's checks *on arrival,* to host. (Membership and deposits *not* refundable but may be applied to a later date at any M.F. home if canceled at least 2 days ahead and reservation rescheduled within a 30-day limit.) Membership is waived for foreign guests—passport number requested. Gift certificates valid for 6 months. Personal help gladly given to members for U.S.A., Canada. Access to over 10,000 B&B accommodations of various types.

Sample Listings:

Monterey Area   about 2 miles from Carmel center

Pines frame this floor-to-ceiling Bay view from inviting bed-sitting room with shower and tub bath, sliding glass door entrance from private deck, king or twin beds, small TV. Thoughtfully decorated, fresh and airy, breakfast in the solarium. 1/$50, 2/$60. Trundle bed for 3rd person in same room, add $10.

Cambria Area   7 miles south of Hearst Castle

Love seat, color TV, private patio with furniture, private entrance, twin beds; or, king bedroom. 1 mile to beach, easy drive to swimming pools, Moonstone Beach and Gardens, Hwy. 46 to wineries, Cambria center's quaint shops. Quiet home at end of the road, flower garden, wildlife. 1/$40, 2/$50.

San Luis Obispo Area

Quiet neighborhood near hills and golf course. Cozy queen room or king master bedroom with glass doors onto patio-garden. Friendly, English hospitality. Local attractions include Old Mission San Luis Obispo de Tolosa (1772), Madonna Inn, historic tour of town, winery, lakes, and parks. Hearst Castle 45 min. No children. 1/$40, 2/$50 for queen.

Most RSOs require guest applications. By now, new RSOs generally copy established RSO forms, so most are similar. Your forms should contain information essential to the guest, such as your RSO policy on delays and cancellations, children, breakfasts, payment by cash, check, credit card, travelers check, and the amount of deposit. Essential to you are the guests' signatures, date signed, date of reservation, selected home, guests' address, telephones, employer, occupation, reference, allergies, special needs, arrival and departure times and dates.

Include a disclaimer of liability. This deters the possibility of lawsuits. To my knowledge, there have been none as of this writing—a great testimonial to both hosts and guests who "do" B&B. B&B/RSO insurance policies are just beginning to be written. Word your guest application carefully to afford you the greatest protection. Here is a sample *Megan's Friends* guest application:

Application

**EXCLUSIVE LISTINGS
NO SMOKING INSIDE**

PRINT NAME: _____
                  Last   First

Reservation
Dates: _____

First Word of Listing;
1st choice _____ 2nd _____ Host _____

    Full breakfasts free at your option. Children by permission, supervised. Usual check-in after 2 PM, check-out by 10 AM. Other hours by arrangement. Notify if delayed over an hour. Reservations held 7 days pending receipt of deposit. Last-minute unpaid reservations held until 4 PM.

    Payment: Personal check in advance for $10 membership fee + 20% deposit for each night's stay. Balance due to host in cash or traveler's check on arrival. (Membership and deposits not refundable, but may be applied to a later date at any home if you cancel at least 2 days in advance and reschedule your reservation within a 30-day limit.) Membership waived for foreign guests on presentation of passport. Personal help and referrals gladly given upon request. Thank you!

PRINT: NAME _____ HOME ADDRESS _____

CITY & STATE _____ ZIP _____

TELEPHONE: HOME _____ BUSINESS _____

OCCUPATION _____ EMPLOYER _____

PERSONAL REFERENCE (someone who knows you well—minister, teacher, employer—who would welcome you as a guest in his own home) NAME, ADDRESS, TELEPHONE: (Print)

_____

ALLERGIES? _____ SPECIAL NEEDS? _____
APPROX. ARRIVAL TIME _____ ARRIVAL DATE _____
DEPARTURE _____

DISCLAIMER: MEGAN'S FRIENDS, agents or host families, shall not be responsible for any damage, injury, or loss incurred by any person as a result of the act, or omission, whether negligent, or not, of any person rendering accommodations offered by this agency. MEGAN'S FRIENDS does not warrant the suitability of hosts or their homes, or vouch for the conduct of participating guests. Accordingly, I hereby release and hold harmless MEGAN'S FRIENDS from all liability arising out of each occurrence of my participation as a guest member. Signature of each party indicates an acceptance of the terms and conditions listed above.

		Each Member
Signatures	**Date Signed**	**of Your Party**
_____	Date _____	Date _____
_____	Date _____	Date _____

If you are already a member, date of your membership: _____
Please enclose a stamped envelope for reservation confirmation, membership card, and directions to your host home. If all arrangements have been made, just mail back this application.

How Did You Discover Megan's Friends?

_____

After you receive a guest application returned by mail with a deposit or a check in full, make the appropriate notations in your booking ledger. Then call the host to confirm the reservation. Then send a confirmation letter to the guest, acknowledging the amount paid and the balance due, repeating the reservation date, and enclosing a map and directions to the house. Here is a chance to convey your personal interest—wish them a safe journey, or a happy anniversary, or reassure them that grandmother will have no steps to climb to reach her room, or whatever is appropriate.

It is a good idea to supply guest evaluation postcards for your hosts to leave in their guest rooms, prepaid (P.O. cards) and addressed to your RSO. Many guests will use these to provide you with compliments or complaints.

Telephones

If you anticipate a busy RSO, you need two lines; one for personal and host calls, and the other for guest and business calls. Or, you may be able to manage with one number featuring call-forwarding and call-waiting. These features are worth their extra cost.

The skillful use of the telephone is most important. You need to extract considerable information from callers, select appropriate homes, convince the callers that this is what they want, and do it all with charm and speed. Callers dislike answering machines; more hurried guests will hang up and dial another B&B. Here is the recorded telephone message I used when I had to be absent from my desk: "Hello! Megan here. I *would* like to talk to you so will you please leave your name, number, address, and message? If this is long distance, may I return your call collect? Regular office hours are . . . (time zone) daily. Thank you!"

Your message needs to be businesslike, informative, short, and friendly. Your prospective guests risk their money and comfort on how you sound over the phone, so you had better sound good. *How* you say it (your tone and manner) is just as important as what you say. It is wise to check your tape occasionally to be sure your message is clear and your voice inviting, relaxed, happy, and efficient. Get a frank evaluation from an objective friend—or stranger!—about this.

Your request for collect return calls will keep your phone bill low. The callers say yes or tell you they'll call again. The caller's message generally includes reservation dates, desired types of lodging, and special needs. Before you call back, do some research.

If you are well organized, you can often nail everything down with the caller's long-distance call followed by your local call to your host. Naturally, whenever possible, you will use "smart phoning" such as evening and weekend calls, to reduce your costs; shop around to see which long-distance phone company offers the best deal.

For a new business, the more live telephone coverage you have, the better. When the other B&Bs are not answering their phones, you can build up your business by keeping *long* hours daily.

Guests often travel on the spur of the moment and pick up the phone from Anywhere, U.S.A., to call your agency for a reservation date *today*, or *tomorrow*. You have no time for a written letter or reference, advance deposit, or applications. In these cases, you need to have people-intuition. Collect as much personal information about the caller as you can.

Here is an example of a typical call from a guest. Have your booking ledger ready and either write directly in it or transfer information from your work pad as soon as you hang up.

1. Listen; answer questions.
2. Get names, address, phone, booking date, occupation, reference if needed.
3. If booking date is far enough ahead, offer to send listings and application.
4. Explain your special rules, like private membership, no smoking, or whatever.
5. After determining guests' preferences, suggest a specific home, describe, make a tentative confirmation pending arrival by the deposit (and membership fee, if applicable).
6. Inform the caller that as soon as his check arrives you will send a map, directions, host's name, address, and firm confirmation of his reservation. Also a list of your B&Bs and application if the guest does not already have one.

Don't increase the caller's long-distance charges with your inefficiency or with long-winded anecdotes. If the caller *wants* to chat, you will sense it. It is good telephone etiquette to let the originator of the call determine its length. (If you are very busy, of course, you can graciously excuse yourself after collecting the necessary data.)

You may reduce inconvenience and lost income if you accept credit card numbers over the phone to confirm deposits on last-minute phone bookings. Decide whether the extra bookkeeping time is worth it.

Publicity and Promotion

Follow the advice given in Chapter 2 for individual B&Bs. Extra ideas for RSO publicity and promotion would include correspondence with far-flung B&Bs, your agency name in publications, inquiries for "hosting" of hosts or from guests who want to become your hosts "back home," and your addition of sidelines using your agency name, such as a recipe book, speeches, paperweights, dolls, etc.

Referrals

Sometimes the honor system of commission-splitting with another B&B works, post guest-stay. Some agencies collect their commission in advance, then refer the guest to you for the remaining payment. Others provide free referrals to save record-keeping time. You may find that you are boosting someone else's business by sending them referrals but not getting any referrals *or* split commissions in return. Keep a short list of reliable B&Bs who will send you 10% per night's stay (the travel industry standard) and concentrate on these referrals.

Write down the names of callers requesting referrals, then give them the appropriate phone number to call, advising them to say at once that you referred them. This record of names, dates, and referred B&Bs will let you determine which B&Bs will reliably send commissions. But realize that some guests will forget to mention you, mistakenly believe they will get a lower price if they don't, or will not follow through on your recommendation.

You may (sweetly!) tell the inquiring callers that you don't have time to research referrals unless the callers make a deposit. If they demur, suggest that they stop at your office to browse through your reference materials.

You will occasionally get a request to arrange an extended tour covering several states. Obtain an advance deposit to cover the cost of your time in case the traveler cancels.

Conclusion

Honesty, reliability, resourcefulness, and courtesy are good management, essential to the continuing success of any business.

Most of your B&B problems can be solved with common sense. If not, pretend that *you* are the guest, or the host, and you will gain insight. If you have the combination of personality and skills needed, you are bound to succeed in this fascinating, personal endeavor.

4

B&B Recipes

The recipes that follow are not to be found in standard cookbooks. Some are original and the measurements are sometimes from the school of "a smidgen of this," "according to taste," and "till done." But they all indicate the host's desire to pamper guests with something special. The most important ingredient is the heartful of love that is as unmeasured as the handful of flour.

We had an overwhelming response to our request for host-contributed favorite breakfast recipes. Although we could not publish them all this time, we will use most of them in future editions. The following represent, as much as possible, regional or ethnic recipes that impart the flavor and variety of B&Bs across the country.

BREADS AND CAKES

Any Fruit Coffee Cake

4 c. chopped apples, apricots, peaches, pineapples, blueberries, or raspberries
1 c. water
2 tbsp. lemon juice
1½ c. sugar
⅓ c. cornstarch

3 c. flour
1 c. sugar
1 tbsp. baking powder
1 tsp. cinnamon

¼ tsp. mace
1 tsp. salt
1 c. butter/margarine
2 slightly beaten eggs
1 c. milk
1 tsp. vanilla

Topping
½ c. sugar
½ c. flour
¼ c. butter
½ c. walnuts

In covered saucepan combine and simmer fruit and water for five minutes. Stir in lemon juice. Stir 1½ cup sugar and cornstarch slowly into fruit mixture; cook, stirring continuously until mixture thickens. Cool. Stir together flour, sugar, baking powder, cinnamon, mace, and salt. Cut in 1 cup butter until mixture is crumbly. Combine eggs, milk, and vanilla, and add to flour mixture and blend. Spread half the batter into one or two pans. Spread fruit mixture over batter. Spread rest of batter over fruit. Combine first three topping ingredients until crumbly, then add nuts and sprinkle over batter. Bake at 350° for 45 to 50 minutes in a 13" × 9" × 2" pan, or 40 to 45 minutes in two 8" × 8" × 2" pans. Cool and remove from pans.

Isaiah B. Hall House, Dennis, Massachusetts

Apple Phyllo Tart

6 sheets phyllo dough
¼ c. unsalted butter, melted
2 apples, peeled, cored, and sliced into eighths
2 tbsp. sugar
2 tbsp. butter
Dash of nutmeg or cinnamon

Filling
¾ c. toasted hazelnuts
½ c. sugar
2 tbsp. butter
1 egg

Sauté the apples in the butter and sugar. Add a dash of freshly grated nutmeg (or cinnamon). Set aside. To prepare filling: in food processor, put sugar and hazelnuts in work bowl and process until well blended. Add butter and egg, process until smooth and creamy. Set aside. Place 1 sheet of phyllo dough in a tart pan and brush on melted butter. Continue in this fashion until you have used all the sheets of dough. Spoon nut filling into tart pan and then arrange sautéed apples on top. Fold phyllo edges over top and brush on butter. Bake at 325° for 25 minutes or until golden brown. Sift powdered sugar on top when cool.

The Carter House, Eureka, California

Cranberry Coffee Cake

½ c. margarine
1 c. sugar
2 eggs
1 c. sour cream
1 tsp. vanilla

1 tsp. baking powder
1 tsp. baking soda
½ c. flour
16 oz. cooked whole cranberries, canned or homemade

Cream margarine and sugar. Add eggs, one at a time, then sour cream and vanilla. Beat well. Add dry ingredients and mix well. Put ½ batter into greased tube pan. Spoon cranberries on top. Pour remaining batter and spoon more berries on top. Bake at 375° for 45 minutes. May be topped with a mixture of powdered sugar, warm water, and almond flavoring.

The Marlborough, Woods Hole, Massachusetts

Cream Cheese Braid

1 c. sour cream
½ c. sugar
1 tsp. salt
½ c. butter
2 pkg. dry yeast
½ c. water
2 eggs, beaten
4 c. bread flour

Cream Cheese Filling
2 8-oz. packages cream cheese, softened
¾ c. sugar
1 egg, beaten
⅛ tsp. salt
2 tsp. vanilla

Glaze
2 c. powdered (10X) sugar
4 tbsp. milk (maybe less)
2 tsp. vanilla

Heat sour cream over low heat. Stir in sugar, salt, and butter, and cool to lukewarm. In a large bowl, sprinkle yeast over the water, stirring well to dissolve. Add sour cream mixture, eggs, and flour. Mix well. Cover tightly and refrigerate overnight. Divide dough into 4 equal parts. On a well-floured work surface, roll each into a 12" × 18" rectangle, flouring work surface well. Make cream cheese filling: Blend cheese and sugar together; add remaining ingredients and mix well. Spread one-fourth of the filling onto each rectangle and then roll up, jelly roll fashion, starting with long side. Pinch edges together, fold ends under slightly, and place seam side down on greased baking sheet. Slit each roll at 1" intervals, ⅔ through dough, to resemble braid. Cover and let rise for 1 hour or more until double in size. Bake at 375° for 12 to 15 minutes. Combine glaze ingredients in small bowl and mix until smooth. Spread glaze while bread is still hot. May be frozen or refrigerated.

The Graustein Inn, Knoxville, Tennessee

Grandma Nettie's Bread Pudding

4 kaiser rolls or half-loaf challah
4 eggs, beaten
½ c. golden raisins
1 tart apple, grated
5 tsp. cinnamon sugar

1 quart milk
6 c. corn flakes
½ c. sugar
1½ tsp. vanilla
boiling and cold water

Soak bread in water and cover. Pour boiling water over raisins and cover. Squeeze water from bread and add eggs. Add sugar, milk, corn flakes, grated apple, and vanilla. Drain raisins and add. Mix together. Spread into 9" × 13" well-greased baking pan. Sprinkle with cinnamon sugar and bake for one hour at 350°. Serve warm with sweet cream.

A Bit o' the Apple, New York City

Plum Nut Bread

1 c. butter
1 tsp. vanilla
3 c. flour
1 tsp. cream of tartar
¾ c. plain yogurt
2 c. diced purple or prune plums in ½" pieces

1 c. chopped walnuts
2 c. sugar
4 eggs
1 tsp. salt
½ tsp. baking soda
1 tsp. grated lemon rind

Cream butter with sugar and vanilla until fluffy. Add eggs, one at a time; beat after each egg. Sift flour, salt, cream of tartar, and baking soda. Blend yogurt and lemon rind. Add to creamed mixture, alternating with dry ingredients. Stir until well blended. Add plums and nuts, mix. Place in 2 greased and floured bread pans. Bake at 350°, 50 to 55 minutes or until done. Loosen sides of bread from pan with a knife and let cool 10 minutes in pan before turning out.

The Colonial House, Weston, Vermont

Strawberry Jam Bread

3 c. all-purpose flour
1 tsp. salt
¾ tsp. cream of tartar
½ tsp. baking soda
1½ c. sugar
1 c. butter or margarine, softened
1 tsp. vanilla extract
¼ tsp. lemon juice
4 eggs
1 c. strawberry jam
½ c. buttermilk
1 c. chopped nuts

Combine flour, salt, cream of tartar, and soda; set aside. Combine sugar, butter, vanilla, and lemon juice in a large mixing bowl; cream until light and fluffy. Add eggs, one at a time, beating well after each addition. Stir together jam and buttermilk; add to creamed mixture alternately with dry ingredients, mixing just until blended. Stir in nuts. Spoon batter into 2 greased 9" × 5" × 3" loaf pans. Bake at 350° for 55 minutes or until bread tests done. Cool 15 minutes; remove from pans onto cooling racks. Yield: 2 loaves.

Parkview House, Amarillo, Texas

Vermont Honey Loaf

1½ c. flour
½ c. brown sugar
½ tsp. salt
½ tsp. baking powder
1 tsp. baking soda
1 tsp. cinnamon
¼ tsp. cloves
½ c. honey, mixed with 1 tbsp. hot water
1 tbsp. molasses
½ c. buttermilk
1 egg

Mix all ingredients together until "satiny." Pour into greased bread pan. Bake at 325° for one hour. Slice and toast before serving.

The Little Lodge at Dorset, Dorset, Vermont

Zucchini Bread

3 eggs
1¼ c. oil
1½ c. sugar
1 tsp. vanilla extract
2 c. grated, unpeeled, raw zucchini
2 c. flour
2 tsp. baking soda
1 tsp. baking powder
1 tsp. salt
1 tsp. cinnamon
½ tsp. cloves
¼ tsp. nutmeg
1 c. raisins
1 c. walnuts (optional)

Preheat oven to 350°. Butter five miniloaf pans. Beat eggs, oil, sugar, and vanilla until light and thick. Fold grated zucchini into egg/oil mixture. Sift dry ingredients, stir into zucchini mixture. Fold in raisins and nuts. Pour batter into pans. Bake for 1¼ hours. Cool slightly. Remove and cool completely on racks. Serve with butter, marmalade butter, or whipped cream cheese.

The Kingsleigh, Southwest Harbor, Maine

EGGS AND CASSEROLES

Apple-Sausage Ring

2 lbs. bulk sausage, cooked & drained
2 eggs, slightly beaten
½ c. milk
1½ c. herb stuffing
¼ c. minced onion
1 c. apples, pared and finely chopped

Preheat oven to 350°. Combine sausage, eggs, milk, stuffing, onion, and apples. Mix thoroughly and press into greased mold. Bake 1 hour. This can be made the day before and partially baked for 30 minutes. Finish baking before serving. Serves 8 to 10.

The Oakwood Inn, Raleigh, North Carolina

Cheese Strata

8 slices day-old bread, cubed
1½ c. cheddar cheese, grated
8 eggs
2 c. milk
4 tbsp. butter, melted
½ tsp. dry mustard

Layer oven-proof Pyrex dish with bread and cheese, ending with cheese. Combine milk, eggs, melted butter, and mustard in blender and blend for 20 seconds. Pour over bread-and-cheese mixture and refrigerate overnight. Bake at 350° until firm in center (about 45 to 60 minutes). Variations: Add minced onion, chopped green chilies, diced ham, cooked and drained bulk sausage, sautéed mushrooms, chopped chives, or scallions.

Refrigerate overnight, turning once. Bake in an electric skillet at low temperature (about 225°) for one hour, turning after 30 minutes. Serve with maple syrup or orange cream.

Orange Cream

Beat together until thick:
1 c. heavy cream
⅓ c. orange juice concentrate
⅓–½ c. sugar

Palmer House Inn, Falmouth, Massachusetts

Puffed Sliced Apple Dish

6 large eggs
1½ c. milk
1 c. flour
3 tbsp. sugar
1 tsp. vanilla extract
1 tsp. cinnamon
¼ tsp. nutmeg
1 stick butter or margarine
2–4 apples
1–2 tbsp. lemon juice
2–3 tbsp. brown sugar

Preheat oven to 350°. Mix eggs, milk, flour, (white) sugar, vanilla, cinnamon, and nutmeg. Core and slice apples; sprinkle with lemon juice. Melt butter in 12" quiche dish in oven. Add apple slices and return to oven until butter sizzles, but does not brown. Remove from oven and pour batter over apples. Sprinkle brown sugar on top, and bake until brown and puffed, about 30 minutes.

Four Seasons B&B, Branchport, New York

Shaw Casserole

1 c. hot cooked grits
1 box jiffy cornbread mix
4 eggs (beaten)
2 lbs. hot bulk sausage, cooked, drained
1 c. grated cheese
1¾ c. hot milk
1 stick of butter
salt & pepper to taste

Mix all ingredients together. Layer sausage, grits mixture, top with cheese. Bake 45 minutes at 325°.

Shaw House, Georgetown, South Carolina

Chili Cheese Casserole

4 eggs
¼ c. flour
½ tsp. baking powder
1½ tsp. dry mustard
1 c. cottage cheese

1 c. Monterey jack cheese, shredded
1 c. cheddar, shredded
¼ c. margarine, melted
14 oz. can chopped green chilies

Beat eggs. Add dry ingredients and beat well. Blend in remaining ingredients. Batter will be lumpy. Lightly grease casserole dish and bake at 350° for 25 to 35 minutes, or until center is firm and top is nicely browned.

La Posada de Chimayó, Chimayó, New Mexico

Mel's Asparagus Cordon Bleu

16 fresh asparagus spears
4 slices Swiss cheese
4 slices boiled ham
3 c. fine bread crumbs
3 tbsp. parsley

¼ tsp. black pepper
1 c. flour
2 eggs, beaten
½ c. butter, melted in skillet

Top each ham slice with a slice of cheese, then 4 asparagus spears. Wrap ham and cheese around asparagus and trim protruding ends of asparagus to fit. Combine bread crumbs with parsley and pepper. Dredge each ham/cheese/asparagus roll in flour, pressing together. Dip each in egg, then bread crumbs. Sauté in melted butter at medium heat for 4 minutes each side, or until golden brown. Serve at once. Top with hollandaise sauce if desired.

Tide Watch Inn, Waldoboro, Maine

Pain Perdue (Custard-Soaked French Toast)

Custard

4 eggs
2 c. milk
⅓ c. sugar

8 oz. orange marmalade
⅓ c. orange juice concentrate
½ oz. brandy extract

Cut French bread into 1" thick slices and place in flat pan. Mix custard ingredients together and cover bread slices with mixture.

Shirred Egg in Bread Basket

Bread Baskets
Use square, white sandwich bread. For each basket: trim crusts, roll flat with rolling pin, butter one side of the bread, place butter side down in muffin tin and bake at 350° till brown (10 to 15 minutes).

Cheese Sauce
One part butter, melted with one part flour. Whisk in four parts of milk and heat until thickened. Add mustard powder (⅙ part). Add favorite cheese and stir till melted.

(Prepare bread baskets and cheese sauce ahead.)
Put bread basket in greased muffin tin. Place slice of ham or smoked turkey in bread basket. Ladle 1 tbsp. of cheese sauce over meat. Carefully crack egg into bread basket. Top with another tbsp. of cheese sauce and bake at 350° for 15 minutes or till yolk is set. Serve topped with cheese sauce.

Beechmont, A Bed and Breakfast Inn, Hanover, Pennsylvania

MUFFINS

Bran Muffins

½ package All-Bran cereal, crushed
2 c. honey
5 c. unbleached white flour or combined whole wheat
5 tsp. baking soda
1 tsp. salt
3 tsp. cinnamon
4 eggs, beaten
1 c. vegetable oil
3 c. buttermilk

Combine first 6 ingredients in large bowl. Mix. Add remaining ingredients. Mix. Bake in preheated oven 15 to 20 minutes at 375°. Store in tight container for up to 6 weeks. Makes about 60 muffins.

Watercourse Way, South Strafford, Vermont

Hearty Blueberry Muffins

1½ c. unsifted all-purpose flour
½ c. unsifted whole wheat flour
½ c. brown sugar (packed)
1 tbsp. baking powder
½ tsp. salt
½ tsp. ground cinnamon
1 c. fresh or frozen (unthawed) blueberries
½ c. (1 stick) butter, melted
½ c. milk
2 large eggs
1 tsp. vanilla

Preheat oven to 425°. Grease 12 muffin cups (or use muffin papers). Makes about a dozen. Combine all dry ingredients in a bowl and blend well. In a separate small bowl, toss 1 tablespoon of the dry ingredients with berries. Cool melted butter a little, then add milk, eggs, and vanilla, and stir. Add wet mixture to dry mixture and stir until just moist. Stir in berries. Spoon batter into muffin cups and sprinkle sugar on top. Bake about 15 minutes until brown on top.

White Lace Inn, Sturgeon Bay, Wisconsin

Jalapeño Muffins

3 c. corn bread mix
2½ c. milk
½ c. salad oil
3 eggs, beaten
1 large onion, grated
2 tbsp. sugar
½ c. finely chopped peppers
1½ c. sharp cheese, shredded
¼ lb. bacon, fried and crumbled
¼ c. chopped pimientoes
½ clove garlic, crushed

Mix first four ingredients, then add remainder. Bake in heavily greased or lined muffin tins. Bake at 400° for approximately 35 minutes. (Yields 4 dozen muffins; freezes well.) Variation for supper use: Decrease milk by ¼ c. and add 2 c. cream-style corn.

Betty Hyde, Dallas, Texas

Pookie Muffins

Sift together:

2 c. all-purpose flour
2 c. whole wheat flour
4 tsp. baking soda
1 tsp salt
4 tsp. ground cinnamon

Combine in a large bowl:

6 eggs, beaten	1 c. buttermilk
¾ c. sugar	1 c. vegetable oil
¾ c. brown sugar	2 tsp. vanilla

Slowly stir dry ingredients into egg mixture (it will be lumpy). Fold in gently the following fruit mixture:

3 c. shredded apple	1 c. nuts, chopped
3 c. shredded carrot	1 c. dates, chopped
1½ c. shredded coconut	1 tbsp. grated orange rind

Spoon batter into greased muffin tins. Bake at 375° for 15 to 20 minutes. Yield: 4 dozen muffins; they freeze well.

Babbling Brook Inn, Santa Cruz, California

Peach Mountain Muffins

2 c. flour	¼ tsp. baking soda
⅓ c. brown sugar	⅛ tsp. nutmeg
1 tbsp. baking powder	¼ tsp. salt

Stir together in bowl, make well in center.

Combine:

1 egg	1 c. chopped peaches (fresh, frozen,
¼ c. cooking oil	or canned)

Add peach mixture all at once to flour mixture. Stir until just moistened. Spoon into greased muffin pan. Temperature: 400°. Bake: 20 to 25 minutes. Yield: 12 muffins.

The Bayberry Inn B&B, Peebles, Ohio

Popovers

2 eggs	1 c. flour
1 c. milk	dash salt

Grease a 12-cup muffin tin and place in freezer to chill. Mix batter; it will be lumpy. Fill muffin cups approximately three-quarters full. Put in cold oven. Turn oven to 450° and bake 20 to

30 minutes. DO NOT OPEN DOOR for 20 minutes. Serve immediately.

Elizabeth Street Guest House, Fort Collins, Colorado

Sara's French Puffs

3 c. flour
1 tbsp. baking powder
1 tsp. salt
½ tsp. ground nutmeg
1 c. sugar
⅔ c. shortening

2 eggs
1 c. milk

Topping
¾ c. melted butter
2 tsp. cinnamon mixed with 1 c. sugar

Stir together flour, baking powder, salt, and nutmeg and set aside. In mixer bowl, cream together the first cup of sugar, shortening, and eggs. Add flour mixture to creamed mixture alternately with milk, beating well after each addition. Fill greased muffin cups ⅔ full. Bake at 350° for 20 to 25 minutes. Dip in melted butter, then in cinnamon-sugar mixture.

Stranahan House, Mercer, Pennsylvania

PANCAKES

Apple Rings

pancake batter
4 McIntosh apples
maple syrup

Prepare one recipe pancake batter (regular or whole wheat). Peel (if desired) and core 4 McIntosh or other soft apples; cut the apples into slices about ¼ inch thick. Use a fork in the center of each apple piece to dip the ring into the pancake batter. Let any excess drip off. Fry the apple rings in butter, margarine, or vegetable oil in a skillet until golden brown on one side. Turn and brown on the other side. Serve hot with maple syrup.

Goose Creek Guesthouse, Southold, New York

Corn Fritters

2 c. sweet corn
3 eggs, separated
2 tbsp. butter

6 tbsp. white or whole wheat flour
dash nutmeg

Beat egg yolks until light and stir into corn. Add flour. Fold in stiffly beaten egg whites. Sauté on hot griddle in 2 tablespoons butter. Turn over gently and cook until lightly browned. Serve with real maple syrup or homemade fruit syrup.

Meadow Spring Farm, Kennett Square, Pennsylvania

Gingerbread Pancakes

Combine in a large bowl:

2½ c. flour
1 tsp. baking soda
1½ tsp. cinnamon
1 tsp. nutmeg

1 tsp. baking powder
½ tsp. salt
1½ tsp. ginger
⅛–¼ tsp. ground cloves

Beat together:

3 eggs
¼ brown sugar

Add to egg mixture, mixing together well:

1 c. buttermilk
¼ c. brewed coffee

1 c. water
¼ c. butter, melted

Add buttermilk mixture to dry ingredients, stirring just until moistened (batter will be slightly lumpy). For each pancake, pour about ¼ c. batter onto a hot, lightly greased griddle. Turn pancakes over when the tops are covered with bubbles and edges appear slightly dry. Serve with warm applesauce, maple syrup, or strawberry sauce.

Strawberry Sauce

1 pint strawberries, hulled
½ c. sugar

2 tbsp. lemon juice

In blender or food processor process all ingredients until smooth. Heat to boiling and cook down until thicker. Add additional whole or halved berries and serve warm over Gingerbread Pancakes.

Lambsgate, Swoope, Virginia

Strawberry Blintzes

1 c. all-purpose flour
3 tbsp. granulated sugar
¼ tsp. salt
3 eggs
1⅓ c. milk
2 eggs

2 (8 oz.) cartons strawberry yogurt
½ c. strawberry preserves
butter/margarine
powdered sugar
strawberry preserves

In medium bowl, mix flour, sugar, and salt. In another medium bowl, mix 3 eggs and milk. Gradually add milk mixture to flour mixture. Beat with electric mixer (medium speed) until blended. Cover and chill 2 to 3 hours. Prepare crêpe pan or shallow skillet. Brush with oil, use 2 tbsp. batter for each crêpe. Cook until brown on bottom. Remove crêpe, stack crêpe between waxed paper. In medium bowl, slightly beat 2 eggs with fork. Stir in yogurt and ½ cup strawberry preserves. Place crêpe brown side up and spoon 1½ tbsp. yogurt mix on center of crêpe. Fold crêpe over—first bottom, then sides, and top—envelope style. Melt butter in pan. Brown blintzes over medium heat on both sides. Sprinkle blintzes with powdered sugar and top with spoonful of strawberry preserves. Makes 10 servings.

The Brafferton Inn, Gettysburg, Pennsylvania

SCONES

Maine Blueberry Scones

2 c. flour
2 tbsp. sugar
3 tsp. baking powder
nutmeg (dash)
¾ tsp. salt

½ stick sweet butter
1 egg, beaten
1 c. blueberries
½ c. medium cream
½–¾ c. milk

Sift dry ingredients. Cut in shortening. Add berries. Combine egg with milk. Add to dry ingredients. Stir just enough to moisten. Pat out dough quickly and gently into a circle about ¾" thick. Cut into pie-shaped wedges. Brush with cream and sprinkle with sugar. Place on cookie sheet and bake in 450° oven for 15 minutes or until golden brown. Serve warm.

Bed & Breakfast Down East, Eastbrook, Maine

Scottish Oat Scones

⅔ c. butter or margarine (melted)
⅓ c. milk
1 egg
1½ c. all-purpose flour
1¼ c. quick Quaker oats, uncooked

⅓ c. sugar
1 tbsp. baking powder
1 tsp. cream of tartar
½ tsp. salt
½ c. raisins or currants

Add butter, milk and egg to combined dry ingredients; mix until just moist. Stir in raisins. Shape dough to form ball; pat out on lightly floured surface to form 8" circle. Cut into 8 to 12 wedges; bake on greased cookie sheet in preheated 425° oven 12 to 15 minutes or until light golden brown. Serve warm with butter, preserves, or honey.

Oak Shores, Swampscott, Massachusetts

FRUITS

Baked Pears

d'Anjou pears
brown or cinnamon sugar
cream

Peel and halve small d'Anjou pears. Generously butter baking dish just large enough to hold desired number of pears. Sprinkle dish with ½ tablespoon brown sugar or cinnamon sugar per pear. Put pears cut side down in dish and sprinkle with additional ½ tablespoon sugar per pear. Bake in 375° oven for 20 minutes. Remove and pour one tablespoon cream over each pear half. Bake an additional 15 minutes. Serve hot or warm.

The Heirloom, Ione, California

French Clafouti

3 c. fresh ripe fruit (sliced peaches, cherries, pears, blueberries—or mixture, don't use strawberries)
½ c. sifted flour
½ c. sugar
3 eggs
1⅓ c. half 'n' half

Mix flour and sugar. Make a well, add eggs and mix. Add half 'n' half as you mix. Butter a rectangular baking dish and line with the fruit. Pour batter over fruit. Bake until golden and puffed for 30 to 35 minutes at 425°. Dust with powdered sugar when cold. Serve warm or cold.

Le Clos Normand Bed & Breakfast, Kennett Square, Pennsylvania

Fruit Crisp

1 qt. of berries (or any mixture of fruit sliced thinly)
⅓ c. water
⅓ c. flour
⅓ c. brown sugar
¾ c. oatmeal
¼ c. lemon juice (over the fruit)
6 tbsp. butter

Cream sugar and butter. Beat in oatmeal. Toss fruit in flour and water. Place in greased baking dish. Crumble oatmeal mixture over the top. Bake 40 minutes at 375°—serves 4 to 6.

The Whistling Swan, Stanhope, New Jersey

Granola

Mix together:

12 c. rolled oats, old-fashioned
1½ c. wheat germ
1 lb. shredded coconut
1 c. sesame seeds
3 c. nuts, chopped

Combine in a saucepan:

1½ c. brown sugar
1½ c. water
1¼ c. safflower oil
½ c. honey
¾ c. molasses
1 tsp. vanilla
1 tsp. salt
1 tbsp. cinnamon

Heat on low until sugar has dissolved (do not boil). Pour over dry ingredients, mixing well. In a 9" × 13" pan, bake at 250° for 25 to 30 minutes per batch (this recipe makes 4 to 6 batches). After cooking add 3 c. (or more) mixed dried fruit (chopped). Serve with milk, yogurt, or as a snack. Freezes well.

Bluebird Haven, Williamsburg, Virginia

Voss Inn
Bozeman, Montana

KEY TO LISTINGS

✪ This star means that rates are guaranteed through December 31, 1989 to any guest making a reservation as a result of reading about the B&B in *BED & BREAKFAST U.S.A.*—1989 edition.

Location: As indicated, unless the B&B is right in town, or its location is clear from the address as stated.
Best time to call: When indicated, the time when the host is usually home to accept calls. Some have telephone answering machines or answering services to cover other times. Remember the differences in times zones when calling.
NOTE: Reservation services are available during normal business hours (9 A.M.–5 P.M., Monday through Friday) unless otherwise indicated.
No. of rooms: Number of *guest* bedrooms.
Double: Rate for two people in one room. Double rooms may be furnished with a standard double bed, queen- or king-sized bed, or twin beds.
Single: Rate for one person in a room.
Suite: Can be either two bedrooms with an adjoining bath, or a living room and bedroom with private bath.
Guest cottage: A separate building that usually has a mini-kitchen and private bath.
pb: Private bath and/or shower.
sb: Shared bath and/or shower.
Max. no. sharing bath: Maximum number of people that might be sharing one bathroom. Keep in mind that some B&Bs have sinks in each bedroom.
Double/pb: Room for two with private bath.
Single/pb: Room for one with private bath.
Double/sb: Room for two with shared bath.
Single/sb: Room for one with shared bath.
NOTE: There is usually an extra charge for an additional person occupying the same room.
Open: As indicated. Keep in mind that many B&Bs are closed for Thanksgiving, Christmas, and Easter.
Breakfast: Included in the room rate unless otherwise stated. A Continental breakfast consists of juice, bread, and hot beverage. Some hosts provide a gourmet breakfast with homemade cakes, breads, and preserves. A full breakfast consists of juice, cereal, eggs, breakfast meat, bread or rolls, and hot beverage. Some are so special, you may not be hungry for lunch!
Credit cards: When reservation services accept them, the deposit can be made with a credit card but the host will still require that the balance due be paid in cash or by check.
Pets: Keep in mind that the host may have resident pets. Always ask if it is convenient to bring yours, to make certain there won't be a conflict with other guests. If you are allergic to animals, inquire before reserving.
Children: If "crib" is noted after the word "welcome," the host can accommodate children under the age of three.
Smoking: If permitted, this means it is allowed *somewhere* inside the house. Some hosts discourage smoking in the breakfast room for the comfort of other guests; some prohibit smoking in bedrooms for safety's sake. Most do not allow cigars or pipes.
Social drinking: Some hosts provide a glass of wine or sherry; other provide setups for bring-your-own.
Airport/station pickup: If "yes" is indicated, the host will pick you up from the closest airport or station for a fee.
Minimum stay: A two-night minimum stay is sometimes required on weekends.

Please enclose a self-addressed, stamped, business-sized envelope when contacting reservation services.

Always mention *Bed & Breakfast U.S.A.* when making reservations!

5
State-by-State Listings

ALABAMA

Bed & Breakfast—Birmingham ○
P.O. BOX 31328, BIRMINGHAM, ALABAMA 35222

Tel: (205) 933-2487
Coordinators: **Bill Shaw and Larry Hanson**
States/Regions Covered: **Auburn, Birmingham, Cullman, Decatur, Dothan, Franklin, Montgomery, Tuscumbia**

Rates (Single/Double):
Modest: $35–$40
Average: $40–$50
Luxury: $50–$65
Credit Cards: **MC, VISA**

Bill and Larry specialize in making compatible placements in host homes where southern hospitality is assured. Their listings range from an exquisite cottage to a classic contemporary. There are Federalist homes, Victorian farmhouses, or cozy vacation hideaways. They are located in a variety of settings: close to lakes, rivers, downtown, in suburbs, or convenient to I-65. All are comfortable accommodations in homes where hosts balance friendliness with respect for privacy.

Montgomery Bed & Breakfast
P.O. BOX 886, MILLBROOK, ALABAMA 36054

Tel: **(205) 285-5421**
Best Time to Call: **Before 9 AM; after 6 PM**
Coordinator: **Helen Maier**
States/Regions Covered: **Hartford, Millbrook, Montgomery, Mt. Meigs, Prattville**

Rates (Single/Double):
  Average: **$36**   **$40**
  Luxury: **$46**   **$40–$56**
Credit Cards: **No**

If you are a history buff, you are sure to love Montgomery, the Cradle of the Confederacy. Helen Maier can put you within easy reach of the sights as a guest in one of her 15 homes. Accommodations range from antebellum to country contemporaries with a typical farmhouse in between. Southern hospitality abounds in each of these diverse homes. All accommodations have private baths, and a hearty breakfast is served at every B&B.

Vincent-Doan Home ✪
1664 SPRINGHILL AVENUE, MOBILE, ALABAMA 36604

Tel: **(205) 433-7121**
Host(s): **Betty M. Doan**
No. of Rooms: **3**
No. of Private Baths: **3**
Double/pb: **$70**
Single/pb: **$50**
Open: **All year**

Breakfast: **Full**
Credit Cards: **MC, VISA**
Pets: **No**
Children: **No**
Smoking: **Permitted**
Social Drinking: **Permitted**
Airport/Station Pickup: **Yes**

The Vincent-Doan Home, built circa 1827, is one of the area's last remaining "summer houses" and the only known example of French Creole architecture in the city. The area, known as the Old Dauphin Way District, is listed on the National Register of Historic Places. The furnishing and decor are subtle but elegant, and reflect the history of the home. It is 15 minutes to Bellingrath Gardens, 10 minutes to Battleship Park, and 30 minutes to deep-sea fishing. Betty will welcome you with a refreshing beverage.

ALASKA

Accommodations Alaska Style—Stay with a Friend ✪
BOX 173, 3605 ARCTIC BOULEVARD, ANCHORAGE, ALASKA 99503

Tel: (907) 344-4006
Coordinator: **Jean Parsons**
States/Regions Covered: **Anchorage, Denali, Fairbanks, Homer, Juneau, Kenai, Seward, Sitka, Valdez, Wasilla**

Rates (Single/Double):
 Modest: **$35–$40**
 Average: **$40–$45**
 Luxury: **$50–$55**
Credit Cards: **MC, VISA**

Anchorage is an eclectic mix of tall buildings, Mt. McKinley, glaciers, and rush-hour traffic. Its frontier spirit and contemporary style always take visitors by surprise. Accommodations include a B&B near a small park with views of the port and Sleeping Lady Mountain; another overlooks Cook Inlet; and a third is an elegant suite where breakfast may be enjoyed on the large deck. Jean will be happy to send you her descriptive directory describing host homes in the towns she serves for $2.

Alaska Private Lodgings ✪
1236 WEST 10TH AVENUE, ANCHORAGE, ALASKA 99511

Tel: **(907) 258-1717**
Best Time to Call: **8 AM–8:30 PM**
Coordinator: **Mary Reardon**
States/Regions Covered: **Anchorage, Fairbanks, Homer, Kenai, Palmer, Seward, Talkeetna, Valdez, Wasilla, Willow**

Rates (Single/Double):
  Modest: **$35–$43**
  Average: **$40–$45**
  Luxury: **$50–$60**
Credit Cards: **MC, VISA**

Alaska hosts are this state's warmest resource! Mary's accommodations range from an original log house of a pioneer's homestead where the host is in the antique-doll business, to a contemporary home with guest quarters on the entire lower level, to a beautiful country guest home offering a spectacular view of the Anchorage Bowl and Cook Inlet. Many are convenient to the University of Alaska and Alaska Pacific University. There's a $5 surcharge for one-night stays.

All the Comforts of Home ✪
12531 TURK'S TURN STREET, ANCHORAGE, ALASKA 99516

Tel: **(907) 345-4279**
Host(s): **Sydnee Mae Stiver and Frank McCurley**
No. of Rooms: **4**
No. of Private Baths: **1**
Max. No. Sharing Bath: **4**
Double/pb: **$100**
Single/pb: **$75**
Double/sb: **$60**
Single/sb: **$50**

Open: **All year**
Reduced Rates: **10%, returning guests**
Breakfast: **Full**
Other Meals: **Available**
Credit Cards: **Discover**
Pets: **No**
Children: **Welcome**
Smoking: **No**
Social Drinking: **Permitted**
Minimum Stay: **2 nights, May 1–Sept. 30**
Airport/Station Pickup: **Yes**

Sydnee Mae and Frank, pioneer Alaskans, invite you to share their quiet hillside home while visiting the "Last Frontier." Goose-down comforters, three fireplaces, a wood-burning sauna, and an outdoor hot tub add to the warm ambience. When the Northern Lights appear, the rear deck provides perfect viewing opportunities, and it isn't unusual to spot a moose ambling through the surrounding five acres. Generous breakfasts feature fresh eggs, compliments of the resident hens. This special B&B, at an elevation of 1,100 feet, overlooks everything but your comfort.

The Green Bough ☼
3832 YOUNG STREET, ANCHORAGE, ALASKA 99508

Tel: **(907) 562-4636**
Best Time to Call: **7 AM–10 AM; 4 PM–8 PM**
Host(s): **Jerry and Phyllis Jost**
Location: **20 min. from airport**
No. of Rooms: **4**
Max. No. Sharing Bath: **4**
Double/sb: **$40–$45**
Single/sb: **$35–$40**

Open: **All year**
Reduced Rates: **Families**
Breakfast: **Continental**
Pets: **Sometimes**
Children: **Welcome**
Smoking: **No**
Social Drinking: **No**

Even on the coldest days, you'll forget about the outside temperature in this comfortable home filled with family furnishings, needlework, and local artifacts. Breakfast features a choice of homemade breads, muffins, and scones served with seasonal fruit and plenty of hot coffee. The Green Bough is located in a quiet residential area close to colleges, shopping, bike trails, and buses. A large yard and deck are available for reading and relaxing. Your hosts have 20 years of experience in this part of the country and they will gladly help you discover its charms. Special arrangements can be made for storing fishing and camping gear.

Wilson's Hostel ☼
BOX 969, BETHEL, ALASKA 99559

Tel: **(907) 543-3841**
Best Time to Call: **Before 8 PM**
Host(s): **Gail and Tom Wilson**
No. of Rooms: **4**
Max. No. Sharing Bath: **4**
Double/sb: **$79**
Single/sb: **$59**
Open: **All year**

Reduced Rates: **Weekly**
Breakfast: **Full**
Credit Cards: **MC, VISA**
Pets: **Sometimes**
Children: **Welcome**
Smoking: **No**
Social Drinking: **No**
Airport/Station Pickup: **Yes**

A third *B* could be added to this B&B: banana splits (!) because Tom and Gail frequently serve them at bedtime as an example of the pampering guests receive here. This is in addition to refrigerator raiding, access to the family library, TV and stereo, laundry facilities, safety pins, and writing paper. You are encouraged to make yourself at home with all the privileges and responsibilities that implies. "Home," accessible only by air to the Bethel jetport, is a chalet made cozy by a fire in the wood stove and comfortable furnishings. Your hearty breakfast might be shared with a family from an Eskimo village, a business traveler, or a vacationer en route to the salmon streams along the nearby Kuskokwim River.

Alaska Bed and Breakfast Association ✪
3/6500 SUITE 169, JUNEAU, ALASKA, 99802

Tel: **(907) 586-2959**
Best Time to Call: **9 AM–5 PM**
Coordinator: **Stephen Hamilton**
States/Regions Covered: **Haines, Juneau, Ketchikan, Petersburg, Sitka, Skagway**

Rates (Single/Double):
Luxury: **$40–$55**
Credit Cards: **MC, VISA**

Visitors can enjoy southeast Alaskan hospitality in a historic inn, a log cabin in the woods, a modern home overlooking the water, or an old Indian village. Mendenhall Glacier, Glacier Bay, and the University of Alaska are nearby. The area is known for fine fishing and great hiking.

Kodiak Bed & Breakfast
P.O. BOX 1729, KODIAK, ALASKA 99615

Tel: **(907) 486-5367**
Best Time to Call: **Evenings; weekends**
Coordinator: **Mary Monroe**
States/Regions Covered: **Kodiak**

Rates (Single/Double):
Average: **$44–$55**
Credit Cards: **No**

Kodiak is one of the nation's top fishing ports, a hunting and sport fishing paradise, the home of the first Russian settlement in America and of the famous Kodiak bear. The people are warm and friendly and look forward to receiving you.

Russell's Bed & Board
HCO1 BOX 6229-R, PALMER, ALASKA 99645

Tel: **(907) 376-7662**
Best Time to Call: **Mornings**
Host(s): **Evelyn and John Russell**
Location: **38 mi. N of Anchorage**
No. of Rooms: **3**
Max. No. Sharing Bath: **4**
Double/sb: **$45**
Single/sb: **35**

Open: **All year**
Breakfast: **Full**
Other Meals: **Available**
Pets: **No**
Children: **Welcome, over 16**
Smoking: **Permitted**
Social Drinking: **Permitted**
Airport/Station Pickup: **Yes**

Discover Alaska's countryside while staying in a modern home in the heart of the Matanuska Valley. The house offers beautiful views, modern furnishings, an art studio, and a two-story glass solarium. Guests may choose from clean, quiet accommodations with twin or full beds. In the morning enjoy a breakfast of sourdough pancakes, homemade breads, and hot coffee. Visit nearby Bradly Lake Barn, Hatcher Pass, and Independence Mine.

Ede Den
BOX 870365, DAVIS ROAD, WASILLA, ALASKA 99687

Tel: **(907) 376-2162**
Host(s): **Jim and Julie Ede**
Location: **45 mi. NE of Anchorage**
No. of Rooms: **1**
No. of Private Baths: **1**
Double/pb: **$55**
Single/pb: **$45**

Open: **All year**
Breakfast: **Full**
Credit Cards: **MC, VISA**
Pets: **Welcome**
Children: **Welcome**
Smoking: **Permitted**
Social Drinking: **Permitted**
Airport/Station Pickup: **Yes**

Guests enjoy the privacy and charm of this scenic Matanuska Valley homestead, furnished with antiques and Alaskan art. A private entrance opens into a cozy bedroom adjoining a luxurious bath that features an artistic rock wall with a waterfall cascading into a hot tub. Breakfast includes sourdough hotcakes, local honey, and homegrown berries in season. Jim and Julie are longtime Alaska village teachers who collect and sell antiques. They'll be happy to arrange sightseeing, fishing, river rafting, and trips to Mt. McKinley.

ARIZONA

Mi Casa-Su Casa Bed & Breakfast ☉
P.O. BOX 950, TEMPE, ARIZONA 85281

Tel: **(602) 990-0682; (800) 456-0682**
Best Time to Call: **8 AM–8 PM**
Coordinator: **Ruth T. Young**
States/Regions Covered: **Flagstaff, Payson, Phoenix, Prescott, Scottsdale, Sedona, Show Low, Sierra Vista, Sun City, Tempe, Tucson, Yuma**

Rates (Single/Double):
Average: **$40–$45**
Luxury: **$55–$110**

Ruth's guest houses are located statewide; the above is only a partial listing. They are located in cities, suburbs, and rural settings, all of which are within easy driving range of canyons, national parks, Indian country, Colorado River gem country, the Mexican border area, historic mining towns, and water recreation areas. Send $3 for her detailed directory. Arizona State University and the University of Arizona are convenient to many B&Bs. $5 surcharge for one night.

Cone's Tourist Home ✪
2804 WEST WARNER, CHANDLER, ARIZONA 85224

Tel: **(602) 839-0369**
Best Time to Call: **After 5 PM**
Host(s): **Howard and Beverly Cone**
Location: **18 mi. SE of Phoenix**
No. of Rooms: **1**
No. of Private Baths: **1**
Double/pb: **$30**

Single/pb: **$30**
Open: **Sept. 1—May 31**
Breakfast: **Continental**
Pets: **Sometimes**
Children: **Welcome**
Smoking: **Permitted**
Social Drinking: **Permitted**

This beautiful contemporary home is situated on two acres. Howard and Beverly offer a large guest room with phone and television, a large parlor for relaxing, and kitchen and barbecue facilities. It is 2 miles from fine restaurants and 12 miles from Sky Harbor airport.

Cedar Bed and Breakfast ✪
425 WEST CEDAR, FLAGSTAFF, ARIZONA 86001

Tel: **(602) 774-1636**
Best Time to Call: **Mornings**
Host(s): **Mary Pickett**
Location: **3 mi. from I-40**
No. of Rooms: **2**
No. of Private Baths: **1**
Max. No. Sharing Bath: **3**
Double/pb: **$40–$45**

Single/pb: **$25**
Open: **All year**
Breakfast: **Full**
Pets: **No**
Children: **Welcome, over 8**
Smoking: **Permitted**
Social Drinking: **Permitted**
Airport/Station Pickup: **Yes**

This attractive contemporary is set among ponderosa pine and gambel oak. The house has a native Malpais stone exterior, with oak floors and wood paneling throughout the interior. Guests are welcome to relax in the large living room, which has plenty of comfortable seating and interesting motifs of glass, Indian rugs, and artifacts. In the colder weather, a fire is always going in the large stone hearth. When the temperatures climb back up, all are welcome to take in the sun on the deck or patio. Flagstaff is the hub of popular tourist attractions including the Grand Canyon, Sunset Crater, Meteor Crater, Walnut Canyon, and Wupatki Indian Ruins. Lowell Observatory, Northern Arizona University, and a branch of the U.S. Geological Survey are located nearby.

Dierker House ✪
423 WEST CHERRY, FLAGSTAFF, ARIZONA 86001

Tel: **(602) 774-3249**
Host(s): **Dorothea Dierker**
No. of Rooms: **3**
Max. No. Sharing Bath: **5**
Double/sb: **$40**
Single/sb: **$26**

Open: **All year**
Breakfast: **Full**
Pets: **Sometimes**
Children: **Welcome, over 12**
Smoking: **Permitted**
Social Drinking: **Permitted**

After a day of touring the Grand Canyon and Indian sites, return to Dorothea's Victorian home and enjoy a glass of wine and fresh fruit in the evening, by the fire in winter or in the pretty garden room. You are welcome to borrow a good book and snuggle in bed under a cozy down comforter. Activities might include a Colorado River raft trip in summer and skiing in winter.

Walking L Ranch ✪
RR 4 BOX 721B, FLAGSTAFF, ARIZONA 86001

Tel: **(602) 779-2219**
Best Time to Call: **8–10 AM; 5–9 PM**
Host(s): **Jerry and Susan Ladhoff**
Location: **7 mi. from I-40 and I-17**
No. of Rooms: **3**
No. of Private Baths: **3**
Double/pb: **$50–$65**
Single/pb: **$30**

Open: **Apr. 1–Oct. 1**
Breakfast: **Full**
Other Meals: **Available**
Pets: **No**
Children: **Welcome, over 12**
Smoking: **Permitted**
Social Drinking: **Permitted**
Airport/Station Pickup: **Yes**

Nestled in the pines of the Coconino National Forest, this ranch house features a lovely plant-filled spa room with hot tub, redwood deck, and patio. The homey, inviting rooms are accented with antiques, collectibles, Indian art, and Susan's handicrafts. Jerry is a retired professor from nearby Northern Arizona University and his hobbies are gardening and woodworking. Hiking, skiing, and walking are popular pastimes after you've had your fill of the Grand Canyon and Sedona.

Villa Galleria ✪
16650 EAST HAWK DRIVE, FOUNTAIN HILLS, ARIZONA 85268

Tel: **(602) 837-1400**
Best Time to Call: **Before 9 AM; after 6 PM**
Host(s): **Allyn and Helmut Fiedler**
Location: **5 mi. E of Scottsdale**
No. of Rooms: **2**
No. of Private Baths: **2**
Double/pb: **$95**
Single/pb: **$85**
Suites: **$100–$110**

Open: **All year**
Breakfast: **Full**
Other Meals: **Available**
Pets: **No**
Children: **No**
Smoking: **No**
Social Drinking: **Permitted**
Minimum Stay: **2 nights**
Foreign Languages: **German**

Villa Galleria is a large, Spanish-style contemporary named for the extensive art collection displayed throughout the house. A spiral staircase leads from the hearth-warmed living room to the loft library and finally to the tower room, where you'll find a fully stocked bar and a panoramic view of the mountains. The lower-level guest suite has a queen-size motionless waterbed, a fireplace, and a private patio. The upper-level room features a queen-size bed and a view of the lush green courtyard and swimming pool. A private tennis court, exercise equipment, and a 50-foot-long pool with massaging swim jet are among the amenities offered here. Your hosts have a repertoire of breakfast specialties, including Belgian waffles, eggs Benedict, and fresh baked breads. The living room of the Villa Galleria is pictured on our back cover.

Bed 'n' Breakfast in Arizona ✪
5995 EAST ORANGE BLOSSOM LANE, PHOENIX, ARIZONA 85018

Tel: **(602) 994-3759**
Best Time to Call: **Mornings, evenings**
Host(s): **Marjorie Ann Lindmark**
Location: **5 mi. from airport**

No. of Rooms: **2**
Double/sb: **$50**
Max. No. Sharing Bath: **2**
Single/sb: **$45**

Suite: **$75**
Open: **All year**
Reduced Rates: **Weekly**
Breakfast: **Full**

Pets: **No**
Children: **No**
Smoking: **Permitted**
Social Drinking: **Permitted**

Marjorie's charming, trilevel home is located in the exclusive Arizona Country Club area. It is furnished in an eclectic mix of contemporary and Indian artifacts. You are welcome to use the swimming pool. The delicious breakfast often features four-egg omelets or unusual waffles. Arizona State University and the fashionable 5th Avenue Scottsdale shops are nearby. There's a $5 surcharge for a one-night stay.

Bed & Breakfast Scottsdale and the West
P.O. BOX 3999, PRESCOTT, ARIZONA 86302-3999

Tel: **(602) 776-1102**
Best Time to Call: **9 AM–6 PM**
Coordinator(s): **Joyce and George Thomson**
States/Regions Covered: **Phoenix, Prescott, Scottsdale, Sedona, Tucson; New Mexico; Utah; Washington**

Rates (Single/Double):
  Modest: **$40**   **$55**
  Average: **$50**   **$65–$75**
  Luxury: **$65**   **$75–$150**
Credit Cards: **No**

The Thomsons have a roster of friendly hosts with homes that have a relaxed atmosphere to complement the easygoing Southwestern lifestyle. Many are close to Paolo Soleri's Bell Foundry, Taliesin West, fine restaurants, shops, galleries, and lively entertainment. Take along plenty of color film to capture the panoramic desert sunset. Discounts available May 1 through September 30.

Ford's Bed & Breakfast ✪
212 SOUTH PLEASANT, PRESCOTT, ARIZONA 86301

Tel: **(602) 776-1564**
Host(s): **David and Joan Ford**
Location: **30 mi. from I-17, Exit Hwy. 69**
No. of Rooms: **2**
Max. No. Sharing Bath: **4**
Double/sb: **$40**
Single/sb: **$25**

Open: **All year**
Breakfast: **Continental**
Pets: **No**
Children: **Welcome**
Smoking: **No**
Social Drinking: **Permitted**
Airport/Station Pickup: **Yes**

The Fords live in a turn-of-the-century frame house on a tree-lined street. Guest rooms are located on the first floor and share a large, connecting bath. Antique furnishings and handmade quilts accent the beauty of the original wood floors and handcarved woodwork. It's a short walk to the lovely park that surrounds the town courthouse, or to several nice shops and good restaurants. Prescott College is nearby.

La Maison de Mettille ✪
P.O. BOX 5282, SCOTTSDALE, ARIZONA 85261

Tel: **(602) 860-8855**
Best Time to Call: **After 6 PM; weekends**
Host(s): **Chuck and Ginny Mettille**
No. of Rooms: **2**
Max. No. Sharing Bath: **4**
Double/sb: **$58**
Single/sb: **$53**
Open: **All year**
Breakfast: **Continental**
Pets: **No**
Children: **Welcome, over 14**
Smoking: **No**
Social Drinking: **Permitted**

Accommodations in this attractive contemporary home are reached by a private stairway to the upstairs deck. Beautifully furnished, the spacious bedrooms are enhanced by mountain views. You are welcome to play billiards, swim in the pool, use the jogging trail, or watch a VCR movie borrowed from Chuck's extensive collection. A full breakfast is served on weekends, when Ginny has time to spoil you with special entrées. Complimentary wine and hors d'oeuvres are served every evening. The Mayo Clinic, restaurants, shops, and golf courses are close by.

Valley o' the Sun Bed & Breakfast
P.O. BOX 2214, SCOTTSDALE, ARIZONA 85252

Tel: **(602)941-1281**
Best Time to Call: **9 AM–5 PM**
Host(s): **Kay Curtis**
Location: **Tempe**
No. of Rooms: **3**
No. of Private Baths: **1**
Max. No. Sharing Bath: **4**
Double/pb: **$40**
Double/sb: **$35**
Single/sb: **$25**

Open: **All year**
Reduced Rates: **Weekly**
Breakfast: **Full, except Sunday**
Minimum stay: **2 nights**
Pets: **No**
Children: **Welcome, over 8**
Smoking: **No**
Social Drinking: **Permitted**
Airport/Station Pickup: **Yes**

The house is ideally located in the college area of Tempe, but is close enough to Scottsdale to enjoy its fine shops and restaurants. From the patio, you can enjoy a beautiful view of the Papago Buttes and McDowell Mountains. Local attractions include swimming at Big Surf, the Phoenix Zoo, and the Scottsdale Center for the Arts.

Old Fueblo Homestays, R.S.O.
P.O. BOX 13603, TUCSON, ARIZONA 85711

Tel: **(602) 790-2399**
Best Time to Call: **9 AM–7 PM**
Coordinators: **Rena Kiekebusch and Dorna Nelson**
States/Regions Covered: **Tucson**

Rates (Single/Double):
Modest: **$25** **$35**
Average: **$35** **$45**
Luxury: **$70** **$80**

There is a wide variety of homes in Tucson proper, close to the desert, in outlying towns, and in more remote desert locations, ranging from "nothing pretentious" to foothills elegance and charm. Most fall into the comfortable middle range. Rena and Dorna will match you with a host home where you'll feel perfectly at home. The weather is always good and you'll find many interests to keep you busy, from playing golf, to visiting Indian missions, to taking a trip south of the border to Nogales, Mexico. The University of Arizona is nearby.

The Bird's Nest ✪
6201 N. PIEDRA SECA, TUCSON, ARIZONA 85718

Tel: **(602) 299-9164**
Best Time to Call: **Evenings**
Host(s): **Vic and Betty Hanson**

Location: **10 mi. from I-10**
No. of Rooms: **1**
No. of Private Baths: **1**

Double/pb: **$35**
Single/pb: **$30**
Open: **Jan. 1–Apr. 30; Oct. 1–Nov. 30**
Breakfast: **Continental**

Pets: **No**
Children: **No**
Smoking: **No**
Social Drinking: **Permitted**

Located in the foothills of the Catalina Mountains, this one-story adobe home has a patio. It's furnished in a pleasant blend of Colonial and Southwestern styles, decorated with lovely plants and original art, and it features beautiful views. Vic and Betty enjoy people and will be happy to help you with your touring plans. They'll also identify the large variety of birds that visit their backyard. The University of Arizona is nearby.

Myers' Blue Corn House ✪
4215 EAST KILMER, TUCSON, ARIZONA 85711

Tel: **(602) 327-4663**
Best Time to Call: **After 5 PM**
Host(s): **Barbara and Vern Myers**
Location: **5 mi. from I-10**
No. of Rooms: **2**
Max. No. Sharing Bath: **4**
Double/sb: **$35**
Single/sb: **$25**

Open: **Sept. 1–May 31**
Reduced Rates: **Families, Seniors**
Breakfast: **Full**
Pets: **Sometimes**
Children: **Welcome (crib)**
Smoking: **No**
Social Drinking: **Permitted**
Airport/Station Pickup: **Yes**

Located on a quiet residential street, it's convenient to downtown Tucson and the University of Arizona via city buses. The family room, decorated with Indian arts and crafts, and filled with history books, has bumper pool and TV. Close to seasonal recreation, it is also handy for tours of Old Tucson, Saguaro National Monument, Kitt Peak Observatory, and Nogales, Mexico. You may use the kitchen for light snacks, and the washing machine, dryer, and barbecue. The University of Arizona is nearby.

O' Desert Dream ✪
825 VIA LUCITAS, TUCSON, ARIZONA 85718

Tel: **(602) 297-1220**
Best Time to Call: **Evenings**
Host(s): **Ken and Nell Putnam**
Location: **6½ mi. from I-10, Exit Ina Rd.**
No. of Rooms: **1**
No. of Private Baths: **1**

Double/pb: **$35**
Open: **All year**
Breakfast: **Continental**
Pets: **No**
Children: **No**
Smoking: **No**
Social Drinking: **Permitted**

Designed to complement its Catalina Mountains setting, this adobe ranch-style house commands a spectacular view of the city in the valley below. The Desert Museum, Sabino Canyon, Pima Air Museum, and the San Xavier Mission are but a few of the not-to-be-missed nearby sights. You are welcome to use the kitchen for light snacks and the spacious patio for your relaxing pleasure.

Redbud House Bed & Breakfast ✪
7002 EAST REDBUD ROAD, TUCSON, ARIZONA 85715

Tel: (602) 721-0218
Host(s): **Ken and Wanda Mayer**
Location: **7 mi. from Rte. 10**
No. of Rooms: **2**
No. of Private Baths: **2**
Double/pb: **$42**
Single/pb: **$36**

Open: **All year**
Breakfast: **Full**
Pets: **No**
Children: **No**
Smoking: **No**
Social Drinking: **Permitted**
Airport/Station Pickup: **Yes**

The Mayers' comfortable ranch-style brick home is on a residential street bordered by tall pines and palm trees. There is a view of the Catalina Mountains from the porch. Local attractions are the Saguaro National Monument, the Arizona Sonora Desert Museum, Kitt Peak National Observatory, and Sabino Canyon. You are welcome to use the bicycles, barbeque, and TV. Several fine restaurants and a dinner theater are nearby.

ARKANSAS

- Eureka Springs
- Fayetteville
- Calico Rock
- Mountain View
- Heber Springs
- Hot Springs

Bed & Breakfast of the Arkansas Ozarks ✪
ROUTE 1, BOX 38, CALICO ROCK, ARKANSAS 72519

Tel: **(501) 297-8764**
Best Time to Call: **7–11 AM**
Coordinator: **Carolyn S. Eck**
States/Regions Covered: **Batesville, Calico Rock, Des Arc, Fayetteville, Fort Smith, Harrison, Mountain Home, Mountain View, Norfolk**

Rates (Single/Double):
  Modest: $23 $35
  Average: $30 $65
  Luxury: $45 $85
Credit Cards: **No**

North-central Arkansas boasts an enviable combination of natural scenic beauty in its forests, rivers, and caves as well as the homespun fun of hootenannies, square dancing, and craft shops. Carolyn's homes include restored Victorians, Colonials, and a log cabin in the mountains.

Bridgeford Cottage B&B ✪
263 SPRING STREET, EUREKA SPRINGS, ARKANSAS 72632

Tel: **(501) 253-7853**
Best Time to Call: **Mornings**
Host(s): **Ken and Nyla Sawyer**
No. of Rooms: **3**
No. of Private Baths: **3**
Double/pb: **$65–$75**
Single/pb: **$55**
Open: **All year**

Reduced Rates: **10% less, Jan.–Mar.**
Breakfast: **Full**
Pets: **No**
Children: **No**
Smoking: **Permitted**
Social Drinking: **Permitted**
Airport/Station Pickup: **Yes**

A stay at the cottage is a step into the quiet elegance of yesterday. It is located in the historic district, where Victorian homes line the charming streets, horse-drawn carriages wind along the avenue, and old-fashioned trolleys carry guests to and fro. Ken and Nyla will pamper you with coffee, tea, and homemade cakes in the afternoon or evening. Breakfast is a real eye-opener of fresh fruit, homemade cinnamon rolls, Ozark ham, and delicious egg casseroles. There's a two-night minimum required on weekends and holidays.

Crescent Cottage Inn ✪
211 SPRING STREET, EUREKA SPRINGS, ARKANSAS 72632

Tel: **(501) 253-6022**
Best Time to Call: **9 AM–8 PM**
Host(s): **Ron and Brenda Bell**
Location: **On Rte. 62**
No. of Rooms: **4**
No. of Private Baths: **3**
Max. No. Sharing Bath: **4**
Double/pb: **$65**

Double/sb: **$55**
Open: **Apr.–Dec.**
Breakfast: **Full**
Credit Cards: **MC, VISA**
Pets: **No**
Children: **No**
Smoking: **No**
Social Drinking: **Permitted**

Crescent Cottage Inn was built in 1881 by Powell Clayton, the first governor of Arkansas. He would still be pleased today with the antique-filled rooms overlooking breathtaking scenes of the valley and East Mountain. Ron and Brenda provide special extras such as nightly turndown service, fresh flowers, and surprise snacks. In the morning they serve homemade rolls, jams, and jellies with a variety of egg dishes. Historic downtown Eureka Springs is just a short walk from here, past lovely springs and shade trees.

Harvest House ✪
104 WALL STREET, EUREKA SPRINGS, ARKANSAS 72632

Tel: **(501) 253-9363**
Best Time to Call: **10 AM–noon; 5–9 PM**
Host(s): **Margaret Conner**
No. of Rooms: **3**
No. of Private Baths: **3**
Double/pb: **$45**
Single/pb: **$35**

Open: **All year**
Breakfast: **Full**
Other Meals: **Available**
Pets: **Sometimes**
Children: **Welcome**
Smoking: **Permitted**
Social Drinking: **Permitted**

This green-and-white Victorian house is furnished with antiques, collectibles, and family favorites. The guest rooms are downstairs, with private entrances. Located in the Ozark Mountains, the scenery is lovely. Homemade surprise snacks are always available. Margaret is a wonderful host and will do everything possible to make your stay pleasant.

Sally's Bed and Breakfast ✪
RR 3, BOX 540, EUREKA SPRINGS, ARKANSAS 72632

Tel: **(501) 253-8430**
Best Time to Call: **9 AM–10 PM**
Host(s): **Sally Major**
No. of Rooms: **2**
Max. No. Sharing Bath: **4**
Double/sb: **$45**
Single/sb: **$30**

Open: **All year**
Reduced Rates: **Dec.–May**
Breakfast: **Full**
Pets: **Small dogs welcome on leash**
Children: **Welcome**
Smoking: **No**
Social Drinking: **No**

Set in the rolling hills of the Ozarks, this B&B is equipped to accommodate wheelchair-bound guests with a ramp on the front porch and a shower large enough for a chair. The great Passion Play and live country-and-western music shows are performed in the area from May to October. Table Rock Lake is popular for fishing, boating, and swimming. There are many walnut trees on the five acres surrounding the large cedar home. A swing set is in the back yard for your children's pleasure. Breakfast often features sausage with gravy, hash browns, eggs, and biscuits. Evening snacks of cake and ice cream are offered along with interesting conversation.

Singleton House Bed & Breakfast ✪
11 SINGLETON, EUREKA SPRINGS, ARKANSAS 72632

Tel: **(501) 253-9111**
Host(s): **Barbara Gavron**
No. of Rooms: **4**
No. of Private Baths: **2**
Max. No. Sharing Baths: **4**
Double/pb: **$55–$65**
Single/pb: **$55**
Double/sb: **$45–$55**
Single/sb: **$45**

Suites: **$55–$65**
Open: **All year**
Reduced Rates: **After 3rd night**
Breakfast: **Full**
Credit Cards: **MC, VISA**
Pets: **No**
Children: **Sometimes**
Smoking: **No**
Social Drinking: **Permitted**

On a hillside overlooking Eureka Springs' historic district, Singleton House is whimsically decorated with an eclectic collection of comfortable antiques and folk art. Each guest room is decorated with handmade quilts, brass-and-iron bedsteads, ceiling fans, and fresh flowers. Breakfast is served on a balcony overlooking a garden with stony paths, a lily-filled fish pond, and flower-covered arches and arbors. This enchanting setting is credited to a one-of-a-kind designer who claims to be an elf. A secluded footpath leads through the woods to quaint shops, cafés, and an active artists' colony. A convenient trolley provides transportation, and guided walking tours are available. Your hostess will help you discover all the best buys and will gladly direct you to popular local attractions, including Beaver Lake.

Eton House ✪
1485 ETON, FAYETTEVILLE, ARKANSAS 72701

Tel: **(501) 521-6344; 443-5481**
Best Time to Call: **10AM–10 PM**
Host(s): **Patricia Parks and Clara Griffith**
Location: **65 mi. N of Ft. Smith**
No. of Rooms: **4**
No. of Private Baths: **4**
Double/pb: **$40**

Single/pb: **$35**
Open: **All year**
Breakfast: **Continental**
Pets: **Sometimes**
Children: **Sometimes**
Smoking: **Permitted**
Social Drinking: **Permitted**
Airport/Station Pickup: **Yes**

This buff brick, ranch-style home has a cathedral ceiling and is furnished in an eclectic blend of white Victorian wicker and more staid European pieces. Your enthusiastic hostesses will be happy to direct you to the University of Arkansas, the Museum of Prehistoric Animals, Beaver Lake, Prairie Grove and Pea Ridge battlefields, plus a wealth of cultural and intellectual events. This area is rich in crafts and antique shops, folk art, and authentic mountain music.

Oak Tree Inn
VINEGAR HILL, HIGHWAY 110 WEST, HEBER SPRINGS, ARKANSAS 72543

Tel: **(501) 362-8870/6111**
Host(s): **David and Freddie Lou Lodge**
Location: **60 mi. N of Little Rock**
No. of Rooms: **5**
No. of Private Baths: **5**
Double/pb: **$55–$65**
Single/pb: **$50–$60**
Open: **All year**

Reduced Rates: **Available**
Breakfast: **Full**
Pets: **No**
Children: **No**
Smoking: **No**
Social Drinking: **Permitted**
Airport/Station Pickup: **Yes**

The Oak Tree Inn is set amid Arkansas oaks next to a 45,000-acre lake. The house was designed for bed and breakfast guests, with all the comforts and elegance of a country retreat. Four of the bedrooms have fireplaces, three have queen-size beds, and each has its own whirlpool bath. Rooms are individually decorated in Oriental, Victorian, and English styles. In town and beyond, taste the renowned mineral waters, visit craft shops, and tour scenic roads; Greers Ferry Lake offers scuba diving, fishing, and boating. In the evening enjoy complimentary desserts with your hosts.

Stillmeadow Farm ✪
111 STILLMEADOW LANE, HOT SPRINGS, ARKANSAS 71913

Tel: **(501) 525-9994**
Host(s): **Gene and Jody Sparling**
Location: **4 mi. S of Hot Springs**
No. of Rooms: **4**
No. of Private Baths: **2**
Max. No. Sharing Bath: **4**
Double/pb: **$45–$50**
Single/pb: **$40–$45**
Double/sb: **$40**
Suites: **$75–$80**
Open: **All year**
Breakfast: **Continental**
Pets: **No**
Children: **Welcome, over 6**
Smoking: **No**
Social Drinking: **Permitted**

Stillmeadow Farm is a reproduction of an 18th-century New England saltbox, set in 75 acres of pine forest with walking trails and an herb garden. The decor is of early country antiques. Your hosts provide homemade snacks and fruit in the guest rooms. For breakfast, freshly baked pastries and breads are served. Hot Springs National Park, Lake Hamilton, the Mid-America Museum, and a racetrack are nearby.

Williams House Bed & Breakfast Inn ✪
420 QUAPAW, HOT SPRINGS, ARKANSAS 71901

Tel: **(501) 624-4275**
Host(s): **Mary and Gary Riley**
Best Time to Call: **9–11 AM; evenings**
Location: **50 mi. SW of Little Rock**
No. of Rooms: **6**
No. of Private Baths: **4**

Max. No. Sharing Bath: **4**
Double/pb: **$60–$75**
Single/pb: **$50–$65**
Double/sb: **$50**
Single/sb: **$45**
Suites: **$70–$75**
Open: **All year**

Breakfast: **Full**
Credit Cards: **MC, VISA**
Pets: **No**
Children: **Welcome, over 7**
Smoking: **Permitted**
Social Drinking: **Permitted**

This Victorian mansion, with its stained-glass and beveled-glass windows, is a nationally registered historical place. The atmosphere is friendly, and the marble fireplace and grand piano invite congeniality. Breakfast menu may include quiche, toast amandine, or exotic egg dishes. Gary and Mary will spoil you with special iced tea, snacks, and mineral spring water. World health experts recognize the benefits of the hot mineral baths in Hot Springs National Park. The inn is within walking distance of Bath House Row. There's a two-night minimum stay on weekends during March and April.

For key to listings, see inside front or back cover.

✪ This star means that rates are guaranteed through December 31, 1989 to any guest making a reservation as a result of reading about the B&B in *BED & BREAKFAST U.S.A.*—1989 edition.

Please enclose a self-addressed, stamped, business-sized envelope when contacting reservation services.

For more details on what you can expect in a B&B, see Chapter 1.

Always mention *Bed & Breakfast U.S.A.* when making reservations!

If no B&B is listed in the area you'll be visiting, use the form on page 693 to order a copy of our "List of New B&Bs."

We want to hear from you! Use the form on page 691.

CALIFORNIA

Mendocino/Wine Country
Sacramento Area
Gold Country
San Francisco Area
Monterey Peninsula
San Joaquin Valley
San Luis Obispo Area
Santa Barbara Area
Desert Area
Los Angeles Area
San Diego and Orange County Area

DESERT AREA

Travellers Repose ✪
P.O. BOX 655, 66920 FIRST STREET, DESERT HOT SPRINGS, CALIFORNIA 92240

Tel: **(619) 329-9584**
Host(s): **Marian and Sam Relkoff**
Location: **12 mi. N of Palm Springs**

No. of Rooms: **3**
No. of Private Baths: **1**
Max. No. Sharing Bath: **4**

Double/pb: **$75**
Double/sb: **$50–$60**
Single/sb: **$45–$54**
Open: **Oct. 1–June 30**
Reduced Rates: **Weekly; 10% families on second room**
Breakfast: **Continental**

Pets: **No**
Children: **Welcome, over 12**
Smoking: **No**
Social Drinking: **Permitted**
Airport/Station Pickup: **Yes**
Foreign Languages: **Russian**

Bay windows, gingerbread trim, stained-glass windows, and a white picket fence decorate this charming Victorian home. The warm look of oak predominates in floors, wainscoting, and cabinetry. Guest rooms are decorated with hearts, dolls, and teddy bears everywhere. There's a rose bedroom with antiques and lace, a blue-and-white room with a heart motif, and a green room decorated with pine furniture hand-crafted by Sam. A patio, pool, and spa complete the amenities. Golf, tennis, museums, galleries, and posh Palm Springs are nearby. Marian graciously serves tea at 4 PM.

Hotel Nipton ✪
72 NIPTON ROAD, NIPTON, CALIFORNIA 92364

Tel: **(619) 856-2335**
Best Time to Call: **9 AM–7 PM**
Host(s): **Jerry and Roxanne Freeman**
Location: **10 mi. from I-15**
No. of Rooms: **4**
Max. No. Sharing Bath: **4**
Double/sb: **$42**
Open: **All year**
Reduced Rates: **Group**

Breakfast: **Continental**
Other Meals: **Available**
Credit Cards: **MC, VISA**
Pets: **No**
Children: **Welcome**
Smoking: **Permitted**
Social Drinking: **Permitted**
Foreign Languages: **Spanish**

The population of Nipton is 30! The recently restored hotel with its foot-thick adobe walls was built in 1904 and is located in the East Mohave National Scenic Area. Nipton is in the heart of gold-mining territory, 30 minutes from Lake Mohave's Cottonwood Cove, and 20 minutes from Searchlight. You are welcome to relax on the porch or in the outdoor Jacuzzi. A home-cooked breakfast including eggs, sausage, hash browns, juice, toast, and coffee is served at the small café next door. Continental breakfast is served in the lobby at your convenience.

Inn at Palm Valley Ranch ✪
67 698 PALM VALLEY SCHOOL ROAD, P.O. BOX 4364, PALM SPRINGS, CALIFORNIA 92263

Tel: **(619) 328-5743**
Best Time to Call: **9 AM–5 PM**
Host(s): **Loris O'Leary**
Location: **5 mi. from I-10**
No. of Rooms: **6**
No. of Private Baths: **6**
Double/pb: **$80–$90**
Single/pb: **$70**
Guest Cottages: **$100–$120 (sleeps 2–4)**
Suites: **$150**
Open: **Oct. 1–July 4**
Reduced Rates: **15%, weekly; 10%, seniors**
Breakfast: **Continental**
Pets: **Sometimes**
Children: **Welcome**
Smoking: **Permitted**
Social Drinking: **Permitted**
Minimum Stay: **2 nights on weekends**
Airport/Station Pickup: **Yes**
Foreign Languages: **Spanish**

The Inn at Palm Valley Ranch is a restored adobe ranch house nestled in a two-acre date grove. The main house has two master bedrooms and a room with twin beds, all furnished with Colonial and contemporary Southwestern furniture. There are several patios for relaxing, in addition to the sun room and large living room with fireplace. Those seeking more privacy can choose from two guest houses, each with its own living room, kitchen, queen-size bed, private phone, and patio. The spacious grounds are landscaped with citrus trees and gardens, and feature a heated pool, spa, outdoor fireplace, and a lighted tennis court. Breakfast is served outside on the spa patio, and your hosts offer cool refreshments by the pool in the afternoon. The inn is just a few blocks from the municipal golf course and is a convenient drive from the Bob Hope Cultural Center and the Oasis Water Park.

GOLD COUNTRY

The Heirloom ✪
P.O. BOX 322, 214 SHAKLEY LANE, IONE, CALIFORNIA 95640

Tel: **(209) 274-4468**
Host(s): **Melisande Hubbs and Patricia Cross**
Location: **35 mi. E of Sacramento**
No. of Rooms: **6**
No. of Private Baths: **4**
Max. No. Sharing Bath: **2**
Double/pb: **$50–$80**
Single/pb: **$45–$80**
Double/sb: **$50–$75**
Single/sb: **$45–$60**
Open: **All year**
Reduced Rates: **Weekly**
Breakfast: **Full**
Pets: **No**
Children: **Welcome, over 10**
Smoking: **Permitted**
Social Drinking: **Permitted**
Airport/Station Pickup: **Yes**

Nestled in the Sierra foothills yet close to the historic gold mines, wineries, antique shops, and museums, this 1863 mansion, with its lovely balconies and fireplaces, is a classic example of antebellum architecture. It is furnished with a combination of family treasures and period pieces. Patricia and Melisande's hearty breakfast includes such delights as quiche, crêpes, soufflé, and fresh fruits. Afternoon refreshments are always offered.

LOS ANGELES AREA

Bed & Breakfast of Los Angeles
32074 WATERSIDE LANE, WESTLAKE VILLAGE, CALIFORNIA 91361

Tel: **(818) 889-8870 or 889-7325**
Best Time to Call: **9–11 AM; 6–9 PM**
Coordinators: **Peg Marshall and Angie Kobabe**
States/Regions Covered: **30 communities in greater Los Angeles**

Rates: (Single/Double):
  Modest: $30 $40
  Average: $35 $50
  Luxury: $40 $85
Credit Cards: **MC, VISA**

Peg and Angie can provide accommodations for you from Ventura in the north to Laguna Beach in the south. There's a guest house in Hollywood, a luxury suite in Beverly Hills, and a contemporary loft in Balboa, to name a few choices. Please send $2 for their directory. B&Bs are located near major colleges in Los Angeles, Orange, and Ventura counties.

El Camino Real Bed & Breakfast ✪
P.O. BOX 7155, NORTHRIDGE, CALIFORNIA 91327-7155

Tel: **(818) 363-6753**
Best Time to Call: **Evenings**
Coordinator: **Claire Reinstein**
States/Regions Covered: **Anaheim, Beverly Hills, Malibu, Ojai, Palm Springs, Pasadena, San Diego, San Fernando Valley**

Rates (Single/Double):
  Modest: $35 $40
  Average: $40–$45 $50–$60
  Luxury: N/A $115
Credit Cards: **No**
Minimum Stay: **2 nights**

This service brings the tradition of California hospitality begun with the Franciscan missions to the present-day traveler. Homes are in beach communities conveniently located to such attractions as Disneyland, Knotts Berry Farm, and the movie studios. Average accommodations are in upper-middle-class homes with swimming pools/spas, except in hilly areas. Claire offers modest apartments with simple furnishings and a luxurious private guest house on an estate with a hot tub and swimming pool. All hosts are longtime residents of California, familiar with the restaurants, tourist attractions, and the best ways of getting to them.

House Guests U.S.A., Inc.
P.O. BOX 1185, HUNTINGTON BEACH, CALIFORNIA 92647

Tel: (714) 891-3736; (800) 333-HOST
Coordinator: Layne Neugart
States/Regions Covered: Los Angeles, Orange County area, Long Beach

Rates (Single/Double):
   Modest: $39 $49
   Average: $49 $59 and up
   Luxury: $59 $69 and up
Credit Cards: AMEX, DC, MC, VISA
Minimum Stay: **3 nights**

Layne invites you to "Wish Upon a Star" and he may have your dream come true. Surely one of his more than 1,000 accommodations will fulfill your desire. Amenities may include a spa, tennis court, spectacular view, or in-room television, and they may be in a beachfront residence or a hillside home. Available at extra cost are a yacht, a car, a chauffeur, or a guide to lead you on a personalized tour. Entertainment and dining discounts are provided. Please note that credit card charges are subject to a 5% surcharge and 60-day advance payment. Hostless homes and condos are also available.

Beautiful Downtown Burbank B&B Service ✪
707 EAST CYPRESS AVENUE, BURBANK, CALIFORNIA 91501

Tel: (818) 841-6479
Best Time to Call: 8 AM–8 PM
Coordinators: Dianne Maritt and Donna Miller
States/Regions Covered: Burbank, Glendale, Pasadena

Rates (Single/Double):
   Modest: $30 $35
   Average: $40 $45
   Luxury: $50 and up $55 and up
Credit Cards: MC, VISA

The B&Bs on this roster are convenient to the media district, including the studios of NBC, Universal, Disney, Warner, and Burbank. If you plan to attend the Rose Bowl game or parade, make your reservations early. There's a wide variety of accommodations to choose from, including one with hosts who have toured the world and delight in serving breakfasts from many cultures. Another host has a lovely Pasadena hillside Victorian with a pool and spa.

Belair ✪
941 NORTH FREDERIC STREET, BURBANK, CALIFORNIA 91505

Tel: **(818) 848-9227**
Best Time to Call: **7 AM–10 PM**
Host(s): **Harry Bell**
Location: **10 mi. N of Los Angeles**
No. of Rooms: **3**
No. of Private Baths: **3**
Double/pb: **$35**
Single/pb: **$25**
Reduced Rates: **Weekly**

Open: **All year**
Breakfast: **Full**
Pets: **No**
Children: **Welcome, over 8**
Smoking: **Permitted**
Social Drinking: **Permitted**
Airport/Station Pickup: **Yes**
Foreign Languages: **French**

Your host, Harry Bell, a retired teacher, musician, adventurer, world traveler, and collector of exotic art, is as interesting as his home is convenient and comfortable. Located in quiet, residential Burbank, it is only 2 miles from studio tours, 5 miles from Hollywood, and 30 miles to beach or mountain resorts. It is also convenient to public bus transportation. The upstairs has a double bed in one room and a dorm with four beds. It is ideal for a family or friends traveling together. The charge for the dorm is $12 per person.

Casablanca Villa ✪
449 NORTH DETROIT STREET, LOS ANGELES, CALIFORNIA 90036

Tel: **(213) 938-4794**
Host(s): **Suzanne Moultout**
No. of Rooms: **1**
Max. No. Sharing Bath: **3**
Double/sb: **$45**
Single/sb: **$35**
Open: **All year**

Breakfast: **Continental**
Pets: **No**
Children: **No**
Smoking: **No**
Social Drinking: **No**
Foreign Languages: **French**

Suzanne Moultout welcomes you to her Spanish-style house located on a quiet, attractive street. Here, guests can enjoy the convenience of being close to West Hollywood, downtown, and Beverly Center, while having a comfortable home base. Your hostess offers an attractive guest room and a shady yard with fruit trees. She will gladly direct you to such nearby sights as Hollywood Hills, CBS Studios, and the beaches. Even if you don't have a car, the area is quite convenient, with a bus stop located within walking distance.

Terrace Manor ✪
1353 ALVARADO TERRACE, LOS ANGELES, CALIFORNIA 90006

Tel: **(213) 381-1478**
Host(s): **Sandy and Shirley Spillman**
Location: **Downtown Los Angeles**
No. of Rooms: **5**
No. of Private Baths: **5**
Double/pb: **$60–$90**
Open: **All year**
Breakfast: **Full**
Credit Cards: **AMEX, MC, VISA**
Pets: **No**
Children: **Welcome, over 10**
Smoking: **No**
Social Drinking: **Permitted**

Nestled in modern downtown Los Angeles, Terrace Manor is one of several historical landmarks surrounding a park. Built in 1902, the Manor contains its original stained-glass and leaded-glass windows, paneled walls, hardwood floors, and an Ionic-columned fireplace with a built-in clock that still chimes on cue. Choose from comfortable rooms each named for its special feature. The Sun Room Suite is decorated in authentic period paper in coral and turquoise and has a queen-size iron-and-brass bed and an attached porch with trundle. Lydia's Room is rich hunter green and mauve, with an ornate king-size bed and Victorian settee. Your hosts serve breakfast in the dining room or outside on the patio. Specialties include seasonal fruit, French toast, fritatta, quiche, and omelets, served with coffee or tea. They also invite you to gather in the parlor or library later for an afternoon social hour with complimentary wine and a light repast.

Casa Larronde ✪
P.O. BOX 86, MALIBU, CALIFORNIA 90265-0086

Tel: **(213) 456-9333**
Best Time to Call: **Mornings**
Host(s): **Jim and Charlou Larronde**
Location: **40 mi. NW of Los Angeles**
No. of Rooms: **1 suite**
No. of Private Baths: **1**
Suite: **$75**
Open: **All year**
Breakfast: **Full**
Pets: **Sometimes**
Children: **Sometimes**
Smoking: **Permitted**
Social Drinking: **Permitted**

The guest suite has a fireplace and color TV, but if you walk down the beach you may get to see the stars live; Rich Little, Ann-Margaret, and the McEnroes are the neighborhood people here on Millionaires' Row. This house is 4,000 square feet of spectacular living space. It has floor-to-ceiling glass, ocean decks, a private beach, and a planter that's two stories high. Jim and Charlou, world travelers, enjoy entertaining, and their gourmet breakfast ranges from Scotch eggs to French toast made with Portuguese sweet bread. Champagne, cocktails, and snacks are complimentary refreshments. Pepperdine College is two miles away. The Getty Museum is a five-minute drive away.

Hideaway House ✪
8441 MELVIN AVENUE, NORTHRIDGE, CALIFORNIA 91324

Tel: **(818) 349-5421**
Best Time to Call: **6–10 PM**
Host(s): **Dean and Dorothy Dennis**
Location: **20 mi. NW of Los Angeles**
No. of Rooms: **1**
No. of Private Baths: **1**
Double/pb: **$55**
Single/pb: **$50**

Open: **All year**
Breakfast: **Full**
Other Meals: **Available**
Pets: **Sometimes**
Children: **No**
Smoking: **No**
Social Drinking: **Permitted**
Airport/Station Pickup: **Yes**

Located in a beautiful Los Angeles suburb, this country ranch home on over an acre in the San Fernando Valley is a good base for exploring southern California. It's 30 minutes to the beach and 50 minutes to Disneyland. Freeways, shops, and restaurants are nearby. Dean and Dorothy welcome you to their art- and antiques-filled home and will provide local guide service by prior arrangement.

The Exley House "By-the-Sea" ✪
4273 PALOS VERDES DRIVE SOUTH, RANCHO PALOS VERDES, CALIFORNIA 90274

Tel: **(213) 377-2113**
Host(s): **Ruth and Earl Exley**
Location: **5 mi. SW of Los Angeles**
No. of Rooms: **2**
No. of Private Baths: **2**
Double/pb: **$50**
Single/pb: **$35**
Open: **All year**

Reduced Rates: **10%, seniors**
Breakfast: **Full**
Other Meals: **Available**
Pets: **Sometimes**
Children: **Welcome**
Smoking: **Yes**
Social Drinking: **Permitted**
Airport/Station Pickup: **Yes**

This gracious ranch-style home in suburban Los Angeles has an unobstructed ocean view. Ruth and Earl belong to a private beach club across the road, and you can use the facilities there. It is close to Marineland, Disneyland, and Hollywood. Ruth's breakfast specialties include honey-baked ham, French toast, or quiche. Your hosts offer you hors d'oeuvres with other pre-dinner refreshments. California State–Dominguez Hills is close by.

Sea Breeze Bed & Breakfast ✪
122 SOUTH JUANITA, REDONDO BEACH, CALIFORNIA 90277

Tel: **(213) 316-5123**
Best Time to Call: **6–10 PM**
Host(s): **Norris and Betty Binding**
Location: **19 mi. S of Los Angeles**
No. of Rooms: **2**
No. of Private Baths: **2**
Double/pb: **$40–$50**
Single/pb: **$30–$35**

Open: **All year**
Reduced Rates: **After 1 night**
Breakfast: **Continental**
Pets: **No**
Children: **Welcome, over 5**
Smoking: **Permitted**
Social Drinking: **Permitted**
Airport/Station Pickup: **Yes**

The welcome mat is out in front of the lovely stained-glass Colonial doors at Norris and Betty's modest home. A patio-garden is just outside the large guest room where you may relax after seeing the sights in the area. The Getty Museum and the Pasadena Rose Bowl are within easy reach. Their beach is the start of 22 miles of the Redondo-to-Pacific Palisades bicycle path, and tennis courts are within walking distance. Provisions are available if you prefer to fix breakfast yourself. You are welcome to use the Jacuzzi and TV. UCLA, USC, and Loyola Marymount are nearby.

Noone Guest House ✪
2755 SONOMA STREET, TORRANCE, CALIFORNIA 90503

Tel: **(213) 328-1837**
Host(s): **Betty and Bob Noone**
Location: **15 mi. SW of Los Angeles**
No. of Rooms: **1 cottage**
No. of Private Baths: **1**
Guest Cottage: **$35; sleeps 2**

Open: **All year**
Breakfast: **Continental**
Pets: **No**
Children: **Welcome**
Smoking: **Permitted**
Social Drinking: **Permitted**

This comfortable guest cottage has a bedroom, bath, kitchen, patio, TV, and laundry facilities, but the special plus is the warm hospitality offered by Betty and Bob. They'll direct you to Disneyland, Knotts Berry Farm, or the beach—all close to "home." Honeymooners love the privacy!

The Whites' House ✪
17122 FAYSMITH AVENUE, TORRANCE, CALIFORNIA 90504

Tel: **(213) 324-6164**
Host(s): **Russell and Margaret White**
Location: **5 mi. S of Los Angeles Intl. Airport**

No. of Rooms: **2**
No. of Private Baths: **2**
Double/pb: **$30–$35**
Single/pb: **$25**

Open: **All year**
Reduced Rates: **Weekly; monthly**
Breakfast: **Continental**
Pets: **No**

Children: **No**
Smoking: **No**
Social Drinking: **Permitted**

This contemporary home with its fireplaces, deck, and patio is located on a quiet street in an unpretentious neighborhood. The airport and lovely beaches are 15 minutes away. Disneyland, Knotts Berry Farm, Universal Studio Tours, and Hollywood are 30 minutes from the door. Use the laundry facilities or kitchen; Russell and Margaret want you to feel perfectly at home.

Hendrick Inn ✪
2124 E. MERCED AVENUE, WEST COVINA, CALIFORNIA 91791

Tel: **(818) 919-2125**
Host(s): **Mary and George Hendrick**
Location: **20 mi. E of Los Angeles**
No. of Rooms: **4**
No. of Private Baths: **1**
Max. No. Sharing Bath: **3**
Double/sb: **$30–$35**
Single/sb: **$25**
Suites: **$40**

Open: **All year**
Breakfast: **Full**
Other meals: **Dinner available**
Pets: **No**
Children: **Welcome, over 5**
Smoking: **Permitted**
Social Drinking: **Permitted**
Foreign Languages: **Spanish**

This lovely home is one hour from the mountains, seashore, and desert. It's less than an hour to Disneyland or busy downtown Los Angeles. The living rooms of this sprawling ranch-style house contain comfortable sitting areas and fireplaces where you may share a nightcap with your hospitable hosts. You will enjoy the backyard swimming pool and the Jacuzzi after a day of touring. There's a three-night minimum in the suite, a two-night minimum in the guest rooms.

Coleen's California Casa ✪
11715 SOUTH CIRCLE DRIVE, WHITTIER, CALIFORNIA 90608

Tel: **(213) 699-8427**
Best Time to Call: **6:30 AM–7:30 AM; 5 PM–9 PM**
Host(s): **Coleen Davis**
Location: **18 mi. E of Los Angeles**
No. of Rooms: **3**
No. of Private Baths: **3**
Double/pb: **$55**
Single/pb: **$45**
Suite: **$55**

Open: **All year**
Breakfast: **Full**
Other meals: **Available**
Pets: **No**
Children: **Welcome**
Smoking: **Permitted**
Social Drinking: **Yes**
Airport/Station Pickup: **Yes**
Foreign Languages: **Spanish**

Only minutes from the freeway system, this tranquil home is nestled into a hillside overlooking the city. It is convenient to Disneyland, Knotts Berry Farm, and all of Los Angeles's attractions. After a day of sightseeing, you'll be welcomed home with wine and hors d'oeuvres. With ample notice, Coleen will be happy to prepare dinner. Otherwise, she'll be pleased to recommend one of the many ethnic restaurants in the neighborhood. Breakfast is served on the deck filled with many exotic plants Coleen has cultivated.

MENDOCINO/WINE COUNTRY/NORTH COAST

Bed & Breakfast Exchange
1458 LINCOLN AVENUE, CALISTOGA, CALIFORNIA 94515

Tel: **(707) 942-5900; in Cal. (800) 654-2992**
Best Time to Call: **9 AM–5 PM**
Coordinators: **Larry M. Paladini and Diane Byrne**
States/Regions Covered: **Napa and Sonoma counties, northern California coast, Gold Rush country**

Rates (Single/Double):
  Modest: **$50–$60**
  Average: **$65–$85**
  Luxury: **$90–$300**
Credit Cards: **MC, VISA**

Some homes are located convenient to the wineries and vineyards. Wine-tasting tours are popular pastimes. Others are in the historic area where gold was discovered, and others are in the spectacular locale of the Pacific. The more expensive accommodations are on fabulous estates with pools, spas, and special services. You may also call Saturday, from 10 AM–5 PM; Sunday, noon–3 PM.

Big Yellow Sunflower Bed & Breakfast ○
235 SKY OAKS DRIVE, ANGWIN, CALIFORNIA 94508

Tel: **(707) 965-3885**
Best Time to Call: **Evenings**
Host(s): **Dale and Betty Clement**
Location: **60 mi. N of San Francisco**
No. of Rooms: **1 suite**
No. of Private Baths: **1**
Double/pb: **$65**
Single/pb: **$55**

Open: **All year**
Breakfast: **Full**
Other Meals: **Available**
Pets: **Sometimes**
Children: **Welcome**
Smoking: **No**
Social Drinking: **Permitted**

Located near the center of the Napa Valley wine area, the guest duplex, a completely private air-conditioned suite with kitchenette, fireplace, TV, videos, and sun deck, is part of Betty and Dale's wood-

and-brick Colonial home. Charmingly decorated with some antiques, lots of plants, and flower baskets, it accommodates seven people. Complimentary snacks and beverages are offered when you arrive. They pride themselves on serving a more-than-you-can-eat breakfast.

Scarlett's Country Inn ✪
3918 SILVERADO TRAIL N., CALISTOGA, CALIFORNIA 94515

Tel: **(707) 942-6669**
Best Time to Call: **9 AM–5 PM**
Host(s): **Scarlett Dwyer**
Location: **75 mi. N of San Francisco; 30 mi. from I-80, Napa Exit**
No. of Rooms: **3**
No. of Private Baths: **3**
Double/pb: **$75**
Single/pb: **$60**
Suites: **$75–$95**

Guest Cottage: **$220, sleeps 6**
Open: **All year**
Breakfast: **Continental**
Credit Cards: **MC, VISA**
Pets: **No**
Children: **Welcome**
Smoking: **Permitted**
Social Drinking: **Permitted**
Foreign Languages: **Spanish**

This inn is an intimate retreat tucked away in a small canyon in the heart of the famed Napa Valley, just minutes away from wineries and spas. Tranquillity, green lawns, and a refreshing swimming pool await you in this peaceful woodland setting. An ample breakfast featuring freshly squeezed juice, sweet rolls, and freshly ground coffee is served on the deck, at poolside, or in your own sitting room. All rooms have separate entrances, queen-size beds, and luxurious linens.

Muktip Manor O
12540 LAKESHORE DRIVE, CLEARLAKE, CALIFORNIA 95422

Tel: (707) 994-9571
Host(s): **Elisabeth and Jerry Schiffman**
Location: **101 mi. N of San Francisco**
No. of Rooms: **1 suite**
No. of Private Baths: **1**
Suite: **$50**
Open: **All year**

Breakfast: **Full**
Pets: **Welcome**
Children: **No**
Smoking: **Permitted**
Social Drinking: **Permitted**
Foreign Languages: **French, Spanish**

Elisabeth and Jerry have traded the often-frenzied San Francisco lifestyle for an uncomplicated existence by the largest lake in the state. They do not offer Victoriana, priceless antiques, or gourmet food. They do provide comfortable accommodations in their unpretentious beach house, a place to relax on the deck, and the use of their private beach and bicycles. They enjoy windsurfing and canoeing and have been known to give instruction to interested guests. Their motto is "If you wish company, we're conversationalists; if you wish privacy, we're invisible."

Pebble Beach B&B
1650 WEST MACKEN AVENUE, CRESCENT CITY, CALIFORNIA 95531

Tel: (707) 464-9086
Best Time to Call: **Mornings, evenings**
Host(s): **Margaret Pappas**
No. of Rooms: **2**
Max. No. Sharing Bath: **4**
Double/sb: **$55–$65**
Open: **All year**

Reduced Rates: **Weekly**
Breakfast: **Full**
Pets: **No**
Children: **Sometimes**
Smoking: **Permitted**
Social Drinking: **Permitted**
Airport/Station Pickup: **Yes**

This quiet and gracious place is just steps away from one of the loveliest beaches on the California coast. Watch the sunset from your room, relax in the guest lounge area, catch up on work at the desk and phone, or enjoy Margaret's extensive collection of compact discs. Wine and hors d'oeuvres are graciously served, and her piano, TV, and laundry facilities are offered for your use as well. Baked French toast made with sour cream and strawberries is a breakfast specialty.

You can walk off the calories on the beach or in the nearby Redwood National Park.

The Carter House ◐
1033 THIRD STREET, EUREKA, CALIFORNIA 95501

Tel: **(707) 445-1390**
Best Time to Call: **Noon–5 PM**
Host(s): **Mark and Christi Carter**
No. of Rooms: **7**
No. of Private Baths: **4**
Max. No. Sharing Bath: **4**
Double/pb: **$65**
Single/pb: **$50**
Double/sb: **$55**
Single/sb: **$45**
Suites: **$120**
Open: **All year**

Reduced Rates: **5%, seniors**
Breakfast: **Full**
Other meals: **Available**
Credit Cards: **AMEX, MC, VISA**
Pets: **No**
Children: **Welcome, over 12**
Smoking: **Permitted**
Social Drinking: **Permitted**
Airport/Station Pickup: **Yes**
Foreign Languages: **French, German, Spanish**

In 1982, this Victorian mansion was precisely reproduced from architectural plans drawn in 1884. The exterior is redwood, and the interior is done in redwood and oak. All trims and moldings are handmade and the chimneys rise to 50 feet. The rooms, each with a view, are furnished with authentic antiques, down comforters, Oriental rugs, original art, and fresh flowers. Christi and Mark pamper you with breakfasts that often include eggs Benedict or unusual pastries, hors d'oeuvres and complimentary wine before dinner, cookies and cordials before bedtime, and (by special arrangement with Mark) limousine service in his 1958 Bentley. Wow! Humboldt State University is nearby.

Campbell Ranch Inn ◐
1475 CANYON ROAD, GEYSERVILLE, CALIFORNIA 95441

Tel: **(707) 857-3476**
Host(s): **Mary Jane and Jerry Campbell**
Location: **1.6 mi. from Rte. 101, Exit Canyon Road**
No. of Rooms: **5**
No. of Private Baths: **3**
Max. No. Sharing Bath: **4**
Double/pb: **$100**
Single/pb: **$90**
Double/sb: **$90**
Single/sb: **$80**
Guest Cottage: **$70; sleeps 4**

Open: **All year**
Reduced Rates: **Weekly; $10 less Dec. 1–Feb. 28**
Breakfast: **Full**
Credit Cards: **MC, VISA**
Pets: **No**
Children: **Welcome, over 13**
Smoking: **No**
Social Drinking: **Permitted**
Minimum Stay: **2 nights on weekends, Mar. 1–Nov. 30**
Airport/Station Pickup: **Yes**

"Spectacular!" "Charming!" are words most often used when guests describe their stay at this picture-perfect hilltop home surrounded by 35 acres. The spacious bedrooms, each with a king-size bed, are handsomely furnished; several have balconies where views of mountains and vineyards are a backdrop to the colorful flower gardens. Breakfast, beautifully served, features a selection of fresh fruit, choice of gourmet egg dishes, homemade breads and cakes, and a variety of beverages. You can burn off the calories on the Campbells' tennis court or in their swimming pool, or borrow a bike to tour the wineries. Water sports and fishing are less than 4 miles away. Jerry will be happy to make your dinner reservations at one of the area's fine restaurants, but leave room for Mary Jane's dessert, always served "at home."

Camellia Inn
211 NORTH STREET, HEALDSBURG, CALIFORNIA 95448

Tel: **(707) 433-8182**
Best Time to Call: **Mornings**
Host(s): **Ray and Del Lewand**
Location: **65 mi. N of San Francisco**
No of Rooms: **9**
No. of Private Baths: **5**
Max. No. Sharing Bath: **4**
Double/pb: **$75–$95**
Double/sb: **$55–$65**
Single/sb: **$65**

Suite: **$95**
Open: **All Year**
Reduced Rates: **Available**
Breakfast: **Full**
Credit Cards: **MC, VISA**
Pets: **No**
Children: **Welcome, over 10**
Smoking: **No**
Social Drinking: **Permitted**

This elegant Italianate Victorian town house (circa 1869) is an architectural delight. It is convenient to the Russian River, wineries, golf, tennis, and more. Ray and Del serve a hearty breakfast buffet in the dining room, and wine is served in the afternoon in the grand parlor or on the pool terrace.

Frampton House
489 POWELL AVENUE, HEALDSBURG, CALIFORNIA 95448

Tel: **(707) 433-5084**	Breakfast: **Full**
Host(s): **Roland and Janette Wilkinson**	Credit Cards: **MC, VISA**
Location: **70 mi. N of San Francisco**	Pets: **No**
No. of Rooms: **3**	Children: **No**
No. of Private Baths: **3**	Smoking: **No**
Double/pb: **$50–$85**	Social Drinking: **Permitted**
Open: **Mar.–Dec.**	Airport/Station Pickup: **Yes**
Reduced Rates: **Available**	Foreign Language: **Spanish**

This turn-of-the-century redwood home is in the heart of Wine Country. The guest rooms offer a choice of queen-size beds or extra-long beds, and two of the baths have tubs-for-two. On chilly evenings, a fire crackles in the fireplace and complimentary vintage wines and cheese are served in the social room. Breakfast might consist of a Finnish oven pancake or apple-sausage casserole, and may be enjoyed in the solarium or at poolside. The Napa and Sonoma valleys are within an easy drive.

The Victorian Farmhouse ✪
7001 NORTH HIGHWAY 1, P.O. BOX 357, LITTLERIVER, CALIFORNIA 95456

Tel: **(707) 937-0697**	Breakfast: **Continental**
Host(s): **George and Carole Molnar**	Pets: **No**
Location: **168 mi. N of San Francisco**	Children: **Welcome, over 10**
No. of Rooms: **10**	Smoking: **Permitted**
No. of Private Baths: **$10**	Social Drinking: **Permitted**
Double/pb: **$75–$90**	Airport/Station Pickup: **Yes**
Open: **All year**	Foreign Language: **Hungarian**

Built in 1877, the farmhouse has been completely renovated and furnished in period antiques to enhance its original beauty and Victorian charm. It's close to Mendocino with its many galleries, boutiques, and restaurants. There's an apple orchard and gardens, and the ocean is a short walk away. Whale-watching in the winter months is popular.

George and Carole will pamper you with breakfast brought to your room, and will invite you to join them for evening sherry. There's a two-night minimum on weekends; three nights on holiday weekends.

The Swiss Chalet ⊙
5128 SWEDBERG ROAD, LOWER LAKE, CALIFORNIA 95457

Tel: **(707) 994-7313**
Host(s): **Robert and Ingrid Hansen**
Location: **60 mi. NE of Santa Rosa**
No. of Rooms: **2**
No. of Private Baths: **1**
Max. No. Sharing Bath: **2**
Double/pb: **$55**
Single/pb: **$45**
Double/sb: **$55**
Single/sb: **$45**

Open: **Apr.–Dec.**
Reduced Rates: **$5 less after 2 nights**
Breakfast: **Full**
Pets: **No**
Children: **No**
Smoking: **Permitted**
Social Drinking: **Permitted**
Airport/Station Pickup: **Yes**
Foreign Languages: **French, German, Italian, Spanish**

Stained-glass windows enhance this Bavarian gem that overlooks an 85-square-mile mountain lake. The interior is immaculate and tastefully furnished with handpainted tole pieces, antiques, and rich woods. The stone fireplace, deck, and private beach are fine sites for relaxation. All seasonal sports are available. Robert and Ingrid will spoil you with such goodies as eggs Benedict or blueberry pancakes. By the way, the second bedroom is available only to friends traveling together.

Wine Country Cottage ⊙
400 MEADOWWOOD LANE, ST. HELENA, CALIFORNIA 94574

Tel: **(707) 963-0852**
Best Time to Call: **Evenings**
Host(s): **Jan Strong**
Location: **In the Napa Valley**
Guest Cottage: **$85; sleeps 2**
Open: **All year**

Breakfast: **Continental**
Pets: **Sometimes**
Children: **Sometimes**
Smoking: **Permitted**
Social Drinking: **Permitted**

A private woodland retreat for two, with a patio under the pines, a comfortable bed-sitting room, private bath with shower, and complete kitchen. Jan will make reservations for you at the nearby spas. Napa Valley wineries, hot-air ballooning, tennis, golf, or swimming facilities are all close by. There are many galleries and renowned restaurants for you to enjoy.

Hilltop House B&B ✪
9550 ST. HELENA ROAD, SANTA ROSA, CALIFORNIA 95404

Tel: **(707) 944-0880**	Reduced Rates: **10%, Jan. 1–Apr. 15**
Host(s): **Annette and Bill Gevarter**	Breakfast: **Continental**
Location: **5 mi. from Rte. 29**	Pets: **No**
No. of Rooms: **2**	Children: **Welcome, over 12**
No. of Private Baths: **2**	Smoking: **No**
Double/pb: **$85**	Social Drinking: **Permitted**
Single/pb: **$75**	Minimum Stay: **2 nights on weekends,**
Open: **All year**	**Apr. 15–Nov. 30**

Annette and Bill built their contemporary country retreat to follow the contours of the Mayacama Mountains. The house is surrounded by 135 acres at the top of the ridge separating the wine regions of Napa and Sonoma. The unspoiled wilderness includes a garden of native plants, shrubs, and the sounds of hummingbirds and other wildlife. A 2,000-square-foot deck with hot tub provides the perfect spot for enjoying the panoramic views. The airy guest rooms are comfortably decorated with a combination of antiques and contemporary pieces, and each has spectacular views and a private entrance onto the deck. Your hosts serve a generous breakfast of fresh fruit, eggs, cheese, and yogurt, with fresh baked breads and muffins. They also welcome you for afternoon snacks and a glass of sherry in the evening. Hilltop House is 12 minutes from St. Helena and 30 minutes from Napa. The historic town of Calistoga, popular for its restorative hot mineral water, mud baths, massages, and fine restaurants, is located nearby.

Oak Knoll Bed & Breakfast ✪
858 SANEL DRIVE, UKIAH, CALIFORNIA 95482

Tel: **(707) 468-5646**	Single/sb: **$45**
Best Time to Call: **8 AM–12 PM; 3 PM–6 PM**	Open: **all year**
	Breakfast: **Full**
Host(s): **Shirley Wadley**	Pets: **No**
Location: **½ mi. from Hwy. 101**	Children: **No**
No. of Rooms: **2**	Smoking: **No**
Max. No. Sharing Bath: **4**	Social Drinking: **Permitted**
Double/sb: **$50**	

Every window of this redwood contemporary offers breathtaking views of the valley and vineyards of Mendocino wine country. Your hostess, Shirley Wadley, has decorated her lovely home with a mixture of modern elegance and rustic charm. The rooms feature exquisite chandeliers and colorful wall coverings. Bedrooms have queen-size beds and fresh flowers to enjoy. Relax on the spacious deck with some cheese, crackers, and a glass of local wine. Guests are welcome to unwind in the large solar spa, play the piano in the living room, or enjoy a movie on a 40-inch screen in the family room. Oak Knoll offers easy access to the coast, the redwoods, Lake Mendocino, and the wineries of Ukiah and Mendocino County.

MONTEREY PENINSULA

Happy Landing Inn ✪
P.O. BOX 2619, CARMEL, CALIFORNIA 93921

Tel: **(408) 624-7917**
Best Time to Call: **8:30 AM–9 PM**
Host(s): **Bob Alberson, Dick Stewart**
Location: **120 mi. S of San Francisco**
No. of Rooms: **7**
No. of Private Baths: **7**
Double/pb: **$85–$135**
Open: **All year**

Breakfast: **Continental**
Credit Cards: **AMEX, MC, VISA**
Pets: **Sometimes**
Children: **Welcome, over 12**
Smoking: **No**
Social Drinking: **Permitted**
Foreign Languages: **Japanese**

Located on Monte Verde between 5th and 6th, this early Comstock-style inn is a charming and romantic place to stay. Rooms with cathedral ceilings open onto a beautiful garden with gazebo, pond, and flagstone paths. Lovely antiques and personal touches, including breakfast served in your room, make your stay special. There's a two-night minimum on weekends.

Unicorn ✪
BOX 1540, PEBBLE BEACH, CALIFORNIA 93953

Tel: **(408) 624-5717**
Best Time to Call: **After 6 PM**
Host(s): **Ingo**
Location: **3 mi. W of Carmel**
No. of Rooms: **1**
No. of Private Baths: **1**
Double/pb: **$75**

Open: **All year**
Breakfast: **Continental**
Pets: **No**
Children: **No**
Smoking: **No**
Social Drinking: **Permitted**
Foreign Languages: **German**

Located in an exclusive area on the magnificent Monterey Peninsula, this lovely home on two acres is just a quarter-mile from the beach. The guest bedroom has an ocean view, and it is quite private because it is separated by two hallways from the main section of the house.

Ingo, a licensed aesthetician and certified massage therapist, will schedule facials and cellulite treatments at her Carmel studio for her women guests.

Babbling Brook Inn
1025 LAUREL STREET, SANTA CRUZ, CALIFORNIA 95060

Tel: **(408) 427-2437**
Best Time to Call: **12 PM–3 PM**
Host(s): **Tom and Helen King**
Location: **2 blocks from Hwy. 1**
No. of Rooms: **12**
No. of Private Baths: **12**
Double/pb: **$85–$125**
Open: **All year**
Reduced Rates: **Available**

Breakfast: **Full**
Credit Cards: **AMEX, Discover, MC, VISA**
Pets: **No**
Children: **Welcome, over 12**
Smoking: **Permitted**
Minimum Stay: **2 nights**
Foreign Languages: **French, Spanish**

Cascading waterfalls, a brook, gardens, and redwood trees surround this country inn. The oldest part of the house was built in 1909 on what was once a tannery and flour mill. Over the years, the house was changed by a number of owners, including the counsel to a czar and a woman known as the countess, who added several rooms and a balcony. When the Kings bought the inn in 1981, they added three two-story structures to make a total of 12 rooms. The result is a rustic, rambling retreat decorated in French country furnishings. Most rooms have a cozy fireplace, private deck, and outside entrance. Your hosts have owned restaurants and hotels in South America and are experts in making 2 people or 100 feel equally at home. Helen is a gourmet cook, as you will see from her breakfast repertoire of omelets, stratas, and fritattas. This historic inn is walking distance from the ocean, boardwalk, shops, and tennis courts.

SACRAMENTO AREA

Annie Horan's ✪
415 WEST MAIN STREET, GRASS VALLEY, CALIFORNIA 95945

Tel: **(916) 272-2418**
Best Time to Call: **Mornings**
Host(s): **Tom and Pat Kiddy**
Location: **45 mi. NW of Sacramento**
No. of Rooms: **4**
No. of Private Baths: **4**
Double/pb: **$55–$85**
Open: **All year**

Breakfast: **Full**
Credit Cards: **MC, VISA**
Pets: **no**
Children: **Welcome**
Smoking: **No**
Social Drinking: **Permitted**
Airport/Station Pickup: **Yes**

Annie Horan's is an elegant Victorian of splendid design and workmanship. Its parlor, entry hall, and guest quarters appear as they did in the opulent Gold Rush days. Tom and Pat have furnished this treasure with antiques that best depict that era. They invite you to enjoy the mountain air on the spacious deck. Nearby activities include panning for gold, swimming, golf, hiking, and nature trails.

The Inn at Shallow Creek Farm ✪
ROUTE 3, BOX 3176, ORLAND, CALIFORNIA 95963

Tel: **(916) 865-4093**
Best Time to Call: **Evenings**
Host(s): **Mary and Kurt Glaeseman**
Location: **3 mi. from I-5**
No. of Rooms: **4**
No. of Private Baths: **2**
Max. No. Sharing Bath: **4**
Double/pb.: **$55**
Double/sb: **$45**
Guest Cottage: **$75; sleeps 2–4**

Open: **All year**
Reduced Rates: **$10 less after 3 nights**
Breakfast: **Continental**
Pets: **No**
Children: **No**
Smoking: **No**
Social Drinking: **Permitted**
Airport/Station Pickup: **Yes**
Foreign Languages: **French, German, Spanish**

The orchards of Shallow Creek Farm are known for mandarin and navel oranges and sweet grapefruit. Luscious berries, fresh garden produce, and a collection of exotic poultry, including rare silver guinea hens and African geese, are quite extraordinary. The inn, a gracious 88-year-old farmhouse, offers airy, spacious rooms furnished with carefully chosen antiques and family heirlooms, combining nostalgia with country comfort. Breakfast features homemade baked goods and jams, and a generous assortment of fresh fruits or juices and hot beverages.

The Feather Bed ✪
542 JACKSON STREET, QUINCY, CALIFORNIA 95971

Tel: **(916) 283-0102**
Host(s): **Chuck and Dianna Goubert**
Location: **70 mi. NW of Reno, Nevada**
No. of Rooms: **7**
No. of Private Baths: **7**
Double/pb: **$55**
Single/pb: **$50**
Suite: **$60**
Separate Cottage: **$75; sleeps 3**

Open: **All year**
Reduced Rates: **10% less on 3rd night**
Breakfast: **Full**
Credit Cards: **AMEX, MC, VISA**
Pets: **No**
Children: **Welcome, over 12**
Smoking: **No**
Social Drinking: **Permitted**
Airport/Station Pickup: **Yes**

CALIFORNIA • 115

This charming Queen Anne was built in 1893 and renovated at the turn of the century. The rooms feature vintage wallpaper, antique furnishings, and charming baths; most have clawfoot tubs. Enjoy a glass of sherry in the parlor or a cool iced tea on the front porch. A breakfast of blended coffee, fresh juices, fruits, and home-baked breads can be served in your room, on the patio, or in the dining room. The inn is convenient to water sports, snowmobiling, hiking, tennis, and skiing. Your hosts offer complimentary bicycles to help you explore beautiful Plumas National Forest and historic downtown Quincy.

Bear Flag Inn ✪
2814 I STREET, SACRAMENTO, CALIFORNIA 95816

Tel: **(916) 448-5417**
Best Time to Call: **Evenings**
Host(s): **Dean and Lisa Wofford**
Location: **½ mile from I-80**
No. of Rooms: **4**
No. of Private Baths: **4**
Double/pb: **$59**
Single/pb: **$54**

Open: **All year**
Breakfast: **Full**
Credit Cards: **AMEX, DC, MC, VISA**
Pets: **No**
Children: **Welcome, over 8**
Smoking: **No**
Social Drinking: **Permitted**

This European-style hostelry is located in a residential neighborhood of downtown Sacramento. It is a handsomely restored California "Arts and Crafts Style" bungalow decorated with Queen Anne furnishings and within walking distance of fine restaurants, Sutters Fort, and "J" Street boutiques.

The Briggs House ✪
2209 CAPITOL AVENUE, SACRAMENTO, CALIFORNIA 95816

Tel: **(916) 441-3214**
Best Time to Call: **9 AM–Noon; 4–9 PM**
Host(s): **Sue Garmston, Barbara Stoltz, Kathy Yeates, Paula Rawles, Leslie Hopper**
Location: **1 mi. from I-80**
No. of Rooms: **7**
No. of Private Baths: **5**
Max. No. Sharing Bath: **2**
Double/pb: **$75–$85**

Double/sb: **$60–$70**
Guest Cottage: **$95**
Open: **All year**
Reduced Rates: **10% less, 6 days**
Breakfast: **Full**
Credit Cards: **AMEX, MC, VISA**
Pets: **No**
Children: **Cottage only**
Smoking: **No**
Social Drinking: **Permitted**

Just a few blocks from the State Capitol, this is an elegantly restored Victorian house surrounded by stately trees. Antiques add to the splendor of the rich wood paneling, inlaid floor, Oriental rugs, and lace curtains. You'll be pampered with flowers in your room and English china and fine silver for your gourmet breakfast. Relax in the spa or sauna after a busy day of sightseeing. Evening treats include wine, fruit, nuts, and unhurried conversation in the living room. California State University–Sacramento is nearby.

SAN DIEGO AND ORANGE COUNTY AREA

American Historic Homes Bed & Breakfast
P.O. BOX 388, SAN JUAN CAPISTRANO, CALIFORNIA 92693

Tel: (714) 496-6953
Coordinator: **Deborah Sakach**
States/Regions Covered: **Nationwide;** in California: Anaheim, Carmel, Cambria, Laguna Beach, Napa, San Diego, San Francisco

Rates (Single/Double):
 Modest: $20 $25–$35
 Average: $30–$35 $36–$55
 Luxury: $50–$60 $56–$105
Credit Cards: **No**

All the homes on Deborah's roster are historically significant. They range from a three-story Victorian in San Francisco to a North Carolina plantation, including sea captains' houses, bayside retreats, Georgian mansions, and Early American Colonials. Many are designated National Landmarks and all share the common element of warmth and hospitality.

Hospitality Plus
P.O. BOX 388, SAN JUAN CAPISTRANO, CALIFORNIA 92693

Tel: **(714) 496-7050**
Best Time to Call: **9 AM–5 PM**
Coordinator: **Deborah Sakach**
States/Regions Covered: **Los Angeles, Laguna Beach, Napa, Pacific Grove, Redondo Beach, Santa Barbara, Solvang**

Rates (Single/Double):
Modest: $20 $30
Average: $30 $45
Luxury: $50 $85

Deborah's computerized service has access to over 1,000 B&Bs throughout California. Her specialty is planning complete coastal, mountain, and desert tours, staying at B&Bs all the way. No matter what your price range, special attention will be given to your needs.

The Blue Door ✪
13707 DURANGO DRIVE, DEL MAR, CALIFORNIA 92014

Tel: **(619) 755-3819**
Best Time to Call: **7 AM–10 PM**
Host(s): **Bob and Anna Belle Schock**
Location: **20 mi. N of San Diego**
No. of Rooms: **1 suite**
No. of Private Baths: **1**
Suites: **$50**

Open: **All year**
Reduced Rates: **After 5 nights**
Breakfast: **Full**
Pets: **No**
Children: **No**
Smoking: **No**
Social Drinking: **Permitted**

Enjoy New England charm in a southern California setting overlooking exclusive Torrey Pines Park. A garden-level suite with wicker accessories and king-size bed is yours; it opens onto a private garden patio. Breakfast is served in the spacious country kitchen or in the dining room warmed by the fire on chilly days. Anna Belle prides herself on creative breakfast menus featuring homemade baked goods. She will gladly direct you to the nearby racetrack, beach, zoo, or University of California at San Diego.

Gulls Nest
12930 VIA ESPERIA, DEL MAR, CALIFORNIA 92014

Tel: **(619) 259-4863**
Best Time to Call: **Before 8:30 AM**
Host(s): **Connie and Mike Segel**
Location: **20 mi. N of San Diego**
No. of Rooms: **2**
No. of Private Baths: **2**
Double/pb: **$50**
Suite: **$65**

Open: **All year**
Breakfast: **Full**
Other Meals: **Available**
Pets: **No**
Children: **Welcome**
Smoking: **No**
Social Drinking: **Permitted**

Gulls Nest is a contemporary wood home surrounded by pine trees. The house boasts a beautiful view of the ocean and a bird sanctuary from two upper decks. Guest accommodations consist of a comfortable, quiet room with queen-size bed, private bath, and patio. The suite has a king-size bed and a sitting room that can accommodate a third person for $10 more. Breakfast is served outdoors, weather permitting, and features fresh-squeezed juice, eggs, ham or bacon, homemade breads, and coffee cake. Great swimming and surfing are three blocks away at Torrey State Beach. Golf, shops, and restaurants are a 5-minute drive and Tijuana and the international border are 40 minutes away.

Country Comfort Bed and Breakfast ✪
5104 EAST VALENCIA DRIVE, ORANGE, CALIFORNIA 92669

Tel: **(714) 532-2802**
Best Time to Call: **Evenings**
Host(s): **Geri Lopker and Joanne Angell**
Location: **5 mi. E of Anaheim**
No. of Rooms: **4**
No. of Private Baths: **1**
Max. No. Sharing Bath: **3**
Double/pb: **$60**
Singie/pb: **$55**
Double/sb: **$50**

Single/sb: **$45**
Open: **All year**
Reduced Rates: **20% less after 3 nights**
Breakfast: **Full**
Other Meals: **Available**
Pets: **Sometimes**
Children: **Welcome**
Smoking: **No**
Social Drinking: **Permitted**
Airport/Station Pickup: **Yes**

Located in a quiet residential area, Geri and Joanne have furnished their home with your comfort and pleasure in mind. It is handicapped-accessible with adaptive equipment available. Amenities include a swimming pool, cable TV and VCR, an atrium, fireplace, and the use of bicycles including one built for two. Breakfast often features delicious cinnamon rolls, Scotch eggs and sausages, along with fruits and assorted beverages. Disneyland and Knotts Berry Farm are less than seven miles away.

Christmas House B&B Inn ✪
9240 ARCHIBALD AVENUE, RANCHO CUCAMONGA, CALIFORNIA 91730

Tel: **(714) 980-6450**
Host(s): **Jay and Janice Ilsley**
Location: **37 mi. E of Los Angeles**
No. of Rooms: **5**
No. of Private Baths: **2**
Max. No. Sharing Bath: **3**
Double/sb: **$55–$65**
Suites: **$95/$125**

Open: **All year**
Reduced Rates: **10%, Sun.–Thur.**
Breakfast: **Continental**
Credit Cards: **MC, VISA**
Pets: **No**
Children: **Welcome, over 13**
Smoking: **No**
Social Drinking: **Permitted**

H. D. Cousins built this late Queen Anne Victorian so that he could raise horses and his wife could entertain their prominent friends in style. Party-giving came naturally here amid the elegant furnishings, red-and-white stained-glass windows, and intricate wood carvings. Yuletide galas became a tradition, and so the name "Christmas House" endured. Your hosts spent two years carefully restoring the rooms and filling them with Old World antiques. Breakfast is served on fine china and linen in the dining room or in your bedroom, where thick terry cloth robes are provided for late morning lounging. On weekend mornings the meal is more elaborate, with choices such as sweet cheese crêpes with fruit sauce, and unique fresh fruit dishes. Afternoon tea is served in the parlor. Southern California's attractions are within easy reach, and your hosts will help with touring plans, picnics, and dinner reservations.

Betty's Bed & Breakfast ✪
3742 ARIZONA STREET, SAN DIEGO, CALIFORNIA 92104

Tel: **(619) 692-1385**
Host(s): **Betty Spiva Simpson**
No. of Rooms: **2**
Max. No. Sharing Bath: **3**
Double/sb: **$35**
Single/sb: **$25–$30**
Open: **All year**

Reduced Rates: **10%, weekly**
Breakfast: **Full**
Pets: **No**
Children: **Welcome, infants (crib)**
Smoking: **Permitted**
Social Drinking: **Permitted**
Airport/Station Pickup: **Yes**

Betty offers clean, comfortable accommodations in an attractive bungalow. The guest rooms are furnished comfortably with tasteful pieces, carpeting, and a ceiling fan. You are welcome to relax in the den or the patio and can feel free to store snacks and beverages in the guest refrigerator. Betty will gladly direct you to nearby Balboa Park, San Diego Zoo, and tennis courts.

E's Inn
3776 HAWK STREET, SAN DIEGO, CALIFORNIA 92103

Tel: **(619) 295-5622**
Host(s): **Erene Rallis**
Location: **½ mi. from US 5 and 8**
No. of Rooms: **2**
No. of Private Baths: **2**
Double/pb: **$45**
Single/pb: **$35**
Open: **All year**
Reduced Rates: **Weekly; 10%, seniors**
Breakfast: **Continental**
Other Meals: **Available**
Pets: **Sometimes**
Children: **Welcome**
Smoking: **Porch and patio only**
Social Drinking: **Permitted**
Airport/Station Pickup: **Yes**
Foreign Languages: **Greek**

On a quiet street in Mission Hills, this gray-and-white cedar-sided home welcomes the visitor with its inviting pillared porch and French doors. Guests are welcomed here with a glass of sherry or a hot cup of coffee or tea. The house is decorated with a blend of Greek antiques, armoires, and modern Dansk pieces, complemented by original paintings, ceramics, and enamels. Your hostess loves to cater to her guests and provides baskets of fresh fruit and flowers in each room. In the evening, she places a tiny surprise under each pillow. Breakfast specialties include bran muffins and Greek and Mexican omelets. E's is close to Balboa Park, the Gaslight District, and beautiful beaches.

Vera's Cozy Corner
2810 ALBATROSS STREET, SAN DIEGO, CALIFORNIA 92103

Tel: **(619) 296-1938**
Best Time to Call: **Before 10 AM; after 5 PM**
Host(s): **Vera V. Warden**
No. of Rooms: **1**
No. of Private Baths: **1**
Double/pb: **$40**
Single/pb: **$30**
Open: **All year**
Reduced Rates: **Weekly; 10%, seniors**
Breakfast: **Continental**
Pets: **No**
Children: **No**
Smoking: **No**
Social Drinking: **Permitted**
Foreign Languages: **French, German**

This crisp white Colonial with black shutters sits on a quiet cul-de-sac overlooking San Diego Bay. Guest quarters consist of a separate cottage with private patio entrance. Vera offers fresh-squeezed juice from her own fruit trees in season as a prelude to breakfast, served in the Wardens' Old World dining room. The house is convenient to local shops and restaurants, and is a mile from the San Diego Zoo.

Loma Vista Bed & Breakfast ✪
33350 LA SERENA WAY, TEMECULA, CALIFORNIA 92390

Tel: **(714) 676-7047**
Best Time to Call: **Mornings**
Host(s): **Betty and Dick Ryan**
Location: **50 mi. N of San Diego**
No. of Rooms: **6**
No. of Private Baths: **6**
Double/pb: **$75–$95**
Open: **All year**
Reduced Rates: **10%, corporate rate Mon.–Thurs.**
Breakfast: **Full**
Pets: **No**
Children: **No**
Smoking: **Permitted**
Social Drinking: **Permitted**

Temecula is a state historic site dating back to the settling of the West. This imposing white Mission-style home, with its red tile roof and numerous arches, sits high on a hill surrounded by lush citrus groves and premium vineyards. Air-conditioned for summer comfort, the beautifully decorated guest rooms are named after local wines, and most have private balconies. A museum, winery tours, shopping, fine dining, boating, fishing, and hot-air ballooning are all favorite pastimes. After a day of pursuing your interests, join your hosts on the patio for a panoramic view, some award-winning Temecula wine, and hors d'oeuvres.

Friends-We-Haven't-Met ✪
10071 STARBRIGHT CIRCLE, WESTMINSTER, CALIFORNIA 92683

Tel: **(714) 531-4269**
Best Time to Call: **7–11 AM**
Host(s): **Bob and Sandy Runkle**
Location: **3 mi. S of Anaheim**
No. of Rooms: **3**
Max. No. Sharing Bath: **5**
Double/sb: **$35**
Single/sb: **$25**
Open: **All year**
Breakfast: **Full**
Pets: **No**
Children: **Welcome, over 12**
Smoking: **Permitted**
Social Drinking: **Permitted**

The Runkles' two-story house offers a private den for reading, playing cards, or listening to music. The delightful backyard patio with flowers and barbecue is yours to enjoy. For those interested in physical fitness, Bob and Sandy are members of a private, 17-acre sports club that you may utilize. You are welcome to help yourself to coffee, wine, and fresh fruit. Long Beach State and the U. of C. at Irvine are nearby. Disneyland, Knotts Berry Farm, and the Queen Mary are minutes away.

SAN FRANCISCO AREA

American Family Inn ✪
P.O. BOX 349, SAN FRANCISCO, CALIFORNIA 94101

Tel: **(415) 931-3083**
Best Time to Call: **9 AM–5 PM**
Coordinators: **Susan and Richard Kreibich**
States/Regions Covered: **Carmel, Monterey, San Francisco, Marin County, Napa, Sonoma (Wine Country)**

Rates (Single/Double):
    Modest: **$40**   **$50**
    Average: **$55**   **$75**
    Luxury: **$75**   **$125**
Credit Cards: **AMEX, DC, MC, VISA**

The San Francisco locations are near all the famous sights, such as Fisherman's Wharf and Chinatown. Many are historic Victorian houses. Some homes offer hot tubs and sun decks; a few are on yachts and houseboats where the tariff ranges $100–$120. There's a two-night stay required.

Bed & Breakfast International—San Francisco ✪
1181-B SOLANO AVENUE, ALBANY, CALIFORNIA 94706

Tel: **(415) 525-4569**
Best Time to Call: **8:30 AM–5 PM**
Coordinator: **Jean Brown**
States/Regions Covered: **California— Berkeley, Palo Alto, San Francisco and the Bay Area, Monterey, Napa Valley, Palm Springs, Lake Tahoe; Las Vegas; Hawaii; N.Y.C.**

Rates (Single/Double):
    Modest: **$34–$52**   **$40–$58**
    Average: **$54–$72**   **$60–$78**
    Luxury: **$74 and up**   **$80 and up**
Credit Cards: **AMEX, DC, MC, VISA**

Jean was the first to bring the concept of a bed and breakfast reservation service to America. Her accommodations range from a town house apartment to a villa above an ocean beach with a private pool. Others are located near the seashore, at a marina, in a redwood forest, by a mountain stream, in the middle of a vineyard, as well as in city neighborhoods and downtown areas. A minimum stay of two nights is required in most homes. A $5 surcharge is made for those accepting one-night stays.

Burlingame B&B ✪
1021 BALBOA AVENUE, BURLINGAME, CALIFORNIA 94010

Tel: **(415) 344-5815**
Host(s): **Joe and Elnora Fernandez**
Location: **½ mi. from Rte. 101**
No. of Rooms: **1**
No. of Private Baths: **1**
Double/pb: **$40**
Single/pb: **$30**
Open: **All year**

Breakfast: **Continental**
Pets: **No**
Children: **Welcome**
Smoking: **No**
Social Drinking: **No**
Airport/Station Pickup: **Yes**
Foreign Languages: **Italian, Spanish**

Located in a pleasantly quiet neighborhood, with San Francisco only minutes away by good public transportation. The house offers the privacy of upstairs guest quarters with a view of a creek and native flora and fauna. It's all very clean and cheerfully decorated. Joe and Elnora will direct you to restaurants and shops to suit your budget.

Lore's Haus ✪
22051 BETLEN WAY, CASTRO VALLEY, CALIFORNIA 94546

Tel: **(415) 881-1533**
Host(s): **Lore Bergman**
Location: **25 mi. SE of San Francisco**
No. of Rooms: **2**
No. of Private Baths: **1**
Max. No. Sharing Bath: **4**
Double/pb: **$50**
Single/pb: **$45**
Double/sb: **$45**
Single/sb: **$35**

Open: **All year**
Breakfast: **Full**
Pets: **No**
Children: **Welcome, over 14**
Smoking: **Permitted**
Social Drinking: **Permitted**
Airport/Station Pickup: **Yes**
Foreign Languages: **French, German**
Minimum Stay: **2 nights**

Lore's Haus is an attractive ranch home on a quiet street, with a large, beautiful garden. Lore was born in Germany and has spent the last 30 years in Castro Valley. She prides herself on offering Americans a true European atmosphere with lots of plants, books, comfortable furnishings, and Oriental rugs. Breakfast includes French Brie, fresh German black bread, homemade jams, cold cuts, and eggs. If you like, tours of the Bay Area, Napa Valley, or anyplace else are available in German, French, or English. If you'd like to venture out on your own, the city center is 25 minutes away via car or rapid transit. After a day of touring, come back to Lore's and enjoy a glass of wine. A two-night stay is required.

Danville Bed & Breakfast ✪
1857 RIDGELAND CIRCLE, DANVILLE, CALIFORNIA 94526

Tel: **(415) 820-9180**
Best Time to Call: **After 5 PM**
Host(s): **Robin Elizabeth Kreske**
Location: **35 mi. SE of San Francisco**
No. of Rooms: **1**
No. of Private Baths: **1**
Double/pb: **$50**

Open: **All year**
Breakfast: **Continental**
Pets: **Sometimes**
Children: **Welcome**
Smoking: **Permitted**
Social Drinking: **Permitted**
Airport/Station Pickup: **Yes**

Situated on a hill overlooking Mt. Diablo, this modern two-story town house is just minutes away from the quaint town of Danville. Robin's home is a restful haven after a hectic day of sightseeing in San Francisco; the tennis courts and a swimming pool are just steps away. Robin is a talented pastry chef and equestrian. She'll be pleased to assist you with your touring plans and dining arrangements.

The Village Green Inn ✪
89 AVENIDA PORTOLA, EL GRANADA, CALIFORNIA 94018

Tel: **(415) 726-3690**
Best Time to Call: **9 AM–3 PM**
Host(s): **Susan Hayward**
Location: **20 mi. S of San Francisco**
No. of Rooms: **2 suites**
No. of Private Baths: **2**
Suites: **$81**
Open: **All year**

Breakfast: **Full**
Other Meals: **Available**
Credit Cards: **MC, VISA**
Pets: **No**
Children: **Welcome**
Smoking: **No**
Social Drinking: **Permitted**

Modeled after an English Tudor country inn, each guest suite has a private entrance, a refrigerator for storing snacks, a view of the Pacific Ocean, and, of course, a teakettle. Both are decorated in the traditional British style, with an abundance of brass, white wicker, hand-rubbed woods, and lace accents. Susan, formerly of Bath, England, serves such British fare as bangers, bacon, scones, and crumpets at breakfast. A half-hour drive from San Francisco and 100 years behind in time, this coastal village offers fishing, hiking, whale-watching, beach strolling, and the nearby historic town of Half Moon Bay. Excellent restaurants abound, and Prohibition-era speakeasies are now operated as colorful cafés.

Montara Bed & Breakfast ✪
P.O. BOX 493, MONTARA, CALIFORNIA 94037

Tel: **(415) 728-3946**
Best Time to Call: **Evenings**
Host(s): **Bill and Peggy Bechtell**
Location: **20 mi. S of San Francisco**
No. of Rooms: **1**
No. of Private Baths: **1**
Double/pb: **$65**
Single/pb: **$55**

Open: **All year**
Reduced Rates: **Weekly**
Breakfast: **Full**
Pets: **Sometimes**
Children: **No**
Smoking: **No**
Social Drinking: **Permitted**

Relax in a California-style contemporary set in a coastal hamlet on scenic Highway 1. Montara is a rural area, yet it's just 20 miles from San Francisco. Guest accommodations are newly remodeled and feature a private entrance that opens onto a redwood deck. Guests have exclusive use of an adjacent sitting room with a fireplace and an ocean view. Breakfast is served in a solarium overlooking the garden. Your hosts serve a variety of specialties along with honey from their beehives. Local activities include playing in the waves at the state beach, wandering the hiking trails at McNee Ranch State Park, or riding on Miramar Beach. There are numerous seafood restaurants to choose from as well as cuisine from Italy, Germany, and Mexico.

Casa Arguello ✪
225 ARGUELLO BOULEVARD, SAN FRANCISCO, CALIFORNIA 94118

Tel: **(415) 752-9482**
Best Time to Call: **10 AM–6 PM**
Host(s): **Emma Baires**
No. of Rooms: **5**
No. of Private Baths: **2**
Max. No. Sharing Bath: **3**
Double/pb: **$50–$60**
Double/sb: **$45**

Suites: **$80 for 4**
Open: **All year**
Breakfast: **Continental**
Pets: **No**
Children: **Welcome, over 7**
Smoking: **No**
Social Drinking: **Permitted**
Foreign Languages: **Spanish**

This spacious duplex has an elegant living room, dining room, and cheerful bedrooms that overlook neighboring gardens. Tastefully decorated with modern and antique furnishings, it is convenient to Golden Gate Park, Golden Gate Bridge, Union Square, and fine shops and restaurants. Mrs. Baires allows her kitchen to be used for light snacks. The University of California Medical School is nearby. There is a two-night minimum stay. Excellent public transportation is close by.

Casita Blanca ✪
330 EDGEHILL WAY, SAN FRANCISCO, CALIFORNIA 94127

Tel: **(415) 564-9339**
Host(s): **Joan Bard**
No. of Rooms: **1 cottage**
No. of Private Baths: **1**
Guest Cottage: **$70; sleeps 2**
Open: **All year**

Pets: **No**
Children: **No**
Smoking: **Permitted**
Social Drinking: **Permitted**
Foreign Languages: **French, Spanish**

Perched on a hill, nestled among trees, and overlooking the city and bay, this unique cottage is separated from the main house, affording you the luxury of privacy. Every detail has been attended to, down to condiments in the kitchen. Though limited to two people at a time, there is a two-day minimum stay. Joan will be happy to direct you to all the nontourist spots that make this city so exciting. The University of California Medical Center is close by. Joan also offers B&B in Carmel Valley, Lake Tahoe, Sonoma, and Palm Desert.

Rancho San Gregorio ✪
ROUTE 1, BOX 54, SAN GREGORIO, CALIFORNIA 94074

Tel: **(415) 747-0810**
Host(s): **Bud and Lee Raynor**
Location: **35 mi. S of San Francisco**
No. of Rooms: **4**
No. of Private Baths: **4**
Double/pb: **$60–$70**
Open: **All year**

Reduced Rates: **Available**
Breakfast: **Full**
Pets: **No**
Children: **Welcome**
Smoking: **No**
Social Drinking: **Permitted**
Airport/Station Pickup: **Yes**

Graceful arches and bright stucco characterize this Spanish Mission home set on 15 wooded acres. Rooms are decorated with American antiques and family pieces. Your hosts, Bud and Lee, are glad to share a snack and a glass of wine or champagne. On weekdays they serve a Continental breakfast; on Saturdays and Sundays a full feast features eggs or pancakes, fresh fruit and breads, and a variety of meats. The atmosphere is relaxing, and guests are welcome to borrow a book from the library, or play the organ. Rancho San Gregorio is close to the beach, horseback riding, and golf. San Francisco, Half Moon Bay, and a variety of state parks and recreational areas are within an hour's drive.

Mrs. "K's" Retreat ✪
14497 NEW JERSEY AVENUE, SAN JOSE, CALIFORNIA 95124

Tel: **(408) 371-0593/559-3828**	Reduced Rates: **Weekly**
Host(s): **Barbara and George Kievlan**	Breakfast: **Full**
Location: **3 mi. E of Hwy. 17**	Credit Cards: **AMEX, MC, VISA**
No. of Rooms: **3**	Pets: **No**
No. of Private Baths: **3**	Children: **Welcome**
Double/pb: **$47.50**	Smoking: **No**
Single/pb: **$37.50**	Social Drinking: **Permitted**
Open: **All year**	

This sprawling ranch-style home is nestled at the base of Blossom Valley, once famous for its orchards. Guest rooms are furnished with flair and boast separate entrances. Your hosts invite you to enjoy the living room fireplace, family room, spa, and adjacent patio, with pool and spacious yard. Those interested in stained glass will surely want to visit the studio on the premises.

Madison Street Inn ✪
1390 MADISON STREET, SANTA CLARA, CALIFORNIA 95050

Tel: **(408) 249-5541**	Reduced Rates: **15% for 4 nights;**
Host(s): **Theresa and Ralph Wigginton**	**15% seniors**
Location: **1½ mi. from Rte. 880**	Breakfast: **Full**
No. of Rooms: **5**	Other Meals: **Available**
No. of Private Baths: **3**	Credit Cards: **AMEX, MC, VISA**
Max. No. Sharing Bath: **4**	Pets: **Sometimes**
Double/pb: **$55–$75**	Children: **Welcome (crib)**
Double/sb: **$55**	Smoking: **No**
Single/sb: **$50**	Social Drinking: **Permitted**
Open: **All year**	

This restored, vintage Queen Anne is furnished with Oriental rugs and museum-quality antiques, including brass beds and tubs for two. Landscaped gardens, a swimming pool, and a hot tub grace the grounds, and a sunny meeting room is available for business gatherings. Belgian waffles or eggs Benedict are often on the breakfast menu. Exciting dinners can be arranged, prepared by Ralph, an accomplished cook. It is convenient to Santa Clara University and San Jose State University.

Gasthaus zum Bären ✪
2113 BLACKSTONE DRIVE, WALNUT CREEK, CALIFORNIA 94598

Tel: **(415) 934-8119**
Best Time to Call: **After 3 PM**
Host(s): **Lois D. Martin**
Location: **33 mi. E of San Francisco**
No. of Rooms: **3**
No. of Private Baths: **1**
Max. No. Sharing Bath: **2**
Double/pb: **$55**
Single/pb: **$50**
Double/sb: **$45**
Single/sb: **$40**

Open: **All year**
Breakfast: **Full**
Pets: **No**
Children: **Welcome, over 6 (must be swimmers)**
Smoking: **No**
Social Drinking: **Permitted**
Airport/Station Pickup: **Yes**
Foreign Languages: **German, Italian, Spanish**

This rambling ranch home is furnished with artifacts from around the world. A huge natural fireplace dominates the living and family rooms. In summer, the large swimming pool becomes the center of activity and a California-style breakfast is served in the garden. Guests are welcome to the Jacuzzi, grill, and bicycles. Your hostess will be happy to provide picnic suppers for performances at the nearby Concord Pavilion, an outdoor concert shell carved into Mount Diablo. Foreign-language tours of San Francisco, Sausalito, Muir Woods, and the Wine Country can be arranged on summer weekends. For nature lovers, Briones Regional Park and numerous wilderness areas are nearby. There's a two-night minimum stay.

SAN JOAQUIN VALLEY

Valley View Citrus Ranch ✪
14801 AVENUE 428, OROSI, CALIFORNIA 93647

Tel: **(209) 528-2275**
Host(s): **Tom and Ruth Flippen**
Location: **20 mi. N of Visalia**
No. of Rooms: **4**
No. of Private Baths: **2**
Max. No. Sharing Bath: **4 (washbasin in each bedroom)**
Double/pb: **$45**
Single/pb: **$42**

Double/sb: **$45**
Single/sb: **$42**
Open: **All year**
Breakfast: **Full**
Pets: **Sometimes**
Children: **Welcome**
Smoking: **Permitted**
Social Drinking: **Permitted**
Foreign Languages: **Spanish**

Located in the San Joaquin Valley (The Fruit Basket of the World), this modern, air-conditioned ranch home is set in the foothills of the Sierra Nevadas. The 70-foot-long porch provides some beautiful views. Tom and Ruth will be happy to plan your itinerary, which might include a visit to Sequoia National Park, Kings Canyon, Crystal Caves, Grants Grove, or you can play tennis on their clay court. Breakfast specialties are served in the delightful gazebo. Complimentary beverages are always available, as is fresh fruit in season.

Tatum's Bed & Breakfast ✪
748 N. EAST AVENUE, REEDLEY, CALIFORNIA 93654

Tel: **(209) 638-4940**
Best Time to Call: **5:30–6 PM**
Host(s): **Dale and Mary Lee Tatum**
Location: **25 mi. S of Fresno**
No. of Rooms: **1 suite**
No. of Private Baths: **1**
Suites: **$50**
Open: **All year**
Reduced Rates: **Weekly**
Breakfast: **Continental**
Pets: **No**
Children: **Welcome, over 5**
Smoking: **No**
Social Drinking: **Permitted**
Airport/Station Pickup: **Yes**

The Tatums have lived in this brown stucco house for 20 years. Now that their three kids are grown and on their own, they have converted the upstairs into a suite that's cozy, private, and comfortable. This area is known as "The Fruit Basket of the World" because of the fruit farms that surround it and is located midway between San Francisco and Los Angeles. Nearby, guests can enjoy the pleasures of the Kings River, which flows through the west side of town, where fishing, picnics, boating, river rafting, and swimming are all appealing possibilities. The Tatums' hospitality has inspired guests to ask them "not to change a thing. We loved staying in your home." General Grant National Park is an hour away.

Larson's Bed 'n Breakfast ✪
718 PHILIPPINE STREET, TAFT, CALIFORNIA 93268

Tel: **(805) 765-2917**
Best Time to Call: **Before 9 AM; evenings**
Host(s): **Patricia Larson**
Location: **38 mi. SW of Bakersfield**
No. of Rooms: **3**
No. of Private Baths: **1**
Max. No. Sharing Bath: **4**
Double/pb: **$40**
Single/pb: **$30**
Double/sb: **$40**
Single/sb: **$30**
Open: **All year**
Reduced Rates: **Available**
Breakfast: **Continental**
Pets: **No**
Children: **No**
Smoking: **Permitted**
Social Drinking: **Permitted**
Airport/Station Pickup: **Yes**

Larson's is a custom-built split-level located in the foothills of the San Joaquin Valley. The house is surrounded by three kinds of fruit trees and has a sun deck overlooking the countryside. Your hostess takes pride in offering amenities such as complimentary wine and cheese and pillow mints. Guests are invited to relax by the olympic-size swimming pool or enjoy a game of billiards in the fireplaced game room. After a lazy day, treat yourself to a manicure or pedicure; Patricia is a licensed manicurist with a business on the premises. For breakfast, a varying selection of freshly baked nut breads, muffins, Belgian waffles, and fresh orange and grapefruit juice are served. Taft is one of the great oil-producing centers of the world.

SAN LUIS OBISPO AREA

Megan's Friends
1776 ROYAL WAY, SAN LUIS OBISPO, CALIFORNIA 93401

Tel: **(805) 544-4406**
Best Time to Call: **11 AM–4 PM; 6–10 PM**
Coordinator: **Joyce Segor**
States/Regions Covered: **Atascadero, Baywood Park, Cambria, King City, Los Osos, Solvang, Sunset Palisades, San Luis Obispo**

Rates (Single/Double):
  Average: $35–$45 $40–$50
  Luxury: $55–$75 $60–$95
Credit Cards: **No**

Joyce has exclusive listings that no other reservation agency has. She is certain to accommodate you in a B&B best suited to your interests and purse; these range from a contemporary showplace to a cozy country cottage. A $10 one-time membership is required, for which you receive a detailed list describing the accommodations. Local attractions include the beaches, wineries, Farmers Market, and Hearst Castle.

The Village Inn ✪
407 EL CAMINO REAL, ARROYO GRANDE, CALIFORNIA 93420

Tel: **(805) 489-5926**
Best Time to Call: **11 AM–4 PM**
Host(s): **Jude and Don Stalker**
Location: **12 mi. S of San Luis Obispo**
No. of Rooms: **7**
No. of Private Baths: **7**
Double/pb: **$59–$85**

Single/pb: **$49–$59**
Open: **All year**
Reduced Rates: **Commercial rate Sun.–Thurs.**
Breakfast: **Full**
Credit Cards: **MC, VISA**
Pets: **No**

Children: **Welcome, over 10**
Smoking: **No**
Social Drinking: **Permitted**

Minimum Stay: **2 nights on holiday weekends**

Each of the inn's spacious, air-conditioned guest rooms is decorated with Laura Ashley bed linens and wall coverings, overstuffed pillows, antique dressers or dressing tables, and attractive bay windows with window seats. Two have small balconies, and several have working fireplaces. Breakfast often features apple pancakes, fluffy omelets, potato latkes with applesauce, or French toast with apple slices and caramel sauce. The sand dunes of Pismo Beach, Hearst Castle, the Great American Melodrama Theater, and 30 wineries are within easy reach.

Gerarda's Bed & Breakfast ✪
1056 BAY OAKS DRIVE, LOS OSOS, CALIFORNIA 93402

Tel: **(805) 528-3973**
Host(s): **Gerarda Ondang**
Location: **10 mi. from Hwy. 101**
No. of Rooms: **6**
No. of Private Baths: **2**
Max. No. Sharing Bath: **4**
Double/pb: **$41.34**
Single/pb: **$26.50**
Double/sb: **$41.34**
Single/sb: **$26.50**

Open: **All year**
Breakfast: **Full**
Pets: **Welcome**
Children: **Welcome**
Smoking: **No**
Social Drinking: **Permitted**
Airport/Station Pickup: **Yes**
Foreign Languages: **Dutch, Indonesian**

When you stay at Gerarda's, you are in for a veritable Dutch treat! Located in a pleasant, quiet neighborhood, the house is surrounded by interesting landscaping and lovely flower beds. This is a simple home comfortably furnished with charm and warmth. Breakfast features Dutch delicacies such as honeycake, jams, and breads. Hearst Castle, Morrow Bay, and San Luis Obispo are within a half hour's drive.

SANTA BARBARA AREA

D & B Schroeder Ranch ✪
1825 CRAVENS LANE, CARPINTERIA, CALIFORNIA 93013

Tel: **(805) 684-1579**
Best Time to Call: **7 AM–9 PM**
Host(s): **Don and Beverly Schroeder**

Location: **10 mi. SE of Santa Barbara**
No. of Rooms: **1**
No. of Private Baths: **1**

Double/pb: **$50–$60**
Single/pb: **$50**
Open: **All year**
Breakfast: **Full**

Pets: **No**
Children: **Welcome (one only)**
Smoking: **No**
Social Drinking: **Permitted**

This wood-and-glass contemporary home is on a ten-acre semitropical fruit ranch and boasts ocean and mountain views. You may pick fruit, play a hand of bridge, or enjoy the use of Bev and Don's spa or bicycles. All the attractions of Santa Barbara are close by. You are welcome to play tennis, swim, or watch a polo match for a modest fee at the Polo and Racquet Club. Be sure to ask Bev to show you the miniature room settings she creates. Fascinating!

George and Jean Harris ✪
1483 ANITA STREET, CARPINTERIA, CALIFORNIA 93013

Tel: **(805) 684-5629**
Host(s): **George and Jean Harris**
Location: **11 mi. E of Santa Barbara**
No. of Rooms: **1**
No. of Private Baths: **1**
Double/pb: **$45**
Single/pb: **$40**

Open: **All year**
Breakfast: **Full**
Pets: **No**
Children: **Welcome, over 11**
Smoking: **No**
Social Drinking: **Permitted**
Airport/Station Pickup: **Yes**

George and Jean have a one-story stucco home at the end of a quiet court. The guest room is decorated in Early American style and features a king-size bed and a mountain view. Special touches, such as a cookie jar filled with homemade goodies and fresh flowers in your room, are sure to help you feel at home. Outside, a spa surrounded by ferns awaits you in the garden. Breakfast specialties include orange-and-blueberry waffles, whole wheat pancakes, eggs, sausages, and fresh seasonal fruit. Carpinteria is known for its flower production, both in greenhouses and in open fields. The Harrises are 11 miles east of Santa Barbara, one mile from the beach, and a half-mile from the mountains.

Hidden Valley Home ✪
939 BARCELONA DRIVE, SANTA BARBARA, CALIFORNIA 93105

Tel: **(805) 687-8799**
Host(s): **Ellie and Kurt Pilgram**
Location: **¼ mi. from Rte. 101**
No. of Rooms: **1**
No. of Private Baths: **1**

Double/pb: **$50–$60**
Single/pb: **$45–$55**
Open: **All year**
Breakfast: **Continental**
Other Meals: **Available**

Pets: **No**
Children: **Welcome**
Smoking: **No**

Social Drinking: **Permitted**
Airport/Station Pickup: **Yes**

The Pilgrims are self-confessed tennis addicts, and for guests who share their enthusiasm, they offer use of the tennis courts and swimming pool at the Tennis Club of Santa Barbara for a small guest fee. Ellie and Kurt live just one mile from the Arroya Burro Beach and four miles from downtown Santa Barbara. Bus service is convenient for those without a car. Guests are welcome to share Ellie's well-tuned piano and her knowledge of the area—she is a docent at the Santa Barbara Historical Museum.

Long's Seaview Bed & Breakfast ✪
317 PIEDMONT ROAD, SANTA BARBARA, CALIFORNIA 93105

Tel: **(805) 687-2947**
Best Time to Call: **Before 6 PM**
Host(s): **LaVerne Long**
Location: **1½ mi. from Hwy. 101**
No. of Rooms: **1**
No. of Private Baths: **1**
Double/pb: **$60–$65**
Single/pb: **$50–$55**

Reduced Rates: **5%, seniors**
Open: **All year**
Breakfast: **Full**
Pets: **No**
Children: **Welcome**
Smoking: **No**
Social Drinking: **Permitted**
Airport/Station Pickup: **Yes**

Overlooking Santa Barbara's prestigious north side, this ranch-style home is in a quiet, residential neighborhood. Breakfast is usually served on the patio where you can see the ocean, Channel Islands, and citrus orchards. Convenient to the beach, Solvang, and Santa Ynez Valley, the large, airy bedroom is cheerfully furnished, with antiques and brass double bed. You are welcome to use the spa. The breakfast menu varies from Southern dishes to Mexican specialties.

Ocean View House ✪
P.O. BOX 20065, SANTA BARBARA, CALIFORNIA 93102

Tel: **(805) 966-6659**
Best Time to Call: **8 AM–5 PM**
Host(s): **Bill and Carolyn Canfield**
Location: **2 mi. from 101 Fwy.**
No. of Rooms: **2**
No. of Private Baths: **1**
Double/pb: **$40–$50**
Suites: **$60–$70 for 4**

Open: **All year**
Breakfast: **Continental**
Pets: **Sometimes**
Children: **Welcome**
Smoking: **No**
Social Drinking: **Permitted**
Airport/Station Pickup: **Yes**

This California ranch house features a guest room furnished with a queen-size bed and antiques. The adjoining paneled den, with double-bed divan and TV, is available together with the guest room as a suite. While you relax on the patio, you can look out at the sailboats on the ocean. It's a short walk to the beach and local shops. Hard-boiled eggs and cheese are always served. There is a two-night minimum.

Primrose Patio Inn ✪
P.O. BOX 60730, SANTA BARBARA, CALIFORNIA 93160

Tel: **(805) 683-1263**
Host(s): **Mildred "Mid" Lamb**
Location: **1½ mi. from Rte. 101**
No. of Rooms: **2**
No. of Private Baths: **1**
Max. No. Sharing Bath: **3**
Double/pb: **$69**
Double/sb: **$50**
Open: **All year**
Breakfast: **Full**
Children: **Welcome**
Smoking: **No**
Social Drinking: **Permitted**
Minimum Stay: **2 nights on weekends, holidays**
Airport/Station Pickup: **Yes**

Mildred's one-story contemporary home is in a garden setting surrounded by lush green lawns. It is beautifully furnished in Oriental simplicity accented with paintings, plants, and sculpture. The guest rooms have a private entrance off the flower-filled patio. The University of Santa Barbara and Goleta Beach and pier are five minutes away. The interesting Danish-inspired town of Solvang is a half-hour's drive. Tennis courts and boat rentals are nearby.

COLORADO

Bed and Breakfast of Colorado, Ltd. ✪
BOX 6061, BOULDER, COLORADO 80306

Tel: **(303) 494-4994**
Coordinators: **Kate and Jim Carey**
States/Regions Covered: **Boulder, Lafayette, Louisville, Longmont**

Rates (Single/Double):
Modest: $23 $30
Average: $32 $50
Luxury: $75–$95
Credit Cards: **MC, VISA**

The Careys' accommodations are quite select; listings range from a "modest" huge bedroom with a double bed, private bath, and separate entrance at the garden level to an "average" one with a living room with a fireplace and a deck overlooking the city. One "luxury" offering is a honeymoon cottage with fireplace, sauna, and hot tub. Don't miss Rocky Mountain National Park, the Shakespeare Festival, and great skiing. There is a $5 surcharge for a one-night stay. Please send $3 for their statewide directory.

A "Skier's" Bed & Breakfast ✪
P.O. BOX 804, COLORADO SPRINGS, COLORADO 80901

Tel: **(719) 630-3433**
Best Time to Call: **9 AM–5 PM**
Coordinator: **Kate Winters**
States/Regions Covered: **Colorado;**
  Ski Areas: **New Mexico, Utah**

Rates (Single/Double):
  Average: **$40–$95 $57–$125**
Credit Cards: **MC, VISA**

Skiers choose "Skier's" because its hosts and reservationists do ski and know best how to help the skier find suitable lodging. Hosts share their knowledge of the best powder runs for the experts and, because many of them instruct at the slopes, help the novice learn the skills of downhill or cross-country. Snowmobiles, sleighs, dogsleds, and snowshoes are some of the fun vehicles you can try. Snow bunnies will be directed to the best spot for sipping hot chocolate and watching the spectacular scenery through lodge windows.

Parrish's Country Squire ✪
2515 PARRISH ROAD, BERTHOUD, COLORADO 80513

Tel: **(303) 772-7678**
Host(s): **Donna and Jess Parrish**
Location: **30 mi. NW of Denver**
No. of Rooms: **2**
No. of Private Baths: **2**
Double/pb: **$55**
Single/pb: **$45**
Open: **Jan. 16–Dec. 14**

Reduced Rates: **10%, seniors**
Breakfast: **Full**
Pets: **No**
Children: **Welcome, over 5**
Smoking: **Permitted**
Social Drinking: **Permitted**
Airport/Station Pickup: **Yes**

Donna and Jess invite you to relax at their comfortable log ranch home located near Estes Park and Carter Lake. You are certain to enjoy the serenity and breathtaking scenery of this 1500-acre cattle ranch. Breakfast features homemade breads, wild plum or chokecherry jellies, as well as other delicious morsels. Horseback riding is available, or try your luck fishing in their stocked trout pond. No license required!

Briar Rose Bed & Breakfast ✪
2151 ARAPAHOE AVENUE, BOULDER, COLORADO 80302

Tel: **(303) 442-3007**
Best Time to Call: **7 AM–9 PM**
Host(s): **Emily Hunter and Kit Riley**
Location: **½ mi. from Hwy. 36**
No. of Rooms: **11**
No. of Private Baths: **6**
Max. No. Sharing Bath: **4**
Double/pb: **$88–$98**
Single/pb: **$68–$78**
Double/sb: **$68**
Single/sb: **$49**

Open: **All year**
Reduced Rates: **10%, after 4 nights**
Breakfast: **Continental**
Credit Cards: **AMEX, DINERS, MC, VISA**
Pets: **Welcome**
Children: **Welcome (crib)**
Smoking: **Permitted**
Social Drinking: **Permitted**
Foreign Languages: **Dutch, French, German, Italian, Polish, Tibetan**

This is a beautiful English country-style inn where hospitality is a studied art. Each comfortable guest room is furnished with antique furniture, fresh flowers, handmade feather comforters, and good books. You will be pampered with chocolates at bedtime, a glass of sherry in the evening, and a tea tray anytime. Adjacent to the University of Colorado campus, it is close to the summer music and Shakespeare festivals, and Bureau of Standards, the Boulder Dinner Theatre, and Rocky Mountain National Park.

Two Ten Casey ✪
BOX 154, 210 CASEY AVENUE, CENTRAL CITY, COLORADO 80427

Tel: **(303) 582-5906**
Best Time to Call: **6 AM–6 PM**
Host(s): **Esther Campbell**
Location: **35 mi. NW of Denver**
No. of Rooms: **1**
No. of Private Baths: **1**
Double/pb: **$35**

Single/pb: **$30**
Open: **Apr. 1–Nov. 1**
Breakfast: **Continental**
Pets: **Sometimes**
Children: **Welcome, over 5**
Smoking: **Permitted**
Social Drinking: **Permitted**

The bay windows of this comfortable clapboard cottage overlook Gregory Gulch, where gold was discovered in 1859. Esther, a retired nurse, will be happy to point out the historic sights. She is an experienced hiker and will lead you along the old trails. Area attractions include ski slopes, museums, shops, and restaurants.

Griffin's Hospitality House ✪
4222 NORTH CHESTNUT, COLORADO SPRINGS, COLORADO 80907

Tel: **(719) 599-3035**
Best Time to Call: **Mornings**
Host(s): **John and Diane Griffin**
Location: **5 mi. N of Colorado Springs**
No. of Rooms: **3**
No. of Private Baths: **1**
Max. No. Sharing Bath: **4**
Double/pb: **$35**
Single/pb: **$25**
Double/sb: **$35**
Open: **All year**
Breakfast: **Full**
Pets: **No**
Children: **Welcome (crib)**
Smoking: **No**
Social Drinking: **Permitted**
Airport/Station Pickup: **Yes**
Minimum Stay: **2 nights**

The welcome mat is always out at Diane and John's house. It's close to Pike's Peak, the Air Force Academy, and the Garden of the Gods. You can use the picnic table, TV, washing machine, and dryer. You will enjoy a fine view of Pike's Peak while eating the bountiful breakfast. In the evening, you are invited to relax in the living room with wine and good conversation. The University of Colorado is 4 miles away.

Holden House—1902
1102 W. PIKE'S PEAK AVENUE, COLORADO SPRINGS, COLORADO 80904

Tel: **(719) 471-3980**
Best Time to Call: **Early AM; evenings**
Host(s): **Sallie and Welling Clark**
Location: **2 mi. from I-25**
No. of Rooms: **3**
No. of Private Baths: **3**
Double/pb: **$46–$50**
Single/pb: **$46–$50**
Open: **All year**
Breakfast: **Full**
Pets: **No**
Children: **No**
Smoking: **No**
Social Drinking: **Permitted**

This stately Victorian home, built in 1902, is located in the historic Old Colorado City area. It has been colorfully and lovingly furnished with many family heirlooms. A breakfast of homemade breads, muffins, jam, and freshly ground coffee is served in the lovely dining room, or on the veranda on warm, sunny mornings. Complimentary sherry is offered in the evening. Sallie and Welling will be pleased to help in planning your itinerary around the area's many attractions.

Katie's Korner ✪
1304 NORTH EL PASO, COLORADO SPRINGS, COLORADO 80903

Tel: **(719) 630-3322**
Best Time to Call: **Mornings**
Host(s): **Katherine Robertson**
No. of Rooms: **2**
No. of Private Baths: **1**
Max. No. Sharing Bath: **4**
Double/pb: **$44**
Single/pb: **$35**
Double/sb: **$40**

Single/sb: **$30**
Open: **All year**
Breakfast: **Continental**
Other Meals: **Available**
Pets: **No**
Children: **Welcome, over 8**
Smoking: **No**
Social Drinking: **Permitted**

Comfortably and attractively decorated with antiques and print wallpapers, this pretty two-story yellow Victorian sits on a corner near Colorado College. There's a private entrance into the guests' sitting room area. Katie is a "people person," sincerely interested in helping her guests get the most out of their visit.

Trout City Inn at Buena Vista ✪
(Mailing address: 12345 LINDSEY LANE, COLORADO SPRINGS, COLORADO 80908)

Tel: **(719) 495-0348**
Best Time to Call: **After 6 PM**
Host(s): **Juel and Irene Kjeldsen**
Location: **75 mi. W of Colorado Springs on Hwy. 24/285**
No. of Rooms: **5**
No. of Private Baths: **5**
Double/pb: **$28**
Suites: **Each room sleeps four**
Open: **June 1–Oct. 15**

Reduced Rates: **10%, seniors over 65**
Breakfast: **Full**
Other Meals: **Available**
Credit Cards: **MC, VISA**
Pets: **No**
Children: **Welcome, over 12**
Smoking: **No**
Social Drinking: **Permitted**
Airport/Station Pickup: **Yes**

Trout City Inn is a historic site on the famous South Park Narrow Gauge Railroad, and is located at the edge of a trout stream. It is an accurate reconstruction of a mountain railroad depot with authentic private rail cars containing Pullman berths. The depot rooms feature Victorian decor, high ceilings, and four-poster or brass beds. Glass doors open onto a deck with views of the 14,000-foot peaks of the Continental Divide. Hiking, biking, panning for gold, and fly-fishing are within steps of the front door; white-water rafting is minutes away. Social-hour snacks are served in the depot "waiting room."

The Claim Jumper Inn ✪
704 WHITEROCK, CRESTED BUTTE, COLORADO 81224

Tel: (303) 349-6471
Host(s): Jim and Nancy Harlow
Location: 28 mi. from US Hwy. 50, Gunnison Exit
No. of Rooms: 3
No. of Private Baths: 1
Max. No. Sharing Bath: 4
Double/pb: $50
Double/sb: $45
Open: All year

Reduced Rates: $5 less in spring and summer
Breakfast: Continental
Pets: No
Children: Welcome, over 12 (in sep. room)
Smoking: No
Social Drinking: Permitted
Airport/Station Pickup: Yes

This beautiful old log home includes a Victorian parlor, breakfast room, and three bedrooms furnished with antiques and queen-size brass-and-iron beds. In addition, Jim and Nancy have added a complete plant-filled redwood hot tub room and sauna for your enjoyment. Some of the unusual antiques are a gramophone from the Arabian peninsula, model wooden sailing ships from the island of Mauritius in the Indian Ocean, and a gold-leaf mirror that hung in the home of the notorious Belle Starr. All were collected by your hosts during their travels throughout the world. From fine skiing in winter to fun at the Center for Performing Arts in summer, a variety of activities are yours for the asking.

Queen Anne Inn ✪
2147 TREMONT PLACE, DENVER, COLORADO 80205

Tel: (303) 296-6666
Best Time to Call: 8 AM–Noon
Host(s): Ann and Charles Hillestad
No. of Rooms: 10
No. of Private Baths: 10
Double/pb: $69–$99
Single/pb: $54–$89

Open: All year
Breakfast: Continental
Credit Cards: MC, VISA
Pets: No
Children: Welcome, over 15
Smoking: No
Social Drinking: Permitted

Located in the residential Clements Historic District, this three-story house built in 1879 faces Benedict Fountain and Park. Decorated in the Queen Anne style, the elegant bedrooms offer a choice of mountain or city views along with such touches as a unique aspen mural, a Roman tub with gold fixtures, a private third-floor deck, and antique writing desks. Fine art, good books, and unobtrusive chamber music provide a lovely backdrop. The Hillestads offer a generous breakfast including seasonal fruits, assorted breads, homemade granola, and a special blend of coffee. The Denver Center Arts Complex, the Denver Art Museum, a shopping mall, and diverse restaurants are within walking distance. You are always welcome to help yourself to fruit, candy, soft drinks, and a glass of sherry. Ann and Charles will be happy to lend you their bike for local touring.

"Little Southfork" Ranch B&B ✪
15247 COUNTY ROAD 22, DOLORES, COLORADO 81323

Tel: **(303) 882-4259**
Host(s): **Gwen M. Taylor**
Location: **7 mi. N of Cortez**
No. of Rooms: **2**
No. of Private Baths: **1**
Max. No. Sharing Bath: **4**
Double/sb: **$30**
Single/sb: **$25**
Guest Cottage: **$40; sleeps 4**

Open: **All year**
Reduced Rates: **10%, off-season; families; weekly**
Breakfast: **Full**
Pets: **Sometimes**
Children: **Welcome, over 7**
Smoking: **Permitted**
Social Drinking: **Permitted**
Airport/Station Pickup: **Yes**

Enjoy a panoramic view of the Rockies in this picturesque rural section of southwestern Colorado. It's minutes to Mesa Verde National Park, Durango and the Silverton Train, river rafting on the Dolores River, the Painted Desert, aspen forests, lakes, and streams. Gwen is an active grandma who will make you feel at home.

Country Sunshine B&B ✪
35130 HIGHWAY 550 N., DURANGO, COLORADO 81301

Tel: **(303) 247-2853; 247-4559**
Best Time to Call: **Before 9 AM; after 3 PM**
Host(s): **Jim and Jill Anderson**
No. of Rooms: **4**
No. of Private Baths: **2**
Max. No. Sharing Bath: **4**
Double/pb: **$45**
Single/pb: **$40**
Double/sb: **$35**
Single/sb: **$30**

Open: **All year**
Reduced Rates: **10%, Nov., Apr., May**
Breakfast: **Full**
Credit Cards: **AMEX, MC, VISA**
Pets: **Sometimes**
Children: **Welcome (crib)**
Smoking: **No**
Social Drinking: **Permitted**
Airport/Station Pickup: **Yes**
Foreign Language: **French**

Nestled below rocky bluffs, there's a spectacular view of the San Juan Mountains from this spacious ranch home. Breakfast of homemade breads, jams, and blackberry pancakes with pure maple syrup is served on the large deck in view of the narrow-gauge train. You may borrow a bicycle for riding the winding roads along the Animas River, which also has excellent trout fishing.

River House B&B ✪
495 COUNTY ROAD 203, DURANGO, COLORADO 81301

Tel: **(303) 247-4775**	Breakfast: **Full**
Host(s): **Mari Carter**	Other Meals: **Available**
No. of Rooms: **6**	Credit Cards: **MC, VISA**
No. of Private Baths: **6**	Pets: **Sometimes**
Double/pb: **$55**	Children: **Welcome**
Single/pb: **$50**	Smoking: **Permitted**
Open: **All year**	Social Drinking: **Permitted**
Reduced Rates: **10%, Mar., May, Oct.**	Airport/Station Pickup: **Yes**

The airy, spacious bedrooms of this large ranch-style house boast beautiful views of the Animas River Valley. Breakfast specialties are egg-and-cheese casseroles, French toast, home-baked bread, and homemade preserves. They are served in the spectacular 900-square-foot atrium featuring eight skylights, a goldfish pond, and a cascading waterfall. Play pool or take a walk along the riverside. In winter, skiers appreciate the indoor storage for their equipment and the warmth of the living room fireplace.

Scrubby Oaks Bed & Breakfast ✪
P.O. BOX 1047, DURANGO, COLORADO 81302

Tel: **(303) 247-2176**	Single/pb: **$40**
Best Time to Call: **Early AM or PM**	Double/sb: **$45**
Host(s): **Mary Ann Craig**	Single/sb: **$30**
Location: **4 mi. from junction 160 and 550**	Open: **All year**
	Breakfast: **Full**
No. of Rooms: **7**	Pets: **No**
No. of Private Baths: **3**	Children: **Welcome**
Max. No. Sharing Bath: **4**	Smoking: **No**
Double/pb: **$55**	Social Drinking: **Permitted**

There's a quiet country feeling to this two-story home set on 10 acres overlooking the spectacular Animas Valley and surrounding mountains. Trees and gardens frame the patios where breakfast is apt to be served. All breads and preserves are homemade, and strawberry Belgian waffles are a specialty. On chilly mornings, the kitchen fireplace is the cozy backdrop for your wake-up cup of coffee or cocoa. You are made to feel part of the family and are welcome to play pool, take a sauna, read a book, watch a VCR movie, or simply take in the crisp air.

Cottonwood House ○
P.O. BOX 1208, ESTES PARK, COLORADO 80517

Tel: **(303) 586-5104**
Best Time to Call: **Mornings; evenings**
Host(s): **Kathleen and Ron Cotten**
Location: **70 mi. NW of Denver**
No. of Rooms: **1 suite**
No. of Private Baths: **1**
Suites: **$47–$70**
Open: **All year**

Reduced Rates: **Weekly**
Breakfast: **Continental**
Pets: **No**
Children: **No**
Smoking: **Permitted**
Social Drinking: **Permitted**
Airport/Station Pickup: **Yes**

A prominent businessman built this three-story mountain home in 1929. The house is set on a quiet, residential street, surrounded by towering spruce and pine. The rooms boast mountain views and have been lovingly restored right down to the oak floors. The Cottens have decorated 1930s style, with a combination of antique and country furnishings, and welcome you to a guest suite privately located on the second floor. The suite consists of a bedroom with a queen-size brass bed and a sitting room with a maple daybed, TV, telephone, and refrigerator. Relax with a lemonade on the porch, or by a cozy fire with a warm drink. Freshly baked muffins, rolls, and a choice of main dishes such as three-cheese quiche and apple-and-sausage crêpes are served each morning. In the warm weather, breakfast can be enjoyed on a sun porch with white wicker furnishings and plants. Cottonwood House is five miles from Rocky Mountain National Park and is convenient to golf, tennis, shops, and restaurants.

Emerald Manor ✪
441 CHIQUITA LANE, P.O. BOX 3592, ESTES PARK, COLORADO 80517

Tel: **(303) 586-8050**
Best Time to Call: **8 AM–8 PM**
Host(s): **Reggie and Maura Fowler**
Location: **65 mi. NW of Denver**
No. of Rooms: **4**
No. of Private Baths: **2**
Max. No. Sharing Bath: **2**
Double/pb: **$55–$65**
Single/pb: **$50–$60**

Double/sb: **$50**
Single/sb: **$45**
Open: **All year**
Breakfast: **Full**
Pets: **No**
Children: **No**
Smoking: **No**
Social Drinking: **Permitted**
Airport/Station Pickup: **Yes**

Every window of this Tudor pioneer home affords a beautiful view of the Rocky Mountains. The house is set on two acres in a quiet estate neighborhood within walking distance of downtown. Your hosts have decorated with comfortable wood furnishings, antiques, fine china, and crystal. Guest rooms are furnished in a variety of styles from western to Victorian, and all have fine linens and lace-trimmed towels. Your hosts invite you to relax in a beamed living room in front of a cozy fire or in a tropical room with indoor heated pool and sauna. They serve a complete Irish breakfast—including eggs and bacon or sausage accompanied by grilled tomatoes and soda bread.

Wanek's Lodge at Estes ✪
P.O. BOX 898, 560 PONDEROSA DRIVE, ESTES PARK, COLORADO 80517

Tel: **(303) 586-5851**
Best Time to Call: **Evenings**
Host(s): **Jim and Pat Wanek**
Location: **71 mi. NW of Denver**
No. of Rooms: **3**
Max. No. Sharing Bath: **4**
Double/sb: **$38–$43**
Single/sb: **$31–$34**

Open: **All year**
Breakfast: **Continental**
Other Meals: **Available**
Pets: **No**
Children: **Welcome, over 10**
Smoking: **No**
Social Drinking: **Permitted**

Jim and Pat invite you to share their modern mountain inn, located on a ponderosa pine-covered hillside, just minutes away from Rocky Mountain National Park. The wood beams, stone fireplace, plants, and beautiful scenery provide a comfortable and relaxed atmosphere. Former educators, your hosts are people oriented, and staying with them is like being with old friends.

Elizabeth Street Guest House ✪
202 EAST ELIZABETH, FT. COLLINS, COLORADO 80524

Tel: **(303) 493-BEDS**
Host(s): **John and Sheryl Clark**
Location: **65 mi. N of Denver**
No. of Rooms: **3**
Max. No. Sharing Bath: **4**
Double/sb: **$39**
Single/sb: **$32**
Open: **All year**

Reduced Rates: **Weekly**
Breakfast: **Full**
Credit Cards: **MC, VISA**
Pets: **No**
Children: **Welcome, over 4**
Smoking: **Permitted**
Social Drinking: **Permitted**

This completely renovated and restored 1905 brick American four-square has leaded windows and oak woodwork. Family antiques, plants, old quilts, and handmade touches add to its charm. All the bedrooms have sinks. It is close to historic Old Town Square, Estes Park, Rocky Mountain National Park, and a block away from Colorado State University. John and Sheryl will spoil you with their special brand of hospitality and homemade treats.

Hardy House
P.O. BOX 0156, GEORGETOWN, COLORADO 80444

Tel: **(303) 569-3388**
Best Time to Call: **After 10 AM**
Host(s): **Sarah M. Schmidt**
Location: **50 mi. W of Denver**
No. of Rooms: **3**
No. of Private Baths: **1**
Max. No. Sharing Bath: **3**
Double/pb: **$65**
Double/sb: **$45**
Single/sb: **$25**

Suites: **$45–$65**
Open: **All year**
Reduced Rates: **Weekly**
Breakfast: **Full**
Other Meals: **Available**
Pets: **Sometimes**
Children: **Welcome, over 10**
Smoking: **Permitted**
Social Drinking: **Permitted**

Back in the 1870s this bright red Victorian, surrounded by a white picket fence, was the home of a blacksmith. Inside you can relax by the potbelly parlor stove, sleep under feather comforters, and wake up to savory breakfast dishes such as waffle cheese strata and coffee cake. Guest quarters range from a two-bedroom suite to rooms with queen-size or twin beds. If you have a special birthday to celebrate, you can stay in the Victorian Suite and be served a candlelight dinner along with champagne, cake, and breakfast the next morning, for $125. In the evening, Sarah serves wine, coffee, and tea. She will also prepare fresh trout for breakfast if you happen to get lucky in the creek across the street. Hardy House is located in the heart of the Historic District, half a block from the shops of Main Street. It is also close to hiking, skiing, and is walking distance from the Loop Railroad. Perhaps the best way to explore the town is on Sarah's six-speed tandem mountain bike, which she will gladly lend.

Sojourner's Inn ✪
1032 COOPER AVENUE, GLENWOOD SPRINGS, COLORADO 81601

Tel: **(303) 945-7162**
Best Time to Call: **After 5 PM**
Host(s): **Clay and Darlene Carrington**
Location: **160 mi. W of Denver**
No. of Rooms: **4**
No. of Private Baths: **4**
Max. No. Sharing Bath: **4**
Double/pb: **$32–$48**
Single/pb: **$27**

Open: **All year**
Reduced Rates: **Available**
Breakfast: **Full**
Credit Cards: **MC, VISA**
Pets: **No**
Children: **Permitted**
Smoking: **Permitted**
Social Drinking: **Permitted**
Airport/Station Pickup: **Yes**

Sojourner's Inn is a large, turn-of-the-century home in a quiet, residential neighborhood. The house is a blending of different styles, but the prevailing one is comfort. Guest rooms are individually designed, featuring television and comfortable queen-size beds. Each morning, the cheerful dining room is the setting for a tempting breakfast, including homemade breads, fresh fruit, and specialty dishes. Hosts Clay and Darlene love their country surroundings and will gladly direct you to skiing, rafting, fishing, and hiking. Downtown Glenwood Springs and the world's largest hot springs pool are just a short walk from the house.

Sunnyside Bed and Breakfast ✪
925 PITKIN AVENUE, GLENWOOD SPRINGS, COLORADO 81601

Tel: **(303) 945-6203**
Best Time to Call: **Mornings; evenings**
Host(s): **Phil Breidenbach and Michelle Dvoryak**
Location: **160 mi. W of Denver**

No. of Rooms: **3**
No. of Private Baths: **1**
Max. No. Sharing Bath: **4**
Double/pb: **$42**
Single/pb: **$32**

Double/sb: **$32**
Single/sb: **$22**
Open: All year
Breakfast: **Full**
Credit Cards: **MC, VISA**

Pets: **No**
Children: **Welcome, over 6**
Smoking: **No**
Social Drinking: **Permitted**
Airport/Station Pickup: **Yes**

Guests are welcomed to Sunnyside with a warm hello and a seasonal drink. The house is a 1905 frame with diverse furnishings and a friendly kitchen filled with copper, baskets, and collectibles. Breakfast specialties include fluffy omelets, homemade jam, and French toast. A sunny deck provides a comfortable spot for summer relaxing and birdwatching; separate cookout and picnic facilities are also available, as is a hot tub. Walk to hot springs pool, shops, restaurants, and the shuttle bus to Sunlight Ski area. Hiking, rafting, fishing, and boating are also nearby.

Talbott House ✪
928 COLORADO AVENUE, GLENWOOD SPRINGS, COLORADO 81601

Tel: **(303) 945-1039**
Host(s): **Cherry Talbott**
Location: **1 mi. from I-70, Exit 116**
No. of Rooms: **4**
Max. No. Sharing Bath: **4**
Double/sb: **$42**
Single/sb: **$27**
Guest Cottage: **$55 up; sleeps 2–5**

Open: **All year**
Breakfast: **Full**
Credit Cards: **MC, VISA**
Pets: **No**
Children: **Welcome**
Smoking: **Permitted**
Social Drinking: **Permitted**
Airport/Station Pickup: **Yes**

This Victorian dates back to the beginning of the century. It's been lovingly restored and features colorful wallpaper, Oriental rugs that cover fir floors, and an assortment of accessories collected from all over the world. Breakfast is served, family-style, in the dining room and typically includes homemade breads, burritos, potatoes, and fresh fruit. Cherry invites you to use the solar-powered, outdoor hot tub in all seasons. Walk to the Hot Springs Pool, Vapor Caves, interesting shops, and restaurants. A free shuttle will wisk you to the slopes of nearby Ski Sunlight.

The Dove Inn ✪
711 14TH STREET, GOLDEN, COLORADO 80401

Tel: **(303) 278-2209**
Host(s): **Ken and Jean Sims**
Location: **10 mi. W of downtown Denver**

No. of Rooms: **6**
No. of Private Baths: **6**
Double/pb: **$39–$59**
Single/pb: **$34–$54**

COLORADO

Open: **All year**
Reduced Rates: **10%, weekly**
Breakfast: **Full**
Credit Cards: **AMEX, DC, MC, VISA**
Pets: **Sometimes**

Children: **Welcome (crib)**
Smoking: **No**
Social Drinking: **Permitted**
Airport/Station Pickup: **Yes**
Foreign Languages: **Spanish**

The Dove Inn is a charming Victorian on grounds beautifully landscaped with decks, walkways, and huge trees. The house has many bay windows, dormers, and angled ceilings; each room is individually decorated with pretty wallpapers and Victorian touches. Breakfast specialties such as cinnamon rolls and fresh fruit compotes are served on the porch in the summertime. This delightful inn is located in the foothills of West Denver in one of the state's most beautiful valleys, yet it is just minutes from downtown Denver, historic Golden, and many other Rocky Mountain attractions. No unmarried couples, please.

The Gate House B&B
2502 NORTH FIRST STREET, GRAND JUNCTION, COLORADO 81501

Tel: **(303) 242-6105**
Best Time to Call: **9–11 AM; 5–9 PM**
Host(s): **Julie Susemihl and Rhonda McClary**
Location: **250 mi. W of Denver**
No. of Rooms: **4**
No. of Private Baths: **2**
Max. No. Sharing Bath: **4**
Double/pb: **$52**
Single/pb: **$40**
Double/sb: **$34–$42**

Single/sb: **$28–$36**
Open: **All year**
Reduced Rates: **10%, after 2 nights; 5%, seniors**
Breakfast: **Full**
Credit Cards: **MC, VISA**
Pets: **No**
Children: **Welcome, over 10**
Smoking: **No**
Social Drinking: **Permitted**
Airport/Station Pickup: **Yes**

Originally built in 1889 as a gatekeeper's house to a castle estate, this Tudor-style home was moved, stone by stone, to its present site in 1945 and was recently restored. The living room is enhanced by solid oak floors, French love seats, and a large window overlooking the rose garden. The bedrooms are large and tastefully furnished. Stroll the spacious grounds, complete with the original wrought-iron gate, past the vine-covered arbor, and relax under giant sycamore trees. Breakfast treats often include fruit-filled French toast and delicious crêpes and coffee cakes. It's less than an hour to the Grand Mesa, Dinosaur Museum, the Center for the Arts, and seasonal sports.

Ye Ole Oasis Bed and Breakfast ✪
3142 J ROAD, P.O. BOX 609, HOTCHKISS, COLORADO 81419

Tel: **(303) 872-3794**
Best Time to Call: **Mornings; late evenings**
Host(s): **Dwight and Rosemarie Ward**
Location: **1 mi. from Rte. 92**
No. of Rooms: **3**
Max. No. Sharing Bath: **4**
Double/sb: **$40–$45**
Single/sb: **$30–$35**

Open: **Oct.–Aug.**
Reduced Rates: **Available**
Breakfast: **Full**
Other Meals: **Available**
Credit Cards: **MC, VISA**
Pets: **Sometimes**
Children: **Welcome, over 6**
Smoking: **No**
Social Drinking: **Permitted**

The Wards welcome you to their restored farmhouse set on the Rodgers Mesa at an elevation of 5,200 feet. They have a 17-acre working farm complete with buggy rides and a turkey named Hillary. The house is filled with antiques of all kinds, including many family heirlooms. Bedrooms have hand-crocheted and quilted spreads, wood furnishings, and period wallpapers. Before retiring, you can take a long soak in the claw-foot tub. On winter mornings, Rosemarie uses an antique wood stove to prepare special dishes such as Swedish-style French toast and New England fruit duffy. The farm is close to swimming at Glenwood Springs, skiing at Powderhorn and Aspen, and over 80 lakes for swimming and fishing.

Onaledge Bed & Breakfast Inn ✪
336 EL PASO BOULEVARD, MANITOU SPRINGS, COLORADO 80829

Tel: **(719) 685-4265**
Best Time to Call: **Afternoons**
Host(s): **Mel and Shirley Podell**
Location: **4 mi. from I-25, Exit 141**
No. of Rooms: **3**
No. of Private Baths: **3**
Double/pb: **$60**
Single/pb: **$60**
Suites: **$85–$95**
Open: **All year**

Reduced Rates: **Oct. 15–Apr. 15 (except holidays); 10%, seniors**
Breakfast: **Full**
Credit Cards: **AMEX, DINERS, MC, VISA**
Pets: **No**
Children: **Welcome (crib)**
Smoking: **Permitted**
Social Drinking: **Permitted**
Airport/Station Pickup: **Yes**

Located on a hill overlooking historic Manitou Springs, this rock-and-frame Tudor-style home was built by a millionaire in 1912. Approximately $75,000 was spent on the garden area alone. The inn boasts unusual copper hardware and light fixtures, a large copper fireplace, and lovely hardwood floors. The spacious bedrooms have large windows framing lovely views of the mountains and Pike's Peak. In warm weather, breakfast may be enjoyed on one of the flowery patios. The cranberry muffins are legend, and guests have been known to give Michael's Western Omelet a standing ovation. For those watching their diet, a "Heart's Delight" low-fat breakfast may be ordered. Downtown Manitou Springs and Garden of the Gods Park are within walking distance.

The Eagle River Inn
145 NORTH MAIN, BOX 100, MINTURN, COLORADO 81645

Tel: **(303) 827-5761**
Best Time to Call: **8 AM–Noon; 3–10 PM**
Host(s): **Beverly Rude and Richard Galloway**
Location: **100 mi. W of Denver**
No. of Rooms: **12**
No. of Private Baths: **12**
Double/pb: **$69–$110**
Single/pb: **$59–$100**
Open: **All year**

Reduced Rates: **$10 less in April**
Breakfast: **Continental**
Credit Cards: **AMEX, MC, VISA**
Pets: **No**
Children: **Welcome, over 12**
Smoking: **Permitted**
Social Drinking: **Permitted**
Minimum Stay: **5 nights Dec. 20–Feb. 12**
Airport/Station Pickup: **Yes**

The inn's adobe facade and decor are fashioned after the historic inns of Santa Fe. The living room is warm and cozy, accented by an authentic beehive fireplace and a view of the river. The guestrooms are furnished in a southwestern mode, each with two double beds.

Minutes away are the slopes of Vail and Beaver Creek. A free ski shuttle stops across the street. You are invited to join your hosts for wine and cheese each afternoon. Prices increase December 21 through January 4 and for Vail Alpine Ski Championship weeks.

Uncompahgre Cabin
8454 5700 ROAD, OLATHE, COLORADO 81425

Tel: (303) 323-6789	Single/sb: $15
Best Time to Call: **Before 8 AM; after 8 PM**	Open: **All year**
	Breakfast: **Continental**
Host(s): **Dean and Ellen Mosher**	Other Meals: **Available**
Location: **15 mi. N of Montrose**	Pets: **Sometimes**
No. of Rooms: 2	Children: **Welcome, over 2**
Max. No. Sharing Bath: 4	Smoking: **No**
Double/sb: $27.50	Social Drinking: **Permitted**

This log cabin home is surrounded by the magnificent vistas of the Grand Mesa, the San Juan Mountains, and the Uncompahgre Plateau. Your hosts have created a rustic hunting lodge atmosphere overlooking the surrounding countryside. Natural, wholesome foods are served here, and guests are welcome to BYOB to a reasonably priced dinner topped off with a homemade dessert. In the morning choose from a Continental or full breakfast with home-baked breads. There is much to do close to home, such as fishing in the stocked ponds or visiting the many farm animals. Dean and Ellen will gladly pack a lunch for those who like to spend the day hunting, bird-watching, hiking or skiing. After a busy day, watch the sunset from a porch rocker, or unwind in the hot tub.

The Main Street House ✪
334 MAIN STREET, OURAY, COLORADO 81427

Tel: (303) 325-4317	Suites: $55
Host(s): **David Vince**	Open: **All year**
Location: **80 mi. from I-70**	Breakfast: **Continental**
No. of Rooms: 3	Pets: **Sometimes**
No. of Private Baths: 3	Children: **Welcome**
Double/pb: $40–$55	Smoking: **Permitted**
Single/pb: $35	Social Drinking: **Permitted**

The second-floor suite occupies an entire floor and features a fully equipped kitchen and two decks. The bedroom has a king-size bed and antique dresser. The living room is decorated in wood tones and the sofa converts to a double bed. One ground-floor suite has a studio room, small greenhouse, and a large deck overlooking Oak Creek Canyon. The other suite contains a double bed and futon couch that can sleep two. It is surrounded by a large deck with views of the San Juan Mountains. All guests are welcome to use the courtyard and children's play area. David is an avid outdoor enthusiast and will be happy to recommend ways for you to best enjoy his hometown.

Ouray 1898 House ○
322 MAIN STREET, P.O. BOX 641, OURAY, COLORADO 81427

Tel: **(303) 325-4871**
Host(s): **Kathy and Lee Bates**
Location: **On Hwy. 550**
No. of Rooms: **3**
No. of Private Baths: **3**
Double/pb: **$45**
Single/pb: **$40**
Open: **May 15–Sept. 15**
Reduced Rates: **10%, seniors; May 15–July 1**
Breakfast: **Full**
Credit Cards: **MC, VISA**
Pets: **No**
Children: **Welcome, over 5**
Smoking: **No**
Social Drinking: **Permitted**

This 90-year-old house has been carefully renovated and combines the elegance of the 19th century with the comfortable amenities of the 20th. Each guest room features a spectacular view of the San Juan Mountains from its private deck. Breakfast is beautifully served on antique china. Jeep trips, horseback riding, hiking, browsing in the many quaint shops, and relaxing in the hot springs are but a few of the local diversions.

Davidson's Country Inn ○
BOX 87, PAGOSA SPRINGS, COLORADO 81147

Tel: **(303) 264-5863**
Host(s): **The Davidson Family**
Location: **On US Hwy. 160**
No. of Rooms: **10**
No. of Private Baths: **2**
Max. No. Sharing Bath: **4**
Double/pb: **$64**
Single/pb: **$52**
Double/sb: **$43.50**
Single/sb: **$36**
Open: **All year**
Breakfast: **Full**
Credit Cards: **MC, VISA**
Pets: **Welcome (outside pen)**
Children: **Welcome**
Smoking: **No**
Social Drinking: **No**

You're sure to enjoy the beautiful Rocky Mountain scenery surrounding the 30 acres of the inn's grounds. Some months bring the deer and elk to graze neaby. There's a natural hot spring in town and the San Juan River flows close by. You are invited to browse in the gift shop, stocked with homemade items; play horseshoes, or use the solarium and library. For the children, there's a full toy chest and sandbox. Family heirlooms, handmade quilts, and lovely paintings enhance the comfortable decor. Seasonal beverages are graciously offered.

Echo Manor Inn ✪
3366 HIGHWAY 84, PAGOSA SPRINGS, COLORADO 81147

Tel: **(303) 264-5646**
Host(s): **Sandy and Virginia Northcutt**
No. of Rooms: **10**
No. of Private Baths: **6**
Max. No. Sharing Bath: **4**
Double/pb: **$59**
Single/pb: **$50**
Double/sb: **$49**
Single/sb: **$40**
Guest Cottage: **$125 for 4**

Suites: **$75**
Open: **All year**
Reduced Rates: **Weekly; families**
Breakfast: **Full**
Pets: **Sometimes**
Children: **Welcome, over 11**
Smoking: **No**
Social Drinking: **Permitted**
Airport/Station Pickup: **Yes**

Known to many locals as "The Castle on 84," Echo Manor is a labyrinth of alcoves, bay windows, and turrets. The house draws from the Queen Anne and Dutch styles and is framed on all sides by the San Juan Mountains. The Royal Suite has a fireplace, a brass bed, and complimentary champagne, while the Courtyard Suite—with living room, stone fireplace, kitchen, and wet bar—is perfect for families. Relax in the wood-beamed game room, where you can enjoy satellite TV and a crackling fire. Just across the way is Echo Lake, where you can bring a picnic lunch or take your chances with the rainbow trout. The healing waters of Pagosa Springs and the slopes of Wolf Creek Ski Area are located within a half-hour's drive. After a day of activity, sit back in the hot tub or enjoy the sunset from the deck. The Northcutts will serve a gourmet breakfast and offer the kind of hospitality that will make your visit feel like a holiday.

Meadow Creek B&B Inn ✪
13438 HIGHWAY 285, PINE, COLORADO 80470

Tel: **(303) 838-4167; 4899**
Best Time to Call: **Before 10 AM; after 4 PM**
Host(s): **Pat and Dennis Carnahan**
Location: **25 mi. SW of Denver**
No. of Rooms: **6**
No. of Private Baths: **6**

Double/pb: **$49–$69**
Open: **All year**
Reduced Rates: **6th night free; 10%, seniors**
Breakfast: **Full**
Other Meals: **Available**
Credit Cards: **MC, VISA**

154 • COLORADO

Pets: **No**
Children: **Welcome, over 12**
Smoking: **Permitted**
Social Drinking: **Permitted**
Minimum Stay: **2 nights on weekends**

Nestled in a secluded meadow surrounded by stone outcroppings and aspen and pine trees, along a spring-fed creek, this rustic mountain retreat is balm for stress. Don't forget your camera as you wander the 65 acres, home to elk, birds, and wildlife. The historically significant house, barn, and outbuildings have been faithfully restored. Omelets and fresh baked cinnamon bread are breakfast specialties. The relaxing hot tub and the parlor fireside are both favorite gathering spots; fruit, beverages, homemade treats, and sherry are graciously served.

Sweet Adeline's ✪
949 F STREET, SALIDA, COLORADO 81201

Tel: **(719) 539-4100**
Best Time to Call: **9 AM–9 PM**
Host(s): **Bob and Adella Schulz**
Location: **132 mi. SW of Denver**
No. of Rooms: **3**
No. of Private Baths: **1**
Max. No. Sharing Bath: **4**
Double/pb: **$55**
Double/sb: **$45**
Single/sb: **$35**
Open: **May–Sept.; Oct.–Apr. for extended stays of 5 nights only**
Breakfast: **Full**
Credit Cards: **MC, VISA**
Pets: **No**
Children: **Welcome, over 12**
Smoking: **No**
Social Drinking: **Permitted**

Listed on the Colorado Inventory of Historic Sites, this Queen Anne home, vintage 1900, has been restored and decorated with country charm. Surrounded by the snow-capped peaks of the Rockies, the area abounds in every imaginable seasonal recreation. Adella enjoys catering to your appetite by serving family recipes that include a variety of homemade breads from Czech kolaches to Southern pecan rolls. The bedrooms are beautifully decorated, and guests may choose from king, double, or extra-long twin beds.

The Alma House ✪
220 EAST 10TH STREET, SILVERTON, COLORADO 81433

Tel: **(303) 387-5336**
Host(s): **Don and Jolene Stott**
Location: **50 mi. N of Durango**
No. of Rooms: **10**
Max. No. Sharing Bath: **4**
Double/sb: **$35**
Open: **June 1–Labor Day**
Breakfast: **Continental**
Credit Cards: **AMEX, MC, VISA**
Pets: **No**
Children: **No**
Smoking: **No**
Social Drinking: **Permitted**

This 1898 stone-and-frame building has been lovingly restored and comfortably updated. Each spacious room has a deluxe queen-size bed, luxurious linens, antique dressers, and special touches. The plumbing in the bathrooms is up-to-date but the brass-and-walnut fixtures are faithful to a day gone by. Don and Jolene have a large videotape library for your evening entertainment. Ride the Durango-Silverton Narrow Gauge Railroad. Silverton retains the flavor of the old Western town it is.

Wilson's Pinto Bean Farm ✪
BOX 252, YELLOW JACKET, COLORADO 81335

Tel: **(303) 562-4476**
Best Time to Call: **Before 8 AM**
Host(s): **Arthur and Esther Wilson**
Location: **18 mi. NW of Cortez**
No. of Rooms: **3**
Max. No. Sharing Bath: **6**
Double/sb: **$33**
Single/sb: **$26**
Open: **March–Nov.**

Reduced Rates: **Available**
Breakfast: **Full**
Other Meals: **Available**
Pets: **Sometimes**
Children: **Welcome**
Smoking: **Permitted**
Social Drinking: **Permitted**
Airport/Station Pickup: **Yes**

Wilson's Pinto Bean Farm is located in the dryland area, with mountains, alfalfa hay, and waving wheat visible in every direction. The farmhouse is surrounded by gardens and trees, with the biggest elm sheltering the backyard smokehouse and picnic table. This is a working farm with chickens, geese, ducks, and cows. Esther enjoys baking bread and has never bought a bakery cake or cookie mix. Breakfast specialties include blueberry or sourdough pancakes, hot cheese biscuits, fresh eggs, and homemade jams. The family would also be pleased to have you join them for supper. They can show children of all ages the delights of farm animals and country living. The farm is 40 miles from Four Corners, where the southwestern states meet in one place.

CONNECTICUT

Bed and Breakfast, Ltd. ✪
P.O. BOX 216, NEW HAVEN, CONNECTICUT 06513

Tel: **(203) 469-3260**
Best Time to Call: **5–9 PM weekdays; anytime weekends**
Coordinator: **Jack Argenio**
States/Regions Covered: **Statewide; Rhode Island—Providence, Newport**

Rates (Single/Double):
  Modest: $35 $45
  Average: $40 $50
  Luxury: $45 $55–$75
Credit Cards: **No**

Whether you plan to visit one of Connecticut's many fine colleges including Trinity, Yale, Wesleyan, or the Coast Guard Academy, the Mystic Seaport, picturesque country villages, theater, opera, fine restaurants, it is always pleasant to return to one of Jack's homes-away-from-home with congenial hosts ready to extend warmth and hospitality.

Covered Bridge Bed & Breakfast
P.O. BOX 701A, MAPLE AVENUE, NORFOLK, CONNECTICUT 06058

Tel: **(203) 542-5944**
Best Time to Call: **9 AM–7 PM**
Coordinator: **Diane Tremblay**
States/Regions Covered:
  Connecticut—Cornwall, Essex, Kent, Litchfield, New Preston, Salisbury, Sharon; Massachusetts—The Berkshires

Rates (Single/Double):
  Modest: **$45–$55**   **$45–$55**
  Average: **$55–$75**   **$55–$75**
  Luxury: **$75–$130**   **$75–$130**
Credit Cards: **No**
Minimum Stay: **2 days/holiday weekends**

If you enjoy historic homes, picture-postcard New England scenery, unsurpassed fall foliage, music festivals, theater, antiquing, auto racing, skiing, white-water rafting, or hiking, call Diane. Host homes are located primarily in the northwest corner of Connecticut, and the Berkshires in western Massachusetts. Williams College and Bennington College are nearby.

Captain Dibbell House ✪
21 COMMERCE STREET, CLINTON, CONNECTICUT 06413

Tel: **(203) 669-1646**
Host(s): **Ellis and Helen Adams**
Location: **21 mi. E of New Haven**
No. of Rooms: **3**
No. of Private Baths: **2 half-baths**
Max. No. Sharing Bath: **4**
Double/pb: **$60**
Single/pb: **$55**
Double/sb: **$50**

Single/sb: **$45**
Open: **All year**
Reduced Rates: **Weekly; 10% seniors**
Breakfast: **Continental**
Pets: **No**
Children: **Welcome, over 14**
Smoking: **Permitted**
Social Drinking: **Permitted**
Airport/Station Pickup: **Yes**

Ellis and Helen fell in love with this piece of Connecticut shore years ago when they used to come from their home in New York to spend the weekend sailing. They liked it so much, in fact, that they bought this sea captain's home, located just one half mile from the shore and marinas and a short drive from the town beach, and converted it into a B&B. Clinton is ideally situated for exploring the Connecticut coast; not far away you'll find Hammonassett State Beach, Mystic Seaport and Aquarium, Gillette Castle, the Goodspeed Opera House, the Essex Steam Train, Long Wharf Theater, and Yale. In order to help you enjoy the Connecticut shore they love so much, the Adamses are happy to lend you their bicycles, beach chairs, beach umbrellas, and inflatable boat.

Shore Inne
54 EAST SHORE ROAD, GROTON LONG POINT, CONNECTICUT 06340

Tel: **(203) 536-1180**
Best Time to Call: **8 AM–8 PM**
Host(s): **Helen Ellison**
Location: **3½ mi. W of Mystic**
No. of Rooms: **7**
No. of Private Baths: **3**
Max. No. Sharing Bath: **4**
Double/pb: **$55**
Double/sb: **$45**

Single/sb: **$40**
Open: **Apr.–Oct.**
Breakfast: **Continental**
Credit Cards: **MC, VISA**
Pets: **No**
Children: **Welcome**
Smoking: **Permitted**
Social Drinking: **Permitted**

Capturing the charm of the Connecticut coast, the inn's gracious rooms command water views. It is within a few miles of Mystic Seaport, the Marine Life Aquarium, Fort Griswold, and the U.S. Submarine Base and Memorial. Connecticut College and the U.S. Coast Guard Academy are close by. Swimming, fishing, biking, and tennis are a few steps from the door, and harbor and day cruises are available. Helen encourages you to enjoy the TV, library, and sunrooms.

Comolli's House ✪
36 BRUGGEMAN PLACE, MYSTIC, CONNECTICUT 06355

Tel: **(203) 536-8723**
Host(s): **Dorothy M. Comolli**
Location: **1 mi. from I-95, Exit 90**
No. of Rooms: **2**
No. of Private Baths: **1**
Max. No. Sharing Bath: **4**
Double/pb: **$75**
Single/pb: **$65**
Double/sb: **$65**

Single/sb: **$60**
Open: **All year**
Breakfast: **Continental**
Pets: **No**
Children: **Welcome, over 12**
Smoking: **Permitted**
Social Drinking: **Permitted**
Airport/Station Pickup: **Yes**

This immaculate home on a quiet hill overlooking Mystic Seaport is convenient to the sights of Olde Mistick Village and the Aquarium. Dorothy caters to discriminating adults who appreciate a homey atmosphere. The guest rooms are cozy in winter and cool in summer. She is pleased to provide information on sightseeing, sporting activities, shopping, and restaurants.

Weaver's House ✪
GREENWOODS ROAD, NORFOLK, CONNECTICUT 06058

Tel: **(203) 542-5108**
Host(s): **Judy and Arnold Tsukroff**
Location: **39 mi. NW of Hartford**
No. of Rooms: **4**
Max. No. Sharing Bath: **4**
Double/sb: **$45**
Single/sb: **$40**
Open: **All year**

Breakfast: **Continental**
Pets: **No**
Children: **Welcome**
Smoking: **No**
Social Drinking: **Permitted**
Airport/Station Pickup: **Yes**
Foreign Languages: **German**

Weaver's House is a turn-of-the-century Victorian facing the Yale Summer School of Music and Art Estate. In the 1930s, it was used as an annex to the Norfolk Inn. The guest rooms are simply decorated with handwoven curtains and rag rugs. Your hostess is a talented weaver, who will gladly display her loom for you. There are concerts and art shows in the summer and two state parks are nearby.

Janse Bed and Breakfast ✪
11 FLAT ROCK HILL ROAD, OLD LYME, CONNECTICUT 06371

Tel: **(203) 434-7269**
Best Time to Call: **Evenings**
Host(s): **Helen and Donald Janse**

Location: **1 mi. SW of New London**
No. of Rooms: **1**
No. of Private Baths: **1**

Double/pb: **$60**
Open: **All year**
Reduced Rates: **15%, seniors**
Breakfast: **Full**
Pets: **No**

Children: **Welcome, over 5**
Smoking: **Permitted**
Social Drinking: **Permitted**
Airport/Station Pickup: **Yes**

This Williamsburg-style saltbox is set on a quiet country road lined with vintage stone walls and century-old maples. The one-acre property includes a back patio and beautifully maintained gardens. Inside you'll find fresh flower arrangements, original art, Oriental rugs, and many antiques. Guest quarters feature pretty wallpaper, carpeting, wooden bed and bureau, and a sitting area with a Victorian love seat. Guests are welcome to relax in the library or living room with fireplace and grand piano. Your hosts serve fruit juice, ham or bacon, eggs, freshly baked muffins, and homemade jams for breakfast. Nearby points of interest include Mystic Seaport, the Goodspeed Opera House, and the Coast Guard Academy, home of the tall ship *Eagle*.

The Old Mill Inn ○
63 MAPLE STREET, SOMERSVILLE, CONNECTICUT 06072

Tel: **(203) 763-1473**
Best Time to Call: **9 AM–9 PM**
Host(s): **Ralph and Phyllis Lumb**
Location: **10 mi. S of Springfield, Mass.**
No. of Rooms: **4**
No. of Private Baths: **2**
Max. No. Sharing Bath: **4**
Double/pb: **$50**
Single/pb: **$50**

Double/sb: **$45**
Single/sb: **$45**
Open: **All year**
Reduced Rates: **10%, seniors**
Breakfast: **Continental**
Pets: **No**
Children: **Welcome**
Smoking: **No**
Social Drinking: **Permitted**
Airport/Station Pickup: **Yes**

Originally built in the 1850s, this comfortable home was enlarged and renovated many years later by the owner of the woolen mill next door. Today the old mill is a place to shop for gifts and furniture, while the house provides cozy lodgings for the traveler. Guest quarters are located on the second floor with bedrooms, baths, and a sitting room with cable TV, books, and a refrigerator. Bedrooms feature twin or full-size beds and comfortable furnishings. Downstairs in the gracious guest living room, you may relax by the fire, read, or listen to the stereo. Breakfast is served in a beautiful dining room with hand-painted walls overlooking the lawn. The Old Mill Inn is minutes from golf, the Basketball Hall of Fame, museums, restaurants, and shops.

The Old Mill Inn

Captain Stannard House ✪
138 SOUTH MAIN STREET, WESTBROOK, CONNECTICUT 06498

Tel: **(203) 399-7565**
Host(s): **Ray and Elaine Grandmaison**
Location: **25 mi. E of New Haven**
No. of Rooms: **9**
No. of Private Baths: **9**
Double/pb: **$60–$80**
Single/pb: **$55–$75**
Open: **All year**

Reduced Rates: **10%, seniors; AAA or Mobil clubs**
Breakfast: **Continental**
Credit Cards: **AMEX, DC, MC, VISA**
Pets: **No**
Children: **Welcome, over 6**
Smoking: **Permitted**
Social Drinking: **Permitted**

This Georgian Federal house with its fan window is the former home of a sea captain. Relax with a book, or browse through the on-premises antique shop. The village and the beach are close by. It is convenient to Mystic Seaport, Goodspeed Opera House, river cruises, fine restaurants, and charming shops. The U.S. Coast Guard Academy, Yale, and Wesleyan are nearby.

DELAWARE

- Wilmington
- New Castle
- Dover
- Rehoboth Beach
- Bethany Beach

The Sand Box & Sea-Vista Villas ✪
BOX 62, BETHANY BEACH, DELAWARE 19930

Tel: **(302) 539-3354 or (703) 820-7633**
Best Time to Call: **9 AM–5 PM**
Host(s): **Dale M. Duvall**
Location: **½ mi. from Rte. 1**
No. of Rooms: **3**
No. of Private Baths: **3**
Double/pb: **$60**

Single/pb: **$55**
Open: **May–Nov. 24**
Breakfast: **Full**
Pets: **Sometimes**
Children: **Welcome at the Sand Box**
Smoking: **Permitted**
Social Drinking: **Permitted**

Your cosmopolitan and most cordial host has two villas in a lovely wooded setting near Rehoboth Beach and Ocean City, Maryland. Guests will find the tennis court, swimming pool, terrace, and superb beach fine therapy after an urban winter. The Sand Box has two double bedrooms with baths, a deluxe kitchen, and a fireplace for chilly times. The Sea-Vista features a double bedroom and bath. Dale offers Happy Hour on the house.

Biddles Bed and Breakfast ✪
101 WYOMING AVENUE, DOVER, DELAWARE 19901

Tel: **(302) 736-1570**
Best Time to Call: **4–9 PM**
Host(s): **Millard and Hattye Mae Biddle**
Location: **½ mi. from US 13**
No. of Rooms: **3**
Max. No. Sharing Bath: **3**
Double/sb: **$40**

Single/sb: **$26**
Open: **All year**
Reduced Rates: **$30, Nov. 1–Apr. 1**
Breakfast: **Full**
Pets: **No**
Children: **No**
Smoking: **No**
Social Drinking: **Permitted**

At Biddles you will find old-fashioned hospitality in a contemporary setting. The guest rooms of this white frame house have been recently redecorated with comfortable furnishings and special touches, such as fruit and mints. Breakfast features hot homemade muffins and biscuits. Your hosts will do all they can to make your stay in the capital city enjoyable. It's a short walk to the sights of the historic district. The beaches are 40 miles away. Dover Air Force Base is nearby.

William Penn Guest House ✪
206 DELAWARE STREET, NEW CASTLE, DELAWARE 19720

Tel: **(302) 328-7736**
Best Time to Call: **After 5 PM**
Host(s): **Mr. and Mrs. Richard Burwell**
Location: **2 mi. from I-95**
No. of Rooms: **4**
Max. No. Sharing Bath: **4**
Double/sb: **$35**
Single/sb: **$35**

Open: **All year**
Breakfast: **Continental**
Pets: **No**
Children: **Welcome, over 3**
Smoking: **Permitted**
Social Drinking: **Permitted**
Foreign Languages: **Italian**

If you're a history buff, perhaps a stay in a 1682 house named for William Penn is what you've been seeking. Located in the heart of New Castle's historic district, the accommodations here are most comfortable. A lovely park for strolling and for the children to play in borders the Delaware shore, just two blocks away. The University of Delaware is 15 minutes from the house.

Tembo Guest House ✪
100 LAUREL STREET, REHOBOTH BEACH, DELAWARE 19971

Tel: (302) 227-3360
Host(s): **Don and Gerry Cooper**
Location: ¾ mi. from US 1
No. of Rooms: **4**
Max. No. Sharing Bath: **4**
Double/sb: **$50**
Open: **All year**

Reduced Rates: **Seasonal**
Breakfast: **Continental**
Pets: **Sometimes**
Children: **Welcome (crib, high chair)**
Smoking: **No**
Social Drinking: **Permitted**
Airport/Station Pickup: **Yes**

This white two-story frame beach cottage, set among old shade trees, is one block from the Atlantic Ocean. The house is surrounded by brick walks and gardens, and a private yard with chaise lounges for relaxing. The living room has a fireplace, hand-braided rugs, and an unusual collection of hand-carved shore birds and elephants. Each bedroom has an antique bureau, rocking chair, and either twin or full-size beds. Breakfast is served on a large enclosed front porch with rockers and swing. In colder weather, homemade muffins and scones are served in the kitchen, with its antique chandelier, butter churn, and coffee grinder. Don and Gerry will gladly direct you to local sights such as the restored Homestead, historic Port Lewes, and the Zwaanendael Museum.

The Boulevard Bed & Breakfast ✪
1909 BAYNARD BOULEVARD, WILMINGTON, DELAWARE 19802

Tel: (302) 656-9700
Host(s): **Charles and Judy Powell**
Location: ½ mi. from I-95, Exit 8
No. of Rooms: **6**
No. of Private Baths: **4**
Max. No. Sharing Bath: **3**
Double/pb: **$65**
Single/pb: **$60**
Double/sb: **$55**
Single/sb: **$50**

Open: **All year**
Reduced Rates: **Corporate; 10%, seniors**
Breakfast: **Full**
Credit Cards: **AMEX, MC, VISA**
Pets: **No**
Children: **Welcome**
Smoking: **Permitted**
Social Drinking: **Permitted**
Airport/Station Pickup: **Yes**

This beautifully restored city mansion was built in 1913 and has earned a place on the National Register of Historic Places. Upon entering, you'll be struck by the impressive foyer and magnificent staircase, leading to a landing complete with a window seat and large leaded-glass windows flanked by 15-foot fluted columns. Breakfast is served in the formal dining room or on the screened-in porch. Although

Baynard Boulevard is a quiet and peaceful street, it's just a short walk away from the downtown business district. Parks are close by, and it's just a short drive to Hagley, Winterthur, the Delaware Natural History or Art Museum, or head for nearby Chadds Ford, Pennsylvania, and the famous Brandywine River Museum.

The Pink Door ✪
8 FRANCIS LANE, WILMINGTON, DELAWARE 19803

Tel: **(302) 478-8325**
Best Time to Call: **Noon–9 PM**
Host(s): **Frank and Mary Wehner**
Location: **4½ mi. N of Wilmington**
No. of Rooms: **2**
No. of Private Baths: **1**
Max. No. Sharing Bath: **3**
Double/pb: **$45–$50**
Single/pb: **$40–$45**
Open: **All year**
Breakfast: **Full**
Pets: **Sometimes**
Children: **Welcome, over 3**
Smoking: **Permitted**
Social Drinking: **Permitted**
Airport/Station Pickup: **Yes**

The Pink Door is a contemporary ranch home on a wooded cul-de-sac. Guests are welcomed with a carafe of wine or pot of tea, and a tray of cookies. The decor is eclectic, ranging from the romantic Queen Anne period to today's modern designs. After a long day of touring the Brandywine Valley, you will appreciate returning to the sounds of crickets and awakening to the chirping of the many birds. Breakfast is served in the dining room or on the screened deck facing the woods. Your hosts will gladly direct you to the nearby Brandywine River Museum, Longwood Gardens, Winterthur, and the Hagley Museum.

Small Wonder B&B ✪
P.O. BOX 25254, WILMINGTON, DELAWARE 19899

Tel: **(302) 764-0789**
Best Time to Call: **After 4:30 PM**
Host(s): **Dot and Art Brill**
Location: **.4 mi. from I-95, Exit 9**
No. of Rooms: **2**
No. of Private Baths: **1**
Max. No. Sharing Bath: **4**
Double/pb: **$60**
Single/pb: **$55**
Double/sb: **$55**
Single/sb: **$45**
Open: **All year**
Breakfast: **Full**
Other Meals: **Available**
Credit Cards: **AMEX, MC, VISA**
Pets: **No**
Children: **Welcome, over 9**
Smoking: **No**
Social Drinking: **Permitted**
Airport/Station Pickup: **Yes**

The Brills describe their area—the Delaware and Brandywine valleys—as "a microcosm of American history and cosmopolitan trends—a blend of 17th-century Swedish and Dutch heritage and 20th-century innovation." They live in a quiet suburb surrounded by the things they love—a piano, an organ (Dot's a music teacher and organist), lots of books, and original paintings by a Delaware artist. Outdoors they have a swimming pool (in use from May through September) and a hot tub set in an award-winning garden. Bellevue State Park, once the estate of William B. du Pont, is nearby—perfect, according to the Brills, for jogging or strolling or for a leisurely dinner served in the mansion on the property. Longwood Gardens, Winterthur, and the Hagley Museum are close by. There's a $5 surcharge for a one-night stay.

For key to listings, see inside front or back cover.

✪ This star means that rates are guaranteed through December 31, 1989 to any guest making a reservation as a result of reading about the B&B in *BED & BREAKFAST U.S.A.*—1989 edition.

Please enclose a self-addressed, stamped, business-sized envelope when contacting reservation services.

For more details on what you can expect in a B&B, see Chapter 1.

Always mention *Bed & Breakfast U.S.A.* when making reservations!

If no B&B is listed in the area you'll be visiting, use the form on page 693 to order a copy of our "List of New B&Bs."

We want to hear from you! Use the form on page 691.

DISTRICT OF COLUMBIA

The Bed & Breakfast League, Ltd. ○
3639 VAN NESS STREET, N.W., WASHINGTON, D.C. 20008

Tel: **(202) 363-7767**
Coordinator: **Millie Groobey**
States/Regions Covered: **Washington, D.C.**

Rates (Single/Double):
  Modest: $30–$35 $40–$45
  Average: $35–$45 $45–$55
  Luxury: $45–$60 $55–$70
Credit Cards: **AMEX, MC, VISA**
Minimum Stay: **2 nights**

Millie's roster includes accommodations in apartment buildings, town houses, large homes, and small inns. Many are in historic areas and all are within easy walking distance of public transportation. Gracious hosts will cheerfully direct you to museums, fine restaurants, and interesting shops. There's a $10 processing fee for each reservation.

Bed 'n' Breakfast Ltd. of Washington, D.C.
P.O. BOX 12011, WASHINGTON, D.C. 20005

Tel: (202) 328-3510
Best Time to Call: **10 AM–5 PM Mon.–Fri.; 10 AM–1 PM Sat.**
Coordinator: **Lisa Stofan**
States/Regions Covered: **Washington, D.C.; Virginia and Maryland suburbs**

Rates (Single/Double):
   Average: **$35–$80 $45–$90**
Credit Cards: **AMEX, MC, VISA**

This service boasts a network of homes in the city's historic districts. Lisa has been on the Washington scene a long time, and she knows that the best places need not cost the most. Several of her accommodations are located in gracious Georgetown and on Dupont Circle. All of the homes are convenient to public transportation. She caters to women and those in the international field. Five-dollar surcharge for one-night stay.

Sweet Dreams & Toast, Inc.
P.O. BOX 4835-0035, WASHINGTON, D.C. 20008

Tel: (202) 483-9191
Best Time to Call: **11 AM–5 PM**
Coordinators: **Ellie Chastain and Amanda Adlon**
States/Regions Covered: **Washington, D.C.; Maryland—Bethesda, Chevy Chase, Silver Spring; Virginia—Alexandria, Arlington**

Rates (Single/Double):
   Average: **$40–$65 $53–$75**
Credit Cards: **MC, VISA**

The capital of the United States is awe-inspiring. You will want to spend several days to take it all in. This is your opportunity to watch history in the making and to visit the glorious monuments erected to memorialize those who shaped America's history. Ellie's hosts will direct you to restaurants and special shops that suit your taste and wallet. The agency is open January 6 to December 17. There's a two-night minimum stay.

FLORIDA

- Pensacola
- Tallahassee
- Jacksonville
- Sunnyside
- St. Augustine
- Gainesville
- Crescent City
- Daytona Beach
- Eastlake Weir
- DeLand
- Orlando
- Winter Park
- Tarpon Springs
- Clearwater
- Indian Shores
- Tampa
- St. Petersburg
- Sarasota
- Hobe Sound
- Jupiter
- Lantana
- Palm Beach
- Fort Myers
- Delray Beach
- Estero
- Fort Lauderdale
- Naples
- Hollywood
- Miami Beach
- Big Pine Key
- Marathon
- Summerland Key

A & A Bed & Breakfast of Florida, Inc. ✪
P.O. BOX 1316, WINTER PARK, FLORIDA 32790

Tel: (305) 628-3233
Best Time to Call: **9 AM–6 PM**
Coordinator: **Brunhilde (Bruni) Fehner**
States/Regions Covered: **Orlando area—Disney World, Epcot; Altamonte Springs, Cape Canaveral (Kennedy Space Center), Maitland, New Smyrna Beach, Sea World, Winter Park; Delray Beach, Ft. Myers, St. Augustine**

Rates (Single/Double):
  Modest: $25 $35
  Average: $25–$35 $36–$45
  Luxury: $40 $65
Credit Cards: **No**
Minimum Stay: **2 nights**

You should allow several days to really savor all this area has to offer. Bruni's hosts will suggest hints on getting the most out of the major attractions, wonderful un-touristy restaurants, and tips on where to shop for unique gifts to take home. All of her homes have a certain "touch of class" to make you delighted with your visit. Rollins College is close by. There is a surcharge of $5 for one night.

Bed & Breakfast Co.—Tropical Florida ✪
P.O. BOX 430262, SOUTH MIAMI, FLORIDA 33243

Tel: **(305) 661-3270**
Coordinator: **Marcella Schaible**
States/Regions Covered: **Boca Raton, Delray Beach, Ft. Lauderdale, Ft. Myers, Melbourne, Miami, Palm Beach, Sanibel Island, The Keys**

Rates (Single/Double):
Modest: $27–$35 $32–$40
Average: $35–$55 $40–$60
Luxury: $55–$145 $60–$150
Credit Cards: **MC, VISA (for deposit only)**

Marcella's roster ranges from a restored Art Deco mansion on an island in Biscayne Bay to a 59-foot Hatteras yacht. Accommodations to suit all budgets, with or without swimming pools, hot tubs, spas, but all with comfortable furniture and traditional hospitality. Many are convenient to the University of Miami, Barry College, and the University of South Florida. There's a $5 surcharge for one-night stays.

Bed & Breakfast Registry of Volusia County
P.O. BOX 573, DE LEON SPRINGS, FLORIDA 32028

Tel: **(904) 985-5068**
Coordinator: **Robin Johnstone**
States/Regions Covered: **Astor, Daytona Beach, De Bary, De Land, De Leon Springs, Deltona, Sanford**

Rates (Single/Double):
Average: $30 $35
Luxury: $40 $45
Credit Cards: **No**

Area attractions include the famed Daytona International Speedway and beach where the auto is king, Spring Garden Ranch where harness horses are trained, De Leon Springs State Park, and Blue Springs State Park, which is home to the manatee, an aquatic mammal. It's also a fine fishing area. Summer rates are reduced by $10 nightly. Keep this in mind should you care to visit Disney World, Sea World, and Epcot, since they are an hour's drive from most host homes.

Central Florida B&B Reservations ✪
719 S.E. 4TH STREET, OCALA, FLORIDA 32671

Tel: (904) 351-1167
Coordinator: **Marcie Gauntlett**
States/Regions Covered: **Cocoa Beach, McIntosh, Melbourne, Micanopy, Naples**

Rates (Single/Double):
Modest: $30 $35
Average: $35 $40
Luxury: $45 $65
Credit Cards: **No**

One of Marcie's B&Bs is decorated with antiques and Oriental rugs bought in the Middle East and Europe. The hostess has a most interesting doll collection as well. Another is a farm located on Lake Fay where you are welcome to try your hand at fishing. The owner, a former horse trainer, has Arabians, quarter horses, and Thoroughbreds. Silver Springs, Wild Waters, the Museum of Drag Racing, and Cross Creek, the home of Marjorie Kinnan Rawlings, are some of the local attractions.

Open House Bed & Breakfast Registry—Gold Coast
P.O. BOX 3025, PALM BEACH, FLORIDA 33480

Tel: (305) 842-5190
Best Time to Call: **Evenings; weekends**
Coordinator(s): **Peggy Maxwell**
States/Regions Covered: **Boca Raton, Bonyton Beach, Delray, Jupiter, Lake Worth, Lantana, Palm Beach, Tequesta, West Palm Beach**

Rates (Single/Double):
Modest: $35 $45
Average: $45 $55
Luxury: $65 $75

Peggy's roster includes many homes within a short walk to ocean beaches. They are all within easy reach of fine restaurants, shops, galleries, museums, theaters, and sports arenas. The service is closed from July 1 to September 30. Rates are reduced for weekly and off-season stays.

The Barnacle ✪
ROUTE 1, BOX 780 A, LONG BEACH ROAD, BIG PINE KEY, FLORIDA 33043

Tel: (305) 872-3298
Best Time to Call: **Before 9 PM**
Host(s): **Wood and Joan Cornell**
Location: **Mile Marker 33**
No. of Rooms: **4**

No. of Private Baths: **4**
Double/pb: $70–$80
Guest Cottage: $80–$90; sleeps 2
Apartment: $75–$85
Open: **All year**

Smoking: **Permitted**
Social Drinking: **Permitted**
Foreign Languages: **French**
Minimum Stay: **2 nights**

Breakfast: **Full**
Pets: **No**
Children: **No**

The ultimate in privacy is the self-contained cottage—a tropical tree house with stained-glass windows and private terrace. The main house guest rooms have ocean views and one overlooks the atrium, hot tub, and lush plants; the mini-apartment has a private entrance and kitchenette. Every detail in and around their home reflects Wood and Joan's taste, attention to detail, and artistic flair. The structure was built to frame their eclectic collection of statuary, tapestries, and art. Their emphasis is on the sun and sea, with warm hospitality offered in abundance. You can scuba dive or fish right off "your own" beach. Bahia Honda State Park and Key West are close by. There's a two-night minimum stay in the guest rooms; three nights in the cottage and apartment.

Bed & Breakfast-on-the-Ocean "Casa Grande" ✪
P.O. BOX 378, BIG PINE KEY, FLORIDA 33043

Tel: **(305) 872-2878**
Host(s): **Jon and Kathleen Threlkeld**
Location: **33 mi. E of Key West**
No. of Rooms: **3**
No. of Private Baths: **3**
Double/pb: **$70**
Single/pb: **$65**

Open: **All year**
Breakfast: **Full**
Pets: **No**
Children: **No**
Smoking: **Permitted**
Social Drinking: **Permitted**

This spectacular Spanish-style home facing the water was custom-designed to suit the natural beauty of the Keys. The large landscaped garden patio is where you'll enjoy Jon and Kathleen's bountiful breakfast. It is also the site of the hot tub/Jacuzzi for relaxing by day or under a moonlit sky. The large and airy guest rooms are comfortably cooled by Bahama fans. Key deer and birds abound. You'll enjoy swimming, fishing, snorkeling, bicycling, and jogging. There's a picnic table, gas grill, hammock, and Windsurfer for guests to use, compliments of the gracious hosts.

Canal Cottage Bed & Breakfast
P.O. BOX 266, BIG PINE KEY, FLORIDA 33043

Tel: **(305) 872-3881**
Best Time to Call: **Evenings**
Host(s): **Dean and Patti Nickless**
No. of Rooms: **1 suite**
No. of Private Baths: **1**
Suites: **$58 for 2**

Open: **All year**
Breakfast: **Full**
Pets: **No**
Children: **Welcome, over 10**
Smoking: **Permitted**
Social Drinking: **Permitted**

You can be self-sufficient in this unusual wood stilt house. Your accommodations are nestled in the trees and consist of a bedroom with a queen-size bed, a bathroom, a living room with sleep space for two, and a kitchen stocked for your breakfast, which you can prepare at leisure and enjoy on the porch. You can dive, snorkel, and fish in the Gulf or the Atlantic. You can launch your boat at the neighborhood ramp and tie it up at your backyard dock, where you may also enjoy swimming. Dean and Patti live on the premises and will make every effort to ensure you a comfortable, enjoyable stay. Two-night minimum stay.

Deer Run ✪
LONG BEACH ROAD, P.O. BOX 431, BIG PINE KEY, FLORIDA 33043

Tel: **(305) 872-2015**
Best Time to Call: **7 AM–9 AM; 6 PM–10 PM**
Host(s): **Sue Abbott**
Location: **33 mi. E of Key West**
No. of Rooms: **2**
No. of Private Baths: **2**
Double/pb: **$75**

Single/pb: **$65**
Open: **All year**
Breakfast: **Full**
Pets: **No**
Children: **No**
Smoking: **No**
Social Drinking: **Permitted**
Airport/Station Pickup: **Yes**

Deer Run is a Florida Cracker-style home nestled among lush native trees on the ocean. The house is beautifully designed with skylights, high ceilings, and Bahama fans. The decor boasts many paintings, artifacts, and antiques to compliment wicker and rattan furnishings. Upstairs each room has French doors that open onto a large veranda. Breakfast is served outside overlooking the water, where you may spot Key deer walking along the beach. Looe Key Coral Reef, Bahia Honda State Park, and Key West are all within easy reach, or you can relax and soak up the rays in the free-form deep spa where there's room for eight.

Bed & Breakfast of Tampa Bay ✪
3234 TERN WAY, FEATHERSOUND, CLEARWATER, FLORIDA 34622

Tel: (813) 573-5825
Best Time to Call: **Before 10 AM; after 6 PM**
Host(s): **Vivian and David Grimm**
Location: **7 mi. W of Tampa**
No. of Rooms: **3**
No. of Private Baths: **1**
Max. No. Sharing Bath: **4**
Double/pb: **$45**
Single/pb: **$35**
Double/sb: **$35**
Single/sb: **$25**
Open: **All year**
Breakfast: **Full**
Pets: **Sometimes**
Children: **Welcome**
Smoking: **Permitted**
Social Drinking: **Permitted**

The lovely gardens of this fine stucco home have an Oriental flair, and the interior is graced with fine Oriental and European art. Whenever Vivian and David travel, they bring home souvenirs to enhance their decor. Busch Gardens, St. Petersburg Fine Arts Museum, and Tarpon Springs are 15 miles away; Disney World, Dali Museum, and Sea World are 65 miles away. If you want to stay close to home, the Grimms will lend you their bikes. You're welcome to use the pool, play the piano, or use the kitchen for light snacks. It's close to the University of South Florida and the University of Tampa.

Sprague House Inn
125 CENTRAL AVENUE, CRESCENT CITY, FLORIDA 32012

Tel: (904) 698-2430
Host(s): **Barry and Elaine Nord**
Location: **75 mi. N of Orlando**
No. of Rooms: **4**
No. of Private Baths: **4**
Double/pb: **$40**
Single/pb: **$35**
Open: **All year**
Reduced Rates: **$5 less, June 1–Aug. 31**
Breakfast: **Full**
Other Meals: **Available**
Credit Cards: **MC, VISA**
Pets: **Sometimes**
Children: **Welcome**
Smoking: **Permitted**
Social Drinking: **Permitted**
Airport/Station Pickup: **Yes**

This one-stoplight town, unspoiled by plastic and neon, is claimed by residents to be "The Bass Capital of the World." Elaine and Barry are professional glass artisans, and their handiwork is visible in the inn's stained-glass windows, tableware, lamps, and accessories; many such items are for sale in their on-premises glass and old print shop. The air-conditioned bedrooms of this steamboat-Gothic-style house are furnished with antiques, old prints, lace accessories, and throw rugs on heart cypress floors; they all open onto the second-story porch, where you may relax on a swing. A tennis court and a lake for swimming are a mile away. You are welcome to borrow one of their cane fishing poles (no license is necessary) or grab a net and try your luck at catching blue crabs.

Lakeside Inn Bed and Breakfast
P.O. BOX 71, EASTLAKE WEIR, FLORIDA 32632

Tel: **(904) 288-1396**
Best Time to Call: **Mornings, evenings**
Host(s): **Bill and Sandy Bodner**
Location: **20 mi. S of Ocala**
No. of Rooms: **6**
No. of Private Baths: **3**
Max. No. Sharing Bath: **4**
Double/pb: **$40**
Single/pb: **$28**
Double/sb: **$38**

Single/sb: **$25**
Open: **All year**
Reduced Rates: **5%, families**
Breakfast: **Full**
Other Meals: **Available**
Pets: **Sometimes**
Children: **Welcome, over 5**
Smoking: **On porch only**
Social Drinking: **Permitted**
Airport/Station Pickup: **Yes**

If you enjoy fascinating homes filled with antiques and collectibles this may be the vacation spot for you. This lovely Victorian Gothic home was built in the 1880s as a hotel. The house is set on beautiful Lake Weir and is complete with dock and sun deck. A huge veranda overlooks the lake on the first floor, as does the screened-in porch upstairs. The rooms are quaint and comfortable, featuring heart-of-pine paneling and floors, plus five fireplaces. Enjoy a hearty Southern breakfast complete with home-baked goodies, then grab a fishing pole or go swimming right off their dock. Lakeside Inn is located in the Silver Springs area, which abounds with numerous lakes, streams, and rollings hills.

Feller House ✪
21102 BUTCHERS HOLLER, ESTERO, FLORIDA 33928

Tel: **(813) 992-4865**
Best Time to Call: **Evenings**
Host(s): **Wayne and Pat Feller**
No. of Rooms: **1**
No. of Private Baths: **1**
Double/pb: **$35**
Single/pb: **$30**

Open: **Oct. 1–June 1**
Breakfast: **Full**
Pets: **No**
Children: **No**
Smoking: **No**
Social Drinking: **Permitted**
Airport/Station Pickup: **Yes**

You are assured of a warm welcome in this attractive home on a creek in a quiet, residential neighborhood. Feel free to use the TV in the den; use the community golf course, tennis courts, and pool, too. Gulf beaches are minutes away. Wayne and Pat, experienced travelers and home exchangers, will supply maps to take you to Everglades National Park, Corkscrew Bird Sanctuary, as well as directions to the fine shops and restaurants in town. Naples is 15 minutes away.

Casa Alhambra B&B Inn ✪
3029 ALHAMBRA STREET, FT. LAUDERDALE, FLORIDA 33304

Tel: **(305) 467-2262**
Host(s): **Vicky Feaman**
Location: **2½ mi. E of I-95**
No. of Rooms: **5**
No. of Private Baths: **3**
Max. No. Sharing Bath: **4**
Double/pb: **$60**
Double/sb: **$50**
Suites: **$75**

Open: **All year**
Reduced Rates: **May 1–Dec. 31**
Breakfast: **Continental**
Credit Cards: **AMEX**
Pets: **No**
Children: **Welcome, over 10**
Smoking: **Permitted**
Social Drinking: **Permitted**
Airport/Station Pickup: **Yes**

Overlooking the Atlantic Ocean, this historic two-story home has been lovingly restored to its original Florida/Mediterranean architecture. All the rooms are air-conditioned and are decorated with your comfort in mind. The deck, spa, and garden area are yours to enjoy. Whether you wish to borrow a bike or a book, or anything else to enhance your stay, Vicky will be pleased to cater to your wishes.

Dolan House
1401 N.E. 5 COURT, FT. LAUDERDALE, FLORIDA 33301

Tel: **(305) 462-8430**
Host(s): **Tom and Sandra Dolan**
Location: **5 mi. from I-95**

No. of Rooms: **4**
No. of Private Baths: **2**
Max. No. Sharing Bath: **4**

Double/pb: **$50**
Single/pb: **$45**
Double/sb: **$50**
Single/sb: **$45**
Open: **All year**
Breakfast: **Continental**

Pets: **No**
Children: **Welcome**
Smoking: **Permitted**
Social Drinking: **Permitted**
Airport/Station Pickup: **Yes**

All the comforts of home—if your home has a hot tub large enough to fit 19! Set right in the heart of Fort Lauderdale, and only two miles from the city's famed beach, the Dolan House offers privacy (it's completely fenced in) and convenience. When the weather's balmy, guests sit out on the large deck; when the nights are cool they can move indoors and enjoy the large coquina fireplace. The Dolans have lived in the area for 30 years and they're anxious to tell you all about it—ask them about the Galleria Shopping Center, the new Riverwalk historic section, Holiday Park, and all the nearby theaters and museums.

Windsong Garden & Art Gallery ✪
5570–4 WOODROSE COURT, FORT MYERS, FLORIDA 33907

Tel: **(813) 936-6378**
Host(s): **Embe Burdick**
No. of Rooms: **2**
No. of Private Baths: **2**
Double/pb: **$50**
Suite: **$50**
Open: **All year**

Breakfast: **Continental**
Pets: **No**
Children: **No**
Smoking: **No**
Social Drinking: **Permitted**
Minimum Stay: **2 nights**

This modern clear-shake-and-brick town house has a private courtyard and balcony for your enjoyment. The spacious combination bedroom-and-sitting room is most comfortable. Embe's varied interests include arts, crafts, and music. It's close to Sanibel and Captiva islands, Ft. Myers Beach, fine shopping, good restaurants, and the University of Florida. You are welcome to use the pool.

Country Meadows ✪
9506 SOUTH WEST 81 WAY, GAINESVILLE, FLORIDA 32608

Tel: **(904) 495-2699**
Best Time to Call: **3–11 PM**
Host(s): **Allene and Orville Higgs**
Location: **10 mi. SW of Gainesville**
No. of Rooms: **2**
No. of Private Baths: **2**

Double/pb: **$30–$35**
Single/pb: **$26–$30**
Open: **All year**
Breakfast: **Continental**
Other Meals: **Available**
Pets: **No**

178 • FLORIDA

Children: **Welcome**
Smoking: **Permitted**
Social Drinking: **Permitted**
Airport/Station Pickup: **Yes**

Country Meadows is a Colonial-style home set on an acre and a half. The house is surrounded by pine trees and has a fenced-in yard for relaxing. The country-style decor consists of comfortable furnishings and lots of handmade craft items. The Higgses enjoy entertaining and are glad to prepare either a Continental breakfast or a larger meal for guests. They will gladly direct you to nearby nature parks, horse farms, and museums.

Meeks B&B on the Gulf Beaches ✪
19506 GULF BOULEVARD #8, INDIAN SHORES, FLORIDA 34635

Tel: **(813) 596-5424**
Best Time to Call: **7 AM–10 PM**
Host(s): **Greta and Bob Meeks**
Location: **10 mi. NW of St. Petersburg**
No. of Rooms: **7**
No. of Private Baths: **5**
Double/pb: **$45**
Single/pb: **$40**
Double/sb: **$40**
Single/sb: **$35**
Open: **All year**
Breakfast: **Full**
Pets: **No**
Children: **Welcome**
Smoking: **No**
Social Drinking: **Permitted**
Airport/Station Pickup: **Yes**

This lovely beach cottage condo is located directly on the Gulf of Mexico. From your room you can step right onto lovely white sand beaches. A bountiful breakfast is served on the sun porch overlooking the pool and Gulf. This B&B is close to seafood restaurants and within walking distance of the Tiki Gardens. Greta is a local real estate agent who can easily guide you to the best sightseeing and dining.

A Sunny Place Guest House ✪
121 NORTH OAK STREET, LANTANA, FLORIDA 33462

Tel: **(407) 586-3596**
Host(s): **Kent and Diane Hager**
Location: **1 mi. from I-95, Lantana Road Exit**
No. of Rooms: **1 apartment**
No. of Private Baths: **1**
Guest Apartment: **$75; sleeps 4**
Open: **All year**
Reduced Rates: **10% weekly, seniors; 25% less May 15–Sept. 15**
Breakfast: **Continental**
Pets: **Sometimes**
Children: **Welcome (crib)**
Smoking: **No**
Social Drinking: **Permitted**
Airport/Station Pickup: **Yes**

A Sunny Place is a casual beach house located in the heart of Florida's Gold Coast, adjacent to South Palm Beach. It is within walking distance of a beautiful stretch of the beach that boasts its own snack bar and picnic and barbeque areas. The apartment is furnished in modern decor, with a bedroom, living room, full kitchen, bath, screened porch, and outdoor deck. It's a pleasant walk to restaurants, unique shops, boat rentals, scuba diving, snorkeling, and the Intracoastal Waterway. It's a short drive to posh Palm Beach and the exclusive shops of Worth Avenue.

Bette Lane
600 N.E. 36TH STREET, APARTMENT 1923, MIAMI, FLORIDA 33137

Tel: **(305) 576-6606**	Reduced Rates: **15%, Mar.–Sept.**
Best Time to Call: **9–10 AM; 6–7 PM**	Breakfast: **Full**
Host(s): **Bette Lane**	Other Meals: **Available**
Location: **20 mi. from airport**	Pets: **No**
No. of Rooms: **1**	Children: **Sometimes**
No. of Private Baths: **1**	Smoking: **No**
Double/pb: **$47**	Social Drinking: **Permitted**
Open: **All year**	

Bette lives on the 19th floor of a high-rise building overlooking downtown Miami and the Bay. The apartment has two bedrooms, two baths, and is furnished in comfortable Floridian style. Breakfast is your choice of pancakes, eggs, and hot or cold cereal, served with toast, coffee, and juice. Guests are welcome to take advantage of the tennis courts, swimming pool, and exercise room located on the premises. This lovely apartment is set at the foot of the bridge to Miami Beach and offers easy access to Miami International Airport, the major highways, and shopping areas.

Action Center of Orlando
6638 CONWAY LAKES DRIVE, ORLANDO, FLORIDA 32812

Tel: **(407) 859-8333**	Suites: **$75 for 4**
Best Time to Call: **8 AM–Noon; 3–10 PM**	Open: **All year**
	Breakfast: **Full**
Host(s): **Trish and Rob Kershner**	Pets: **Welcome**
Location: **1 mi. from Beeline 528**	Children: **Welcome**
No. of Rooms: **3**	Smoking: **Permitted**
Max. No. Sharing Bath: **4**	Social Drinking: **Permitted**
Double/sb: **$55**	Minimum Stay: **2 nights**
Single/sb: **$40**	Airport/Station Pickup: **Yes**

Rob and Trish's contemporary home is furnished in a pleasant mix of past and present accented by unusual silk flower arrangements. It is accessible to all of the area's attractions, including Disney World, Epcot and Sea World. Cape Canaveral, home of the United States space program, is less than an hour's drive; Orlando International Airport is minutes away.

Bed & Breakfast of Orlando ✪
8205 BANYAN BOULEVARD, ORLANDO, FLORIDA 32819

Tel: **(407) 352-9257**
Host(s): **Bobbie Jean Havlish**
Location: **2 mi. from I-4**
No. of Rooms: **2**
Max. No. Sharing Bath: **4**
Double/sb: **$55**
Single/sb: **$45**
Open: **All year**

Reduced Rates: **10%, seniors from Sept.–Nov.**
Breakfast: **Full**
Pets: **No**
Children: **Welcome**
Smoking: **Permitted**
Social Drinking: **No**
Airport/Station Pickup: **Yes**

Located in Sand Lake Hills, close to the country clubs of Bay Hills and Orange Tree, is Bobbie's lovely home. Weather permitting, breakfast is served in the screened-in Florida room overlooking orange groves. It is all very quiet and peaceful, yet minutes away from Epcot, Disney World, the Orange County Convention Center, and the Factory Outlet Mall. A two-night minimum stay is required.

Esther's B&B ✪
2411 VIRGINIA DRIVE, ORLANDO, FLORIDA 32803

Tel: **(407) 896-9916**
Best Time to Call: **5:30 PM–9:30 PM**
Host(s): **Esther Allen**
Location: **2½ mi. from I-4**
No. of Rooms: **2**
Max. No. Sharing Bath: **4**
Double/sb: **$45**

Single/sb: **$35**
Open: **All year**
Breakfast: **Continental**
Pets: **No**
Children: **No**
Smoking: **No**
Social Drinking: **Permitted**

The house is attractively furnished and features lovely needlepoint "paintings" by the Old Masters. In the morning, enjoy a special array of homemade muffins, breads, or coffee cake along with cheese, fruit, and beverages. It's close to the famous attractions of Disney World, Epcot, Boardwalk and Baseball, and Cypress Gardens. The Loch Haven Art Center, Winter Park shops, and Harry Leu Gardens are also nearby. You are welcome to enjoy the swimming pool.

Jarman's Friendly Inn ✪
567 HEWETT DRIVE, ORLANDO, FLORIDA 32807

Tel: **(407) 282-6388**
Best Time to Call: **Evenings**
Host(s): **Jo Ellen and Bert Jarman**
Location: **1 block from Hwy. 436**
No. of Rooms: **3**
No. of Private Baths: **1**
Max. No. Sharing Bath: **4**
Double/pb: **$55–$65**
Single/pb: **$45–$55**
Double/sb: **$45–$55**
Single/sb: **$35–$45**
Open: **All year**
Reduced Rates: **10%, families, seniors**
Breakfast: **Continental**
Pets: **No**
Children: **Welcome (crib)**
Smoking: **No**
Social Drinking: **Permitted**
Minimum Stay: **Two nights**
Airport/Station Pickup: **Yes**

Six children grew up in this ranch-style home, and the Jarmans say there is plenty of love left to welcome your kids. There is also plenty of space. The house spans 5,100 square feet, including a large screened-in pool with patio area. A contemporary Florida room with hanging plants and spa is available for your enjoyment. The Victorian Rose Room has an old-fashioned wooden bed with floral spread, ceiling fan, couch, and colorful quilted wall hanging. The Gold Room has a canopy bed with handmade spread, antique dresser, and Oriental rug. If you're traveling with a small child, a third bedroom features a three-quarter oak bed, baby bed, and changing table. House specialties such as sausage-mushroom casserole and homemade biscuits are served on the patio or in a cheery breakfast room. The Jarmans are within 45 minutes of Sea World, Disney World, and Epcot.

Rinaldi House ✪
502 LAKE AVENUE, ORLANDO, FLORIDA 32801

Tel: **(407) 425-6549**
Best Time to Call: **Evenings**
Host(s): **Victor C. Brown**
No. of Rooms: **2**
Max. No. Sharing Bath: **4**
Double/sb: **$47**
Single/sb: **$39**
Guest Cottage: **$39; sleeps 2**
Open: **All year**
Breakfast: **Full**
Other Meals: **Available**
Pets: **Welcome**
Children: **Welcome**
Smoking: **Permitted**
Social Drinking: **Permitted**
Airport/Station Pickup: **Yes**

A lovely 1895 restoration in the Lake Cherokee Historic District, this two-story Colonial is furnished with many antiques, including an 1886 reed organ. The landscaping features an ornate, Victorian-style gazebo. It's a 12-minute walk to downtown Orlando, Eola Park, the

Historic Church Street Station Entertainment Complex, and fine restaurants. Disney World is a 30-minute drive. Complimentary wine and cheese are graciously served by Victor, whose hospitality is legend.

The Rio Pinar House ✪
532 PINAR DRIVE, ORLANDO, FLORIDA 32825

Tel: **(407) 277-4903**
Host(s): **Victor and Delores Freudenburg**
Location: **½ mi. from E-W Expy., Chickasaw Exit**
No. of Rooms: **3**
No. of Private Baths: **2**
Max. No. Sharing Bath: **4**
Double/pb: **$40**
Single/pb: **$35**
Double/sb: **$35**
Single/sb: **$30**
Suites: **$60 (family)**
Open: **All year**
Breakfast: **Full**
Other Meals: **Available**
Pets: **No**
Children: **Welcome**
Smoking: **No**
Social Drinking: **Permitted**

This home is located in a quiet neighborhood across from the Rio Pinar Golf Course. The rooms are furnished comfortably with both antiques and Americana. Breakfast is served on the porch overlooking a garden and trees. The house is a 30-minute drive from Disney World and nine miles from downtown Orlando. Your hosts recommend an outing to beautiful Rock Springs and the nearby Church Street Station Complex.

The Spencer Home ✪
313 SPENCER STREET, ORLANDO, FLORIDA 32809

Tel: **(407) 855-5603**
Host(s): **Neal and Eunice Schattauer**
Location: **2 mi. from I-4**
No. of Rooms: **1 suite**
No. of Private Baths: **1**
Suites: **$50 for 2; $60 for 4**
Double/sb: **$40**
Max. No. Sharing Bath: **4**
Open: **All year**
Breakfast: **Full**
Other Meals: **Available**
Pets: **No**
Children: **Welcome**
Smoking: **No**
Social Drinking: **Permitted**
Airport/Station Pickup: **Yes**

The guest suite of this neat, ranch-style house has a private entrance and consists of a bedroom with a double bed, a living room with a sleeper for two, a full bathroom, and is completely air-conditioned. You are welcome to freshen your traveling duds in the laundry room and yourselves in the swimming pool. Eunice will start your day with breakfast and Neal would be pleased to have you join in harmony singing whenever the mood is right.

Sunshine Inn
508 DECATUR AVENUE, PENSACOLA, FLORIDA 32507

Tel: **(904) 455-6781**	Breakfast: **Full**
Best Time to Call: **Evenings**	Pets: **No**
Host(s): **The Jablonskis**	Children: **Welcome**
Location: **8 mi. from I-10**	Smoking: **No**
No. of Rooms: **1 suite**	Social Drinking: **Permitted**
No. of Private Baths: **1**	Airport/Station Pickup: **Yes**
Suite: **$35**	Foreign Languages: **German**
Open: **All year**	

Sun yourself on the whitest sand, swim in the Gulf of Mexico, and return to the Sunshine Inn for a dip in the pool. Or, walk a block to the bayou for fishing. Feel free to relax in the living room and seek touring advice from your knowledgeable hostess Renate. The University of West Florida is nearby.

Carriage Way Bed & Breakfast ☉
70 CUNA STREET, ST. AUGUSTINE, FLORIDA 32084

Tel: **(904) 829-2467**	Breakfast: **Continental**
Best Time to Call: **8:30 AM–4:30 PM**	Other Meals: **Available**
Host(s): **Karen Burkley**	Credit Cards: **MC, VISA**
No. of Rooms: **6**	Pets: **Sometimes**
No. of Private Baths: **6**	Children: **Sometimes**
Double/pb: **$47–$87**	Smoking: **Permitted**
Single/pb: **$47–$87**	Social Drinking: **Permitted**
Open: **All year**	Airport/Station Pickup: **Yes**
Reduced Rates: **10%, seniors; Sun.–Thurs., off-season**	

This B&B, located in the heart of the historic district, is a restored Victorian built in 1883. Unique shops, museums, Castillo de San Marcos, fine restaurants, carriage tours, and the waterfront are within an easy walk. The atmosphere is leisurely and casual, in keeping with the feeling of Old St. Augustine. In addition to breakfast, Karen generously includes newspapers, wine, cookies, cordials, and dessert on Friday and Saturday evenings.

Casa de la Paz ☉
22 AVENIDA MENENDEZ, ST. AUGUSTINE, FLORIDA 32084

Tel: **(904) 829-2915**	Host(s): **Brenda and Harry Stafford**
Best Time to Call: **10 AM–4 PM**	Location: **7 mi. from I-95**

No. of Rooms: **5**
No. of Private Baths: **5**
Double/pb: **$75–$95**
Suites: **$105–$150**
Open: **All year**
Breakfast: **Continental**
Credit Cards: **AMEX, MC, VISA**

Pets: **No**
Children: **Welcome, over 9**
Smoking: **No**
Social Drinking: **Permitted**
Airport/Station Pickup: **Yes**
Foreign Languages: **French**

Overlooking historic Matanzas Bay in the heart of Old St. Augustine is this three-story Mediterranean-style stucco home. The rooms are comfortably furnished in a pleasant blend of the old and new. Amenities in each room include ceiling fans, central air-conditioning and heat, high-quality linens, cable TV, and complimentary sherry or wine. The veranda rooms have private entrances. Guests are welcome to use the private, walled courtyard, well-stocked library, and delightful parlor. It is central to all attractions and convenient to fine restaurants and shops.

Casa de Solana O
21 AVILES STREET, ST. AUGUSTINE, FLORIDA 32084

Tel: **(904) 824-3555**
Best Time to Call: **8 AM–9 PM**
Host(s): **Faye and Jim McMurry**
No. of Rooms: **4 suites**
No. of Private Baths: **4**
Suites: **$100–$125**
Open: **All year**

Breakfast: **Full**
Credit Cards: **AMEX, MC, VISA**
Pets: **No**
Children: **Welcome**
Smoking: **No**
Social Drinking: **Permitted**

This is a gorgeous Colonial home built in 1763. It is located in the heart of the historic area, within walking distance of restaurants, museums, and quaint shops. Some of the antique-filled suites have fireplaces, while others have balconies that overlook the lovely garden, or a breathtaking view of Matanzas Bay. Jim and Faye include cable TV, chocolates, a decanter of sherry, and the use of their bicycles in the rate.

Kenwood Inn O
38 MARINE STREET, ST. AUGUSTINE, FLORIDA 32084

Tel: **(904) 824-2116**
Best Time to Call: **8 AM–8 PM**
Host(s): **Mark, Kerrianne, and Caitlin Constant**

Location: **40 mi. S of Jacksonville**
No. of Rooms: **15**
No. of Private Baths: **15**
Double/pb: **$55–$75**

Single/pb: **$45**
Open: **All year**
Breakfast: **Continental**
Credit Cards: **MC, VISA**

Pets: **No**
Children: **Welcome, over 8**
Smoking: **Permitted**
Social Drinking: **Permitted**

If you are to discover a Victorian building in Florida, how appropriate that it should be in the historic section of St. Augustine, the oldest city in the U.S. This New England-style inn is a rarity in the South; this one has old-fashioned beds with color-coordinated touches right down to the sheets and linens. Breakfast may be taken in your room, in the courtyard surrounded by trees, or by the swimming pool. Tour trains, the waterfront shops, restaurants, and museums are within walking distance. Flagler College is three blocks away.

St. Francis Inn ✪
279 ST. GEORGE STREET, ST. AUGUSTINE, FLORIDA 32084

Tel: **(904) 824-6068**
Host(s): **Marie Register**
Location: **2 mi. from US 1**
No. of Rooms: **11**
No. of Private Baths: **11**
Double/pb: **$42–$75**
Guest Cottage: **$90; sleeps 4–6**
Open: **All year**

Breakfast: **Continental**
Credit Cards: **MC, VISA**
Pets: **No**
Children: **Welcome (crib)**
Smoking: **Permitted**
Social Drinking: **Permitted**
Airport/Station Pickup: **Yes**

Built in 1791, the inn is a Spanish Colonial structure with a private courtyard and garden, located in the center of the restored part of town. Balconies are furnished with rocking chairs, and the swimming pool is a great cooling-off spot. The building is made of coquina, a limestone made of broken shells and coral. Due to its trapezoidal shape, there are no square or rectangular rooms. All of St. Augustine's historic and resort activities are within a three-mile radius.

Victorian House Bed & Breakfast ✪
11 CADIZ STREET, ST. AUGUSTINE, FLORIDA 32084

Tel: **(904) 824-5214**
Host(s): **Daisy Morden**
No. of Rooms: **6**
No. of Private Baths: **6**
Double/pb: **$50–$75**
Open: **All year**

Breakfast: **Continental**
Credit Cards: **AMEX, MC, VISA**
Pets: **No**
Children: **In cottage only**
Smoking: **Permitted**
Social Drinking: **Permitted**

From its location in the heart of the historic district, it's a short walk to fine restaurants, the waterfront, shops, museums, and the plaza. The rooms are charming, with brass and canopy beds, handwoven coverlets, handmade quilts, stenciled walls and floors. The house is comfortably air-conditioned, but the warmth of your hostess is quite special.

Bayboro House on Old Tampa Bay ✪
1719 BEACH DRIVE S.E., ST. PETERSBURG, FLORIDA 33701

Tel: **(813) 823-4955**
Host(s): **Gordon and Antonia Powers**
Location: **½ mi. from I-275, Exit 9**
No. of Rooms: **3**
No. of Private Baths: **3**
Double/pb: **$50–$60**
Open: **All year**

Breakfast: **Continental**
Credit Cards: **MC, VISA**
Pets: **No**
Children: **No**
Smoking: **No**
Social Drinking: **Permitted**

A unique three-story Queen Anne with airy, high-ceilinged rooms and a wraparound veranda in view of Tampa Bay, it is graced with antique furniture plus tropical plants and flowers. It is the ideal spot for sunning, beachcombing, and fishing. Relax in the hammock or visit unusual shops, fine restaurants, the Sunken Gardens, or the Salvador Dali museum.

Crescent House
459 BEACH ROAD, SIESTA KEY, SARASOTA, FLORIDA 34242

Tel: **(813) 346-0857**	Reduced Rates: **Weekly; less Jun.–Oct.**
Host(s): **Patricia and Jean-Marc Murre**	Breakfast: **Continental**
Location: **10 mi. from Sarasota**	Pets: **No**
No. of Rooms: **4**	Children: **Welcome**
No. of Private Baths: **2**	Smoking: **No**
Max. No. Sharing Bath: **4**	Social Drinking: **Permitted**
Double/pb: **$70**	Airport/Station Pickup: **Yes**
Double/sb: **$35**	Foreign Languages: **French, Spanish**
Open: **All year**	

This lovely, 70-year-old home has been fully restored and furnished with comfortable antiques. Breakfast specialties include freshly squeezed Florida orange juice, homemade muffins, scones, and freshly ground coffee. Relax in the hot tub, sunbathe on a spacious wood deck, or step across the street to a white sandy beach and cool off in the Gulf of Mexico. The house is located within a short walk of Siesta Village and Pavilion, with its many restaurants, quaint shops, tennis courts, and public beach. Your hosts specialize in European service and hospitality, and will gladly guide you to fine dining and sailboat and water sporting gear rentals.

Knightswood ✿
P.O. BOX 151, SUMMERLAND KEY, FLORIDA 33042

Tel: **(305) 872-2246**	Open: **All year**
Host(s): **Chris and Herb Pontin**	Breakfast: **Full**
Location: **26 mi. E of Key West**	Pets: **No**
No. of Rooms: **1**	Children: **No**
No. of Private Baths: **1**	Smoking: **No**
Double/pb: **$75**	Social Drinking: **Permitted**
Single/pb: **$55**	

Knightswood overlooks one of the loveliest views in the Keys. Guest accommodations include a bed and bath, kitchenette, rec room, and screened-in porch with barbecue. Snorkeling, fishing, and boating can be enjoyed from a private dock, and guests are welcome to swim in the freshwater pool. Your hosts will gladly point the way to fine dining and nightlife in Key West.

Cobb's Gulf View Inn ✪
21722 WEST HIGHWAY 98, P.O. BOX 199, SUNNYSIDE, FLORIDA 32461

Tel: **(904) 234-6051 Mar. 1–Sept. 10;**
  (912) 435-0178 Sept. 11–Apr. 30
Host(s): **Bill and Tina Cobb**
Location: **2 mi. W of Panama City Beach**
No. of Rooms: **5**
No. of Private Baths: **5**
Double/pb: **$55**
Single/pb: **$50**
Suite: **$75**
Open: **Mar. 1–Sept. 10**
Breakfast: **Continental**
Pets: **No**
Children: **Welcome**
Smoking: **Permitted**
Social Drinking: **Permitted**

Cobb's Gulf View Inn is a new two-story beach house painted Cape Cod blue with cream lattice trim. The decor is eclectic with white wicker furnishings on the downstairs porches and modern touches in the bedrooms. Guest quarters have private entrances, TV, carpeting, and ceiling fans. In the morning, dine on the upstairs sun deck or porch overlooking the panoramic Gulf of Mexico. Homemade breads and jellies are specialties of the house. It's just 200 feet across the road to the white, sandy beaches of Sunnyside. Bill and Tina are located convenient to fishing, sailing, golf, tennis, restaurants, and water parks for the children are within easy reach. There's a three-night minimum on holiday weekends.

Fiorito's Bed & Breakfast ✪
421 OLD EAST LAKE ROAD, TARPON SPRINGS, FLORIDA 34689

Tel: **(813) 937-5487**
Best Time to Call: **8–9 PM**
Host(s): **Dick and Marie Fiorito**
Location: **2 mi. E of US 19**
No. of Rooms: **1**
No. of Private Baths: **1**
Double/pb: **$40**
Single/pb: **$35**
Open: **All year**
Breakfast: **Full**
Pets: **Sometimes**
Children: **No**
Smoking: **Permitted**
Social Drinking: **Permitted**
Airport/Station Pickup: **Yes**

Just off a quiet road that runs along Lake Tarpon's horse country, this meticulously maintained home on 2½ acres offers respite for the visitor. The guest room and bath are decorated in tones of blue, enhanced with beautiful accessories. Fresh fruit, cheese omelet, homemade bread and jam, and choice of beverages, are the Fioritos' idea of breakfast. It is beautifully served on the tree-shaded, screened terrace. Busch Gardens and Clearwater Beach are ½ hour away. It's an hour to Cypress Gardens, 1½ hours to Disney World.

Spring Bayou Inn ✪
32 WEST TARPON AVENUE, TARPON SPRINGS, FLORIDA 34689

Tel: **(813) 938-9333**
Best Time to Call: **11 AM–9 PM**
Host(s): **Ron and Cher Morrick**
Location: **2 mi. W of US 19**
No. of Rooms: **4**
No. of Private Baths: **2**
Max. No. Sharing Bath: **4**
Double/pb: **$55–$65**
Single/pb: **$50–$60**
Double/sb: **$45–$50**
Single/sb: **$40–$45**
Open: **Oct. 1–Aug. 15**
Breakfast: **Continental**
Pets: **No**
Children: **No**
Smoking: **No**
Social Drinking: **Permitted**

This large, comfortable home was built around 1900. It is unique in having architectural details of the past combined with up-to-date conveniences. You will enjoy relaxing on the porch or in the courtyard to take in the sun. The parlor is a favorite gathering place, offering informal atmosphere, complimentary wine, music, books, and games, and the opportunity to make new friends. The fireplace chases the chill on winter evenings. Tarpon Springs is the sponge capital of the world and the nearby sponge docks are interesting to visit. The area is known for its excellent restaurants and variety of shops.

GEORGIA

Bed & Breakfast—Atlanta ☯
1801 PIEDMONT AVENUE NE, SUITE 208, ATLANTA, GEORGIA 30324

Tel: **(404) 875-0525**
Best Time to Call: 9 AM–Noon; 2–5 PM
Coordinator(s): **Madalyne Eplan, Paula Gris**
States/Regions Covered: **Atlanta, Decatur, Dunwoody, Jonesboro, Marietta, McDonough, Savannah, St. Simons, Smyrna, Stone Mountain**

Rates (Single/Double):
  Modest: $28–$36 $32–$40
  Average: $40–$48 $44–$52
  Luxury: $52–$72 $56–$100
Credit Cards: AMEX, MC, VISA

Visit one of America's most gracious cities, with the advantage of being a houseguest. Madalyne and Paula have been carefully selecting accommodations for fortunate travelers since 1979. They consider transportation and language needs as well as other personal preferences in making your reservation. Lodging is offered in the city's most desirable locations. There is an $8 surcharge for a one-night stay. Georgia Tech, Emory University, and Georgia State University are close by.

Quail Country Bed & Breakfast, Ltd. ✪
1104 OLD MONTICELLO ROAD, THOMASVILLE, GEORGIA 31792

Tel: **(912) 226-7218 or 226-6882**
Coordinator(s): **Mercer Watt, Kathy Lanigan**
States/Regions Covered: **Georgia—Thomas County, Thomasville**

Rates (Single/Double):
    Average: **$30**   **$40**
    Luxury: **$40**   **$50**
Credit Cards: **No**

Mercer and Kathy have a wide selection of homes, several with swimming pools, in lovely residential areas. There's lots to see and do, including touring historic restorations and plantations. Enjoy the Pebble Hill Plantation museum, historic Glen Arven Country Club, and the April Rose Festival. Five-dollar surcharge for one-night stay.

Layside ✪
611 RIVER STREET, BLAKELY, GEORGIA 31723

Tel: **(912) 723-8932**
Best Time to Call: **8:30 AM–11 PM**
Host(s): **Ted and Jeanneane Lay**
Location: **1½ mi. from US 27**
No. of Rooms: **3**
Max. No. Sharing Bath: **4**
Double/sb: **$35**
Single/sb: **$25**

Open: **All year**
Reduced Rates: **10%, seniors over 60**
Breakfast: **Continental**
Pets: **No**
Children: **Welcome, over 10**
Smoking: **Permitted**
Social Drinking: **Permitted**

Layside is a southern Colonial, dating back to the turn of the century. Spend the night in a queen-size bed and wake up to homemade bread, jams, and coffee. State parks, Indian burial grounds, good fishing and boating are all nearby attractions. The 60-foot-long front porch is a fine place to relax after a day of touring.

Schlemmer's Bed & Breakfast ✪
ROUTE 4, BOX 4655, CLEVELAND, GEORGIA 30528

Tel: **(404) 845-5897**
Host(s): **John and Karla Schlemmer**
No. of Rooms: **5**
No. of Private Baths: **5**
Double/pb: **$45–$60**
Open: **Apr. 15–Nov. 30**
Reduced Rates: **August; after 3 nights**

Breakfast: **Continental**
Pets: **No**
Children: **Sometimes**
Smoking: **No**
Social Drinking: **Permitted**
Airport/Station Pickup: **Yes**
Foreign Languages: **German**

This cozy, Bavarian-style home is nestled in the woods on a hillside overlooking the clear water of the Chattahoochee River. The bedrooms are attractively furnished and each has an outside entrance. In summer, a 2-bedroom efficiency apartment is available. Surrounded by trees and flowers, there's plenty of room for leisurely strolls, or just relax on the deck with a good book. Alpine Helen, with its quaint shops, restaurants, entertainment, festivals, and friendly people, is just 20 minutes away. Babyland Hospital, home of the Cabbage Patch Kids, is nearby. You have to see it to believe it!

The Mountain Top Lodge ✪
ROUTE 3, BOX 173, DAHLONEGA, GEORGIA 30533

Tel: **(404) 864-5257**
Best Time to Call: **12–6 PM**
Host(s): **David Middleton**
Location: **70 mi. N of Atlanta**
No. of Rooms: **8**
No. of Private Baths: **8**
Double/pb: **$60–$70**
Single/pb: **$50–$60**

Suites: **$70–$80**
Open: **All year**
Breakfast: **Full**
Pets: **No**
Children: **Welcome, over 12**
Smoking: **Permitted**
Social Drinking: **Permitted**

Flanked by porches and decks, this gambrel-roofed, rustic cedar lodge is a secluded rural retreat on 40 acres with a 360° mountain view. Decorated with art and antiques, the pine furniture and accessories made by mountain craftsmen add to the charm. Dahlonega was the site of America's first gold rush and nature buffs will appreciate the Chattahoochee National Forest and Amicalola Falls State Park. Rafting, hiking, and horseback riding are all nearby. Don't miss the "Alpine village" of Helen, Georgia, only 30 minutes away. The higher rates quoted apply during October for the fall foliage season.

Hilltop Haus
P.O. BOX 154, CHATTAHOOCHEE STREET, HELEN, GEORGIA 30545

Tel: **(404) 878-2388**
Host(s): **Frankie Tysor and Barbara Nichols**
Location: **60 mi. from I-85**
No. of Rooms: **5**
No. of Private Baths: **3**
Max. No. Sharing Bath: **3**
Double/pb: **$40–$55**
Single/pb: **$35–$45**
Double/sb: **$35–$50**
Single/sb: **$30–$40**
Suite: **$50–$65**
Open: **All year**
Breakfast: **Full**
Credit Cards: **MC, VISA**
Reduced Rates: **10%, seniors**
Pets: **No**
Children: **Welcome, over 12**
Smoking: **Permitted**
Social Drinking: **Permitted**

This contemporary split-level overlooks Alpine Helen and the Chattahoochee River. It is near the foothills of the Smoky Mountains, six miles from the Appalachian Trail. Rich wood paneling and fireplaces create a homey atmosphere for the traveler. Guests may choose a private room or the efficiency cottage with separate entrance. Each morning a hearty breakfast includes homemade biscuits and preserves. Your hostess will direct you to many outdoor activities and sights.

Blue and Grey Bed and Breakfast ✪
511 KINGSWOOD AVENUE, MARIETTA, GEORGIA 30066

Tel: **(404) 425-0392**
Best Time to Call: **After 6 PM**
Host(s): **John and Connie Kone**
Location: **25 mi. N of Atlanta**
No. of Rooms: **2**
Max. No. Sharing Bath: **4**
Double/sb: **$35**
Single/sb: **$30**
Open: **All year**
Reduced Rates: **10%, seniors**
Breakfast: **Continental**
Pets: **No**
Children: **Welcome, over 8**
Smoking: **No**
Social Drinking: **Permitted**

This rambling Cape Cod-style home is set in a quiet neighborhood surrounded by trees. The house is warmly decorated, featuring comfortable, extra-large guest quarters. Your hosts are local history buffs, fond of sharing their knowledge of the area. Nearby attractions include Marietta Square, Kennesaw Mountain National Battlefield Park, restaurants, and the new Town Center, one of the largest shopping and entertainment centers in the Southeast.

Parrott-Camp-Soucy House ✪
15 GREENVILLE STREET, NEWNAN, GEORGIA 30263

Tel: **(404) 253-4846**
Host(s): **Chuck and Doris Soucy**
Location: **25 mi. SW of Atlanta**
No. of Rooms: **3**
No. of Private Baths: **1**
Max. No. Sharing Bath: **4**
Double/pb: **$70**
Single/pb: **$60**
Double/sb: **$60**
Single/sb: **$50**
Open: **All year**
Breakfast: **Continental**
Pets: **No**
Children: **No**
Smoking: **No**
Social Drinking: **Permitted**

This extraordinary Second Empire mansion, listed on the National Register of Historic Places, is a brilliant example of Victorian-French Mansard architecture. It took two years to restore it to its original elegance. For example, the fireplace in the front hall is surrounded by tiles that depict characters from the Robin Hood legend, and the magnificent grand staircase is lit by beautiful stained-glass windows. It is no surprise that the house is furnished entirely in antiques. The surprise is that it is so comfortable. You are certain to enjoy the formal gardens, swimming pool and spa, and the game room with its 1851 Brunswick pool table. If you can tear yourself away, Warm Springs, Callaway Gardens, and Atlanta are within easy reach.

R.S.V.P. Savannah—B&B Reservation Service ✪
417 EAST CHARLTON STREET, SAVANNAH, GEORGIA 31401

Tel: **(912) 232-7787**
 Best Time to Call: **8:30 AM–6 PM**
 Coordinator: **Alan Fort**
 States/Regions Covered: **Georgia— Savannah, St. Simons Island, Tybee Island; South Carolina—Beaufort, Charleston**
	Rates (Single/Double):
	   Modest: **$50** **$65**
	   Average: **$60** **$80**
	   Luxury: **$90** **$175**
	 Credit Cards: **AMEX, MC, VISA**

Alan's accommodations include elegantly restored inns, guest houses, private homes, and even a villa on the water. They're located in the best historic districts as well as along the coast, from South Carolina's Low Country to Georgia's Sea Islands and beyond. A special blend of cordial hospitality, comfort, and services is provided. All are air-conditioned in the summer. Facilities for children and the handicapped are often available. Please note that while most hosts accept credit cards, some do not.

Bed & Breakfast Inn
117 WEST GORDON AT CHATHAM SQUARE, SAVANNAH, GEORGIA 31401

Tel: **(912) 238-0518** Host(s): **Robert McAlister** No. of Rooms: **11** No. of Private Baths: **4** Max. No. Sharing Bath: **4** Double/pb: **$65** Single/pb: **$50** Double/sb: **$38–$42** Single/sb: **$30–$34**	Open: **All year** Breakfast: **Full** Credit Cards: **AMEX, MC, VISA** Pets: **No** Children: **Welcome (crib)** Smoking: **Permitted** Social Drinking: **Permitted** Airport/Station Pickup: **Yes** Foreign Languages: **German, Spanish**

Located in the heart of the historic district, the inn is a Federalist row house built in 1853. It is decorated with a few period pieces and many appropriate reproductions. Some of the bedrooms have poster beds, and all rooms are air-conditioned. The outstanding courtyard, with its profusion of trees and colorful flowers, has twice been photographed by *Southern Living* magazine. Bob is active in a variety of historical organizations and Scottish Heritage groups. He is also the Budget Director of Savannah.

The Culpepper House
P.O. BOX 462, BROAD AT MORGAN, SENOIA, GEORGIA 30276

Tel: **(404) 599-8182**
Best Time to Call: **7 PM–10 PM**
Host(s): **Mary A. Brown**
Location: **37 mi. S of Atlanta**
No. of Rooms: **4**
No. of Private Baths: **1**
Max. No. Sharing Bath: **4**
Double/pb: **$55**
Double/sb: **$50**
Single/sb: **$45**

Open: **All year**
Reduced Rates: **10%, families**
Breakfast: **Full**
Credit Cards: **No**
Pets: **No**
Children: **Welcome, over 10 and infants**
Smoking: **Permitted**
Social Drinking: **Permitted**
Airport/Station Pickup: **Yes**

This Queen Anne Victorian was built in 1871. Gingerbread trim, stained glass, sliding doors, bay windows, and provincial furnishings re-create that turn-of-the-century feeling. Snacks and setups are offered. Your hostess will gladly direct you to surrounding antique and craft shops, state parks, and gardens.

HAWAII

Bed & Breakfast—Hawaii ✪
P.O. BOX 449, KAPAA, HAWAII 96746

Tel: **(808) 822-7771**
Best Time to Call: **8:30 AM–4:30 PM**
Coordinators: **Evie Warner and Al Davis**
States/Regions Covered: **All of the Hawaiian Islands**

Rates (Single/Double):
  Modest: **$35**   **$35**
  Average: **N/A**   **$45–$55**
  Luxury: **N/A**   **$80**
Credit Cards: **No**

Hawaii is a group of diverse islands offering traditional warmth and hospitality to the visitor through this membership organization. For a $10 membership fee, you will receive a descriptive directory of accommodations on all five islands. Some are separate units; others are in the main house. Most have private baths. Minimum stay is two nights. The University of Hawaii at Oahu is convenient to many B&Bs.

Bed & Breakfast Honolulu and Statewide ✪
3242 KAOHINANI DRIVE, HONOLULU, HAWAII 96817

Tel: (808) 595-7533; (800) 367-8047 from the Continental U.S.
Best Time to Call: 8 AM–8 PM
Coordinators: **Gene Bridges and Mary Lee**
States/Regions Covered: **Island of Oahu: Honolulu, Waikiki, Kailua; Islands of Maui, Molokai, Kauai, Hawaii, Lanai**

Rates (Single/Double):
  Modest: $25 $35
  Average: $40 $50
  Luxury: $50 up $60 up
Credit Cards: **No**
Minimum Stay: **3 nights**

Gene is a local attorney as well as a Unitarian minister. His roster includes many lovely residential areas where rainbows can often be seen against the green cliffs. Some B&Bs are near or on the beach; some have private swimming pools. They range from homes that are simply furnished to those that are luxuriously decorated. All are comfortable and promise warm, personal attention by attentive hosts.

Bed and Breakfast "Maui Style" ✪
P.O. BOX 886, KIHEI, HAWAII 96753

Tel: (808) 879-7865
Coordinator: **Jeanne Rominger**
States/Regions Covered: **Kauai, Hawaii, Maui, Molokai, Oahu**

Rates (Single/Double):
  Average: $30 $40–$55
  Luxury: $65 $95
Credit Cards: **No**
Minimum Stay: **3 nights**

Jeanne's host homes range from tranquil, up-country spots to a house in Lahaina with a pool, private lanais off the bedroom, car, and three meals included in the price. Another is a quiet studio with a hot tub; another an old plantation home in Haiku. Hosts have a variety of interests and range from an avid chess player to an astrologist to a massage therapist. There is no public transportation on Maui, so plan to arrange a car rental. A $5–$10 surcharge is imposed for a one-night stay.

Mahina Kai
BOX 699, ANAHOLA BAY, ANAHOLA, KAUAI, HAWAII 96703

Tel: (808) 822-9451
Host(s): **Dale Matlock and Rick Herold**

No. of Rooms: 3
No. of Private Baths: 1

Max. No. Sharing Bath: **4**
Double/pb: **$75**
Single/pb: **$65**
Double/sb: **$70**
Single/sb: **$60**
Guest Cottage: **$125 for 4**
Open: **All year**

Breakfast: **Continental**
Pets: **No**
Children: **No**
Smoking: **Permitted**
Social Drinking: **Permitted**
Minimum Stay: **3 nights**
Foreign Languages: **French, Italian**

This unusual villa, surrounded by terraced hillside gardens, overlooks beautiful Anahola Bay; it's handsomely decorated with a deft blend of Far Eastern grace and Western comfort. Located 200 yards from the ocean, the 23 steps leading up to the house make it unsuitable for people who might have a problem with the climb. Hiking on mountain trails, swimming, and snorkeling are just a few of the recreational pleasures. Rick is an artist who will be happy to show you the art treasures collected from his extensive world travels. A guest wing provides privacy with individual lanais centered around a dramatic redwood-beamed living room and library. After a good night's sleep you'll enjoy breakfast served in a tropical atmosphere, with the sounds of a fountain, birds singing, and the sea.

Adrienne's Bed & Breakfast Paradise ○
RR 1, BOX 8E, CAPTAIN COOK, BIG ISLAND, HAWAII 96704

Tel: **(808) 328-9726**
Host(s): **Adrienne and Reg Ritz**
Location: **18 mi. S of Kailua-Kona**
No. of Rooms: **3**
No. of Private Baths: **2**
Max. No. Sharing Bath: **4**
Double/pb: **$45**
Single/pb: **$35**
Double/sb: **$40**

Single/sb: **$30**
Open: **All year**
Reduced Rates: **Families; weekly**
Breakfast: **Continental**
Pets: **No**
Children: **Welcome (crib)**
Smoking: **No**
Social Drinking: **Permitted**
Airport/Station Pickup: **Yes**

This custom cedar home, surrounded by gardens, has an unobstructed view of the ocean that can even be seen from the lanai's hot tub. The light and airy rooms are decorated with local artwork. Breakfast of Kona coffee, local fruits, and home-baked muffins and popovers is served on a covered lanai. Adrienne and Reg are former New Yorkers who feel they've found paradise and are pleased to share their special discoveries with you. She's an international archery champion who will direct you to places for swimming and snorkeling.

Haikuleana ✪
69 HAIKU ROAD, HAIKU, MAUI, HAWAII 96708

Tel: **(808) 575-2890**
Best Time to Call: **8 AM–7 PM**
Host(s): **Clark and Denise Champion**
Location: **12 mi. E of Kahului**
No. of Rooms: **2**
Max. No. Sharing Bath: **4**
Double/sb: **$55**

Single/sb: **$45**
Open: **All year**
Breakfast: **Continental**
Pets: **Sometimes**
Children: **Welcome**
Smoking: **Permitted**
Social Drinking: **Permitted**

Experience the real feeling of aloha as a guest in an 1850s Hawaiian plantation home. Haikuleana is set in the agricultural district, close to secluded waterfalls and beautiful beaches. The house is built in the old style, with high ceilings, a porch, and gardens of Hawaiian plants and flowers. The rooms are cool and tropical, with wood motifs, antiques, and quilts. Swimming ponds, fine photographic sites, and the world's foremost windsurfing spot are all nearby.

Bob & Val's Sunset Beach B&B on Oahu ✪
P.O. BOX 487, HALEIWA, OAHU, HAWAII 96712

Tel: **(808) 638-7258**
Host(s): **Bob and Val Brasch**
Location: **40 mi. N of Honolulu**
No. of Rooms: **3**
No. of Private Baths: **3**
Double/pb: **$45**
Suites: **$55 for 2**

Open: **All year**
Breakfast: **Full**
Pets: **No**
Children: **Welcome, over 16**
Smoking: **Permitted**
Social Drinking: **Permitted**

Just an hour's drive from Honolulu you'll find Bob and Val's beautiful two-story pole house with decks that overlook the North Shore's best wind-surfing beaches. Bob, a retired engineer, and Val, a nurse, had their own dance band in California, but the music you'll hear outside your window is more likely to be the songs of jungle birds greeting the day rather than swing. Val takes great pride in her table settings and the special touches she gives her breakfasts. Bob and Val offer guests a choice of three facilities—the largest with its own full-sized kitchen and living room, and the two others with private entrances and baths, small refrigerators, and television/VCRs.

Holualoa Inn ○
P.O. BOX 222A, HOLUALOA, BIG ISLAND, HAWAII 96725

Tel: **(808) 324-1121**
Best Time to Call: **8 AM–5 PM**
Host(s): **Desmond and Karen Twigg-Smith**
Location: **4 mi. E of Kailua-Kona**
No. of Rooms: **3**
No. of Private Baths: **3**
Double/pb: **$75–$85**

Open: **June–Apr.**
Breakfast: **Continental**
Credit Cards: **MC, VISA**
Pets: **No**
Children: **Welcome, over 12**
Smoking: **No**
Social Drinking: **Permitted**

Experience country elegance on a private, 30-acre estate overlooking Kailua and the Kona Coast of the Big Island. The house is constructed entirely of cedar, with beautiful red eucalyptus floors. Guests may choose from the Bali, Oriental, or Polynesian rooms, each with a different decor and either queen, king, or twin beds. During your visit, feel free to take a swim in their pool, shoot a game of billards, sip a drink from the wet bar, or simply stroll in the garden. When the sun sets, you'll want to be in the rooftop gazebo overlooking the pastures, coffee orchards, and ocean. Your hosts offer delicious Kona coffee and fresh fruit each morning. They will gladly show you the way to the beach, galleries, restaurants, entertainment, and a full range of water sports.

Bed & Breakfast Waikiki Beach
P.O. BOX 89080, HONOLULU, HAWAII 96830

Tel: **(808) 923-5459**
Host(s): **Carol and Franz Schaier**
No. of Rooms: **1**
No. of Private Baths: **1**
Double/pb: **$45–$55**
Single/pb: **$35–$45**
Open: **All year**

Breakfast: **Continental**
Pets: **No**
Children: **No**
Smoking: **No**
Social Drinking: **Permitted**
Foreign Languages: **French, German, Spanish, Swiss**

The Schaiers' home is a condominium, not two blocks from the beach, where their guest bedroom looks exactly like one you'd find in a small country guest house in Switzerland. The reason? Franz is Swiss, a pastry chef by profession. Breakfast is served out on a small terrace overlooking the Waikiki skyline, on a bistro set that the Schaiers brought with them from Switzerland. "We serve cappuccino and espresso with tiny jars of Swiss confitures that our family sends from the Alps, sweet butter, sugar with a vanilla bean in it, and a basket full of croissants, brioches, or some other special Swiss pastry."

Bev & Monty's Bed & Breakfast
4571 UKALI STREET, HONOLULU, HAWAII 96818

Tel: **(808) 422-9873**
Best Time to Call: **7 AM–9 PM**
Host(s): **Bev and Monty Neese**
Location: **4½ mi. from airport**
No. of Rooms: **2**
Max. No. Sharing Bath: **4**
Double/sb: **$40**
Single/sb: **$30**

Open: **All year**
Reduced Rates: **Weekly**
Breakfast: **Continental**
Pets: **No**
Children: **Welcome**
Smoking: **Permitted**
Social Drinking: **Permitted**
Airport/Station Pickup: **Yes**

This typical Hawaiian home is convenient to many of Hawaii's most popular attractions. Bev and Monty are just a mile above historic Pearl Harbor, and the Arizona Memorial can be seen from their veranda. They enjoy sharing an Hawaiian aloha, for a convenient overnight stay or a long vacation where they can share their favorite places with you. This comfortable home is just off the access road leading east to Honolulu and Waikiki or west to the North Shore beaches, sugar plantations, and pineapple fields. Good hiking country as well as city entertainment and shopping centers are located nearby.

Papaya Paradise
395 AUWINALA ROAD, KAILUA, OAHU, HAWAII 96734

Tel: **(808) 261-0316**
Best Time to Call: **7 AM–8 PM**
Host(s): **Bob and Jeanette Martz**
Location: **10 mi. E of Honolulu**
No. of Rooms: **2**
Double/pb: **$50**
Open: **All year**

Breakfast: **Full**
Pets: **No**
Children: **No**
Smoking: **Permitted**
Social Drinking: **Permitted**
Minimum Stay: **3 nights**

Bob and Jeanette Martz are located on the windward side of Oahu, miles from high rises and hotels. Their one-story Hawaiian-style home is surrounded by a papaya grove, tropical plants, and flowers. Each guest room has two beds and its own private entrance for your privacy and comfort. Breakfast is served on the lanai overlooking the pool and Jacuzzi. Jeanette offers something different every day, but papaya fresh from the family grove is always on the menu. A four-mile-long white sandy beach without rocks or coral is just a five-minute drive away. Lanikai Beach, known as the windsurfing capital of the world, is also nearby. Papaya Paradise is removed from the hectic activity of Waikiki, but those craving an evening on the town can be there in 20 minutes.

Kay Barker's Bed & Breakfast ✪
P.O. BOX 740, KAPAA, KAUAI, HAWAII 96746

Tel: **(808) 822-3073**
Best Time to Call: **Before noon**
Host(s): **Kay Barker**
No. of Rooms: **4**
No. of Private Baths: **4**
Double/pb: **$30–$40**
Single/pb: **$25–$40**

Open: **All year**
Breakfast: **Full**
Pets: **Sometimes**
Children: **Welcome, over 10**
Smoking: **Permitted**
Social Drinking: **Permitted**

Kauai, the Garden Island, is most beautiful, with its powdery sand beaches and lush waterfalls. Kay, a longtime resident, knows the out-of-the-way places that others dream about. Her home is located on the slopes of the Sleeping Giant, with sweeping views of pastures and mountains. There is a separate TV room, an extensive library, a large lanai, and beautiful gardens. Breakfast often features macadamia nut waffles and pancakes.

Poipu Bed and Breakfast Inn ✪
2720 HOONANI ROAD, RR1 BOX 308B, KOLOA, KAUAI, HAWAII 96756

Tel: **(808) 742-1146**
Best Time to Call: **7 AM–10 PM**
Host(s): **Dotti Cichon**
Location: **12 mi. SW of Lihue**
No. of Rooms: **4**
No. of Private Baths: **4**
Double/pb: **$65–$100**
Single/pb: **$60–$95**
Suites: **$140–$155**

Open: **All year**
Reduced Rates: **10%, weekly, seniors**
Breakfast: **Continental**
Credit Cards: **MC, VISA**
Pets: **No**
Children: **Welcome**
Smoking: **No**
Social Drinking: **Permitted**
Foreign Languages: **French, German**

Built in 1935, this authentic plantation house has been restored and renovated; the handcrafted wood interiors and shady lanais are the perfect complement to the white wicker and antique pine furnishings. Your hostess is an avid collector of local art and handcrafts. Guest rooms have either king-size or queen-size beds, color TVs, refrigerators, and new luxurious baths, two with whirlpool tubs. If you want to sleep in, a breakfast of fresh fruit, rolls, and cereals or yogurt can be served in your room; then catch up with other guests during afternoon tea in the great room or out on the lanai. Dotti invites you to be her guest at the nearby tennis club and will also direct you to golf and a wide selection of water sports at the nearby beaches.

Kilohana
212 KAWEHI PLACE, KULA, MAUI, HAWAII 96790

Tel: **(808) 878-6086**
Best Time to Call: **8 AM–6 PM**
Host(s): **Jody Baldwin and Charles Hansen**
Location: **16 mi. NW of Kahului Airport**
No. of Rooms: **1**
No. of Private Baths: **1**
Double/pb: **$55**
Single/pb: **$45**
Open: **All year**
Reduced Rates: **Weekly**
Breakfast: **Continental**
Pets: **No**
Children: **No**
Smoking: **No**
Social Drinking: **Permitted**

Drive up, up, up, along the slopes of Haleakala, past cabbage and flower fields, and you will come to Jody and Charles's home—a modernized plantation house surrounded by 12 acres of wooded land, with a sweeping view of the islands of Lanai and Molokai. "The quiet and coolness of the countryside bring our visitors back again and again." Must-sees while you're in the "Kula" district are the sunrise from the summit of the crater, the Tedeschi Winery, and exotic Protea Farms. The beach and windsurfing are a half-hour away, and restaurants just 5 to 15 minutes by car. You'll be greeted with refreshments when you arrive, and in the morning after the sun enters your spacious guest room, you'll get up to a breakfast of fresh fruit, homemade pastry, coffee, tea, and "fresh Hawaiian juice."

Victoria Place
P.O. BOX 930, LAWAI, KAUAI, HAWAII 96765

Tel: **(808) 332-9300**
Host(s): **Edee Seymour**
No. of Rooms: **3**
No. of Private Baths: **1**
Max. No. Sharing Bath: **3**
Double/pb: **$70**
Double/sb: **$60**
Single/sb: **$50**
Open: **All year**

Reduced Rates: **$10 less, Easter–Dec. 14**
Breakfast: **Continental**
Pets: **No**
Children: **No**
Smoking: **No**
Social Drinking: **Permitted**
Minimum Stay: **2 nights**
Airport/Station Pickup: **Yes**

Perched high in the lush hills of southern Kauai, overlooking the thick jungle, cane fields, and the Pacific, Victoria Place promises an oasis of pampered comfort and privacy. The guest rooms, located in one wing of this spacious skylit home, open directly through glass doors onto the pool area, which is surrounded by flower gardens. Edee, a former Michigan native, will direct you to nearby attractions, including the resort beaches of Poipu, the Pacific Tropical Botanical Gardens, Spouting Horn geyser, open-air markets, boutiques, and ethnic restaurants, all within minutes of the house. There is a $5 surcharge for one-night stays.

IDAHO

Bed and Breakfast of Idaho
P.O. BOX 7323, BOISE, IDAHO 83702

Tel: **(208) 336-5174**
Best Time to Call: **6–9 PM**
Coordinator: **Lynda Rule**
States/Regions Covered: **Boise, Coeur d'Alene, Kellogg**

Rates (Single/Double):
  Modest: $20 $25
  Average: $30 $35
  Luxury: $60 $65
Credit Cards: **AMEX, MC, VISA**

Lynda is prepared to arrange a stay to suit your purse and preference. In the "modest" classification, you might stay in a contemporary home with a mountain view; an "average" selection might be an inn located close to a lovely lake; and a "luxury" setting is a large suite with a sunken tub in the bathroom and a fireplace in the sitting area. All the hosts have a genuine desire to share their knowledge of where to eat and what to do in their area. A $5 surcharge is imposed for a one-night stay.

Idaho Heritage Inn
109 WEST IDAHO, BOISE, IDAHO 83702

Tel: **(208) 342-8066**
Host(s): **Tom and Phyllis Lupher**
No. of Rooms: **4**
Double/pb: **$50**
Double/sb: **$45–$50**
Suites: **$65**
Open: **All year**

Breakfast: **Continental**
Credit Cards: **AMEX, MC, VISA**
Pets: **No**
Children: **Welcome, over 15**
Smoking: **Permitted**
Social Drinking: **Permitted**
Airport/Station Pickup: **Yes**

Over the years a governor, a senator, and a merchant have all called this 1904 Colonial house home. After careful restoration by the Luphers, it is now listed on the National Register. The spacious common rooms feature French doors, oak flooring, Oriental carpets, and comfortable seating. Guest rooms are decorated in period furnishings and crisp linens; two of the bedrooms open out onto a veranda. Enjoy fresh-squeezed juice, seasonal fruits, and oven-warmed breads in your private quarters each morning. A glass of wine, a soft drink, and a good book are always on hand when you want them. The inn is set in the historic Warm Springs district, just five blocks from the fine shops, theaters, and restaurants in downtown Boise.

Greenbriar Bed and Breakfast Inn ✪
315 WALLACE, COEUR d'ALENE, IDAHO, 83814

Tel: **(208) 667-9260**
Best Time to Call: **Before 10 PM**
Host(s): **Kris McIluenna**
Location: **30 mi. E of Spokane, Washington**
No. of Rooms: **7**
No. of Private Baths: **4**
Max. No. Sharing Bath: **4**
Double/pb: **$49–$54**
Single/pb: **$44–$49**
Double/sb: **$35–$45**
Single/sb: **$35–$40**

Suites: **$65**
Open: **All year**
Reduced Rates: **10%, seniors**
Breakfast: **Continental**
Other Meals: **Available**
Credit Cards: **MC, VISA**
Pets: **Sometimes**
Children: **Welcome (crib)**
Smoking: **No**
Social Drinking: **Permitted**
Airport/Station Pickup: **Yes**

The Greenbriar is located on the north shore of Lake Coeur d'Alene, four blocks from the beach. The house was built in 1908 and is now listed on the National Register of Historic Places. The interior is unique, with mahogany woodwork, winding staircases, and gracefully arched ceilings. The bedrooms feature gabled ceilings and dormers with mahogany window seats, and are furnished in antiques and genuine linen-covered down comforters, direct from Ireland. Kris's gourmet breakfasts feature eggs in pastry, sourbread French toast, and Swedish pancakes. She will gladly pack picnic lunches and arrange for canoe and bike rentals. An outdoor hot tub invites you to relax after a day of exploring.

Inn The First Place ✪
509 NORTH 15TH STREET, COEUR d'ALENE, IDAHO 83814

Tel: **(208) 667-3346**
Best Time to Call: **7 AM–11:30 PM**
Host(s): **Tom and Lois Knox**
Location: **30 mi. E of Spokane, Washington**
No. of Rooms: **3**
Max. No. Sharing Bath: **4**
Double/sb: **$35**
Single/sb: **$25**
Open: **All year**

Reduced Rates: **Available**
Breakfast: **Full**
Other Meals: **Available**
Credit Cards: **MC, VISA**
Pets: **No**
Children: **Welcome, over 12**
Smoking: **Permitted**
Social Drinking: **Permitted**
Airport/Station Pickup: **Yes**

Tom and Lois welcome you to their unusual home, which was once a grocery store. The guest rooms, located on the second floor, are decorated attractively, with wood paneling or country wallpaper, coordinating quilts, and a smattering of crafts and collectibles. The large living room and fully equipped kitchen are available to guests. In the morning, you can look forward to Lois's specialties, such as stuffed French toast or quiche. The inn is a mile away from beautiful Lake Coeur d'Alene, famous for fishing, swimming, and day cruises.

The Sleeping Place of the Wheels ✪
P.O. BOX 5273, 3308 LODGEPOLE ROAD, COEUR d'ALENE, IDAHO 83814

Tel: **(208) 765-3435**
Host(s): **Donna and Wallace Bedord**
Location: **1 mi. from I-90**
No. of Rooms: **3**
Max. No. Sharing Bath: **2**
Double/sb: **$25–$35**
Single/sb: **$20**
Open: **All year**

Reduced Rates: **10% less, Nov. 1– Mar. 31**
Breakfast: **Full**
Other Meals: **Available**
Pets: **Welcome**
Children: **Welcome**
Smoking: **No**
Social Drinking: **No**
Airport/Station Pickup: **Yes**

Wagon wheels mark the entrance to Donna and Wallace's home, which is surrounded by tall pines and pretty flower gardens. Raspberries, strawberries, plums, and cherries are yours for the picking. Children will delight in the special playhouse with its fireman's slide, swing, and sandbox. Wallace enjoys making burled-wood tables and plant stands made of iron; Donna enjoys quilting and reading. The handstitched quilts and handcrafted wood and iron items are for sale.

Heritage Inn
510 LENA STREET, SALMON, IDAHO 83467

Tel: **(208) 756-3174**
Best Time to Call: **6 PM–9 PM**
Host(s): **Audrey Nichols**
Location: **½ mi. from Hwy. 93**
No. of Rooms: **5**
Max. No. Sharing Bath: **3**
Double/sb: **$25**
Single/sb: **$20**

Suites: **$40**
Open: **All year**
Breakfast: **Continental**
Credit Cards: **MC, VISA**
Pets: **No**
Children: **Welcome, over 4**
Smoking: **On porch only**
Social Drinking: **Permitted**

This 100-year-old Victorian farmhouse is set in a valley, surrounded by mountains and pine trees. In the old days, this was a cozy stopover for those traveling by stagecoach. The Heritage has since been lovingly restored and decorated with many antiques. Enjoy a cool drink on the glassed-in sun porch while you enjoy the quiet of this pretty neighborhood. The River of No Return is just half a mile away, and it's just a mile to the city park and swimming pool. Your hostess serves homemade muffins and jams in the sunny dining room or on the porch each morning. She is a native of Salmon and can gladly direct you to restaurants within walking distance, nearby ghost towns, and other places of historic or cultural interest.

Smith House Bed & Breakfast
49 SALMON RIVER ROAD, SHOUP, IDAHO 83469

Tel: **(208) 756-2098**
Best Time to Call: **Early mornings; evenings**
Host(s): **Aubrey and Marsha Smith**
Location: **50 mi. N of Salmon**
No. of Rooms: **6**
No. of Private Baths: **2**
Max. No. Sharing Bath: **4**
Double/pb: **$54**
Double/sb: **$40**
Single/sb: **$35**

Open: **All year**
Reduced Rates: **Weekly**
Breakfast: **Full**
Other Meals: **Available**
Credit Cards: **MC, VISA**
Pets: **Sometimes**
Children: **Welcome**
Smoking: **No**
Social Drinking: **Permitted**
Airport/Station Pickup: **Yes**

Located on the Salmon River and adjoining a wilderness area, Smith House is a dream come true. Aubrey and Marsha vacationed here 11 years ago and fell in love with the constantly changing scenery. They sold their Florida house and built their dream log home, which they enjoy sharing with their guests. Marsha enjoys pampering people with such breakfast creations as hash-brown quiche, buttermilk scones, or wheat French toast with homemade fruit topping. Meals are served underneath the dining room skylight. Recreational opportunities include white-water rafting, fishing, hunting, and hiking. Visit the nearby ghost town or restored gold mine, then come "home" to relax in the hot tub.

For key to listings, see inside front or back cover.

✪ This star means that rates are guaranteed through December 31, 1989 to any guest making a reservation as a result of reading about the B&B in *BED & BREAKFAST U.S.A.*—1989 edition.

Please enclose a self-addressed, stamped, business-sized envelope when contacting reservation services.

For more details on what you can expect in a B&B, see Chapter 1.

Always mention *Bed & Breakfast U.S.A.* when making reservations!

If no B&B is listed in the area you'll be visiting, use the form on page 693 to order a copy of our "List of New B&Bs."

We want to hear from you! Use the form on page 691.

ILLINOIS

Bed & Breakfast/Chicago, Inc. ✪
P.O. BOX 14088, CHICAGO, ILLINOIS 60614

Tel: (312) 951-0085
Coordinator: Mary Shaw
States/Regions Covered: Arlington Heights, Chicago, Deerfield, Evanston, Glencoe, Northfield, Oak Park, Wilmette

Rates: (Single/Double):
 Modest: $40 $50
 Average: $55 $65
Credit Cards: AMEX, MC, VISA
Minimum Stay: 2 nights

Mary welcomes you to midwestern hospitality in the "windy city" and its suburbs. Discover, on foot, Chicago's outdoor sculpture plazas, shop world-famous Marshall Fields, or observe the skyline from the top of the Sears Tower. Follow the happenings on the campuses of Northwestern, University of Chicago, Loyola, and the University of Illinois. There is a three-night minimum stay for apartments without hosts in residence, and a $10 surcharge if you stay only one night in hosted B&Bs.

Curly's Corner ✪
R.R. 2, BOX 85B, ARCOLA, ILLINOIS 61910

Tel: **(217) 268-3352**
Best Time to Call: **Mornings; after 5 PM**
Hosts: **Warren and Maxine Arthur**
Location: **35 mi. S of Champaign; 5 mi. from I-57**
No. of Rooms: **3**
No. of Private Baths: **2**
Max. No. Sharing Bath: **3**
Double/pb: **$40–$50**
Single/sb: **$30**
Open: **March–Nov.**
Breakfast: **Full**
Pets: **No**
Children: **Welcome, over 10**
Smoking: **No**
Social Drinking: **No**
Airport/Station Pickup: **Yes**

This ranch-style farmhouse is located in a quiet Amish community. Your hosts are dedicated to cordial hospitality and will gladly share information about the area or even take you on a tour. They offer comfortable bedrooms, one with a king-size water bed. In the morning, enjoy a wonderful breakfast of homemade biscuits, apple butter, fresh country bacon, and eggs. Curly's Corner is a half mile from beautiful Rockome Gardens.

Country House
ROUTE 1, BOX 61, CISCO, ILLINOIS 61830

Tel: **(217) 669-2291**
Host(s): **Carol and Don Padgett**
Location: **17 mi. E of Decatur**
No. of Rooms: **2**
No. of Private Baths: **1**
Max. No. Sharing Bath: **4**
Double/sb: **$35**
Single/sb: **$30**
Suites: **$45**
Open: **All year**
Breakfast: **Continental**
Pets: **No**
Children: **No**
Smoking: **Permitted**
Social Drinking: **No**

This 100-year-old country home is located in the heart of prairie farmland. Your hosts, Carol and Don, have decorated the rooms with a blend of traditional, wicker, and antique furnishings. In the warmer weather, a leisurely breakfast may be served on the porch overlooking the flower garden. During cooler months, guests are served in the rustic family room or gracious dining room. Down the road is the private fishing pond with a dock for sunbathing. The city of Monticello is for shopping and dining. The Country House is a short distance from Robert Allerton Park for picnicking, skiing, and biking. Guests are always welcome to relax with a game of pool or a traditional round of horseshoes back at the house. The University of Illinois at Champaign is close by.

The Golds
R.R.3, BOX 69, CHAMPAIGN, ILLINOIS 61821

Tel: **(217) 586-4345**
Best Time to Call: **Evenings**
Host(s): **Bob and Rita Gold**
Location: **6 mi. W of Champaign**
No. of Rooms: **3**
No. of Private Baths: **1**
Max. No. Sharing Bath: **4**
Double/pb: **$40**
Single/pb: **$35**
Double/sb: **$35–$40**

Single/sb: **$30**
Open: **All year**
Reduced Rates: **15% weekly**
Breakfast: **Continental**
Pets: **Sometimes**
Children: **Welcome**
Smoking: **No**
Social Drinking: **Permitted**
Airport/Station Pickup: **Available**

One of the most beautiful views in Champaign County is yours from the deck of this restored farmhouse. The house is set on six acres surrounded by prime central Illinois farmland. Inside you'll find country antiques, complemented by beautiful wainscoting. An open walnut stairway leads to bedrooms decorated with four-poster beds, handmade quilts, and Oriental rugs. Guests can relax by the living room wood stove or enjoy a glass of wine on the deck. Bob and Rita offer garden fruits and cider for breakfast, served with homemade jams, muffins, and coffee cakes. The Golds is two miles from Lake of the Woods, known for golf, fishing, and boating. Shopping and restaurants are also within easy reach.

Hamilton House ✪
500 WEST MAIN STREET, DECATUR, ILLINOIS 62522

Tel: **(217) 429-1669**
Best Time to Call: **After 4 PM**
Hosts: **Nancy and Dave Phillips**
Location: **30 mi. E of Springfield**
No. of Rooms: **5**
No. of Private Baths: **1**
Max. No. Sharing Bath: **4**
Double/pb: **$45–$50**
Double/sb: **$45**
Open: **All year**

Reduced Rates: **10%, seniors**
Breakfast: **Full (except Sunday)**
Credit Cards: **AMEX, MC, VISA**
Pets: **Sometimes**
Children: **Welcome (crib)**
Smoking: **Permitted**
Social Drinking: **Permitted**
Airport/Station Pickup: **Yes**
Foreign Languages: **Dutch, French, German**

Hamilton House is a brick Victorian mansion located in the Abraham Lincoln historic area. It was built in 1892 and is listed on the National Register of Historic Places. The house has been beautifully maintained and still boasts its original woodwork fireplaces. The guest rooms are decorated with period furnishings and each has a different style antique bed. Nancy and Dave also specialize in simple, elegant lunches. Their gift shop specializes in fine treasures of Victorian and American design.

Aldrich Guest House ✪
900 THIRD STREET, GALENA, ILLINOIS 61036

Tel: **(815) 777-3323**
Host(s): **Judy Green**
Location: **¼ mi. from Rte. 20**
No. of Rooms: **4**
No. of Private Baths: **3**
Max. No. Sharing Bath: **4**
Double/pb: **$60–$65**
Single/pb: **$55–$60**
Double/sb: **$55**
Single/sb: **$50**
Suites: **$115**
Open: **All year**
Breakfast: **Full**
Credit Cards: **MC, VISA**
Pets: **No**
Children: **Welcome, over 6**
Smoking: **Permitted**
Social Drinking: **Permitted**

George Washington didn't sleep here, but Ulysses S. Grant was entertained in the spacious double parlors of this elegant 1845 home. Throughout the house, period decor, antiques, and some reproductions harmonize effectively. Centrally air-conditioned for summer comfort, the house is convenient to all the historic sites. Judy's hearty breakfasts include fresh fruit salads and entrées such as pancakes or egg dishes.

Avery Guest House
606 SOUTH PROSPECT STREET, GALENA, ILLINOIS 61036

Tel: **(815) 777-3883**
Best Time to Call: **9 AM–9 PM**
Host(s): **Flo and Roger Jensen**
Location: **15 mi. E of Dubuque, Iowa**
No. of Rooms: **4**
Max. No. Sharing Bath: **4**
Double/sb: **$45**
Single/sb: **$40**
Open: **All year**

Reduced Rates: **10%, 3-day stays; seniors**
Breakfast: **Continental**
Pets: **No**
Children: **Welcome (crib, high chair)**
Smoking: **No**
Social Drinking: **Permitted**
Airport/Station Pickup: **Yes**

This spacious, 140-year-old home is located two blocks from historic downtown Galena. Enjoy the view of bluffs and Victorian mansions from an old-fashioned porch overlooking the Galena River Valley. Your hosts welcome you to use the piano or bring your own instrument and join them in chamber music. Enjoy delicious homemade muffins and breads along with cheeses and jams each morning. Flo and Roger will gladly direct you to Grant's home and other interesting sights in the historic district.

Ahern's Bed & Breakfast
8553 WEST OGDEN AVENUE, LYONS, ILLINOIS 60534

Tel: **(312) 442-1170**
Host(s): **Richard and Brigid Ahern**
Location: **18 mi. W of Chicago**
No. of Rooms: **1**
No. of Private Baths: **1**
Double/pb: **$50**
Single/pb: **$40**

Open: **All year**
Reduced Rates: **10%, seniors**
Breakfast: **Full**
Pets: **No**
Children: **No**
Smoking: **No**
Social Drinking: **Permitted**

A beautiful penthouse apartment is your home base while you are guests of the Aherns. Their apartment has plenty of room—it's 2,000 square feet in all. Your hostess, a native of Ireland, has furnished her home with lovely antiques. The guest room features comfortable furnishings, a walk-in closet, and a television. A whirlpool bath is also available in your hosts' bathroom. Richard and Brigid are very knowledgeable about Chicago and can direct you to many local attractions and restaurants. The Brookfield Zoo is two miles away, and the Chicago loop is just a 20-minute ride. Before a day of touring you'll get a fresh start with a healthy breakfast of eggs, whole wheat toast, and fresh fruit.

Die Blaue Gans (The Blue Goose) ✪
9 S 265 ROUTE 59, NAPERVILLE, ILLINOIS 60565

Tel: **(312) 355-0835**
Best Time to Call: **Early mornings**
Host(s): **Molly Konrad**
Location: **35 mi. W of Chicago**
No. of Rooms: **3**
No. of Private Baths: **1**
Max. No. Sharing Bath: **3**
Double/pb: **$50**
Double/sb: **$45**

Single/sb: **$45**
Open: **All year**
Breakfast: **Full**
Pets: **No**
Children: **Welcome (crib)**
Smoking: **Permitted**
Social Drinking: **Permitted**
Airport/Station Pickup: **Yes**
Foreign Languages: **German**

Only 45 minutes from Chicago's Loop is the open prairie with fields of corn and wildflowers. It is in this setting that you will find an Austrian flag marking the spacious yard of this charming home. Painted dressers, ceiling borders, a French brass bed, and Bavarian tea service set the tone. The roof deck, gazebo, and fireplace are perfect spots for relaxing. Visit the Naper Settlement, stroll the Riverwalk where you may picnic and watch the mallard ducks. The band concert is a must on Thursday nights. On a summer's evening you may hear the renowned voices of the Konrad Family singers practicing for a concert.

Toad Hall Bed & Breakfast House ✪
301 NORTH SCOVILLE AVENUE, OAK PARK, ILLINOIS 60302

Tel: **(312) 386-8623**
Best Time to Call: **Evenings**
Host(s): **Cynthia Mungerson**
Location: **5 mi. from Chicago Loop**
No. of Rooms: **2**
No. of Private Baths: **1**
Max. No. Sharing Bath: **3**
Double/sb: **$45**
Single/sb: **$40**

Suites: **$50 for 2; $75 for 3**
Open: **All year**
Reduced Rates: **Weekly**
Breakfast: **Full**
Pets: **No**
Children: **Welcome, over 12**
Smoking: **No**
Social Drinking: **Permitted**

Built in 1912 and carefully maintained and restored, this gracious home is furnished with Victorian antiques, Oriental rugs, and Laura Ashley wallpapers. Guest rooms have comfortable reading chairs, luxurious linens, television, and air-conditioning. You are welcome to relax in the wicker on the porches, picnic on the sun deck, or curl up near a fireplace with a book. Breakfast, a British-style feast, is served in the oak-paneled dining room; in the same tradition, afternoon tea and evening brandy and sweets are offered. Centrally located in the

Frank Lloyd Wright Historic District, it is within walking distance of 25 Wright masterpieces, dozens of architecturally significant buildings, and the Ernest Hemingway home and lovely shops and restaurants.

The Kaufmann House
1641 HAMPSHIRE, QUINCY, ILLINOIS 62301

Tel: **(217) 223-2502**
Best Time to Call: **Noon–9 PM**
Host(s): **Emery and Bettie Kaufmann**
Location: **100 mi. W of Springfield**
No. of Rooms: **3**
No. of Private Baths: **1**
Max. No. Sharing Bath: **4**
Double/pb: **$60**
Single/pb: **$50**
Double/sb: **$40–$50**
Single/sb: **$30**
Open: **All year**
Breakfast: **Continental**
Pets: **No**
Children: **Welcome (crib)**
Smoking: **No**
Social Drinking: **No**
Airport/Station Pickup: **Yes**

History buffs will remember Quincy, set right on the Mississippi River, as the scene of the famous Lincoln-Douglas debates, while architecture buffs will be attracted to the town's feast of Victorian styles—Greek Revival, Gothic Revival, Italianate, and Richardsonian. The Kaufmann House was built 100 years ago, and the owners have been careful to maintain its "country" feeling. Guests may enjoy breakfast in the Ancestor's Room, on a stone patio, or at a picnic table under the trees. They are invited to play the piano, watch television, or enjoy popcorn by the fire. The Kaufmanns describe themselves as "Christians who have a love for God, people, nature, and life."

Victoria's B&B
201 NORTH 6TH STREET, ROCKFORD, ILLINOIS 61107

Tel: **(815) 963-3232**
Best Time to Call: **7 AM–9 PM**
Host(s): **Martin Lewis**
Location: **90 mi. W of Chicago**
No. of Rooms: **4**
No. of Private Baths: **4**
Double/pb: **$69**
Suites: **$135–$150**
Open: **All year**
Reduced Rates: **Weekly; 10%, seniors**
Breakfast: **Continental**
Credit Cards: **MC, VISA**
Pets: **No**
Children: **Welcome, over 12**
Smoking: **Permitted**
Social Drinking: **Permitted**

This is Rockford's first Bed and Breakfast, part of the town's "Victorian Village" area, 20 turn-of-the-century homes that have been restored and converted to boutiques and restaurants. Victoria's features a winding staircase, stained-glass windows, two fireplaces, and the kind of woodwork that you seldom see nowadays. Although the ambience is Victorian, the comforts are most definitely modern—television, air-conditioning, and refrigerators in each room, and even a Jacuzzi in some.

Top o' the Morning
1505 19TH AVENUE, ROCK ISLAND, ILLINOIS 61201

Tel: **(309) 786-3513**
Best Time to Call: **After 5 PM**
Host(s): **Sam and Peggy Doak**
Location: **1½ mi. from Rte. 92, 18th Ave. Exit**
No. of Rooms: **2**
No. of Private Baths: **2**

Double/pb: **$35–$45**
Open: **All year**
Breakfast: **Full**
Pets: **No**
Children: **Welcome**
Smoking: **Permitted**
Social Drinking: **Permitted**

Sam and Peggy welcome you to their country estate, set on a bluff overlooking the Mississippi River, near the center of the Quad Cities area. The 18-room mansion is situated at the end of a winding drive on three acres of lawn, orchards, and gardens. The guest rooms, graced with lovely chandeliers and Oriental rugs, command a spectacular view of the cities and river. The parlor, with its grand piano and fireplace, is an inviting place to relax. Local attractions are Mississippi River boat rides, harness racing, Rock Island Arsenal, Black Hawk State Park, and Augustine and Marycrest colleges.

The Stagecoach Inn
41 WEST 278 WHITNEY ROAD, ST. CHARLES, ILLINOIS 60175

Tel: **(312) 584-1263**
Host(s): **Pat and Bud Koecher**
Location: **41 mi. W of Chicago**
No. of Rooms: **2**
No. of Private Baths: **2**
Double/pb: **$45–$50**
Single/pb: **$35**

Open: **All year**
Reduced Rates: **Available**
Breakfast: **Continental**
Pets: **No**
Children: **Welcome (high chair)**
Smoking: **No**
Social Drinking: **Permitted**

The Stagecoach Inn is situated on picturesque Lake Campton in a scenic area five miles west of St. Charles. The house is a spacious ranch with a porch for sunning and relaxing. Year-round activities such as ice skating and fishing can be enjoyed just steps from your door. Biking, riding, and antiquing are also within easy reach. Your hosts, Pat and Bud, serve assorted muffins, toast, or sweet rolls, with plenty of coffee and tea for breakfast. They also are glad to offer snacks and soft drinks later in the day.

Mischler House ✪
718 SOUTH 8TH STREET, SPRINGFIELD, ILLINOIS 62703

Tel: **(217) 523-3714**
Host(s): **Rhonda and Mark Daniels**
Location: **¼ mi. from I-55**
No. of Rooms: **2**
Max. No. Sharing Bath: **4**
Double/sb: **$40**
Open: **All year**

Reduced Rates: **After 3 nights; 10%, seniors**
Breakfast: **Continental**
Pets: **Sometimes**
Children: **Welcome**
Smoking: **Permitted**
Social Drinking: **Permitted**
Airport/Station Pickup: **Yes**

Built around 1880, the house is a comfortable blend of old and new. It is located two blocks from the restored Abraham Lincoln Home, and just three blocks from downtown Springfield, where Lincoln's law office and the Old State Capitol are open to visitors. Upon arrival, guests are served coffee or tea, then escorted to one of the comfortable guest rooms. Guests are free to lounge or curl up with a book in one of the parlors after a day of sightseeing. You are welcome to use the TV, laundry facilities, patio barbecue, and the kitchen for light snacks.

INDIANA

Indiana Homes Bed & Breakfast, Inc. ✪
1431 ST. JAMES COURT, LOUISVILLE, KENTUCKY 40208

Tel: (502) 635-7341
Best Time to Call: 8 AM–Noon
Coordinator(s): Lillian Marshall and John Dillehay
States/Regions Covered: **Indiana**— Corydon, Evansville, Indianapolis, Paoli, Washington, West Baden

Rates (Single/Double):
  Modest: $33 $38
  Average: $45 $50
  Luxury: $65 and up $65 and up
Credit Cards: MC, VISA (deposit only)

Moving south from the Indianapolis Museum of Art and the Indy 500 racetrack, leave the Interstate for a true view of "Middle America." Traverse rolling hills past the famous stone quarries in Bedford and head for historic Corydon, the state's original capital city. Tour the cave systems, canoe the Blue River, and explore Wyandotte Woods.

Wherever you decide to stop, you can be assured of a hearty welcome and pleasant surroundings.

Gray Goose Inn ☉
350 INDIAN BOUNDARY ROAD, CHESTERTON, INDIANA 46304

Tel: **(219) 926-5781**
Host(s): **Tim Wilk and Charles Ramsey**
Location: **60 mi. E of Chicago**
No. of Rooms: **5**
No. of Private Baths: **5**
Double/pb: **$60–$65**
Single/pb: **$55–$60**
Double/sb: **$48**
Single/sb: **$45**
Suites: **$75**

Open: **All year**
Reduced Rates: **10%, seniors**
Breakfast: **Full**
Credit Cards: **AMEX, Discover, MC, VISA**
Pets: **No**
Children: **Welcome, over 12**
Smoking: **Permitted**
Social Drinking: **Permitted**
Foreign Languages: **Polish**

Elegant accommodations await you in this English country–style home overlooking a 30-acre lake. Guest rooms feature canopied four-poster beds, fine linens, and thick fluffy towels. All rooms are decorated in Williamsburg style, and some have a fireplace. Enjoy a quiet moment in the common room or relax with a cup of coffee on the screened-in porch. Take long walks beside the shady oaks or feed the Canada geese and wild ducks. The Gray Goose is five minutes from Dunes State and National Lakeshore parks. Swimming, canoeing down the Little Calumet River, hiking, and fishing on Lake Michigan are all within easy reach. Dining, weekend entertainment, and miniature golf are within walking distance.

The Kintner House Inn ☉
CAPITOL AND CHESTNUT, CORYDON, INDIANA 47112

Tel: **(812) 738-2020**
Best Time to Call: **8 AM–9 PM**
Host(s): **Mary Jane Bridgwater**
Location: **1½ mi. from I-64**
No. of Rooms: **14**
No. of Private Baths: **14**
Double/pb: **$50–$80**

Open: **All year**
Breakfast: **Full**
Credit Cards: **AMEX, MC, VISA**
Pets: **No**
Children: **Welcome, (crib, high chair)**
Smoking: **No**
Social Drinking: **Permitted**

The elegant experience at this restored 1800s inn begins in the reception area where guests sign in on a unique inlaid registration desk. From there, you'll be shown to your choice of sleeping quarters, ranging in decor from country to formal. A typical bedroom has floral wallpaper, colorful quilt with coordinating curtains, antique wood or poster bed, and a blend of wood tables and love seats. Conversation or cable TV can be enjoyed in the fireplaced parlor, which is decorated with Victorian furnishings. Breakfast is served in a large dining room with antique wood sideboard, sterling silver service, and fine bone china. The inn is located in the center of a small country town, and you can watch it all go by from a pillared veranda that runs the length of the Federal-style building. Your hosts will gladly direct you to nearby caves and a wild and scenic river.

Brigadoon Bed & Breakfast Inn
1201 SOUTH EAST 2ND STREET, EVANSVILLE, INDIANA 47713

Tel: **(812) 422-9635**
Host(s): **Kathee Forbes**
Location: **1 mi. from Hwy. 41**
No. of Rooms: **4**
No. of Private Baths: **2**
Max. No. Sharing Bath: **4**
Double/pb: **$40**
Single/pb: **$35**
Double/sb: **$40**
Single/sb: **$35**

Open: **All year**
Reduced Rates: **Families**
Breakfast: **Full**
Other Meals: **Sometimes**
Credit Cards: **MC, VISA**
Pets: **Sometimes**
Children: **Welcome (baby-sitter)**
Smoking: **Permitted**
Social Drinking: **Permitted**
Airport/Station Pickup: **Yes**

Brigadoon is a white frame Victorian with a gingerbread porch. The inn was built in 1892 and has been thoroughly renovated by the Forbes family. Four fireplaces, original parquet floors, and beautiful stained-glass windows have been lovingly preserved. Modern baths and a country eat-in kitchen have been added. Bedrooms are large and sunny with accents of lace and ruffles, floral wallpapers, and antique furnishings. Guests are welcome to relax in the parlor or library. Breakfast specialties change daily and can include a soufflé or quiche served with lots of homemade breads, jams, and apple butter. This charming Victorian getaway is close to the Historic Preservation area, restaurants, the riverfront, antique shops, the University of Southern Indiana, and the University of Evansville.

Old Hoosier House ✪
ROUTE 2, BOX 299-1, KNIGHTSTOWN, INDIANA 46148

Tel: **(317) 345-2969**
Host(s): **Tom and Jean Lewis**
Location: **30 mi. E of Indianapolis**
No. of Rooms: **4**
No. of Private Baths: **3**

Max. No. Sharing Bath: **3**
Double/pb: **$55**
Single/pb: **$45**
Double/sb: **$45**
Single/sb: **$35**

INDIANA • 223

Open: **May 1–Nov. 1**
Reduced Rates: **10%, seniors**
Breakfast: **Full**
Pets: **No**

Children: **Welcome (crib)**
Smoking: **No**
Social Drinking: **No**
Airport/Station Pickup: **Yes**

The Old Hoosier House takes you back more than 100 years, when the livin' was easier. The rooms are large, with high ceilings, arched windows, antiques, and mementos. A library and patio are available for your pleasure. In the morning you'll wake to the aroma of homemade rolls and coffee. Golfers will enjoy the adjoining golf course, while antique buffs will be glad to know there are hundreds of local dealers in the area. The cities of Anderson and Richmond are close by and the Indianapolis 500 is within an hour's drive.

Old Madison House
517 MULBERRY STREET, MADISON, INDIANA 47250

Tel: **(812) 265-6874**
Host(s): **Sherley and Jack Baugh**
Location: **50 mi. SW of Cincinnati, Ohio**
No. of Rooms: **2**
Max. No. Sharing Bath: **4**
Double/sb: **$35**

Single/sb: **$28**
Open: **All year**
Breakfast: **Full**
Pets: **Sometimes**
Children: **Welcome**
Smoking: **Permitted**
Social Drinking: **Permitted**

Located a block away from Main Street, this three-story Federal-style house dates back to 1900. It is comfortably furnished and accented with cherished antiques. Sherley prides herself on her country breakfast of eggs, hashed brown potatoes or grits, and fried apples. Jack will be happy to show you his collection of beer cans. Madison, situated on the banks of the Ohio River, is known for its splendid examples of Federal, Classic Revival, and Italian villa–inspired architecture.

The Rock House ✪
380 WEST WASHINGTON STREET, MORGANTOWN, INDIANA 46160

Tel: **(812) 597-5100**
Host(s): **Doug and Marcia Norton**
Location: **32 mi. S of Indianapolis**
No. of Rooms: **5**
No. of Private Baths: **2**
Max. No. Sharing Bath: **4**
Double/pb: **$55**

Single/pb: **$45**
Double/sb: **$45**
Single/sb: **$35**
Suites: **$80**
Open: **All year**
Reduced Rates: **10%, seniors**
Breakfast: **Full**

Pets: **No**　　　　　　　　　　Smoking: **Permitted**
Children: **Welcome**　　　　　Social Drinking: **Permitted**

The Rock House was built in the 1890s by James Smith Knight. He used concrete blocks years before they were popular, but it's the way he used them that made him an innovator. Before the concrete dried, Knight embedded in it rocks, seashells, dishes, and jewelry collected as souvenirs from 48 states. The result is spectacular, drawing many sightseers to the house. Inside, guests will find a homey atmosphere and comfortable furnishings. Your hosts will gladly direct you to such local attractions as Lake Monroe, Ski World, and Little Nashville Opry.

Allison House
90 SOUTH JEFFERSON STREET, P.O. BOX 546, NASHVILLE, INDIANA 47448

Tel: **(812) 988-4673**
Best Time to Call: **9 AM–9 PM**
Host(s): **Tammy and Bob Galm**
Location: **50 mi. S of Indianapolis**
No. of Rooms: **5**
No. of Private Baths: **5**
Double/pb: **$65–$75**

Open: **All year**
Reduced Rates: **10% after 2 nights**
Breakfast: **Continental**
Pets: **No**
Children: **Welcome, over 12**
Smoking: **No**
Social Drinking: **No**

Allison House is a fully restored Victorian located in the heart of Nashville. Tammy and Bob have filled the house with a blend of old mementos and new finds from the local arts and crafts colony. The artisans are quite famous in this area, and they are located within walking distance. Tammy and Bob offer a light breakfast of home-baked goods.

Sunset House ✪
RURAL ROUTE 3, BOX 127, NASHVILLE, INDIANA 47448

Tel: **(812) 988-6118**
Host(s): **Mary Margaret Baird**
Location: **18 mi. from I-65**
No. of Rooms: **3**
No. of Private Baths: **3**
Double/pb: **$50**
Single/pb: **$50**

Suites: **$60**
Open: **Feb.–Nov.**
Breakfast: **Continental**
Pets: **No**
Children: **Welcome (crib)**
Smoking: **Permitted**
Social Drinking: **Permitted**

Mary's home is a magnificent contemporary house with a deck and patio for relaxing. The guest rooms have separate entrances and all are furnished in fine cherry wood. The master suite has a handsome stone fireplace. Although there are many things to keep you busy, the Little Nashville Opry is a major attraction each Saturday, with country-and-western stars entertaining. Indiana University is nearby.

Braxtan House Inn B&B ✪
210 NORTH GOSPEL STREET, PAOLI, INDIANA 47454

Tel: **(812) 723-4677**
Best Time to Call: **6–8 PM**
Host(s): **Terry and Brenda Cornwell**
Location: **45 mi. S of Bloomington**
No. of Rooms: **8**
No. of Private Baths: **4**
Max. No. Sharing Bath: **4**
Double/pb: **$40–$50**
Single/pb: **$35–$45**
Double/sb: **$30–$40**
Single/sb: **$25–$35**

Suites: **$60**
Open: **All year**
Reduced Rates: **10%, seniors**
Breakfast: **Continental**
Pets: **Sometimes**
Children: **Welcome, over 10**
Smoking: **Permitted**
Social Drinking: **Permitted**
Minimum Stay: **2 nights ski season and Kentucky Derby weekend**

This Queen Anne Victorian was built in 1893. The original cherry, oak, and walnut woodwork is still evident in many of the 21 rooms. Terry and Brenda have carefully refurbished the mansion and decorated with lovely antiques, many of which are for sale. The dining room, with its original wainscoting and wide-plank floors, is where pecan pancakes with a variety of fruit toppings are on the breakfast menu. Paoli Peaks, a ski resort, is 2 miles away, and it's 15 miles to Patoka, the second largest lake in the state. Coffee, tea, and snacks are graciously offered.

The Rockport Inn ✪
THIRD AT WALNUT, ROCKPORT, INDIANA 47635

Tel: **(812) 649-2664**
Best Time to Call: **8 AM–6PM**
Host(s): **Emil and Carolyn Ahnell**
Location: **40 mi. E of Evansville**
No. of Rooms: **6**
No. of Private Baths: **6**
Double/pb: **$35–$45**
Single/pb: **$25–$35**
Open: **All year**

Reduced Rates: **30%, weekly**
Breakfast: **Continental**
Other Meals: **Available**
Pets: **Sometimes**
Children: **Welcome (crib)**
Smoking: **Permitted**
Social Drinking: **Permitted**
Foreign Languages: **German, Swedish**

Built in 1855, this white frame two-story residence has a porch and landscaped yard. It's furnished with antiques; plants and flowers add to its cozy atmosphere. Lincoln State Park, Santa Claus Land, and Kentucky Wesleyan College are nearby.

Country Roads Guesthouse ✪
2731 WEST 146TH STREET, WESTFIELD, INDIANA 46074

Tel: (317) 846-2376
Host(s): **Phil Pegram**
Location: **15 mi. N of Indianapolis; 10 mi. from I-465**
No. of Rooms: **2**
No. of Private Baths: **2**
Double/pb: **$50**
Single/pb: **$36**
Open: **All year**
Breakfast: **Continental**
Pets: **No**
Children: **Welcome**
Smoking: **No**
Social Drinking: **No**

This 100-year-old farmhouse is situated on four acres, has high ceilings, a kitchen fireplace, and is furnished with antiques. It's air-conditioned for your summer comfort, and guests are welcome to use the swimming pool and basketball court. The country setting is fine for walking, jogging, or bicycling, and the area is filled with antique shops, historic sites, and fine restaurants. The Herb Barn Country Store and Gardens, and Conner Prairie, a pioneer settlement, are nearby attractions.

IOWA

Bed and Breakfast in Iowa, Ltd. ✪
BOX 430, PRESTON, IOWA 52069

Tel: **(319) 689-4222**
Best Time to Call: **Mornings; evenings**
Coordinator: **Wilma Bloom**
States/Regions Covered: **Statewide**

Rates (Single/Double):
Modest:	$20	$35
Average:	$25	$35–$40
Luxury:	$35	$65

Credit Cards: **No**

Wilma has a vast variety of accommodations, some of which are on the National Register of Historic Places. Travelers' interests, including cultural, historic, sports, and crafts, as well as fairs and festivals, can be easily satisfied. The University of Iowa, Iowa State, and Drake University are close to several homes. Please send $1 for her directory.

B&B on Ash ✪
517 ASH AVENUE, AMES, IOWA 50010

Tel: (515) 292-9382
Host(s): **Helen and Keith McRoberts**
Location: **30 mi. N of Des Moines**
No. of Rooms: **2**
No. of Private Baths: **1½**
Double/pb: **$35**
Single/pb: **$30**

Open: **All year**
Breakfast: **Full**
Pets: **No**
Children: **Welcome**
Smoking: **No**
Social Drinking: **Permitted**

Built in 1913, this beige frame and stucco home is comfortably furnished. Wood beams, a stone fireplace, and the front porch with its wicker furniture spell welcome. The breakfast of omelets, Danish pastry, and freshly ground coffee is an instant eye-opener and may be enjoyed on the backyard deck. Iowa State University campus and the Iowa State Center for cultural activities and sports events are nearby.

Calmar Guesthouse
RR 1, BOX 206, CALMAR, IOWA 52132

Tel: (319) 562-3851
Best Time to Call: **6–8 AM**
Host(s): **Art and Lucille Kruse**
Location: **10 mi. S of Decorah**
No. of Rooms: **4**
Max. No. Sharing Bath: **4**
Double/sb: **$29**
Single/sb: **$24**

Open: **All year**
Breakfast: **Full**
Pets: **No**
Children: **Welcome**
Smoking: **Permitted**
Social Drinking: **Permitted**
Airport/Station Pickup: **Yes**

A recent guest reports that: "The Calmar Guesthouse is a spacious, lovely, newly remodeled Victorian home located on the edge of town. The atmosphere is enhanced by the friendly, charming manner of Lucille, who made us feel right at home. The rooms were comfortable, private, and pretty. After a peaceful night's sleep, we were served a delicious breakfast of fresh farm eggs with ham and cheeses, croissants with butter and jam, homemade cinnamon rolls, and coffee. I would recommend it to anyone visiting the area." Nearby points of interest include Lake Meyer, the world's smallest church, and Spillville, where the hand-carved Billy Bros. Clocks are made.

IOWA • 229

River Oaks Inn ◐
1234 EAST RIVER DRIVE, DAVENPORT, IOWA 52803

Tel: **(319) 326-2629**
Best Time to Call: **8 AM–8 PM**
Host(s): **Bill and Suzanne Pohl; Ron and Mary Jo Pohl**
Location: **2 mi. from I-80**
No. of Rooms: **4**
No. of Private Baths: **3**
Double/pb: **$45**
Suites: **$60**
Open: **All year**

Reduced Rates: **Available**
Breakfast: **Full**
Credit Cards: **MC, VISA**
Pets: **Sometimes**
Children: **Welcome**
Smoking: **In designated areas**
Social Drinking: **Permitted**
Airport/Station Pickup: **Yes**
Foreign Languages: **Spanish**

Abner Davison combined Italianate, Victorian, and Prairie architecture when he built his home back in the 1850s. The house is situated on a rolling lot that still shows evidence of the original carriage drive. Choose from a suite with king-size bed, sun porch, and dressing room; the Ambrose Fulton Room, with double bed and garden view; the Mississippi Room, with queen-size bed and window seat; or the Abner Davison Room, which has twin beds and a bay window. Breakfast is served in the dining room or out on the deck in the warm weather. High tea is served in the afternoon, and guests are welcome to enjoy it outside in the gazebo. The inn is located one block from river boat rides, and is convenient to many area attractions such as Historic Rock Island Arsenal and the village of East Davenport.

Rainbow H Ranch and Campground ◐
ROUTE 1, ELK HORN, IOWA 51531

Tel: **(712) 764-8272**
Best Time to Call: **Mornings; after 6 PM**
Host(s): **Mark and Cherie Hensley**
Location: **60 mi. E of Omaha, Neb.**
No. of Rooms: **2**
Max No. Sharing Bath: **4**
Double/sb: **$32**
Single/sb: **$26**

Open: **All year**
Reduced Rates: **10% after 1 night**
Breakfast: **Full**
Pets: **Sometimes**
Children: **Welcome**
Smoking: **Permitted**
Social Drinking: **No**
Airport/Station Pickup: **Yes**

Enjoy the charm of the Iowa countryside as a guest in this grand brick home. The decor is country French and features a spacious recreation room with fireplace and beamed ceilings. The bedrooms have full or twin-size beds, color TVs; there is a private entrance and outdoor patio for your use. Your hosts raise longhorn cattle and will gladly give you and the kids a tour of the farm. If you prefer, the Hensleys also have a small campground nearby in a parklike setting. The Elk Horn community is home to the largest Danish settlement in the United States. The town has a working windmill and is home to the National Danish Museum and the Tivoli Festival.

The Morton House ✪
#7 HIGHPOINT, FORT MADISON, IOWA 52627

Tel: **(319) 372-9501**
Best Time to Call: **11 AM–9 PM**
Host(s): **Dennis and Carole Morton**
Location: **1 mi. E of Fort Madison**
No. of Rooms: **2**
No. of Private Baths: **2**
Double/pb: **$60**
Single/pb: **$45**
Open: **Apr. 1–Nov. 1**
Reduced Rates: **Available**
Breakfast: **Continental**
Credit Cards: **MC, VISA**
Pets: **Sometimes**
Children: **Welcome, over 16**
Smoking: **Permitted**
Social Drinking: **Permitted**
Airport/Station Pickup: **Yes**

This 17-room house, perched 120 feet above the Mississippi, was built for the Sheaffer Pen family in the 1920s. The three-story stone and wood-frame home is located off a private road on a two-acre lot surrounded by a variety of trees. The Mortons have decorated the large rooms with antique furniture to complement the rich oak floors and stained glass. Each guest room has a breathtaking view, as does the breakfast room, where you will be served a variety of fresh fruit, pastries, and plenty of hot coffee each morning. Guests may enjoy the river room, screened-in-porch, and the outdoor patio, all overlooking the water. The Morton House is five miles from historic Nauvoo and convenient to many Mississippi River regional events and festivals.

Loy's Bed and Breakfast ✪
R.R. 1, MARENGO, IOWA 52301

Tel: **(319) 642-7787**
Best Time to Call: **7 AM, noon, 6 PM**
Host(s): **Loy and Robert Walker**
Location: **3 mi. from I-80**
No. of Rooms: **3**
No. of Private Baths: **3**
Max. No. Sharing Bath: **4**
Double/sb: **$40**
Single/sb: **$25**
Open: **All year**
Pets: **If caged**
Children: **Welcome**
Smoking: **No**
Social Drinking: **Permitted**

The Walkers invite you to visit their contemporary farmhouse in the heartland of rural Iowa. Enjoy the peaceful surroundings of a large lawn, gardens, and patio. The rooms are furnished in modern and refinished pieces. Guests are welcome to relax in the family room by the fire or to stop by the rec room for a game of shuffleboard or pool, and a treat from the snack bar. If they are not busy with the harvest, your hosts will gladly take you on day trips. Tours may include Plum Grove, Iowa City, Brucemore Mansion, and Herbert Hoover's birthplace. A visit to the nearby lakes is recommended and a take-along lunch can be arranged. The Amana Colonies is right here and shouldn't be missed.

For key to listings, see inside front or back cover.

✪ This star means that rates are guaranteed through December 31, 1989 to any guest making a reservation as a result of reading about the B&B in *BED & BREAKFAST U.S.A.*—1989 edition.

Please enclose a self-addressed, stamped, business-sized envelope when contacting reservation services.

For more details on what you can expect in a B&B, see Chapter 1.

Always mention *Bed & Breakfast U.S.A.* when making reservations!

If no B&B is listed in the area you'll be visiting, use the form on page 693 to order a copy of our "List of New B&Bs."

We want to hear from you! Use the form on page 691.

KANSAS

Bed & Breakfast Kansas City—Missouri & Kansas ✪
P.O. BOX 14781, LENEXA, KANSAS 66215

Tel: **(913) 888-3636**
Coordinator: **Edwina Monroe**
States/Regions Covered: **Kansas—**
  Leawood, Lenexa, Topeka;
  Missouri—Grandview,
  Independence, Kansas City,
  Parkville, St. Joseph

Rates (Single/Double):
  Average: **$35** $40
  Luxury: **$55** $60
Credit Cards: **No**

You will enjoy visiting such places as the Truman Library and home, Crown Center, Country Club Plaza, Arrowhead Stadium, Royals Stadium, Kemper Arena, and the Missouri Repertory Theatre. A directory fully describing all of the host homes is available. Please send a self-addressed envelope with 39¢ postage. Jewell College, Parkville College, the University of Missouri, and Central Missouri State are close by.

Balfours' House
ROUTE 2, ABILENE, KANSAS 67410

Tel: **(913) 263-4262**
Best Time to Call: **After 5 pm**
Host(s): **Gilbert and Marie Balfour**
Location: **2¼ mi. S of Abilene**
No. of Rooms: **2**
No. of Private Baths: **1**
Max. No. Sharing Bath: **4**
Double/pb: **$35**
Single/pb: **$25**
Double/sb: **$30**

Single/sb: **$20**
Open: **All year**
Breakfast: **Continental**
Credit Cards: **MC, VISA**
Pets: **Sometimes**
Children: **Welcome**
Smoking: **Permitted**
Social Drinking: **Permitted**
Airport/Station Pickup: **Sometimes**

Gilbert and Marie Balfour welcome you to their modern, cottage-style home, set on a hillside. The house is located on just over two acres, and has a spacious yard. Guests have their own private entrance into the family room, which includes a fireplace, piano, and TV. The main attraction of the house is a hexagonal recreation room that has a built-in swimming pool, spa, and dressing area with shower. Start your day off with a cup of coffee and Bubble Bread, the specialty of the house. Your hosts will gladly direct you to the Eisenhower Museum, Greyhound Hall of Fame, and many old historic mansions.

Country Quarters ✪
ROUTE 5, BOX 80, FORT SCOTT, KANSAS 66701

Tel: **(316) 223-2889**
Host(s): **Marilyn McQuitty**
Location: **2 mi. S of Fort Scott**
No. of Rooms: **2**
Max. No. Sharing Bath: **4**
Double/sb: **$25**

Open: **All year**
Breakfast: **Full**
Pets: **No**
Children: **Welcome**
Smoking: **Permitted**
Social Drinking: **Permitted**

Marilyn McQuitty welcomes you to a real working farm located outside a charming Victorian town. Her 100-year-old farmhouse is furnished with comfortable family pieces. While you're sitting by the fire, ask to hear the story behind the 100-year-old hearth and hand-carved mantelpiece. Guests are welcome to relax on the porch or visit the ceramic shop located on the premises. There is easy access to the Fort Scott Lake, Gunn Park, and the Fort Scott National Historic Site, an authentically restored military fort dating back to 1892. Downtown you can drive past the magnificent old homes, browse through antiques stores, and visit a one-room schoolhouse.

Schoolhouse Inn ✪
106 EAST BECK, BOX 175, MELVERN, KANSAS 66510

Tel: **(913) 549-3473**
Best Time to Call: **After 5 PM**
Host(s): **Bill and Mary Fisher**
Location: **80 mi. SW of Kansas City, Mo.**
No. of Rooms: **4**
No. of Private Baths: **2**
Max. No. Sharing Bath: **4**
Double/pb: **$40**
Single/pb: **$35**
Double/sb: **$37.50**
Single/sb: **$32.50**
Open: **All year**
Credit Cards: **AMEX, MC, VISA**
Reduced Rates: **10%, seniors**
Breakfast: **Full**
Pets: **Sometimes**
Children: **Welcome, over 5**
Smoking: **No**
Social Drinking: **Permitted**

The Schoolhouse was built in 1870 of heavy timbers, and stone from nearby quarries. It is on the National Register of Historic Places. Today the house has been completely restored to serve as an elegant retreat in a pastoral setting. The second-floor guest rooms are large, with high ceilings, queen-size beds, and comfortable furnishings. The Schoolhouse is four miles from Melvern Lake and is convenient to state and federal parks and antique shops.

Krause House ✪
ROUTE 1, BOX 9, MODOC, KANSAS 67866

Tel: **(316) 379-4627**
Host(s): **Paul and Merilyn Krause**
Location: **13 mi. W of Scott City**
No. of Rooms: **2**
No. of Private Baths: **1**
Max. No. Sharing Bath: **4**
Double/pb: **$35**
Single/pb: **$25**
Double/sb: **$35**
Single/sb: **$25**
Open: **All year**
Reduced Rates: **Families**
Breakfast: **Full**
Other Meals: **Available**
Pets: **Sometimes**
Children: **Welcome**
Smoking: **No**
Social Drinking: **No**
Airport/Station Pickup: **Available**

Experience a working grain farm in the western Kansas countryside. Paul and Merilyn Krause have a remodeled farmhouse surrounded by tall shade trees. Guest rooms are located on the second floor and are decorated with country furnishings. Breakfast specialties such as egg casseroles, homemade breads, and cinnamon rolls are served on the glassed-in patio overlooking the flowers and greenery. On weekends, you're invited to a full-course dinner in the formal dining room. Krause House is 25 miles from Scott County State Park, where you may fish, boat, hunt for fossils, and see the Indian remains.

Almeda's Inn
BOX 103, 220 SOUTH MAIN, TONGANOXIE, KANSAS 66086

Tel: **(913) 845-2295**
Best Time to Call: **Before 9 AM; after 6 PM**
Host(s): **Almeda and Richard Tinberg**
Location: **20 mi. W of Kansas City**
No. of Rooms: **7**
No. of Private Baths: **1**
Max. No. Sharing Bath: **4**
Double/pb: **$30**

Double/sb: **$30**
Single/sb: **$25**
Open: **All year**
Breakfast: **Continental**
Pets: **No**
Children: **Welcome, over 4**
Smoking: **Permitted**
Social Drinking: **Permitted**

Located in a picturesque small town, and made a designated Historical Site in 1983, the inn dates back to World War I. You are welcome to sip a cup of coffee at the unique stone bar in the room once used as a bus stop in 1930. In fact, this room was the inspiration for *Bus Stop*. Almeda and Richard will be happy to direct you to the golf course, swimming facilities, the Starlight Theatre, or the University of Kansas at Lawrence.

The Barn Bed and Breakfast Inn ✪
RR #2, BOX 87, VALLEY FALLS, KANSAS 66088

Tel: **(913) 945-3303**
Host(s): **Tom and Marcella Ryan**
Location: **23 mi. NE of Topeka**
No. of Rooms: **9**
No. of Private Baths: **9**
Double/pb: **$54**
Single/pb: **$46**
Open: **All year**

Reduced Rates: **Available**
Breakfast: **Full**
Other Meals: **Available**
Pets: **No**
Children: **Welcome**
Smoking: **No**
Social Drinking: **No**
Airport/Station Pickup: **Yes**

The Barn is a real American farm original, dating back over 100 years. It has been converted into a large, gracious home with motifs of wood and plenty of windows. The rooms are decorated with comfortable furnishings, king-size beds, and many antiques. A lovely living room with fireplace takes the chill out of winter nights, and if you like plants, the glassed-in sun deck is the place for you. The Ryans raise their own food and bake their own bread. They offer a farm-style breakfast including pecan rolls, buttermilk pancakes, and bacon and eggs. They love people and would be pleased if your family joined theirs for lunch or dinner. The Barn has its own swimming hole, fishing ponds, and plenty of space for long walks.

Thistle Hill ✪
ROUTE 1, BOX 93, WAKEENEY, KANSAS 67672

Tel: **(913) 743-2644**
Best Time to Call: **Evenings**
Host(s): **Dave and Mary Hendricks**
Location: **1½ mi. from I-70, Exit 120**
No. of Rooms: **2**
No. of Private Baths: **2**
Double/pb: **$40**
Single/pb: **$35**

Open: **All year**
Reduced Rates: **Families**
Breakfast: **Full**
Pets: **Sometimes**
Children: **Welcome**
Smoking: **Permitted**
Social Drinking: **Permitted**
Airport/Station Pickup: **Yes**

The entry of this weathered wood country house sets the hospitable tone of this B&B located 325 miles west of Kansas City or the same distance east of Denver, Colorado. Seasonal wreaths, an Early American bench, antique lanterns, and a big sign saying, "Welcome to Thistle Hill" are the Hendrickses way of saying they're glad you've come to visit. They're anxious to share with you the pleasures of their rural life, which include cooking, restoring antiques, and working with their team of draft horses. A varied breakfast often includes country fresh eggs, breakfast meats, fresh baked breads, or hotcakes made with whole wheat from their own wheat fields. On chilly mornings it is served near the fireplace. Cedar Bluff Reservoir, for fishing, is 30 miles away; pheasant, waterfowl, and deer roam 10,000 acres of public hunting land nearby.

KENTUCKY

Bluegrass Bed & Breakfast ✪
ROUTE 1, BOX 263, VERSAILLES, KENTUCKY 40383

Tel: **(606) 873-3208**
Coordinator: **Betsy Pratt**
States/Regions Covered: **Greensburg, Harrodsburg, Lexington, Midway, Versailles**

Rates (Single/Double):
  Modest: $36
  Average: $48
  Luxury: $60

Most of Betsy's B&Bs are in beautiful old houses that grace the country roads of the area. You may choose among a stone house built in 1796, or a turreted Victorian in downtown Lexington, or a country home where your bedroom windows look out on Thoroughbred horses. Visit Shakertown, where weavers, smiths, and woodworkers display their skills in an 1839 restored village. Take a ride on the winding Kentucky River in a paddlewheel boat. Tour exquisite historic mansions of see the picturesque homes of such Derby winners as Secretariat and Seattle Slew. And don't miss the 1,000-acre Kentucky Horse Park that includes a theater, museum, track, barns, and hundreds of horses. You may even take a horseback ride, because this place will inspire you.

Kentucky Homes Bed & Breakfast, Inc.
1431 ST. JAMES COURT, LOUISVILLE, KENTUCKY 40208

Tel: **(502) 635-7341**
Best Time to Call: **8 AM–Noon**
Coordinators: **Lillian Marshall and John Dillehay**
States/Regions Covered: **Kentucky—Bardstown, Danville, Lexington, Louisville; S.Indiana—Corydon, Indianapolis, Paoli**

Rates (Single/Double):
  Modest: **$33–$39**   **$38–$44**
  Average: **$41–$50**   **$46–$55**
  Luxury: **$55–$75**   **$60–$80**
Credit Cards: **MC, VISA (deposit only)**

Lillian and John cordially invite you to be a guest in friendly Kentucky at one of dozens of host homes. Fish in spectacular lakes, visit Mammoth Cave, drop in on Shakertown at Pleasant Hill, or reserve early and assure yourself of a spot at the next running of the Kentucky Derby (held the first Saturday in May). Stay in a gorgeous turn-of-the-century home in restored old Louisville, or a dairy farm that boards and trains racehorses, or many comfortable choices in between. Ask about their unique "prepaid voucher" plan.

Bowling Green Bed & Breakfast ✪
659 EAST 14TH AVENUE, BOWLING GREEN, KENTUCKY 42101

Tel: **(502) 781-3861**
Best Time to Call: **Evenings; early AM**
Host(s): **Dr. and Mrs. Norman Hunter**
Location: **4 mi. from I-65, Exit 22**
No. of Rooms: **3**
No. of Private Baths: **1**
Max. No. Sharing Bath: **4**
Double/pb: **$40**
Single/pb: **$30**

Double/sb: **$40**
Single/sb: **$30**
Open: **All year**
Breakfast: **Continental**
Pets: **No**
Children: **Welcome, over 14**
Smoking: **No**
Social Drinking: **Permitted**
Airport/Station Pickup: **Yes**

This trim, gray-shingled, comfortably furnished, two-story home is situated on a wooded lot. You are welcome to watch TV, select a book from the library, crank out a tune on the old Victrola, or play Ping-Pong in the recreation room. It is an easy drive to state parks, Opryland, and Mammoth Cave. Ronna Lee and Norman teach at nearby Western Kentucky University.

Olde Kantucke Bed and Breakfast ✪
210 EAST FOURTH STREET, FRANKFORT, KENTUCKY 40601

Tel: **(502) 227-7389**
Best Time to Call: **9 AM–7 PM**
Host(s): **Patty and Dan Smith**
Location: **30 mi. W of Lexington**
No. of Rooms: **5**
No. of Private Baths: **5**
Double/pb: **$45**
Single/pb: **$35**
Open: **All year**

Reduced Rates: **3rd night free with advance reservations**
Breakfast: **Continental**
Credit Cards: **MC, VISA**
Pets: **No**
Children: **No**
Smoking: **Permitted**
Social Drinking: **Permitted**
Airport/Station Pickup: **Available**

Guests often say that visiting this 100-year-old white frame home is like going back to Grandma's house. Two large maple trees shade the porch, where tea is served each afternoon beside the tall white columns. Inside, you'll find touches of the Victorian era in the lovingly restored rooms. Each bedroom overlooks the Capitol dome and is cooled by a ceiling fan. Homemade muffins and biscuits, fresh fruit, and a choice of hot drinks are served in an open kitchen–dining area. The Olde Kantucke is one block from the Frankfort Walking Tour, 15 minutes from the beautiful bluegrass and horse country, and half an hour from Lexington.

Log Cabin Bed and Breakfast ✪
350 NORTH BROADWAY, GEORGETOWN, KENTUCKY 40324

Tel: **(502) 863-3514**
Host(s): **Clay and Janis McKnight**
Location: **10 mi. N of Lexington**
No. of Rooms: **2**
No. of Private Baths: **1**
Guest Cottage: **$60 for 2**

Open: **All year**
Breakfast: **Continental**
Pets: **Welcome**
Children: **Welcome**
Smoking: **Permitted**
Social Drinking: **Permitted**

This rustic log cabin was built, circa 1809, with a shake shingle roof and chinked logs. Inside, the living room is dominated by a huge fieldstone fireplace. The master bedroom and bath are on the ground floor and a loft bedroom will sleep an additional two with ease. The house has been fully restored and air-conditioned by the McKnights and is filled with period furnishings. The dining-kitchen wing is equipped with all new appliances and modern amenities. The Log Cabin is located in a quiet neighborhood close to Kentucky Horse Park, Keeneland, and many other historic places. This is the perfect spot to bring the kids and give them a taste of authentic American tradition.

Three Deer Inn ✪
P.O. DRAWER 299, GRAYS KNOB, KENTUCKY 40829

Tel. (606) 573-6666
Best Time to Call: 8 AM–6 PM
Host(s): C. V. and Blanche Bennett
Location: 10 mi. N of Harlan
No. of Rooms: 5
No. of Private Baths: 5
Double/pb: $49
Single/pb: $39
Suites: $45
Open: **All year**
Reduced Rates: **20%, seniors, families**
Breakfast: **Continental**
Credit Cards: **AMEX, MC, VISA**
Pets: **Sometimes**
Children: **Welcome**
Smoking: **Permitted**
Social Drinking: **Permitted**
Airport/Station Pickup: **Yes**

Three Deer Inn is nestled in the base of Black Mountain and is surrounded by forest. The house is a newly built cedar A-frame with beautiful workmanship that includes a lovely cathedral ceiling. Your hosts want you to learn firsthand about the beauty, splendor, and hospitality found in the mountains of eastern Kentucky. They want to share good food, clean surroundings, and friendliness. Among the local attractions are the Little Shepard trail, a beautiful mountaintop gravel road that offers tremendous views of eastern Kentucky; the Hensley Settlement, a village located on the top of Stone Mountain; Daniel Boone National Forest; and Stone Canyon.

Ehrhardt's B&B ✪
285 SPRINGWELL LANE, PADUCAH, KENTUCKY 42001

Tel. (502) 554-0644
Best Time to Call: 7–9 AM; 4–6 PM
Host(s): Eileen and Phil Ehrhardt
Location: 1 mi. from I-24
No. of Rooms: 2
Max. No. Sharing Bath: 4
Double/sb: $35
Single/sb: $30
Open: **All year**
Reduced Rates: **10%, seniors**
Breakfast: **Full**
Other Meals: **Available**
Pets: **No**
Children: **Welcome, over 12**
Smoking: **Permitted**
Social Drinking: **Permitted**
Airport/Station Pickup: **Yes**

This brick Colonial ranch home is just a mile off I-24, which is famous for its beautiful scenery. Your hosts hope to make you feel at home in antique-filled bedrooms and a fireplaced den. Homemade biscuits, jellies, country ham and gravy are breakfast specialties. Enjoy swimming in the Ehrhardts' pool and boating at nearby Lake Barkley, Ky Lake, and Land between the Lakes. Paducah features quarterhorse racing from June through November and the National Quilt Show in April.

For key to listings, see inside front or back cover.

✪ This star means that rates are guaranteed through December 31, 1989 to any guest making a reservation as a result of reading about the B&B in *BED & BREAKFAST U.S.A.*—1989 edition.

Please enclose a self-addressed, stamped, business-sized envelope when contacting reservation services.

For more details on what you can expect in a B&B, see Chapter 1.

Always mention *Bed & Breakfast U.S.A.* when making reservations!

If no B&B is listed in the area you'll be visiting, use the form on page 693 to order a copy of our "List of New B&Bs."

We want to hear from you! Use the form on page 691.

LOUISIANA

Southern Comfort Bed & Breakfast
2856 HUNDRED OAKS, BATON ROUGE, LOUISIANA 70808

For Information: (504) 346-1928 or 928-9815
For Reservation: 800-523-1181, #, Dial Tone, 722
Best Time to Call: 8 AM–8 PM
Coordinators: **Susan Morris and Helen Heath**
States/Regions Covered: **Louisiana—Statewide; Mississippi—Natchez, Vicksburg, Port Gibson; New Mexico—Taos**

Rates (Single/Double):
  Modest: $30–$40 $35–$45
  Average: $45–$55 $50–$60
  Luxury: $65–$80 $65–$150
Credit Cards: MC, VISA

Susan and Helen offer you the best of the old and the new South with hosts in urban and rural areas. The above is only a sample list. Special attractions are Civil War and other historic sites; fabulous New Orleans; Acadian (Cajun) country; sports, deep-sea fishing, and racetracks in Louisiana and New Mexico. Their descriptive directory is $3.

Joy's B&B ✪
4920 PERKINS ROAD, BATON ROUGE, LOUISIANA 70808

Tel: **(504) 766-2291**
Best Time to Call: **6 AM–Noon**
Host(s): **Joy Robinson**
Location: **85 mi. from New Orleans**
No. of Rooms: **2**
No. of Private Baths: **1**
Max. No. Sharing Bath: **4**
Double/sb: **$47.50**
Single/sb: **$37.50**

Open: **All year**
Reduced Rates: **15%, seniors**
Breakfast: **Full**
Pets: **No**
Children: **Welcome, over 12**
Smoking: **Permitted**
Social Drinking: **Permitted**
Airport/Station Pickup: **Yes**

This charming stucco home is furnished with antiques and collectibles. Guest quarters are on the second floor and feature a family room, TV, and kitchen facilities. Joy serves a hearty, Southern breakfast with pride. She will gladly direct you to interesting nearby sites including the Atchafalaya basin, the largest hardwood swamp in the South. Louisiana State University is five minutes away.

Plantation Bell Guest House ✪
204 WEST 24TH AVENUE, COVINGTON, LOUISIANA 70433

Tel: **(504) 892-1952**
Best Time to Call: **Before 8 AM**
Host(s): **Lila Rapier**
Location: **35 mi. N. of New Orleans**
No. of Rooms: **3**
No. of Private Baths: **3**
Double/pb: **$40**
Single/pb: **$35**

Open: **All year**
Reduced Rates: **$5 less on 2nd night**
Breakfast: **Full**
Pets: **Sometimes**
Children: **Welcome**
Smoking: **Permitted**
Social Drinking: **Permitted**

This late Victorian house has an old-fashioned porch with rocking chairs overlooking a quiet street. Inside, the ceilings are 13 feet high, and the old-time fans add to the nostalgic motif. The guest rooms are decorated with cheerful wallpapers and are comfortably air-conditioned. Local possibilities include canoeing, cycling, and shopping in Covington. You are welcome to use the kitchen for light snacks.

Ti Frere's House ✪
1905 VEROT SCHOOL ROAD, LAFAYETTE, LOUISIANA 70508

Tel: **(318) 984-9347**
Best Time to Call: **After 3 PM**
Host(s): **Charles and Peggy Mosley**
Location: **2 mi. E of Lafayette**
No. of Rooms **3**
No. of Private Baths: **3**
Double/pb: **$55**
Single/pb: **$45**

Open: **All year**
Breakfast: **Full**
Credit Cards: **MC, VISA**
Pets: **Sometimes**
Children: **No**
Smoking: **No**
Social Drinking: **Permitted**
Airport/Station Pickup: **Yes**

This Cajun-style Victorian was built in 1880 by Oneziphore Comeaux. "Ti-Frere," as he was known to his friends, constructed the house with handmade bricks and cypress. After its restoration by Charles and Peggy Mosley, the house stands as a beautiful landmark in the heart of Cajun country. Inside you'll find fresh flowers, cozy fireplaces, and a mixture of Louisiana, French, and American antiques. Your hosts provide true hospitality with handmade soap and terry cloth robes in the bathroom, mint juleps on the porch, and a Jacuzzi to unwind in. The rooster crows in the morning to awaken you, but if that doesn't work the smell of homemade bread, farm fresh eggs, and coffee will coax you down for breakfast in the formal dining room. In the afternoon, tea can be enjoyed in the parlor, the garden room, or the gazebo. Ti Frere's is located on the plantation side of Lafayette, near gourmet restaurants that feature fresh seafood and Cajun music.

Bed & Breakfast, Inc.—New Orleans ✪
1360 MOSS STREET, BOX 52257, NEW ORLEANS, LOUISIANA 70152-2257

Tel: **(504) 525-4640 or 800-228-9711/ Dial Tone: 184**
Coordinator: **Hazell Boyce**
States/Regions Covered: **New Orleans**

Rates (Single/Double):
  Modest: **$25–$35**   **$35–$40**
  Average: **$35–$60**   **$40–$60**
  Luxury: **$50 and up**   **$60 and up**
Credit Cards: **No**

New Orleans is called the "City That Care Forgot." You are certain to be carefree, visiting the French Quarter, taking Mississippi riverboat rides, taking plantation tours, as well as dining in fine restaurants or attending jazz concerts. Hazell's hosts, many with historic properties along the streetcar line and in the French Quarter, will help you get the most out of your stay.

New Orleans Bed & Breakfast ✪
P.O. BOX 8163, NEW ORLEANS, LOUISIANA 70182

Tel: **(504) 822-5038 or 5046**
Best Time to Call: **8 AM–7 PM**
Coordinator: **Sarah-Margaret Brown**
States/Regions Covered: **Louisiana—Covington, Jeanevette, Lafayette, Mendeville, New Iberia, New Orleans**

Rates (Single/Double):
  Modest: **$25–$35**   **$30–$45**
  Average: **$35–$55**   **$45–$55**
  Luxury: **$55 and up**   **$55–$150**
Credit Cards: **AMEX, MC, VISA (for deposits only)**

Sarah-Margaret offers a range from the youth-hostel type for the backpacker crowd, to modest accommodations in all areas of the city, to deluxe B&Bs in lovely and historic locations. If the past intrigues you, treat yourself to an overnight stay in a great Louisiana plantation home. Rates increase during Mardi Gras, Jazz Fest, Sugar Bowl; decrease for longer stays.

Jensen's Bed & Breakfast ✪
1631 SEVENTH STREET, NEW ORLEANS, LOUISIANA 70115

Tel: **(504) 897-1895**
Best Time to Call: **7 AM–10 AM; 6 PM–9 PM**
Host(s): **Shirley, Joni, and Bruce Jensen**
No. of Rooms: **5**
Max. No. Sharing Bath: **4**
Double/sb: **$45**

Single/sb: **$40**
Open: **All year**
Breakfast: **Continental**
Pets: **No**
Children: **Welcome**
Smoking: **Permitted**
Social Drinking: **Permitted**

Your hosts have drawn on their backgrounds as an interior decorator, piano teacher, and renovator of vintage homes, to restore this Victorian mansion. Stained glass, 12-foot alcove ceilings, antiques, a grand piano, raised-panel-pocket doors, and carefully chosen furnishings enhance the mansion. Located across the street from the Garden District, an area famed for its lovely homes, it is just a block to the trolley, which will whisk you to the French Quarter, Audubon Park, the zoo, or Tulane University. Breakfast is likely to feature banana cornbread or fried bananas, seasonal fruit, and Louisiana-style coffee. The mansion is air-conditioned for your summer comfort, and you are welcome to use the piano, and TV. Rates increase to $75 during Mardi Gras and the Jazz Festival.

246 • LOUISIANA

The Levee View ✪
39 HENNESEY COURT, NEW ORLEANS, LOUISIANA 70123

Tel: **(504) 737-5471**
Host(s): **Jack and Clemence Devereaux**
No. of Rooms: **2**
No. of Private Baths: **1**
Max. No. Sharing Bath: **4**
Double/pb: **$30**
Single/pb: **$25**
Double/sb: **$25**
Single/sb: **$20**
Suites: **$45**

Open: **All year**
Reduced Rates: **20%, seniors; 10%, weekly**
Breakfast: **Continental**
Pets: **No**
Children: **Welcome**
Smoking: **Permitted**
Social Drinking: **Permitted**
Airport/Station Pickup: **Yes**

The Devereauxs welcome you to their contemporary home, located in a convenient residential suburb of New Orleans. The house is large and attractive, with comfortable family furnishings. Guest quarters are located in a two-story wing with separate entrance, ensuring visitors plenty of privacy and quiet. Breakfast specialties include homemade breads, croissants, and plenty of hot coffee. If you like, you can relax outside on the patio or sip a drink in the gazebo. The levee bordering the Mississippi River is less than 100 feet from the house; many lovely plantation homes are also located nearby. Your hosts will gladly guide you to the best restaurants and shops and will occasionally baby-sit for the kids while you go out on the town.

Terrell House ✪
1441 MAGAZINE STREET, NEW ORLEANS, LOUISIANA 70130

Tel: **(504) 524-9859**
Host(s): **Counce Hightower**
Location: **½ mi. from I-10**
No. of Rooms: **10**
No. of Private Baths: **10**
Double/pb: **$50–$85**
Suites: **$100**
Guest Cottage: **$50, for 2**

Open: **All year**
Breakfast: **Continental**
Credit Cards: **AMEX, MC, VISA**
Pets: **No**
Children: **Welcome, over 13**
Smoking: **Permitted**
Social Drinking: **Permitted**

Built in 1858, this faithfully restored mansion offers antique furnishings with modern conveniences. The twin parlors and the formal dining room, with gas chandeliers, gold mirrors, marble mantels, and period furnishings, capture the grace of yesteryear. All the guest rooms open onto balconies and the landscaped courtyard. They all have telephones, color television, and central air conditioning. Located in the historic Lower Garden District, it's convenient to public transportation that will bring you to the French Quarter. Complimentary cocktails and other refreshments are graciously offered.

Cottage Plantation ✪
HC 68, BOX 425, ST. FRANCISVILLE, LOUISIANA 70775

Tel: **(504) 635-3674**
Host(s): **Mr. & Mrs. H. M. Brown**
Location: **35 mi. N of Baton Rouge**
No. of Rooms: **6**
No. of Private Baths: **6**
Double/pb: **$70**
Single/pb: **$50**
Open: **All year**

Breakfast: **Full**
Credit Cards: **MC, VISA**
Other Meals: **Available**
Pets: **No**
Children: **Welcome**
Smoking: **Permitted**
Social Drinking: **Permitted**

This sprawling antebellum home is a working plantation listed on the National Register of Historic Places. Andrew Jackson once slept here, and today you can see much of the same furnishings he did. A full Southern-style breakfast is offered. Guests are welcome to tour the original outbuildings built over a century ago. Nearby attractions include Audubon Memorial Park and the historic sites of St. Francisville.

The St. Francisville Inn ✪
118 NORTH COMMERCE, DRAWER 1369, ST. FRANCISVILLE, LOUISIANA 70775

Tel: **(504) 635-6502**
Host(s): **Florence and Dick Fillet**
Location: **24 mi. N of Baton Rouge**
No. of Rooms: **9**
No. of Private Baths: **9**
Double/pb: **$55**
Single/pb: **$45**
Suite: **$55**
Open: **All year**

Reduced Rates: **10%, seniors**
Breakfast: **Continental**
Other Meals: **Available**
Credit Cards: **AMEX, MC, VISA**
Pets: **No**
Children: **Welcome (crib)**
Smoking: **Permitted**
Social Drinking: **Permitted**

The St. Francisville Inn is located in the heart of plantation country in a town that is listed on the National Register of Historic Places. The inn is a Victorian Gothic known as the Wolf-Schlesinger House, built circa 1880. The air-conditioned guest rooms are furnished in lovely antiques and each opens onto a New Orleans–style courtyard out back. Breakfast includes fabulous pastries from a local bakery. Florence is an antique-print dealer whose specialty is Audubon.

The Columns on Jordan
615 JORDAN, SHREVEPORT, LOUISIANA 71101

Tel: **(318) 222-5912**
Best Time to Call: **11 AM; After 5 PM**
Host(s): **Judith and Edwin Simonton**
Location: **½ mi. from I-20**
No. of Rooms: **5**
No. of Private Baths: **3**
Max. No. Sharing Bath: **4**
Double/pb: **$68**
Single/pb: **$64**
Double/sb: **$58**
Single/sb: **$54**

Open: **All year**
Reduced Rates: **10%, clergy; faculty; seniors**
Breakfast: **Full**
Credit Cards: **AMEX, MC, VISA**
Pets: **Sometimes**
Children: **No**
Smoking: **Permitted**
Social Drinking: **Permitted**
Foreign Languages: **Spanish**

At the Columns, you will sleep in the splendor of a spacious room, authentically furnished with period pieces. You'll awaken to enjoy your morning coffee and newspaper on the upstairs porch overlooking the stately magnolias or in the garden at poolside. Breakfast is graciously served in the morning room. Located within the Highland Restoration area, the house is listed on the National Register of Historic Places. The atmosphere is that of Southern charm and thoughtful hospitality as evidenced by the hair dryer, iron, and ironing board in each bedroom.

Fairfield Place ✪
2221 FAIRFIELD AVENUE, SHREVEPORT, LOUISIANA 71104

Tel: **(318) 222-0048**
Host(s): **Janie Lipscomb**
Location: **½ mi. from I-20**
No. of Rooms: **6**
No. of Private Baths: **6**
Double/pb: **$65–$85**
Single/pb: **$55–$75**
Open: **All year**

Breakfast: **Continental**
Credit Cards: **AMEX, MC, VISA**
Pets: **No**
Children: **Sometimes**
Smoking: **No**
Social Drinking: **Permitted**
Airport/Station Pickup: **Yes**

You will enjoy this elegant 1900s inn where the legendary hospitality of the Deep South rings true. Begin your day with New Orleans coffee, croissants and strawberry butter, and French pastries. Janie's home features lambskin rugs, king-size beds, 19th-century paintings, Swedish crystal, and designer sheets and linens. It is located in the beautiful Highland Historical Restoration District, convenient to the business district, medical center, and airport. Louisiana Downs Racetrack is minutes away.

MAINE

Bed & Breakfast Down East, Ltd.
BOX 547, MACOMBER MILL ROAD, EASTBROOK, MAINE 04634

Tel: (207) 565-3517
Coordinator: **Sally B. Godfrey**
States/Regions Covered: **Maine (statewide)**

Rates (Single/Double):
Modest: $30 $40
Average: $40–$45 $45–$60
Luxury: $50–$55 $80–$140
Credit Cards: **AMEX, MC, VISA**

There are delightful accommodations waiting for you, from Eliot near the New Hampshire border to "way down East" in Eastport, near F.D.R.'s Campobello Island in New Brunswick, Canada. You are certain to enjoy Bar Harbor, Acadia National Park, the rugged coastline, and inland forests and streams. All of Sally's hosts will make you feel welcome. A surcharge for one-night stays is imposed July through September.

"Glad II"
60 PEARL STREET, BATH, MAINE 04530

Tel: **(207) 443-1191**
Host(s): **Gladys Lansky**
Location: **.7 mi. from US 1**
No. of Rooms: **3**
Max. No. Sharing Bath: **3**
Double/sb: **$40–$45**
Open: **All year**

Breakfast: **Continental**
Pets: **No**
Children: **Welcome, over 8 (in own room)**
Smoking: **No**
Social Drinking: **Permitted**

This spic-and-span white house with its crisp green trim is comfortable and attractively furnished. Gladys delights in pleasing her guests with breakfasts featuring fresh, homemade treats. You are welcome to play the piano, borrow a book from her library, and visit or watch TV in the parlors. It's an easy walk to the Maritime Museum, a short drive to Popham Beach, Reid State Park, Boothbay Harbor, L. L. Bean, and the Brunswick Naval Air Station. Bowdoin College is eight miles away.

Horatio Johnson House ✪
36 CHURCH STREET, BELFAST, MAINE 04915

Tel: **(207) 338-5153**
Host(s): **Helen and Gene Kirby**
Location: **30 mi. S of Bangor**
No. of Rooms: **3**
No. of Private Baths: **3**
Double/pb: **$40**
Open: **All year**

Breakfast: **Full**
Pets: **No**
Children: **No**
Smoking: **Permitted**
Social Drinking: **Permitted**
Airport/Station Pickup: **Yes**

While the rest of the world is rushing ahead, the small seafaring town of Belfast is rediscovering its past. The waterfront and old town buildings are being refurbished to reflect the way things used to be. Your hosts offer good company and comfortable lodging in a 19th-century home five minutes from the ocean. The Kirbys offer a variety of breakfast specialties such as Belgian waffles and blueberry pancakes. They will glady recommend flea markets, antique shops, and restaurants galore.

Kenniston Hill Inn
ROUTE 27, BOOTHBAY, MAINE 04537

Tel: **(207) 633-2159**
Host(s): **Paul and Ellen Morissette**

Location: **50 mi. N of Portland**
No. of Rooms: **8**

252 • MAINE

No. of Private Baths: **8**
Double/pb: **$60–$80**
Open: **Apr.–Nov.**
Breakfast: **Full**
Credit Cards: **MC, VISA**

Pets: **No**
Children: **Welcome, over 12**
Smoking: **No**
Social Drinking: **Permitted**

Kenniston Hill Inn is a white clapboard mansion dating back to 1786. The house is warm and gracious, with a large front porch and open-hearth fireplace. The bedrooms, four with fireplaces, are tastefully decorated with handmade quilts, delicately colored wallpapers, and fresh flowers. Your hosts are former restaurant owners from Vermont. They offer sumptuous breakfast specialties such as zucchini-and-walnut pancakes and a vegetable frittata. The inn is surrounded by woods and gardens, but is within easy reach of shops, restaurants, boat rides, horseback riding, and tennis.

L'ermitage ✪
219 MAIN STREET, BUCKSPORT, MAINE 04416

Tel: **(207) 469-3361**
Host(s): **Veronique and Richard Melsheimer**
Location: **19 mi. E of Bangor; .8 mi. from US 1**
No. of Rooms: **3**
Max. No. Sharing Bath: **2**
Double/sb: **$40**
Single/sb: **$30**
Open: **All year**

Reduced Rates: **20%, off-season**
Breakfast: **Full**
Other Meals: **Available**
Credit Cards: **MC, VISA**
Pets: **No**
Children: **No**
Smoking: **Permitted**
Social Drinking: **Permitted**
Foreign Languages: **French**

L'ermitage is a 19th-century white Colonial with black shutters, dating back to the 1830s. Your hosts, Veronique and Richard Melsheimer, have patterned their inn after those found in Europe. The spacious rooms are furnished in period antiques, Oriental carpets, and collectibles. A small, reasonably priced restaurant is on the premises and features an extensive wine list. L'ermitage is on Penobscot Bay, near Ft. Knox.

Blue Harbor House ✪
67 ELM STREET, ROUTE 1, CAMDEN, MAINE 04843

Tel: **(207) 236-3196**
Host(s): **Connie and Bob Hood**
Location: **85 mi. NE of Portland**

No. of Rooms: **6**
No. of Private Baths: **4**
Max. No. Sharing Bath: **4**

Double/pb: **$80–$90**
Single/pb: **$75–$85**
Double/sb: **$70**
Single/sb: **$65**
Open: **All year**
Reduced Rates: **$40–$70, Nov.–Mar.**
Breakfast: **Full**

Credit Cards: **MC, VISA**
Pets: **No**
Children: **Welcome, over 8**
Smoking: **No**
Social Drinking: **Permitted**
Airport/Station Pickup: **Yes**

Camden is one of the prettiest coastal villages in New England. This 1835 Cape Cod house has been completely renovated and captures the essence of a bygone era. Each room is decorated in country antiques, stenciled walls, and handmade quilts. Guests enjoy visiting with each other in the common room, furnished with comfortable chairs and accented by antique stoneware, samplers, and folk art. The spacious dining room with its views of Mt. Battie is the setting for the generous breakfast that features homemade breads, delicious egg dishes, and Maine blueberries. It's a few minutes' walk to many fine restaurants, unique shops, and the famous Windjammer fleet.

Hawthorn Inn
9 HIGH STREET, CAMDEN, MAINE 04843

Tel: **(207) 236-8842**
Best Time to Call: **9 AM–8 PM**
Host(s): **Pauline and Brad Staub**
Location: **On Rte. 1, 150 mi. N of Boston**
No. of Rooms: **7**
No. of Private Baths: **4**
Max. No. Sharing Bath: **3**
Double/pb: **$75–$85**
Double/sb: **$65–$75**

Open: **All year**
Reduced Rates: **$10 less daily, Nov. 1–May 25**
Breakfast: **Full**
Credit Cards: **MC, VISA**
Pets: **No**
Children: **Welcome, over 10**
Smoking: **Permitted**
Social Drinking: **Permitted**
Airport/Station Pickup: **Yes**

254 • MAINE

The airy rooms of this Victorian inn are an elegant mixture of the old and the new. Guests are welcome to wine or coffee while relaxing on the deck or getting warm by the fire. Breakfast is served in a sunny dining room. All rooms overlook either Mt. Battie or Camden Harbor. A score of sports can be enjoyed in the area, and shops and restaurants are a short walk away.

Maine Stay Bed and Breakfast ✪
22 HIGH STREET, CAMDEN, MAINE 04843

Tel: **(207) 236-9636**
Best Time to Call: **1–7 PM**
Host(s): **Sally and Bob Tierney**
Location: **97 mi. NE of Portland**
No. of Rooms: **8**
Max. No. Sharing Bath: **4**
Double/sb: **$65**
Single/sb: **$40**

Open: **All year**
Reduced Rates: **Off season; weekly**
Breakfast: **Full**
Pets: **No**
Children: **Welcome, over 7**
Smoking: **Permitted**
Social Drinking: **Permitted**
Foreign Languages: **French**

This is one of Camden's treasured Colonials, built in 1813. Choose from eight bedrooms decorated with period pieces. Relax with a cup of coffee or catch up on a book in one of the spacious parlors. Breakfast is served on an attractive deck in warm weather. It's only a five-minute walk to the shops, restaurants, and Camden Harbor. Windjammer cruises, a Shakespeare theater, skiing, and Camden Hills State Park are just a few of the local attractions.

Ricker House ✪
PARK STREET, P.O. BOX 256, CHERRYFIELD, MAINE 04622

Tel: **(207) 546-2780**
Host(s): **William and Jean Conway**
Location: **32 mi. E of Ellsworth**
No. of Rooms: **3**
Max. No. Sharing Bath: **5**
Double/sb: **$40**
Single/sb: **$35**
Open: **All year**

Reduced Rates: **Available**
Breakfast: **Full**
Pets: **No**
Children: **Welcome (crib)**
Smoking: **No**
Social Drinking: **Permitted**
Airport/Station Pickup: **Yes**

Built in 1803, this comfortable Federal Colonial has grounds that border the Narraguagus River, one of the best salmon rivers in the States. The village is quaint and historic, and it is fun to tour it on foot or by bike. Reasonable restaurants offer great menus and all feature fabulous local lobster. Your hosts have canoed every river, swum every lake, climbed every mountain, and visited every village in their hometown area and they will be pleased to help you get the most out of your visit.

Brannon-Bunker Inn ✪
HCR 64, BOX 045L, DAMARISCOTTA, MAINE 04543

Tel: **(207) 563-5941**
Host(s): **Jeanne and Joseph Hovance**
No. of Rooms: **7**
No. of Private Baths: **4**
Max. No. Sharing Bath: **3**
Double/pb: **$55**
Single/pb: **$50**
Double/sb: **$40–$45**
Single/sb: **$35–$40**
Suites: **$60–$100**
Open: **All year**
Reduced Rates: **Available**
Breakfast: **Continental**
Credit Cards: **MC, VISA**
Pets: **No**
Children: **Welcome**
Smoking: **No**
Social Drinking: **Permitted**

The Brannon-Bunker Inn is an informal, relaxing inn, ideally situated in rural, coastal Maine. Guests may choose from accommodations in the main 1820 Cape House, the 1900 converted barn, or the carriage house across the stream. Each room is individually decorated in styles ranging from Colonial to Victorian. Hosts Jeanne and Joseph Hovance will help you plan your days over breakfast. Nearby activities include golf, ocean swimming at Pemaquid Beach Park, and fishing on the Damariscotta River.

Isaac Randall House ✪
INDEPENDENCE DRIVE, FREEPORT, MAINE 04032

Tel: **(207) 865-9295**
Best Time to Call: **Noon**
Host(s): **Glynrose and Jim Friedlander**
Location: **16 mi. NE of Portland**
No. of Rooms: **8**
No. of Private Baths: **6**
Max. No. Sharing Bath: **4**
Double/pb: **$75–85**
Double/sb: **$60**
Open: **All year**
Reduced Rates: **Off season**
Breakfast: **Full**
Pets: **Sometimes**
Children: **Welcome (crib)**
Smoking: **Limited**
Social Drinking: **Permitted**
Airport/Station Pickup: **Yes**
Foreign Languages: **Spanish**

One hundred sixty years ago, this Federal-style farmhouse was built as a wedding gift for Isaac Randall, Jr., and his young bride. It later became a stop-over on the underground railroad and then a Depression-era dance hall. Today, guests are welcomed to a charming, antique-filled home set on five wooded acres. The grounds include a spring-fed pond, perfect for ice skating. Hiking and cross-country ski trails start at the front door. Breakfast specialties such as fruit compote, homemade breads, blueberry pancakes, coffee, and assorted teas are served in the country kitchen. Downtown Freeport, home of L. L. Bean, is within walking distance. Maine's beautiful coast, summer theater, Bowdoin College, and Freeport Harbor are just a short drive away. After a day of activity, join your hosts for an evening snack back at the inn.

Arundel Meadows Inn ☉
P.O. BOX 1129, KENNEBUNK, MAINE 04043

Tel: **(207) 985-3770**
Best Time to Call: **Before 5 PM**
Host(s): **Mark Bachelder, Murray Yaeger**
Location: **2 mi. N of Kennebunk**
No. of Rooms: **6**
No. of Private Baths: **6**
Double/pb: **$60–80**
Suites: **$80–$120**
Open: **All year**
Breakfast: **Full**
Pets: **Sometimes**
Children: **Welcome, over 11**
Smoking: **Permitted**
Social Drinking: **Permitted**

The Arundel Meadows Inn is situated on three and a half acres next to the Kennebunk River. Murray, a professor at Boston University, and Mark, a professional chef, have always loved this area, and it is a dream come true for them to watch others enjoy it. They renovated this 165-year-old house themselves and meticulously planned the decor. Several guest rooms have fireplaces and one suite sleeps four. Mark's beautifully prepared breakfast specialties, such as brioche, quiche, eggs Benedict, or French toast, are the perfect start for your day. It's just three minutes to the center of town and about ten to Kennebunk Beach. In the afternoon, come back to the inn for tea and enjoy pâtés, homemade sweets, and beverages.

1802 House Bed & Breakfast Inn ☉
LOCKE STREET, P.O. BOX 646-A, KENNEBUNKPORT, MAINE 04046

Tel: **(207) 967-5632**
Best Time to Call: **8 AM–9 PM**
Host(s): **Sal and Pat Ledda**
Location: **22 mi. S of Portland**
No. of Rooms: **8**
No. of Private Baths: **8**
Double/pb: **$74–$94**
Single/pb: **$74–79**
Open: **All year**
Reduced Rates: **10%, weekly**
Breakfast: **Full**
Credit Cards: **AMEX, MC, VISA**
Pets: **No**
Children: **Welcome, over 12**
Smoking: **Permitted**
Social Drinking: **Permitted**

Tastefully decorated in Colonial style, some of the bedrooms have working fireplaces. The sound of a ship's bell will beckon you to a sumptuous breakfast that might feature sesame French toast or a stack of pancakes with blueberry sauce. In spring, visit the Rachel Carson Wildlife Refuge; in fall, the foliage is glorious; in winter, cross-country ski from the doorstep and return for mulled cider by the fireside; in summer, take in the theater, or swim at the shore. Sal and Pat will pamper you in all seasons. There is a two-night minimum on weekends.

The Green Heron Inn
P.O. BOX 2578, OCEAN AVENUE, KENNEBUNKPORT, MAINE 04046

Tel: **(207) 967-3315**
Best Time to Call: **Noon–8 PM**
Host(s): **Charles and Elizabeth Reid**
Location: **4½ mi. from US 1**
No. of Rooms: **10**
No. of Private Baths: **10**
Double/pb: **$50–$70**
Single/pb: **$35–$55**

Guest Cottage: **$53–$78; sleeps 4**
Open: **Apr. 15–Dec. 12**
Reduced Rates: **Weekly; Families**
Breakfast: **Full**
Pets: **Sometimes**
Children: **Welcome (crib)**
Smoking: **Permitted**
Social Drinking: **Permitted**

This immaculate inn (circa 1908) with its inviting porch and striped awnings, furnished simply and comfortably, is located between the river and the ocean in this Colonial resort village. The full Yankee breakfast is a rib-buster! This is a saltwater fisherman's heaven, with boating, golf, swimming, and tennis all nearby, close to shops and galleries.

The Inn at Harbor Head ✪
RR2, BOX 1180, PIER ROAD, CAPE PORPOISE, KENNEBUNKPORT, MAINE 04046

Tel: **(207) 967-5564**
Host(s): **Joan and David Sutter**
Location: **7 mi. from I-95, Exit 3**
No. of Rooms: **4**
No. of Private Baths: **4**
Double/pb: **$90–$105**
Single/pb: **$80–$95**
Suites: **$100–$150**
Open: **Dec.–Oct.**

Reduced Rates: **15%, Jan. 1–May 23**
Breakfast: **Full**
Credit Cards: **Discover, MC, VISA**
Pets: **No**
Children: **Welcome, over 12**
Smoking: **No**
Social Drinking: **Permitted**
Minimum Stay: **2 nights summer, fall, holidays**

A romantic getaway awaits you on the edge of an ocean inlet on Cape Porpoise. This farmhouse recently celebrated its 100th birthday with a top-to-bottom renovation. The result combines elegance with comfort. Share a shady hammock for two or enjoy a swim from the dock at high tide. Historic old homes, the Goat Island lighthouse, a trolley museum, art galleries, excellent restaurants, and charming shops abound.

Harbour Watch ✪
FOLLETT LANE, RFD 1, BOX 42, KITTERY POINT, MAINE 03905

Tel: **(207) 439-3242**
Host(s): **Marian and Robert Craig**
Location: **50 mi. N of Boston**
No. of Rooms: **4**
Max. No. Sharing Bath: **4**
Double/sb: **$55**

Open: **Apr.–Oct.**
Breakfast: **Continental**
Pets: **No**
Children: **Welcome, over 14**
Smoking: **No**
Social Drinking: **Permitted**

This beautiful sea captain's house has been in Marian's family since 1797. The harbor views from the property are an ever-changing panorama of lobstermen pulling their traps, sailboat races, and the boat that cruises to the Isle of Shoals. It's a 10-minute drive to Portsmouth, New Hampshire, with historic Strawbery Banke and the Prescott Park summer art and theater series. York Beach is only nine miles away along the coast.

Old Tavern Inn ✪
POST ROAD, P.O. BOX 445, LITCHFIELD, MAINE 04350

Tel: **(207) 268-4965**
Host(s): **Virginia Albert**
Location: **12 mi. SW of Augusta**
No. of Rooms: **6**
No. of Private Baths: **2**
Max. No. Sharing Bath: **4**
Double/pb: **$40**
Double/sb: **$35**

Single/sb: **$30**
Open: **All year**
Breakfast: **Full**
Credit Cards: **MC, VISA**
Pets: **Sometimes**
Children: **Welcome**
Smoking: **Permitted**
Social Drinking: **Permitted**

Virginia's home was built as a tavern in 1808, and the hitching posts that flank it go back to the time when stagecoach horses were tethered there. Furnished with traditional pieces, comfortable antiques, and plants, it is warm and cozy. There's a heated in-ground pool and a pond for fishing; it's an easy walk to Tacoma Lake for boating and fishing. Bates College is nearby.

Black Friar Inn ✪
10 SUMMER STREET, BAR HARBOR, MT. DESERT ISLAND, MAINE 04609

Tel: **(207) 288-5091**
Host(s): **Barbara and Jim Kelly**
No. of Rooms: **6**
No. of Private Baths: **4**
Max. No. Sharing Bath: **4**
Double/pb: **$75–$85**
Single/pb: **$70–$80**
Double/sb: **$58–$65**
Single/sb: **$53–$60**
Open: **May–Oct.**

Reduced Rates: **May 1–June 15**
Breakfast: **Full**
Credit Cards: **MC, VISA**
Pets: **No**
Children: **Welcome, over 12**
Smoking: **No**
Social Drinking: **Permitted**
Minimum Stay: **2 nights July and Aug.**
Airport/Station Pickup: **Yes**

Fine woodwork, mantels, bookcases, and tasteful furnishings enhance the fine restoration of this vintage Victorian. The full English breakfast, afternoon tea, and refreshments are graciously served in the Greenhouse, a room paneled in cypress and embossed tin salvaged from an old Maine church. Opportunities for hiking, biking, swimming, boating, photography, nature watching, and antiquing abound.

Hearthside Inn ✪
7 HIGH STREET, BAR HARBOR, MT. DESERT ISLAND, MAINE 04609

Tel: **(207) 288-4533**
Host(s): **Susan and Barry Schwartz**
No. of Rooms: **9**
No. of Private Baths: **7**
Max. No. Sharing Bath: **4**
Double/pb: **$70–$90**
Double/sb: **$60**
Open: **All year**

Reduced Rates: **No**
Breakfast: **Continental**
Credit Cards: **MC, VISA**
Pets: **No**
Children: **Welcome, over 10**
Smoking: **No**
Social Drinking: **Permitted**

On a quiet street, just a short walk to town, is this gracious home, recently redecorated in the manner of a country cottage. You are invited to share the special ambience of a living room with a cozy fireplace and brimming with books. Some rooms have a balcony or a fireplace. Complimentary iced tea, cheese, crackers, and wine are offered. Two-night minimum stay required during July and August.

Holbrook House ✪
74 MOUNT DESERT STREET, BAR HARBOR, MT. DESERT ISLAND, MAINE 04609

Tel: **(207) 288-4970**
Host(s): **Dorothy and Mike Chester**
Location: **15 mi. from Rte. 1, Exit Rte. 3**
No. of Rooms: **10**
No. of Private Baths: **10**
Double/pb: **$75–$100**
Guest Cottage: **Available**
Open: **June 15–Oct. 15**

Reduced Rates: **$15 less after Labor Day; seniors**
Breakfast: **Full**
Credit Cards: **AMEX, MC, VISA**
Pets: **No**
Children: **Welcome, over 8**
Smoking: **No**
Social Drinking: **Permitted**
Minimum Stay: **2 nights**
Airport/Station Pickup: **Yes**

In 1876 Nathan Ash built Holbrook House to provide lodging for wealthy Easterners seeking the social diversions of Bar Harbor. The 19-room house has been fully restored, but summer still brings the guests, who seek many of the same things: afternoon tea in china cups, evenings on an 80-foot porch, and conversations in the parlor. Victorian floral wallpapers, lace, chintz, and flowers complement the period furnishings and memorabilia found throughout the house. After spending the night in a four-poster bed, you'll waken in time for breakfast in the sun room. House specialties include fruit flans, blueberry buckle, French toast, cheese-and-egg pudding, and eggs Holbrook. In the afternoon, Dorothy and Mike serve wine, cheese, tea, and other refreshments. Holbrook House is located in the historic part of town, a five-minute walk from restaurants, shops, and the seashore. Acadia National Park is just one mile away.

The Kingsleigh ✪
P.O. BOX 1426, 100 MAIN STREET, SOUTHWEST HARBOR, MT. DESERT ISLAND, MAINE 04679

Tel: **(207) 244-5302**
Host(s): **Jim and Kathy King**
Location: **45 mi. E of Bangor**
No. of Rooms: **7**
No. of Private Baths: **5**
Max. No. Sharing Bath: **4**
Double/pb: **$65–$85**
Double/sb: **$55**

Open: **All year**
Reduced Rates: **$15–$20 less, May 1– June 30, Sept. 8–Oct. 30**
Breakfast: **Full**
Pets: **No**
Children: **Welcome, over 12**
Smoking: **No**
Social Drinking: **Permitted**

Built at the turn of the century, the Kingsleigh is a shingled and pebble-dash Colonial revival. The house is set high on a knoll overlooking magnificent Southwest Harbor, where generations of boatbuilders and fishermen have earned their living. Waverly wall coverings, lace window treatments, plush carpeting, and period furnishings provide a comfortable blend of the old and new. Afternoon tea is served on a wraparound porch overlooking the harbor, while you relax in a white wicker chair. Your hosts serve fresh coffee, imported teas, country omelets, oatmeal pancakes, and other specialties for breakfast. They take pleasure in welcoming you to Mt. Desert Island, and will gladly direct you to swimming, hiking, fishing expeditions, whale-watching, restaurants, and shopping.

Lindenwood Inn ✪
P.O. BOX 1328, SOUTHWEST HARBOR, MT. DESERT ISLAND, MAINE 04679

Tel: **(207) 244-5335**
Host(s): **Gardiner and Marilyn Brower**
No. of Rooms: **7**
No. of Private Baths: **3**
Max. No. Sharing Bath: **4**
Double/pb: **$65–$80**
Double/sb: **$50–$60**
Guest Cottage: **$95; sleeps 4**

Open: **All year**
Reduced Rates: **Nov. 1—June 1**
Breakfast: **Full**
Pets: **No**
Children: **Welcome, over 12 in inn; any age in cottage**
Smoking: **Permitted**
Social Drinking: **Permitted**

Built at the turn of the century as a sea captain's home, the inn derives its name from the stately linden trees that line the front lawn. Most rooms have fine harbor views, and all are comfortably furnished. Cool mornings are warmed by the glowing fireplace in the dining room, where you can enjoy a hearty breakfast. You are welcome to relax on the shaded porch or enjoy the pleasures of a good book or music in the parlor. You can explore the wonders of Acadia National Park by car, bicycle, hiking, or sailing.

Penury Hall ✪
BOX 68, MAIN STREET, SOUTHWEST HARBOR, MT. DESERT ISLAND, MAINE 04679

Tel: **(207) 244-7102**
Host(s): **Gretchen and Toby Strong**
No. of Rooms: **3**
Max. No. Sharing Bath: **3**
Double/sb: **$50**
Single/sb: **$40**
Open: **All year**

Reduced Rates: **Available Sept. 16–June 15**
Breakfast: **Full**
Pets: **No**
Children: **Welcome, over 16**
Smoking: **Permitted**
Social Drinking: **Permitted**
Airport/Station Pickup: **Yes**

This gray frame house has a red door and a crisp, welcoming air. Built in 1830, it is comfortably furnished with traditional pieces, antiques, and original art. Gretchen and Toby are cosmopolitan and cordial. Their motto is: "Each guest is an honorary member of the family," and you'll soon feel at home. Knowledgeable about the area's highlights, they'll direct you to special shops and restaurants and all the best things do see and do.

Two Seasons ✪
BOX 829, SOUTHWEST HARBOR, MT. DESERT ISLAND, MAINE 04679

Tel: (207) 244-9627
Host(s): **Dorothy M. Lazareth**
No. of Rooms: **4**
No. of Private Baths: **2**
Max. No. Sharing Bath: **4**
Double/pb: **$60–$65**
Double/sb: **$50–$55**
Open: **June 15–Oct. 31**

Reduced Rates: **$10 less June, Oct.**
Breakfast: **Continental**
Pets: **No**
Children: **No**
Smoking: **Permitted**
Social Drinking: **Permitted**
Minimum Stay: **3 nights, July & Aug.**

Dorothy offers bright, airy rooms in a spacious Colonial home overlooking the harbor. Southwest Harbor is a small fishing village; locally this B&B is called the "doctor's house" and its blue shutters still bear the caduceus symbol. Breakfast, served in the sun room, consists of fresh fruit, cereal, local breads, muffins, homemade jams, and beverages. Shops and restaurants are within an easy stroll; yacht builders, golf courses, and Acadia National Park are a few miles away. Guests always remark about the comfortable beds and spic-and-span condition of the house.

The Gazebo ✪
P.O. BOX 668, ROUTE 1, OGUNQUIT, MAINE 03907

Tel: (207) 646-3733
Host(s): **Tony Fontes**
Location: **63 mi. N of Boston**
No. of Rooms: **10**
No. of Private Baths: **8**
Max. No. Sharing Bath: **4**
Double/pb: **$85**
Double/sb: **$60–$70**
Suite: **$100**

Open: **Feb. 1–Dec. 31**
Reduced Rates: **Oct. 16–May 16**
Breakfast: **Full**
Credit Cards: **AMEX, MC, VISA**
Pets: **No**
Children: **Welcome, over 12**
Smoking: **Permitted**
Social Drinking: **Permitted**

You'll recognize this 150-year-old farmhouse by its Victorian gazebo on the front lawn. Inside, there are lovely rooms with antique beds and old-fashioned furnishings. In the morning, a gourmet breakfast is served by candlelight on fine china and crystal. House specialties include stuffed French toast served with apricot-orange sauce, and ham-and-egg croquettes topped with tomato-basil sauce. The Gazebo is walking distance of the beach and Ogunquit's many recreational activities. There's a swimming pool on the grounds.

Morning Dove Bed and Breakfast
5 BOURNE LANE, OGUNQUIT, MAINE 03907

Tel: **(207) 646-3891**
Host(s): **Peter and Eeta Schon**
Location: **75 mi. N of Boston**
No. of Rooms: **6**
No. of Private Baths: **3**
Max. No. Sharing Bath: **4**
Double/pb: **$70–$85**
Suite: **$60–$70**

Double/sb: **$55–$70**
Open: **All year**
Breakfast: **Continental**
Credit Cards: **AMEX, MC, VISA**
Pet: **No**
Children: **Welcome, over 12**
Smoking: **Permitted**
Social Drinking: **Permitted**

The Morning Dove is a restored farmhouse dating back to the 1860s. The airy rooms feature antiques, luxurious towels, and fresh garden flowers. At night handmade chocolates are placed on the pillows. Breakfast is served on the Victorian porch or in the elegant dining room. The house is within walking distance of beaches, a busy harbor for fishing and boating, and the Marginal Way, a clifftop path along the edge of the ocean. Restaurants, art galleries, and the trolley stop are just a few steps away. A two-night minimum stay is required; three nights on summer holiday weekends.

Broad Bay Inn & Gallery ✪
MAIN STREET, P.O. BOX 607, WALDOBORO, MAINE 04572

Tel: **(207) 832-6668**
Host(s): **Jim and Libby Hopkins**
Location: **80 mi. N of Portland**
No. of Rooms: **5**
No. of Private Baths: **3**
Max. No. Sharing Bath: **4**
Double/sb: **$40–$60**
Single/sb: **$35–$55**
Open: **All year**

Breakfast: **Full**
Other Meals: **Available Fri. & Sat.**
Credit Cards: **MC, VISA**
Pets: **No**
Children: **Welcome, over 12**
Smoking: **Permitted**
Social Drinking: **Permitted**
Foreign Languages: **French**

The inn, located in a charming mid-coast village, is a classic Colonial with light, airy, handsomely decorated rooms. Some of the guest rooms have canopy beds, and all have Victorian furnishings. There's a large deck on which to enjoy afternoon tea or sherry. This is a convenient base from which to enjoy the quaint fishing villages, the Camden Shakespeare Theatre, the Waldo summer-stock theater, and the Maine Seafood Festival. A sumptuous breakfast often includes quiche, crêpes, baked eggs in sausage, or herbed cheese omelets. Guests never go hungry because beverages are served on arrival, wine and cheese are available each afternoon, and snacks are frequently offered. Jim and Libby are retired commercial artists and have a gallery in the barn. They plan art workshops for interested guests.

Tide Watch Inn ✪
P.O. BOX 94, PINE STREET, WALDOBORO, MAINE 04572

Tel: (207) 832-4987
Best Time to Call: **Before 10 AM; after 2 PM**
Host(s): **Mel and Cathy Hanson**
Location: **62 mi. N of Portland; 1 7/16 mi. from Rte. 1**
No. of Rooms: **3**
No. of Private Baths: **1**
Max. No. Sharing Bath: **4**
Double/pb: **$45**
Single/pb: **$35**
Double/sb: **$40**
Single/sb: **$30**
Open: **All year**
Breakfast: **Full**
Pets: **No**
Children: **Welcome**
Smoking: **Permitted**
Social Drinking: **Permitted**
Airport/Station Pickup: **Yes**

Built in 1850, this twin Colonial home is located on the shore of the Medomac River. The first five-masted schooners were crafted right by the inn. You are welcome to bring your boat or canoe, or just watch the local fishermen sail with the tide. Catherine's forte is keeping the inn "ship-shape" and guests comment on the comfortable ambience she's created. Mel's talent as a retired chef is evident in the ambitious and delicious breakfasts that might include asparagus cordon bleu and a hearty, welcome bowl of clam chowder.

The Wild Rose of York B&B
78 LONG SANDS ROAD, YORK, MAINE 03909

Tel: **(207) 363-2532**
Best Time to Call: **Before 8 AM; afternoons and evenings**
Host(s): **Fran and Frank Sullivan**
Location: **10 mi. N of Portsmouth, N.H.**
No. of Rooms: **4**
No. of Private Baths: **2**
Max. No. Sharing Bath: **4**
Double/pb: **$55**
Single/pb: **$45**
Double/sb: **$48**
Single/sb: **$40**
Suites: **$75, for 3**
Open: **All year**
Reduced Rates: **Oct. 16–May 31**
Breakfast: **Full**
Pets: **No**
Children: **Welcome (crib)**
Smoking: **No**
Social Drinking: **Permitted**
Airport/Station Pickup: **Yes**

This handsome house, built in 1814, sits high on a hill within easy range of the ocean breezes. The bedrooms are cozy, with antique beds, patchwork quilts, fireplaces, and Fran's special artistic touches. Breakfast is special and may feature peach pancakes or nut waffles. In summer, an old-fashioned trolley will take you to the beach. Deep-sea fishing, golf, hiking, shops, galleries, and factory outlets are nearby diversions. Frank, a biology professor, often conducts nature and tidepool walks. In winter, sledding, skating, and cross-country skiing are all fun. An art gallery, featuring works by local artists, is literally on the drawing board for this B&B. Complimentary tea, cookies, and sherry are always offered.

MARYLAND

Betsy's Bed and Breakfast
1428 PARK AVENUE, BALTIMORE, MARYLAND 21217

Tel: (301) 383-1274
Best Time to Call: **8:30 AM–5:30 PM**
Host(s): **Betsy Grater**
No. of Rooms: **3**
No. of Private Baths: **2**
Max. No. Sharing Bath: **4**
Double/pb: **$65**
Single/pb: **$60**
Double/sb: **$60**

Single/sb: **$45**
Open: **All year**
Reduced Rates: **10–15%, weekly**
Breakfast: **Full**
Credit Cards: **AMEX, MC, VISA**
Pets: **No**
Children: **Welcome**
Smoking: **No**
Social Drinking: **Permitted**

This four-story B&B is located in Bolton Hill, a neighborhood listed on the National Register of Historic Places. This is a charming 115-year-old town house, with elegant features such as a hallway floor inlaid with alternating strips of oak and walnut. There are six marble fireplaces, the most elaborate of which is in the dining room. Other decorations include heirloom quilts, displayed on the walls, and an interesting assortment of antique kitchen tools. Guests are welcome to relax in the spacious, high-ceilinged living room with French doors opening out to the garden. Betsy's is convenient to Meyerhoff Symphony Hall, the Lyric Opera House, the Inner Harbor, and some of the city's finest restaurants.

Mulberry House ✪
111 WEST MULBERRY STREET, BALTIMORE, MARYLAND 21201

Tel: **(301) 576-0111**	Pets: **No**
Host(s): **Charlotte and Curt Jeschke**	Children: **Welcome, over 16 (in separate room)**
No. of Rooms: **4**	
Max. No. Sharing Bath: **4**	Smoking: **Permitted**
Double/sb: **$65**	Social Drinking: **Permitted**
Open: **All year**	Airport/Station Pickup: **Yes**
Breakfast: **Full**	Foreign Languages: **German**

Mulberry House, in downtown Baltimore, was built circa 1830 as a Federal-period town house. Over the years a fourth floor and a courtyard were added and a painstaking restoration has now taken place. The owners have added special touches like leaded glass in first-floor transoms, fan windows, and needlepoint cushions from 19th-century wallpaper designs. Guests may choose from the Victorian, Far East, Federal, and Pineapple rooms, all professionally decorated. Guests are treated like old friends and are welcome to relax in the sitting room with its grand piano, sofa, and fireplace. A sumptuous breakfast is served at an 18th-century banquet table each morning. The house is within walking distance of many shops, museums, restaurants, historic sights, and the waterfront area.

The Winslow Home ✪
8217 CARAWAY STREET, CABIN JOHN, BETHESDA, MARYLAND 20818

Tel: **(301) 229-4654**	Open: **All year**
Best Time to Call: **After 5PM**	Reduced Rates: **Seniors; families**
Host(s): **Jane Winslow**	Breakfast: **Full**
Location: **7 mi. W of D.C.**	Pets: **Welcome**
No. of Rooms: **2**	Children: **Welcome**
Max. No. Sharing Bath: **4**	Smoking: **No**
Double/sb: **$40**	Social Drinking: **No**
Single/sb: **$30**	Airport/Station Pickup: **Yes**

You may enjoy the best of two worlds while staying at Jane's. This comfortable home is located in a lovely residential section of Bethesda, just 20 minutes from downtown Washington, D.C. Imagine touring the capital with some extra pocket money saved on high hotel costs. You are welcome to use the kitchen, laundry facilities, and piano. Georgetown, George Washington, and American universities are close by. There's a $5 surcharge for one-night stays.

The Taylors' B&B ✪
P.O. BOX 238, BURTONSVILLE, MARYLAND 20866

Tel: **(301) 236-4318**
Best Time to Call: **9–11 AM; 7–9 PM**
Host(s): **Ruth and Fred Taylor**
Location: **10 mi. NNE of Baltimore**
No. of Rooms: **1**
No. of Private Baths: **1**
Double/pb: **$60**

Open: **All year**
Breakfast: **Continental**
Pets: **No**
Children: **No**
Smoking: **No**
Social Drinking: **Permitted**
Foreign Languages: **French**

This gracious two-story Colonial home offers a breath of fresh country air just 45 minutes from Washington, D.C., and Baltimore's Inner Harbor district. Guests can enjoy the grand piano, the extensive collection of books in the library, and Ruth's paintings. In warm weather, cool drinks are served in the gazebo; in winter, guests gather by the fireplace in the family room. Both your hosts are retired. Ruth likes to read, sew, paint, and cook; Fred enjoys reading, writing, history, and music. They've traveled extensively and know how to make guests feel welcome. Tennis courts, horseback riding, and nature trails are nearby.

Inn at Mitchell House ✪
BOX 329, R.D. 2, ROUTE 21, CHESTERTOWN, MARYLAND 21620

Tel: **(301) 778-6500**
Best Time to Call: **Evenings**
Host(s): **Tracy and Jim Stone**
Location: **78 mi. E of Washington, D.C.**
No. of Rooms: **6**
No. of Private Baths: **5**
Max. No. Sharing Bath: **2**
Double/pb: **$75–$85**
Single/pb: **$70–$80**

Suite: **$90**
Open: **All year**
Breakfast: **Full**
Credit Cards: **MC, VISA**
Pets: **No**
Children: **Sometimes**
Smoking: **Permitted**
Social Drinking: **Permitted**
Minimum Stay: **2 nights on holiday weekends**

This brick Federal-style inn is known as the "Mitchell Mansion," and is listed on the Maryland Register of Historic Homes. The house, set on 10 acres, dates back to 1743 and boasts seven fireplaces, guest parlors, and a dining room with the original beamed ceiling and exposed brick floors. Tracy and Jim enjoy providing extra touches like wine and cheese at cocktail time. They want you to have a restful night amid period antiques, designer sheets, and authentic rope beds. Breakfast is always a hearty offering that often includes homemade granola and unusual French toast. Guests have bathing privileges at a private beach on Chesapeake Bay, just one half mile from the house.

Radcliffe Cross ✪
QUAKER NECK ROAD, ROUTE 3, BOX 360, CHESTERTOWN, MARYLAND 21620

Tel: **(301) 778-5540**
Host(s): **Dan and Marge Brook**
No. of Rooms: **2**
No. of Private Baths: **2**
Double/pb: **$60**
Open: **All year**

Breakfast: **Full**
Pets: **Sometimes**
Children: **Welcome, infants or over 10**
Smoking: **No**
Social Drinking: **Permitted**

This pre-Revolutionary white brick Colonial, situated on 28 acres, is appropriately furnished with Early American antiques. A unique hanging spiral staircase rises from the center hall to the third floor. Each room boasts its own fireplace. Guests rave about Marge's puff pastries, muffins, and coffee cakes. Coffee, tea, and soft drinks are always available. Reserve well in advance for the popular Chestertown Tea Party Festival in May or the Candlelight Walking Tour of Historic Charleston in September.

Chevy Chase Bed & Breakfast ✪
6815 CONNECTICUT AVENUE, CHEVY CHASE, MARYLAND 20815

Tel: **(301) 656-5867**
Best Time to Call: **Before 9 AM**
Host(s): **S. C. Gotbaum**
Location: **1 mi. N of Washington, D.C.**
No. of Rooms: **2**
No. of Private Baths: **1**
Double/pb: **$50**
Single/pb: **$45**

Single/sb: **$35**
Open: **All year**
Reduced Rates: **Weekly; families**
Breakfast: **Continental**
Pets: **No**
Children: **Welcome**
Smoking: **Permitted**
Social Drinking: **Permitted**

Enjoy the convenience of being close to the sights of Washington, D.C., while staying at a relaxing country-style house outside the city. Rooms have beamed ceilings and are filled with rare tapestries, Oriental rugs, baskets, copperware, and native crafts from Mexico to the Mideast. Your hostess is a sociologist with a private consulting business. For breakfast she offers homemade muffins, jams, pancakes, French toast, and a special blend of Louisiana coffee. When you want to take a break from touring, a quiet backyard and garden will relax you. Tennis courts and a swimming pool are nearby.

Country Hosting
DAMERON, MARYLAND 20628

Tel: **(301) 862-2589**
Coordinator: **Carolyn Lepper**

Rates (Single/Double):
Average: **$50**   **$48–$65**

Most of Carolyn's B&Bs are in the historic section of St. Marys County, within 90 miles of Washington D.C. They range from manor houses to a small country inn run by friendly people who are eager to see that you have a pleasant visit. Some hosts are fluent in French, Spanish, or Swedish. Calvert Cliffs, St. Marys City, the Civil War Museum, and the Calvert Marine Museum are nearby. The Amish Market, held on Wednesday and Saturday, is particularly interesting. Only children over the age of 12 are accommodated. $5 is charged for each booking.

The Garden Cottage at Sinking Springs Herb Farm ✪
234 BLAIR SHORE ROAD, ELKTON, MARYLAND 21921

Tel: **(301) 398-5566**
Best Time to Call: **8 AM–8 PM**
Host(s): **Ann and Bill Stubbs**
Location: **4½ mi. from Rte. 40**
No. of Rooms: **2**
No. of Private Baths: **2**
Double/pb: **$55**
Guest Cottage: **$65; sleeps 3**
Open: **All year**

Reduced Rates: **5%, seniors**
Breakfast: **Continental**
Credit Cards: **MC, VISA**
Other Meals: **Available**
Pets: **Sometimes**
Children: **Welcome**
Smoking: **No**
Social Drinking: **Permitted**
Airport/Station Pickup: **Yes**

Guests frequently comment on the peaceful beauty of the farm's setting. You may opt to stay in the main house, furnished with antiques in Early American style, or in the garden cottage, with its sitting room and fireplace adjoining the bedroom. Breakfast features coffee ground from organically grown beans, herbal teas, and homemade buns, fruit, and juice. A full country breakfast prepared with unprocessed food fresh from the farm is available at no extra charge.

Lectures on herbs and craft classes are available, and a gift shop is on the premises. Longwood Gardens and the famed Winterthur Museum are close by.

Hayland Farm ○
5000 SHEPPARD LANE, ELLICOTT CITY, MARYLAND 21043

Tel: (301) 531-5593 or (301) 596-9119
Host(s): **Louis and Dorothy Mobley**
Location: **Bet. Baltimore & D.C.**
No. of Rooms: **3**
No. of Private Baths: **1**
Max. No. Sharing Bath: **4**
Double/pb: **$45**
Single/pb: **$35**
Double/sb: **$35**
Single/sb: **$25**
Open: **All year**
Breakfast: **Full**
Pets: **No**
Children: **No**
Smoking: **No**
Social Drinking: **Permitted**

When you breathe the country-fresh air, it may surprise you that Baltimore and Washington, D.C., are only a short drive away. At Hayland Farm you will find gracious living in a large manor house furnished in a handsome yet comfortable style. Louis and Dorothy are retired and have traveled extensively. They enjoy sharing conversation with their guests. In warm weather, the 20' by 50' swimming pool is a joy.

The Stockmans ○
P.O. BOX 125, TAYLOR LANDING ROAD, GIRDLETREE, MARYLAND 21829

Tel: (301) 632-3299
Best Time to Call: **After 6 PM**
Host(s): **John and Joan Stockman**
Location: **6 mi. S of Snow Hill**
No. of Rooms: **2**
Max. No. Sharing Bath: **4**
Double/sb: **$45**
Single/sb: **$40**
Open: **Mar.–Dec.**
Breakfast: **Continental**
Pets: **No**
Children: **Welcome, over 4**
Smoking: **No**
Social Drinking: **Permitted**

This large Victorian country house is comfortably furnished with a blend of antiques and charm. Fishing, crabbing, and swimming are nearby, as well as interesting historic sites. The coffeepot is usually full, and you are welcome to enjoy a cup while relaxing on the front porch.

Lewrene Farm B&B ✪
RD 3, BOX 150, HAGERSTOWN, MARYLAND 21740

Tel: (301) 582-1735
Host(s): **Lewis and Irene Lehman**
Location: 3½ mi. from I-70 and I-81
No. of Rooms: **6**
No. of Private Baths: **3**
Max. No. Sharing Bath: **4**
Double/pb: **$55–$65**
Double/sb: **$40**

Suites: **$65**
Open: **All year**
Breakfast: **Full**
Pets: **Sometimes**
Children: **Welcome**
Smoking: **No**
Social Drinking: **No**
Foreign Languages: **Spanish**

Lewis and Irene will help you discover the peaceful beauty of their 125-acre farm located in a historic area near the Antietam Battlefield. Guests are treated like old friends and are welcome to lounge in front of the fireplace or to play the piano in the Colonial-style living room. You're invited to enjoy snacks and a video in the evening. Harpers Ferry, Fort Frederick, the C&O Canal, and Gettysburg are nearby. Irene sells antiques and collectibles on the premises.

Oakwood ✪
4566 SOLOMONS ISLAND ROAD, HARWOOD, MARYLAND 20776

Tel: (301) 261-5338
Host(s): **Dennis and Joan Brezina**
Location: **10 mi. S of Annapolis**
No. of Rooms: **2**
Max. No. Sharing Bath: **4**
Double/sb: **$60**
Single/sb: **$55**

Open: **Mar. 1–Nov. 30**
Breakfast: **Full**
Pets: **No**
Children: **Welcome, over 12**
Smoking: **Permitted**
Social Drinking: **Permitted**

This elegant antebellum manor house, featured on Maryland House Tours, has six fireplaces, 11-foot ceilings, and handmade rugs. Guests are welcome to relax on the veranda or stroll in the terraced gardens. Your hosts serve an English-style breakfast in the open-hearthed kitchen. They are happy to advise on day trips to Washington, D.C., or nearby Chesapeake Bay and Annapolis.

Vandiver Inn ✪
301 SOUTH UNION AVENUE, HAVRE DE GRACE, MARYLAND 21078

Tel: (301) 939-5200
Best Time to Call: **8 AM–5 PM**
Host(s): **Charles Rothwell**

Location: **35 mi. NE of Baltimore**
No. of Rooms: **8**
No. of Private Baths: **6**

Max. No. Sharing Bath: **4**
Double/pb: **$65–$85**
Double/sb: **$65–$85**
Open: **All year**
Breakfast: **Full**
Credit Cards: **AMEX, MC, VISA**

Pets: **No**
Children: **Welcome, over 12**
Smoking: **Permitted**
Social Drinking: **Permitted**
Airport/Station Pickup: **Yes**

Built in 1886, the Vandiver Inn is located in the Havre de Grace historic district, two blocks from the Chesapeake Bay. Today its graceful porches, stained glass, and rich woodwork have earned it a place on the National Register of Historic Places. Guest rooms are furnished with antiques and most have fireplaces individually styled with imported tile. The inn is well known for its meals, prepared by your host, Charles Rothwell. He is an award-winning chef trained at Baltimore's International Culinary Institute. Specialties such as roast rack of New England lamb, fresh Norwegian salmon, and broiled tenderloin of beef are served in the gracious dining room. The inn is the perfect base for exploring the Concord Point lighthouse or enjoying the water sports on the bay.

St. Michael's Manor B&B ✪
ST. MICHAEL'S MANOR, SCOTLAND, MARYLAND 20687

Tel: **(301) 872-4025**
Host(s): **Joe and Nancy Dick**
Location: **9 mi. S of St. Marys City**
No. of Rooms: **2**
Max. No. Sharing Bath: **4**
Double/sb: **$50**
Open: **All year**

Reduced Rates: **10%, after Labor Day**
Breakfast: **Full**
Pets: **No**
Children: **Welcome (crib, high chair)**
Smoking: **Downstairs only**
Social Drinking: **Permitted**

St. Michael's Manor was built in 1805 on land patented to Leonard Calvert during the 17th century. Today, the white stucco manor home on picturesque Long Neck Creek is included on the state's Pilgrimage Tour. The beautifully handcrafted woodwork has been preserved and is complemented with antiques and handcrafts. Guests are sure to enjoy the added touches, such as fresh fruit and flowers in the rooms. For breakfast, choose from a tasty array of homemade muffins, jellies, and farm-fresh fruit in season. Your hosts offer the use of their boat and bicycles for touring this lovely area. The Manor House is near Point Lookout State Park, half a mile from Chespeake Bay, and close to many historic sites.

Inn at Antietam ✪
220 EAST MAIN STREET, P.O. BOX 119, SHARPSBURG, MARYLAND 21782

Tel: **(301) 432-6601**
Best Time to Call: **Mornings; Evenings**
Host(s): **Betty and Cal Fairbourn**
Location: **15 mi. SW of Hagerstown**
No. of Rooms: **5**
No. of Private Baths: **5**
Double/pb: **$55–$85**
Suites: **$85–$105**

Open: **Jan. 2–Dec. 23**
Reduced Rates: **5%, seniors**
Breakfast: **Continental**
Credit Cards: **AMEX**
Pets: **No**
Children: **Welcome, over 6**
Smoking: **Permitted**
Social Drinking: **Permitted**

This classic Victorian, located next to the historic Antietam Battlefield, was built in 1908. The wraparound porch with its rockers and swing is a great place to relax. The house is decorated in a pleasant mix of styles with Victorian accents. Coffee and cookies are always available. It is close to the C & O Canal, Harpers Ferry, and less than an hour from Gettysburg. Shepherd College in Shepherdstown, West Virginia, is four miles away. Children are not accepted on weekends.

Blue Bear Bed & Breakfast ✪
ROUTE 2, BOX 378, HOLIDAY DRIVE, SMITHSBURG, MARYLAND 21783

Tel: **(301) 824-2292**
Best Time to Call: **After 4 PM**
Host(s): **Ellen Panchula**
Location: **6 mi. from I-70, Exit 35**
No. of Rooms: **2**
Max. No. Sharing Bath: **4**
Double/sb: **$40**
Single/sb: **$30**

Open: **July 1–Aug. 31; weekends, Apr.–June, Sept.–Dec.**
Breakfast: **Continental**
Pets: **No**
Children: **Welcome, over 12**
Smoking: **No**
Social Drinking: **Permitted**

Ellen is a full-time schoolteacher from September through June, so she can entertain guests during the week only in July and August; during the school year it's strictly weekends only. Her home is decorated in an informal country mode, with several antiques complementing the decor. Smithsburg is located in apple and peach country. It is convenient to the Antietam Battlefield in Sharpsburg and to many fine restaurants in Hagerstown. Homemade breads, coffee cakes, quiche, fresh fruit, and beverages comprise the breakfast menu. Snacks, dessert, and wine and cheese are generously offered in the evenings.

Long Way Hill ✪
7406 SPRINGFIELD AVENUE, SYKESVILLE, MARYLAND 21784

Tel: **(301) 795-8129**	Double/sb: **$50**
Best Time to Call: **After 7 PM**	Single/sb: **$40**
Host(s): **Anita-Barbara Huddlestun**	Open: **All year**
Location: **20 mi. W of Baltimore**	Breakfast: **Full (except Sunday)**
No. of Rooms: **3**	Pets: **Sometimes**
No. of Private Baths: **1**	Children: **Welcome (high chair)**
Max. No. Sharing Bath: **4**	Smoking: **Permitted**
Double/pb: **$50**	Social Drinking: **Permitted**
Single/pb: **$40**	

Anita-Barbara Huddlestun's entire block is listed on the National Register of Historic Places. She welcomes you to her cottage Victorian, set on five and a half landscaped acres. The property includes fruit trees, flowers, woods, and a swimming pool to enjoy in the summer months. The rooms are decorated with charming pieces ranging in period from the 1900s to the 1930s, with lovely wallpapers, wood furnishings, and fine linens. Breakfast specialties such as homemade cinnamon-raisin buns, eggs, and bacon are served in a sunny dining room with floral wallpaper and an old-fashioned curio cabinet. Long Way Hill is located in a rural area, yet is close to fine dining, shopping, and a movie theater. Columbia and Newmarket, the antiques capital of the state, are just a short drive from the house.

The Tavern House ✪
111 WATER STREET, P.O. BOX 98, VIENNA, MARYLAND 21869

Tel: **(301) 376-3347**	Reduced Rates: **After 1 night**
Host(s): **Harvey and Elise Altergott**	Breakfast: **Full**
Location: **15 mi. NW of Salisbury**	Credit Cards: **MC, VISA**
No. of Rooms: **3**	Pets: **No**
Max. No. Sharing Bath: **4**	Children: **No**
Double/sb: **$55–$60**	Smoking: **Permitted**
Single/sb: **$45–$55**	Social Drinking: **Permitted**
Open: **All year**	Foreign Languages: **German, Spanish**

Vienna is a quiet little town where one can escape the stress of the 20th century. Careful restoration has brought back the simple purity of this Colonial tavern. The stark white "lime, sand, and hair" plaster accents the authentic furnishings. This is a place for those who enjoy looking at the river and marshes, watching an osprey, or taking a leisurely walk. Days begin with fruits of the season and end with complimentary cheese and wine. For the sports minded, there's tennis, boating, and flat roads for bicycling, all within easy reach. This is an excellent base for exploring the Eastern Shore, interesting small towns and antique shops, and Blackwater National Wildlife Refuge.

Winchester Country Inn ✪
430 SOUTH BISHOP STREET, WESTMINSTER, MARYLAND 21157

Tel: **(301) 876-7373**
Best Time to Call: **7 AM–7 PM**
Host(s): **Phyllis Karrer**
Location: **35 mi. NW of Baltimore**
No. of Rooms: **5**
No. of Private Baths: **3**
Max. No. Sharing Bath: **4**
Double/pb: **$65**
Single/pb: **$60**
Double/sb: **$60**
Single/sb: **$55**
Open: **All year**
Reduced Rates: **10% weekly; 10% seniors**
Breakfast: **Full**
Credit Cards: **MC, VISA**
Pets: **No**
Children: **Welcome, over 6**
Smoking: **Permitted**
Social Drinking: **Permitted**

Built in the 1760s, this inn is one of the most historic inns in Carroll County. It is furnished with period antiques that enhance the interior. It is only a quarter of a mile to the historic Carroll County Farm Museum, which houses special events such as the Maryland Wine Festival. It is within walking distance to the Farmers Market, where produce, flowers, and crafts may be bought. Breakfast includes farm-fresh eggs and country sausage or ham. In the afternoon, Phyllis offers complimentary sherry or tea.

MASSACHUSETTS

Pineapple Hospitality, Inc. ✪
47 NORTH SECOND STREET, NEW BEDFORD, MASSACHUSETTS 02740

Tel: (508) 990-1696 or 1798
Best Time to Call: Winter: 11 AM–7 PM; Summer: 9 AM–7 PM
Coordinator: Judy Mulford
States/Regions Covered: Connecticut, Maine, Massachusetts, New Hampshire, Rhode Island, Vermont

Rates (Single/Double):
 Modest: $30–$36　$36–$40
 Average: $33–$45　$48–$60
 Luxury: $48–$75　$60–$165
Credit Cards: AMEX, MC, VISA

The pineapple has been the symbol of rare hospitality since early Colonial days, and the host homes on Judy's roster personify this spirit. They are located in cities and in the countryside, at beach resorts and lakeside communities, in historic districts and near hundreds of schools and colleges; you are bound to find just the spot to call home. Send $5.95 for a descriptive directory so that you may make your choices. There's a $5 processing fee.

Bed & Breakfast Associates—Bay Colony, Ltd. ✪
P.O. BOX 166, BABSON PARK, BOSTON, MASSACHUSETTS 02157

Tel: **(617) 449-5302**
Best Time to Call: **10 AM–12:30 PM; 1:30–5 PM**
Coordinators: **Arline Kardasis, Marilyn Mitchell**
States/Regions Covered: **Boston, Brookline, Cambridge, Concord, Framingham, Gloucester, Lexington, Marblehead, Newton, Wellesley**

Rates (Single/Double):
Modest: **$35–$40**   **$45–$50**
Average: **$40–$50**   **$50–$55**
Luxury: **$55–$75**   **$60–$100**
Credit Cards: **MC, VISA**
Minimum Stay: **2 nights**

A wide variety of 100 host homes is available in the city, in the country, and at the shore. They range from a historic brownstone to contemporary condominiums. Many are convenient to the major colleges and universities. Send $3 for the descriptive directory. There's a $10 surcharge for one-night stays.

Bed & Breakfast Marblehead & North Shore ✪
P.O. BOX 172, BEVERLY, MASSACHUSETTS 01915

Tel: **(508) 921-1336**
Best Time to Call: **Mon.–Sat. 7:30 AM–8 PM**
Coordinator: **Helena Champion**
States/Regions Covered: **Beverly, Burlington, Cape Ann, Danvers, Gloucester, Lynn, Manchester, Marblehead, Peabody, Salem, Swampscott; Maine, New Hampshire, Vermont**

Rates (Single/Double):
Modest: **$36–$42**   **$42–$50**
Average: **$45–$55**   **$55–$70**
Luxury: **$60–$120**   **$75–$125**
Credit Cards: **AMEX, MC, VISA (5% surcharge)**

Ranging from the reasonable to the regal, Helena's B&Bs all assure the warm, friendly atmosphere of a private home. This service has many accommodations within 30 minutes of Boston, yet they are in quaint seaside towns, on the ocean, or in ski areas. Her descriptive directory costs $3. This is a membership organization with annual dues of $25. Nonmembers are charged $10 to $15 for each booking.

Bed & Breakfast in Minuteman Country ✪
P.O. BOX 665, CAMBRIDGE, MASSACHUSETTS 02140

Tel: **(617) 576-2112**
Coordinators: **Tally and Pamela Carruthers**
States/Regions Covered:
　Massachusetts: Arlington, Bedford, Boston, Brookline, Cambridge, Concord, Lexington, Sudbury, Waltham, Winchester

Rates (Single/Double):
　Average:　$40　　$66
　Luxury:　　$50　　$86
Credit Cards: **AMEX, MC, VISA**
Minimum Stay: **2 nights**

Tally and Pamela can place you in host homes convenient to historic Lexington and Concord, downtown Boston, or in Cambridge. Many are close to Harvard and MIT, Leahy Clinic, historic Wright Tavern, Emerson's home, Walden Pond, and the Charles River. Unusual restaurants, specialty shops, and cultural happenings abound. Just tell your host about your interests and you will be assured of excellent advice. There's a $6 surcharge for one-night stays.

Be Our Guest Bed & Breakfast, Ltd. ✪
P.O. BOX 1333, PLYMOUTH, MASSACHUSETTS 02360

Tel: **(617) 837-9867**
Coordinators: **Diane Gillis and Mary Gill**
States/Regions Covered: **Boston, Cohasset, Duxbury, Falmouth, Hanover, Kingston, Marshfield, Plymouth, Sandwich, Scituate**

Rates (Single/Double):
　Modest:　$32　　$45
　Average:　$38　　$50
　Luxury:　　$65　　$65
Credit Cards: **AMEX, MC, VISA**

The homes range from historic to traditional New England style. Some are in private settings; others are surrounded by tourist activities. A few have commanding views of the waterfront. All are hosted by people who are dedicated to making certain that you enjoy your visit. Don't miss Plymouth Rock, the Mayflower, the Wax Museum, and winery tours. If you enjoy the sea, whale watching, deep-sea fishing, and sailing are all available. Send $1 for their descriptive directory.

BOSTON AREA

Greater Boston Hospitality ✪
P.O. BOX 1142, BROOKLINE, MASSACHUSETTS 02146

Tel: **(617) 277-5430**
Coordinator: **Lauren A. Simonelli**
States/Regions Covered: **Boston, Brookline, Cambridge, Gloucester, Lexington, Marblehead, Needham, Newton, Wellesley, Winchester**

Rates (Single/Double):
  Modest: $35 $45
  Average: $45 $55
  Luxury: $55 $100
Credit Cards: **MC, VISA**

Lauren's homes are convenient to many of the 75 colleges and universities in the greater Boston area. What a boon it is for people applying to school, and to parents visiting undergrads, to have a home-away-from-home nearby. There's a $10 surcharge for one-night stays.

Host Homes of Boston ✪
P.O. BOX 117, WABAN BRANCH, BOSTON, MASSACHUSETTS 02168

Tel: **(617) 244-1308 Telex: 136575**
Best Time to Call: **9:30 AM–12:30 PM; 1:30 PM–4:30 PM**
Coordinator: **Marcia Whittington**
States/Regions Covered: **Boston, Brookline, Cambridge, Concord, Framingham, Marblehead, Needham, Newton, Wellesley, Weymouth**

Rates (Single/Double):
  Modest: $40–$45 $45–$50
  Average: $45–$48 $50–$55
  Luxury: $55–$80 $60–$94
Credit Cards: **AMEX, MC, VISA**
Minimum Stay: **2 nights**

Marcia has culled a variety of select private homes in excellent areas convenient to good public transportation. Most hosts prepare a full breakfast, although only Continental breakfast is required. It's their special way of saying welcome to their city of colleges, universities, museums, and cultural life. Ask Marcia for her free directory of the B&Bs on her roster.

Williams Guest House ✪
136 BASS AVENUE, GLOUCESTER, MASSACHUSETTS 01930

Tel: **(508) 283-4931**
Best Time to Call: **8 AM–9 PM**
Host(s): **Betty Williams**
Location: **30 mi. N of Boston**
No. of Rooms: **7**

No. of Private Baths: **5**
Max. No. Sharing Bath: **4**
Double/pb: **$48–$50**
Double/sb: **$40–$42**
Guest Cottage: **$400 (week); sleeps 4**

Open: **May 1–Nov. 1**
Reduced Rates: **Off-season, before June 17 and after Labor Day**
Breakfast: **Continental**
Pets: **No**

Children: **Sometimes**
Smoking: **Permitted**
Social Drinking: **Permitted**
Airport/Station Pickup: **Yes**

Located five miles from Rockport and one and a half miles from Rocky Neck, Gloucester is a quaint fishing village on the North Shore. Betty's Colonial Revival house borders the finest beach, Good Harbor. The guest rooms are furnished with comfort in mind, and her homemade breakfast muffins are delicious. Betty will be happy to suggest many interesting things to do, such as boat tours, sport fishing, whale-watching trips, sightseeing cruises around Cape Ann, the Hammond Castle Museum, and the shops and galleries of the artist colony.

Checkerberry Corner
5 CHECKERBERRY CIRCLE, SUDBURY, MASSACHUSETTS 01776

Tel: **(508) 443-8660**
Best Time to Call: **Evenings**
Host(s): **Stuart and Irene MacDonald**
Location: **20 mi. W of Boston**
No. of Rooms: **2**
Max. No. Sharing Bath: **4**
Double/sb: **$50–$60**
Single/sb: **$45–$50**

Open: **All year**
Reduced Rates: **10%, families**
Breakfast: **Full**
Pets: **No**
Children: **Welcome, over 12**
Smoking: **No**
Social Drinking: **Permitted**

Checkerberry Corner is a classic Colonial with stained-glass entry windows, red doors, and a large porch. The rooms are tastefully decorated with traditional mahogany furnishings and comfortable Colonial accents. Beverages and snacks are always available. Stuart and Irene serve breakfast on fine china in the dining room. Homemade muffins, jams, and coffee cakes are specialties of the house. This charming Colonial is located in a historic district, close to the Lexington Minuteman Statue, the Old North Bridge, the homes of Louisa Mae Alcott, Hawthorne, and Emerson, and Longfellow's Wayside Inn.

Marshall House ✪
11 EASTERN AVENUE, SWAMPSCOTT, MASSACHUSETTS 01907

Tel: **(617) 595-6544**
Host(s): **Pat and Al Marshall**
Location: **10 mi. N of Boston**

No. of Rooms: **2**
Max. No. Sharing Bath: **4**
Double/sb: **$50–$60**

Single/sb: **$40–$50**
Open: **All year**
Reduced Rates: **10%, seniors**
Breakfast: **Continental**
Credit Cards: **AMEX, MC, VISA**

Pets: **No**
Children: **Welcome, over 6**
Smoking: **No**
Social Drinking: **Permitted**
Airport/Station Pickup: **Yes**

Marshall House, built circa 1900, is located just a short walk from the beaches of the North Shore. The many porches of this spacious home offer salty breezes and an ocean view. Inside, the rooms are decorated with country furnishings, some cherished antiques, and accents of wood and stained glass. The bedrooms have modern amenities such as color televisions and refrigerators. Guests are welcome to relax in the common room and warm up beside the wood stove. This B&B is located ten miles from Logan International Airport. Pat and Al will gladly direct you to nearby restaurants, historic seacoast villages, and popular bicycle touring routes.

Oak Shores ✪
64 FULLER AVENUE, SWAMPSCOTT, MASSACHUSETTS 01907

Tel: **(617) 599-7677**
Best Time to Call: **5 PM–8 PM**
Host(s): **Marjorie McClung**
Location: **13 mi. N. of Boston**
No. of Rooms: **2**
Max. No. Sharing Bath: **4**
Double/sb: **$50**

Single/sb: **$45**
Open: **Apr. 1–Dec. 1**
Breakfast: **Continental**
Pets: **No**
Children: **Welcome, over 9**
Smoking: **No**
Social Drinking: **Permitted**

This 58-year-old Dutch Colonial is located on Boston's lovely North Shore. Enjoy rooms filled with fine restored furniture and sleep in the comfort of old brass and iron beds. Relax in the private shady garden, on the deck, or take a two-block stroll to the beach. Swampscott was

Orleans Bed & Breakfast Associates ☉
P.O. BOX 1312, ORLEANS, MASSACHUSETTS 02653

Tel: **(508) 255-3824**	Rates (Single/Double):
Best Time to Call: **8 AM–8 PM**	Modest: **N/A** **$45**
Coordinator: **Mary Chapman**	Average: **N/A** **$50**
States/Regions Covered: **Cape Cod:**	Luxury: **N/A** **$80**
Brewster, Chatham, Harwich,	Credit Cards: **AMEX, MC, VISA**
Orleans, Truro, Wellfleet	Minimum Stay: **2 nights**

Mary offers a variety of accommodations with a diversity of styles, and guests may choose from historic to contemporary houses, all compatible with the atmosphere of the Cape. The fine reputation this service enjoys is largely due to the attitude of the host to the guest. Under Mary's direction, hosts meet regularly to share experiences, role-play B&B situations, and tour member homes. Each host is aware that a guest's experience reflects on the association as a whole. We applaud the professionalism of this organization! A descriptive directory is $1. A $5 booking fee is charged per reservation.

Thomas Huckins House ☉
2701 MAIN STREET (Route 6A), P.O. BOX 515, BARNSTABLE, MASSACHUSETTS 02630

Tel: **(508) 362-6379**	Reduced Rates: **$55–$75, Nov. 1– May 15**
Host(s): **Burt and Eleanor Eddy**	Breakfast: **Full**
Location: **2 mi. from Rte. 6, Exit 6**	Credit Cards: **MC, VISA**
No. of Rooms: **3**	Pets: **No**
No. of Private Baths: **3**	Children: **Welcome, over 6**
Double/pb: **$75–$85**	Smoking: **Permitted**
Suites: **$95**	Social Drinking: **Permitted**
Open: **All year**	

Located in the historic district, which is less crowded and less commercial than much of the Cape, the house (circa 1705) has all the privacy and charm of a small country inn. Each bedroom has a small sitting area and a four-poster bed with canopy top. The parlor is comfortably furnished with antiques and handmade reproductions. It's a short walk to a small beach, boat ramp, and the inlet that overlooks the dunes of Sandy Neck. Whale watching, the Nantucket ferry, the Sandwich Glass Museum, and Plimoth Plantation are but 15 minutes away. Eleanor loves to garden, and the jam served at breakfast is literally the fruits of her labor. Breakfast is served in the original keeping room in front of the fireplace. Banana pancakes and Cape Cod cranberry muffins are two favorites.

the summer White House of Calvin Coolidge. It is a convenient place to begin tours of nearby Marblehead, birthplace of the United States Navy, and Salem, famous for its witch trials. Marjorie is glad to help with travel plans, and has an ample supply of maps and brochures.

CAPE COD/MARTHA'S VINEYARD

Bed & Breakfast—Cape Cod
P.O. BOX 341, W. HYANNISPORT, MASSACHUSETTS 02672

Tel: **(508) 775-2772**
Best Time to Call: **9:30 AM–7:30 PM**
Coordinator: **Clark Diehl**
States/Regions Covered: **Cape Cod, Martha's Vineyard, Nantucket; Boston Area: Cape Ann, Gloucester**

Rates (Single/Double):
  Modest: **$32**   **$42**
  Average: **$40**   **$58**
  Luxury: **$60**   **$105**
Credit Cards: **AMEX, MC, VISA**
Minimum Stay: **2 nights**

It is just a little over an hour's drive from sophisticated Boston to the relaxed, quaint charm of the Cape. Year-round, you can choose from Clark's roster of 60 homes. The B&B you stay in may be a Victorian inn, a sea captain's home, or an oceanfront house. Your hosts will direct you to the restaurants and shops off the tourist trail. There is a $5 surcharge for a one-night stay. There is no charge for Clark's descriptive directory.

House Guests—Cape Cod and the Islands ✪
BOX 1881, ORLEANS, MASSACHUSETTS 02653

Tel: **(508) 896-7053**
Best Time to Call: **10 AM–4 PM**
Coordinator: **Richard Griffin**
States/Regions Covered: **Cape Cod, Martha's Vineyard, Nantucket**

Rates (Single/Double):
  Modest: **$40**   **$48–$58**
  Average: **$45**   **$59–$75**
  Luxury: **$55**   **$76–$187**
Credit Cards: **AMEX, MC, VISA**
Minimum Stay: **2 nights Memorial Day weekend–Columbus Day**

Richard's accommodations range from a simple single bedroom with shared bath to historic homes furnished with antiques. Some are on the ocean; others are in wooded country areas. There are even a few self-contained guest cottages on private estates. A seven-day vacation with stays at three B&Bs can be arranged. His descriptive directory is $3.50. There is a $15 booking fee.

Old Cape House ✪
108 OLD MAIN STREET, BASS RIVER, MASSACHUSETTS 02664

Tel: **(508) 398-1068**
Host(s): **George and Linda Arthur**
Location: **5 mi. E of Hyannis**
No. of Rooms: **6**
No. of Private Baths: **2**
Max. No. Sharing Bath: **3**
Double/pb: **$50–$60**
Double/sb: **$40–$45**
Single/sb: **$30**

Open: **May–Oct.**
Reduced Rates: **Off-season**
Breakfast: **Continental**
Pets: **No**
Children: **Welcome, over 15**
Smoking: **No**
Social Drinking: **Permitted**
Foreign Languages: **French, Italian**

This fine Greek Revival home was built in 1815 and is convenient to fine beaches, restaurants, and scenic attractions of Cape Cod. You will enjoy home-baked items at breakfast, plus the use of a spacious porch and garden. All the rooms are charmingly decorated in New England style. It's a great place to stay in the fall for visits to antique shops and craft fairs. Linda is from London, and George also lived in Europe for many years, so they know how to bring the bed-and-breakfast tradition here. There is a two-night minimum on holiday weekends and during July and August.

Old Sea Pines Inn ✪
2553 MAIN STREET, BREWSTER, MASSACHUSETTS 02631

Tel: (508) 896-6114
Host(s): **Michele and Steve Rowan**
Location: **16 mi. E of Hyannis**
No. of Rooms: **14**
No. of Private Baths: **9**
Max. No. Sharing Bath: **3**
Double/pb: **$40–$75**
Suites: **$80**
Open: **Apr.1–Nov. 30**

Reduced Rates: **Off-season**
Breakfast: **Continental**
Credit Cards: **AMEX, DC, MC, VISA**
Pets: **No**
Children: **Welcome, over 8**
Smoking: **Permitted**
Social Drinking: **Permitted**
Airport/Station Pickup: **Yes**
Foreign Languages: **German, Italian**

Originally a women's finishing school, this sprawling inn has kept many of its turn-of-the-century features, such as brass and iron beds, plus antique and wicker furniture. A breakfast of homemade specialties is served on the porch or in the sunny dining room. Located on over three acres, the inn is close to beaches, bike paths, shops, and restaurants.

Copper Beech Inn on Cape Cod ✪
497 MAIN STREET, CENTERVILLE, MASSACHUSETTS 02632

Tel: (508) 771-5488
Best Time to Call: **8:30 AM–5:30 PM**
Host(s): **Joyce Diehl**
Location: **4 mi. W of Hyannis**
No. of Rooms: **3**
No. of Private Baths: **3**
Double/pb: **$75**
Open: **All year**

Breakfast: **Full**
Credit Cards: **AMEX, MC, VISA**
Pets: **No**
Children: **Welcome, over 11**
Smoking: **Permitted**
Social Drinking: **Permitted**
Airport/Station Pickup: **Yes**

Home of the largest copper beech tree in Cape Cod, the inn is set in the heart of historic Centerville amid private estates and vintage homes. It features traditional furnishings, formal parlors, well-kept grounds with sunning areas, and a duck pond. Golf, tennis, fishing, sailing, and swimming are available nearby; Craigville Beach is less than a mile away. In summer, the Cape Cod Melody tent featuring stars of stage and screen is four miles away.

Isaiah B. Hall House ✪
152 WHIG STREET, DENNIS, MASSACHUSETTS 02638

Tel: (508) 385-9928
Best Time to Call: **8 AM–10 PM**
Host(s): **Marie and Dick Brophy**
Location: **7 mi. E of Hyannis**

No. of Rooms: **11**
No. of Private Baths: **10**
Max. No. Sharing Bath: **3**
Double/pb: **$55–$78**

MASSACHUSETTS • 287

Single/pb: **$40–$60**
Double/sb: **$46**
Single/sb: **$38**
Open: **Mar. 15–Nov. 15**
Breakfast: **Continental**
Credit Cards: **AMEX, MC, VISA**

Pets: **No**
Children: **Welcome, over 7**
Smoking: **Permitted (5 nonsmoking rooms)**
Social Drinking: **Permitted**

This Cape Cod farmhouse built in 1857 offers casual country living on the quiet, historic northside. The house is decorated in true New England style with quilts, antiques, and Oriental rugs. Four rooms have balconies and one has a fireplace. Within walking distance are the beach, good restaurants, the Cape Playhouse, and countless antique and craft shops. It is also close to freshwater swimming, bike paths, and golf.

The Penny House
P.O. BOX 238, ROUTE 6, EASTHAM, MASSACHUSETTS 02651

Tel: **(508) 255-6632**
Host(s): **Bill and Margaret Keith**
No. of Rooms: **12**
Max. No. Sharing Bath: **4**
Double/sb: **$65–$75**
Open: **All year**
Reduced Rates: **$50–$65 Sept.–June**

Breakfast: **Full**
Credit Cards: **MC, VISA**
Pets: **No**
Children: **No**
Smoking: **Permitted**
Social Drinking: **Permitted**

Back in 1751, Captain Isiah Horton built the Penny House and crowned it with a shipbuilder's bow roof. She has weathered many a storm, but this spacious cape just gets more charming. The rooms have wide-pine floors and are decorated with a blend of antiques and country accents. Your hosts provide special treats in the public room, where beautiful old wooden beams provide a sense of nostalgia. The Penny House is five minutes from National Seashore Park and just as convenient to the warm waters off Cape Cod Bay.

The Parsonage ✪
P.O. BOX 1016, 202 MAIN STREET, EAST ORLEANS, MASSACHUSETTS 02643

Tel: **(508) 255-8217**
Best Time to Call: **9 AM–9 PM**
Host(s): **Chris and Lloyd Shand**
Location: **90 mi. SE of Boston**

No. of Rooms: **6**
No. of Private Baths: **2**
Max. No. Sharing Bath: **4**
Double/pb: **$50**

Single/pb: **$45**
Double/sb: **$50**
Single/sb: **$45**
Suites: **$60**
Open: **All year**
Reduced Rates: **20%, Nov.–Apr.**

Breakfast: **Continental**
Credit Cards: **MC, VISA**
Pets: **No**
Children: **Welcome**
Smoking: **Permitted**
Social Drinking: **Permitted**

The Parsonage is located on the road to Nauset Beach, a street lined with lovely old homes of early settlers and sea captains. This spacious Cape Cod, circa 1770, has old wavy glass windows, low ceilings, and is decorated with antiques. Enjoy a homemade breakfast on a tray in your room or outside in the sunny courtyard. Cranberry muffins are the specialty of the house. The Parsonage is located between the Atlantic Ocean and Cape Cod Bay. Bike trails, restaurants, sailing, fishing, and swimming are minutes away.

The Arbor ☉
222 UPPER MAIN STREET, P.O. BOX 1628, EDGARTOWN, MARTHA'S VINEYARD, MASSACHUSETTS 02539

Tel: **(508) 627-8137**
Best Time to Call: **8 AM–8PM**
Host(s): **Peggy Hall**
Location: **7 mi. SE of Woods Hole Ferry**
No. of Rooms: **10**
No. of Private Baths: **8**
Max. No. Sharing Bath: **4**
Double/pb: **$85–$90**
Double/sb: **$70–$85**

Open: **May 1–Oct. 31**
Reduced Rates: **May 1–June 14; Sept. 16–Oct. 30**
Breakfast: **Continental**
Credit Cards: **MC, VISA**
Pets: **No**
Children: **Welcome, over 12**
Smoking: **Permitted**
Social Drinking: **Permitted**

This turn-of-the-century guest house offers island visitors a unique experience in comfort and charm. The house is walking distance from downtown, and at the same time provides the feeling of being away from it all. Relax in a hammock, enjoy tea on the porch, and retire to a cozy room filled with the smell of fresh flowers. Peggy provides setups and mixers at cocktail time, and will gladly direct you to unspoiled beaches, walking trails, sailing, fishing, and the delights of Martha's Vineyard. There's a three-night minimum stay required in season.

Captain Tom Lawrence House—1861 ✪
75 LOCUST STREET, FALMOUTH, MASSACHUSETTS 02540

Tel: (508) 540-1445 or 548-9178
Best Time to Call: 8 AM till noon
Host(s): Barbara Sabo
Location: 67 mi. S of Boston
No. of Rooms: 6
No. of Private Baths: 4
Max. No. Sharing Bath: 4
Double/pb: $58–$75
Double/sb: $45–$60
Open: All year
Reduced Rates: Off-season
Breakfast: Full
Credit Cards: MC, VISA
Pets: No
Children: Welcome, over 11
Smoking: Permitted
Social Drinking: Permitted
Airport/Station Pickup: Yes
Foreign Languages: German

Captain Lawrence was a successful whaler in the 1800s. When he retired from the sea, he built himself a town residence on Locust Street. Today, the house remains much as he left it, including the original hardwood floors, circular stairwell, high ceilings, and antique furnishings. In the morning, Barbara serves a hearty breakfast of fruit and creative entrées. Her Black Forest bread and Belgian waffles are truly special. She grinds her own flour from organically grown grain. She will gladly help you get around town—it's half a mile to the beach, a short walk to downtown Falmouth, and four miles to Woods Hole Seaport.

Palmer House Inn ✪
81 PALMER AVENUE, FALMOUTH, MASSACHUSETTS 02540

Tel: (508) 548-1230
Best Time to Call: After 2 PM
Host(s): Phyllis Niemi and Bud Peacock
Location: 1 block from Rte. 28
No. of Rooms: 8
No. of Private Baths: 8
Double/pb: $80–$95
Single/pb: $70–$85
Open: All year
Reduced Rates: Off-season
Breakfast: Full
Credit Cards: MC, VISA
Pets: No
Children: Welcome, over 14
Smoking: Permitted
Social Drinking: Permitted

Warmth and charm are evident in this turn-of-the-century Victorian home, with its stained-glass windows, soft warm wood, antiques, and collectibles. Centrally located within the Historic District, it is convenient to recreational diversions, miles of sandy beaches, ferries, and Woods Hole. Guests rave about breakfast entrées such as Pain Perdue with orange cream and Vermont maple syrup, Belgian waffles with honey butter, or Finnish pancake and strawberry soup served in the dining room on fine linen, china, and crystal. Return from your afternoon activities and enjoy a glass of lemonade in a rocker on the front porch. Spend your after-dinner hours relaxing before the fireplace or sampling theater offerings close by.

Village Green Inn ✪
40 WEST MAIN STREET, FALMOUTH, MASSACHUSETTS 02540

Tel: **(508) 548-5621**
Host(s): **Linda and Don Long**
Location: **15 mi. S of Bourne Bridge**
No. of Rooms: **5**
No. of Private Baths: **5**
Double/pb: **$80**
Suites: **$95**
Open: **All year**
Reduced Rates: **20%, Nov. 15– Memorial Day**
Breakfast: **Full**
Pets: **No**
Children: **No**
Smoking: **No**
Social Drinking: **Permitted**
Airport/Station Pickup: **Yes**

This lovely Victorian is located on Falmouth's village green. Feel free to relax on the outdoor porch or in the parlor. Four of the guest rooms have fireplaces to take the chill out of blustery evenings. Breakfast is a treat that includes hot, spiced fruit, eggs Mornay, homemade breads and muffins, and freshly ground coffee. Linda and Don look forward to pampering you with such delights as sherry, cordials, lemonade, fresh flowers, and sinfully delicious chocolates.

Wyndemere House ✪
718 PALMER AVENUE, FALMOUTH, MASSACHUSETTS 02540

Tel: **(508) 540-7069**
Best Time to Call: **Mornings; evenings**
Host(s): **Carole Railsback**
Location: **8 mi. from Rte. 28 South**
No. of Rooms: **6**
No. of Private Baths: **4**
Max. No. Sharing Bath: **4**
Double/pb: **$85**
Single/pb: **$75**
Double/sb: **$75**
Single/sb: **$65**
Suite: **$95**
Open: **May–Oct.**
Reduced Rates: **Weekly**
Breakfast: **Full**
Pets: **No**
Children: **Welcome, over 12**
Smoking: **Permitted**
Social Drinking: **Permitted**
Airport/Station Pickup: **Yes**

This Paul Revere Colonial was built at the end of the 18th century and was completely renovated in 1980. Its bright, airy rooms are filled with English furnishings, elegant antiques, and chintz accents. Guests are encouraged to make themselves at home in the reading areas and library, TV room, and on the patio. In the afternoon, tea is served on the terrace, along with coffee and sangria. Your hostess also provides setups for cocktails. In the morning such breakfast delights as eggs Benedict or apple Dutch pancakes are offered in the main dining room. Wyndemere House is nestled in a cool, wooded area off the beaten track, yet is close to downtown Falmouth and is a few minutes from two beautiful beaches. A minimum two-night stay is required.

The Coach House ○
74 SISSON ROAD, HARWICH PORT, MASSACHUSETTS 02646

Tel: **(508) 432-9452**
Host(s): **Sara and Cal Ayer**
Location: **1 mi. from Rtes. 39 and 124**
No. of Rooms: **2**
No. of Private Baths: **2**
Double/pb: **$60**
Single/pb: **$60**

Open: **Apr.–Oct.**
Breakfast: **Continental**
Credit Cards: **AMEX, MC, VISA**
Pets: **No**
Children: **No**
Smoking: **Permitted**
Social Drinking: **Permitted**

Built in 1909, the Coach House was the original barn of one of Cape Cod's old estates. In the mid-1950s the barn was fully converted into a lovely Cape Cod home. The rooms are quiet and elegant, and guests may choose from king- and queen-size beds. A breakfast of fresh fruit compote, home-baked muffins, coffee cake, or croissants is served in the dining room each morning. Enjoy three picturesque harbors, beautiful beaches, sailing, windsurfing, golf, and tennis. A 21-mile hard-surface bike trail will take you through the scenic woods and cranberry bogs to the National Seashore. Your hosts will gladly recommend shops, museums, fine restaurants, and summer theater.

The Inn on Bank Street ○
88 BANK STREET, HARWICH PORT, MASSACHUSETTS 02646

Tel: **(508) 432-3206**
Best Time to Call: **8 AM–10 PM**
Host(s): **Arky and Janet Silverio**
Location: **85 mi. S of Boston**
No. of Rooms: **6**
No. of Private Baths: **6**
Double/pb: **$50–$65**
Single/pb: **$45–$60**
Open: **Apr. 1–Nov. 30**

Reduced Rates: **Available**
Breakfast: **Continental**
Credit Cards: **MC, VISA**
Pets: **No**
Children: **Welcome, over 7**
Smoking: **Permitted**
Social Drinking: **Permitted**
Airport/Station Pickup: **Yes**
Foreign Languages: **Italian, Spanish**

This contemporary, sprawling Cape is set in a quaint old town named after an English village. The main house has a large living room and library, with a fine selection of vacation reading. Guest rooms are decorated with comfortable country-style modern pieces. In the morning, breakfast is served on the sun porch or outdoors on the shady grounds where the roses grow wild. Specialties of the house include cranberry crisp, French toast, and fresh-baked breads. The ocean is a five-minute walk from the inn, and you can bike the paved trails for a closer look at Harwich Port. Restaurants, art galleries, and a movie theater are also within walking distance.

Hawthorn Hill ✪
P.O. BOX 777, SANDWICH, MASSACHUSETTS 02563

Tel: **(508) 888-3333**
Best Time to Call: **Evenings**
Host(s): **Maxime Caron**
Location: **60 mi. S of Boston**
No. of Rooms: **2**
No. of Private Baths: **2**
Double/pb: **$60–$65**
Open: **May–Nov.**

Breakfast: **Continental**
Pets: **Sometimes**
Children: **Sometimes**
Smoking: **Permitted**
Social Drinking: **Permitted**
Airport/Station Pickup: **Yes**
Foreign Languages: **German**

This rambling English country house, off Grove Street, is set on a hill surrounded by trees, with both the conveniences of an in-town location and the pleasantness of a country setting. The property has a spring-fed pond for boating and swimming, and there is plenty of space for long walks through the woods. Inside, your hosts welcome you to large, sunny rooms, comfortably furnished. Hawthorn Hill is close to beaches, fishing, museums, and shops, and is adjacent to the Heritage Plantation. Maxime will gladly help plan sightseeing in this historic town or day trips to many nearby points of interest.

"Glen Cara"—An Irish B&B ✪
285 REDEMPTION ROCK TRAIL (Route 140), STERLING, MASSACHUSETTS 01564

Tel: **(508) 422-6678**
Best Time to Call: **8 AM–Noon**
Host(s): **Rita O'Brien**
Location: **50 mi. W of Boston**
No. of Rooms: **2**
Max. No. Sharing Bath: **4**
Double/sb: **$65**
Single/sb: **$60**

Open: **All year**
Breakfast: **Continental**
Pets: **Sometimes**
Children: **Welcome, over 10**
Smoking: **No**
Social Drinking: **Permitted**
Airport/Station Pickup: **Yes**
Foreign Languages: **French**

Rita has brought a touch of Erin to her spanking clean B&B. Located on a small, two-acre glen, it is contemporary in style and accented with Irish arts and crafts, lace curtains, and appropriate antiques. Irish soda bread made from an old family recipe is a breakfast treat. A brook for fishing and an above-ground swimming pool are pleasant diversions; fine horseback riding and cross-country ski trails are nearby. It's 10 minutes to the Mt. Wachusett Ski Area and the bird sanctuary, and Sturbridge Village and the Worcester Centrum are less than an hour's drive. Closer by are 15 antique shops.

Little Harbor Guest House ✪
20 STOCKTON SHORTCUT, WAREHAM, MASSACHUSETTS 02571

Tel: **(508) 295-6329**	Open: **All year**
Host(s): **Dennis and Ken**	Reduced Rates: **20%, Nov. 1–May 1**
Location: **20 mi. S of Plymouth**	Breakfast: **Continental**
No. of Rooms: **5**	Pets: **No**
Max. No. Sharing Bath: **4**	Children: **Welcome**
Double/sb: **$57**	Smoking: **Permitted**
Single/sb: **$47**	Social Drinking: **Permitted**
Suites: **$67**	

The Little Harbor Guest House is set on three acres surrounded by a lovely 18-hole golf course. The house is a rambling Cape Cod, dating back to 1703. The large, sunny rooms are comfortable and quiet, furnished in antiques, wicker, and lots of plants. Dennis and Ken prepare a lovely breakfast, featuring many types of homemade breads. They have bicycles to lend, a pool, and will gladly give directions to local attractions. The beach is less than a half mile away, and it's just 20 minutes to Plymouth and Hyannis.

Mulberry Bed and Breakfast
257 HIGH STREET, WAREHAM, MASSACHUSETTS 02571

Tel: **(508) 295-0684**	Reduced Rates: **15%, weekly**
Host(s): **Frances Murphy**	Breakfast: **Continental**
Location: **52 mi. S of Boston**	Pets: **No**
No. of Rooms: **3**	Children: **Welcome, over 10**
Max. No. Sharing Bath: **4**	Smoking: **No**
Double/sb: **$38–$45**	Social Drinking: **Permitted**
Open: **All year**	Airport/Station Pickup: **Yes**

Frances Murphy welcomes you to her vintage Cape Cod home, built in 1847. The house is one and a half stories and is painted white with red shutters. It is named for the mulberry tree in the yard that attracts many birds and provides shade from the summer sun. Frances has created a home-away-from-home atmosphere where guests can relax in a small living room with a piano, or join her in a larger living-dining area with fireplace. Spend the night in an Early American-style bedroom and have breakfast on the spacious private deck. Home-baked breads and muffins, casseroles, and fresh fruit are served with jams and jellies made from Frances's fruit trees. In the afternoon, snacks and cool drinks are served. Mulberry Bed and Breakfast is located in the historic part of town, ten minutes from the beach.

The Manor House
57 MAINE AVENUE, WEST YARMOUTH, MASSACHUSETTS 02673

Tel: **(508) 771-9211**
Host(s): **Sherry Braun**
Location: **1 mi. E of Hyannis**
No. of Rooms: **6**
No. of Private Baths: **6**
Double/pb: **$60–$65**
Open: **All year**

Reduced Rates: **Off-season**
Breakfast: **Continental**
Pets: **No**
Children: **Welcome, over 6**
Smoking: **No**
Social Drinking: **Permitted**

This large, white Dutch Colonial is one block from the beach on Lewis Bay. It is decorated with lovely antiques, handmade quilts, plants, and dried flower arrangements. It is close to golf, tennis, antique shops, fine restaurants, and the ferry dock, although it is in a quiet seaside area.

CENTRAL/WESTERN/SOUTHERN MASSACHUSETTS

House of Amacord ✪
1797 UPPER STREET, BUCKLAND, MASSACHUSETTS 01338

Tel: **(413) 625-2975; 625-2697**
Best Time to Call: **Evenings; weekends**
Host(s): **Janet Turley**
Location: **13 mi. from Rte. 91, Exit 26**
No. of Rooms: **3**
No. of Private Baths: **3**
Double/pb: **$58**

Single/pb: **$42**
Open: **Jan. 2–Oct. 31**
Breakfast: **Full**
Pets: **No**
Children: **No**
Smoking: **Permitted**
Social Drinking: **Permitted**

This white, center-hall Colonial (circa 1797) has a lovely screened-in porch for summer enjoyment and four fireplaces for cozy winter pleasure. Prestigious Deerfield Academy, Old Deerfield, Sturbridge Village, and the historic sights of Pioneer Valley are all close by. The University of Massachusetts, Smith, Amherst, and Williams are convenient to Janet's home. Sensational breakfast treats include stuffed croissants, mushroom paté, and special casseroles, along with fresh fruit and breakfast meats.

Chalet d'Alicia ✪
EAST WINDSOR ROAD, PERU, MASSACHUSETTS 01235

Tel: **(413) 655-8292**
Host(s): **Alice and Richard Halvorsen**
Location: **15 mi. E of Pittsfield**
No. of Rooms: **3**
Max. No. Sharing Bath: **4**
Double/sb: **$45**

Open: **All year**
Breakfast: **Full**
Pets: **Sometimes**
Children: **Welcome**
Smoking: **Permitted**
Social Drinking: **Permitted**

Chalet d'Alicia is set high in the Berkshire Mountains overlooking the majestic countryside. This Swiss chalet-style home offers a private, casual atmosphere. The large front deck is a perfect spot for reading, sunning, or chatting. Alice and Richard are proud to make everyone feel at home. For breakfast they serve homemade muffins, and jams made from local wild berries. The property has a pond and plenty of places for cross-country skiing. Tanglewood, Jacob's Pillow, and the Williamstown Theatre Festival are all within easy reach.

Perryville Inn ✪
157 PERRYVILLE ROAD, REHOBOTH, MASSACHUSETTS 02769

Tel: **(508) 252-9239**
Best Time to Call: **8 AM–10 PM**
Host(s): **Tom and Betsy Charnecki**
Location: **8 mi. E of Providence, R.I.**
No. of Rooms: **5**
No. of Private Baths: **3**
Max. No. Sharing Bath: **4**
Double/pb: **$55–$75**

Double/sb: **$40**
Open: **All year**
Breakfast: **Continental**
Credit Cards: **AMEX, MC, VISA**
Pets: **Sometimes**
Children: **Welcome**
Smoking: **Permitted**
Social Drinking: **Permitted**

This 19th-century restored Victorian, listed on the National Register of Historic Places, is located on 4½ acres featuring a quiet brook, stone walls, and shaded paths. You are welcome to use your hosts' bikes for local touring. There's a public golf course across the road. It's a short drive to antique shops, museums, and fine seafood restaurants. Don't miss a traditional New England clambake. All rooms are furnished with antiques and accented with colorful, handmade quilts. Brown University, Wheaton College, and the Rhode Island School of Design are within a 10-mile radius of the inn.

Lakeshore Bed and Breakfast ✪
94 SOUTH SHORE DRIVE, STURBRIDGE, MASSACHUSETTS 01566

Tel: (508) 347-9495
Host(s): **Paul and Jeannette Baillargeon**
Location: **50 mi. W of Boston**
No. of Rooms: **3**
Max. No. Sharing Bath: **3**
Double/sb: **$50**
Single/sb: **$45**

Open: **May 1–Oct. 31**
Breakfast: **Full**
Pets: **No**
Children: **Welcome**
Smoking: **Permitted**
Social Drinking: **Permitted**
Foreign Languages: **French**

This lakeside contemporary is on one of Massachusetts's cleanest lakes, Quacumquasit. Enjoy fishing, boating, swimming, sunbathing, and beautiful sunsets on a private beach, just steps from your room. A hearty breakfast is served on the terrace each morning. In the evening, you are welcome to use the grill and picnic tables for a barbecue. Lakeshore is four miles from Old Sturbridge Village and shopping areas. Your hosts are happy to help make sightseeing plans for you.

The Golden Goose ✪
MAIN ROAD, BOX 336, TYRINGHAM, MASSACHUSETTS 01264

Tel: **(413) 243-3008**
Best Time to Call: **8 AM–8 PM**
Host(s): **Lilja and Joseph Rizzo**
Location: **4 mi. from Mass. Tpk., Exit 2-Lee**
No. of Rooms: **5**
No. of Private Baths: **3**
Max. No. Sharing Bath: **4**
Double/pb: **$65–$75**
Single/pb: **$60–$70**

Double/sb: **$55–$65**
Single/sb: **$50–$60**
Suites: **$75–$85**
Open: **All year**
Reduced Rates: **Available**
Breakfast: **Continental**
Pets: **No**
Children: **Welcome in apt. suite**
Smoking: **Permitted**
Social Drinking: **Permitted**

The inn lies between Stockbridge and Lenox in the Berkshires. Antique beds with firm new mattresses, and washstands are in each bedroom. Lilja and Joseph serve hors d'oeuvres and drinks by the fireside in the two common rooms. In warm weather, you may play croquet, volleyball, badminton, hike the Appalachian Trail, or fish for trout in the brook across the street and barbecue it at "home." In summer, the cultural attractions of Tanglewood and Jacob's Pillow are nearby. Skiing is popular in winter. There's a two-night weekend minimum during the Tanglewood season, and a three-night minimum on holidays. A $5 surcharge is added for one-night stays.

The Wildwood Inn ✪
121 CHURCH STREET, WARE, MASSACHUSETTS 01082

Tel: **(413) 967-7798**
Best Time to Call: **5–8 PM**
Host(s): **Margaret and Geoffrey Lobenstine**
Location: **70 mi. W of Boston**
No. of Rooms: **5**
Max. No. Sharing Bath: **3**
Double/sb: **$33–$61**

Open: **All year (Nov.–Apr., weekends only)**
Reduced Rates: **10%, weekly**
Breakfast: **Full**
Pets: **No**
Children: **Welcome, over 6**
Smoking: **No**
Social Drinking: **Permitted**

Everything about this old-fashioned country home with its rambling two acres is designed to help you unwind. There's a swing on the porch, a hammock under the firs, a blazing fire in the winter, a Norman Rockwell-esque brook-fed swimming hole in the summer. Your hosts have furnished their guest rooms with heirloom quilts and American primitive antiques, all of which work to spell welcome. Homemade bread and Margaret's own peach butter and "country yummies" are included with breakfast. Sturbridge Village, Old Deerfield, and Amherst offer recreational activities that are all close by. You can stroll to the tennis court or borrow the canoe, or visit in the parlor for stimulating conversation. Margaret does her best to spoil you.

NANTUCKET

Lynda Watts Bed & Breakfast ✪
10 UPPER VESTAL STREET, NANTUCKET, MASSACHUSETTS 02554

Tel: **(617) 228-3828**
Host(s): **Lynda and David Watts**
No. of Rooms: **2**
Max. No. Sharing Bath: **4**
Double/sb: **$60**
Open: **All year**

Reduced Rates: **20%, Jan. 1–Apr. 15**
Breakfast: **Continental**
Pets: **No**
Children: **Welcome**
Smoking: **Permitted**
Social Drinking: **Permitted**

Lynda and David's 12-year-old saltbox house is located on a quiet street in a residential neighborhood, only a seven-minute walk to town. It is simply furnished and guest rooms are equipped with TVs. Weather permitting, breakfast is served on the sunny patio. A two-night minimum stay is required.

MICHIGAN

The Olde Bricke House ✪
P.O. BOX 211, ALLEN, MICHIGAN 49227

Tel: **(517) 869-2349**
Host(s): **Erma and Al Jones**
Location: **On Rte. 12**
No. of Rooms: **4**
Max. No. Sharing Bath: **4**
Double/sb: **$45**
Single/sb: **$40**

Open: **All year**
Breakfast: **Continental**
Credit Cards: **MC, VISA**
Pets: **No**
Children: **Welcome, over 13**
Smoking: **Permitted**
Social Drinking: **Permitted**

This Victorian house, built in 1873, was recently renovated by Erma and Al, whose humor and eclectic tastes are reflected in its decor. If you are an antiques buff, spend the day browsing the fabulous shops (75 at last count) that have made Allen the "Antiques Capital" of Michigan. Several lakes for boating, swimming, and fishing are nearby, and Hillsdale College is 10 miles away. You are welcome to join your hosts for afternoon refreshments on the porch or in the library or living room.

Windermere Inn ✪
747 CRYSTAL DRIVE, BEULAH, MICHIGAN, 49617

Tel: **(616) 882-7264**
Best Time to call: **1–6 PM**
Host(s): **Loralee and Bill Ludwig**
Location: **200 mi. NW of Detroit**
No. of Rooms: **4**
No. of Private Baths: **4**
Double/pb: **$65**
Open: **Apr. 1–Feb. 28**

Reduced Rates: **10%, weekly**
Breakfast: **Continental**
Credit Cards: **MC, VISA**
Pets: **No**
Children: **No**
Smoking: **Permitted**
Social Drinking: **Permitted**

Set among century-old pine trees, this many-gabled white farmhouse is delightfully decorated with antiques. Loralee and Bill put fruit and flowers in each room daily, and coffee and snacks are always available. There's a fine view of Crystal Lake, and you're close to Sleeping Bear Dunes National Lakeshore and Interlochen Arts Academy. Recreational activities are plentiful in all seasons.

Celibeth House
ROUTE 1, BOX 58A, M-77 BLANEY PARK ROAD, BLANEY PARK, MICHIGAN 49836

Tel: **(906) 283-3409**
Host(s): **Elsa Strom**
Location: **60 mi. W of MacKinaw Bridge**
No. of Rooms: **8**
No. of Private Baths: **8**
Double/pb: **$35**
Single/pb: **$30**
Open: **May 1–Dec. 1**

Reduced Rates: **10% less on 3rd night**
Breakfast: **Continental**
Credit Cards: **No**
Pets: **No**
Children: **Welcome**
Smoking: **Permitted**
Social Drinking: **Permitted**

Located on Michigan's upper peninsula, this large 24-room mansion, built in 1890, overlooks a lake. Elsa enjoys traveling and collecting antiques. She has done a lovely job of decorating the house with special mementos. A retired personnel manager, she thoroughly enjoys visiting with her guests. Gardening and reading are her pleasures.

The Calumet House ✪
1159 CALUMET AVENUE, P.O. BOX 126, CALUMET, MICHIGAN 49913

Tel: **(906) 337-1936**
Host(s): **George and Rose Chivses**
Location: **10 mi. N of Hancock-Houghton**
No. of Rooms: **2**
Max. No. Sharing Bath: **4**
Double/sb: **$25**
Single/sb: **$21**

Open: **May 15–Sept. 15**
Breakfast: **Full**
Pets: **No**
Children: **No**
Smoking: **No**
Social Drinking: **Permitted**
Airport/Station Pickup: **Yes**
Foreign Languages: **Finnish**

The Calumet House is set in a historic old mining town, known for its clean air and scenic vistas. Built in 1895, the house boasts its original woodwork and is filled with local antique furnishings. In the morning, you're in for a treat with Rose's home cooking. Breakfast specialties include English scones, pancakes, local berries in season, and homemade jam. Calumet House is within walking distance of the village, with its opera house, museum, and antique shops. Your hosts will also direct you to local hunting and fishing, as well as to places that any botanist would call paradise. It's 10 miles north of Michigan Technological University and Suomi College

Bannicks B&B ✪
4608 MICHIGAN ROAD, DIMONDALE, MICHIGAN 48821

Tel: **(517) 646-0224**
Host(s): **Pat and Jim Bannick**
Location: **5 mi. SW of Lansing**
No. of Rooms: **2**
Max. No. Sharing Bath: **3**
Double/sb: **$30**
Single/sb: **$20**

Open: **all year**
Breakfast: **Full**
Pets: **No**
Children: **Welcome**
Smoking: **No**
Social Drinking: **No**

This large ranch-style home features a stained-glass entry, nautical-style basement, and a Mona Lisa bathroom. Guest accommodations consist of comfortable bedrooms and a den-TV room. your hosts invite you to share a cup of coffee anytime. They will be happy to advise on the sights of Michigan's capital city, just five minutes away. Michigan State University is eight miles away.

Rosemont Inn
83 LAKESHORE DRIVE, P.O. BOX 541, DOUGLAS, MICHIGAN 49406

Tel: **(616) 857-2637**
Best Time to Call: **8 AM–8 PM**
Host(s): **Ric and Cathy Gillette**
Location: **10 mi. S of Holland**
No. of Rooms: **14**
No. of Private Baths: **14**
Double/pb: **$75**
Open: **All year**

Reduced Rates: **Weekly; off-season**
Breakfast: **Continental**
Credit Cards: **MC, VISA**
Pets: **No**
Children: **Welcome**
Smoking: **Permitted**
Social Drinking: **Permitted**

The Rosemont is a Victorian inn with gingerbread trim. It began receiving guests in 1886 and still maintains a tradition of country living and hospitality. The house is furnished in country prints and antiques reproductions, with fireplaces in ten of the guest rooms. On a large porch, enjoy the cool breezes from Lake Michigan, whose beaches are directly across the street. Or swim in the inn's heated pool. Your hosts will gladly supply information on boat trips, golf, and the sights of Saugatuck.

Hidden Pond Farm ✪
5975 128TH AVENUE, FENNVILLE, MICHIGAN 49408

Tel: **(616) 561-2491**
Host(s): **Edward Kennedy**
Location: **40 mi. SW of Grand Rapids**
No. of Rooms: **2**
No. of Private Baths: **2**
Double/pb: **$75–$90**
Open: **All year**

Reduced Rates: **Sun–Thurs.**
Breakfast: **Full**
Pets: **No**
Children: **Welcome, over 12**
Smoking: **Permitted**
Social Drinking: **Permitted**
Airport/Station Pickup: **yes**

Hidden Pond Farm is set on 28 acres of woods, perfect for bird-watching, hiking, and cross-country skiing. Your host designed the sprawling, 13-room house to provide for the privacy and relaxation of visitors. Seven rooms on the entry level are for the exclusive use of guests and include the bedrooms and baths, a living room with fireplace, dining room, den, kitchen, and breakfast porch. Edward Kennedy is a retired insurance executive who enjoys pleasing guests and creating an atmosphere of quiet elegance. There are no schedules, and breakfast is served when you wake up. Behind the house is a ravine with a pond where you may see a deer or two. An outdoor deck and patio are available for relaxing and taking in the sun. This lovely retreat is near the beaches on Lake Michigan, the boutiques of Saugatuck, and the winery and cider mill in Fennville.

Frankenmuth Bed & Breakfast Reservations ✪
337 TRINKLEIN STREET, FRANKENMUTH, MICHIGAN 48734

Tel: **(517) 652-8897**
Coordinator: **Beverley J. Bender**
States/Regions Covered: **Bay City, Bridgeport, Frankenmuth, Harbor Beach, Trenton**

Rates (Single/Double):
  Modest: **N/A**   **$35–$40**
  Average: **N/A**   **$40–$45**
  Luxury: **N/A**   **$45**
Credit Cards: **AMEX, MC, VISA**

Dating back to the mid-1800s, this area has a distinctive German flavor. There's a Bavarian Festival in June, Volkslaufe races in July, a Polka Festival in August, an Oktoberfest, and a shopping spree in any season at Bronners Christmas Wonderland. To assure that you feel more like a friend than a paying guest, you will receive the name and address of your host after first meeting Beverley. Instead of paying the host, payment is made directly to the reservation service. She usually escorts you to the B&B personally to make the introductions.

Wellock Inn ✪
404 SOUTH HURON AVENUE, HARBOR BEACH, MICHIGAN 48441

Tel: **(517) 479-3645**
Host(s): **Bill and Lavonne Cloutier**
Location: **125 mi. N of Detroit**
No. of Rooms: **4**
No. of Private Baths: **2**
Max. No. Sharing Bath: **4**
Double/pb: **$43**
Double/sb: **$37–$40**
Open: **All year**

Reduced Rates: **Weekly; seniors**
Credit Cards: **MC, VISA**
Breakfast: **Continental**
Pets: **Welcome**
Children: **Welcome**
Smoking: **Permitted**
Social Drinking: **Permitted**
Airport/Station Pickup: **Local marina**

Beautiful oak woodwork, antique furnishings, and the artful use of beveled glass add to the charm of Lavonne and Bill's gracious home. You may enjoy breakfast in the privacy of your room or with the other guests in the dining room. Afterward, stroll to the nearby beach, browse through local shops or historic sites, fish from the breakwall, launch your boat, or play tennis or have a picnic in the park. Or, just relax at the inn and feel free to use the kitchen, living room, porch, laundry facilities, picnic table, and barbecue.

Shadowlawn Manor ✪
84 UNION STREET, HILLSDALE, MICHIGAN 49242

Tel: **(517) 437-2367**
Host(s): **Art Young and Al Paskevich**
Location: **90 mi. SW of Detroit**
No. of Rooms: **5**
No. of Private Baths: **1**
Max. No. Sharing Bath: **4**
Double/pb: **$50**
Double/sb: **$45**
Single/sb: **$35**

Open: **All year**
Reduced Rates: **10%, Jan., Feb., Dec.; weekly; 10%, seniors**
Breakfast: **Continental**
Pets: **No**
Children: **No**
Smoking: **No**
Social Drinking: **Permitted**
Airport/Station Pickup: **Yes**

Built in 1860, Shadowlawn Manor has been restored and refurbished with your comfort in mind. Art and Al have been collecting furniture, silverware, crystal, and antique accessories for years, and they have used it all to great advantage at Shadowlawn. They will be happy to direct you to the lake, beach, golf course, or Hillsdale College's arboretum. You are welcome to relax on the screened-in porch where, in springtime, the lilacs perfume the air.

Dutch Colonial Inn ✪
560 CENTRAL AVENUE, HOLLAND, MICHIGAN 49423

Tel: **(616) 396-3664**
Best Time to Call: **After 5 PM**
Host(s): **Bob and Pat Elenbaas**
Location: **30 mi. W of Grand Rapids**
No. of Rooms: **3**
Max. No. Sharing Bath: **4**
Double/sb: **$50**

Open: **all year**
Breakfast: **Full**
Other Meals: **Available**
Pets: **No**
Children: **Welcome, over 10**
Smoking: **No**
Social Drinking: **No**
Airport/Station Pickup: **Yes**

Bob and Pat Elenbaas invite you to experience Dutch hospitality in their spacious Colonial inn. The house is set in a quiet, residential section, with a large yard and lovely sun porch. Rooms are furnished with traditional family antiques, some dating back to the 1830s. Choose from a bedroom with lovely candlewicking on the drapes, comforters, and pillow shams; a suite with Victorian furnishings and its own sitting area; or the Jenny Lind Room, with its antique beds and dusty rose accents. Breakfast specialties such as quiche, homemade rolls, and muffins are served in the formal dining room. The Elenbaases are centrally located in a beautiful city, famous for its tulip festival, original Dutch windmill, and miles of sandy beaches on Lake Michigan.

Hall House
106 THOMPSON STREET, KALAMAZOO, MICHIGAN 49007

Tel: **(616) 343-2500**
Best Time to Call: **Noon–8 PM**
Host(s): **Pamela and Terry O'Connor**
Location: **150 mi. E of Detroit**
No. of Rooms: **5**
No. of Private Baths: **3**
Max. No. Sharing Bath: **4**
Double/pb: **$63**
Single/pb: **$54**
Double/sb: **$44**

Single/sb: **$38**
Open: **All year**
Reduced Rates: **10%, weekly**
Breakfast: **Continental**
Credit Cards: **AMEX, Discover, MC, VISA**
Pets: **No**
Children: **Welcome, over 12**
Smoking: **Permitted**
Social Drinking: **Permitted**

This stately Georgian Revival Colonial, with its spacious rooms and architecturally significant details, is located midway between Chicago and Detroit. It is less than an hour from winter skiing, the Lake Michigan shore, and the Midwest's largest wine-producing region. Pamela and Terry have tastefully furnished with an artful blend of contemporary and period styles. They will be happy to assist with your plans for theater, music, or sporting events. There are several fine restaurants nearby, and they'll reserve a table for you. It's just four blocks to Western Michigan University and Kalamazoo's business district.

Seven Oaks Farm ✪
7891 HOLLISTER ROAD, LAINGSBURG, MICHIGAN 48848

Tel: **(517) 651-5598**
Host(s): **Terry and Mary Brock**
Location: **15 mi. NE of East Lansing**
No. of Rooms: **3**
Max. No. Sharing Bath: **4**
Double/sb: **$40**
Single/sb: **$20**
Open: **All year**

Breakfast: **Full**
Other Meals: **Available**
Pets: **Welcome**
Children: **Welcome (crib)**
Smoking: **Permitted**
Social Drinking: **Permitted**
Airport/Station Pickup: **Yes**

Seven Oaks is a large, comfortable home on a quiet country road. There are 100 acres to roam, a fishing pond, and ample opportunity for bird-watching, snowmobiling and cross-country skiing. The house dates back 100 years, with spacious, double-bedded rooms now newly remodeled. Guests are invited to browse in the library or relax on the screened-in porch. Nearby are country auctions, bowling, movies, golf, and museums, as well as Michigan State University.

The Stagecoach Stop ☼
0-4819 LEONARD ROAD WEST, P.O. BOX 18, LAMONT, MICHIGAN 49430

Tel: **(616) 677-3940**
Host(s): **Marcia Ashby**
Location: **3 mi. from I-96**
No. of Rooms: **3**
No. of Private Baths: **1**
Max. No. Sharing Bath: **4**
Double/pb: **$55**
Single/pb: **$50**
Double/sb: **$50**

Single/sb: **$45**
Open: **All year**
Breakfast: **Continental**
Credit Cards: **MC, VISA**
Pets: **Sometimes**
Children: **Welcome (crib)**
Smoking: **Permitted**
Social Drinking: **No**

Built in 1859, this clapboard house was a thriving stagecoach stop for many years. Its location, midway between Grand Rapids and Grand Haven, made it ideal for the weary traveler. While much has been added over time, the original section of the house remains unchanged. The decor is a blend of Early American furnishings and turn-of-the-century antiques. Guest quarters are extra large and located in a separate wing of the house. This picturesque village overlooking the Grand River has much to offer sightseers. After a day of activity, relax on the front-porch swing or inside an enclosed porch furnished in wicker and warmed by a wood stove.

Governor's Inn ☼
LEXINGTON, MICHIGAN 48450

Tel: **(313) 359-5770**
Host(s): **Jane and Bob MacDonald**
Location: **20 mi. N of Port Huron**
No. of Rooms: **3**
No. of Private Baths: **3**
Double/pb: **$40**
Single/pb: **$40**

Open: **May 1–Sept. 30**
Breakfast: **Continental**
Pets: **No**
Children: **Welcome, over 12**
Smoking: **Permitted**
Social Drinking: **Permitted**

A handsome residence built in 1859, it is located near the shore of Lake Huron. It has been refurbished to its original "summer home" style. Wicker furniture, rag rugs, iron beds, and green plants accent the light, airy decor. You can stroll to the nearby beach, browse through interesting shops, fish from the breakwater, or play golf or tennis. Jane and Bob, both educators, look forward to sharing their quaint village surroundings with you.

Vickie Van's Bed and Breakfast
5076 SOUTH LAKESHORE ROAD, LEXINGTON, MICHIGAN 48450

Tel: **(313) 359-5533**
Best Time to Call: **Mornings**
Host(s): **Vickie Van**
Location: **80 mi. N of Detroit**
No. of Rooms: **4**
No. of Private Baths: **2**
Max. No. Sharing Bath: **4**
Double/pb: **$43–$50**
Single/pb: **$38–$45**
Double/sb: **$43–$50**
Single/sb: **$38–$45**
Open: **All year**
Reduced Rates: **Weekly**
Breakfast: **Continental**
Pets: **No**
Children: **Welcome, over 11**
Smoking: **Permitted**
Social Drinking: **Permitted**

Vickie Van's is a big old white farmhouse with three porches. The house is situated on five acres right across the street from Lake Huron. The comfortable rooms are furnished with antiques, wicker, and canopy beds. Breakfast is served in the bright, colorful dining room, and includes fresh-picked berries, homemade muffins, hot croissants, served on fine linen and silver. Your hostess offers lemonade or iced tea in the afternoon. She will gladly direct you to the nearby marina, flea market, orchards, golf course, and much more.

Bed and Breakfast at Ludington ✪
2458 SOUTH BEAUNE ROAD, LUDINGTON, MICHIGAN 49431-9327

Tel: **(616) 848-9768**
Host(s): **Grace and Robert Schneider**
Location: **½ mi. from US 31**
No. of Rooms: **4**
No. of Private Baths: **2**
Max. No. Sharing Bath: **4**
Double/pb: **$49**
Single/pb: **$42**
Double/sb: **$36**
Single/sb: **$29**
Guest Cottage: **$63; sleeps 4**
Open: **All year**
Reduced Rates: **10%, after 1st night**
Breakfast: **Full**
Pets: **Welcome**
Children: **Welcome**
Smoking: **No**
Social Drinking: **Permitted**

Robert and Grace Schneider invite you to their spacious contemporary home, set on 15 acres and surrounded by trees. The house is two miles from Lake Michigan and 10 miles from two state parks. You don't have to leave the grounds to enjoy beautiful nature trails along the creek and a pond that is perfect for trout fishing in summer and ice skating in winter. Your hosts also have toboggans, snowshoes, and a snurfboard to lend. After a day of activity, relax in the hot tub or enjoy a game of darts or table tennis. A hearty breakfast featuring pancakes, sausage, fruit, and plenty of coffee is served at your convenience.

Blue Lake Lodge ⊙
9765 BLUE LAKE LODGE LANE, P.O. BOX 1, MECOSTA, MICHIGAN 49332

Tel: **(616) 972-8391**
Host(s): **Frank and Elaine Huisgen**
Location: **65 mi. NE of Grand Rapids**
No. of Rooms: **6**
Max. No. Sharing Bath: **6**
Double/sb: **$35**
Single/sb: **$30**
Open: **All year**

Reduced Rates: **10%, seniors**
Breakfast: **Continental**
Credit Cards: **MC, VISA**
Pets: **Sometimes**
Children: **Welcome (crib)**
Smoking: **No**
Social Drinking: **Permitted**
Airport/Station Pickup: **Yes**

This is a large, informal home built in 1913 and located on the shore of a beautiful lake. All lakeside activities, such as swimming, boating, and fishing, are available. It's close to restaurants, but cooking grills, guest refrigerator, and picnic tables will help you cut down on dining costs.

Raymond House Inn ⊙
111 SOUTH RIDGE STREET, M-25, PORT SANILAC, MICHIGAN 48469

Tel: **(313) 622-8800**
Host(s): **Shirley Denison**
Location: **30 mi. N of Port Huron**
No. of Rooms: **7**
No. of Private Baths: **7**
Double/pb: **$50**
Open: **May 1–Oct. 31**

Reduced Rates: **10%, seniors**
Breakfast: **Continental**
Pets: **No**
Children: **Welcome, over 12**
Smoking: **Permitted**
Social Drinking: **Permitted**

Shirley will put you right at ease in her antique-filled inn with the conveniences of today and the ambience of 1895. Each bedroom is furnished with period furniture, brightly colored spreads, and lace curtains. There's an old-fashioned parlor and a dining room where you are served breakfast. Sport fishermen and sailboat enthusiasts will enjoy this area; cultural activities, quilting bees, and the annual summer festival are longtime traditions here. There is a pottery and sculpture gallery in the inn.

Twin Gables Country Inn ⊙
900 LAKE STREET, P.O. BOX 881, SAUGATUCK, MICHIGAN 49453

Tel: **(616) 857-4346**
Best Time to Call: **Afternoons**
Host(s): **Michael and Denise Simcik**

Location: **9 mi. S of Holland**
No. of Rooms: **14**
No. of Private Baths: **14**

Double/pb: **$49–$89**
Open: **All year**
Reduced Rates: **$34–$68, off-season**
Breakfast: **Continental**
Credit Cards: **MC, VISA**
Pets: **No**

Children: **Welcome, over 12**
Smoking: **Permitted**
Social Drinking: **Permitted**
Airport/Station Pickup: **Yes**
Foreign Languages: **French, Italian, Maltese**

Built in 1865, the inn, a registered State Historic Site, overlooks Lake Kalamazoo. The guest rooms are attractively furnished with wicker, brass, and antiques. The embossed tin ceilings add to the charm. In summer, guests enjoy the outdoor pool; in all seasons the indoor hot tub is appreciated. It's a short walk to the beach, marinas, museum, and theater. There is a two-night weekend minimum May 1 through Labor Day. Michael and Denise specialize in old-fashioned hospitality.

Rummel's Tree Haven ✪
41 NORTH BECK STREET, M-25, SEBEWAING, MICHIGAN 48759

Tel: **(517) 883-2450**
Best Time to Call: **Afternoons; evenings**
Host(s): **Carl and Erma Rummel**
Location: **28 mi. NE of Bay City**
No. of Rooms: **2**
Max. No. Sharing Bath: **4**
Double/sb: **$40**

Single/sb: **$30**
Open: **All year**
Breakfast: **Full**
Pets: **Sometimes**
Children: **Welcome (crib)**
Smoking: **Permitted**
Social Drinking: **Permitted**
Airport/Station Pickup: **Yes**

A tree grows right through the porch and roof of this charming old home that was built by the Beck family in 1878. Guests can relax in large, airy rooms furnished with twin beds and comfortable family pieces. City dwellers are sure to enjoy the small-town friendliness and the quiet of the countryside. Saginaw Bay offers fine fishing, hunting, boating, bird-watching, or just plain relaxing. Carl and Erma offer color TV, videocassettes, and the use of the barbecue and refrigerator. They love having company and will do all they can to make you feel welcome and relaxed.

The Victorian Villa Guesthouse ✪
601 NORTH BROADWAY STREET, UNION CITY, MICHIGAN 49094

Tel: **(517) 741-7383**
Host(s): **Ron Gibson**
Location: **20 mi. S of Battle Creek**
No. of Rooms: **8**

No. of Private Baths: **6**
Max. No. Sharing Bath: **4**
Double/pb: **$70–$75**
Single/pb: **$65–$70**

Double/sb: **$60**
Single/sb: **$55**
Open: **All year**
Breakfast: **Full**
Credit Cards: **MC, VISA**

Pets: **No**
Children: **Welcome**
Smoking: **No**
Social Drinking: **Permitted**
Airport/Station Pickup: **Yes**

The Victorian Villa is a 19th-century estate house furnished with antiques. Guests may choose from eight private chambers, all elegantly appointed. Chilled champagne, wine, cheese, and a private "tea-for-two" can be arranged. Fancy chocolates, a specialty of the house, are placed on the pillows at night. Your host will help make your visit as sparkling as you like, directing you to summer theater, museums, antique shops, and restaurants. Ask Ron about the special "getaway" weekends, including cross-country skiing, Sherlock Holmes mystery themes, a Victorian Christmas, and fun-filled "Summer-Daze."

Villa Hammer ✪
3133 BENSTEIN, WALLED LAKE, MICHIGAN 48088

Tel: **(313) 624-1071**
Best Time to Call: **Evenings**
Host(s): **Veronica and Reinhold Hammer**
Location: **5 mi. N of Novi**
No. of Rooms: **1**
No. of Private Baths: **1**
Double/pb: **$45**

Single/pb: **#35**
Open: **All year**
Reduced Rates: **10%, weekly**
Breakfast: **Full**
Pets: **Sometimes**
Children: **Welcome, over 12**
Smoking: **No**
Social Drinking: **Permitted**

A Tudor house set on three secluded acres on the Huron River, the house is furnished in a contemporary fashion accented with lots of plants. Veronica and Reinhold invite you to relax in the hot tub and sauna. They offer a hearty breakfast; waffles are the house specialty. The Hammers are happy to acquaint you with the delights of the Lake Region and its many recreational activities. The Villa Hammer is 20 miles from Greenfield Village and Ann Arbor.

Williamston Bed and Breakfast ✪
3169 SOUTH WILLIAMSTON ROAD, WILLIAMSTON, MICHIGAN 48895

Tel: **(517) 655-1061**
Best Time to Call: **Mornings; evenings**
Host(s): **Coleen Stone**

Location: **18 mi. E of Lansing**
No. of Rooms: **3**
No. of Private Baths: **1**

Max. No. Sharing Bath: **4**
Double/pb: **$55**
Double/sb: **$45**
Single/sb: **$38**
Open: **All year**
Breakfast: **Continental**

Other Meals: **Available**
Credit Cards: **MC, VISA**
Pets: **No**
Children: **Welcome**
Smoking: **Permitted**
Social Drinking: **Permitted**

Colleen Stone welcomes you to her 1916 farmhouse located at the edge of historic Williamston. This is a town filled with craftsmen, and your hostess is no exception. Colleen's basketry and primitive country landscapes accent each room. The bedrooms are decorated with antique beds and matching wood dressers, spanking white quilts and curtains. The breakfast specialty of the house is bran bread served with plenty of fresh coffee. In the afternoon wine and cheese can be enjoyed by the living room fire or outside on the porch. Antique dealers, shops, and fine restaurants are within walking distance of the house.

MINNESOTA

Bed & Breakfast Registry Ltd.
P.O. BOX 80174, ST. PAUL, MINNESOTA 55108

Tel: **(612) 646-4238**
Best Time to Call: **9 AM–5 PM**
Coordinator: **Gary Winget**
States/Regions Covered: **Statewide and national**

Rates (Single/Double):
  Modest: **$25** $30
  Average: **$40** $45
  Luxury: **$85** $155
Credit Cards: **MC, VISA**

The Twin City attractions of the Guthrie Theater, Walker Art Center, Art Institute, Omni Theater, and Science Center attract visitors from all over the country. There are delightful urban accommodations on Gary's roster, as well as more rural B&Bs for quiet serenity. He will be happy to offer vacation packages for your entire itinerary throughout North America. There is a $6 surcharge for a one-night stay.

Gabrielson's B&B
RURAL ROUTE 1, BOX 269, DASSEL, MINNESOTA 55325

Tel: **(612) 275-3609**
Best Time to Call: **Evenings**
Host(s): **Elaine and Don Gabrielson**
Location: **65 mi. W of Minneapolis**
No. of Rooms: **1**
Max. No. Sharing Bath: **3**
Double/sb: **$42**
Single/sb: **$37**
Open: **All year**
Breakfast: **Continental**
Pets: **Sometimes**
Children: **Welcome, over 9**
Smoking: **No**
Social Drinking: **Permitted**

Perched on a hilltop, this 1910 white clapboard farmhouse, decorated in Early American style, overlooks a private lake. You are welcome to use the paddleboat for getting to the little island, where you can picnic. Or, try your hand at archery, trap shooting, or pond fishing. Elaine and Don are busy raising corn and beans but they'll happily arrange a farm tour of Meeker County. Wine, cheese, and rolls are stocked in the guest refrigerator. The University of Minnesota is nearby. A hot tub and central air-conditioning add to your comfort.

Glenview B&B
RR #1, GLENVIEW, GARVIN, MINNESOTA 56132

Tel: **(507) 629-4808**
Best Time to Call: **6–8 AM; 5:30–9 PM**
Host(s): **Caryl Keith and Charles Reinert**
Location: **166 mi. SW of Minneapolis**
No. of Rooms: **2**
No. of Private Baths: **2**
Double/pb: **$36**
Single/pb: **$31**
Suites: **$36–$41**
Open: **All year**
Breakfast: **Continental**
Other Meals: **Available**
Pets: **Sometimes**
Children: **Welcome (crib)**
Smoking: **No**
Social Drinking: **Permitted**
Airport/Station Pickup: **Yes**

A local architect designed this cedar-sided home as a modern prairie retreat. It is set on 100 acres, with woods and open spaces to hike, ski, bike, and explore. A two-story stone fireplace is the showpiece of the gathering room, where you can relax and enjoy a hot drink. Choose from a guest room with queen-size feather bed, country furnishings, and a private entrance or a spacious suite with king-size water bed, plush carpeting, and modern furnishings. Your hosts offer fresh baked muffins, breads, gourmet coffee, and local honey on the private deck each morning, and will gladly supply other meals with advance notice. Glenview is within easy reach of lakes, antique stores, horseback riding, and Southwest Minnesota State University.

Red Gables Inn
403 NORTH HIGH STREET, LAKE CITY, MINNESOTA 55041

Tel: **(612) 345-2605**
Host(s): **Bill and Bonnie Saunders**
Location: **60 mi. SE of Twin Cities**
No. of Rooms: **4**
No. of Private Baths: **2**
Double/pb: **$68**
Single/pb: **$63**
Double/sb: **$48**
Single/sb: **$43**
Open: **All year**

Reduced Rates: **Available**
Breakfast: **Full**
Other Meals: **Available**
Credit Cards: **MC, VISA**
Pets: **No**
Children: **Welcome, over 13**
Smoking: **Permitted**
Social Drinking: **Permitted**
Airport/Station Pickup: **Yes**

Red Gables Inn is located in the Hiawatha Valley on the shores of Lake Pepin. The inn was built in 1865 by a wealthy merchant and is a mixture of Italianate and Greek Revival styles. The original pine floors, white-pine woodwork, and large windows have been carefully restored; and each bedroom has an old-fashioned iron, brass, or walnut bed, antique wood wardrobe, Victorian wall coverings, and ceiling fan. A breakfast buffet of fruit specialties, cheeses, home-baked breads, quiches, eggs, jams, and coffee is served on the screened-in porch or in the fireside dining room, and hors d'oeuvres are served in the parlor. Your hosts are also happy to assist with gourmet picnic lunches, chilled champagne in your room, and reservations for dining. They have bicycles to lend for exploring the nearby marina, antique shops, and nature trails.

Carrolton Country Inn & Cottage
ROUTE 2, BOX 139, LANESBORO, MINNESOTA 55949

Tel: **(507) 467-2257**
Best Time to Call: **Evenings**
Host(s): **Charles and Gloria Ruen**
Location: **35 mi. SE of Rochester**
No. of Rooms: **4**
No. of Private Baths: **2**
Max. No. Sharing Bath: **4**
Double/sb: **$45**
Single/sb: **$35**
Separate Guest Cottage: **$15 per person; sleeps 9**

Suites: **$50–$55**
Open: **All year**
Reduced Rates: **$5 less Sun.–Thurs.; weekly**
Breakfast: **Full**
Pets: **Welcome (in kennel)**
Children: **Welcome**
Smoking: **No**
Social Drinking: **Permitted**
Airport/Station Pickup: **Yes**
Foreign Languages: **Scandinavian**

Charles and Gloria Ruen welcome you to their country farmhouse, circa 1882. Nestled among the hills in an open valley, this is the perfect spot to enjoy the fresh air and the changing of the seasons. The house is decorated, country style, with antiques and still boasts the original milk-painted woodwork, dumbwaiter in the butler's pantry, and the old potbelly stove. Homemade muffins, jams, and plenty of wholesome cereal, eggs, meats, and fruit are served at breakfast, and snacks are offered later in the day. Antique stores, craft shops, a winery, and the largest state fish hatchery are nearby. Hiking, biking, fishing, canoeing, and cross-country skiing can all be enjoyed within steps of the front door.

Creekside Bed & Breakfast ✪
P.O. BOX 19164, MINNEAPOLIS, MINNESOTA 55419

Tel: **(612) 922-9142**
Host(s): **John and Jeanne Banovetz**
Location: **1½ mi. from I-35W, Diamond Lake Exit**
No. of Rooms: **2**
No. of Private Baths: **1**
Max. No. Sharing Bath: **4**
Double/pb: **$40**
Single/pb: **$30**
Double/sb: **$35**
Single/sb: **$25**
Open: **All year**
Reduced Rates: **Weekly; family**
Breakfast: **Full**
Pets: **No**
Children: **Welcome**
Smoking: **Permitted**
Social Drinking: **Permitted**
Airport/Station Pickup: **Yes**

This Country-French brick and stucco three-story home is located within minutes of the Walker Art Center, Guthrie Theater, antique shops, lakes, recreational sports, and Minnehaha Falls. You are welcome to relax in the living room, which features a cozy, book-lined window seat, fireplace, piano, and several antique pieces. The French doors lead to a screened porch. Breakfast is served in the formal dining room and features homemade breads, jams, fresh fruit, and granola. You are welcome to use the laundry facilities. John and Jeanne graciously offer afternoon snacks.

Evelo's Bed & Breakfast ✪
2301 BYRANT AVENUE SOUTH, MINNEAPOLIS, MINNESOTA 55405

Tel: **(612) 374-9656**
Best Time to Call: **After 4 PM**
Host(s): **David and Sheryl Evelo**
No. of Rooms: **4**
Max. No. Sharing Bath: **6**
Double/sb: **$30–$35**
Single/sb: **$20–25**

Open: **All year**
Breakfast: **Full**
Pets: **No**
Children: **Welcome**
Smoking: **Permitted**
Social Drinking: **Permitted**

Located in the historic Lowry Hill East neighborhood, this 1837 Victorian has one of the best-preserved interiors in the area and is furnished with fine period pieces. David and Sheryl are both school-teachers. Breakfast often features quiche or egg casseroles. The house is within walking distance of the Guthrie Theater and the Walker Art Center.

Red Pine Log B&B ✪
ROUTE 2, BOX 154, NORTH BRANCH, MINNESOTA 55056

Tel: **(612) 583-3226**
Best Time to Call: **After 5 PM; weekends**
Host(s): **Lowell and Gloria Olson**
Location: **45 mi. N of St. Paul**
No. of Rooms: **3**
No. of Private Baths: **1**
Max. No. Sharing Bath: **4**
Double/pb: **$69**
Double/sb: **$69**

Single/sb: **$60**
Open: **All year**
Reduced Rates: **10%, weekly; Mar.– Apr.**
Breakfast: **Full**
Pets: **No**
Children: **Welcome, over 12**
Smoking: **No**
Social Drinking: **Permitted**

If Abe Lincoln had known log homes could look like this, he would have had second thoughts about heading for the White House! Lowell Olson handcrafted this lodge-style home in 1985. His professional training as a log home designer is obvious from the exposed logs and trusses throughout the house. Loft bedrooms are richly paneled and feature country furnishings, skylights, ceiling fans, and a balcony. Your hosts invite you for wine and cheese in the living room, which boasts a 26-foot-high ceiling and an antique parlor stove. You will find the kitchen an equally cozy place with its antique harvest table and ash cabinets. Here you can relax over Gloria's homemade breads and jams, served with plenty of fresh coffee. The Olsons have 30 acres for you to explore, and they are within easy reach of downhill skiing, Taylors Falls, and Wild River State Park.

Canterbury Inn Bed & Breakfast ✪
723 SECOND STREET S.W., ROCHESTER, MINNESOTA 55902

Tel: **(507) 289-5553**
Host(s): **Mary Martin and Jeffrey Van Sant**
Location: **90 mi. SE of Minneapolis**
No. of Rooms: **4**
No. of Private Baths: **4**
Double/pb: **$65**
Single/pb: **$55**
Open: **All year**
Breakfast: **Full**
Credit Cards: **MC, VISA**
Pets: **No**
Children: **Sometimes**
Smoking: **Permitted**
Social Drinking: **Permitted**
Airport/Station Pickup: **Yes**
Foreign Languages: **Italian**

This is a Victorian structure, just three blocks from the Mayo Clinic, with polished hardwood floors, stained-glass windows, and a cozy fireplace complete with carved mantel. Lace curtains and eclectic furnishings give it an air in keeping with its age. Enjoy games, music, and conversation in the parlor. Breakfast is served in the formal dining room and may include such delicious fare as eggs Benedict and German apple pancakes. Afternoon tea at 5:30 generally lingers into the evening.

Chatsworth Bed and Breakfast ✪
984 ASHLAND AVENUE, ST. PAUL, MINNESOTA 55104

Tel: **(612) 227-4288**
Best Time to Call: **Noon–5 PM**
Host(s): **Donna and Earl Gustafson**
Location: **½ mi. from I-94**
No. of Rooms: **5**
No. of Private Baths: **2**
Max. No. Sharing Bath: **4**
Double/pb: **$85**

Single/pb: **$75**
Double/sb: **$52–58**
Single/sb: **$42–48**
Open: **All year**
Reduced Rates: **Weekly**
Breakfast: **Continental**

Pets: **No**
Children: **Welcome**
Smoking: **No**
Social Drinking: **Permitted**
Airport/Station Pickup: **Yes**

This spacious 1902 Victorian is located on a large corner lot surrounded by maple and basswood trees. The setting is quiet and residential, but is just a few blocks from shops, restaurants, and the governor's mansion. Guest rooms are decorated in international motifs and are located on a separate floor from your hosts' quarters. The Victorian Room features a handcarved wood bed, floral rug, lace curtains, and antiques, while the Scandinavian Room uses pine furnishings, white curtains, and matching spread to create a light and airy feeling. Guests may prefer the room with a four-poster bed and private double whirlpool bath, or the one with Afro-Asian furnishings, whirlpool bath, and adjoining porch. The Gustafsons serve breakfast in a beautifully paneled formal dining room. They also invite you to relax in the living room, where you may enjoy the library, the piano, and a roaring fire.

Chase's Bed & Breakfast
508 NORTH HURON, SPRING VALLEY, MINNESOTA 55975

Tel: **(507) 346-2850**
Host(s): **Bob and Jeannine Chase**
Location: **26 mi. S of Rochester**
No. of Rooms: **5**
No. of Private Baths: **2**
Max. No. Sharing Bath: **3**
Double/pb: **$50**
Single/pb: **$50**
Double/sb: **$35**
Single/sb: **$30**

Open: **Feb.–Dec.**
Reduced Rates: **15%, weekly**
Breakfast: **Full**
Credit Cards: **MC, VISA**
Pets: **No**
Children: **Sometimes**
Smoking: **No**
Social Drinking: **Permitted**
Airport/Station Pickup: **Yes**

William H. Strong built this Second Empire–style home in 1879 for $8,000. At the time, it was considered to be the most handsome home in the county. Over the years, the house has been an office, motel, and rest home, but is now listed on the National Register of Historic Places. Guests will find elegant rooms furnished in period antiques, many of which are for sale. Bob and Jeannine serve a hearty breakfast and offer snacks and setups in the evening. Nearby activities include swimming, tennis, golf, trout fishing, and hiking. Chase's is 18 miles from the airport and 28 miles from the Mayo Clinic. The Amish area is nearby.

Kings Oakdale Park Guest House ✪
6933 232 AVENUE N.E., STACY, MINNESOTA 55079

Tel: **(612) 462-5598**
Host(s): **Donna and Charles Solem**
Location: **38 mi. N of St. Paul**
No. of Rooms: **3**
No. of Private Baths: **2**
Double/pb: **$28**
Single/pb: **$25**
Double/sb: **$26**
Single/sb: **$23**

Suites: **$28**
Open: **All year**
Breakfast: **Continental**
Pets: **Sometimes**
Children: **No**
Smoking: **Permitted**
Social Drinking: **Permitted**
Foreign Languages: **French**

This comfortable home is situated on four landscaped acres on the banks of Typo Creek. The picinc tables, volleyball net, and horseshoe game are sure signs of a hospitable country place. It is a serene retreat for people on business trips to the Twin Cities. The Wisconsin border and the scenic St. Croix River, where boat trips are offered, are minutes from the house. Charles and Donna will direct you to the most reasonable restaurants in town. For late snacks, refrigerators in the bedrooms are provided.

MISSISSIPPI

- Holly Springs
- Columbus
- Vicksburg
- Port Gibson
- Natchez
- Jackson
- Meridian
- Brookhaven
- Woodville

Lincoln, Ltd. Bed & Breakfast—Mississippi Reservation Service ✪
DEPT. T, P.O. BOX 3479, MERIDIAN, MISSISSIPPI 39303-3479

Tel: **(601) 482-5483**
Best Time to Call: **9 AM–4:30 PM**
Coordinator: **Barbara Lincoln Hall**
States/Regions Covered: **Aberdeen, Brookhaven, Columbus, Como, Holly Springs, Jackson, Meridian, Natchez, Oxford, Mississippi Gulf Coast, Port Gibson, Vicksburg**

Rates (Single/Double):
 Average: $45–$65 $55–$65
 Luxury: $65–$105 $65–$140
Credit Cards: **MC, VISA**

For the traveling business person or for the vacationer, a stay with one of Barbara's hosts offers a personal taste of the finest Southern hospitality. All rooms have private baths. Mississippi abounds with historic-house tours, called "pilgrimages," in March and April, and Natchez and Vicksburg have similar pilgrimages in autumn. In May, Meridian is host to the Jimmie Rodgers Festival. There's a $3.50 charge for her descriptive directory.

Hamilton Place ✪
105 EAST MASON AVENUE, HOLLY SPRINGS, MISSISSIPPI 38635

Tel. (601) 252-4368	Open: **All year**
Host(s): **Linda and Jack Stubbs**	Breakfast: **Full**
Location: **35 mi. SE of Memphis, TN**	Credit Cards: **MC, VISA**
No. of Rooms: 3	Pets: **No**
No. of Private Baths: 3	Children: **Welcome**
Double/pb: $65	Smoking: **Permitted**
Single/pb: $50	Social Drinking: **Permitted**
Guest cottage: $75	Airport/Station Pickup: **Yes**

On the National Historic Register, this antebellum home, circa 1838, is furnished with heirloom antiques. In fact, Linda and Jack have a delightful antique shop on the premises featuring furniture, china, and cut glass. Breakfast can be enjoyed on the veranda or in the garden gazebo. You'll love the taste of the homemade biscuits with strawberry or honey-lemon butter. You are welcome to use the sauna or swimming pool.

Oak Square Plantation ✪
1207 CHURCH STREET, PORT GIBSON, MISSISSIPPI 39150

Tel: (601) 437-4350 or 437-5771	Single/pb: $50–$60
Best Time to Call: **Mornings; evenings**	Open: **All year**
Host(s): **Mr. and Mrs. William D. Lum**	Breakfast: **Full**
Location: **On Hwy. 61 between Natchez and Vicksburg**	Credit Cards: **AMEX, MC, VISA**
	Pets: **No**
No. of Rooms: 8	Children: **Welcome**
No. of Private Baths: 8	Smoking: **Permitted**
Double/pb: $65–$75	Social Drinking: **Permitted**

Port Gibson is the town that Union General Ulysses S. Grant said was "too beautiful to burn." Oak Square is the largest and most palatial antebellum mansion (circa 1850) in Port Gibson, and is listed on the National Historic Register. The guest rooms are all furnished with family heirlooms, and most have canopied beds. Guests will enjoy the courtyard, gazebo, and beautiful grounds. A chairlift for upstairs rooms is available. You will enjoy the delightful Southern breakfast and tour of the mansion. Your hosts offer complimentary wine, tea, or coffee, and will enlighten you on the many historic attractions in the area. Oak Square has been awarded a four-star rating by AAA.

Square Ten Inn ✪
242 DEPOT STREET, P.O. BOX 371, WOODVILLE, MISSISSIPPI 39669

Tel: **(601) 888-3993**
Host(s): **Elizabeth M. Treppendahl**
Location: **35 mi. S of Natchez**
No. of Rooms: **3**
No. of Private Baths: **3**
Double/pb: **$34**
Suites: **$39.50**

Open: **All year**
Reduced Rates: **25%, 5-day stay**
Breakfast: **Continental**
Pets: **No**
Children: **Welcome, over 6**
Smoking: **Permitted**
Social Drinking: **Permitted**

This inn is an 1830 town house listed on the National Register of Historic Places. It features a New Orleans-style courtyard and antique furnishings. Other amenities include a stocked breakfast pantry, complimentary wine, and fresh fruit. Woodville was chosen by Harvard University as the city best typifying the Old South in appearance, customs, and traditions. Rosemont, the boyhood home of Jefferson Davis, is nearby.

MISSOURI

Ozark Mountain Country B&B Service ✪
BOX 295, BRANSON, MISSOURI 65616

Tel: **(417) 334-4720; 5077**
Best Time to Call: **5–10 PM**
Coordinators: **Linda Johnson, Kay Cameron**
States/Regions Covered: **Missouri—Branson, Brighton, Camdenton, Hollister, Kimberling City, Rogersville; Arkansas—Eureka Springs; Oklahoma—Marionville, Tulsa**

Rates (Single/Double):
  Modest: **$30–$35** **$30–$35**
  Average: **$40–$50** **$40–$50**
  Luxury: **$55** **$55–$80**
Credit Cards: **MC, VISA (5% surcharge)**

Linda and Kay will send you a complimentary copy of their descriptive listing of 33 homes, so you can select the host of your choice; they'll take care of making your reservation. They would appreciate your sending them a self-addressed, stamped envelope.

Borgman's Bed & Breakfast ✪
ARROW ROCK, MISSOURI 65320

Tel: **(816) 837-3350**
Best Time to Call: **7–9 AM**
Host(s): **Helen and Kathy Borgman**
Location: **100 mi. E of Kansas City**
No. of Rooms: **4**
Max. No. Sharing Bath: **4**
Double/sb: **$35–$40**
Single/sb: **$30**

Open: **All year**
Reduced Rates: **10%, 3 nights**
Breakfast: **Continental**
Other Meals: **Dinner (winter only)**
Pets: **Sometimes**
Children: **Welcome**
Smoking: **No**
Social Drinking: **Permitted**

This 1860 home is spacious and comfortable, and it is furnished with cherished family pieces. Helen is a seamstress, artisan, and baker. Wait till you taste her fresh breads! Daughter Kathy is a town tour guide, so you will get firsthand information on this National Historic Landmark town at the beginning of the Santa Fe Trail. A fine repertory theater, the Lyceum, is open in summer. Craft shops, antique stalls, and the old country store are fun places to browse in. Good restaurants are within walking distance.

Mansion Hill Country Inn
MANSION HILL DRIVE, BONNE TERRE, MISSOURI 63628

Tel: **(314) 731-5003**
Best Time to Call: **9 AM–8 PM**
Host(s): **Doug and Cathy Goergens**
Location: **60 mi. S of St. Louis**
No. of Rooms: **7**
No. of Private Baths: **3**
Max. No. Sharing Bath: **4**
Double/pb: **$60–$80**
Double/sb: **$60**

Single/sb: **$60**
Open: **All year**
Breakfast: **Continental**
Other Meals: **Available**
Credit Cards: **AMEX, MC, VISA**
Pets: **No**
Children: **Welcome**
Smoking: **Permitted**
Social Drinking: **Permitted**

The president of the St. Joseph Lead Company built this 32-room mansion in the early 1900s. The grounds span 130 acres, including a stocked fishing lake and nature and ski trails. Antiques from both Spain and New Orleans, plus nautical artifacts, complement the Victorian style of the rooms. In summer, enjoy a glass of wine in the garden with its 45-mile view of the Ozark foothills. On winter nights, guests gather around the fire at Goosby's Pub, named in honor of the family goose. You don't have to leave the grounds to enjoy chateaubriand, blackened shrimp, and pecan pie. A four-star restaurant on the premises will surely please all gourmets. It is just four blocks from the house to Bonne Terre Mine, the largest manmade cavern in the world. Guests are also welcome to golf at the local PGA course, take a carriage ride, or take a walking tour of the mine.

Country Gardens B&B ✪
P.O. BOX 537, LAKESHORE DRIVE, BRANSON, MISSOURI 65616

Tel: **(417) 334-6262**
Host(s): **Bob and Pat Cameron**
Location: **39 mi. from I-44**
No. of Rooms: **3**
No. of Private Baths: **3**
Double/pb: **$45**
Single/pb: **$40**
Guest Cottage: **$55, sleeps 4**
Suites: **$80**

Open: **All year**
Reduced Rates: **20%, Nov. 1–Apr. 1**
Breakfast: **Full**
Credit Cards: **MC, VISA**
Pets: **No**
Children: **Welcome (crib)**
Smoking: **Permitted**
Airport/Station Pickup: **Yes**

A parklike setting of gardens and a waterfall surround this wood-frame-and-rock home, located on beautiful Lake Taneycomo. The Camerons have a variety of accommodations with private entrances. The Rose Suite consists of three rooms and features a large bathroom spa. The Bittersweet Room is decorated with antiques and has a private deck overlooking the water. Dogwood has a single whirlpool tub and kitchen for those who like to prepare light meals. Breakfast specialties such as waffles with strawberries, and hot biscuits with eggs are served in the garden room overlooking the garden. Bob and Pat invite you to swim in the pool and enjoy a picnic under the trees. They say the best trout fishing around is right on the lake, and they have boats and fishing docks for anglers. Music lovers will be glad to know that there are 22 different country music shows in the area.

Lakeside Guest House ✪
R.R. 2, BOX 41, NORMAC, CAMDENTON, MISSOURI 65020

Tel: **(314) 346-3767**
Best Time to Call: **Evenings**
Host(s): **Virginia Dyck**
Location: **170 mi. SE of Kansas City**
No. of Rooms: **2**
No. of Private Baths: **2**
Double/pb: **$40**

Single/pb: **$35**
Open: **May 1–Oct. 31**
Breakfast: **Continental**
Pets: **No**
Children: **No**
Smoking: **No**
Social Drinking: **Permitted**

Virginia's lovely home is a bilevel, modified A-frame just 50 feet from the Lake of the Ozarks, with cathedral ceilings and many glass doors opening onto the patio and deck. You will be lulled to sleep by the sound of lapping water. HaHa Tonka Ruins and Trails, Bridal Cave, country music shows, antique shops, and many fine restaurants are all close by.

Ramblewood Bed and Breakfast O
402 PANORAMIC DRIVE, CAMDENTON, MISSOURI 65020

Tel: (314) 346-3410 or (816) 479-5698
Best Time to Call: **After 5 PM**
Host(s): **Mary Massey**
Location: **90 mi. S of Columbia**
No. of Rooms: **2**
Max. No. Sharing Bath: **4**
Double/sb: **$40**

Single/sb: **$35**
Open: **Apr. 15–Oct. 31**
Breakfast: **Full**
Pets: **Sometimes**
Children: **No**
Smoking: **No**
Social Drinking: **Permitted**

Ramblewood is a pilgrim-red home with white trim. Set on a quiet, wooded lot, it has the feel of an English country cottage. Spend the night in an attractive, comfortable room and awaken to breakfast served on a sunny deck. Ham-and-cheese omelets and homemade breads are specialties of the house. The inn is minutes from Lake of the Ozarks, HaHa Tonka State Park and Castle, and antique shops, malls, and restaurants to suit any taste. After a busy day, enjoy a cool drink on the porch.

Brewer's Maple Lane Farms B&B O
RR 1, CARTHAGE, MISSOURI 64836

Tel:(417) 358-6312
Best Time to Call: **6–10 PM**
Host(s): **Arch and Renee Brewer**
Location: **4 mi. from Rte. 96, Exit 10**
No. of Rooms: **4**
Max. No. Sharing Bath: **4**
Double/pb: **$40**
Guest Cottage: **$60, sleeps 4**
Open: **May 1–Dec. 15**

Reduced Rates: **15%, weekly**
Breakfast: **Full**
Other Meals: **Available**
Pets: **Sometimes**
Children: **Welcome (crib)**
Smoking: **Permitted**
Social Drinking: **No**
Airport/Station Pickup: **Yes**

Built in 1900, this stone Victorian with its red tile roof is situated on farm property encompassing 676 acres. The reception parlor, dining room, and stairway are oak-paneled. Each of the 200 stair rails in the banister was hand turned, and one can see from the main floor up to the third. A climb to the ballroom on the third floor will reward you with views of the 22-acre lake surrounded by trees. The rooms are large and comfortable, furnished with many family heirlooms. Bird's-eye maple was used in the woodwork and Italian marble in the fireplaces. Facilities include fishing ponds, game hunting, farm and exotic animals, a playground, and a picnic area. Carthage hosts a country or craft fair almost every month of the year.

The Fountains ✪
12610 BLUE RIDGE, GRANDVIEW, MISSOURI 64030

Tel: **(816) 763-6260**
Best Time to Call: **9 AM–9 PM**
Host(s): **Sally J. Stewart**
Location: **1½ mi. W of Rte. 71**
No. of Rooms: **4**
Max. No. Sharing Bath: **4**
Double/sb: **$35**
Single/sb: **$30**

Open: **Jan. 11–Dec. 9**
Reduced Rates: **15%, weekly; 10% Tues.–Thurs.; 15%, seniors**
Breakfast: **Continental**
Pets: **Sometimes**
Children: **Welcome, over 9**
Smoking: **Permitted**
Social Drinking: **Permitted**

Sally's home is convenient to the Truman Library and home, the Nelson-Atkins Art Gallery, Starlight Theatre, Worlds of Fun park, and the famous plaza of Kansas City. The guest quarters has its own private entrance, dining room with fireplace, and kitchen. You are welcome to use the patio, barbecue, and gazebo. Sally enjoys having guests, and her good humor and warm hospitality will make you feel welcome immediately.

Lingerlong ✪
RR 3, BOX 338-D, GRAVOIS MILLS, MISSOURI 65037

Tel: **(314) 372-2481**
Best Time to Call: **8 AM**
Host(s): **Carl and Min Blochberger**
No. of Rooms: **2**
No. of Private Baths: **1**
Max. No. Sharing Bath: **4**
Double/pb: **$55**
Single/pb: **$26.50**
Double/sb: **$30**

Single/sb: **$15**
Open: **Apr. 1–Oct. 31**
Reduced Rates: **10%, seniors; after 2 nights**
Breakfast: **Full**
Pets: **No**
Children: **Welcome, over 12**
Smoking: **No**
Social Drinking: **Permitted**

While most of Carl and Min's guests arrive by car, a good many come via boat because this lovely cedar-and-glass B&B is situated in beautiful Wolff Harbor Cove in the famed Lake of the Ozarks. One of the two decks extends over the water for fishing or sunning. The living room with its comfortable rattan furniture, imported from Hawaii, is the spot for evening snacks and fireside conversation. Guests enjoy all the comforts of home including air-conditioning and a washing machine and dryer. Nearby recreational activities are golf, bowling, horseback riding, and water sports; it's just minutes to restaurants, shops, and theater.

Garth Woodside Mansion ✪
NEW LONDON GRAVEL ROAD, RR1, HANNIBAL, MISSOURI 63401

Tel: **(314) 221-2789**
Best Time to Call: **10 AM–4 PM**
Host(s): **Irv and Diane Feinberg**
Location: **99 mi. N of St. Louis**
No. of Rooms: **8**
No. of Private Baths: **4**
Max. No. Sharing Bath: **4**
Double/pb: **$50–$58**
Single/pb: **$45–$53**

Double/sb: **$45**
Single/sb: **$40**
Open: **All year**
Breakfast: **Full**
Credit Cards: **MC, VISA**
Pets: **No**
Children: **Welcome, over 12**
Smoking: **Permitted**
Social Drinking: **Permitted**

A lifetime friend of Mark Twain built this country estate home in 1871. John Garth had someone a bit more sophisticated than Huck Finn in mind when he designed this Second Empire Victorian with its three-story flying staircase, 14-foot-high ceilings, and eight handcarved marble fireplaces. The rooms are furnished with Victorian antiques, many of them dating back to the original owners. Your hosts want you to feel completely at home here, and they offer such touches as nightshirts and turndown service. Breakfast is served in the formal dining room and features French toast, egg casseroles, and quiches. In the afternoon, Irv and Diane serve tea and homemade snacks on the veranda. They will help you plan your visit with restaurant, theater, and riverboat ride suggestions. When it's time to relax, there are four porches, a rose garden, and 39 acres for picnicking and croquet.

Frisco House ✪
P.O. BOX 118, CORNER CHURCH AND ROLLA STREETS, HARTVILLE, MISSOURI 65667

Tel: **(417) 741-7304 or 833-0650**
Best Time to Call: **7–9 AM; 6–10 PM**
Host(s): **Betty and Charley Roberts**
Location: **50 mi. E of Springfield**
No. of Rooms: **4**
Max. No. Sharing Bath: **4**
Double/sb: **$35**
Single/sb: **$30**
Open: **All year**

Reduced Rates: **5%, after 3 nights; 5%, seniors**
Breakfast: **Full**
Pets: **Sometimes**
Children: **Welcome, over 15**
Smoking: **No**
Social Drinking: **Permitted**
Airport/Station Pickup: **Yes**

Located in the noncommercial historic area of the Missouri Ozarks, this 1890 Victorian, listed on the National Historic Register, has been completely restored, retaining absolute authenticity while being unobtrusively outfitted with central air-conditioning, and up-to-date plumbing and heating systems. Many of the furnishings are third- and fourth-generation family heirlooms, including oil paintings, Oriental rugs, and hanging lamps, as well as china, brass, and wooden artifacts. Most bedrooms have marble-topped sinks. The wainscoted dining room is furnished in oak and decorated with railroad pictures and maps. This is where you'll be served refreshments on arrival, and a bountiful breakfast. The interesting Amish community is close by.

Woodstock Inn ✪
1212 W. LEXINGTON, INDEPENDENCE, MISSOURI 64050

Tel: **(816) 833-2BED**
Host(s): **Lane and Ruth Harold**
Location: **10 mi. E of Kansas City**
No. of Rooms: **11**
No. of Private Baths: **11**
Double/pb: **$38.50–$42.50**
Single/pb: **$33.50–$37.50**
Open: **All year**
Reduced Rates: **10%, after 2 nights**

Breakfast: **Full**
Credit Cards: **MC, VISA**
Pets: **No**
Children: **Welcome**
Smoking: **No**
Social Drinking: **Permitted**
Airport/Station Pickup: **Yes**
Foreign Languages: **German**

This inn is convenient to all the historic and cultural sites in President Harry Truman's hometown. The guest rooms offer a choice of queen, double, or twin beds; all are tastefully appointed with individual decor and are handicapped accessible. Individual heat and air-conditioning controls add to the comfort. Breakfast is served at a handsome oak table, and special dietary needs can be met. The living room has a TV, a piano, and a variety of reading material. Woodstock Inn is also on the city tourist shuttle bus route.

Pridewell ✪
600 WEST 50TH STREET, KANSAS CITY, MISSOURI 64112

Tel: **(816) 931-1642**
Best Time to Call: **4–9 PM**
Host(s): **Edwin and Louann White**
No. of Rooms: **1**
No. of Private Baths: **1**
Double/pb: **$58**
Single/pb: **$49**

Open: **All year**
Breakfast: **Full**
Pets: **No**
Children: **No**
Smoking: **No**
Social Drinking: **Permitted**
Airport/Station Pickup: **Yes**

This fine Tudor residence is situated in a wooded residential area on the battlefield of the Civil War's Battle of Westport. The Nelson Art Gallery, the University of Missouri at Kansas City, and the Missouri Repertory Theatre are close by. It is adjacent to the Country Club Plaza shopping district, which includes several four-star restaurants, tennis courts, and a park.

Grey Goose House ✪
121 NORTH EIGHTH, LOUISIANA, MISSOURI 63353

Tel: **(314) 754-5836**
Host(s): **Don and Joan Mogensen**
Location: **55 mi. N of St. Louis**
No. of Rooms: **4**
No. of Private Baths: **1**
Max. No. Sharing Bath: **4**
Double/pb: **$65**
Double/sb: **$55**
Single/sb: **$40**

Open: **All year**
Breakfast: **Full**
Other Meals: **Available**
Credit Cards: **MC, VISA**
Pets: **Sometimes**
Children: **Welcome**
Smoking: **No**
Social Drinking: **Permitted**

Be prepared to be pampered when you're a guest at Joan and Don's restored 1850s brick home, in an ambience of cheerful country comfort. Breakfast is a bountiful spread that always includes a soufflé, crêpes, or a special omelet, served at the guests' convenience. You'll enjoy the fluffy feather pillows, the use of the VCR, and a selection of books and games. Your hosts will be pleased to show you their workshop, in which they repair, restore, and refinish antiques, and to assist you with your sightseeing plans. A beverage or wine and cheese are graciously offered.

Wardell Guest House ✪
1 WARDELL ROAD, MACON, MISSOURI 63552

Tel: **(816) 385-4352**
Best Time to Call: **After 5 PM**
Host(s): **Larry and Marie Hyde**
Location: **1 mi. from US 36**
No. of Rooms: **4**
No. of Private Baths: **2**
Max. No. Sharing Bath: **4**
Double/pb: **$55**
Single/pb: **$50**
Double/sb: **$45**
Single/sb: **$40**

Open: **All year**
Reduced Rates: **Sun.–Thurs.**
Breakfast: **Full**
Other Meals: **Available**
Credit Cards: **MC, VISA**
Pets: **No**
Children: **Welcome, over 12**
Smoking: **No**
Social Drinking: **Permitted**
Airport/Station Pickup: **Yes**

Built in 1890, this gracious Victorian is listed on the National Register of Historic Places. It is located on eight acres in the heart of a city that is known for its peace, tranquillity, and natural beauty. Spend the day on one of the many surrounding lakes or visit the boyhood homes of Mark Twain, Walt Disney, or General John Pershing. Closer to "home," you are welcome to play croquet during spring and summer, enjoy the beautiful fall foliage, or share an old-fashioned Christmas in this beautiful old mansion.

Down-to-Earth Lifestyles
ROUTE 22, PARKVILLE, MISSOURI 64152

Tel: **(816) 891-1018**
Host(s): **Lola and Bill Coons**
Location: **15 mi. N of downtown Kansas City**
No. of Rooms: **4**
No. of Private Baths: **4**
Double/pb: **$60**
Single/pb: **$50**
Open: **All year**

Reduced Rates: **Families**
Breakfast: **Full**
Other Meals: **Available**
Pets: **No**
Children: **Welcome**
Smoking: **Permitted**
Social Drinking: **Permitted**
Airport/Station Pickup: **Yes**

This spacious new earth-integrated home, with its picture windows and skylights, emphasizes close contact with nature. It's located on an 85-acre ranch where there are horses and cows, a fishing pond, and lots of space for mind and soul. The furnishings complement the country setting, and the heated indoor pool, exercise room, and jogging and walking trails will keep you in shape. Lola and Bill will be pleased to suggest nearby places of interest if you can bear to tear yourself away from this restorative haven.

Anchor Hill Lodge ✪
ANCHOR HILL RANCH, ROUTE 1, ROGERSVILLE, MISSOURI 65742

Tel: **(417) 753-2930**
Best Time to Call: **After 7 PM**
Host(s): **Mrs. T. E. Atkinson**
Location: **23 mi. SE of Springfield**
No. of Rooms: **2**
No. of Private Baths: **2**
Double/pb: **$40**
Single/pb: **$30**

Open: **All year**
Breakfast: **Continental**
Pets: **Horses only**
Children: **Welcome (crib)**
Smoking: **Permitted**
Social Drinking: **Permitted**
Airport/Station Pickup: **Yes**

If your horse hasn't taken a vacation in a while, he's most welcome to accompany you to this rural ranch in the foothills of the Ozark

Mountains. For $5 he will have a box stall and all he can eat, while you enjoy the comfort of an old-fashioned country home. Your hosts breed and ride Arabian horses and there are miles of trails for you to enjoy. In addition, there's lots to do and see, including an exotic animal farm, theater, museums, water sports, hiking, and craft fairs. Enjoy the relaxing on-premises hot tub as well as the beautiful views.

Lafayette House
2156 LAFAYETTE AVENUE, ST. LOUIS, MISSOURI 63104

Tel: **(314) 772-4429**
Host(s): **Sarah and Jack Milligan**
No. of Rooms: **5**
No. of Private Baths: **2**
Max. No. Sharing Bath: **4**
Double/pb: **$50**
Double/sb: **$40**
Suite: **$55**

Open: **All year**
Breakfast: **Full**
Pets: **Sometimes**
Children: **Welcome (crib)**
Smoking: **Permitted**
Social Drinking: **Permitted**
Airport/Station Pickup: **Yes**
Minimum Stay: **2 nights in suite**

This 1876 Queen Anne mansion is located in the historic district overlooking Lafayette Park. the house is furnished comfortably with several antiques and features a deck overlooking the famous Arch. The suite on the third floor, accommodating six, has a private bath and kitchen. Your hosts serve a special egg dish and homemade breads each morning, and offer wine, cheese, and crackers later. They will gladly take you on tour or can direct you to the Botanical Gardens, Convention Center, and other nearby attractions.

Stelzer Bed & Breakfast
7106 GENERAL SHERMAN LANE, ST. LOUIS, MISSOURI 63123

Tel: **(314) 843-5757**
Best Time to Call: **Mornings; evenings**
Host(s): **Pat and Anita Stelzer**
Location: **10 mi. W of St. Louis**
No. of Rooms: **2**
No. of Private Baths: **1**
Max. No. Sharing Bath: **4**
Double/pb: **$30**
Single/pb: **$20**
Double/sb: **$25**
Single/sb: **$18**
Open: **All year**
Breakfast: **Continental**
Pets: **No**
Children: **Welcome**
Smoking: **No**
Social Drinking: **No**
Airport/Station Pickup: **Yes**

Pat and Anita Stelzer have a corner house with green siding and window awnings. The lot is quite spacious, with lovely trees and flowers. Inside, you'll find a mixture of Windsor chairs, old-fashioned rockers, books, and family treasures such as the old spoon collection mounted on the wall. Breakfast on fresh fruit, biscuits, cereals, eggs, and bacon. The Stelzers are located ten miles from the riverfront and within easy reach of the Botanical Garden, fine dining, and shops.

Tower Grove House
4662 TOWER GROVE PLACE, ST. LOUIS, MISSOURI 63110

Tel: **(314) 772-8404**
Best Time to Call: **After 6 PM; weekends**
Host(s): **Michael and Alison Cohen**
Location: **1 mi. from Rte. 44**
No. of Rooms: **1**
No. of Private Baths: **1**
Double/pb: **$35**
Single/pb: **$30**
Open: **All year**
Reduced Rates: **20%, seniors; families with hospitalized members at Medical Center**
Breakfast: **Continental**
Other Meals: **Available**
Pets: **Sometimes**
Children: **Welcome**
Smoking: **Permitted**
Social Drinking: **Permitted**
Airport/Station Pickup: **Yes**

This air-conditioned brick Victorian is home to gracious hosts who are knowledgeable about their city and enjoy sharing it with you. It borders "The Hill," a famous Italian neighborhood known for its fabulous restaurants and bakeries and is within walking distance of the Missouri Botanical Garden and Tower Grove Park. Forest Park, home of the zoo, art museum, and three golf courses, and Washington University Medical Center are five minutes away by car. Alison is a registered nurse at Children's Hospital; Michael is a scrap metal dealer. The guest suite is furnished with a blend of contemporary and antique pieces and includes a private kitchen. You are welcome to use the laundry facilities. Home-baked breads and pastries are featured at breakfast; wine and cheese are served with compliments of the hosts.

The Schwegmann House B&B Inn ✪
438 WEST FRONT STREET, WASHINGTON, MISSOURI 63090

Tel: **(314) 239-5025**
Host(s): **George, Barbara, and Cathy**
Location: **50 mi. W of St. Louis**
No. of Rooms: **9**
No. of Private Baths: **7**
Max. No. Sharing Bath: **4**
Double/pb: **$60**
Single/pb: **$50**
Double/sb: **$45**
Single/sb: **$35**
Open: **All year**
Breakfast: **Continental**
Credit Cards: **MC, VISA**
Pets: **No**
Children: **Welcome**
Smoking: **Permitted**
Social Drinking: **Permitted**

A three-story 1861 Georgian brick house included on the National Historic Register, it is located on the Missouri River. It is tastefully furnished with antiques; handmade quilts complement the decor of each guest room. It is close to Daniel Boone's home, Meramec Caverns, Missouri's Rhineland wineries, antiques shops, and fine restaurants. Relax in the graceful parlor by the fireside or stroll the gardens that overlook the river. George, Barbara, and Cathy serve a bountiful breakfast including fresh-ground coffee, imported cheeses, croissants, and grape juice from Missouri's vineyards.

Benner House Bed and Breakfast ✪
645 MAIN STREET, WESTON, MISSOURI 64098

Tel: **(816) 386-2616**
Host(s): **Ken and Karen West**
Location: **30 mi. NW of Kansas City**
No. of Rooms: **4**
Max. No. Sharing Bath: **4**
Double/sb: **$65**
Single/sb: **$58**
Open: **All year**
Breakfast: **Full**
Pets: **No**
Children: **Welcome, over 12**
Smoking: **No**
Social Drinking: **Permitted**
Airport/Station Pickup: **Yes**

Listed on the National Register of Historic Places, this fine example of steamboat Gothic architecture is just a short walk from the historic downtown shopping district. Ken and Karen invite you to relax on the charming wraparound porch, tour the hills of Weston in their 1929 automobile, or enjoy the many antebellum homes in their neighborhood. Their beautifully decorated home is accented by a fine collection of antiques. Enjoy relaxed conversation in the main parlor or slip away to the sitting room, where you can curl up in a rocking chair with a book. Karen is likely to spoil you with her delicious brownies at snack time.

For key to listings, see inside front or back cover.

✪ This star means that rates are guaranteed through December 31, 1989 to any guest making a reservation as a result of reading about the B&B in *BED & BREAKFAST U.S.A.*—1989 edition.

Please enclose a self-addressed, stamped, business-sized envelope when contacting reservation services.

For more details on what you can expect in a B&B, see Chapter 1.

Always mention *Bed & Breakfast U.S.A.* when making reservations!

If no B&B is listed in the area you'll be visiting, use the form on page 693 to order a copy of our "List of New B&Bs."

We want to hear from you! Use the form on page 691.

MONTANA

O'Duach'Ain Country Inn ✪
675 FERNDALE DRIVE, BIGFORK, MONTANA 59911

Tel: (406) 837-6851
Best Time to Call: **Before Noon**
Host(s): **Margot and Tom Doohan**
Location: **17 mi. S of Kalispell**
No. of Rooms: **5**
Max. No. Sharing Bath: **4**
Double/sb: **$50**
Single/sb: **$42.50**
Separate Guest Cottage: **$70–$75**

Open: **All year**
Breakfast: **Full**
Other Meals: **Available**
Credit Cards: **MC, VISA**
Pets: **Welcome**
Children: **Welcome, over 12**
Smoking: **No**
Social Drinking: **Permitted**
Airport/Station Pickup: **Yes**

O'Duach'Ain is a gracious three-level log home set on five beautiful acres. Inside, you'll find a casual atmosphere of open wood logs, stone fireplaces, antiques, and artwork. Guests are welcome to relax on the deck and take in the spectacular view. In the morning, your hosts provide a gourmet breakfast, featuring freshly prepared international dishes. Margot and Tom will gladly take you on a one-day tour of the area in their luxury van; the fee includes an outdoor picnic lunch. Your hosts will also direct you to nearby Glacier National Park, Swan Lake, Big Mountain Ski Area, and Flatland Lake.

Sky View ✪
BOX 408, BIG SANDY, MONTANA 59520

Tel: **(406) 378-2549; 386-2464**	Guest Cottage: **$35–$60**
Best Time to Call: **Before 11 AM; after 6 PM**	Open: **May 1–Dec. 1**
	Reduced Rates: **Families**
Host(s): **Ron and Gay Pearson and family**	Breakfast: **Full**
	Other Meals: **Available**
Location: **75 mi. N of Great Falls**	Pets: **Sometimes**
No. of Rooms: **3**	Children: **Welcome**
Max. No. Sharing Bath: **6**	Smoking: **Permitted**
Double/sb: **$35**	Social Drinking: **Permitted**
Single/sb: **$26**	Airport/Station Pickup: **Yes**

Sky View is a working ranch located in an area known for its wild and rugged ambience, sparse population, and spectacular scenery. It's in the heart of Lewis and Clark country, just off a major highway to Glacier National Park. The Pearson family enjoys people of all ages and looks forward to sharing its life-style with guests, keeping you informed of local rodeos, Indian powwows, river float trips, tours, and hunting and fishing opportunities. Children enjoy their playground, and baby-sitters are available. A public swimming pool and tennis courts are nearby.

Voss Inn ✪
319 SOUTH WILLSON, BOZEMAN, MONTANA 59715

Tel: **(406) 587-0982**	Reduced Rates: **Business travelers, Sun.–Thurs.**
Best Time to Call: **10 AM–9 PM**	
Host(s): **Ken and Ruthmary Tonn**	Breakfast: **Full**
Location: **3 mi. from I-90**	Credit Cards: **MC, VISA**
No. of Rooms: **6**	Pets: **No**
No. of Private Baths: **6**	Children: **Sometimes**
Double/pb: **$50–$70**	Smoking: **Permitted**
Single/pb: **$40–$60**	Social Drinking: **Permitted**
Open: **All year**	

This handsome 100-year-old brick mansion flanked by Victorian gingerbread porches is set like a gem on a tree-lined street in historic Bozeman. The bedrooms are elegantly wallpapered and furnished with brass and iron beds, ornate lighting, Oriental throw rugs over polished hardwood floors . . . a perfect spot for a first or second honeymoon. The parlor has a good selection of books, as well as a chess set for your pleasure. It's north of Yellowstone, on the way to Glacier, with trout fishing, mountain lakes, and skiing within easy reach. Don't miss the Museum of the Rockies on the Montana State University campus 10 blocks away.

Ballymurray B&B
206 FOURTH AVENUE EAST, KALISPELL, MONTANA 59901

Tel: **(406) 755-7080**
Best Time to Call: **9–11 AM; 5–10 PM**
Host(s): **Bryce and Bette Baker**
No. of Rooms: **3**
No. of Private Baths: **1**
Max. No. Sharing Bath: **4**
Double/pb: **$50**
Single/pb: **$35**

Single/sb: **$35**
Open: **All year**
Breakfast: **Full**
Pets: **No**
Children: **Welcome, over 6**
Smoking: **Permitted**
Social Drinking: **Permitted**
Airport/Station Pickup: **Yes**

Bette, the Irish half of the Baker family, is an artist who named their B&B after the village in Ireland where her mother lived. Bryce, who is Irish through inclination, invites you to fish the many lakes, rivers, and streams in Flathead Valley. On mornings when fishing's been good, he's likely to fix you a special fisherman's breakfast, served in the formal dining room or the cheery sun room. You'll enjoy a visit to historic Conrad Mansion or Woodland Park, where you can see exotic birds, swim, or skate. Within a short drive, you can climb the peaks of Glacier National Park, ski the slopes of Big Mountain, waterski on Flathead Lake, try white-water rafting, or play golf on one of five challenging courses. Afterwards, relax in the living room, where the crackling fire takes the chill off cool evenings.

Whitetail Lodge O
1705 BROWNS MEADOW ROAD, KILA, MONTANA 59920

Tel: **(406) 755-3904**
Best Time to Call: **After 5 PM**
Host(s): **Cyndi Westbrook**
Location: **5 mi. from Hwy. 2**
No. of Rooms: **1**
No. of Private Baths: **1**
Double/pb: **$30**
Single/pb: **$20**
Open: **All year**

Reduced Rates: **10%, weekly**
Breakfast: **Full**
Other Meals: **Available**
Pets: **No**
Children: **Welcome**
Smoking: **No**
Social Drinking: **Permitted**
Airport/Station Pickup: **Yes**

Surrounded by 10 secluded acres of woods, Whitetail Lodge is a hand-hewn log home with split-log staircases and hardwood floors. The multilevel house is furnished with oak and pine antiques, animal pelts and antlers, a Lincoln Range wood stove. The rustic guest room features a four-poster bed and spectacular views. The kids will enjoy sleeping in the cozy loft overlooking the main room. Cyndi serves a country breakfast featuring homemade bread, her own Montana potato pancakes, eggs, biscuits, and gravy. The lodge is close to Glacier National Park and Flathead Lake. After a day of activities you can enjoy a cold drink on the sun deck and watch grazing deer.

Mission Mountains B&B
RR BOX 183A, ST. IGNATIUS, MONTANA 59865

Tel: **(406) 745-4331**
Best Time to Call: **9 AM–5 PM**
Host(s): **Doris Peterson**
Location: **¼ mi. W of Hwy. 93**
No. of Rooms: **2**
Max. No. Sharing Bath: **4**
Double/sb: **$33**
Single/sb: **$29**

Open: **All year**
Reduced Rates: **10%, seniors**
Breakfast: **Full**
Other Meals: **Available**
Pets: **No**
Children: **Welcome (crib, high chair)**
Smoking: **No**
Social Drinking: **No**

A casual, comfortable atmosphere awaits you in this quiet, rural ranch house. The views are spectacular, with the Mission Mountains five miles to the east, the Cabinet Mountains 10 miles to the west, and the National Bison Range to the south. Nine Pipe National Wildlife Refuge is just north of here and the St. Ignatius Church, a National Historic Monument, is located in town, just a short drive away. Your host loves catering to guests and offer snacks and fresh tea or coffee. In the morning they serve a breakfast of Swedish pancakes, homemade breads, coffee cake, and jams. Activities such as fishing, hiking, boating, white-water rafting, golf, and skiing can all be enjoyed within a 30-mile drive.

Country Caboose ✪
852 WILLOUGHBY ROAD, STEVENSVILLE, MONTANA 59870

Tel: **(406) 777-3145**
Host(s): **Lisa Thompson**
Location: **35 mi. S of Missoula**
No. of Rooms: **1**
No. of Private Baths: **1**
Double/pb: **$35**
Single/pb: **$35**

Open: **May–Sept.**
Breakfast: **Full**
Other Meals: **Available**
Pets: **No**
Children: **Welcome**
Smoking: **No**
Social Drinking: **Permitted**

If you enjoy romantic train rides, why not spend the night in an authentic caboose? This one dates back to 1923, is made of wood, and is painted red, of course. It is set on real rails in the middle of the countryside. The caboose sleeps two and offers a spectacular view of the Bitterroot Mountains, right from your pillow. In the morning, breakfast is served at a table for two. Specialties include huckleberry pancakes, quiche, and strawberries in season. Local activities include touring St. Mary's Mission, hiking the mountain trails, fishing, and hunting.

Duck Inn ✪
1305 COLUMBIA AVENUE, WHITEFISH, MONTANA 59937

Tel: **(406) 862-DUCK**
Host(s): **Ken and Phyllis Adler**
Location: **25 mi. from Glacier Nat'l. Park**
No. of Rooms: **10**
No. of Private Baths: **10**
Double/pb: **$50**
Single/pb: **$45**
Open: **All year**

Reduced Rates: **5%, seniors**
Breakfast: **Continental**
Credit Cards: **AMEX, DC, MC, VISA**
Pets: **No**
Children: **Welcome**
Smoking: **Permitted**
Social Drinking: **Permitted**
Airport/Station Pickup: **Yes**

The Duck Inn is on the Whitefish River, eight miles from Big Mountain Ski Area. Each guest room features a brass or white iron bed, cozy fireplace, deep soak tub, and a balcony. A large living room with a view of Big Mountain and the river is a relaxing spot. Your hosts offer a different kind of fresh-baked bread each morning, and can provide information on Glacier National Park, wilderness areas, and spots to swim, sail, and fish. A Jacuzzi is available after a heavy day of touring.

For key to listings, see inside front or back cover.

✪ This star means that rates are guaranteed through December 31, 1989 to any guest making a reservation as a result of reading about the B&B in *BED & BREAKFAST U.S.A.*—1989 edition.

Please enclose a self-addressed, stamped, business-sized envelope when contacting reservation services.

For more details on what you can expect in a B&B, see Chapter 1.

Always mention *Bed & Breakfast U.S.A.* when making reservations!

If no B&B is listed in the area you'll be visiting, use the form on page 693 to order a copy of our "List of New B&Bs."

We want to hear from you! Use the form on page 691.

NEBRASKA

Bed & Breakfast of the Great Plains ✪
P.O. BOX 2333, LINCOLN, NEBRASKA 68502

Tel: (402) 423-3480	Rates (Single/Double):
Coordinator: **Rose Ann Foster**	Modest: $20–$25 $30
States/Regions Covered: **Nebraska—**	Average: $25–$30 $35–$45
Statewide; Iowa & Kansas borders	Luxury: $40–$50 $55–$80
	Credit Cards: **MC, VISA**

Rose Ann's ever-growing roster includes a modest home within blocks of Interstate-80, an air-conditioned farmhouse where the alarm clock is a rooster, and a mansion on the National Register of Historic Places. The friendly hosts will be delighted to direct guests to rodeos, ethnic festivals, museums, state or county fairs, lakeside recreation areas, Indian powwows, concerts, Cornhusker football, and Boys' Town. Tell them your interests and they will custom-tailor an itinerary to suit you.

The Georges ✪
ROUTE 1, BOX 50, DIXON, NEBRASKA 68732

Tel: **(402) 584-2625**
Best Time to Call: **6:30 AM–6 PM**
Host(s): **Harold and Marie George**
Location: **35 mi. W of Sioux City, Iowa**
No. of Rooms: **3**
Max. No. Sharing Bath: **4**
Double/sb: **$35**
Single/sb: **$25**

Open: **All year**
Breakfast: **Full**
Other Meals: **Available**
Pets: **Sometimes**
Children: **Welcome**
Smoking: **No**
Social Drinking: **Permitted**
Airport/Station Pickup: **Yes**
Foreign Languages: **Swedish**

The Georges have a large, remodeled farmhouse with a spacious backyard. They offer the opportunity to see a farming operation at first hand, right down to the roosters crowing and the birds singing in the morning. Harold and Marie are now full-time farmers after careers in social work and engineering. They prepare a hearty country breakfast featuring homemade jellies and jams. The Georges are close to Wayne State College and Ponca State Park.

Bundy's Bed and Breakfast ✪
16906 SOUTH 255, GRETNA, NEBRASKA 68028

Tel: **(402) 332-3616**
Best Time to Call: **7 AM–9 PM**
Host(s): **Bob and Dee Bundy**
Location: **30 mi. S of Omaha**
No. of Rooms: **4**
Max. No. Sharing Bath: **4**
Double/sb: **$25**

Single/sb: **$15**
Open: **All year**
Breakfast: **Full**
Pets: **Sometimes**
Children: **No**
Smoking: **No**
Social Drinking: **No**

The Bundys have a pretty farmhouse painted white with black trim. Here you can enjoy country living just 30 minutes from downtown Lincoln and Omaha. The rooms are decorated with antiques, attractive wallpapers, and collectibles. In the morning, wake up to farm-fresh eggs and homemade breads. The house is just a short walk from a swimming lake and is three miles from a ski lodge.

The Rogers House ✪
2145 B STREET, LINCOLN, NEBRASKA 68502

Tel: **(402) 476-6961**
Best Time to Call: **12–4 PM**
Host(s): **Nora Houtsma**

No. of Rooms: **8**
No. of Private Baths: **8**
Double/pb: **$45–$55**

Single/pb: **$40–$50**
Open: **All year**
Reduced Rates: **10% on 3rd and 4th night; 15% thereafter**
Breakfast: **Full**

Credit Cards: **AMEX, MC, VISA**
Pets: **No**
Children: **Welcome, over 12**
Smoking: **Permitted**
Social Drinking: **Permitted**

This Jacobean Revival-style brick mansion was built in 1914 and is a local historic landmark. There are three sun porches, attractively furnished with wicker and plants, and the air-conditioned house is decorated with lovely antiques. Nora will direct you to the diverse cultural attractions available at the nearby University of Nebraska, the surrounding historic district, and antique shops. Don't miss a visit to the Children's Zoo and the beautiful Sunken Gardens. Breakfast is hearty and delicious. A professional staff of 5 is eager to serve you.

Watson Manor Inn ✪
410 SOUTH SYCAMORE, P.O. BOX 458, NORTH PLATTE, NEBRASKA 69103

Tel: **(308) 532-1005**
Host(s): **Ron and Patty Watson**
Location: **2 mi. N of I-80**
No. of Rooms: **3**
No. of Private Baths: **1**
Max. No. Sharing Bath: **4**
Double/pb: **$45**
Single/pb: **$40**
Double/sb: **$40**
Single/sb: **$35**

Suites: **$60**
Open: **All year**
Breakfast: **Continental**
Credit Cards: **AMEX, MC, VISA**
Pets: **No**
Children: **Welcome, over 10**
Smoking: **No**
Social Drinking: **Permitted**
Airport/Station Pickup: **Yes**

This is a beautiful two-story brick home with white shutters, stately pillars, and a manicured lawn. Ron and Patty have furnished it with carefully chosen antiques and comfortable decor. Breakfast often features omelets, French toast, or quiche, and is always served with a smile that says, "We're glad you're here!" The area was once the home of Colonel William "Buffalo Bill" Cody. His ranch, Scouts Rest, has been reconstructed as part of a historical park. You're welcome to relax on the deck and refresh yourself in the spa, and have some wine and cheese before going out to dinner and perhaps taking in the local color at the nightly rodeo.

The Offutt House ✪
140 NORTH 39TH STREET, OMAHA, NEBRASKA 68131

Tel: **(402) 553-0951**
Host(s): **Jeannie K. Swoboda**
Location: **1 mi. from I-80**
No. of Rooms: **7**
No. of Private Baths: **5**
Max. No. Sharing Bath: **4**
Double/pb: **$60**
Single/pb: **$50**
Double/sb: **$50**

Single/sb: **$40**
Suites: **$70**
Open: **All year**
Reduced Rates: **After 5 nights**
Breakfast: **Continental**
Pets: **Sometimes**
Children: **Welcome**
Smoking: **Permitted**
Social Drinking: **Permitted**

This comfortable mansion (c. 1894) is part of the city's Historic Gold Coast, a section of handsome homes built by Omaha's wealthiest residents. Offering peace and quiet, the rooms are air-conditioned, spacious, and furnished with antiques; some have fireplaces. Jeannie will direct you to nearby attractions such as the Joslyn Museum or the Old Market area, which abounds with many beautiful shops and fine restaurants. She graciously offers coffee or wine in late afternoon.

NEVADA

Winters Creek Ranch
1201 US 395 NORTH, CARSON CITY, NEVADA 89701

Tel: **(702) 849-1020**
Best Time to Call: **Mornings**
Host(s): **Myron Sayan and Susan Hannah**
Location: **14 mi. S of Reno**
No. of Rooms: **4**
No. of Private Baths: **4**
Double/pb: **$75**
Single/pb: **$75**

Separate Guest Cottage: **$85 for 4**
Open: **All year**
Breakfast: **Full**
Credit Cards: **MC, VISA**
Pets: **Sometimes**
Children: **Welcome, over 13**
Smoking: **No**
Social Drinking: **Permitted**
Foreign Languages: **Spanish**

Established in 1865, this historic horse ranch is nestled among ponderosa pines and meadows on 50 acres. You may choose Oliver's Nook, a delicate blend of lavender and lace, the Colonial Room with its cozy fireplace, or the Nevada Room with a lovely deck. Enjoy the beautiful countryside from the back of a horse. Other activities include fishing, ice skating, hiking, and picnicking. Your hosts invite you to use the hot tub, and offer complimentary wine and hors d'oeuvres in the afternoon. Carson City, Reno, Virginia City, and Lake Tahoe are minutes away.

Haus Bavaria ✪
P.O. BOX 3308, 593 NORTH DYER CIRCLE, INCLINE VILLAGE, LAKE TAHOE, NEVADA 89450

Tel: (702) 831-6122 or (800) GO-TAHOE
Best Time to Call: **9 AM–8 PM**
Host(s): **Wolfgang and Anna Zimmermann**
Location: **35 mi. SW of Reno**
No. of Rooms: **5**
No. of Private Baths: **5**
Double/pb: **$70**

Single/pb: **$60**
Open: **All year**
Breakfast: **Full**
Pets: **No**
Children: **No**
Smoking: **No**
Social Drinking: **Permitted**
Foreign Languages: **German**

This immaculate residence is framed by the mountains and convenient to the lake. It's hard to believe you're not in the Swiss Alps! Each guest room opens onto a balcony. Continental hosts Wolfgang and Anna set a breakfast table with bountiful platters of cold cuts, imported cheeses, sliced fruits, boiled eggs, cake, rolls, and endless cups of delicious coffee or tea. It's close to the gambling casinos and shows, all water sports, and, in winter, the challenging slopes of Mount Rose and Heavenly Valley. There is a two-night minimum stay required.

Las Vegas B&B
CONTACT; BED AND BREAKFAST INTERNATIONAL, 1181-B SOLANO AVENUE, ALBANY, CALIFORNIA 94706

Tel: (415) 525-4569
Best Time to Call: **8:30 AM–5 PM**
Host(s): **Jean Brown**
No. of Rooms: **2**
No. of Private Baths: **1**
Max. No. Sharing Bath: **3**
Double/pb: **$55**
Single/pb: **$50**

Double/sb: **$50**
Single/sb: **$45**
Open: **All year**
Breakfast: **Full**
Pets: **No**
Children: **Swimmers only**
Smoking: **Permitted**
Social Drinking: **Permitted**

Located a few minutes from the fabled "Strip" of hotels, casinos, and restaurants is this two-story contemporary home. The quiet, residential neighborhood is a welcome respite from the 24-hour hoopla available nearby. You are welcome to use your host's swimming pool.

B&B—Northern Nevada ✪
136 ANDREW LANE, RENO, NEVADA 89511

Tel: **(702) 849-0772**
Best Time to Call: **Mornings**
Host(s): **Caroline Walters and Robert McNeill**
Location: **⅛ mi. from Hwy. 395 South**
No. of Rooms: **3**
No. of Private Baths: **1**
Max. No. Sharing Bath: **4**
Double/pb: **$64**
Double/sb: **$54**
Single/sb: **$38**
Open: **Apr. 1–Nov. 1**
Breakfast: **Full**
Pets: **No**
Children: **Welcome**
Smoking: **No**
Social Drinking: **Permitted**
Minimum Stay: **2 nights**

Situated in Steamboat Valley and surrounded by unbroken vistas of the 10,000-foot-high Mt. Rose and Slide Mountains is this rustic home with its beamed ceilings and Early American decor. The atmosphere is casual and unhurried, and one can really revel in the simple life. Breakfast is ranch-sized and always includes one of Caroline's delicious apple–nut creations along with the bacon and eggs. Depending on your mood and the season, you can ski; revisit the gold rush days in Virginia City; gamble, dine, or be entertained at a posh hotel; cruise magnificent Lake Tahoe; or stay "home" and swim in the backyard pool.

Edith Palmer's Country Inn
SOUTH "B" STREET, P.O. BOX 756, VIRGINIA CITY, NEVADA 89449

Tel: **(702) 847-0707**
Host(s): **Erlene Brown**
Location: **23 mi. S of Reno**
No. of Rooms: **5**
No. of Private Baths: **3**
Max. No. Sharing Bath: **4**
Double/pb: **$60–75**
Single/pb: **$70**
Double/sb: **$70**
Single/sb: **$65**
Open: **All year**
Breakfast: **Full**
Other Meals: **Available**
Credit Cards: **MC, VISA**
Pets: **No**
Children: **No**
Smoking: **No**
Social Drinking: **Permitted**
Airport/Station Pickup: **Yes**

One of Nevada's first wine merchants built this country Victorian over 100 years ago. What was once a stone wine cellar is now a gourmet restaurant with rock walls and a fireplace crafted from local ores and gemstones. Spend the night in a comfortable bedroom and wake up to a breakfast of freshly ground coffee and a variety of hot breads and egg dishes. Outside, the pretty gardens are often used for wedding receptions. Many celebrities find this inn a wonderful escape spot. Even if you're not a star, you'll be treated like one. Edith Palmer's is within walking distance from the historic sights of Virginia City and close to Lake Tahoe and Reno.

For key to listings, see inside front or back cover.

✪ This star means that rates are guaranteed through December 31, 1989 to any guest making a reservation as a result of reading about the B&B in *BED & BREAKFAST U.S.A.*—1989 edition.

Please enclose a self-addressed, stamped, business-sized envelope when contacting reservation services.

For more details on what you can expect in a B&B, see Chapter 1.

Always mention *Bed & Breakfast U.S.A.* when making reservations!

If no B&B is listed in the area you'll be visiting, use the form on page 693 to order a copy of our "List of New B&Bs."

We want to hear from you! Use the form on page 691.

NEW HAMPSHIRE

New Hampshire Bed & Breakfast ✪
RFD 3, BOX 53, LACONIA, NEW HAMPSHIRE 03246

Tel: **(603) 279-8348**
Best Time to Call: **10 AM–5 PM**
Coordinator: **Martha W. Dorais**
States/Regions Covered: **Statewide**

Rates (Single/Double):
  Modest: $25–$30 $35–$40
  Average: $35–$40 $40–$50
  Luxury: $50 $55–$85
Credit Cards: MC, VISA
Minimum Stay: **2 nights holidays and Fall Foliage**

New Hampshire is a haven for the sports-minded, having facilities for every type of recreation. Shoppers will find it a bargain haven since there's no sales tax on merchandise. Martha's roster ranges from an

18th-century Cape house where the hostess makes her own cheese, to a mountainside home overlooking Lake Winnipesaukee with its own pool and tennis court, to a contemporary home convenient to the Manchester factory outlets. Send $1 for her descriptive directory, make your selection, and she will make the reservation for you.

The Mulburn Inn ☉
MAIN STREET, BETHLEHEM, NEW HAMPSHIRE 03574

Tel: **(603) 869-3389**
Best Time to Call: **9 AM–9 PM**
Host(s): **Bob and Cheryl Burns, Moe and Linda Mulkigian**
Location: **20 mi. SE of St. Johnsbury**
No. of Rooms: **7**
No. of Private Baths: **7**
Double/pb: **$50–$65**
Single/pb: **$35**
Open: **All year**
Reduced Rates: **10%, weekly**
Breakfast: **Full**
Other Meals: **Available**
Credit Cards: **AMEX, MC, VISA**
Pets: **No**
Children: **Welcome (crib)**
Smoking: **No**
Social Drinking: **Permitted**
Airport/Station Pickup: **Yes**

Back in the early 1900s, this sprawling Tudor home was known as the Ivie Estate, a family summer retreat. It boasts original oak staircases, stained-glass windows, rounded-corner architecture, three tile fireplaces, and even has an elevator. There is plenty of room here, with three enclosed wraparound porches for relaxing and a large living room for reading and fireside chats. Breakfast is served by the fire in a sunny dining room. In the afternoon, your hosts offer seasonal snacks such as soup or cider and cheese. If you are visiting in March or April, you'll be treated to fresh syrup right from the family maples. This lively inn is located in the heart of the White Mountains, near Franconia Notch, the Old Man in the Mountain, Mt. Washington, plus places to ski, shop, and dine.

Mountain-Fare Inn
BOX 553, CAMPTON, NEW HAMPSHIRE 03223

Tel: **(603) 726-4283**
Best Time to Call: **After 5 PM**
Host(s): **Susan and Nick Preston**
Location: **40 mi. N of Concord**
No. of Rooms: **9**
No. of Private Baths: **5**
Max. No. Sharing Bath: **4**
Double/pb: **$56**
Single/pb: **$35**
Double/sb: **$48**
Single/sb: **$31**
Open: **All year**
Reduced Rates: **10% less, Apr.–June; families**
Breakfast: **Full**
Other Meals: **Dinner available in ski season**
Pets: **Sometimes**

Children: **Welcome**
Smoking: **No**

Social Drinking: **Permitted**

Built in the 1800s, this white clapboard farmhouse is located in the foothills of the White Mountains, just minutes away from Franconia Notch and the Waterville Valley Resort. Susan and Nick are professional skiers and into physical fitness. Their enthusiasm is contagious! Generous seasonal snacks are offered. During the ski season, you are invited to have a family-style dinner for $8.50 per person. Plymouth State College is nearby. There is a two-day minimum stay on weekends.

Blanche's B&B ✪
RFD 1, BOX 75, ROUTE 116, EASTON, NEW HAMPSHIRE 03580

Tel: **(603) 823-7061**
Best Time to Call: **Evenings**
Host(s): **Brenda Shannon and John Vail**
Location: **5 mi. SW of Franconia**
No. of Rooms: **5**
Max. No. Sharing Bath: **4**
Double/sb: **$50**
Single/sb: **$30**
Open: **All year**
Reduced Rates: **Weekly**

Breakfast: **Full**
Other Meals: **Available**
Pets: **No**
Children: **Welcome**
Smoking: **No**
Social Drinking: **Permitted**
Minimum Stay: **2 nights, holiday weekends, fall foliage season**
Airport/Station Pickup: **Yes**

Set in a meadow near the Appalachian Trail, this steep-gabled, Victorian farmhouse (c. 1887) is decorated with family pieces and auction finds. Brenda and John provide cotton linens on comfortable beds, a breakfast hearty enough to allow you to skip lunch, and good advice about the nearby hiking and cross-country ski trails. Franconia Notch and Cannon Mountain are a 10-minute drive. Your hosts will be happy to suggest the best spots for antiques, crafts, bird-watching, or help you discover the simple pleasures of life in the White Mountains.

Maria W. Atwood Inn
R.F.D. #2, ROUTE 3A NORTH, FRANKLIN, NEW HAMPSHIRE 03235

Tel: **(603) 934-3666**
Best Time to Call: **Mornings; afternoons**
Host(s): **Philip and Irene Fournier**
Location: **21 mi. N of Concord**
No. of Rooms: **8**
No. of Private Baths: **8**
Double/pb: **$58**
Single/pb: **$48**

Open: **All year**
Breakfast: **Full**
Credit Cards: **AMEX, MC, VISA**
Pets: **No**
Children: **Welcome, over 11**
Smoking: **Permitted**
Social Drinking: **Permitted**
Airport/Station Pickup: **Yes**

At the turn of the century, Maria Atwood and her husband bought this brick, Federal-style home along with 200 acres. Over the years, the house became known for its quality restorations and impeccable maintenance. The grounds feature formal gardens and acres of fields for walking or cross-country skiing. Today the inn features new plumbing and electrical systems, but restoration has been made according to original designs, and the locks still take an old turnkey. The decor features period antiques, and bedrooms all have old-fashioned beds and fine linens. Your hosts offer complimentary snacks and invite you to BYOB if you like. This lovely inn is within ten minutes of swimming and boating and half an hour from the ski slopes.

Webster Lake Inn ✪
WEBSTER AVENUE, FRANKLIN, NEW HAMPSHIRE 03235

Tel: **(603) 934-4050**
Host(s): **Shirley and Henry McCue and Roland and Cheryl Tyner**
No. of Rooms: **8**
No. of Private Baths: **2**
Max. No. Sharing Bath: **4**
Double/pb: **$53–$60**
Double/sb: **$44**

Single/sb: **$35**
Open: **All year**
Breakfast: **Full**
Pets: **No**
Children: **Welcome**
Smoking: **Permitted**
Social Drinking: **Permitted**

This country inn, modeled after a Swiss chalet, is set on picturesque Webster Lake. Enjoy a quiet moment in a lovely waterfront gazebo or by the great fireplace in the sitting room. Bedrooms feature panoramic views and original, handcrafted furnishings. Your hosts serve a country-style breakfast in a fireplaced dining room overlooking the water. Nearby activities include swimming, fishing, hiking, golf, skiing, and snowmobiling. There are many regional events throughout the year such as Winter Carnival and an assortment of country fairs. Webster Lake Inn is a short drive from Lake Winnipesaukee and less than an hour from the White Mountains.

Cartway House Inn ✪
OLD LAKE SHORE ROAD, GILFORD, NEW HAMPSHIRE 03246

Tel: **(603) 528-1172**
Host(s): **The Shortway family**
Location: **33 mi. N of Concord**
No. of Rooms: **7**
Max. No. Sharing Bath: **4**
Double/sb: **$52–$58**

Single/sb: **$45**
Open: **All year**
Breakfast: **Full**
Other Meals: **Available**
Credit Cards: **MC, VISA**
Pets: **No**

Children: **Welcome**
Smoking: **Permitted**
Social Drinking: **Permitted**

Airport/Station Pickup: **Yes**
Foreign Languages: **French, Italian**

This clapboard Colonial, built in 1771, is set on a hill overlooking fields and mountains. Recent renovations include a French country kitchen where special desserts are served Saturday nights. Some of the guest rooms have bunk beds, suitable for groups of skiers and hikers. The more private rooms have double beds, and there is a suite with separate entrance. Breakfast specialties include eggs Benedict and French toast. Afternoon tea is served to wind down your busy day. Ski areas, a private beach, and Lake Winnipesaukee are just a few of the area attractions.

The Gables ✪
139 MAIN, GORHAM, NEW HAMPSHIRE 03581

Tel: **(603) 466-2876**
Host(s): **Bill and Dot Dunton**
No. of Rooms: **4**
No. of Private Baths: **2**
Max. No. Sharing Bath: **4**
Double/pb: **$45–$50**
Single/pb: **$30**
Double/sb: **$40–$45**

Single/sb: **$25**
Open: **All year**
Breakfast: **Full**
Credit Cards: **AMEX**
Pets: **No**
Children: **Welcome**
Smoking: **Permitted**
Social Drinking: **Permitted**

The Gables is a New England clapboard farmhouse painted antique blue. This village home is decorated in country style, with old family pieces and antique furnishings. Guests are welcome to gather around the living room fireplace to share a cup of coffee and perhaps some conversation. Bill and Dot serve a hearty breakfast featuring homemade bran muffins. They are just a short walk from antique shops, restaurants, and a shopping plaza. Mount Washington is just west of town, in the Presidential Range of the White Mountains. You can reach the summit by foot, auto, or the famous Cog Railway.

Roy Family Bed & Breakfast ✪
473 OCEAN BOULEVARD, HAMPTON BEACH, NEW HAMPSHIRE 03842

Tel: **(603) 926-7893 or 926-5505**
Best Time to Call: **After 1 PM**
Host(s): **Debbie and Richard Roy**
Location: **50 mi. N of Boston**

No. of Rooms: **6**
Max. No. Sharing Bath: **4**
Double/sb: **$45–$60**
Open: **May 15–Sept. 15**

Reduced Rates: **Available**
Breakfast: **Continental**
Credit Cards: **AMEX, MC, VISA**
Pets: **No**
Children: **Welcome, over 12**
Smoking: **Permitted**
Social Drinking: **Permitted**
Foreign Languages: **French**

The Atlantic Ocean is right at your feet when you stay at this comfortable, New England–style home. The house is decorated in a mixture of traditional, Victorian, and casual pieces. Bedrooms are immaculate and furnished Colonial-style. Choose from two spacious decks to enjoy the sun and the ocean view. There is a television room furnished in white wicker for rainy days. The beach is one and a half miles long, and includes boardwalk shops, boutiques, and restaurants. A short drive away are many discount shopping areas, Seabrook Raceway, and Portsmouth Harbor.

The Inn on Golden Pond ✪
ROUTE 3, BOX 680, HOLDERNESS, NEW HAMPSHIRE 03245

Tel: **(603) 968-7269**
Best Time to Call: **Evenings**
Host(s): **Bill and Bonnie Webb**
Location: **4 mi. from I-93**
No. of Rooms: **9**
No. of Private Baths: **7**
Max. No. Sharing Bath: **4**
Double/pb: **$75**
Single/pb: **$55**
Double/sb: **$65**
Single/sb: **$45**
Open: **All year**
Breakfast: **Full**
Credit Cards: **MC, VISA**
Pets: **No**
Children: **Welcome, over 12**
Smoking: **No**
Social Drinking: **Permitted**
Airport/Station Pickup: **Yes**

If you saw the film *On Golden Pond*, you are familiar with the beauty of the countryside surrounding this inn. Built in 1879 on 55 acres, the house is across the street from Squam Lake, the setting for the movie. The rooms are bright and airy, decorated in a warm, homey style. Breakfast specialties include apple pancakes with local maple syrup, and a sausage, egg, and cheese casserole. Nearby are two golf courses, Waterville Valley, and Loon Mountain.

The Forest—A Country Inn ✪
ROUTE 16A, P.O. BOX 37, INTERVALE, NEW HAMPSHIRE 03845

Tel: **(603) 356-9772**
Best Time to Call: **After Noon**
Host(s): **Rae and Ken Wyman**
Location: **50 mi. from Rte. 93**
No. of Rooms: **13**
No. of Private Baths: **7**
Max. No. Sharing Bath: **4**
Double/pb: **$48–$70**

Double/sb: **$44–$66**
Single/sb: **$37–$48**
Guest Cottage: **$56–$80, sleeps 4**
Open: **May 1–Mar. 31**
Reduced Rates: **Oct. 23–Dec. 22;
　May 1–June 30**
Breakfast: **Full**

Other Meals: **Available**
Credit Cards: **AMEX, MC, VISA**
Pets: **No**
Children: **Welcome**
Smoking: **Permitted**
Social Drinking: **Permitted**

Reigning over 25 wooded acres in the White Mountains, this three-story Victorian inn has been in continuous operation since the late 1800s. Inside, the inn has the feel of a big country home—full of braided rugs, comfortable chairs, antiques, crafts, and country collectibles. The stone cottage has a fireplace and is a favorite of honeymooners. Outside, you're close to all of the wonderful recreational possibilities that the valley has to offer—downhill skiing, hiking, biking, canoeing, kayaking, tennis, golf, and more. In back of the inn is a swimming pool and, in winter, all you have to do is go across the street to the Intervale Nordic Learning Center where you can use the cross-country ski trails at no extra cost.

The Galway House
OLD PETERBOROUGH ROAD, JAFFREY, NEW HAMPSHIRE 03452

Tel: **(603) 532-8083**
Host(s): **Joe and Marie Manning**
Location: **1 mi. from US 202**
No. of Rooms: **2**
Max. No. Sharing Bath: **4**
Double/sb: **$45**
Single/sb: **$35**

Open: **Aug. 15–June 30**
Breakfast: **Full**
Pets: **No**
Children: **Welcome (crib)**
Smoking: **Permitted**
Social Drinking: **Permitted**
Airport/Station Pickup: **Yes**

This new, oversize Cape with a spacious yard and sun deck is situated on a rural road surrounded by acres of woodland. It is located at the foot of 3,165-foot Grand Monadnock, in the center of the Monadnock Region, known as the "Currier and Ives" corner of the state. Picturesque in every season, the area will make sports enthusiasts revel in the choice of activities. Joe and Marie welcome you to a warm hearth, a suitable beverage, and comfortable accommodations! From June through September they offer B&B on board their sailing sloop.

The Jefferson Inn ✪
ROUTE 2, RFD 1, BOX 63A, JEFFERSON, NEW HAMPSHIRE 03583

Tel: **(603) 586-7998**
Host(s): **Greg Brown and Bertie Koelewijn**
Location: **20 mi. from Rte. 93, Exit 35**
No. of Rooms: **7**
No. of Private Baths: **1**
Max. No. Sharing Bath: **4**
Double/pb: **$57**
Double/sb: **$39–$49**
Single/sb: **$36–$46**
Suites: **$75**
Open: **Dec.–Mar.; May–Oct.**

Reduced Rates: **Families; winter weekdays**
Breakfast: **Full**
Credit Cards: **AMEX, MC, VISA**
Pets: **No**
Children: **Welcome**
Smoking: **Permitted**
Social Drinking: **Permitted**
Airport/Station Pickup: **Yes**
Foreign Languages: **Dutch, French, German**

Built in 1896, this B&B is situated in the White Mountain National Forest and boasts beautiful valley and mountain views. Its location is ideal for outdoor activities, including hiking, swimming, canoeing, and golf in summer; downhill and cross-country skiing, skating, and snowshoeing in winter. The village of Jefferson sits within the shadows of Mt. Washington and the Presidential Range, with hiking trails starting near the inn's door. Decorated simply with period antiques, each impeccably clean room has a distinctive character. Relax on the porch in warm weather and end the day with a soothing cup of tea.

Ferry Point House ✪
R-1 BOX 335, LACONIA, NEW HAMPSHIRE 03246

Tel: **(603) 524-0087**
Best Time to Call: **After 6 PM**
Host(s): **Diane and Joe Damato**
Location: **90 mi. N of Boston**
No. of Rooms: **4**
No. of Private Baths: **4**
Double/pb: **$55–$65**
Single/pb: **$45–$55**
Open: **Memorial Day—Labor Day; Weekends during fall foliage**

Reduced Rates: **15%, weekly**
Breakfast: **Full**
Pets: **No**
Children: **Welcome**
Smoking: **Downstairs only**
Social Drinking: **Permitted**
Airport/Station Pickup: **Yes**
Foreign Languages: **French**

New England's past is well preserved in this 150-year-old Victorian located on picturesque Lake Winnisquam. Enjoy breathtaking views of the water and the mountains from a 60-foot veranda. Of course, the view is even more enjoyable when you're sipping lemonade or the house blend of coffee. Guest rooms overlook the lake and are furnished with antiques, collectibles, and fresh flowers. Breakfast is served in a Victorian-style dining room, and your hosts take pride in offering unusual dishes, such as cheese baked apples, crêpes, or Gran Marnier French toast. Ferry Point House is minutes from regional activities such as boating, skiing, dinner cruises, and a large selection of fine restaurants.

The Tin Whistle Inn ○
1047 UNION AVENUE, LACONIA, NEW HAMPSHIRE 03246

Tel: **(603) 528-4185**
Host(s): **Maureen C. Blazok**
Location: **10 mi. from Rte. 93**
No. of Rooms: **4**
Max. No. Sharing Bath: **4**
Double/sb: **$55–$65**
Single/sb: **$42–$52**
Open: **All year**

Reduced Rates: **20%, Mar.–Apr.**
Breakfast: **Full**
Credit Cards: **AMEX, MC, VISA**
Pets: **Sometimes**
Children: **Welcome, over 8**
Smoking: **Permitted**
Social Drinking: **Permitted**
Airport/Station Pickup: **Yes**

Step back to the Victorian age where you can relax in a quiet, homey atmosphere in front of a crackling fire. It is minutes away from a multitude of activities for the adventurous as well as the more inhibited. Try your hand at para sailing, scuba diving, water slides, hiking, skiing, and snowmobiling. You are welcome to play the piano, watch TV, or just relax on the large veranda overlooking Paugus Bay on Lake Winnipesaukee.

The Beal House Inn
247 WEST MAIN STREET, LITTLETON, NEW HAMPSHIRE 03561

Tel: **(603) 444-2661**
Best Time to Call: **10 AM–10 PM**
Host(s): **Jim and Ann Carver**
Location: **1 mi. I-93**
No. of Rooms: **14**
No. of Private Baths: **10**
Max. No. Sharing Bath: **4**
Double/pb: **$45–$95**
Single/pb: **$40–$75**
Double/sb: **$40–$45**

Suites: **$70–$125**
Open: **All year**
Reduced Rates: **Groups**
Breakfast: **Continental**
Credit Cards: **AMEX, DC, MC, VISA**
Pets: **No**
Children: **Welcome (crib)**
Smoking: **Permitted**
Social Drinking: **Permitted**

Jim and Ann have an antiques shop and have furnished their Federal-style home with choice pieces. The decor is constantly changing since so many guests buy these pieces and take them away. Breakfast features hot popovers served by the fireside. The inn is conveniently accessible to six great ski areas, Franconia Notch, and the famed Old Man of the Mountain. Popcorn, cheese, and crackers are complimentary. Tea is always available.

Peep-Willow Farm ✪
BIXBY STREET, MARLBOROUGH, NEW HAMPSHIRE 03455

Tel: (603) 876-3807
Best Time to Call: 7:30 PM–8 AM
Host(s): **Noel Aderer**
Location: **7 mi. E of Keene**
No. of Rooms: 3
Max. No. Sharing Bath: **4**
Double/sb: **$35**
Single/sb: **$20**

Open: **All year**
Breakfast: **Full**
Pets: **No**
Children: **Welcome**
Smoking: **No**
Social Drinking: **Permitted**
Airport/Station Pickup: **Yes**

Noel Aderer has a new Colonial farmhouse on a working Thoroughbred horse farm. She raises and trains horses for competition, and while there is plenty of room for petting and admiring, guests are not permitted to ride. Peep-Willow is named after horses number one and two, respectively. It is a charming place with lots of wood accents and antiques. Breakfast specialties include French toast, with local maple syrup, and bacon and eggs. Guests are welcome to watch farm chores, visit the horses, and enjoy a cup of coffee with Noel, who has done everything from working on a kibbutz to training polo ponies for a maharajah.

Blue Goose Inn ✪
ROUTE 103B, P.O. BOX 182, MT. SUNAPEE, NEW HAMPSHIRE 03772

Tel: (603) 763-5519
Host(s): **Bobbie and Dennis Giacino**
Location: **10 mi. from I-89**
No. of Rooms: 5
No. of Private Baths: **4**
Max. No. Sharing Bath: **3**
Double/pb: **$45**
Single/pb: **$40**
Double/sb: **$45**

Single/sb: **$40**
Open: **All year**
Breakfast: **Full**
Credit Cards: **MC, VISA**
Pets: **No**
Children: **Welcome**
Smoking: **Permitted**
Social Drinking: **Permitted**
Airport/Station Pickup: **Yes**

This cozy, early 19th-century Colonial farmhouse is located at the base of Mt. Sunapee on scenic Lake Sunapee. The guest rooms are quiet and spacious, adorned with handmade quilts and attractive antiques.

Whether you're coming here for the greening of spring, the long lush summer, the autumn foliage, or the white-blanketed backdrop for skiing or sleighing, you'll be treated to Bobbie's breakfast specialty: a combination of bacon, eggs, and cheese, baked in a maple flavored biscuit. It is served on the enclosed porch, which is enhanced by skylights and hanging plants. You're invited to join your hosts and other guests for wine, fruit, and cheese served on the porch or by the fireplace in the common room.

The Inn at Coit Mountain
HCR 63, BOX 3, NEWPORT, NEW HAMPSHIRE 03773

Tel: **(603) 863-3583 or (800) 367-2364**	Breakfast: **Full**
Host(s): **Dick and Judi Tatem**	Other Meals: **Available**
Location: **8 mi. S of Rte. 89**	Credit Cards: **MC, VISA**
No. of Rooms: **5**	Pets: **No**
Max. No. Sharing Bath: **4**	Children: **Welcome (crib)**
Double/sb: **$55–$85**	Smoking: **Permitted**
Single/sb: **$45–$75**	Social Drinking: **Permitted**
Open: **All year**	Airport/Station Pickup: **Yes**
Reduced Rates: **Weekly**	

This elegant Georgian home was built in 1790. It was later purchased by the Corbins, wealthy entrepreneurs known for developing Coney Island. The romantic history of the inn is well blended with the comforts of today. The library, with its massive granite fireplace, offers year-round warmth. Just off the library is the Stoneagle Frame Studio, whose large arched window is modeled after the one in Independence Hall in Philadelphia. The bedrooms are comfortable and spacious, some with cozy fireplaces. The Lake Sunapee area provides much to see and do, including swimming, boating, cross-country skiing, hiking, and golfing.

The Foothills Farm ○
P.O. BOX 1904, NORTH CONWAY, NEW HAMPSHIRE 03818

Tel: **(207) 935-3799**	Single/sb: **$32**
Best Time to Call: **Early evenings**	Open: **Apr. 16–Mar. 14**
Host(s): **Kevin Early and Theresa Rovere**	Reduced Rates: **Available; 10%, seniors**
Location: **40 mi. W of Portland, Me.**	Breakfast: **Full**
No. of Rooms: **4**	Pets: **Welcome**
Max. No. Sharing Bath: **4**	Children: **Welcome**
Double/sb: **$42–$48**	Smoking: **Permitted**

Social Drinking: **Permitted**
Minimum Stay: **2 nights weekends during fall foliage and holidays**

Airport/Station Pickup: **Yes**

This restored 1850s clapboard farmhouse is located on a quiet back road in the foothills of the White Mountains. The house is surrounded by flowers, a vegetable garden, and asparagus fields. The well-groomed grounds also include a trout stream and plenty of room to bike or cross-country ski. Bedrooms are furnished in period antiques, and one has a fireplace. Guests are welcome to relax in the den, where they'll find books and a crackling fire. In warmer weather, the screened-in porch overlooking the fields and gardens is a favorite spot. Breakfast specialties such as eggs Benedict with home fries, and blueberry pancakes with sausage are served in a country kitchen with antique stove and pine paneling. Kevin and Theresa have bicycles to lend and are glad to direct you to the sights of this scenic region. Scores of restaurants, factory outlets, and canoeing, hiking, and ski areas are also nearby.

Meadow Farm
JENNESS POND ROAD, NORTHWOOD, NEW HAMPSHIRE 03261

Tel: **(603) 942-8619**
Host(s): **Douglas and Janet Briggs**
Location: **18 mi. E of Concord**
No. of Rooms: **3**
Max. No. Sharing Bath: **3**
Double/sb: **$45**
Single/sb: **$35**

Open: **All year**
Reduced Rates: **Families**
Breakfast: **Full**
Pets: **Sometimes**
Children: **Welcome**
Smoking: **Permitted**
Social Drinking: **Permitted**

Meadow Farm is set on 50 acres of quiet woods and horse pastures. The house is an authentic New England Colonial dating back to 1770, with wide pine floors, beamed ceilings, and old fireplaces. In the morning, a country breakfast of homemade breads, seasonal fruit, and local syrup is served in the keeping room. Guests are invited to relax on the private beach on an adjacent lake. The property also has plenty of wooded trails for long walks or cross-country skiing. Meadow Farm is an ideal location for those en route to Concord, the seacoast, or the mountains.

Crab Apple Inn ✪
ROUTE 25, PLYMOUTH, NEW HAMPSHIRE 03264

Tel: **(603) 536-4476**
Best Time to Call: **Mornings; evenings**
Host(s): **Bill and Carolyn Crenson**
Location: **4 mi. from Rte. 93**
No. of Rooms: **4**
No. of Private Baths: **2**
Max. No. Sharing Bath: **4**
Double/pb: **$65–$70**
Double/sb: **$60–$65**
Suites: **$70–$75**
Open: **All year**
Breakfast: **Full**
Credit Cards: **MC, VISA**
Pets: **No**
Children: **Welcome, over 8**
Smoking: **Permitted**
Social Drinking: **Permitted**

Located in the beautiful Baker River Valley at the gateway to the White Mountain region, the inn is an 1835 brick building of Federal design situated beside a small brook at the foot of Tenny Mountain. The bedrooms on the second floor have fireplaces; those on the third floor have a panoramic view of the mountains. All are tastefully furnished. There are several fine restaurants nearby, and the inn is within a 10-minute drive of Plymouth State College. Gift studios and handcraft and antique shops in the area provide treasures for both the discerning and casual buyer.

Leighton Inn ✪
69 RICHARDS AVENUE, PORTSMOUTH, NEW HAMPSHIRE 03801

Tel: **(603) 433-2188**
Host(s): **Catherine Stone**
Location: **1 mi. from I-95**
No. of Rooms: **5**
No. of Private Baths: **3**
Max. No. Sharing Bath: **4**
Double/pb: **$75**
Single/pb: **$65**
Double/sb: **$65**
Single/sb: **$55**
Open: **All year**
Reduced Rates: **Nov.–Apr.**
Breakfast: **Full**
Credit Cards: **MC, VISA**
Pets: **No**
Children: **Welcome**
Smoking: **Permitted**
Social Drinking: **Permitted**
Airport/Station Pickup: **Yes**
Foreign Languages: **French**

In 1809, cabinetmaker Samuel Wyatt built himself a Federal-style home, sparing no expense. Now named for a prominent Portsmouth family who lived there in the 1800s, the inn is just a short walk from Strawbery Banke, a "living museum" that traces the history of this colorful waterfront city through four centuries. Swimming, boating, and fishing are just a short drive away, and whale-watch cruises can easily be arranged. In summer, guests breakfast on the porch that overlooks the inn's formal gardens; in winter, they sit in front of a fire in the pine-paneled country kitchen. And, if you're musically inclined, Catherine invites you to sit down at the 1913 Steinway concert grand piano in the library and play as long as you'd like.

Grassy Pond House
RINDGE, NEW HAMPSHIRE 03461

Tel: **(603) 899-5166/5167**
Best Time to Call: **Mornings**
Host(s): **Carmen Linares and Robert Multer**
Location: **60 mi. NW of Boston**
No. of Rooms: **3**
No. of Private Baths: **2**
Max. No. Sharing Bath: **4**
Double/pb: **$65**
Double/sb: **$60**

Single/sb: **$40**
Open: **All year**
Breakfast: **Full**
Pets: **No**
Children: **Welcome, over 14**
Smoking: **No**
Social Drinking: **Permitted**
Airport/Station Pickup: **Yes**
Foreign Languages: **Spanish**

This secluded 19th-century farmhouse is set among 150 acres of woods and fields. The house has been restored, enlarged, and decorated in period pieces. Guest quarters, overlooking the gardens and lake, feature a private entrance and a living room with fireplace. Breakfast specialties include pancakes with local maple syrup, fresh eggs and bacon, and plenty of good Colombian coffee. This setting high in the Monadnock region is perfect for hiking, skiing, boating, fishing, and swimming.

The Tokfarm ✪
BOX 229, WOOD AVENUE, RINDGE, NEW HAMPSHIRE 03461

Tel: **(603) 899-6646**
Best Time to Call: **Early AM, evenings**
Host(s): **Mrs. W. B. Nottingham**
Location: **50 mi. NW of Boston**
No. of Rooms: **5**
Max. No. Sharing Bath: **4**
Double/sb: **$35–$45**
Single/sb: **$18**
Open: **Apr. 16–Nov. 14**

Breakfast: **Continental**
Pets: **No**
Children: **No**
Smoking: **No**
Social Drinking: **Permitted**
Airport/Station Pickup: **Yes**
Foreign Languages: **Dutch, French, German**

This 150-year-old farmhouse has a spectacular view of three states from its 1,400-foot hilltop. Mt. Monadnock, the second most climbed peak in the world (Mt. Fuji is first), is practically in its backyard! Mrs.

Nottingham raises Christmas trees, is a world traveler, and loves to ski. She'll recommend things to keep you busy. Don't miss the lovely Cathedral of the Pines. Franklin Pierce College is nearby.

The Hilltop Inn ✪
MAIN STREET, P.O. BOX 9, SUGAR HILL, NEW HAMPSHIRE 03585

Tel: **(603) 823-5695**
Host(s): **Mike and Meri Hern**
Location: **2½ mi. W of Franconia**
No. of Rooms: **5**
No. of Private Baths: **2**
Max. No. Sharing Bath: **4**
Double/sb: **$50–$60**
Single/sb: **$40**
Suites: **$35–$100**
Open: **All year**
Breakfast: **Full**
Pets: **Welcome**
Children: **Welcome (crib)**
Smoking: **Permitted**
Social Drinking: **Permitted**
Airport/Station Pickup: **Yes**

The Hilltop Inn is a sprawling, 19th-century Victorian located in a small, friendly village. Inside, you'll find a warm, cozy atmosphere, comfortable furnishings, and lots of antiques. The kitchen is the heart of the house in more ways than one. In the morning, homemade muffins are served fresh from the old-fashioned Garland stove. In the evening, the sunsets from the deck are breathtaking. Your hosts are professional caterers and are pleased to cater to you. Join them for wine and cheese after a day of activities. Local attractions include Franconia Notch, White Mountain National Forest, North Conway, great skiing, and spectacular foliage.

Times Ten Inn ✪
ROUTE 103B, BOX 572, SUNAPEE, NEW HAMPSHIRE 03782

Tel: **(603) 763-5120**
Host(s): **Audrey and Dick Kelly**
Location: **90 mi. NW of Boston**
No. of Rooms: **3**
Max. No. Sharing Bath: **4**
Double/sb: **$42**
Single/sb: **$30**
Open: **All year**
Reduced Rates: **Families**
Breakfast: **Full**
Pets: **No**
Children: **Welcome**
Smoking: **Permitted**
Social Drinking: **Permitted**
Airport/Station Pickup: **Yes**

An 1820 New England farmhouse, with floor-to-ceiling living room windows overlooking a wildlife preserve, it's 25 miles to Dartmouth College, recreational Lake Sunapee, and skiing. Audrey and Dick offer a huge breakfast of Swedish pancakes, real maple syrup, homemade preserves, bacon, or sausage. Complimentary cheese snacks and good conversation are always on tap.

Suncook House ✪
62 MAIN STREET, SUNCOOK, NEW HAMPSHIRE 03275

Tel: **(603) 485-8141**
Best Time to Call: **Mornings**
Host(s): **Gerry and Evelyn Lavoie**
Location: **6 mi. S of Concord**
No. of Rooms: **4**
No. of Private Baths: **2**
Max. No. Sharing Bath: **3**
Double/pb: **$50**
Single/pb: **$44**
Double/sb: **$42**

Single/sb: **$35**
Open: **All year**
Reduced Rates: **10%, seniors**
Breakfast: **Full**
Pets: **No**
Children: **Welcome, over 12**
Smoking: **No**
Social Drinking: **Permitted**
Airport/Station Pickup: **Yes**

Suncook House is a spacious brick Georgian set on three beautifully maintained acres. The house is newly renovated and its comfortable rooms are furnished with period pieces. A formal living room, sun parlor, den, and an excellent organ are available for your relaxation and pleasure. This country home allows one the benefits of feeling away from it all while still being able to enjoy the convenience of a main road that leads to the mountains and lakes. Walk to village churches, restaurants, and tennis courts. New Hampshire College and Bear Brook State Park are both within a five-mile drive.

Isaac Springfield House ✪
RFD 1, ROUTE 28 SOUTH, WOLFEBORO, NEW HAMPSHIRE 03894

Tel: **(603) 569-3529**
Best Time to Call: **Mornings; evenings**
Host(s): **Rose LeBlanc and Andrew Terragni**
Location: **2 mi. S of Wolfeboro**
No. of Rooms: **4**
Max. No. Sharing Bath: **4**
Double/sb: **$60**
Single/sb: **$55**

Open: **All year**
Reduced Rates: **Available**
Breakfast: **Full**
Credit Cards: **MC, VISA**
Pets: **Sometimes**
Children: **Welcome**
Smoking: **Permitted**
Social Drinking: **Permitted**

Isaac Springfield built this spacious Victorian back in 1871. It is painted a warm yellow and has a large, old-fashioned, wraparound porch. Inside, the rooms are decorated with antique and brass furnishings. There is a cozy parlor with fireplace and piano where guests may want to bring a bottle of wine. Rose and Andrew will gladly provide ice and glasses at any time. Each morning, they serve homemade muffins, fresh fruit, eggs, and pancakes in a spacious dining room. This lovely home is five minutes from beautiful Lake Winnipesaukee and from the quaint shops and attractions in town. Wolfeboro is a center of seasonal activities including boating, hiking, ice sailing, and much more.

Tuc' Me Inn
68 NORTH MAIN STREET, P.O. BOX 657, WOLFEBORO, NEW HAMPSHIRE 03894

Tel: **(603) 569-5702**
Host(s): **Irma and Walter Limberger**
Location: **25 mi. from I-93, Rte. 104 Exit**
No. of Rooms: **7**
No. of Private Baths: **3**
Max. No. Sharing Bath: **4**
Double/pb: **$75**
Single/pb: **$70**
Double/sb: **$70**

Single/sb: **$65**
Open: **All year**
Reduced Rates: **Available**
Breakfast: **Full**
Credit Cards: **MC, VISA**
Pets: **No**
Children: **No**
Smoking: **Permitted**
Social Drinking: **Permitted**
Airport/Station Pickup: **Yes**

This early 1800s Colonial is located in the town that is known as the oldest summer resort in America. Wolfeboro is situated on the eastern shore of Lake Winnipesaukee, a beautiful spot in any season. At the inn, guests will enjoy a homey atmosphere and tastefully furnished rooms. In the morning, wake up to the aroma of freshly brewed coffee and everything that goes with it. You can walk to town or take a cruise on the *Mt. Washington*. After a day of activity, enjoy a cool drink on one of the sun porches back at your home away from home.

For key to listings, see inside front or back cover.

✪ This star means that rates are guaranteed through December 31, 1989 to any guest making a reservation as a result of reading about the B&B in *BED & BREAKFAST U.S.A.*—1989 edition.

Please enclose a self-addressed, stamped, business-sized envelope when contacting reservation services.

For more details on what you can expect in a B&B, see Chapter 1.

Always mention *Bed & Breakfast U.S.A.* when making reservations!

If no B&B is listed in the area you'll be visiting, use the form on page 693 to order a copy of our "List of New B&Bs."

We want to hear from you! Use the form on page 691.

NEW JERSEY

Stanhope •
Denville •
• Midland Park
• Lyndhurst
Milford •
Princeton •
• Spring Lake
Jobstown •
• Atlantic City
Dennisville •
• North Wildwood
• Cape May

Bed & Breakfast of New Jersey, Inc.
SUITE 132, 103 GODWIN AVENUE, MIDLAND PARK, NEW JERSEY 07432

Tel: **(201) 444-7409**
Best Time to Call: **9 AM–3 PM**
States/Regions Covered: **New Jersey**

Rates (Single/Double):
Average: $35 $65
Luxury: $70 $135
Credit Cards: **AMEX, MC, VISA**

Whether you crave the sound of lazy waves gently slapping the side of a boat, or the tranquillity of rolling country hills, you'll find it all in New Jersey. Indulge yourself, and take in the lavish elegance of a high-rise condo with a perfect view of the Manhattan skyline. Stay in a restored mountain mansion, in a villa by a great golf course, in an

1889 artist's studio, or in any of hundreds of traditional, well-maintained homes. From the Meadowlands, to Princeton University, to Cape May, to Edison's home in Menlo Park, to the Pine Barrens, you will find that the Garden State has much to offer. Please send $5 for the descriptive directory.

Bed & Breakfast of Princeton—A Reservation Service
P.O. BOX 571, PRINCETON, NEW JERSEY 08450

Tel: **(609) 924-3189**
Coordinator: **John W. Hurley**
States/Regions Covered: **Princeton**

Rates (Single/Double):
Average: **$30–$55 $40–$65**
Credit Cards: **No**

Princeton is a lovely town; houses are well set back on carefully tended lawns, screened by towering trees. Some of John's hosts live within walking distance of Princeton University. Nassau Hall (circa 1756) is its oldest building; its chapel is the largest of any at an American university. Nearby corporate parks include national companies such as RCA, Squibb, and the David Sarnoff Research Center. Restaurants feature every imaginable cuisine, and charming shops offer a wide variety of wares. Personal checks accepted for deposit or total payment in advance, cash or traveler's checks are required for any balance due.

Albert G. Stevens Inn ✪
127 MYRTLE AVENUE, CAPE MAY, NEW JERSEY 08204

Tel: **(609) 884-4717**
Host(s): **Paul and Alice Linden**
Location: **40 mi. S of Atlantic City**
No. of Rooms: **6**
No. of Private Baths: **4**
Max. No. Sharing Bath: **4**
Double/pb: **$85**
Double/sb: **$70**

Suites: **$95**
Open: **Feb. 1–Dec. 31**
Breakfast: **Full**
Credit Cards: **MC, VISA**
Pets: **No**
Children: **No**
Smoking: **No**
Social Drinking: **Permitted**

This 87-year-old Victorian is located next door to historic Wilbrahan Mansion and three blocks from the beach. The antique decor includes mother-of-pearl inlay in the parlor suite, an oak mantel, and other treasures throughout. The wraparound veranda is a wonderful place for sipping your second cup of coffee or for relaxing later in the day. Breakfast often features ham and cheese quiche or waffles with whipped cream. There is a minimum stay of two nights on weekends and three nights for the Fourth of July, Memorial Day, and Labor Day weekends.

Barnard-Good House ✪
238 PERRY STREET, CAPE MAY, NEW JERSEY 08204

Tel: **(609) 884-5381**
Best Time to Call: **8 AM–9 PM**
Host(s): **Nan and Tom Hawkins**
No. of Rooms: **6**
No. of Private Baths: **3**
Max. No. Sharing Bath: **2**
Double/pb: **$85**
Single/pb: **$67.50**
Double/sb: **$75**
Single/sb: **$58.50**
Suites: **$85**
Open: **Apr.–Nov.**
Breakfast: **Full**
Pets: **No**
Children: **No**
Smoking: **No**
Social Drinking: **Permitted**
Airport/Station Pickup: **Yes**

Nan and Tom cordially invite you to their Second Empire Victorian cottage (circa 1869), just two blocks from the "swimming" beach. They love antiques and are continually adding to their collection. They use them generously to create the warm and comfortable atmosphere. Nan's breakfast includes homemade exotic juices, delicious home-baked breads, and unusual preserves. In spring and fall, added gourmet entrées and side dishes make for an epicurean feast. Iced tea and snacks are served evenings. There's a two-night minimum stay in spring and fall; three nights in summer.

Columns-by-the-Sea ✪
1513 BEACH DRIVE, CAPE MAY, NEW JERSEY 08204

Tel: **(609) 884-2228**
Best Time to Call: **11 AM–10 PM**
Host(s): **Barry and Cathy Rein**
No. of Rooms: **11**
No. of Private Baths: **11**
Double/pb: **$89–$115**
Single/pb: **$79–$105**
Open: **Apr.–Oct.**
Reduced Rates: **10% weekly; 20% Mon.–Wed. in June, Sept., Oct.**
Breakfast: **Full**
Other Meals: **Available**
Credit Cards: **MC, VISA**
Pets: **No**
Children: **Welcome, over 12**
Smoking: **No**
Social Drinking: **Permitted**
Minimum Stay: **3 nights on weekends**
Airport/Station Pickup: **Yes**
Foreign Languages: **German**

A prominent Philadelphia physician built this grand Victorian back when a summer "cottage" had 20 rooms, two fireplaces, and hand-carved 12-foot ceilings. Dr. Davis combined a whimsical Italian palazzo style with fluted columns on the veranda and Colonial Revival accents. Inside, a three-story staircase leads to large, airy rooms with ocean views. Your hosts have decorated the rooms with Victorian, modern, and Chinese pieces collected over years of world travel. Gourmet soufflés and stratas are served in a formal dining room with antique wood sideboards and lace curtains. In the afternoon, tea and sherry are offered on the seaside veranda. The Reins have bikes to lend, and they will gladly direct you to charming streets lined with vintage Victorians, shops, and restaurants.

The Mainstay Inn ✪
635 COLUMBIA AVENUE, CAPE MAY, NEW JERSEY 08204

Tel: **(609) 884-8690**
Best Time to Call: **10 AM–4 PM**
Host(s): **Tom and Sue Carroll**
No. of Rooms: **12**
No. of Private Baths: **12**
Double/pb: **$90–$115**
Single/pb: **$80–$105**
Suites: **$95–$115**

Open: **Mar. 15–Dec. 15**
Reduced Rates: **Off-season; weekdays**
Breakfast: **Full**
Pets: **No**
Children: **Welcome, over 12**
Smoking: **No**
Social Drinking: **Permitted**

Located in the heart of the historic district, this 116-year-old mansion was originally built as a private gambling club. Except for a few 20th-century concessions, it still looks much as it did when the gamblers were there, with 14-foot ceilings, elaborate chandeliers, and outstanding Victorian antiques. Tom and Sue serve breakfast either in the formal dining room or on the veranda; afternoon tea and homemade snacks are a ritual. Breakfast often features ham and apple pie, or corn quiche with baked ham. Continental breakfast is served in summer. Rock on the wide veranda; enjoy croquet in the garden; or retreat to the cupola. Minimum stay is three nights in season.

The Henry Ludlam Inn ✪
DENNISVILLE, NEW JERSEY (CAPE MAY COUNTY, RD 3, BOX 298, WOODBINE, NEW JERSEY 08270)

Tel: **(609) 861-5847**
Best Time to Call: **After 5 PM**
Host(s): **Ann and Marty Thurlow**
Location: **18 mi. N of Cape May**
No. of Rooms: **6**
No. of Private Baths: **2**
Max. No. Sharing Bath: **4**
Double/pb: **$75**
Double/sb: **$65**

Suite: **$75**
Open: **All year**
Reduced Rates: **Weekly**
Breakfast: **Full**
Pets: **No**
Children: **Welcome, over 12**
Smoking: **Permitted**
Social Drinking: **Permitted**
Airport/Station Pickup: **Yes**

Built in 1803, Ann and Marty's home is furnished with antiques, handmade quilts, plants, and other nice touches to complete the decor. It's located in Dennisville, on a 55-acre lake that's 20 minutes from the Stone Harbor beaches. During cold months, breakfast is served in the Keeping Room; in warm months, on the porch overlooking the lake. All the bedrooms have working fireplaces for cozy comfort. Afternoon tea and wine are served.

Lakeside B&B ✪
11 SUNSET TRAIL, DENVILLE, NEW JERSEY 07834

Tel: **(201) 625-5129**
Host(s): **Annette and Al Begins**
Location: **35 mi. W of New York City**
No. of Rooms: **1**
No. of Private Baths: **1**
Double/pb: **$40**
Single/pb: **$30**

Open: **All year**
Breakfast: **Full**
Pets: **No**
Children: **No**
Smoking: **Permitted**
Social Drinking: **Permitted**

Just off Route 80, midway between Manhattan and the Pocono Mountains, is this modern, two-story home with private guest quarters on the ground level. There's a stunning view of the bay leading to Indian Lake. Al and Annette, both teachers, will provide you with a rowboat and beach passes, as well as wine and cheese afterward. Relax on the deck overlooking the bay, or explore the unspoiled towns and points of interest off the tourist trail. Good restaurants of every variety and price range abound.

Daffodil ✪
R.D. 1, BOX 420, JOBSTOWN, NEW JERSEY 08041

Tel: **(609) 723-5364**
Host(s): **Lyd Sudler**

Location: **5 miles from N.J. Tpke., Exit 7**

No. of Rooms: **3**
Max. No. Sharing Bath: **4**
Double/sb: **$40**
Suites: **$65**
Open: **All year**
Breakfast: **Full**

Other Meals: **Available**
Pets: **No**
Children: **Welcome**
Smoking: **Permitted**
Social Drinking: **Permitted**

This spacious, contemporary farmhouse was built in 1961 and is attractively furnished with family heirlooms. From the porch, there's a spectacular view of the pastures with the cows grazing and the deer that come out of the woods at dusk. It's situated in the heart of Burlington County, where every little town, including Burlington, Bordentown, and Mt. Holly, is a pre-Revolutionary gem. It is a half hour to Philadelphia or Princeton. Lyd enjoys music, gardening, and pampering her guests.

Jeremiah J. Yereance House ✪
410 RIVERSIDE AVENUE, LYNDHURST, NEW JERSEY 07071

Tel: **(201) 438-9457**
Best Time to Call: **After 6 PM**
Host(s): **Evelyn and Frank Pezzolla**
Location: **12 mi. W of New York City**
No. of Rooms: **1 suite**
No. of Private Baths: **1**
Suites: **$70–$75**
Open: **All year**

Reduced Rates: **Weekly; 15%, seniors**
Breakfast: **Continental**
Pets: **No**
Children: **Welcome, over 12**
Smoking: **No**
Social Drinking: **Permitted**
Airport/Station Pickup: **Yes**

Evelyn and Frank Pezzolla fell in love with this wood-frame Colonial when they first saw it in 1984. After a year of rewiring and replacing the roof and just about everything else, the house began to look like the historical landmark it is. In 1986 the government agreed and placed it on the state and national registers. The house is set in a quiet neighborhood across from a riverside park with jogging paths, bike trails, and picnic areas. The guest suite occupies the south wing of the house and consists of a small parlor with fireplace and an adjoining bedroom and private bath. In the morning, a help-yourself buffet of hot drinks, homemade breads, muffins, and fresh fruits awaits you. The Jeremiah J. Yereance House is just five minutes from the Meadowlands Sports Complex.

Chestnut Hill on-the-Delaware ◐
63 CHURCH STREET, MILFORD, NEW JERSEY 08848

Tel: **(201) 995-9761**
Host(s): **Linda and Rob Castagna**
Location: **15 mi. from Rte. 78**
No. of Rooms: **5**
No. of Private Baths: **2**
Max. No. Sharing Bath: **4**
Double/pb: **$75–$80**
Double/sb: **$60**

Single/sb: **$50**
Open: **All year**
Reduced Rates: **Weekly**
Breakfast: **Full**
Pets: **No**
Children: **Welcome**
Smoking: **No**
Social Drinking: **Permitted**

The veranda of this 1860 Neo-Italianate Victorian overlooks the peaceful Delaware River. Linda, Rob, and teenage son Michael have refurbished and restored their home with charm, grace, and beauty. The historic countryside is great for antique hunting, water sports, art shows, and restaurants. It's only minutes to New Hope and Bucks County delights, and to dozens of factory outlets.

Candlelight Inn ◐
2310 CENTRAL AVENUE, NORTH WILDWOOD, NEW JERSEY 08260

Tel: **(609) 522-6200**
Best Time to Call: **8 AM–11 PM**
Host(s): **Paul DiFilippo and Diane Buscham**
Location: **40 mi. S of Atlantic City**
No. of Rooms: **9**
No. of Private Baths: **7**
Max. No. Sharing Bath: **4**
Double/pb: **$60–$90**
Double/sb: **$50–$65**
Suite: **$80–$100**

Open: **Feb.–Dec.**
Reduced Rates: **10%, seniors**
Breakfast: **Full**
Credit Cards: **AMEX, MC, VISA**
Pets: **No**
Children: **No**
Smoking: **No**
Social Drinking: **Permitted**
Airport/Station Pickup: **Yes**
Foreign Languages: **French**
Minimum Stay: **3 nights July and Aug.**

Leaming Rice, Sr., built this Queen Anne Victorian at the turn of the century. The house remained in the family until Diane and Paul restored it and created a bed and breakfast. Large oak doors with beveled glass invite you into the main vestibule, which has a fireplace nook. A wide variety of original gas lighting fixtures may be found throughout the house. Guest rooms have fresh flowers and are furnished with period pieces and antiques. Breakfast is served in the dining room with a built-in oak breakfront, and chestnut picket doors. A hot tub and sun deck are special spots for relaxing. In the afternoon, enjoy tea and cookies on the wide veranda. This elegant inn is convenient to the beaches, boardwalk, and historic Cape May.

Home Suite Home ✪
1410 SURF AVENUE, NORTH WILDWOOD, NEW JERSEY 08260

Tel: **(609) 729-6625**
Host(s): **Jim and Connie Costa**
Location: **40 mi. S of Atlantic City**
No. of Rooms: **4**
No. of Private Baths: **2**
Max. No. Sharing Bath: **4**
Double/pb: **$65–$85**
Single/pb: **$50–$65**
Double/sb: **$60–$75**
Single/sb: **$45–$60**
Open: **Mar. 1–Dec. 31**
Reduced Rates: **10%, seniors; weekly**
Breakfast: **Full**
Credit Cards: **MC, VISA**
Pets: **No**
Children: **Welcome, over 12**
Smoking: **Permitted**
Social Drinking: **Permitted**
Foreign Languages: **Italian, Polish**
Minimum Stay: **3 nights July and Aug.**

Jim and Connie Costa welcome you to their white marble executive-style home located one block from the beach. The house is decorated in a Grecian motif with comfortable furnishings and family pieces. There is plenty to do in this resort town, and you're just one and a half blocks from the boardwalk when you stay with the Costas. They can suggest bicycle routes, recommend restaurants, and direct you to even more activities in nearby Atlantic City.

Ashling Cottage ✪
106 SUSSEX AVENUE, SPRING LAKE, NEW JERSEY 07762

Tel: **(201) 449-3553**
Host(s): **Goodi and Jack Stewart**
Location: **6 mi. from Garden State Pky., Exit 98**
No. of Rooms: **10**
No. of Private Baths: **8**
Max. No. Sharing Bath: **4**
Double/pb: **$67–$102**
Single/pb: **$63–$91**
Double/sb: **$58–$75**

Single/sb: **$54–$71**
Open: **Mar.–Dec.**
Reduced Rates: **Sept. 15–May 15**
Breakfast: **Continental**
Pets: **No**

Children: **No**
Smoking: **Permitted**
Social Drinking: **Permitted**
Airport/Station Pickup: **Yes**

The Jersey shore is a block away from this three-story, mansard-roofed cottage with bay windows, overhangs, nooks, and a small romantic balcony. Each guest room is different, with such features as dormer windows, wainscoting, and individual porches. A buffet breakfast is served in the glass-enclosed solarium with views of the ocean and boardwalk to the east. To the west is the willow-bordered Spring Lake, popular for boaters, with its wooden foot bridges, ducks, and geese. A two- to three-night minimum stay is required on weekends from May through August.

Whistling Swan Inn ✪
BOX 791, 110 MAIN STREET, STANHOPE, NEW JERSEY 07874

Tel: **(201) 347-6369**
Best Time to Call: **9 AM–6 PM**
Host(s): **Paula Williams and Joe Mulay**
Location: **45 mi. W of New York City**
No. of Rooms: **10**
No. of Private Baths: **10**
Double/pb: **$60–$75**
Open: **All year**

Reduced Rates: **Weekly; 10%, seniors**
Breakfast: **Full**
Credit Cards: **AMEX, MC, VISA**
Pets: **No**
Children: **Welcome, over 12**
Smoking: **No**
Social Drinking: **Permitted**
Airport/Station Pickup: **Yes**

You'll feel like you're back in grandmother's house when you visit this lovely Queen Anne Victorian located in a small, historic village. The massive limestone wraparound porch leads to comfortable rooms filled with family antiques. Your hosts have labored tirelessly to make the ornate woodwork, huge fireplace, old-fashioned fixtures, and even the dumbwaiter look like new. Take a bubble bath in a claw-footed tub and then wrap yourself in a fluffy robe before retiring. Your room will be individually decorated in an Oriental art decor or brass motif. Breakfast includes homemade muffins, breads, and fruit, along with a hot egg, cheese, or fruit dish. Special arrangements are easily made for corporate guests who need to eat early or require the use of a private telephone, copy service, or meeting room. The inn is close to the International Trade Zone, Waterloo Village, Lake Musconetcong, restaurants, and state parks and forests.

NEW MEXICO

Bed & Breakfast Rocky Mountains—New Mexico ✪
P.O. BOX 804, COLORADO SPRINGS, COLORADO 80901

Tel: (719) 630-3433
Best Time to Call: **May 15–Sept. 15, 9 AM–5 PM; 1–5 PM other times**
Coordinator: **Kate Peterson Winters**
States/Regions Covered:
  Albuquerque, Santa Fe, Taos

Rates (Single/Double):
  Modest: $35 $45
  Average: $60 $65
  Luxury: $60 $98
Credit Cards: **MC, VISA**

The Southwest is a "Land of Enchantment," where folks are able to maintain their bond with a slower, more relaxed pace. Experience southwestern art galleries, sculptures, ethnic foods, and Indian pueblos. Visit the hot-air balloon festival and the Taos Art Festival; go to the Santa Fe opera; ski in winter. B&Bs are in old thick-walled adobes, lovely suites, modest homes, or unhosted apartments. There is a $4.50 charge for Kate's directory.

The Corner House ☉
9121 JAMES PLACE NE, ALBUQUERQUE, NEW MEXICO 87111

Tel: **(505) 298-5800**	Open: **All year**
Host(s): **Jean Thompson**	Reduced Rates: **10%, families; seniors**
Best Time to Call: **After 5 PM**	Breakfast: **Full**
Location: **8 mi. NE of Albuquerque**	Other Meals: **Available**
No. of Rooms: **2**	Pets: **Sometimes**
No. of Private Baths: **1**	Children: **Welcome**
Max. No. Sharing Bath: **2**	Smoking: **Permitted**
Double/pb: **$40**	Social Drinking: **Permitted**
Double/sb: **$30**	

Jean welcomes you to her handsome Southwestern-style home, decorated in a delightful mix of antiques, handmade collectibles, and family mementos. A complimentary bottle of wine will make you feel right at home. Breakfast specialties include Jean's homemade muffins and Albuquerque's own Monday Goody Company delights. The Corner House is located in a quiet residential neighborhood just minutes from the significant Sandia Mountains. It is convenient to Old Town Albuquerque, Santa Fe, and many Indian pueblos.

Santa Fe Casita
P.O. BOX 287, CEDAR CREST, NEW MEXICO 87008

Tel: **(505) 281-3597**	Reduced Rates: **Weekly in winter**
Best Time to Call: **10 AM–4 PM**	Breakfast: **Continental**
Host(s): **Trisha Ambrose**	Credit Cards: **AMEX, MC, VISA**
Location: **½ mi. from Rte. 285**	Pets: **No**
Guest Cottage: **$85, sleeps 2**	Children: **Welcome**
Suite: **$125**	Smoking: **No**
Open: **All year**	Social Drinking: **Permitted**

The Ambrose family welcomes you to their Santa Fe Territorial-style home, located in the downtown historic district. Guests can choose from two accommodations, each with private entrance. The Artists Suite consists of two bedrooms and a sleeping loft. You can relax on the enclosed private patio or next to the kiva fireplace. The private adobe casita features a comfortable bedroom, a kitchen, a wood stove, and a private patio. Your hosts are interior decorators and have created a charming southwestern atmosphere with Santa Fe furnishings, Mexican tile floors, Hand-quilted linens, and down pillows. Greet each morning with French-roast coffee and fresh flowers in your room. This southwestern retreat is within walking distance of shops, galleries, and fine restaurants.

La Posada de Chimayó ✪
P.O. BOX 463, CHIMAYÓ, NEW MEXICO 87522

Tel: **(505) 351-4605**
Host(s): **Sue Farrington**
Location: **30 mi. N of Santa Fe**
No. of Rooms: **2**
No. of Private Baths: **2**
Double/pb: **$65**
Single/pb: **$55**
Open: **All year**
Reduced Rates: **Weekly in winter**
Breakfast: **Full**
Credit Cards: **MC, VISA (for deposits)**
Pets: **Sometimes**
Children: **Welcome**
Smoking: **Permitted**
Social Drinking: **Permitted**
Foreign Languages: **Spanish**

Chimayó is known for its historic old church and its tradition of fine Spanish weaving. This is a typical adobe home with brick floors and *viga* ceilings. The suite is comprised of a small bedroom and sitting room and is made cozy with Mexican rugs, handmade quilts, comfortable furnishings, and traditional corner fireplaces. Sue's breakfasts are not for the fainthearted and often feature stuffed French toast or chilies rellenos. Wine or sun tea are graciously offered after you return from exploring Bandelier National Monument Park, the Indian pueblos, and cliff dwellings on the "High Road" to Taos.

The Elms ✪
1110 CARVER RD, P.O. BOX 1176, MESILLA PARK, NEW MEXICO 88047

Tel: **(505) 524-1513**
Best Time to Call: **After 5 PM**
Host(s): **Margaret B. Dalton**
Location: **2 mi. from I-10, I-25**
No. of Rooms: **4**
No. of Private Baths: **2**
Max. No. Sharing Bath: **4**
Double/pb: **$50–$75**
Double/sb: **$40**
Single/sb: **$30**
Open: **All year**
Reduced Rates: **10% less after 5 nights**
Breakfast: **Continental**
Pets: **No**
Children: **Welcome**
Smoking: **No**
Social Drinking: **Permitted**

This large redwood-and-stucco house is set on five acres and shaded by 100-year-old elm trees. Guest rooms are furnished with solid oak antiques and Oriental rugs. Your hosts offer homemade breads and preserves for breakfast. They will gladly direct you to historic sights, White Sands National Monument, Juarez, and the Gila Cliff Dwellings National Monument.

Wilderness Inn ✪
P.O. BOX 1040, PECOS, NEW MEXICO 87552

Tel: (505) 757-6351
Best Time to Call: 7–11 AM; 6–11 PM
Host(s): **Bob Hattle and Cate Smock**
Location: **25 mi. E of Santa Fe**
No. of Rooms: **7**
No. of Private Baths: **7**
Double/pb: **$27.50–$50**
Single/pb: **$25–$45**
Suites: **$75**

Open: **Apr. 15–Jan. 8**
Breakfast: **Continental**
Credit Cards: **MC, VISA**
Pets: **Sometimes**
Children: **Welcome**
Smoking: **No**
Social Drinking: **Permitted**
Airport/Station Pickup: **Yes**

This 175-year-old adobe hacienda has an inner courtyard where the original town well still stands. It is also a chartered American Youth Hostel, and your breakfast companions might be visitors from all over the world. This town is the gateway to the Pecos Wilderness, where hiking, bird-watching, trout fishing, and gold panning are things to do. The Pecos National Monument marks the ruins of a Pueblo Indian community. In summer, the inn keeps llamas as pack animals for wilderness treks that it organizes.

The Boellner House
508 NORTH MISSOURI AVENUE, ROSWELL, NEW MEXICO 88201

Tel: (505) 625-9206
Host(s): **Barbara and John Evans**
No. of Rooms: **4**
No. of Private Baths: **2**
Max. No. Sharing Bath: **4**
Double/pb: **$55**
Single/pb: **$47**
Double/sb: **$47**

Single/sb: **$39**
Open: **All year**
Reduced Rates: **5%, seniors**
Breakfast: **Full**
Pets: **No**
Children: **Welcome, over 12**
Smoking: **No**
Social Drinking: **Permitted**

Victorian style and grace are in evidence here, from the elegant furniture to the exquisite gardens. Listed in the National Register of Historic Places and located in the downtown historic district, the house was built in 1910 by Dr. L. B. Boellner, who was a self-taught hybridizer. His love of horticulture is still evident in the beautiful flowers, shrubs, and trees of vast variety that still grace the lawn. Guests often return for the Evanses' warm hospitality that makes strangers feel like longtime friends. John is a consulting geologist; Barbara is a gourmet cook and interior decorator.

Bed & Breakfast of Santa Fe ✪
218 EAST BUENA VISTA, SANTA FE, NEW MEXICO 87501

Tel: **(505) 982-3332**	Rates (Single/Double):
Best Time to Call: **9 AM–5 PM**	Modest: **$40** **$45**
Coordinator: **Star Jones**	Average: **$50** **$55**
States/Regions Covered: **Santa Fe**	Luxury: **$60** **$100**
	Credit Cards: **No**
	Minimum Stay: **2 nights**

Do come and enjoy the Santa Fe Opera in summer, the vibrant colors of the aspens in autumn, or skiing in winter. Don't miss the nearby Indian pueblos and ancient cliff dwellings, the national forest areas, art colonies, museums, and nearby Taos. Santa Fe still retains the traditions of its early Spanish history, and is blessed with an average of 300 days of sunshine a year. Send for Star's free descriptive list of accommodations.

Water Street Inn ✪
427 WEST WATER STREET, SANTA FE, NEW MEXICO 87501

Tel: **(505) 984-1193**	Reduced Rates: **10%, Nov.–Feb.; after 2 nights**
Best Time to Call: **9 AM–5 PM**	Breakfast: **Continental**
Host(s): **Dolores and Albert Dietz**	Credit Cards: **MC, VISA**
No. of Rooms: **5**	Pets: **No**
No. of Private Baths: **5**	Children: **Welcome, over 12**
Double/pb: **$75–$85**	Smoking: **No**
Open: **All year**	Social Drinking: **Permitted**

The Water Street Inn is part of an award-winning adobe restoration project in the downtown historic area. Guest rooms combine the best of old and new, with private baths, cable TV, and a decor of southwestern furnishings and antiques; some rooms have Jacuzzi tubs or fireplaces. In the morning, a breakfast tray will be brought to your room, and in the afternoon complimentary wine is served. The inn is four blocks from the Plaza and convenient to the city's best shops, restaurants, and galleries. Your host took part in New Mexico's economic development effort and is glad to share his knowledge of the state.

American Artists Gallery-House ✪
FRONTIER ROAD, P.O. BOX 584, TAOS, NEW MEXICO 87571

Tel: (505) 758-4446
Best Time to Call: **Mornings; evenings**
Host(s): **Benjamin and Myra Carp**
Location: **3 blocks from Rte. 68**
No. of Rooms: **3**
No. of Private Baths: **3**
Double/pb: **$55–$75**
Single/pb: **$50–$70**
Separate Guest Cottage: **$55**
Open: **All year**
Breakfast: **Full**
Pets: **No**
Children: **Welcome (crib)**
Smoking: **No**
Social Drinking: **Permitted**
Airport/Station Pickup: **Yes**

This charming adobe-style home is filled with artwork by American artists. A large, comfortable bedroom with a splendid view of Taos Mountain awaits you. Your hosts, gallery owners, will gladly advise on local craft shops and boutiques. Their home is close to Rio Grande Gorge State Park, 900-year-old Taos Pueblo, and places to go fishing and rafting. Complimentary refreshments are served in the evening. Fireplaces, the outdoor hot tub, gardens, and a sculpture courtyard will delight you.

Harrison's B&B ✪
P.O. BOX 242, TAOS, NEW MEXICO 87571

Tel: (505) 758-2630
Host(s): **Jean and Bob Harrison**
Location: **1½ mi. from Rte. 3**
No. of Rooms: **3**
No. of Private Baths: **2**
Max. No. Sharing Bath: **4**
Double/pb: **$50**
Single/pb: **$40**
Double/sb: **$30–$40**
Single/sb: **$20–$30**
Open: **All year**
Reduced Rates: **10%, after 4 nights**
Breakfast: **Full**
Pets: **No**
Children: **Welcome (crib)**
Smoking: **No**
Social Drinking: **Permitted**

The Harrisons have lived in this large adobe home just outside of Taos for 25 years. The house overlooks town from the foot of the western mesa and, framed by trees and bushes, boasts with lovely mountain views. Inside, original works of art enhance the styling and the use of native materials. In the warm weather, breakfast is served at an umbrella table on a patio surrounded by flowers. Breakfast pie and homemade coffee cakes are specialties of the house, but your hosts will gladly prepare choices tailored to your preferences. The Harrisons are just over two miles from the Taos plaza and are conveniently located near many outdoor pursuits, including skiing, hiking, fishing, and river rafting.

Two Pipe Bed & Breakfast ○
BOX 52, TALPA ROUTE, RANCHOS DE TAOS, NEW MEXICO 87557

Tel: **(505) 758-4770**
Host(s): **Dusty and Babs Davis**
Location: **4 mi. SE of Taos**
No. of Rooms: **2**
No. of Private Baths: **2**
Double/pb: **$60**
Single/pb: **$50**
Guest Cottage: **$70**
Open: **All year**

Reduced Rates: **10%, 2-day stays May–Oct.**
Breakfast: **Continental**
Pets: **No**
Children: **Welcome, over 5**
Smoking: **No**
Social Drinking: **Permitted**
Airport/Station Pickup: **Yes**

Beautiful gardens and mountain views surround this 275-year-old adobe hacienda. The house includes many traditional adobe features such as kiva fireplaces and *viga* ceilings along with many antiques and family furnishings. Guests are welcome to relax in the hot tub or curl up in front of a cozy fire. Your hosts offer complimentary snacks, wine, and beverages, and will do all they can to make you feel welcome. Five ski areas are located less than an hour from here, and a special hearty skiers' breakfast is served in season. Art galleries, museums, Indian pueblos, and Rio Grande Gorge, as well as great hunting and fishing, can all be enjoyed nearby.

NEW YORK

CATSKILLS

Maplewood ✪
PARK ROAD, P.O. BOX 40, CHICHESTER, New York 12416

Tel: (914) 688-5433
Best Time to Call: **After 7 PM**
Host(s): **Nancy and Albert Parsons**
Location: **25 mi. NW of Kingston, N.Y.**
No. of Rooms: **4**
Max. No. Sharing Bath: **4**
Double/sb: **$55**
Single/sb: **$40**

Open: **All year**
Breakfast: **Full**
Pets: **Sometimes**
Children: **Welcome**
Smoking: **Permitted**
Social Drinking: **Permitted**
Airport/Station Pickup: **Yes**

A Colonial manor on a quiet country lane nestled among stately maples is the site of this charming B&B; each spacious bedroom has a view of the Catskills. In summer, you can swim in the in-ground pool, or play badminton, croquet, or horseshoes. In winter, ski Belleayre, Hunter, and Cortina, all only 12 miles away. In any season, enjoy the art galleries, boutiques, great restaurants, and theater at Woodstock, 20 minutes away. After a great day outdoors, come home to a glass of wine and good conversation. After a good night's sleep, you'll enjoy freshly squeezed orange juice, homemade breads and pastries, and freshly ground coffee.

Scudder Hill House ✪
SCUDDER HILL ROAD, ROXBURY, NEW YORK 12474

Tel: **(607) 326-4215 or 4364**	Open: **All year**
Host(s): **Carol and Phil O'Beirne**	Breakfast: **Full**
Location: **50 mi. W of Kingston, N.Y.**	Credit Cards: **MC, VISA**
No. of Rooms: **5**	Pets: **No**
No. of Private Baths: **5**	Children: **Welcome, over 12**
Double/pb: **$55–$70**	Smoking: **Permitted**
Single/pb: **$55**	Social Drinking: **Permitted**

Within minutes of five major Catskill ski centers, hiking trails, golf courses, and antiques shops, Roxbury is home base for music, art, and country fairs. This 130-year-old Federal-style farmhouse is attractively furnished for comfort, quiet, and relaxation. Carol and Phil enjoy music, books, farming, and cooking. Breakfast breads are homemade; ham, bacon, and eggs are homegrown. You're apt to be spoiled with sherry whenever you wish, and with snacks if you look hungry.

The Eggery Inn
COUNTY ROAD 16, TANNERSVILLE, NEW YORK 12485

Tel: **(518) 589-5363**	Breakfast: **Full**
Best Time to Call: **10 AM–8 PM**	Credit Cards: **AMEX, MC, VISA**
Host(s): **Julie and Abe Abramczyk**	Other Meals: **Available**
No. of Rooms: **13**	Pets: **No**
No. of Private Baths: **13**	Children: **Welcome**
Double/pb: **$70–$80**	Smoking: **Permitted**
Single/pb: **$60**	Social Drinking: **Permitted**
Open: **May 16–Sept. 7;** **Sept. 15–Apr. 1**	Minimum Stay: **2 nights weekends; 3 nights holiday weekends**
Reduced Rates: **Families; off-season**	

The inn, with its wraparound porch, is nestled amid the majestic ridges of the Catskills at an elevation of 2,200 feet. The sitting room is enhanced by a beautiful oak balustrade leading to cozy guest rooms furnished with antiques, rockers, and warm comforters. The player piano, Mission Oak furnishings, and abundance of plants lend a homey atmosphere. It is in the Catskill Game Preserve, and convenient to Hunter, Cortina, and Windham mountains for Alpine skiing, hiking, and seasonal recreational activities. On weekends and holiday periods the above rates change, since dinner is included.

Sunrise Inn ✪
RD 1, BOX 232B, WALTON, NEW YORK 13856

Tel: **(607) 865-7254**
Best Time to Call: **9 AM–11 PM**
Host(s): **James and Adele Toth**
Location: **135 mi. NW of N.Y.C.; 25 mi. from Rte. 17**
No. of Rooms: **2**
Max. No. Sharing Bath: **4**
Double/sb: **$34**

Single/sb: **$29**
Open: **All year**
Reduced Rates: **10%, seniors**
Breakfast: **Continental**
Pets: **No**
Children: **Welcome (crib)**
Smoking: **No**
Social Drinking: **Permitted**

Relax and enjoy the sound of the bubbling brook that borders the landscape of this 19th-century farmhouse. You'll awaken to the aroma of Irish soda bread and other homemade goodies, which you are invited to enjoy in the dining area or, weather permitting, on the wraparound porch. Afterward, browse through the antiques shop adjoining the inn. Area activities include fishing, canoeing, golfing, skiing, country fairs, and fine dining. End the day in quiet and homey comfort around the parlor wood stove.

CENTRAL NEW YORK/LEATHERSTOCKING AREA

Bed & Breakfast—Leatherstocking ✪
389 BROCKWAY ROAD, FRANKFORT, NEW YORK 13340

Tel: **(315) 733-0040**
Best Time to Call: **7 AM–10 PM**
Coordinator: **Floranne McCraith**
States/Regions Covered: **Central NY—Booneville, Cooperstown, Fort Plain, Hamilton, Norwich, Oneida, Rome, Utica, Waterville**

Rates (Single/Double):
  Average: **$30**   **$50**
  Luxury: **$50**   **$75**
Credit Cards: **MC, VISA**

Leatherstocking Country is an 11-county region of New York that extends from the Catskills across the Mohawk Valley to the Central Adirondacks. It's a region to be visited in all seasons for all reasons, and its residents warmly welcome visitors. Recreational sports and activities, outlet shopping, antiques, fairs, and fine dining are waiting for you, and your B&B host will tell you where to find the best of everything. Send $2 for her descriptive directory. There is a $3 booking fee.

Jericho Farm Inn ✪
155 EAST MAIN STREET, AFTON, NEW YORK 13730

Tel: **(607) 639-1842**
Best Time to Call: **1–10 PM**
Host(s): **Patricia and Donald Fabricius**
Location: **25 mi. NE of Binghamton**
No. of Rooms: **5**
Max. No. Sharing Bath: **4**
Double/sb: **$40–$45**
Single/sb: **$35**
Suites: **$55**
Open: **All year**
Breakfast: **Full**
Pets: **Sometimes**
Children: **Welcome (crib, stroller)**
Smoking: **Permitted**
Social Drinking: **Permitted**
Airport/Station Pickup: **Yes**

Right out of a Norman Rockwell painting is the way you might describe this 200-year-old Colonial mansion, situated on the Susquehanna River. Step through an entrance graced by four massive pillars and you'll find comfortable rooms and plenty of hospitality. Breakfast is served in the common room overlooking the river. When the sun is shining, take your coffee outside to the courtyard, which has an impressive outdoor fireplace. The six-acre property is great for lawn games, picnicking, sunning, and offers easy access to fishing and canoeing on the river. In warm weather, Patricia and Donald invite you to use their Jacuzzi.

B&B Adagio ✪
4 CIRCLE DRIVE, BINGHAMTON, NEW YORK 13905

Tel: **(607) 724-5803**
Host(s): **Jean Adagio**
No. of Rooms: **3**
Max. No. Sharing Bath: **4**
Double/sb: **$45**
Single/sb: **$35**
Open: **All year**
Breakfast: **Continental**
Pets: **No**
Children: **Welcome**
Smoking: **No**
Social Drinking: **Permitted**

Located in a quiet, residential area, Jean's home has a lovely screened porch for restful relaxation. It's only minutes to the tennis courts at Broome Community College, and SUNY-Binghamton is nearby. Jean loves to quilt, and her bedrooms show samples of her fine handiwork.

Creekside Bed & Breakfast ✪
RD 1, BOX 206, COOPERSTOWN, NEW YORK 13326

Tel: (607) 547-8203
Host(s): **Fred and Gwen Ermlich**
No. of Rooms: **4**
No. of Private Baths: **4**
Double/pb: **$50–$60**
Suites: **$60**
Guest Cottage: **$95, sleeps 2**

Open: **All year**
Breakfast: **Full**
Pets: **No**
Children: **Welcome (crib)**
Smoking: **No**
Social Drinking: **Permitted**
Foreign Languages: **French, German**

This 200-year-old Colonial is perfect for a romantic escape. The Bridal Suite features an antique brass bed, skylights and a private deck. The three-room cottage has a wet bar, HBO, and a private deck overlooking the stream. The Ermlichs perform with the Glimmerglass Opera.

The Inn at Brook Willow Farm ✪
R.D. 2, BOX 514, MIDDLEFIELD CENTER ROAD, COOPERSTOWN, NEW YORK 13326

Tel: (607) 547-9700
Best Time to Call: **After 6 PM**
Host(s): **Joan and Jack Grimes**
No. of Rooms: **4**
No. of Private Baths: **4**
Double/pb: **$50**

Open: **All year**
Breakfast: **Full**
Pets: **No**
Children: **Welcome (crib)**
Smoking: **Permitted**
Social Drinking: **Permitted**

Located on 14 acres of meadow and woods, nestled among the pines and willows, this charming Victorian cottage with its restored barn is furnished with lovely antiques, wicker, and plants. Enjoy homemade blueberry muffins at breakfast, and wine, fresh fruit, and fresh flowers in your room. The world-famous Baseball Hall of Fame is here, as well as countless historic and cultural sites to visit. Recreational activities abound on unspoiled Otsego Lake.

The Inn at Mill Pond ✪
P.O. BOX 167, COOPERSTOWN, NEW YORK 13326

Tel: (315) 858-1654 or (607) 293-7980
Best Time to Call: **After 5 PM**
Host(s): **Gail and Ed Newton-Condon**
Location: **On Rte. 80**
No. of Rooms: **3**

No. of Private Baths: **1**
Max. No. Sharing Bath: **4**
Double/pb: **$55**
Single/pb: **$50**
Double/sb: **$45**

Single/sb: **$40**
Open: **May 1–Oct. 31**
Breakfast: **Full**
Pets: **No**

Children: **No**
Smoking: **No**
Social Drinking: **Permitted**
Airport/Station Pickup: **Yes**

This inn is perfectly situated for anyone planning their vacation around Cooperstown's many attractions: the Glimmerglass Opera, Cooperstown Theater Festival, the Baseball Hall of Fame, nearby golf courses, museums, and picturesque Otsego Lake. Furnished with local antiques and folk art, the inn reflects Gail and Ed's interests in woodworking, gardening, antiques, herbs, and painting. A nice feature is the late-afternoon tea—just right after a day of sightseeing in the surrounding hills of Central New York State.

Litco Farms Bed and Breakfast ✪
P.O. BOX 1048, COOPERSTOWN, NEW YORK 13326

Tel: **(607) 547-2501**
Host(s): **Margaret and Jim Wolff**
Location: **2 mi. NW of Cooperstown**
No. of Rooms: **2**
Max. No. Sharing Bath: **4**
Double/sb: **$45**
Suites: **$85**
Open: **All year**

Reduced Rates: **Families; off-season**
Breakfast: **Full**
Pets: **No**
Children: **Welcome**
Smoking: **Permitted**
Social Drinking: **Permitted**
Airport/Station Pickup: **Yes**

Seventy acres of unspoiled meadows and woodlands are yours to explore at Litco Farms. The day begins with fresh-baked breads, fresh eggs, milk, and local bacon, served in the dining room–library. Borrow a canoe to fish on Canadarago Lake, which is stocked with freshwater salmon. There are other places to paddle, including Glimmerglass, the lake made famous by James Fenimore Cooper. After spending a day at the Baseball Hall of Fame, guests may relax and unwind around the large in-ground pool. Your hosts recommend a visit to the Cider Mill and the quaint craft and antique shops.

Whisperin Pines Chalet ✪
RD #3, BOX 248, COOPERSTOWN, NEW YORK 13326

Tel: **(607) 547-5640**
Best Time to Call: **11 AM**
Host(s): **Joyce and Gus Doucas**
No. of Rooms: **7**
No. of Private Baths: **3**

Max. No. Sharing Bath: **4**
Double/pb: **$75**
Single/pb: **$70**
Double/sb: **$45–$55**
Single/sb: **$30**

Suites: **$100**
Open: **All year**
Breakfast: **Full**
Pets: **No**
Children: **Welcome**

Smoking: **Permitted**
Social Drinking: **Permitted**
Airport/Station Pickup: **Yes**
Foreign Languages: **French, Greek**

Guests may choose from a variety of accommodations, including some with canopy beds, fireplaces, private balconies—even a bubble bath for two. The country setting offers a private walking trail, waterfalls, and a brook from which the lucky can catch a trout for breakfast. The chalet is equipped with a wheelchair ramp and electric chairlift. A delicious country breakfast is served in the cozy dining room featuring country-fresh eggs, milk, and butter; homemade sausage and bacon; and Vermont maple syrup.

Jonathan House ✪
39 EAST MAIN STREET, P.O. BOX 9, RICHFIELD SPRINGS, NEW YORK 13439

Tel: **(315) 858-2870**
Host(s): **Jonathan and Peter Parker**
Location: **14 mi. N of Cooperstown**
No. of Rooms: **3**
No. of Private Baths: **2**
Max. No. Sharing Bath: **4**
Double/pb: **$55**
Single/pb: **$50**
Double/sb: **$45**
Single/sb: **$40**
Suites: **$65**

Open: **All year**
Reduced Rates: **$10 less, Nov. 1–May 1; weekly**
Breakfast: **Full**
Other Meals: **Available**
Credit Cards: **MC, VISA**
Pets: **Sometimes**
Children: **Welcome**
Smoking: **Permitted**
Social Drinking: **Permitted**
Airport/Station Pickup: **Yes**

The Parker brothers enjoy cooking and entertaining so, when they were both widowed, their friends suggested that they open a B&B in the house they share with their mother. The 1883 house, a hybrid of the Eastlake and Stick styles, has three full floors plus a tower room on a fourth level—a total of 17 rooms in all. The house is elegantly decorated with antiques (some that belonged to the brothers' great-grandparents and grandparents), fine paintings, and Oriental rugs. Breakfast is served in the dining room—with bone china, damask linen, and English silver. The Parkers also serve candlelight dinners, presented just as regally.

CHAUTAUQUA/ALLEGHENY AREA

Rainbow Hospitality—Chautauqua ✪
758 RICHMOND AVENUE, BUFFALO, NEW YORK 14222

Tel: **(716) 386-3066 or 7361**
Best Time to Call: **10 AM–6 PM, Mon.–Fri.; 10 AM–Noon, Sat.**
Coordinator: **Shirley Ingraham**
States/Regions Covered: **Chautauqua, South Dayton, Little Valley**

Rates: (Single/Double):
  Modest: **$35**   **$45**
  Average: **$55**   **$65**
  Luxury: **$60**   **$75**
Credit Cards: **No**

This area boasts an infinite variety of cities and farm towns, of colleges and commerce, of skiing and sailing, of attractions both natural and man-made. Chautauqua is famous for the cultural, educational, and religious activities of the summer colony on the lake, as well as for its topnotch recreational diversions. Send $1 for Shirley's descriptive directory of accommodations.

Hitchcock House ✪
15 SOUTH MAIN STREET, ALFRED, NEW YORK 14802

Tel: **(607) 587-9102**
Best Time to Call: **8 AM–11 PM**
Host(s): **June and Bob Hitchcock**
Location: **75 mi. S of Rochester**
No. of Rooms: **3**
No. of Private Baths: **1**
Max. No. Sharing Bath: **4**
Double/pb: **$48**
Double/sb: **$35**
Open: **All year**
Reduced Rates: **15%, weekly**
Breakfast: **Full**
Pets: **No**
Children: **Welcome**
Smoking: **Permitted**
Social Drinking: **Permitted**

Bob and June Hitchcock welcome you to the heart of Alfred's Village Historic District. Their house was built in 1932 in the Colonial Revival style by a hometown physician; the small wing of the house that once was the doctor's office has been remodeled for guests. Guest quarters feature a private entrance and bath, queen-size bed, and lace curtains. The kitchen is stocked with eggs, juice, coffee, toast, and muffins for a make-it-yourself breakfast. A large backyard with lounge chairs and a picnic table is available for relaxing. Hitchcock House is located on a quiet, tree-lined street, just a short walk from activities at Alfred University and the state college.

Green Acres ✪
ROUTE 474, ASHVILLE, NEW YORK 14710

Tel: **(716) 782-4254**
Best Time To Call: **Mornings**
Host(s): **Lowell and Mary Ann Green**
Location: **8 mi. W of Jamestown**
No. of Rooms: **2**
Max. No. Sharing Bath: **4**
Double/sb: **$55**

Single/sb: **$35**
Open: **All year**
Breakfast: **Full**
Pets: **No**
Children: **Welcome, over 12**
Smoking: **No**
Social Drinking: **No**

Lowell and Mary Ann once owned an antique store, and their country Colonial is the perfect setting for their old treasures. The rooms feature hand-hewn beams, paneled walls, and stone fireplaces. Guests are welcome to relax in the comfortable living room or curl up on an old porch rocker. A heated pool is located on the three-acre property, and it is in use from June through September. Just beyond the pool lie the woods, where you can hike, fish in a large stocked pond, and cross-country ski. The breakfast specialty of the house is blueberry pancakes and sausages; the berries are as fresh as you can get, because they grow right out back. Your hosts will gladly direct you to local attractions including skiing, Panama Rocks, and the Chautauqua Institution.

Mansard Inn ✪
RD 1, BOX 633, GERRY LEVANT ROAD, FALCONER, NEW YORK 14733

Tel: **(716) 665-2352 or 4558**
Host(s): **Frank and Debra Viramontes**
Location: **1 mi. from Rte. 17, Exit 13—Falconer**
No. of Rooms: **4**
No. of Private Baths: **2**
Max. No. Sharing Bath: **4**
Double/pb: **$55**
Single/pb: **$50**
Double/sb: **$40**

Single/sb: **$35**
Suites: **$50**
Open: **All year**
Reduced Rates: **10%, seniors**
Breakfast: **Continental**
Pets: **No**
Children: **Welcome**
Smoking: **Permitted**
Social Drinking: **Permitted**
Airport/Station Pickup: **Yes**

To keep the workers of his brickyard busy during a mid-1800s economic slump, Reuben Neate, an early settler of the area, had them build this villa for his family. The house is surrounded by open pastures, woods, and large flower gardens. The interior of the house re-creates the feel of the Victorian era. Debra loves flowers and, if the season is right, you're bound to find flowers in your room; Frank is an "outdoors type"—just ask him about fishing in the area. Nearby, guests will find horseback riding, hiking, the Chautauqua Institution, and lots of antiques shops.

Napoli Stagecoach Inn ✪
NAPOLI CORNERS, LITTLE VALLEY, NEW YORK 14755

Tel: **(716) 938-6735, 358-3928**	Breakfast: **Full**
Host(s): **Emmett and Marion Waite**	Credit Cards: **No**
Location: **60 mi. S of Buffalo**	Pets: **No**
No. of Rooms: **3**	Children: **Welcome, over 10**
Max. No. Sharing Bath: **4**	Smoking: **No**
Double/sb: **$35**	Social Drinking: **No**
Single/sb: **$25**	Airport/Station Pickup: **Yes**
Open: **All year**	Foreign Languages: **Spanish**
Reduced Rates: **Weekly**	

Located in the foothills of the Allegheny Mountains, this residence was originally built as a stagecoach inn in 1830. It is now part of a seven-acre fruit and vegetable farm where you can enjoy uncrowded comfort and warm hospitality. Emmett and Marion have many hobbies such as antique collecting, building grandfather clocks, china painting, doll making, and quilting. The inn is close to Holiday Valley Ski Area, Kinzua Dam and Reservoir, Chautauqua Institution, and the Seneca-Iroquois National Museum. Their 4,000-volume library is a fine place to browse.

The Village Inn B&B ✪
ROUTE 394, 111 SOUTH ERIE STEET, MAYVILLE, NEW YORK 14757

Tel: **(716) 753-3583**	Open: **All year**
Best Time to Call: **After 5 PM**	Reduced Rates: **Weekly**
Host(s): **Dean R. Hanby**	Breakfast: **Full**
Location: **55 mi. SW of Buffalo**	Pets: **Sometimes**
No. of Rooms: **3**	Children: **Welcome (baby-sitter)**
Max. No. Sharing Bath: **4**	Smoking: **Permitted**
Double/sb: **$45**	Social Drinking: **Permitted**
Single/sb: **$30**	Airport/Station Pickup: **Yes**

Built around 1900, this Victorian home is furnished in antiques and trimmed with handcrafted woodwork. The 18-room house features stained glass, a mirrored Victorian fireplace, Oriental rugs, and an open staircase. In the morning you'll get to sample the family recipe for cinnamon nut kuchen, served along with coffee and waffles cooked on a cast-iron Griswald. The inn is a five-minute walk from Chautauqua Lake, and eight miles from Lake Erie. Chautauqua Institution, the resort community known for its concerts, lectures, and educational activities, is three miles away. Your hosts will guide you to boat rides, golf courses, wineries, and ski trails. After a busy day, a glass of wine or a hot drink will await you back at the inn.

Klartag Farms
P.O. BOX 98, WEST BRANCH ROAD, RUSHFORD, NEW YORK 14777

Tel: **(716) 437-2946**
Host(s): **Jerry and Shirley Thorington**
Location: **50 mi. SE of Buffalo**
No. of Rooms: **2**
Max. No. Sharing Bath: **4**
Double/sb: **$38**
Single/sb: **$30**
Open: **All year**

Reduced Rates: **15%, weekly**
Breakfast: **Full**
Other Meals: **Available**
Pets: **No**
Children: **Welcome (crib)**
Smoking: **No**
Social Drinking: **Permitted**
Airport/Station Pickup: **Yes**

Jerry and Shirley welcome you to their 600-acre working dairy farm in the countryside. Their spacious red farmhouse is trimmed with black shutters and set on a beautifully manicured lawn. Inside, you'll find comfortable rooms with some special antiques such as an old player piano. Your hosts serve a farm-style breakfast including home-cured bacon and sausage, homemade jams, and breads. They invite you for complimentary coffee, tea, or wine in the afternoon. The farm is within 30 minutes of several ski areas and a state park. Farm tours are gladly given, and fishing and hunting can be enjoyed on the premises.

Town & Country Bed & Breakfast ✪
P.O. BOX 208, PINE STREET, SOUTH DAYTON, NEW YORK 14138

Tel: **(716) 988-3340**
Best Time to Call: **After 5 PM**
Host(s): **Rick and Jeanne Easterly**
Location: **12 mi. from NYS Thruway, Exit 58**
No. of Rooms: **2**
Max. No. Sharing Bath: **4**
Double/sb: **$35**

Single/sb: **$25**
Open: **All year**
Breakfast: **Continental**
Pets: **No**
Children: **Welcome**
Smoking: **No**
Social Drinking: **Permitted**

Aptly named because of its location in a small, rural village, this restored Victorian is decorated with family treasures and special "finds" that were refinished by Rick and Jeanne. He's a computer engineer; she's a secretary. They offer a simple breakfast weekdays and a full feast on weekends. It is close to the Amish community, 12 miles to Cockaigne Ski Area, 10 miles to local wineries, and 50 miles to Niagara Falls. In fruit-picking season, bring your own baskets and literally go home with the fruits of your labor.

FINGER LAKES/ROCHESTER AREA

Bed & Breakfast—Rochester ✪
P.O. BOX 444, FAIRPORT, NEW YORK 14450

Tel: **(716) 223-8877**	Rates (Single/Double):
Best Time to Call: **2–5 PM**	Modest: **$30–$35** **$35–$40**
Coordinator: **Beth Kinsman**	Average: **$35–$40** **$45–$50**
States/Regions Covered: **Rochester Area**	Luxury: **$65–$80**
	Credit Cards: **No**

Friendly hosts offer a variety of accommodations ranging from a contemporary on Lake Ontario to a traditional suburban home. A full breakfast is always included. All will be happy to advise you on the sights and "doings" in their areas. Don't miss the International Museum of Photography at George Eastman House, or the Strong Museum. The University of Rochester and SUNY-Brockport are local campuses. A non-refundable $3 fee is charged per booking.

The Country House ✪
37 MILL STREET, CANASERAGA, NEW YORK 14822

Tel: **(607) 545-6439**	Single/sb: **$20**
Best Time to Call: **11 AM–1 PM, 5–7 PM**	Open: **All year**
	Breakfast: **Full**
Host(s): **Robert and Renée Coombs**	Pets: **Welcome**
Location: **50 mi. S of Rochester**	Children: **Welcome (crib)**
No. of Rooms: **6**	Smoking: **Permitted**
Max. No. Sharing Bath: **4**	Social Drinking: **Permitted**
Double/sb: **$35**	Airport/Station Pickup: **Yes**

This 100-year-old Victorian home stands on a quiet street in a charming rural village. Guest rooms are comfortably furnished with antiques and all are for sale. Home-baked pastries and fresh fruit are served each morning in the breakfast room or dining room. Your hosts will happily direct you to the many valleys, forests, and streams nearby for hunting, fishing, hiking, and scenic solitude. Swain Ski Center slopes, Corning Glassworks, and Letchworth State Park are minutes away.

1865 White Birch Bed & Breakfast
69 EAST FIRST STREET, CORNING, NEW YORK 14830

Tel: **(607) 962-6355**
Host(s): **Fran and Lois Gehl**
Location: **Off Rte. 17**
No. of Rooms: **3**
No. of Private Baths: **1**
Max. No. Sharing Bath: **4**
Double/pb: **$60**
Single/pb: **$55**
Double/sb: **$50**
Single/sb: **$45**

Suites: **$65**
Open: **All year**
Breakfast: **Continental**
Credit Cards: **MC, VISA**
Pets: **No**
Children: **Welcome**
Smoking: **Downstairs only**
Social Drinking: **Permitted**
Airport/Station Pickup: **Yes**

The red-carpet treatment awaits you at this spacious 1865 Victorian home that has been restored to show off the beautifully crafted winding staircase and hardwood floors. Guests are welcome to choose a game or enjoy television by the fire in the common room. After a good night's sleep in a comfortable queen-size bed, you'll wake to the smell of homemade breads, muffins, and plenty of hot coffee. The

White Birch is located in a residential area just two blocks from restored downtown Corning and near such attractions as the Corning Glass Center, Rockwell Museum, and many fine wineries.

Rosewood Inn ○
134 EAST FIRST STREET, CORNING, NEW YORK 14830

Tel: **(607) 962-3253**	Suites: **$95**
Host(s): **Winnie and Dick Peer**	Open: **All year**
Location: **1 block off Rte. 17**	Reduced Rates: **Weekly; families**
No. of Rooms: **6**	Breakfast: **Full**
No. of Private Baths: **4**	Credit Cards: **DC, MC, VISA**
Max. No. Sharing Bath: **4**	Pets: **Sometimes**
Double/pb: **$73**	Children: **Welcome (crib)**
Single/pb: **$65**	Smoking: **Permitted**
Double/sb: **$63**	Social Drinking: **Permitted**
Single/sb: **$55**	Airport/Station Pickup: **Yes**

This two-story stucco English Tudor is decorated with both antiques and originality. Each guest room is named for a famous person and the accessories echo the personality of that individual's era. It's within walking distance of the Corning Glass Museum and the Rockwell-Corning Museum of Western Art. Winnie taught school, and Dick was the editor of the daily newspaper. Retired, they look forward to your arrival and greet you with refreshments.

Lakeside Terrace ○
RD 1, BOX 197, 660 EAST WANETA LAKE ROAD, DUNDEE, NEW YORK 14837

Tel: **(607) 292-6606**	Open: **All year**
Host(s): **Chris and George Patnoe**	Breakfast: **Continental**
Location: **30 mi. S of Geneva**	Credit Cards: **MC, VISA**
No. of Rooms: **2**	Pets: **Sometimes**
Max. No. Sharing Bath: **4**	Children: **Welcome, over 10**
Double/sb: **$49**	Smoking: **Permitted**
Single/sb: **$35**	Social Drinking: **Permitted**

It's only 30 miles to the Corning Glass Works, or 10 miles to the Hammondsport wineries, and this rustic, air-conditioned house is the perfect spot for relaxation. Swim, fish, sail, sunbathe, or just relax on the beach. The house is located on a picturesque lake and is near the major attractions of the Finger Lakes area.

Willow Cove ✪
77 SOUTH GLENORA ROAD, R.D. 1, BOX 87, DUNDEE, NEW YORK 14837

Tel: **(607) 243-8482**
Best Time to Call: **After 4:30 PM**
Host(s): **George and Joan Van Heusen**
Location: **10 mi. N of Watkins Glen**
No. of Rooms: **4**
Max. No. Sharing Bath: **4**
Double/sb: **$40**

Single/sb: **$35**
Open: **Apr.–Oct. 31**
Breakfast: **Continental**
Pets: **No**
Children: **Welcome (crib)**
Smoking: **Permitted**
Social Drinking: **Permitted**

Located on the western side of Seneca Lake, this 200-year old inn is a comfortable home base for the many activities the area offers. Wineries, auctions, country fairs, antique shops, music festivals, and art galleries are but a few of the diversions. George and Joan offer wine and cheese in the evening as well as the use of their kitchen for light snacks.

American House ✪
39 MAIN STREET, GENESEO, NEW YORK 14454

Tel: **(716) 243-5483**
Host(s): **Harry and Helen Wadsworth**
Location: **30 mi. S of Rochester**
No. of Rooms: **6**
No. of Private Baths: **2**
Max. No. Sharing Bath: **4**
Double/pb: **$55**
Single/pb: **$50**
Double/sb: **$45–$50**
Single/sb: **$40–$45**

Suites: **$60**
Open: **All year**
Reduced Rates: **10%, seniors**
Breakfast: **Continental**
Pets: **No**
Children: **Welcome**
Smoking: **Permitted**
Social Drinking: **Permitted**
Airport/Station Pickup: **Yes**

American House is an 1897 Victorian on the site of the old American Hotel, known throughout the state for its fine accommodations. The hotel burned down in 1885, but Harry and Helen carry on its tradition of warm hospitality. They offer comfortable bedrooms furnished with antiques. Guests are welcome to relax on the sun porch. Most of the village is listed on the National Register of Historic Places; this B&B is close to a state park and Conesus Lake, and is one block from the State University at Geneseo.

The Cobblestones ✪
1160 ROUTES 5 & 20, GENEVA, NEW YORK 14456

Tel: (315) 789-1896
Best Time to Call: 7–9:30 PM
Host(s): **The Lawrence Graceys**
Location: 3½ mi. W of Geneva on Rtes. 5 and 20 on north side of road
No. of Rooms: **4**
Max. No. Sharing Bath: **5**
Double/sb: **$15 and up**

Single/sb: **$10**
Open: **All year**
Breakfast: **No**
Pets: **Sometimes**
Children: **Welcome (crib)**
Smoking: **Permitted**
Social Drinking: **Permitted**

Located in the heart of the Finger Lakes area, this inspired example of Greek Revival cobblestone architecture was built in 1848. The four large fluted columns crowned by Ionic capitals at the front entrance add to its beauty. There are precious antiques and Oriental rugs, which reflect the fine taste of your gracious hosts. Tours are available at nearby wineries. Hobart and William Smith colleges are right in town.

Buttermilk Falls Bed & Breakfast ✪
110 EAST BUTTERMILK FALLS ROAD, ITHACA, NEW YORK 14850

Tel: (607) 273-3947; 272-6767
Best Time to Call: 7–8 AM
Host(s): **Margie Rumsey**
No. of Rooms: **6**
No. of Private Baths: **2**
Max. No. Sharing Bath: **4**
Double/pb: **$75–$95**
Single/pb: **$50–$60**
Double/sb: **$50–$70**
Single/sb: **$40–$50**

Guest Cottage: **$125 for 4**
Open: **All year**
Reduced Rates: **Available**
Breakfast: **Full**
Credit Cards: **MC, VISA**
Pets: **No**
Children: **Welcome**
Smoking: **No**
Social Drinking: **Permitted**
Airport/Station Pickup: **Yes**

Built in 1825, this white brick Federal-style home has been the Rumsey homestead for five generations. The house is decorated comfortably and elegantly with Early American antiques, Persian carpets, and family heirlooms. Margie's breakfast specialties include hot wholegrain cereal, cheese soufflés, popovers, and fresh fruit. In the afternoon, a glass of wine by the fire or a cup of coffee and conversation await you. The house is directly across the street from the beautiful Buttermilk Falls. You can swim at the foot of the falls or follow the gorge up to imposing Pinnacle Rock. Wooded trails, downhill skiing, and a score of water sports on the Finger Lakes are all nearby.

Glendale Farm
224 BOSTWICK ROAD, ITHACA, NEW YORK 14850

Tel: **(607) 272-8756**
Best Time to Call: **Evenings**
Host(s): **Jeanne Marie Tomlinson**
Location: **2 mi. S of Ithaca**
No. of Rooms: **6**
No. of Private Baths: **4**
Max. No. Sharing Bath: **4**
Double/pb: **$60**
Single/pb: **$40**
Double/sb: **$50**

Suites: **$100**
Separate Guest Cottage: **$75–$100**
Open: **All year**
Breakfast: **Full**
Credit Cards: **MC, VISA**
Pets: **Sometimes**
Children: **Welcome**
Smoking: **Permitted**
Social Drinking: **Permitted**
Airport/Station Pickup: **Yes**

Glendale Farm is nestled in the heart of the Finger Lakes region on a hundred acres of rolling hills, woods, and meadows. Built in 1865, the house is large and comfortable, filled with antiques and Oriental rugs. In winter, a fire always burns in the wood stove; in warmer weather, the large screened-in-porch provides a relaxing spot. Your hosts offer popovers hot from the oven, croissants, assorted cheeses, and homemade jams in the morning. They will gladly direct you to nearby wineries, ski areas, lakes, and parks.

Peregrine House
140 COLLEGE AVENUE, ITHACA, NEW YORK 14850

Tel: **(607) 272-0919**
Host(s): **Nancy Falconer and Susan Vance**
No. of Rooms: **8**
No. of Private Baths: **9**
Double/pb: **$69–$89**
Open: **All year**

Reduced Rates: **Available**
Breakfast: **Full**
Credit Cards: **MC, VISA**
Pets: **No**
Children: **Welcome, over 12**
Smoking: **Permitted**
Social Drinking: **Permitted**

This three-story brick home with mansard roof dates back to 1874. Its faux-marble fireplaces and carved-wood ceilings have been beautifully preserved and are accented with Victorian oak furnishings. Pick a good book in the library and relax in a wing chair, or watch some television in your air-conditioned bedroom. At five o'clock your hosts have a sherry hour, and they invite you to plan your evening over a drink. Mexican, Italian, Greek, and Indian food can all be enjoyed with a short walk from here. Peregrine House is two blocks from the Cornell campus and only a few blocks from the Ithaca Commons. Cayuga Lake's wonderful boating and swimming, the wine country, biking, hiking, and cross-country skiing are all close by.

The Historic Cook House B&B ✪
167 MAIN STREET, NEWFIELD, NEW YORK 14867

Tel: **(607) 564-9926**	Single/sb: **$45**
Host(s): **Mildred and Dewitt Zien**	Suites: **$120–$140**
Location: **8 mi. SW of Ithaca**	Guest Cottage: **$260, sleeps 9**
No. of Rooms: **7**	Open: **All year**
No. of Private Baths: **4**	Breakfast: **Full**
Max. No. Sharing Bath: **4**	Pets: **No**
Double/pb: **$50–$60**	Children: **No**
Single/pb: **$50–$60**	Smoking: **No**
Double/sb: **$40–$45**	Social Drinking: **Permitted**

High on a hill above Main Street, overlooking the small village of Newfield, is this brick Victorian built more than 100 years ago. The gracious curved staircase, handsome arched doorways, high ceilings, chestnut cabinetry, and pedestal sinks in all the bedrooms are reminders of its grand past. Although many antiques are used throughout, the atmosphere is friendly and informal. Guests always comment on the marvelous mattresses and bountiful breakfasts. Mildred and Dewitt are retired teachers with interest in flying, cycling, travel, skiing, and reading. A two-night minimum is requested for special college weekends since Cornell University and Ithaca College are close by.

Strawberry Castle Bed & Breakfast ✪
1883 PENFIELD ROAD, PENFIELD, NEW YORK 14526

Tel: **(716) 385-3266**	Open: **All year**
Best Time to Call: **Evenings**	Reduced Rates: **15%, weekly**
Host(s): **Charles and Cynthia Whited**	Breakfast: **Continental**
Location: **8 mi. E of Rochester**	Credit Cards: **AMEX, MC, VISA**
No. of Rooms: **3**	Pets: **No**
Max. No. Sharing Bath: **4**	Children: **Welcome, over 12**
Double/sb: **$60–$70**	Smoking: **Permitted**
Single/sb: **$50–$60**	Social Drinking: **Permitted**
Suites: **$70**	Airport/Station Pickup: **Yes**

An outstanding example of the Italian villa style of architecture, the Whiteds' home (circa 1878) features columned porches, heavy plaster moldings, high sculptured ceilings, and a white marble fireplace, and is appropriately furnished with antiques and brass beds. Wander the lawns and gardens, sun on the patio, or take a dip in the pool. Charles and Cynthia will direct you to fine restaurants, golf courses, and all the nearby Rochester attractions.

The Wagener Estate Bed & Breakfast ✪
351 ELM STREET (ROUTE 54-A), PENN YAN, NEW YORK 14527

Tel: (315) 536-4591
Host(s): **Norm and Evie Worth**
Location: **20 mi. from NYS Thruway, Exit 42, Geneva**
No. of Rooms: **5**
No. of Private Baths: **1**
Max. No. Sharing Bath: **4**
Double/pb: **$60**
Single/pb: **$50**
Double/sb: **$50**
Single/sb: **$40**
Open: **All year**
Breakfast: **Full**
Credit Cards: **MC, VISA**
Pets: **No**
Children: **Welcome, over 5**
Smoking: **No**
Social Drinking: **Permitted**

The Worths raised their family in this 16-room historic house located at the edge of the village on four scenic acres with shaded lawns, apple trees, and gentle breeze. The pillared veranda is a perfect spot for quiet reflection, conversation, and refreshments. Once the home of Abraham Wagener, the founder of Penn Yan, this B&B is perfectly situated for visits to wine country, the Corning Glass Museum, Watkins Glen, and beautiful Keuka Lake. The Worths are retired now and "have always loved to travel. Now we feel we are still traveling, because people from other states and countries bring the world to our door."

Lake View Farm Bed & Breakfast ✪
4761 ROUTE 364, RUSHVILLE, NEW YORK 14544

Tel: (716) 554-6973
Best Time to Call: **After 4 PM**
Host(s): **Betty and Howard Freese**
Location: **15 mi. from NYS Thruway, Exit 44**
No. of Rooms: **2**
Max. No. Sharing Bath: **4**
Double/sb: **$45**
Single/sb: **$35**
Reduced Rates: **10%, after 2 nights; weekly**
Breakfast: **Full**
Pets: **No**
Children: **Welcome, over 10**
Smoking: **No**
Social Drinking: **Permitted**

Several rooms have a view of Canandaigua Lake, a Seneca Indian word meaning "The Chosen Place." The simple architecture and bright and airy atmosphere create a pleasant background for family antiques and pictures. Stroll the grounds, rest in a hammock, or play horseshoes or badminton. Take the time to explore the 170 acres; in winter, cross-country ski. In summer the marina and public beach are just minutes away.

Sage Cottage ✪
BOX 121, 112 EAST MAIN STREET, TRUMANSBURG, NEW YORK 14886

Tel: **(607) 387-6449**
Host(s): **Dorry Norris**
Location: **10 mi. N of Ithaca**
No. of Rooms: **4**
No. of Private Baths: **2**
Max. No. Sharing Bath: **4**
Double/pb: **$45**
Single/pb: **$41**
Double/sb: **$39**
Single/sb: **$34**
Open: **All year**
Breakfast: **Full**
Pets: **No**
Children: **Welcome**
Smoking: **No**
Social Drinking: **Permitted**

This Gothic Revival home built in 1855 has a graceful circular staircase as its focal point. The spacious guest rooms are furnished with period furniture and adorned with treasured family pieces. Greet the morning with a hearty country breakfast on the cheery sun porch. When winter winds blow, relax in front of a cozy fire with a hot cup of tea. The kitchen garden provides the basis for the herb dishes that are so evident in Dorry's delicious cooking. It is convenient to Watkins Glen, Cayuga and Seneca lakes, and fine wineries. A two-night minimum stay is required on Cornell University and Ithaca College "big" weekends and graduation.

HUDSON VALLEY/ALBANY/KINGSTON AREA

The American Country Collection
984 GLOUCESTER PLACE, SCHENECTADY, NEW YORK 12309

Tel: **(518) 370-4948**
Best Time to Call: **10 AM–Noon; 1–5 PM**
Coordinator: **Beverly K. Walsh**
States/Regions Covered: **New York—Albany, Cooperstown, Saratoga, upper Hudson Valley; Vermont—Statewide; Massachusetts—Berkshires**

Rates (Double):
  Modest: **$30–$45**
  Average: **$45–$55**
  Luxury: **$55–$105**
Credit Cards: **AMEX, MC, VISA**

The American Country Collection offers comfortable lodging in private homes and small inns. Accommodations range from a 1798 farmhouse where guests are treated to a pancake breakfast with homegrown maple syrup to a stately Georgian home with canopy beds, fireplaces, and Oriental rugs. Each host offers distinctive touches such as fresh flowers in the room or breakfast in bed. Many homes have lakefront property, swimming pools, and tennis courts. All are in areas of scenic and cultural interest, convenient to such attractions as the Baseball Hall of Fame, Empire State Plaza, Saratoga Racetrack, and ski areas. Send $3 for her directory.

Bed & Breakfast, U.S.A., Ltd. ✪
P.O. BOX 606, CROTON-ON-HUDSON, NEW YORK 10520

Tel: **(914) 271-6228**
Best Time to Call: **10 AM–4 PM**
Coordinator: **Barbara Notarius**
States/Regions Covered: **Hudson Valley, Westchester County, Upstate New York, NYC, Long Island, Finger Lakes**

Rates (Single/Double):
  Modest: **$20–$30** **$30–$40**
  Average: **$35** **$45–$55**
  Luxury: **$50** **$60–$130**
Credit Cards: **MC, VISA**

Barbara's extensive network includes host homes convenient to colleges, corporate headquarters, historic sites, recreational activities, and cultural events. The ambience ranges from a simple cabin to an elegant mansion, with many choices in between. This is a membership organization; annual dues $35 for entry to B&B's in many states. A surcharge of $15 is imposed for each booking for nonmembers. Sarah Lawrence, Manhattanville, Russell Sage, Vassar, West Point, and Skidmore are but a few of the major colleges nearby. Send $4 for her descriptive directory.

Riell's Bed and Breakfast ✪
40 LOCUST PARK, ALBANY, NEW YORK 12205

Tel: **(518) 869-5239**
Host(s): **James and Dolores Riell**
Location: **6 mi. W of Albany**
No. of Rooms: **2**
No. of Private Baths: **1**
Max. No. Sharing Bath: **4**
Double/pb: **$30**
Single/pb: **$25**
Double/sb: **$30**

Single/sb: **$25**
Open: **All year**
Breakfast: **Full**
Pets: **No**
Children: **Welcome, over 10**
Smoking: **Permitted**
Social Drinking: **Permitted**
Airport/Station Pickup: **Yes**

The Riells welcome you to a cozy Cape Cod home in the heart of New York State's capital district. Guests have a separate entrance leading to the second-floor bedrooms. One room features a wicker sitting area and the other a small office area with desk and chair. Both have wall-to-wall carpeting and coordinating linens, and you'll always find a bowl of fresh fruit. Your hosts welcome you to relax at the family room bar or in the lovely backyard with patio. Saratoga Racetrack, Empire State Plaza, and numerous shopping centers and colleges are nearby.

Ananas Hus Bed and Breakfast ✪
ROUTE 3, P.O. BOX 301, AVERILL PARK, NEW YORK 12018

Tel: **(518) 766-5035**
Host(s): **Thelma and Clyde Tomlinson**
Location: **6 mi. from Rte. 22**
No. of Rooms: **3**
Max. No. Sharing Bath: **4**
Double/sb: **$50**
Single/sb: **$40**
Open: **All year**

Breakfast: **Full**
Pets: **No**
Children: **Welcome, over 12**
Smoking: **No**
Social Drinking: **Permitted**
Foreign Languages: **Norwegian**
Minimum Stay: **2 nights on holiday weekends**

The welcome mat is out at this hillside ranch home on 30 acres, with a panoramic view of the Hudson River Valley. It is informally furnished in the Early American style, accented with mementos from your hosts' international travels and Thelma's lovely needlework. Thelma is a former schoolteacher; Clyde was in the food business. They are serious amateur photographers who compete internationally. It is 15 minutes to Jiminy Peak and Brodie Mountain ski areas; 30 minutes to Tanglewood, Williamstown Theatre Festival, and Clark Art Institute in Massachusetts.

The Gregory House Inn
P.O. BOX 401, ROUTE 43, AVERILL PARK, NEW YORK 12018

Tel: **(518) 674-3774**
Best Time to Call: **5 PM**
Host(s): **Bette and Bob Jewell**
Location: **10 mi. E of Albany**
No. of Rooms: **12**
No. of Private Baths: **12**
Double/pb: **$50–$60**
Single/pb: **$45 and up**
Open: **All year**

Reduced Rates: **Weekly**
Breakfast: **Continental**
Other Meals: **Available**
Credit Cards: **AMEX, DC, MC, VISA**
Pets: **No**
Children: **Welcome, over 6**
Smoking: **Permitted**
Social Drinking: **Permitted**

The Gregory House is a clapboard Colonial, dating back to 1830. Your hosts purchased the house in 1964 and opened a small restaurant. Recently, the building was expanded to include beautifully appointed guest rooms and a common room, all in keeping with a relaxed, country style. The house is surrounded by the Catskill, Adirondack, Berkshire, and Green mountains, affording year-round beauty and recreation. The inn is also near the Saratoga Performing Arts Center,

Tanglewood, Hancock Shaker Village, and Saratoga Springs. Your hosts invite you to explore their beautifully landscaped property and to join them for fine dining in the restaurant.

Battenkill Bed and Breakfast Barn ✪
ROUTE 313, R.D. 1, CAMBRIDGE, NEW YORK 12816

Tel: **(518) 677-8868**	Open: **All year**
Host(s): **Veronica and Walter Piekarz**	Breakfast: **Full**
Location: **30 mi. E of Saratoga**	Other Meals: **Available**
No. of Rooms: **2**	Pets: **No**
Max. No. Sharing Bath: **4**	Children: **Welcome**
Double/sb: **$40**	Smoking: **Permitted**
Single/sb: **$30**	Social Drinking: **Permitted**

The post-and-beam structure of this Yankee barn contemporary can be spotted throughout its interior. Guests will enjoy the gourmet meals served by their hosts, who are interested in music and a back-to-basics way of life. Bromley Mountain; Saratoga Performing Arts Center; Manchester, Vermont; and Bennington College in Vermont are close by. Canoe and tube rentals are available for use in the Battenkill River.

The Lace House
ROUTE 22 AT TUNNEL HILL ROAD, CANAAN, NEW YORK 12029

Tel: **(518) 781-4669**	Breakfast: **Full**
Best Time to Call: **After 6 PM**	Credit Cards: **MC, VISA**
Host(s): **John and Sheila Clegg**	Pets: **No**
Location: **1 mi. from I-90**	Children: **Welcome, over 12**
No. of Rooms: **7**	Smoking: **Permitted**
Max. No. Sharing Bath: **4**	Social Drinking: **Permitted**
Double/sb: **$60**	Airport/Station Pickup: **Yes**
Open: **All year**	

The Lace House got its name from the intricately detailed rosettes and oval carvings over the windows and doors. The house was built in 1806 in the Federal style. In 1922, a Victorian section was added. The result is a unique combination of architectural styles that has placed The Lace House in the National Register of Historic Places. The house has been completely restored and furnished with antiques and period pieces. An elegant sitting room with Oriental rug and Victorian furnishings is available for private relaxing. In the morning, fresh-baked muffins and blueberry pancakes are favorites, served in one of three dining areas. The Lace House is minutes from Tanglewood, Jacob's Pillow, Williamstown Theatre Festival, many ski areas, and fine restaurants.

One Market Street
COLD SPRING, NEW YORK 10516

Tel: **(914) 265-3912**
Host(s): **Philip and Esther Baumgarten**
Location: **50 mi. N of New York City**
No. of Rooms: **1 suite**
No. of Private Baths: **1**
Suites: **$65**
Open: **All year**

Reduced Rates: **Weekly**
Breakfast: **Continental**
Credit Cards: **VISA**
Pets: **No**
Children: **Welcome, over 10**
Smoking: **Permitted**
Social Drinking: **Permitted**

This beautiful Federal-style building dates back to the 1800s and looks out on the Hudson, surrounding mountains, and the foliage of the valley. The suite's kitchenette is stocked with rolls, juice, tea, and coffee for a make-it-at-your-leisure breakfast. Don't miss nearby West Point, Vassar College, and the Vanderbilt Mansion. Philip and Esther will direct you to the fine restaurants and antiques shops in their historic town.

Golden Eagle Inn ✪
GARRISON'S LANDING, GARRISON, NEW YORK 10524

Tel: **(914) 424-3067**
Host(s): **George and Stephanie Templeton**
Location: **50 mi. N of New York City**
No. of Rooms: **4**
No. of Private Baths: **2**
Max. No. Sharing Bath: **4**
Double/pb: **$80**
Double/sb: **$65**

Suite: **$125**
Open: **Apr. 1–Jan. 31**
Breakfast: **Continental**
Credit Cards: **AMEX, MC, VISA**
Pets: **No**
Children: **No**
Smoking: **Permitted**
Social Drinking: **Permitted**

Built on the high banks of the Hudson River, this gracious brick mansion (circa 1848) is listed on the National Register of Historic Places. It's close to West Point, Boscobel, and Hyde Park. The rooms are decorated with antiques and original artwork. The Templetons will direct you to some of the best restaurants in the area. A two-night minimum is required on weekends; three nights on holiday weekends.

House on the Hill ✪
P.O. BOX 86, OLD ROUTE 213, HIGH FALLS, NEW YORK 12440

Tel: **(914) 687-9627**
Best Time to Call: **Before 8 PM**
Host(s): **Shelley and Sharon Glassman**
Location: **10 mi. S of Kingston**
No. of Rooms: **3 suites**
Suites: **$65–$75**
Open: **All year**

Breakfast: **Full**
Pets: **No**
Children: **Welcome**
Smoking: **No**
Social Drinking: **Permitted**
Airport/Station Pickup: **Yes**

A bowl of fruit, a bouquet of flowers, and handmade quilts give the suites in this spacious Colonial a special charm. Breakfast is served by the fireside in the living room, or on the glass porch facing the pond. There are woods to explore, lawns for the children to play on, and ice skating on the pond in winter. Tennis, golf, and fine skiing are all nearby. Lake Mohonk and historic Kingston are minutes away. Complimentary wine and cheese are served, and Shelley and Sharon will direct you to the two four-star restaurants within walking distance of their home. SUNY-New Paltz is nearby.

Elaine's Guest House ✪
P.O. BOX 27, JOHNSON, NEW YORK 10933

Tel: **(914) 355-8811**
Host(s): **Elaine Scott**
Location: **10 mi. from I-84**
No. of Rooms: **2**
No. of Private Baths: **1**
Max. No. Sharing Bath: **2**
Double/pb: **$30**
Single/pb: **$15**

Double/sb: **$30**
Single/sb: **$15**
Open: **All year**
Breakfast: **Full**
Pets: **Welcome**
Children: **Welcome**
Smoking: **No**
Social Drinking: **Permitted**

Located ten minutes from Middletown, between Westtown and Slate Hill, Elaine's home features hospitality and comfort. It is furnished with choice items from her on-premises antique and collectibles shop. She will be pleased to direct you to the area's points of special interest and will suggest good places to dine, suited to your budget.

Bed-N-Breakfast Reservation Services of Greater New York ✪
P.O. BOX 1015, PEARL RIVER, NEW YORK 10965

Tel: **(914) 735-4857**
Coordinator: **David J. Rosen**
States/Regions Covered: **Clarkstown, Haverstraw, Orangetown, Ramapo, Stony Point**

Rates (Single/Double):
Modest: **$25–$35 $35–$45**
Average: **$35–$45 $45–$55**

Rich in history, opportunities for recreational diversions within the many public parks, and cultural experiences, this area is only 25 miles north of New York City. Most of David's B&Bs are within easy reach of public transportation, large shopping centers, and corporate park areas. Bear Mountain, the Hudson River, and the Palisades are just a few popular points of interest.

Sunrise Farm ✪
RD #1, BOX 433A, PINE BUSH, NEW YORK 12566

Tel: **(914) 361-3629**
Best Time to Call: **Evenings**
Host(s): **Fred and Janet Schmelzer**
Location: **70 mi. N of New York City**
No. of Rooms: **1**
No. of Private Baths: **1**
Double/pb: **$45**
Single/pb: **$30**
Open: **All year**

Reduced Rates: **Families; weekly**
Breakfast: **Full**
Pets: **No**
Children: **Welcome**
Smoking: **No**
Social Drinking: **Permitted**
Minimum Stay: **2 nights on weekends, except in winter**

Scotch Highland cattle are raised on this 30-acre farm. A restful night is assured in the comfortable second-floor guest room, where, on clear nights, the stars can be seen through the skylight. Breakfast features homemade preserves, honey from the farm's hives, and organically grown fruit. In winter, a wood stove and solar greenhouse keep the house cozy. Cross-country skiing, hiking, canoeing, downhill skiing, horseback riding, golf, house tours, museums, wineries, and antiquing are favorite diversions.

Maggie Towne's B&B ✪
PHILLIPS ROAD, PITTSTOWN, NEW YORK (Mailing address: Box 82, RD 2, Valley Falls, New York 12185)

Tel: **(518) 663-8369; 686-7331**
Host(s): **Maggie Towne**

Location: **14 mi. E of Troy**
No. of Rooms: **3**

Max. No. Sharing Bath: **4**
Double/sb: **$35**
Single/sb: **$25**
Open: **All year**
Reduced Rates: **10% seniors; families**
Breakfast: **Full**

Other Meals: **Available**
Pets: **Sometimes**
Children: **Welcome (crib)**
Smoking: **No**
Social Drinking: **Permitted**

This lovely old Colonial is located amid beautiful lawns and trees. Enjoy a cup of tea or glass of wine before the huge fireplace in the family room. Use the music room or curl up with a book on the screened-in porch. Mornings, your hostess serves home-baked goodies. She will gladly prepare a lunch for you to take on tour or enjoy at the house. It's 20 miles to historic Bennington, Vermont, and 30 to Saratoga.

Ridgebury Inn and Hunt Club
RD 1, BOX 342, SLATE HILL, NEW YORK 10973

Tel: **(914) 355-HUNT**
Host(s): **Bob and Jean Yonelunas**
Location: **60 mi. NW of New York City**
No. of Rooms: **5**
Max. No. Sharing Bath: **4**
Double/sb: **$55–$60**
Single/sb: **$45**
Suites: **$80–$90**

Open: **All year**
Breakfast: **Full**
Credit Cards: **AMEX, MC, VISA**
Pets: **Horses only ($10 per night)**
Children: **Welcome (crib)**
Smoking: **Permitted**
Social Drinking: **Permitted**
Airport/Station Pickup: **Yes**

This 1840 farmhouse has been added onto many times over the years, and currently totals 34 rooms. It is furnished in English country decor with lots of oak and glass, many antiques, equestrian art, and a century-old baby grand piano and is located on a 90-acre horse farm with miles of riding trails and a lovely pond that's home to a variety of fish, turtles, and waterfowl. You are invited to bring your horse along; there's a lovely barn to accommodate him, as well as a complete saddle-and-gift shop geared to the English rider, and even a fox hunt club. Many guests come to take hot-air balloon rides with the local balloon company—the sight of a dozen balloons drifting over the farm is delightful. Theater, wineries, West Point, Hudson River cruises, and the Goshen Hall of Fame are just a few diversions within a half hour's drive. Wine and cheese along with music and laughter are part of the evening entertainment.

LAKE GEORGE AREA
Hayes's B&B Guest House ☯
P.O. BOX 537, 7161 LAKESHORE DRIVE, BOLTON LANDING, NEW YORK 12814

Tel: **(518) 644-5941**
Best Time to Call: **9 AM–9 PM**
Host(s): **Dick Hayes, Mrs. Martha Hayes**
Location: **250 mi. N of New York City**
No. of Rooms: **3**
No. of Private Baths: **3**
Double/pb: **$60**
Single/pb: **$45**
Suites: **$70–$80**
Open: **All year**
Breakfast: **Continental**
Pets: **No**
Smoking: **No**
Social Drinking: **Permitted**
Minimum Stay: **2 nights**

Close to the shores of Lake George, this elegantly appointed 1920s Cape Cod estate is located across from the town beach, picnic area, and public docks. A five-minute walk to town brings you to tennis courts, shops, and fine restaurants. The Hayes family will arrange boat tours and a picnic lunch for a nominal fee in summer and fall. Cable TV and HBO are available. It's only 40 minutes to Saratoga and its famous racetrack. There's a private trout stream on the property, so pack your fishing gear.

Hilltop Cottage ☯
P.O. BOX 186, 6883 LAKESHORE DRIVE, BOLTON LANDING, NEW YORK 12814

Tel: **(518) 644-2492**
Host(s): **Anita and Charlie Richards**
Location: **8 mi. from I-87**
No. of Rooms: **3**
Max. No. Sharing Bath: **6**
Double/sb: **$35**
Single/sb: **$30**
Open: **All year**
Breakfast: **Full**
Pets: **No**
Children: **Welcome, over 4**
Smoking: **Permitted**
Social Drinking: **Permitted**
Foreign Languages: **German**

Hilltop Cottage is a two-story farmhouse furnished in comfortable, traditional style. The newly decorated guest rooms are located on the second floor, apart from the family living quarters. Breakfast usually includes a German dish and is served on the screened porch in the warm weather. Your hosts will gladly help you discover the delights of the Lake George area, including "Millionaire's Row" located along

Route 9. Beaches, marinas, museums, restaurants, and shops in the town center of Bolton Landing are just a ten-minute walk from the house.

The Crislip's Bed and Breakfast
RD 1, BOX 57, RIDGE ROAD, GLENS FALLS, NEW YORK 12801

Tel: **(518) 793-6869**
Best Time to Call: **6 PM**
Host(s): **Ned and Joyce Crislip**
Location: **Off I-87**
No. of Rooms: **4**
No. of Private Baths: **3**
Max. No. Sharing Bath: **2**
Double/pb: **$55**
Single/pb: **$45**
Single/sb: **$45**

Open: **All year**
Reduced Rates: **Weekly**
Breakfast: **Full**
Credit Cards: **MC, VISA**
Pets: **Sometimes**
Children: **Welcome, over 4**
Smoking: **No**
Social Drinking: **Permitted**
Airport/Station Pickup: **Yes**

This restored Federal-style home is on a parklike lawn surrounded by trees. The house boasts fine woodwork and such collectibles as a grandfather clock, Chippendale desk, and Hepplewhite chest. The spacious bedrooms feature four-poster beds and down comforters. A country breakfast of buttermilk pancakes, scrambled eggs, and sausages is served each morning. Your hosts invite you to relax on the front porch and enjoy the mountain views. Lake George, Saratoga, and Glens Falls are minutes from the house. Winter ski rates are $25 per person.

LAKE PLACID/ADIRONDACKS AREA

North Country B&B Reservation Service ✪
THE BARN, BOX 286, LAKE PLACID, NEW YORK 12946

Tel: **(518) 523-9474**	Rates (Single/Double):
Best Time to Call: **10 AM–10 PM**	Modest: **$15** **$30–$40**
Coordinator: **Lyn Witte**	Average: **$20** **$45–$60**
States/Regions Covered: **Adirondack Mountains**	Luxury: **$40** **$65–$100**

Lyn has dozens of hosts waiting to show you Adirondack Mountain hospitality. Your choice may be convenient to Champlain Valley, Revolutionary War forts, John Brown's farm, or Camp Sagamore. Lake Placid, the Olympic Village, and Lake George offer an endless choice of sports in all seasons. St. Lawrence University, Clarkson, SUNY-Potsdam, and Plattsburgh are nearby.

Highland House ✪
3 HIGHLAND PLACE, LAKE PLACID, NEW YORK 12946

Tel: **(518) 523-2377**	Guest Cottage: **$70–$110, sleeps 2–6**
Best Time to Call: **Mornings**	Open: **All year**
Host(s): **Teddy and Cathy Blazer**	Reduced Rates: **Apr.–May; Nov.**
Location: **25 mi. from Rte. 87, Exit 30**	Breakfast: **Full**
No. of Rooms: **9**	Pets: **No**
No. of Private Baths: **3**	Children: **Welcome**
Max. No. Sharing Bath: **4**	Smoking: **Permitted**
Double/pb: **$45–$55**	Social Drinking: **Permitted**
Double/sb: **$40–$45**	Airport/Station Pickup: **Yes**
Single/sb: **$25–$35**	

Located in a lovely section of Lake Placid, Highland House is within walking distance of everything in town. Cathy and Teddy have created a warm and comfortable atmosphere that guests notice upon entering this 1910 house. Every bedroom is furnished with a large, wooden bunk bed as well as a double bed, each adorned with a bright, fluffy comforter. After a good night's rest, you may look forward to a breakfast of blueberry pancakes or French toast, plus hot cereals, eggs, and beverages.

LONG ISLAND

A Reasonable Alternative ✪
117 SPRING STREET, PORT JEFFERSON, NEW YORK 11777

Tel: **(516) 928-4034**
Best Time to Call: **10 AM–2 PM**
Coordinator: **Kathleen B. Dexter**
States/Regions Covered: **Long Island, Westchester**

Rates (Single/Double):
  Modest: **$32**   **$40**
  Average: **$36**   **$48**
  Luxury: **$40**   **$52–$125**
Credit Cards: **MC, VISA**
Minimum Stay: **2 nights in summer at Hamptons; 3 nights holiday weekends**

Bounded by Long Island Sound and the Atlantic Ocean, from the New York City border to Montauk 100 miles to the east, the cream of host homes has been culled by Kathleen for you. There's much to see and do, including museums, historic homes, theater, horse racing, and the famous beaches, including Jones Beach, Fire Island, Shelter Island, and the exclusive Hamptons. (The Hamptons require a two-day minimum stay in July and August.) Adelphi College, Hofstra University, C. W. Post, Stony Brook, and St. Joseph's are a few of the nearby schools.

Hampton-on-the-Water ✪
BOX 106, HAMPTON BAYS, NEW YORK 11946

Tel: **(516) 728-3560**
Best Time to Call: **8–9 AM, 8–9 PM**
Host(s): **Miss Ute**
Location: **100 mi. E of New York City**
No. of Rooms: **3**
No. of Private Baths: **2**
Max. No. Sharing Bath: **3**
Double/pb: **$65–$85**
Single/pb: **$55–$75**
Double/sb: **$45**

Single/sb: **$35–$50**
Open: **May–Nov.**
Reduced Rates: **Off-season**
Breakfast: **Full**
Pets: **No**
Children: **No**
Smoking: **Permitted**
Social Drinking: **Permitted**
Foreign Languages: **French, German, Spanish**

A spanking-white ranch-style home right on the water of Shinnecock Bay awaits your visit. There's a terrace and large garden for relaxing when you aren't clamming, fishing, or swimming, and kitchen privileges for light meals. Miss Ute permits you to use her Windsurfer, small motorboat, or bicycles when the mood strikes you. It's only seven miles from the shops of Southampton. Minimum stay is three nights in July and August; two nights the rest of the time. Miss Ute also has a fabulous spot in Acapulco, Mexico, available from January 15 until April 15.

Duvall Bed and Breakfast On-the-Garden City-Line ✪
237 CATHEDRAL AVENUE, HEMPSTEAD, NEW YORK 11550

Tel: **(516) 292-9219**
Best Time to Call: **6–9 PM**
Host(s): **Wendy and Richard Duvall**
Location: **20 mi. E of New York City**
No. of Rooms: **4**
No. of Private Baths: **3**
Double/pb: **$50–$75**
Suite: **$100 for 4**
Open: **All year**
Breakfast: **Continental**
Pets: **No**
Children: **Welcome (crib)**
Smoking: **No**
Social Drinking: **Permitted**
Foreign Languages: **German, Spanish**

Guests feel right at home in this charming Dutch Colonial with four-poster beds and antique reproductions. Wine or soft drinks are served on arrival and breakfast features homemade breads, puff pancakes, and fresh fruit. Jones Beach, Fire Island, and New York City are nearby. Guests are welcome to use the patio, garden, and barbecue. Adelphi and Hofstra universities are close by. Nassau Coliseum is less than a mile away.

Mattituck Bed & Breakfast ✪
795 PIKE STREET, MATTITUCK, NEW YORK 11952

Tel: **(516) 298-8785**
Best Time to Call: **Before 6 PM**
Host(s): **Michael Z. Herbert**
Location: **14 mi. from L. I. Expressway, Exit 73**
No. of Rooms: **6**
No. of Private Baths: **1**
Max. No. Sharing Bath: **3**
Double/pb: **$60–$85**
Double/sb: **$60–$65**
Single/sb: **$45–$50**

Open: **All year**
Breakfast: **Continental**
Credit Cards: **MC, VISA**
Pets: **No**
Children: **Welcome, over 8**
Smoking: **Permitted**
Social Drinking: **No**
Minimum Stay: **2 nights June 1–Sept. 5**
Airport/Station Pickup: **Yes**

This rambling, turn-of-the-century Victorian manor house is located on Long Island's North Fork, just steps away from the prestigious Love Lane shopping district. Wicker, stained glass, and Michael's collection of Victorian memorabilia enhance the spacious interior. The grounds and wraparound porch are comfortable spots for relaxing after touring the nearby vineyards, museums, beaches, and antique stores. The breakfast buffet includes fresh fruit salad, cereal, croissants, and a variety of beverages.

Seafield House ✪
2 SEAFIELD LANE, WESTHAMPTON BEACH, NEW YORK 11978

Tel: **(516) 288-1559**
Best Time to Call: **After 4 PM**
Host(s): **Elsie Collins**
Location: **90 mi. E of New York City**
No. of Rooms: **3 suites**
No. of Private Baths: **3**
Suites: **$150**

Open: **All year**
Reduced Rates: **$75, Sept. 6–May 26**
Breakfast: **Full**
Pets: **No**
Children: **No**
Smoking: **No**
Social Drinking: **Permitted**

This 100-year-old home in posh Westhampton is five blocks from the beach but boasts its own pool and tennis court. Victorian lounges, a caned rocker, piano, hurricane lamps, Shaker benches, Chinese porcelain all combine to create the casual, country inn atmosphere. When the sea air chills Westhampton Beach, the parlor fire keeps the house toasty warm. The aromas of freshly brewing coffee and Mrs. Collins' breads and rolls baking in the oven are likely to wake you in time for breakfast. You'll leave this hideaway relaxed, carrying one of Mrs. Collins' homemade goodies.

NEW YORK CITY AREA
Bed & Breakfast (& Books)
35 WEST 92ND STREET, NEW YORK, NEW YORK 10025

Tel: **(212) 865-8740**	Rates (Single/Double):
Best Time to Call: **Mon.–Fri. 10 AM–3 PM; 7–8 PM**	Average: **$62.50** **$72.50**
Coordinator: **Judith Goldberg Lewis**	Luxury: **N/A** **$125**
States/Regions Covered: **Manhattan**	Credit Cards: **No**
	Minimum Stay: **2 nights**

Accommodations are conveniently located in residential areas near transportation and within walking distance of many cultural attractions. Hosts are photographers, psychologists, lawyers, dancers, teachers, and artists. They are pleased to share their knowledge of fine shops, reasonable restaurants, galleries, theater, and bookstores.

Bed & Breakfast Network of New York ✪
134 WEST 32ND STREET, SUITE 602, NEW YORK, NEW YORK 10001

Tel: **(212) 645-8134**	Rates (Single/Double):
Best Time to Call: **8 AM–Noon; 2–6 PM**	Modest: **$40** **$60**
	Average: **$50** **$70–$80**
Coordinator: **Mr. Leslie Goldberg**	Luxury: **$60** **$90**
States/Regions Covered: **New York City**	Credit Cards: **No**

Accommodations appropriate to your purpose and purse are available, from the chic East Side to the arty West Side; from SoHo to Greenwich Village. They range from a historic brownstone where the host is an artist to a terraced apartment near Lincoln Center. Leslie's hosts are enthusiastic about the Big Apple and happy to share their insider information with you.

City Lights B&B, Ltd.
P.O. BOX 20355 CHEROKEE STATION, NEW YORK, NEW YORK 10028

Tel: **(212) 737-7049**	Rates (Single/Double):
Coordinators: **Yedida Mielsen and Dee Staff**	Modest: **$30–$40** **$35–$50**
	Average: **$45–$50** **$50–$65**
States/Regions Covered: **New York City**	Luxury: **$50–$60** **$65–$75**
	Credit Cards: **MC, VISA**

From the tony East Side to the yuppie West Side; from the downtown New York University and Greenwich Village areas to uptown neighborhoods near Columbia University and the Museum of Natural History, accommodations range from simple to opulent. Many of the hosts are from the theater and the arts; all of them are anxious to make your stay in their town memorable. Unhosted apartments range from $65 to $180 per night, depending upon the location, ambience, and number of people staying. A two-night minimum is required in all B&Bs; a $10 surcharge is imposed for a one-night stay.

Hosts & Guests, Inc. ✪
P.O. BOX 6798, FDR STATION, NEW YORK, NEW YORK 10150

Tel: **(212) 874-4308**
Best Time to Call: **9–11 AM; 4–7 PM (Mon.–Fri.)**
Coordinator: **David M. Gottlieb**
States/Regions Covered: **Manhattan**

Rates (Single/Double):
Average: $50–$60 $65
Luxury: $65 $75
Credit Cards: **MC, VISA**

David has an exclusive roster of hosts who live in fashionable neighborhoods all over town. Most are in high-rise, luxury buildings with the security of 24-hour doormen, and practically all have private baths. Many B&Bs are in the posh area of Lincoln Center, where understanding hosts are willing to accept one-night reservations to accommodate guests from the tri-state area who enjoy attending performances without having to leave before the last act is over in order to catch a commuter train. We applaud them!

Judith Mol Agency ✪
357 WEST 37TH STREET, NEW YORK, NEW YORK 10018

Tel: **(212) 971-9001**
Coordinator: **Judith Bodeutsch**
States/Regions Covered: **Manhattan**

Rates (Single/Double):
Modest: $45 $55
Average: $65 $80
Luxury: $100 $120
Credit Cards: **No**
Minimum Stay: **2 nights**

Judith's listings are as diverse as the city. An apartment in the old-world area of Gramercy Park has a queen-size bed and antique decor; one that's close to Columbia University has a loft bed, suitable for one, with a great view of the Hudson River. Another, on the chic East Side, is decorated in contemporary style accented with beautiful art. It has a Jacuzzi in the bathroom and a color TV and VCR in the bedroom. There is a 10% surcharge for a one-night stay.

New World Bed & Breakfast ✪
150 FIFTH AVENUE, SUITE 711, NEW YORK, NEW YORK 10011

Tel: (212) 675-5600 or (800) 443-3800 (outside N.Y. State)
Coordinator: **Laura Tilden**
States/Regions Covered: **Manhattan**

Rates (Single/Double):
Modest: $40 $50
Average: $60 $75
Luxury: $65 $90
Credit Cards: **AMEX, MC, VISA**
Minimum Stay: **2 nights**

Offering a unique cross section of accommodations in Manhattan, Laura's specialties are residential sections such as Greenwich Village, Chelsea, Gramercy Park, the Upper East Side, and the Upper West Side. Business visitors who want to be convenient to Midtown, culture buffs who are happiest near Museum Mile or Lincoln Center, and those who come for theater or shopping, are all accommodated. The toll-free phone allows you the luxury of personally discussing your needs and receiving suggestions and descriptions of places on the phone without waiting to receive a descriptive list.

Urban Ventures ✪
P.O. BOX 426, NEW YORK, NEW YORK 10024

Tel: (212) 594-5650
Best Time to Call: **9 AM–5 PM on Sat.**
Coordinator: **Mary McAulay**
States/Regions Covered: **Manhattan, New Jersey**

Rates (Single/Double):
Modest: $34–$40 $45–$60
Average: $50–$55 $65–$80
Luxury: $65–$80 $90–$120
Credit Cards: **AMEX, MC, VISA**
Minimum Stay: **2 nights in B&Bs; 3 nights in unhosted apartments**

The biggest bargains since the Indians sold Manhattan for $24 are offered by this registry. Mary has bedrooms and complete apartments located throughout the best areas of New York City, including landmarked historic districts. She'll be happy to help with theater tickets, restaurant information, current museum exhibits, as well as special tours. Unhosted apartments range from $65 to $120 for two.

A Bit o' the Apple—New York City ✪
Contact: TRAILS END, RD 2, BOX 355A, GREENTOWN, PENNSYLVANIA 18426

Tel: (212) 321-2930 or (717) 857-0856
Best Time to Call: **After 7 PM**

Location: **Manhattan**
No. of Rooms: **2 Suites**

No. of Private Baths: **2**
Suites: **$85–$100 for 2**
Open: **All year**
Reduced Rates: **Weekly**
Breakfast: **Continental**

Pets: **No**
Children: **Welcome, over 5**
Smoking: **No**
Social Drinking: **Permitted**

Situated in a luxury high-rise building on the Hudson River, the suites are within walking distance of the World Trade Center, Trinity Church, the Wall Street Stock Exchanges, the Statue of Liberty ferry, and the South Street Seaport. The accommodations are comfortably furnished with traditional furniture, antiques, and lots of plants. You will enjoy the spectacular city or water views. Your hosts, native New Yorkers, live next door and will be happy to direct you to special restaurants and shops off the tourist trail that will make your visit affordable and memorable. A garage, health club, and delightful promenade are on the premises.

NIAGARA/BUFFALO AREA

Rainbow Hospitality ✪
758 RICHMOND AVENUE, BUFFALO, NEW YORK 14222

Tel: **(716) 881-9977 or 283-4794**
Best Time to Call: **9 AM–3 PM**
Coordinators: **Georgia Brannon and Cheryl Biggie**
States/Regions Covered: **Buffalo, Chautauqua, Lewiston, Niagara Falls, Olcott, Youngstown**

Rates (Single/Double):
  Modest: **$30**   **$35**
  Average: **$40**   **$45**
  Luxury: **$50**   **$80**
Credit Cards: **No**

The scenic splendor of Niagara Falls is only the beginning of the attractions in this area. Georgia and Cheryl welcome travelers with a wide variety of activities to keep everyone interested and busy. Lewiston is the home of Artpark, a 200-acre park and open-air theater featuring productions from May through September. Fishing and antiquing are popular pastimes too. The best things in the area are the hosts, who open their homes to extend the hand of friendship.

B&B of Niagara Frontier ✪
440 LE BRUN ROAD, BUFFALO, NEW YORK 14226

Tel: **(716) 836-0794**
Best Time to Call: **Evenings**
Host(s): **Virginia Trinidad**

Location: **2½ mi. from I-90**
No. of Rooms: **2**
Max. No. Sharing Bath: **4**

Double/sb: **$45**
Single/sb: **$30**
Open: **All year**
Reduced Rates: **Weekly; 15%, families**
Breakfast: **Full (on weekends)**
Pets: **No**

Children: **Welcome, over 6**
Smoking: **No**
Social Drinking: **Permitted**
Airport/Station Pickup: **Yes**
Foreign Languages: **Filipino**

Virginia is a health professional who enjoys traveling, music, and meeting people. You are cordially invited to share her sprawling brick ranch-style home located in a prime suburban section of Buffalo. Elegantly furnished and centrally air-conditioned, it is surrounded by parklike grounds where you can jog, toss a frisbee, play badminton, or cross-country ski, depending upon the season. It is only 16 miles to Niagara Falls; four miles to the Albright Knox Gallery; five miles to Buffalo's theater district. Don't forget to sample the famous Buffalo chicken wings, which can be delivered from a nearby restaurant, and which you are welcome to enjoy in Virginia's kitchen. You'll enjoy the comfort of this home as you would your own.

The Eastwood House ✪
45 SOUTH MAIN STREET, CASTILE, NEW YORK 14427

Tel: **(716) 493-2335**
Best Time to Call: **After 6 PM**
Host(s): **Joan Ballinger**
Location: **63 mi. SE of Buffalo on Rte. 39**
No. of Rooms: **2**
Max. No. Sharing Bath: **4**
Double/sb: **$25**

Single/sb: **$21**
Open: **All year**
Breakfast: **Continental**
Pets: **Sometimes**
Children: **Welcome, over 5**
Smoking: **No**
Social Drinking: **Permitted**

This comfortable house is a few minutes' drive from Letchworth State Park. Your hostess offers coffee, fresh fruit, and juice on arrival. Hot biscuits, freshly whipped cream, and jam are featured at breakfast each morning. Local sights include the Historical Society and the Indian Museum.

The Davidson House ✪
2447 BAUER ROAD, EDEN, NEW YORK 14057

Tel: **(716) 627-5543**
Best Time to Call: **After 3 PM**
Host(s): **Jim and Dolores Davidson**
Location: **15 mi. SW of Buffalo**

No. of Rooms: **2**
Max. No. Sharing Bath: **4**
Double/sb: **$30**
Single/sb: **$25**

Open: **All year**
Reduced Rates: **15%, weekly; 10%, seniors, families**
Breakfast: **Continental**
Pets: **No**

Children: **Welcome, over 12**
Smoking: **Permitted**
Social Drinking: **Permitted**
Airport/Station Pickup: **Yes**

Jim and Dolores welcome you to their large Colonial-style home set on three acres. The house is surrounded by a lovely lawn, gardens, and a pond where deer can often be seen. The house is decorated with many homemade accessories and comfortable family furnishings. Guests are welcome to relax on the porch swing or sit by the fireplace and enjoy homemade wine and snacks. Breakfast specialties include home-baked breads, jams, and plenty of hot coffee. This quiet rural setting is close to skiing, Niagara Falls, and Lake Erie. The Davidsons love flying and extend a special welcome to private pilots. They also invite you to take advantage of their beauty shop to freshen up on your arrival or before an evening out.

The Fox's Den ✪
88 JAMESTOWN STREET, ROUTE 62, GOWANDA, NEW YORK 14070

Tel: **(716) 532-4252**
Best Time to Call: **Evenings**
Host(s): **Janet Fox Mansfield**
Location: **35 mi. SE of Buffalo**
No. of Rooms: **3**
Max. No. Sharing Bath: **6**
Double/sb: **$35**
Single/sb: **$30**

Open: **All year**
Reduced Rates: **10%, seniors; families**
Breakfast: **Continental**
Pets: **No**
Children: **Welcome (crib)**
Smoking: **Permitted**
Social Drinking: **Permitted**

A gracious welcome awaits you at this 100-year-old Gothic Revival home, painted white with green shutters. The large and comfortable rooms are decorated with Early American furnishings. Janet makes her own bran muffins and serves them with fresh fruit for breakfast. On weekends, the meal includes her special recipe for pineapple fritters. In the evening, guests can relax with wine and cheese around the living room fireplace. The Fox's Den is located in a quiet area, close to hiking, boating, skiing, the Seneca Nation of Indians, and the Amish country.

Chestnut Ridge Inn ✪
7205 CHESTNUT RIDGE, LOCKPORT, NEW YORK 14094

Tel: **(716) 439-9124**
Best Time to Call: **Evenings**

Host(s): **Frank and Lucy Cervoni**
Location: **20 mi. E of Niagara Falls**

No. of Rooms: **4**
No. of Private Baths: **4**
Double/pb: **$65**
Single/pb: **$60**
Suite: **$65–$85 for 2–4**
Open: **All year**

Breakfast: **Full**
Pets: **No**
Children: **Welcome, over 12**
Smoking: **No**
Social Drinking: **Permitted**
Foreign Languages: **Italian**

This handsome white Federal mansion built in 1826 boasts 22 rooms. Surrounded by eight acres, it has a circular staircase, library, several fireplaces, and appropriate antique and Chippendale furniture. The bedrooms have queen-size beds and are decorated with Laura Ashley fabrics. Both Lucy and Frank are gourmet cooks and will take pleasure in pampering you with wine, cheese, and special snacks. The inn is centrally air-conditioned for your summer comfort.

THOUSAND ISLANDS AREA

Battle Island Inn ☉
BOX 176, RD #1, FULTON, NEW YORK 13069

Tel: **(315) 593-3699**
Host(s): **Joyce and Richard Rice**
Location: **30 mi. N of Syracuse**
No. of Rooms: **6**
Max. No. Sharing Bath: **6**
Double/pb: **$50**
Single/pb: **$45**

Open: **All year**
Breakfast: **Full**
Pets: **No**
Children: **Welcome**
Smoking: **No**
Social Drinking: **Permitted**

The Rice family welcomes you to their pre-Civil War estate, which they restored themselves with lots of love and hard work. The inn is across the street from a golf course and is surrounded by fields and orchards. The rooms feature Victorian antiques and marble fireplaces. Guest bedrooms are spacious and elegant with imposing high-backed beds. Joyce is a full-time hostess who will tempt your palate with homemade rolls, biscuits, and crêpes. Richard is a systems analyst who oversees the challenges of an 1840s house. Whether you're enjoying the privacy of your room or socializing in the formal front parlor, you are sure to appreciate the friendly family atmosphere.

For key to listings, see inside front or back cover.

✪ This star means that rates are guaranteed through December 31, 1989 to any guest making a reservation as a result of reading about the B&B in *BED & BREAKFAST U.S.A.*—1989 edition.

Please enclose a self-addressed, stamped, business-sized envelope when contacting reservation services.

For more details on what you can expect in a B&B, see Chapter 1.

Always mention *Bed & Breakfast U.S.A.* when making reservations!

If no B&B is listed in the area you'll be visiting, use the form on page 693 to order a copy of our "List of New B&Bs."

We want to hear from you! Use the form on page 691.

NORTH CAROLINA

Charlotte Bed and Breakfast ✪
P.O. BOX 220802, CHARLOTTE, NORTH CAROLINA 28222

Tel: (704) 868-3762
Best Time to Call: 9 AM–5 PM
Coordinator: Mrs. Ruth Foell Hill
States/Regions Covered: Asheville, Beaufort, Chapel Hill, Charlotte, Elkin, Raleigh, Southern Pines, Winston-Salem

Rates (Single/Double):
Modest: $25 $30
Average: $30 $40
Luxury: $40 $65–$80
Credit Cards: No

Ruth is devoted to giving her personal attention to every B&B guest with a sincere effort to place you in a suitable environment. Charlotte, the state's largest city, is a base for international commerce, and is home to Queens College and the University of North Carolina. The Mint Museum of Art and History, the Charlotte Symphony, and Discovery Place are popular attractions. One of her accommodations is in a decorator's home in the Cotswold area; another is a Victorian that was featured in *Travel/Leisure* magazine. Send for Ruth's free brochure. There is a $5 booking surcharge; a $10 surcharge for a double placement.

Cedar Crest Victorian Inn ✪
674 BILTMORE AVENUE, ASHEVILLE, NORTH CAROLINA 28803

Tel: **(704) 252-1389**
Best Time to Call: **Mornings**
Host(s): **Jack and Barbara McEwan**
Location: **1¼ mi. from I-40**
No. of Rooms: **13**
No. of Private Baths: **9**
Max. No. Sharing Bath: **4**
Double/pb: **$78–$90**
Single/pb: **$72–$84**
Double/sb: **$60–$65**
Single/sb: **$55–$60**
Open: **All year**
Breakfast: **Continental**
Credit Cards: **AMEX, Discover, MC, VISA**
Pets: **No**
Children: **Welcome, over 12**
Smoking: **Permitted**
Social Drinking: **Permitted**

Built in 1891 and listed on the National Register of Historic Places, Cedar Crest is one of the largest and most opulent residences to survive Asheville's boom period. Enter the grand foyer and you'll find the rich warmth of hardwood paneling, lace window treatments, and an intricately carved fireplace. A massive oak staircase leads to the guest rooms, decorated with Victorian antiques and fine linens. Your hosts serve tea or lemonade on the spacious veranda in the summer months. In the cold weather, enjoy hot drinks by the fire. This lovely Queen Anne is located close to the Blue Ridge Parkway, the Biltmore House, and downtown Asheville. Your hosts will be glad to recommend local eateries and invite you back to the inn for hot chocolate and cookies in the evening.

Cornerstone Inn ✪
230 PEARSON DRIVE, ASHEVILLE, NORTH CAROLINA 28801

Tel: **(704) 253-5644**
Host(s): **Lonnie and Evelyn Wyatt**
No. of Rooms: **3**
No. of Private Baths: **3**
Double/pb: **$50–$60**
Single/pb: **$45**
Open: **All year**
Breakfast: **Full**
Credit Cards: **MC, VISA**
Pets: **No**
Children: **Welcome, over 12**
Smoking: **No**
Social Drinking: **No**

The Dutch Tudor home is surrounded by hemlocks and is located in the heart of the historic area. Lonnie and Evelyn have furnished with family heirlooms, antiques, and treasures collected while living and traveling in Europe. It is a brief walk to the Botanical Garden at the University of North Carolina, and a short distance to shops, restaurants, and cultural events. Depending upon the weather, breakfast may be enjoyed on the covered side porch, in the formal dining room, or in the rock-walled garden amid local wildflowers.

Flint Street Inns ✪
100 & 116 FLINT STREET, ASHEVILLE, NORTH CAROLINA 28801

Tel: **(704) 253-6723**
Host(s): **Rick, Lynne and Marion Vogel**
Location: **¼ mi. from Rte. 240**
No. of Rooms: **8**
No. of Private Baths: **8**
Double/pb: **$65**
Single/pb: **$50**
Open: **All year**

Breakfast: **Full**
Credit Cards: **AMEX, Discover, MC, VISA**
Pets: **No**
Children: **No**
Smoking: **Permitted**
Social Drinking: **Permitted**

These turn-of-the-century homes on an acre of century-old trees are listed on the National Register of Historic Places. Stained glass, pine floors, and a claw-footed bathtub are part of the Victorian decor. The bedrooms are air-conditioned for summer comfort; some have fireplaces for winter coziness. Guests are served wine, coffee, and soft drinks. The Blue Ridge Parkway is close by.

The Ray House ✪
83 HILLSIDE STREET, ASHEVILLE, NORTH CAROLINA 28801

Tel: **(704) 252-0106**
Best Time to Call: **10 AM–9 PM**
Host(s): **Will and Alice Curtis**
Location: **5 mi. from I-40**
No. of Rooms: **4**
No. of Private Baths: **2**
Max. No. Sharing Bath: **4**
Double/pb: **$52**
Single/pb: **$42**
Double/sb: **$42**

Single/sb: **$32**
Open: **All year**
Reduced Rates: **Weekly**
Breakfast: **Continental**
Pets: **Sometimes**
Children: **Welcome**
Smoking: **Permitted**
Social Drinking: **Permitted**
Airport/Station Pickup: **Yes**
Foreign Languages: **French**

This restored 1891 home sits on an acre of towering trees that provide leafy privacy in a parklike setting. Interior features include windows of unusual design, beamed ceilings, and handsome woodwork. A breakfast of homemade breads, sweet cakes, and jellies is served in the formal dining room or on the shaded wraparound porch

Bath Guest House ○
SOUTH MAIN STREET, BATH, NORTH CAROLINA 27808

Tel: **(919) 923-6811**
Best Time to Call: **9 AM–9 PM**
Host(s): **Paul and Irene Komarow**
No. of Rooms: **5**
No. of Private Baths: **1**
Max. No. Sharing Bath: **4**
Double/pb: **$48**
Single/pb: **$43**

Double/sb: **$43**
Single/sb: **$38**
Open: **All year**
Breakfast: **Full**
Pets: **No**
Children: **Welcome**
Smoking: **Permitted**
Social Drinking: **Permitted**

This is a fine historic home, on the beautiful Pamlico River. You can absorb the abundant history of the town, join the sailing enthusiasts, enjoy hunting and fishing, or just relax on the back porch rocking chairs and watch the sun set over the river. Everything is within walking distance, but bicycles are available for your use. There's no charge for the use of small boats or for docking your own. Special duck-hunting packages are available in season, including experienced guide service and meals. Paul and Irene's Southern breakfasts are special.

The Blackberry Inn ○
P.O. BOX 965, BLACK MOUNTAIN, NORTH CAROLINA 28711

Tel: **(704) 669-8303**
Best Time to Call: **10 AM–9 PM**
Host(s): **Roy and Barbara DeHaan Miller**
Location: **15 mi. E of Asheville**
No. of Rooms: **6**
No. of Private Baths: **6**
Double/pb: **$45–$65**
Single/pb: **$40**

Open: **All year**
Reduced Rates: **10%, weekly**
Breakfast: **Continental**
Pets: **No**
Children: **Welcome (crib)**
Smoking: **Permitted**
Social Drinking: **Permitted**
Airport/Station Pickup: **Yes**

The Blackberry Inn is a red brick Colonial set on a secluded hilltop surrounded by oaks and evergreens. The house was built in the 1930s, and though it has been renovated, it retains its original charm, with hardwood floors upstairs and polished brass throughout. The rooms have an American country theme and are furnished with antiques of all kinds. The inn is a short drive from the Blue Ridge Parkway and the Biltmore House. Rustic mountain trails, brilliant foliage, and relaxed hospitality are sure to lure you back to this charming inn.

The Inn at Brevard
410 EAST MAIN STREET, BREVARD, NORTH CAROLINA 28712

Tel: **(704) 884-2105**
Best Time to Call: **10 AM–8 PM**
Host(s): **Bertrand and Eileen Bourget**
Location: **25 mi. W of Hendersonville**
No. of Rooms: **15**
No. of Private Baths: **15**
Double/pb: **$46–$60**
Single/pb: **$40–$50**
Suite: **$85**

Open: **Mar. 1–Dec. 31**
Reduced Rates: **Weekly**
Breakfast: **Full**
Other Meals: **Available**
Pets: **No**
Children: **Welcome**
Smoking: **Permitted**
Social Drinking: **Permitted**

This white-columned inn is listed on the National Register of Historic Places and has retained the original brass hardware, carved fireplace mantels, and antique furnishings to recall old-time Southern charm. The bedrooms are comfortable and the clear air and mountain breezes will refresh you. Explore the many splendors of this Land of Waterfalls, and return to spend a peaceful evening with other guests on the porch or sitting room.

Hamrick Inn ✪
7787 HIGHWAY 80, BURNSVILLE, NORTH CAROLINA 28714

Tel: **(704) 675-5251**
Best Time to Call: **Mornings**
Host(s): **Neal and June Jerome**
Location: **55 mi. NE of Asheville; 16 mi. from I-40, Exit 72**
No. of Rooms: **4**
No. of Private Baths: **4**
Double/pb: **$45–$50**

Single/pb: **$35–$45**
Open: **All year**
Reduced Rates: **Weekly**
Breakfast: **Continental**
Pets: **No**
Children: **Welcome**
Smoking: **Permitted**
Social Drinking: **Permitted**

This charming three-story Colonial-style stone inn is nestled at the foot of Mt. Mitchell, the highest mountain east of the Mississippi River. Much of the lovely furniture was built by Neal and June. The den has a fine selection of books as well as a TV set for your enjoyment. There is a private porch off each bedroom where you may take in the view and the cool mountain breezes. Golfing, hiking, fishing, rock hounding, craft shopping, and fall foliage are local activities. Pisgah National Park, Linville Caverns, Crabtree Meadows, and the Parkway Playhouse are area diversions.

The Homeplace ✪
5901 SARDIS ROAD, CHARLOTTE, NORTH CAROLINA 28226

Tel: **(704) 365-1936**
Host(s): **Peggy and Frank Dearien**
Location: **10 mi. from I-77; I-85**
No. of Rooms: **4**
No. of Private Baths: **2**
Max. No. Sharing Bath: **4**
Double/pb: **$65**
Single/pb: **$60**
Double/sb: **$55**

Single/sb: **$50**
Open: **All year**
Reduced Rates: **10%, 4 nights**
Breakfast: **Full**
Credit Cards: **AMEX, MC, VISA**
Pets: **No**
Children: **Welcome, over 10**
Smoking: **No**
Social Drinking: **No**

The warm and friendly atmosphere hasn't changed since 1902. The minute you arrive at this country Victorian and walk up to the wraparound porch with its rockers, you'll feel you've "come home." The handcrafted staircase, 10-foot beaded ceilings, and heart-of-pine floors add to the interior's beauty. Complimentary appetizers or desserts are served evenings in the parlor. The Homeplace's porch is pictured on our back cover.

The Inn on Providence
6700 PROVIDENCE ROAD, CHARLOTTE, NORTH CAROLINA 28226

Tel: **(704) 366-6700**
Host(s): **Darlene and Dan McNeill**
No. of Rooms: **5**
No. of Private Baths: **3**
Max. No. Sharing Bath: **4**
Double/pb: **$70**
Double/sb: **$55**
Open: **All year**
Reduced Rates: **Available**
Breakfast: **Full**
Credit Cards: **MC, VISA**
Pets: **No**
Children: **Welcome, over 11**
Smoking: **No**
Social Drinking: **Permitted**
Airport/Station Pickup: **Yes**

The Inn on Providence is a large, three-story Colonial nestled in South Charlotte, close to many amenities to the Queen City. The walnut-paneled library, sitting room with fireplace, and oak-floored dining room will make both vacationers and business executives feel at home. The bedrooms are decorated with Early American antiques, and each features something special, such as a canopy bed or a sitting room. In warm weather, breakfast is served on the screened veranda, which is decorated with white wicker and paddle fans. The veranda is also a great place to sip afternoon tea while overlooking the gardens and swimming pool.

The Overcarsh House ✪
326 WEST EIGHTH STREET, CHARLOTTE, NORTH CAROLINA 28202

Tel: **(704) 334-8477**
Host(s): **Dennis Cudd and George Brown**
Location: **1 mi. from I-77**
No. of Rooms: **1 suite**
No. of Private Baths: **1**
Suites: **$65–$80 (2–4)**
Open: **All year**
Reduced Rates: **10%, corporate**
Breakfast: **Continental**
Pets: **No**
Children: **Welcome**
Smoking: **Permitted**
Social Drinking: **Permitted**

The Library Suite is a Victorian-style retreat in the luxurious Overcarsh House. The private entrance into the suite leads to a wraparound gallery overlooking Fourth Ward park. The adjoining sleeping quarters feature a draped Savannah plantation bed. Your hosts have stocked the floor-to-ceiling bookcases with plenty of books and periodicals. They also provide wine and a wet bar, fresh flowers, cable TV, and coffeemaker. Overcarsh House is listed on the National Register of Historic Places, and is close to the uptown area, the performing arts center, shopping, and restaurants.

Arrowhead Inn ✪
106 MASON ROAD, DURHAM, NORTH CAROLINA 27712

Tel: **(919) 477-8430**
Host(s): **Jerry and Barbara Ryan**
Location: **6.8 mi. from I-85, Exit Roxboro**
No. of Rooms: **8**
No. of Private Baths: **4**
Max. No. Sharing Bath: **4**
Double/pb: **$70–$90**
Double/sb: **$60**

Open: **Jan. 1–Dec. 22**
Reduced Rates: **10% after 4 nights**
Breakfast: **Full**
Credit Cards: **AMEX, MC, VISA**
Pets: **No**
Children: **Welcome**
Smoking: **Permitted**
Social Drinking: **Permitted**
Foreign Languages: **French**

Arrowhead Inn is a 200-year-old columned manor house in Durham County's tobacco country. Its rooms reflect various moments in the house's history, from Colonial through Tidewater and Victorian. Stroll the nearly four acres, or visit the historic district, the Museum of Life and Science, Duke University, or famous Research Triangle Park. After dinner at one of the area's fine restaurants, join the other guests for VCR, Scrabble, or conversation.

Buttonwood Inn ✪
190 GEORGIA ROAD, FRANKLIN, NORTH CAROLINA 28734

Tel: **(704) 369-8985**
Best Time to Call: **After 5 PM**
Host(s): **Liz Oehser**
Location: **75 mi. SW of Asheville**
No. of Rooms: **4**
No. of Private Baths: **2**
Max. No. Sharing Bath: **4**
Double/pb: **$50–$58**
Single/pb: **$40**

Double/sb: **$48**
Single/sb: **$38**
Suites: **$85**
Open: **May 15–Dec.**
Breakfast: **Full**
Pets: **No**
Children: **Welcome, over 10**
Smoking: **Permitted**
Social Drinking: **Permitted**

The Buttonwood is a small country inn surrounded by towering pines, a spacious lawn, and mountain views. The original residence was a small cottage built in the late 1920s adjacent to the greens of the Franklin golf course. Years later, a new wing was added with rustic, charming rooms. Guests may choose from comfortable bedrooms decorated with antiques, cozy quilts, and handcrafts, many of which are offered for sale. Breakfast selections include sausage-apple ring, eggs Benedict, or cheese frittata, with coffee cake and plenty of hot coffee or tea. Golfers will be glad to be so close to the beautiful fairways and Bermuda grass greens right next door. Nearby there are also craft shops, hiking trails, the Blue Ridge Parkway, gem mines, and plenty of places to swim and ride.

Mountain High ✪
BIG RIDGE ROAD, GLENVILLE, NORTH CAROLINA 28736

Tel: **(704) 743-3094**
Host(s): **Margaret and George Carter**
Location: **2 mi. from Rte. 107**
No. of Rooms: **3**
No. of Private Baths: **1**
Max. No. Sharing Bath: **4**
Double/sb: **$33**
Single/sb: **$18**

Open: **July–Nov.**
Reduced Rates: **Weekly**
Breakfast: **Full**
Pets: **No**
Children: **No**
Smoking: **No**
Social Drinking: **Permitted**

It is located 4,200 feet high in the Smoky Mountains, only a short distance from the Carolina Highlands. Margaret and George offer warm hospitality to their guests. You are welcome to use the kitchen for light snacks, and may freshen your wardrobe in the washer and dryer. Western Carolina University–Cullowhee is nearby.

College Hill Bed & Breakfast ✪
922 CARR STREET, GREENSBORO, NORTH CAROLINA 27403

Tel: **(919) 852-1487; 274-6829**
Host(s): **Tom and Ann Martin**
Location: **12 mi. SW of High Point**
No. of Rooms: **4**
No. of Private Baths: **1**
Max. No. Sharing Bath: **4**
Double/sb: **$40**
Single/sb: **$30**
Suites: **$50–$60**
Open: **Sept. 1–June 15**

Breakfast: **Continental**
Credit Cards: **AMEX, MC, VISA**
Pets: **No**
Children: **Welcome, over 12**
Smoking: **Permitted**
Social Drinking: **Permitted**
Minimum Stay: **3 nights, Oct. 15–Apr. 15**
Airport/Station Pickup: **Yes**
Foreign Languages: **German**

High-ceilinged rooms, antiques, accessories collected in Europe, lace curtains, pretty quilts, area rugs framed by oak floors, and a fireplace in each room enhance the decor of this 85-year-old home located in the historic district. Greensboro College and the University of North Carolina at Greensboro are within walking distance. High Point, the mecca for discount home furnishings, is only 20 minutes away. Imported teas, blended coffee, homemade preserves, muffins, and fresh fruit will get your day off to a fine start.

Greenwood ☉
205 NORTH PARK DRIVE, GREENSBORO, NORTH CAROLINA 27401

Tel: **(919) 274-6350**	Single/sb: **$30**
Best Time to Call: **Mornings**	Open: **All year**
Host(s): **Jo Anne Green**	Breakfast: **Continental**
No. of Rooms: **5**	Credit Cards: **AMEX, MC, VISA**
No. of Private Baths: **3**	Pets: **No**
Max. No. Sharing Bath: **4**	Children: **Welcome**
Double/pb: **$45–$55**	Smoking: **Permitted**
Single/pb: **$30**	Social Drinking: **Permitted**
Double/sb: **$35**	

Located in the historic district, this 1905 house has been lovingly restored and air-conditioned for your comfort. Inside the house, the decor includes wood carvings and art from all over the world. Guests are welcome to relax by the fireside and enjoy wine or soft drinks. Breakfast features fresh fruit, cereals, homemade muffins, and jam. Golf, tennis, boating, and hiking are nearby, in Bryan Park. UNC-Greensboro is nearby. There's a swimming pool on the premises.

Gingerbread Inn ☉
103 SOUTH CHURCH STREET, HERTFORD, NORTH CAROLINA 27944

Tel: **(919) 426-5809**	Breakfast: **Full**
Host(s): **Jenny Harnisch**	Credit Cards: **MC, VISA**
Location: **68 mi. SW of Norfolk**	Pets: **No**
No. of Rooms: **3**	Children: **Welcome**
No. of Private Baths: **3**	Smoking: **Permitted**
Double/pb: **$40**	Social Drinking: **Permitted**
Single/pb: **$35**	Foreign Languages: **German, Russian**
Open: **All year**	

This beautifully restored turn-of-the-century home is on the local historic tour and boasts a wraparound porch with paired columns. The comfortably furnished rooms are spacious with queen- or king-size beds and plush carpeting. The aroma of freshly baked gingerbread is something you can't miss during your stay. Your hostess even offers a souvenir cookie for the ride home.

The Hickory Bed & Breakfast ✪
464 7TH STREET SOUTH WEST, HICKORY, NORTH CAROLINA 28602

Tel: **(704) 324-0548**
Host(s): **Jane and Bill Mohney**
Location: **36 mi. N of Charlotte**
No. of Rooms: **4**
No. of Private Baths: **1**
Max. No. Sharing Bath: **6**
Double/pb: **$40**
Single/pb: **$30**
Double/sb: **$35**
Single/sb: **$25**
Open: **All year**
Breakfast: **Full**
Pets: **No**
Children: **Welcome (crib)**
Smoking: **Permitted**
Social Drinking: **Permitted**
Airport/Station Pickup: **Yes**

Bill and Jane Mohney invite you to their Georgian-style home, built in 1908. Downstairs there are three large rooms for relaxing. The parlor is a cozy room with comfortable furniture, and there is a library in the living room where you may choose from a variety of books. The dining room has a fireplace and is a lovely spot to enjoy a breakfast of homemade bread, bacon, and eggs. Sleeping quarters have fresh flowers in season and are furnished in a range of styles, from traditional to contemporary. Your hosts invite you to relax on the porches, and in the summer months, a swimming pool surrounded by bushes, oaks, and grape vineyards is a fine place to spend the afternoon. The Hickory is near a lake, and is walking distance from downtown shops and restaurants.

Colonial Pines Inn ✪
ROUTE 1, BOX 22B, HICKORY STREET, HIGHLANDS, NORTH CAROLINA 28741

Tel: **(704) 526-2060**
Best Time to Call: **10 AM–10 PM**
Host(s): **Chris and Donna Alley**
Location: **80 mi. SW of Asheville**
No. of Rooms: **7**
No. of Private Baths: **7**
Double/pb: **$60**
Single/pb: **$55**
Suites: **$70**
Guest Cottage: **$75, sleeps 4**
Open: **All year**
Reduced Rates: **Weekly**
Breakfast: **Full**
Credit Cards: **MC, VISA**
Pets: **No**
Children: **Welcome**
Smoking: **No**
Social Drinking: **Permitted**

Located in a charming, uncommercial mountain resort town, this white Colonial is flanked by tall columns and is surrounded by two acres. The scenic view may be enjoyed from comfortable rocking chairs on the wide veranda. Donna, a former interior decorator, has furnished with antiques, art, and interesting accessories. Chris is a classical guitarist, woodworker, and great cook. The hearty breakfast includes a variety of homemade breads.

Greenfield B&B ✪
ROUTE #1, BOX 206A, LEICESTER, NORTH CAROLINA 28748

Tel: **(704) 683-2128**
Best Time to Call: **9 AM–5 PM**
Host(s): **Mahlon and Janet Green**
Location: **5 mi. NW of Asheville**
No. of Rooms: **3**
No. of Private Baths: **1**
Max. No. Sharing Bath: **4**
Double/pb: **$45**
Single/pb: **$40**

Double/sb: **$40**
Single/sb: **$35**
Open: **Apr.–Oct.**
Breakfast: **Continental**
Pets: **No**
Children: **No**
Smoking: **Permitted**
Social Drinking: **Permitted**

This southern country estate is set on a hilltop surrounded by lawns and seven acres of pine and hardwood forest. The grounds include over 100 dogwood trees, walking paths, and a pond. The house is a columned Colonial, furnished wth a mixture of antiques, traditional furnishings, and artwork. Breakfast is served on the second-story deck, with its 360-degree panorama of the mountains. On colder days home-baked breads, muffins, and coffee cakes are served in the dining room beside the open brick hearth. The Greens are located near the Great Smoky Mountains National Park and the Blue Ridge Parkway. After a day of touring enjoy a glass of wine or champagne, and a snack on the deck.

Woodside Inn
P.O. BOX 197, NC 575, MILTON, NORTH CAROLINA 28305

Tel: **(919) 234-8646; 694-4450**
Best Time to Call: **Before 8 AM; after 4 PM**
Host(s): **Tom and Lib McPherson**
Location: **12 mi. E of Danville, Va.; 5 mi. from US 58**
No. of Rooms: **4**
No. of Private Baths: **4**
Double/pb: **$52**
Single/pb: **$47**

Open: **All year**
Reduced Rates: **15% less weekly**
Breakfast: **Full**
Other Meals: **Available**
Credit Cards: **MC, VISA**
Pets: **Small pets welcome**
Children: **Welcome**
Smoking: **Permitted**
Social Drinking: **Permitted**
Airport/Station Pickup: **Yes**

Built on a hill overlooking the rolling countryside, this 1838 Greek Revival manor house is furnished with elegant late Federal and American Empire antiques. The large bedrooms are air-conditioned for summer comfort and have fireplaces for chilly winter nights. Breakfast treats are southern raised biscuits, quick breads, country ham, and pancakes. Complimentary beverages are offered, and laundry facilities are available. Tom is a County Supervisor; Lib directs a school nutrition program. They share interests in history, music, travel, golf, reading, and bridge. The on-premises restaurant serves lunch and dinner.

Pine Ridge B&B Inn
2893 WEST PINE STREET, MT. AIRY, NORTH CAROLINA 27030

Tel: **(919) 789-5034**
Host(s): **Ellen and Manford Haxton**
Location: **2 mi. from I-77**
No. of Rooms: **7**
No. of Private Baths: **5**
Max. No. Sharing Bath: **4**
Double/pb: **$75**
Double/sb: **$40**
Open: **All year**

Reduced Rates: **10% Jan.–Mar.**
Breakfast: **Continental**
Other Meals: **Available**
Credit Cards: **MC, VISA**
Pets: **No**
Children: **Welcome (crib)**
Smoking: **Permitted**
Social Drinking: **Permitted**
Airport/Station Pickup: **Yes**

Luxury and elegance await you in this 40-year-old mansion set on eight acres in the shadow of the Blue Ridge Mountains. Each guest room is attractively decorated and has a telephone and cable TV. Read in the wood-paneled library, soak in the hot tub, work out on the Nautilus equipment in the exercise room, or swim in the backyard pool. Golf and tennis are available nearby. A few miles away are outlet stores, the world's largest open-face granite quarry, and the famous frescoes of Ashe County.

Harmony House Inn ✪
215 POLLOCK STREET, NEW BERN, NORTH CAROLINA 28560

Tel: **(919) 636-3810**
Best Time to Call: **9 AM–9 PM**
Host(s): **A. E. and Diane Hansen**
Location: **110 mi. SE of Raleigh**
No. of Rooms: **9**
No. of Private Baths: **9**
Double/pb: **$70**
Single/pb: **$49**

Open: **All year**
Breakfast: **Full**
Other Meals: **Available**
Credit Cards: **AMEX, MC, VISA**
Pets: **Sometimes**
Children: **Welcome**
Smoking: **Permitted**
Social Drinking: **Permitted**

Built in 1850, the inn is located in the historic district just four blocks from Tryon Palace and one block from the confluence of the Trent and Neuse rivers. About 7,000 square feet in area, the house is graced with spacious hallways and an aura of elegance. The air-conditioned guest accommodations are furnished with antiques and fine reproductions. You are welcome to help yourself to soft drinks and ice from the well-stocked guest refrigerator. Relax in the parlor, on the front porch with its rockers and swings, or in the pretty backyard.

Kings Arms Inn
212 POLLOCK STREET, NEW BERN, NORTH CAROLINA 28560

Tel: **(919) 638-4409**	Open: **All year**
Best Time to Call: **8 AM–8 PM**	Breakfast: **Continental**
Host(s): **David and Diana Parks**	Credit Cards: **AMEX, MC, VISA**
No. of Rooms: **8**	Pets: **Only Seeing-Eye dog**
No. of Private Baths: **8**	Children: **Welcome (crib)**
Double/pb: **$63–$65**	Smoking: **Permitted**
Single/pb: **$45**	Social Drinking: **Permitted**

The Kings Arms is named for an old town tavern said to have hosted members of the First Continental Congress. The inn boasts its own historic significance, as many of its rooms date back to the early 1800s. Today its rooms are available to those seeking superior accommodations in the historic district. The bedrooms have fireplaces, antiques, brass, canopied, or poster beds, plus color TV. Homemade biscuits and banana bread are brought to guests each morning. Your hosts will gladly direct you to the waterfront, Tryon Palace, and fine restaurants.

New Berne House Bed and Breakfast Inn ✪
709 BROAD STREET, NEW BERN, NORTH CAROLINA 28560

Tel: **(919) 636-2250**	Reduced Rates: **25%, seniors; 15%, weekly, families**
Host(s): **Joel and Shan Wilkins**	Breakfast: **Full**
Location: **1 mi. from Hwy. 70**	Credit Cards: **AMEX, MC, VISA**
No. of Rooms: **6**	Pets: **Sometimes**
No. of Private Baths: **6**	Children: **Welcome (crib)**
Double/pb: **$68**	Smoking: **Permitted**
Single/pb: **$50**	Social Drinking: **Permitted**
Suites: **$110**	Airport/Station Pickup: **Yes**
Open: **All year**	

Located in the heart of New Bern's historic district, this brick Colonial was home to the Taylor family for generations. Today Joel and Shan Wilkins have furnished the inn in the style of an English country manor with a mixture of antiques, traditional pieces, and attic treasures. Guests are pampered with afternoon tea served in the formal parlor or the library. A sweeping stairway leads upstairs, where you may choose from the romantic Masters Chamber or the whimsical

Nursery, with its pink claw-foot tub and a brass bed reportedly rescued in 1897 from a burning brothel. Breakfast specialties such as honey-glazed ham, praline muffins, and homemade breads can be enjoyed downstairs or in your private quarters. New Berne House is within walking distance of Tryon Palace, North Carolina's Colonial Capitol, and the governor's mansion.

The Oakwood Inn ✪
411 NORTH BLOODWORTH STREET, RALEIGH, NORTH CAROLINA 27604

Tel: **(919) 832-9712**
Best Time to Call: **8 AM–Noon; 3–10 PM**
Host(s): **Diana Newton**
No. of Rooms: **6**
No. of Private Baths: **6**
Double/pb: **$65–$80**
Single/pb: **$55–$70**

Open: **All year**
Breakfast: **Full**
Credit Cards: **AMEX, MC, VISA**
Pets: **No**
Children: **Welcome, over 12**
Smoking: **Permitted**
Social Drinking: **Permitted**

Built in 1871, the inn is listed on the National Register of Historic Places. Recently restored to their prior elegance, all the rooms are enhanced by the tasteful use of antique furnishings, appropriate draperies, and accessories. The inn is located within the 20-square-block area of homes built from 1879 to 1920, and visiting it is really like taking a step back in time into an era of horse-drawn carriages and gingerbread architecture. There are six colleges nearby offering cultural opportunities, and a number of museums for history buffs.

Rowan Oak House ✪
208 SOUTH FULTON STREET, SALISBURY, NORTH CAROLINA 28144

Tel: **(704) 633-2086**
Host(s): **Bill and Ruth Ann Coffey**
Location: **1 mi. from I-85**
No. of Rooms: **3**
No. of Private Baths: **3**
Double/pb: **$55–$75**
Single/pb: **$50–$70**
Open: **Mar.–Nov.**

Reduced Rates: **10%, seniors**
Breakfast: **Continental**
Pets: **Sometimes**
Children: **Welcome, over 12**
Smoking: **Permitted**
Social Drinking: **Permitted**
Airport/Station Pickup: **Yes**
Foreign Languages: **Spanish**

Milton Brown built the Rowan Oak House for his bride, Fannie, in 1902. Set in the heart of the West Square historic district, this Queen Anne features a cupola, a wraparound porch, and a carved oak door. Step through the dark wood entry to see the intricate woodwork and stained glass. The original fixtures are well preserved and complemented by period furnishings and reproductions. Ruth Ann and Bill invite you to choose from three lavishly appointed guest rooms, including the master bedroom, which features a double Jacuzzi and a fireplace in the bathroom. Breakfast is served in your private quarters or downstairs in the formal dining room, beneath the painting of Queen Louise of Prussia. In the afternoon, tea or a glass of wine can be enjoyed in the garden, on the porch, or in the sitting room amid the curios and Victorian knickknacks. Your hosts can guide you to Salisbury's antebellum architecture and an abundance of nearby lakes, parks, and golf courses.

Eli Olive's ○
3719 US 70 WEST, SMITHFIELD, NORTH CAROLINA 27577

Tel: **(919) 934-9823; 934-0246**
Host(s): **Kay and Taylor Jolliff**
Location: **½ mi. W of I-95**
No. of Rooms: **7**
No. of Private Baths: **7**
Double/pb: **$49**
Single/pb: **$42**
Open: **All year**
Reduced Rates: **10%, seniors**

Breakfast: **Full**
Other Meals: **Available**
Credit Cards: **MC, VISA**
Pets: **No**
Children: **Welcome**
Smoking: **Permitted**
Social Drinking: **Permitted**
Airport/Station Pickup: **Yes**

One of Johnston County's most celebrated citizens was Eli Olive, who in his day was famous for riding down the streets scattering silver coins for the children. The inn named in his honor is a restored two-story plantation home with fireplaces, handcrafts, and antebellum charm. Each guest room is named for a celebrated local and features North Carolina furnishings, linens, candles, and soaps. In the dining room, menu selections highlight specialties such as Smithfield ham, corn pudding, beer-battered Vidalia onions, fresh seafood, and peaches-and-cream pie. Your hosts will direct you to local sights such as the Ava Gardner Museum, Southland Winery, and Bentonville Battleground.

Turby Villa B&B ○
EAST WHITEHEAD STREET, SPARTA, NORTH CAROLINA 28675

Tel: **(919) 372-8490**
Host(s): **Mr. and Mrs. R. E. Turbiville**
No. of Rooms: **3**
No. of Private Baths: **1**

Max. No. Sharing Bath: **4**
Double/pb: **$40**
Single/pb: **$25**
Double/sb: **$40**

Single/sb: **$25**
Open: **All year**
Breakfast: **Full**
Pets: **No**

Children: **Welcome, over 7**
Smoking: **Permitted**
Social Drinking: **Permitted**

At an altitude of 3,000 feet, this contemporary two-story brick home is the centerpiece of a 20-acre farm. The house is surrounded by an acre of trees and manicured lawns, and the lovely views are of the scenic Blue Ridge Mountains. Breakfast is served either on the enclosed porch with its white wicker furnishings or in the more formal dining room with its Early American–style furnishings. The Turbivilles take justifiable pride in their attractive, well-maintained B&B.

The Richmond Inn
101 PINE AVENUE, SPRUCE PINE, NORTH CAROLINA 28777

Tel: **(704) 765-6993**
Best Time to Call: **7 AM–7 PM**
Host(s): **Barbara and Dave Richmond**
Location: **4 mi. from Blue Ridge Pkwy., Exit 331**
No. of Rooms: **7**
No. of Private Baths: **7**
Double/pb: **$50–$60**
Single/pb: **$40–$45**

Open: **All year**
Breakfast: **Full**
Credit Cards: **MC, VISA**
Pets: **No**
Children: **Welcome**
Smoking: **Permitted**
Social Drinking: **Permitted**
Foreign Languages: **French, German**

Surrounded by towering pines, this white wooden house trimmed with black window shutters has a stone terrace and rock walls. It is furnished in a comfortable blend of antiques and family treasures. Dave is originally from England, so it is no surprise that a full British breakfast is often served. Most mornings, Barbara fixes a Southern repast with bacon, eggs, and grits. Spruce Pine is the mineral capital of the world, and panning for gemstones such as garnets and amethysts is a popular pastime. Hiking the Appalachian Trail, playing golf, or working out at your hosts' community spa will keep you in shape. Internationally known artists schedule shows throughout the year.

Scott's Keep
308 WALNUT STREET, P.O. BOX 1425, SWANSBORO, NORTH CAROLINA 28584

Tel: **(919) 326-1257**
Best Time to Call: **After 3:30 PM**

Host(s): **Frank and Norma Scott**
Location: **150 mi. SE of Raleigh**

NORTH CAROLINA • 441

No. of Rooms: **2**
Max. No. Sharing Bath: **4**
Double/sb: **$30**
Single/sb: **$30**
Open: **Apr. 1–Dec. 31**
Reduced Rates: **15%, weekly**

Breakfast: **Full**
Credit Cards: **MC, VISA**
Pets: **No**
Children: **Welcome, over 6**
Smoking: **Permitted**
Social Drinking: **Permitted**

This simple contemporary is located on a quiet street two blocks from the waterfront. Your hosts want you to feel right at home in the bright, spacious living room and comfortable guest rooms. The larger bedroom is decorated with wicker and features an antique trunk, a queen-size bed, and a colorful quilt. The smaller bedroom is furnished in classic maple with a double bed and grandmother's quilt. For breakfast, Norma serves blueberry or apple spice muffins with fruit and homemade jellies. This historic seaside village is filled with inviting shops and waterside seafood restaurants. Your hosts will point the way to beautiful beaches, waterskiing, sailing, and windsurfing.

Little Warren ✪
304 EAST PARK AVENUE, TARBORO, NORTH CAROLINA 27886

Tel: **(919) 823-1314**
Host(s): **Patsy and Tom Miller**
Location: **20 mi. E of Rocky Mount**
No. of Rooms: **3**
No. of Private Baths: **3**
Double/pb: **$58–$65**
Single/pb: **$48–$58**
Open: **All year**

Breakfast: **Full**
Credit Cards: **AMEX, MC, VISA**
Pets: **No**
Children: **Welcome, over 4**
Smoking: **Permitted**
Social Drinking: **Permitted**
Airport/Station Pickup: **Yes**
Foreign Languages: **Spanish**

Little Warren is actually a large and gracious family home built in 1913. It is located along the Albemarle Trail in Tarboro's Historic District. The deeply set, wraparound porch overlooks one of the last originally chartered town commons still in existence. Inside, you'll find rooms of beautiful antiques from England and America, many of which can be purchased. In the morning, choose from a full English, Southern, or Continental breakfast.

Mill Farm Inn ✪
P.O. BOX 1251, TRYON, NORTH CAROLINA 28782

Tel: **(704) 859-6992**
Best Time to Call: **Mornings**
Host(s): **Chip and Penny Kessler**
Location: **45 mi. SE of Asheville**

No. of Rooms: **8**
No. of Private Baths: **8**
Double/pb: **$48**
Single/pb: **$40**

Suites: **$70–$90**
Open: **All year**
Reduced Rates: **10%, seniors**
Breakfast: **Continental**
Pets: **No**

Children: **Welcome**
Smoking: **Permitted**
Social Drinking: **Permitted**
Foreign Languages: **French**

The Pacolet River flows past the edge of this three-and-one-half-acre property in the foothills of the Blue Ridge Mountains. Sitting porches and the living room with fireplace are fine spots to relax. A hearty breakfast of fresh fruit, cereal, English muffins, preserves, and coffee is served. Craft shops, galleries, and antiquing will keep you busy.

Bluestone Lodge ✪
SR 1112, P.O. BOX 736, VALLE CRUCIS, NORTH CAROLINA 28691

Tel: **(704) 963-5177**
Best Time to Call: **9 AM–5 PM**
Host(s): **Merry Lee Mears and Rich Brainard**
Location: **70 mi. NW of Charlotte**
No. of Rooms: **4**
No. of Private Baths: **4**
Double/pb: **$45–$70**
Suites: **$95**
Open: **All year**

Reduced Rates: **Mar., Apr., Nov.; weekly**
Breakfast: **Full**
Credit Cards: **MC, VISA**
Pets: **No**
Children: **Welcome**
Smoking: **Permitted**
Social Drinking: **Permitted**
Minimum Stay: **2 nights in season**

Nestled 3,000 feet atop Bluestone Hollow, this rustic cedar lodge is surrounded by trees, blackberry bushes, and wild flowers. The lodge rooms, both with kitchens, feature sliding glass doors opening onto the deck, where you can enjoy breathtaking mountain views. The spacious third-floor suite has vaulted ceilings, skylights, a fireplace, a whirlpool bath and a kitchen with a Jenn-Air range. The cozy loft room has twin beds and is perfect for both kids and adults. All rooms are highlighted by family quilts and antiques. Guests are invited to gather around the fireplace in the living room or relax in the hammock, sauna, or hot tub. The outdoor pool, rec room, and barbecue will make it tough to leave this mountain hideaway. Your hostess will start your day off with a breakfast buffet and will be happy to offer you afternoon iced tea, hot seasonal drinks, or chilled champagne. Trout-filled streams, gourmet restaurants, craft shops, ski areas, and scenic vistas are all nearby.

Anderson Guest House ✪
520 ORANGE STREET, WILMINGTON, NORTH CAROLINA 28401

Tel: **(919) 343-8128**	Open: **All year**
Best Time to Call: **8 AM–5 PM**	Breakfast: **Full**
Host(s): **Landon and Connie Anderson**	Pets: **Sometimes**
No. of Rooms: **2**	Children: **Welcome**
No. of Private Baths: **2**	Smoking: **Permitted**
Double/pb: **$60**	Social Drinking: **Permitted**
Single/pb: **$50**	Airport/Station Pickup: **Yes**

This 19th-century town house has a private guest house overlooking a garden. The bedrooms have ceiling fans, fireplaces, and air-conditioning. Enjoy cool drinks upon arrival and a liqueur before bed. Breakfast specialities are eggs Mornay, blueberry cobbler, and crêpes. Your hostess can point out the sights of this historic town and direct you to the beaches.

Murchison House B&B Inn
305 SOUTH 3RD STREET, WILMINGTON, NORTH CAROLINA 28401

Tel: **(919) 343-8580**	Breakfast: **Full**
Best Time to Call: **Before 5 PM**	Credit Cards: **AMEX, MC, VISA**
Host(s): **Mr. and Mrs. Joseph Curry**	Pets: **No**
No. of Rooms: **3**	Children: **Welcome**
No. of Private Baths: **3**	Smoking: **Permitted**
Double/pb: **$60**	Social Drinking: **Permitted**
Single/pb: **$55**	Airport/Station Pickup: **Yes**
Open: **All year**	

Built in 1876, Murchison House is an example of modified Victorian Gothic architecture. The back of the house faces a formal garden and courtyard. The Chippendale influence is reflected in all the interior woodwork and trim. Antiques and reproductions, along with the elegant parquet floors and the many unusual fireplaces throughout, lend charm and warmth. Feel welcome to curl up with a book in the mission oak–paneled library. Located in the heart of the Wilmington historic district, it is within easy walking distance of shops, restaurants, churches, and the Cape Fear River.

Pilgrims Rest ✪
600 WEST NASH STREET, WILSON, NORTH CAROLINA 27893

Tel: **(919) 243-4447**
Host(s): **Doug and June Stewart**
Location: **50 mi. E of Raleigh**
No. of Rooms: **3**
No. of Private Baths: **1**
Max. No. Sharing Bath: **4**
Double/pb: **$49**
Single/pb: **$49**
Double/sb: **$39**
Single/sb: **$39**
Open: **All year**
Breakfast: **Continental**
Credit Cards: **MC, VISA**
Pets: **Sometimes**
Children: **Welcome**
Smoking: **Permitted**
Social Drinking: **Permitted**
Airport/Station Pickup: **Yes**

The Stewarts welcome you to their large Victorian surrounded by flowering shrubs and old trees. The house is in Wilson's historic district and is listed on the National Register of Historic Places. After a day of sightseeing you're welcome to pull up a comfortable chair on the beautiful porch. Your hosts will gladly direct you to a famous tobacco market, museums, and numerous places to find interesting antiques.

NORTH DAKOTA

• Stanley

• Bismarck

The Triple T Ranch
ROUTE 1, BOX 93, STANLEY, NORTH DAKOTA 58784

Tel: **(701) 628-2418**
Best Time to Call: **8 AM–Noon**
Host(s): **Joyce and Fred Evans**
Location: **60 mi. W of Minot**
No. of Rooms: **2**
Max. No. Sharing Bath: **4**
Double/sb: **$30**
Single/sb: **$25**

Open: **All year**
Reduced Rates: **Available**
Breakfast: **Full**
Pets: **Sometimes**
Children: **Welcome (crib)**
Smoking: **No**
Social Drinking: **No**

You're warmly invited to come to Joyce and Fred's rustic ranch home, where you're welcome to take a seat in front of the stone fireplace, put your feet up, and relax. There's a lovely view of the hills and the valley, and their herd of cattle is an impressive sight. Lake Sakakawea, for seasonal recreation such as fishing and swimming, is 11 miles away. Indian powwows, area rodeos, and hunting for Indian artifacts are fun. The State Fair is held every July.

OHIO

Ohio Valley Bed & Breakfast ✪
6876 TAYLOR MILL ROAD, INDEPENDENCE, KENTUCKY 41051

Tel: **(606) 356-7865**
Best Time to Call: **8 AM–Noon;
   6–8 PM**
Coordinator: **Nancy Cully**
States/Regions Covered: **Northern Kentucky; Greater Cincinnati, Ohio; Southeastern Indiana**

Rates (Single/Double):
   Modest: $25 $30
   Average: $30 $40
   Luxury: $40 $65
Credit Cards: **MC, VISA**

Convenient to the attractions of Cincinnati and Dayton, Ohio, which include professional football and baseball, cultural activities, the University of Cincinnati, Xavier University, and Northern Kentucky University. Regattas and paddleboat cruises are delightful Ohio River pastimes. B&B host homes are also available in rural settings and in Metamora, Indiana, a historic town well known for its antique shops.

Helen's Hospitality House ✪
1096 PALMETTO, AKRON, OHIO 44306

Tel: **(216) 724-7151; 3034**
Best Time to Call: **8 AM–8 PM**
Host(s): **Helen Claytor**
Location: **1 mi. from I-77 S, Exit 123B**
No. of Rooms: **2**
No. of Private Baths: **1**
Max. No. Sharing Bath: **4**
Double/pb: **$30**
Single/pb: **$25**
Double/sb: **$30**

Single/sb: **$25**
Open: **All year**
Reduced Rates: **Weekly**
Breakfast: **Full**
Pets: **No**
Children: **Welcome, over 10**
Smoking: **No**
Social Drinking: **Permitted**
Airport/Station Pickup: **Yes**

Located in a quiet neighborhood on a dead-end street, Helen's centrally air-conditioned house is a bit of country in the city. It is a renovated old farmhouse furnished with antiques and reproductions. On warm days, breakfast is served on the screened, glass-enclosed porch. Quaker Square, Akron University, the Firestone PGA, and Portage Lakes are just a few of the local attractions. Helen is a retired teacher who enjoys being a B&B hostess.

Portage House ✪
601 COPLEY ROAD, STATE ROUTE 162, AKRON, OHIO 44320

Tel: **(216) 535-9236**
Best Time to Call: **Before 11 PM**
Host(s): **Jeanne and Harry Pinnick**
Location: **2 mi. from I-77**
No. of Rooms: **5**
No. of Private Baths: **1½**
Max. No. Sharing Bath: **6**
Double/pb: **$28**
Single/pb: **$22**
Double/sb: **$28**

Single/sb: **$22**
Open: **Feb. 1–Nov. 30**
Reduced Rates: **$3 off after 1st night**
Breakfast: **Full**
Pets: **Yes**
Children: **Welcome (crib)**
Smoking: **Permitted**
Social Drinking: **Permitted**
Foreign Languages: **French, Spanish**

Steeped in history, nestled in a parklike setting, this gracious Tudor home dates back to 1917. There is a stone wall down the street that was the western boundary of the United States in 1785. Harry is a physics professor at the university, and Jeanne is a gracious hostess. The coffeepot is always on, refreshments are available, and if bread is being baked, you'll be given some with butter. It's close to Akron University.

Vickery's Bed & Breakfast ✪
4942 STATE ROUTE 7 NORTH, ANDOVER, OHIO 44003

Tel: **(216) 293-6875**
Host(s): **Robert and Ruth Vickery**
Location: **60 mi. E of Cleveland**
No. of Rooms: **2**
Max. No. Sharing Bath: **4**
Double/sb: **$25**
Single/sb: **$18**

Open: **All year**
Breakfast: **Full**
Pets: **Sometimes**
Children: **Welcome**
Smoking: **Permitted**
Social Drinking: **Permitted**

Painted yellow and trimmed with white shutters, this 100-year-old home is set on 100 acres where there's something for everyone. You may play volleyball or horseshoes or take a ride on the pond in a paddleboat. If you prefer, just walk the land and breathe deeply of fresh air. The bedrooms have floral wallpaper, tie-back curtains, and antique dressers. Breakfast specialties, such as blueberry pancakes and bacon, are served in the cozy dining room. It is five minutes from Pymatuning Lake, where a spectacular spillway of fish and ducks attracts many visitors. You are welcome to use the kitchen for light snacks and the laundry to freshen your travel wardrobe.

A French Creek House
37511 DETROIT ROAD, AVON, OHIO 44011

Tel: **(216) 934-5195**
Host(s): **June and Jack Kearney**
Location: **25 mi. W of Cleveland**
No. of Rooms: **2**
Max. No. Sharing Bath: **4**
Double/sb: **$35–$50**
Open: **All year**

Breakfast: **Full**
Pets: **No**
Children: **No**
Smoking: **Permitted**
Social Drinking: **Permitted**
Airport/Station Pickup: **Yes**

June and Jack Kearney welcome you to their 100-year-old farmhouse located in the heart of Lorain County. Guests may choose from a large bedroom with two antique brass double beds or a smaller room with canopy bed. Breakfast specialties such as blueberry pancakes with locally made syrup are served in the privacy of your room or downstairs in the dining room. The Kearneys invite you to play the piano in the living room or relax with a drink in the cozy sitting room, beside the wood-burning stove. Lorain County is a haven for antique lovers, with more than 14 shops nearby. Three public golf courses are within a five-minute drive, and the activities in Westlake, Sheffield Lake, and downtown Cleveland are all close by.

Williams House ✪
249 VINEWOOD, AVON LAKE, OHIO 44012

Tel: **(216) 933-5089**	Open: **Closed Christmas, Easter weeks**
Best Time to Call: **4–9 PM**	Reduced Rates: **20%, seniors**
Host(s): **Margaret Williams**	Breakfast: **Full**
Location: **20 mi. W of Cleveland**	Pets: **No**
No. of Rooms: **1**	Children: **No**
No. of Private Baths: **1**	Smoking: **No**
Double/pb: **$40**	Social Drinking: **Permitted**
Single/pb: **$25**	Airport/Station Pickup: **Yes**

Located a mile from the Lake Erie public beach, Margaret lives in a quiet residential neighborhood. The house is comfortably decorated in a harmonious blend of styles. She serves beverages and snacks upon your arrival, and will help you plan a pleasant visit. Breakfast is a dandy, from juice to cereal to eggs to bacon to coffee or tea.

Das Winkeljohn Haus ✪
416 EAST ANTHONY, CELINA, OHIO 45822

Tel: **(419) 586-2155**	Single/sb: **$30**
Best Time to Call: **After 5 PM**	Open: **Apr.–Sept.**
Host(s): **Mary Ellen Winkeljohn**	Breakfast: **Continental**
Location: **70 mi. NW of Dayton**	Pets: **No**
No. of Rooms: **2**	Children: **No**
Max. No. Sharing Bath: **4**	Smoking: **No**
Double/sb: **$35**	Social Drinking: **Permitted**

Located on a quiet, residential street where a leisurely stroll may still be enjoyed, this neat-as-a-pin B&B furnished in Early American style personifies our "4 C's": Comfort, Cleanliness, Cordiality, and Cost-value! Mary Ellen has traveled widely and knows exactly how to please guests. She enjoys crafts, sewing, and baking, and her idea of a pleasant evening is talking with her visitors and serving cold drinks and hot popcorn. She'll be happy to direct you to some exceptional museums in the area as well as a most interesting Amish settlement in nearby Berne, Indiana.

Berry Hill House ✪
9694 BERRY HILL DRIVE, CINCINNATI, OHIO 45241

Tel: **(513) 777-4613; 528-6751**	Open: **All year**
Best Time to Call: **9 AM–5 PM**	Breakfast: **Full**
Host(s): **Ed and Inge Roll**	Pets: **Sometimes**
Location: **3 mi. from I-75**	Children: **Welcome**
No. of Rooms: **1**	Smoking: **Permitted**
No. of Private Baths: **1**	Social Drinking: **Permitted**
Double/pb: **$30**	Airport/Station Pickup: **Yes**
Single/pb: **$25**	Foreign Languages: **German**

When you arrive at this brick ranch-style house, be prepared for an abundance of hospitality. Ed and Inge have travelled extensively and know exactly how to make a guest's stay special. Centrally located, it is within easy reach of the city's historic areas, cultural activities, sports attractions, and excellent dining possibilities. Complimentary snacks are ready and waiting when you return from a day of pursuing your interests.

Private Lodgings, Inc. ✪
P.O. BOX 18590, CLEVELAND, OHIO 44118

Tel: **(216) 321-3213**
Best Time to Call: **9 AM–Noon; 3–5 PM**
Coordinator: **Roberta Cahen**
States/Regions Covered: **Cleveland**

Rates (Single/Double):
- Modest: **$25** **$30**
- Average: **$45** **$55**
- Luxury: **$65** **$85**

Credit Cards: **No**

This is a city with world-renowned cultural and biomedical resources, as well as major corporations and recreational areas. Special attention is given to the needs of relocating and visiting professionals, out-patients, and relatives of hospital in-patients, as well as vacationers. Every effort is made to accommodate persons with physical handicaps. Discounted rates are provided for extended stays. Case Western Reserve, John Carroll, and Cleveland State universities are convenient to the B&Bs.

The Sarah Frisch House ✪
1564 SOUTH TAYLOR ROAD, CLEVELAND, OHIO 44118

Tel: **(216) 321-5694**
Host(s): **Sarah Frisch**
Location: **4 mi. from I-90**
No. of Rooms: **2**
No. of Private Baths: **1**
Max. No. Sharing Bath: **3**
Double/pb: **$45**
Single/pb: **$35**
Double/sb: **$40**
Single/sb: **$25–$35**

Open: **All year**
Reduced Rates: **Available**
Breakfast: **Continental**
Other Meals: **Available**
Pets: **Sometimes**
Children: **Welcome**
Smoking: **No**
Social Drinking: **Permitted**
Airport/Station Pickup: **Yes**

Sarah's brick-and-shingle, comfortably furnished bungalow has a large yard and pretty garden. Sarah will make you feel at home. It is convenient to good shopping, fine restaurants, sports facilities, and all the cultural activities that Cleveland is famous for. Complimentary fruit and cheese are offered.

Columbus Bed & Breakfast
763 S. THIRD STREET, GERMAN VILLAGE, COLUMBUS, OHIO 43206

Tel: **(614) 443-3680 or 444-8888**
Coordinator(s): **Fred Holdridge, Howard Burns**
States/Regions Covered: **Columbus**

Rates (Single/Double):
 Average: **$35**   **$45**
Credit Cards: **No**

Historic German Village is a registered National Historic Area. It's close to downtown Columbus but a century away in character. Small brick houses, brick sidewalks and streets, and wrought-iron fences combine to create an Old World atmosphere. Charming shops and restaurants are within easy walking distance.

Studio 12 Bed and Breakfast ✪
2850 BAILEY ROAD, CUYAHOGA FALLS, OHIO 44221

Tel: **(216) 928-5843**
Host(s): **Edith L. Stinaff**

Location: **6 mi. N of Akron; 7 mi. from I-80**

No. of Rooms: **2**
Max. No. Sharing Bath: **4**
Double/sb: **$30**
Single/sb: **$22**
Open: **All year**
Reduced Rates: **10%, seniors; after 1 night**

Breakfast: **Full**
Pets: **Sometimes**
Children: **Welcome (crib)**
Smoking: **No**
Social Drinking: **Permitted**

Edith Stinaff offers attractive accommodations for guests in the new addition to her home, a 1930s brick bungalow. Guest quarters consist of two bedrooms on the second floor with a studio living room and bath. In the morning your hostess serves a hearty breakfast of scrambled eggs, fresh fruit, bacon, and warm muffins or toast. Studio 12 is convenient to the University of Akron, Kent State University, Blossom Music Center, and Hale Farm.

Hill View Acres ✪
7320 OLD TOWN ROAD, EAST FULTONHAM, OHIO 43735

Tel: **(614) 849-2728**
Host(s): **Jim and Dawn Graham**
Location: **10 mi. SW of Zanesville**
No. of Rooms: **2**
Max. No. Sharing Bath: **4**
Double/sb: **$32**
Single/sb: **$25**
Open: **All year**

Reduced Rates: **10%, after 2 nights; seniors**
Breakfast: **Full**
Other Meals: **Available**
Pets: **Sometimes**
Children: **Sometimes**
Smoking: **Permitted**
Social Drinking: **Permitted**

Hill View is a comfortable, large white house situated on 21 acres with a fishing pond. Homemade breads and specialties such as crispy-apple-sausage bake are breakfast fare. You are welcome to relax on the deck, play the piano, or watch TV. Dawn is a former teacher; Jim is a retired personnel specialist. Their interests are cooking, genealogy, and square dancing. Antique shops, potteries, the famous Y Bridge, and the *Lorena* sternwheeler are some of the area's attractions.

Quiet Country
14758 TR 453, LAKEVILLE, OHIO 44638

Tel: **(216) 378-3882**
Best Time to Call: **Mornings**
Host(s): **Jane Bowman**
Location: **70 mi. SW of Cleveland**
No. of Rooms: **3**
Max. No. Sharing Bath: **3**
Double/sb: **$60**

Single/sb: **$60**
Open: **Spring–Fall**
Breakfast: **Full**
Pets: **No**
Children: **No**
Smoking: **No**
Social Drinking: **Permitted**

Located between Millersburg and Loudonville, this lovely restored farmhouse is set among 100 acres of rolling hills and woods. Relax on the patio and watch the swallows over the pond or spend some time on the versatile sport court. Inside you'll find a quiet, comfortable atmosphere that features many of the original floors and windows, Williamsburg wallpapers, and a smattering of antiques. Breakfast is served in the kitchen, complete with fireplace and rocker, or in the dining room overlooking the old barn and grazing horses. Farm-fresh eggs, local meats, and seasonal fruits are usuals on the menu. Two state parks and the Amish area, with its quaint shops and restaurants, are within easy reach.

Grandma Betty's
ROUTE 1, BOX 60A, LEWISVILLE, OHIO 43754

Tel: **(614) 567-3465**
Best Time to Call: **5:30–10:30 PM**
Host(s): **Betty and Coy Hogue**
Location: **4 mi. W of Woodsfield; 26 mi. from I-77**
No. of Rooms: **3**
Max. No. Sharing Bath: **5**
Double/sb: **$35**
Single/sb: **$30**

Open: **All year**
Reduced Rates: **10%, seniors**
Breakfast: **Full**
Credit Cards: **MC, VISA**
Pets: **Sometimes**
Children: **Welcome**
Smoking: **Permitted**
Social Drinking: **Permitted**

This two-story, spic-and-span country home is surrounded by the scenic beauty of Monroe County. It is attractively decorated with an artful mix of traditional and Early American furniture, handmade quilts, plants, and dried-flower arrangements. Guests may choose between a conventional bed or a water bed. Betty, who looks too young to be a grandma, and Coy provide a game room complete with stereo, exercise equipment, and pool table; treat yourself to a visit to the on-premises beauty salon. In summer, the backyard swimming pool is a popular gathering spot. Nearby attractions include the Parry Museum, Piatt Park, Monroe Lake, and Hannibal Locks and Dam.

Happy Hill ✪
1 LEXINGTON-ONTARIO ROAD, ROUTE 8, MANSFIELD, OHIO 44904

Tel: **(419) 884-3916**
Host(s): **Bill and Sam Masur**
Location: **4 mi. from I-71, Exit Rte. 13**
No. of Rooms: **3**
No. of Private Baths: **2**
Max. No. Sharing Bath: **4**

Double/pb: **$50**
Single/pb: **$35**
Double/sb: **$45**
Single/sb: **$30**
Open: **All year**
Breakfast: **Continental**

Pets: **Sometimes**
Children: **Welcome (crib)**
Smoking: **No**
Social Drinking: **Permitted**

This sprawling brick ranch home is set on six acres in the picturesque village of Lexington. The rooms are elegantly appointed with antiques. After a day at the local racetrack, come home for a swim in a huge private swimming pool. In winter, enjoy a hot drink in front of the fire after a day on the ski slopes. Your hosts grows berries on the grounds, and you can taste them in the Blueberry Buckel, the breakfast specialty of the house.

Mulberry Inn ✪
53 NORTH FOURTH STREET, MARTINS FERRY, OHIO 43935

Tel: **(614) 633-6058**
Host(s): **Shirley Probst**
Location: **5 mi. W of Wheeling, W.Va.**
No. of Rooms: **3**
Max. No. Sharing Bath: **5**
Double/sb: **$30**
Single/sb: **$25**
Open: **All year**
Reduced Rates: **Jan.–Mar.; after 4 nights; 5% seniors**
Breakfast: **Full**
Pets: **No**
Children: **Welcome, over 12**
Smoking: **Permitted**
Social Drinking: **Permitted**

Built in 1868, this frame Victorian is on a tree-lined street within walking distance of a Civil War cemetery and the Sedgwick Museum. (Martins Ferry is the oldest settlement in Ohio.) Beautiful woodwork and mantels grace the large rooms, and overhead fans cool the bedrooms on warm summer nights. A retired medical secretary, Shirley devotes her time to making her guests feel comfortable and welcome, tempting them with her unusual French toast recipe. Dog races, recreational activities, the Fostoria Glass Outlet, the Jamboree-in-the-Hills, Ohio University, and Bethany College are less than 10 miles away.

Locust Hill ✪
1659 EAST US 22-3, MORROW, OHIO 45152

Tel: **(513) 899-2749**
Best Time to Call: **Evenings**
Host(s): **Gail Istler**
Location: **10 mi. NE of Cincinnati**
No. of Rooms: **3**
No. of Private Baths: **2**
Max. No. Sharing Bath: **2**
Double/pb: **$45**
Single/pb: **$35**
Double/sb: **$45**
Single/sb: **$35**
Open: **All year**

Breakfast: **Full**
Pets: **No**
Children: **Welcome, over 10**

Smoking: **Permitted**
Social Drinking: **Permitted**
Airport/Station Pickup: **Yes**

Locust Hill is a Victorian house and farm, complete with fields, family pets, and barns. Your hostess loves crafts and has decorated the house with stenciling, quilts, wicker, and many antiques. A sailboat is available for your use at Cowan Lake, which is a 20-minute drive from the house. Bicycles are available for exploring the 27 miles of winding trail along the Miami River. Picnic lunches will gladly be provided. Other local activities include antiquing, canoeing, and touring the Fort Ancient Park and Indian Museum. A grill and picnic table are available on the patio, and everyone is welcome to cook out. Enjoy a view of the rolling hills from the backyard gazebo. It is ten minutes to historic Lebanon and the Kings Island Amusement Park.

St. George House ✪
33941 LORAIN ROAD, NORTH RIDGEVILLE, OHIO 44039

Tel: **(216) 327-9354**
Best Time to Call: **Early morning; evenings until 9 PM**
Host(s): **Helen Bernardine and Muriel Dodd**
Location: **30 mi. W of Cleveland**
No. of Rooms: **4**
No. of Private Baths: **1**
Max. No. Sharing Bath: **5**
Double/pb: **$40**
Single/pb: **$37**
Double/sb: **$35**

Single/sb: **$30**
Open: **All year**
Reduced Rates: **Weekly**
Breakfast: **Continental**
Pets: **Sometimes**
Children: **Welcome, over 12**
Smoking: **Permitted**
Social Drinking: **Permitted**
Airport/Station Pickup: **Yes**

This gray Colonial house with its bright red shutters is decorated with furnishings artfully restored by Helen and Muriel. The surrounding property includes barns, a bird sanctuary, and a pond that is home to a variety of wild ducks and frogs. The game room is the evening gathering place and your hosts will gladly join in the fun. Within 35 miles are Case Western Reserve and John Carroll universities, and the famed Cleveland Clinic. Oberlin College is 10 miles away. Closer by are the clean beaches of Lake Erie, a zoo, and a variety of theaters.

The Bayberry Inn ✪
25675 STATE ROUTE 41 NORTH, PEEBLES, OHIO 45660

Tel: **(513) 587-2221**
Host(s): **Marilyn and Larry Bagford**
Location: **75 mi. E of Cincinnati**
No. of Rooms: **3**
Max. No. Sharing Bath: **6**
Double/sb: **$35**
Single/sb: **$25**

Open: **May 15–Oct. 15**
Breakfast: **Full**
Pets: **Sometimes**
Children: **Welcome**
Smoking: **No**
Social Drinking: **Permitted**

If you expect to find warm hospitality, cozy accommodations with comfortable appointments, and a front porch on which to relax after a hearty old-fashioned breakfast, you won't be disappointed in Marilyn and Larry's Victorian farmhouse. It's located in Adams County, the hub for those with geological, historical, recreational, and agricultural interests. You are certain to enjoy Serpent Mound, Seven Caves, winery tours, riverboat rides, and outdoor theater productions.

Tudor Country Inn ✪
BOX 113, PETTISVILLE, OHIO 43553

Tel: **(419) 445-2351**
Best Time to Call: **8:30 AM–9 PM**
Host(s): **LeAnna and Dale Gautsche**
Location: **30 mi. W of Toledo; 5 mi. from Ohio Tpk.**
No. of Rooms: **2**
Max. No. Sharing Bath: **4**
Double/sb: **$40**

Single/sb: **$35**
Open: **All year**
Breakfast: **Full**
Pets: **Sometimes**
Children: **Welcome**
Smoking: **No**
Social Drinking: **No**

LeAnna and Dale were restaurant owners until they opened this English Tudor inn. It is set on the edge of a small village, surrounded by farmland in the heart of the Mennonite community. Besides soaking in the hot tub, you may lounge in the great room, where snacks are served in the evenings and a fire burns in winter. Breakfast often includes "Belly Stickers," a creamy-bottom tart, and homemade raised donuts. Local attractions include a farm and craft village, a country store, and an ice-cream parlor and restaurant, all in the Pennsylvania Dutch style.

Inn at the Green ○
500 SOUTH MAIN STREET, POLAND, OHIO 44514

Tel: **(216) 757-4688**
Best Time to Call: **After 12 PM**
Host(s): **Ginny and Steve Meloy**
Location: **7 mi. SE of Youngstown**
No. of Rooms: **4**
No. of Private Baths: **2**
Max. No. Sharing Bath: **4**
Double/pb: **$50**
Single/pb: **$45**
Double/sb: **$40**

Single/sb: **$35**
Open: **All year**
Breakfast: **Continental**
Other Meals: **No**
Credit Cards: **MC, VISA**
Pets: **No**
Children: **Welcome, over 10**
Smoking: **Permitted**
Social Drinking: **Permitted**

The Inn at the Green is an 1876 Victorian town house located on the south end of the village green. The rooms have the grandeur of bygone days, with original moldings, 12-foot ceilings, and original poplar floors. There are five Italian marble fireplaces and extensive public rooms furnished with gracious antiques. Guests are welcome to relax in the parlor, sitting room, and library. Sleeping quarters are air-conditioned, and are furnished with poster beds, Sealy Posturepedic mattresses, and antiques. Coffee, croissants, muffins, and French jam are served in the greeting room in winter and on the wicker-furnished porch during moderate weather. Enjoy a glass of sherry on the porch overlooking the garden before dinner. Your hosts will gladly direct you to gourmet dining as well as cross-country ski trails, golf, tennis, and the Butler Institute, home of one of the nation's finest American art collections.

The Vineyard ○
BOX 283, PUT-IN-BAY, OHIO 43456

Tel: **(419) 285-6181**
Host(s): **Barbi and Mark Barnhill**
Location: **An island 35 mi. E of Toledo**
No. of Rooms: **3**
No. of Private Baths: **2**
Max. No. Sharing Bath: **4**
Double/pb: **$75**
Double/sb: **$60**

Single/sb: **$60**
Open: **All year**
Breakfast: **Full**
Pets: **Sometimes**
Children: **No**
Smoking: **No**
Social Drinking: **Permitted**
Airport/Station Pickup: **Yes**

This 130-year-old wood frame house is set on 20 acres of island seclusion. Your hosts grow Catawba grapes for the local winery, which

458 • OHIO

is part of the region's famous wine industry. Guests are greeted with wine and cheese and shown to newly renovated bedrooms furnished with family antiques. You are invited to sun and swim on a private beach after a day of touring. Local attractions include a picturesque harbor and a monument offering a view of Lake Erie's islands.

Colonial Manor ✪
6075 BUFFHAM ROAD, SEVILLE, OHIO 44273

Tel: (216) 769-3464	Single/sb: $30
Best Time to Call: 8 AM; after 5 PM	Open: May–Nov. 1
Host(s): **Jane and Herman Perry**	Breakfast: **Full**
Location: **15 mi. W of Akron**	Pets: **Welcome**
No. of Rooms: **2**	Children: **Welcome**
Max. No. Sharing Bath: **4**	Smoking: **Permitted**
Double/sb: $35	Social Drinking: **Permitted**

Spend the night in a comfortable room away from noisy highways. There are 63 acres of farmland to wander and an endless amount of fresh air to breathe. Your hosts enjoy entertaining in their 100-year-old Colonial, and serve specialties of the house for breakfast each morning. The manor is close to the Amish country, several historical sights, and small towns.

3 B's Bed 'n' Breakfast ✪
103 RACE STREET, SPRING VALLEY, OHIO 45370

Tel: **(513) 862-4241 or 862-4278**	Reduced Rates: **15%, weekly**
Best Time to Call: **Noon; after 5 PM**	Breakfast: **Full**
Host(s): **Pat and Herb Boettcher**	Other Meals: **Available**
Location: **16 mi. SE of Dayton**	Pets: **Sometimes**
No. of Rooms: **5**	Children: **Welcome, over 4**
Max. No. Sharing Bath: **4**	Smoking: **Permitted**
Double/sb: **$38–$42**	Social Drinking: **Permitted**
Single/sb: **$30–$35**	Airport/Station Pickup: **Yes**
Open: **All year**	

This restored 19th-century farmhouse and adjacent Victorian home are combined to make one very special B&B. The rooms are spacious and airy, and abound with family heirlooms and homemade crafts. The quilts on the beds are handmade. Nearby attractions include historic Lebanon, Kings Island, Dayton's Air Force Museum, and the antique shops at Waynesville. Pat and Herb are retired from the Air

Force and look forward to visiting with you. Wright State University, Antioch, and Cedarville colleges are nearby.

Shirlee's Chambers ○
535 ADELAIDE NORTH EAST, WARREN, OHIO 44483

Tel: **(216) 372-1118**	Reduced Rates: **10%, seniors**
Host(s): **Shirlee and Wayne Chambers**	Breakfast: **Full**
Location: **7 mi. from I-80**	Pets: **No**
No. of Rooms: **3**	Children: **Welcome, over 12**
Max. No. Sharing Bath: **3**	Smoking: **Permitted**
Double/sb: **$35**	Social Drinking: **Permitted**
Single/sb: **$29**	Airport/Station Pickup: **Yes**
Open: **All year**	

Shirlee welcomes you to her Colonial home with wine, cheese, or tea and cookies. Her guest rooms are comfortably furnished. Start the day with a French mushroom omelet, the specialty of the house. Your hosts can direct you to the many nearby antique shops. Local attractions include summer theater and fine dining.

Locust Lane Farm ○
5590 KESSLER COWLESVILLE ROAD, WEST MILTON, OHIO 45383

Tel: **(513) 698-4743**	Single/pb: **$35**
Best Time to Call: **Early morning; late evening**	Double/sb: **$35**
	Single/sb: **$30**
Host(s): **Ruth Shoup**	Open: **All year**
Location: **7 mi. SW of Troy**	Breakfast: **Full**
No. of Rooms: **2**	Pets: **No**
No. of Private Baths: **1**	Children: **Welcome (high chair)**
Max. No. Sharing Bath: **4**	Smoking: **No**
Double/pb: **$40**	Social Drinking: **Permitted**

Enjoy a peaceful night in a big old farmhouse, tucked away in a locust grove, set on 58 acres in the country. This air-conditioned house is tastefully decorated with family antiques. Your host offers fluffy bath towels, extra pillows, and goodies such as hot spiced cider, quick breads, and iced tea in the afternoon. Ruth loves entertaining and serves a farm-style breakfast of fresh fruit, muffins, eggs, homemade breads, and sweet rolls. In the warmer weather, breakfast is served on a lovely screened porch. Locust Lane is convenient to Milton and Troy, and four restaurants are located within two miles.

Priscilla's Bed & Breakfast ☉
5 SOUTH WEST STREET, WESTERVILLE, OHIO 43081

Tel: **(614) 882-3910**	Open: **All year**
Best Time to Call: **10 AM–5 PM**	Reduced Rates: **15%, weekly**
Host(s): **Priscilla H. Curtis**	Breakfast: **Continental**
Location: **10 mi. N of Columbus**	Pets: **Sometimes**
No. of Rooms: **2**	Children: **Welcome**
Max. No. Sharing Bath: **3**	Smoking: **Permitted**
Double/sb: **$35**	Social Drinking: **Permitted**
Single/sb: **$30**	Airport/Station Pickup: **Yes**

Located in a historic area adjacent to Otterbein Campus, this 1854 home, surrounded by a white picket fence, abounds with antiques and collectibles. Guests are welcome to borrow bicycles, use the patio, enjoy concerts in the adjoining park, walk to the Benjamin Hanby Museum or the quaint shops, or just stay "home" and relax. Priscilla is an authority on miniatures and dollhouse construction. Everyone enjoys browsing through her on-premises shop.

The Howey House
340 NORTH BEVER STREET, WOOSTER, OHIO 44691

Tel: **(216) 264-8231**	Suites: **$45**
Host(s): **James and Jo Howey**	Open: **All year**
Location: **60 mi. S of Cleveland**	Breakfast: **Continental**
No. of Rooms: **4**	Pets: **No**
No. of Private Baths: **1**	Children: **Welcome, over 12**
Max. No. Sharing Bath: **6**	Smoking: **No**
Double/sb: **$34**	Social Drinking: **Permitted**
Single/sb: **$24**	

This 139-year-old Victorian Gothic Revival home is located on Route 30 between Canton and Mansfield. The house has been recently restored, and each room is furnished with comfortable family pieces. Your hosts offer an assortment of pastries, fruit juice, fresh fruit, and freshly brewed coffee for breakfast. Howey House is located near the College of Wooster, the Ohio Agricultural Research and Development Center, and the Amish Country. Several fine restaurants and downtown Wooster are within walking distance.

OKLAHOMA

Bed & Breakfast—Oklahoma City ✪
11621 HASTINGS AVENUE, YUKON, OKLAHOMA 73099

Tel: (405) 373-2733
Coordinator: **Esther Pahlka**
States/Regions Covered: **Greater Oklahoma City**

Rates (Single/Double):
Average: $38 $42

Most of Esther's hosts are located in the lovely suburban, country club area. All are warm, hospitable people who will help you plan a delightful stay. The homes are all air-conditioned, have private bath accommodations, and TVs in the guest rooms. Many have swimming pools and hot tubs. Beef is king in Oklahoma City, and there are dozens of great restaurants that serve excellent steak dinners. Don't miss the Cowboy Hall of Fame, Indian City (site of the Artifacts of the Five Civilized Tribes), and a tour of the Oklahoma State Capitol and Pioneer Museum.

Country Inn
ROUTE 3, BOX 1925, CLAREMORE, OKLAHOMA 74017

Tel: **(918) 342-1894**
Best Time to Call: **2–10 PM**
Host(s): **Leland Jenkins**
Location: **25 mi. NE of Tulsa**
No. of Rooms: **2**
No. of Private Baths: **2**
Double/pb: **$35**
Single/pb: **$30**

Open: **All year**
Reduced Rates: **15%, seniors**
Breakfast: **Continental**
Other Meals: **Available**
Pets: **Sometimes**
Children: **No**
Smoking: **No**
Social Drinking: **Permitted**

Leland looks forward to making you feel right at home in the charming barn-style guest quarters, separate from the main house. He invites you to enjoy the swimming pool, improve your suntan, or just sit back in the shade and enjoy a cool drink. He'll be pleased to serve a charcoal steak dinner and a bottle of wine for an additional charge. The Will Rogers Memorial, the J. M. Davis Gun Museum, the 29,500-acre Oologah Lake, and Oral Roberts University are close by.

Clayton Country Inn
ROUTE 1, BOX 8, HIGHWAY 271, CLAYTON, OKLAHOMA 74536

Tel: **(918) 569-4165 or 627-1956**
Best Time to Call: **7 AM–10 PM**
Host(s): **Gary and Edna Colwell, Betty Lundgren**
Location: **140 mi. SE of Tulsa**
No. of Rooms: **11**
No. of Private Baths: **11**
Double/pb: **$30**
Single/pb: **$24**

Guest Cottage: **$32–$50; sleeps 5**
Open: **All year**
Breakfast: **Continental**
Other Meals: **Available**
Credit Cards: **MC, VISA**
Pets: **No**
Children: **Welcome**
Smoking: **Permitted**
Social Drinking: **Permitted**

Perched on a hill amid 135 acres and surrounded by the Kiamichi Mountains is this 42-year-old, two-story, stone and wood inn. It's furnished in a simple, traditional style with a beamed ceiling and fireplace. The restaurant on-premises is noted for its fine cooking. Bass fishing at Lake Sardis is two miles away, and an 18,000-acre game preserve is just across the highway. Feel free to bring your horse and enjoy trail rides under the vast western skies.

Robin's Nest Bed & Breakfast ✪
1700A UTICA SQUARE, SUITE 250, TULSA, OKLAHOMA 74114

Tel: **(918) 446-8700**
Host(s): **Dale and Robin Pressnall**
No. of Rooms: **2**
No. of Private Baths: **2**
Double/pb: **$45**
Single/pb: **$40**
Open: **All year**
Reduced Rates: **10%, seniors**
Breakfast: **Full**
Pets: **Sometimes**
Children: **Welcome, over 12**
Smoking: **No**
Social Drinking: **Permitted**
Airport/Station Pickup: **Yes**

Built in 1987, this five-level hillside home is located on a woodsy cul-de-sac overlooking a 600-acre forest. Furnished in Queen Anne style, it features 10-foot-high ceilings with crown moldings, a fireplace, and a grand piano in the living room. Both the guest rooms have sitting areas, cable TV, private telephones, and a fine view of the Tulsa skyline. Chocolates, fresh flowers, and homemade dessert highlight each evening.

Sunrise Bed and Breakfast ✪
4510 EAST 32ND PLACE, TULSA, OKLAHOMA 74135

Tel: **(918) 743-4234**
Best Time to Call: **Before 8 AM; after 5 PM**
Host(s): **Sue Sark**
Location: **4 mi. from I-244**
No. of Rooms: **1**
No. of Private Baths: **1**
Double/pb: **$35**
Single/pb: **$25**
Open: **Jan. 15–Nov. 15**
Breakfast: **Continental**
Pets: **No**
Children: **No**
Smoking: **Permitted**
Social Drinking: **Permitted**

Sunrise Bed and Breakfast is a comfortable ranch-style home, minutes from downtown Tulsa. The atmosphere is clean and homey and relaxed. In the morning, enjoy Sue's coffee and homemade cinnamon rolls. The Sarks will gladly direct you to the nearby Philbrook and Gilcrease museums and Oral Roberts University, as well as to places to shop and dine.

OREGON

Northwest Bed and Breakfast Travel Unlimited
610 SW BROADWAY, SUITE 609, PORTLAND, OREGON 97205

Tel: (503) 243-7616
Coordinators: **Laine Friedman, Gloria Shaich, and Sarah Stadler**
States/Regions Covered: **Washington, Oregon, California, Hawaii, Idaho; Canada—British Columbia**

Rates (Single/Double):
   Modest: **$22** $30
   Average: **$30** $40
   Luxury: **$40** $75
Credit Cards: **No**

Laine, Gloria, and Sarah have a network established in 1979 of hundreds of host homes throughout the Pacific Northwest and Canada. They charge an annual membership fee of $25. Upon joining, you will receive a directory of all the lodgings, which range from city to suburban to rural to coast, mountains, and desert. There is just a $5 processing fee for those who will only use the service once. The directory charge is $8.50.

Chanticleer ✪
120 GRESHAM STREET, ASHLAND, OREGON 97520

Tel: **(503) 482-1919**	Open: **All year**
Host(s): **Jim and Nancy Beaver**	Breakfast: **Full**
Location: **2 mi. from I-5, Exit 14**	Pets: **No**
No. of Rooms: **7**	Children: **Welcome**
No. of Private Baths: **7**	Smoking: **No**
Double/pb: **$70–$105**	Social Drinking: **Permitted**
Suites: **$115–$130**	Airport/Station Pickup: **Yes**

The Chanticleer overlooks Bear Creek Valley and the Cascade foothills. A large living room with a stone fireplace, a sunny patio, and French country furnishings create a comfortable atmosphere. Guests are welcome to juices, coffee, and sherry. Some of the specialty breakfast items include Italian-roast coffee, blintzes, and cheese-baked eggs. Shops, restaurants, and the site of the Shakespeare Festival are a short walk away. Mount Ashland ski area and the Rogue River are a 30-minute drive from the house. Southern Oregon State College is nearby.

The Coach House Inn ✪
70 COOLIDGE STREET, ASHLAND, OREGON 97520

Tel: **(503) 482-2257**	Pets: **No**
Best Time to Call: **Evenings**	Children: **Welcome, over 12**
Host(s): **Pamela and Jack Evans**	Smoking: **No**
No. of Rooms: **4**	Social Drinking: **Permitted**
No. of Private Baths: **4**	Airport/Station Pickup: **Yes**
Double/pb: **$49**	Foreign Languages: **German**
Open: **June–Oct.**	Minimum Stay: **2 nights**
Breakfast: **Continental**	

The guest rooms at this Victorian inn are air-conditioned, decorated with antiques, and offer mountain views. Enjoy a game of croquet on the spacious lawn. Breakfast features fresh fruit cobblers and homemade jams. Guests are welcome to join daily picnic tours of the local creamery and vineyards. The Shakespeare Theatre, historic homes, and antique shops are all nearby.

Mt. Ashland Inn
550 MT. ASHLAND ROAD, P.O. BOX 944, ASHLAND, OREGON 97520

Tel: **(503) 482-8707**	Host(s): **Elaine and Jerry Shanafelt**
Best Time to Call: **After 7 PM Mon.–Thurs.; 2–5 PM Fri.–Sun.**	Location: **6 mi. from I-5, Exit 5**
	No. of Rooms: **4**

No. of Private Baths: **4**
Double/pb: **$60–$70**
Single/pb: **$50–$60**
Open: **All year**
Breakfast: **Full**
Other Meals: **Available**

Pets: **No**
Children: **Welcome, over 12**
Smoking: **No**
Social Drinking: **Permitted**
Airport/Station Pickup: **Yes**

Nestled among tall evergreens, this beautifully handcrafted log structure is situated on a mountain ridge with views of the Cascade Mountains, including majestic Mt. Shasta. Inside, handcarvings, Oriental rugs, homemade quilts, antiques, and finely crafted furniture provide an atmosphere of comfort and elegance. Breakfasts are hearty to satisfy the appetites of skiers and hikers who take advantage of nearby trails. For quiet relaxation, you are welcome to enjoy the sunny deck or curl up with a book by the large stone fireplace.

Neil Creek House ✪
341 MOWETZA DRIVE, ASHLAND, OREGON 97520

Tel: **(503) 482-1334**
Best Time to Call: **After 10 AM**
Host(s): **Edith and Thomas Heumann**
No. of Rooms: **2**
No. of Private Baths: **2**
Double/pb: **$75**
Single/pb: **$70**
Open: **All year**

Reduced Rates: **10%, weekly; $10 less, Nov.–Feb.**
Breakfast: **Full**
Pets: **No**
Children: **No**
Smoking: **No**
Social Drinking: **Permitted**
Foreign Languages: **French, German**

This country house is set on five wooded acres with a duck pond and creek for boating. Guests are welcome to relax by the swimming pool or on the decks. Afternoon tea and coffee are served. Breakfast treats may include homemade jams and syrups, ranch eggs, sausage, bacon, or ebelskivers. The guest rooms overlook the creek or mountains, and are furnished with antiques and 19th-century art. Skiing, sailing, river rafting, and Shakespeare performances are nearby.

Royal Carter House ✪
514 SISKIYOU BOULEVARD, ASHLAND, OREGON 97520

Tel: **(503) 482-5623**
Best Time to Call: **Mornings**
Host(s): **Alyce and Roy Levy**
No. of Rooms: **4**
No. of Private Baths: **4**

Double/pb: **$44–$55**
Suites: **$60**
Open: **Feb. 1–Nov. 1**
Breakfast: **Full**
Pets: **No**

Children: **Welcome, over 7** Social Drinking: **Permitted**
Smoking: **No** Airport/Station Pickup: **Yes**

This beautiful 1909 Craftsman home is listed on the National Historic Register. Located four blocks from Ashland's famous Shakespeare Theatre, it is surrounded by lovely old trees in a parklike setting. It is suitably modernized but retains the original room structure. Alyce has added decorator touches of vintage hats and old periodicals to the antique furnishings. The Levys have traveled extensively abroad and will share stories of their experiences with you. Southern Oregon State College is six blocks away.

Cedar Crest Inn ✪
64169 HIGHWAY 20, BEND, OREGON 97701

Tel: **(503) 382-5052** Open: **All year**
Best Time to Call: **9 AM–1 PM; after 6 PM** Reduced Rates: **Available**
Host(s): **Kaye and Dean Kine** Breakfast: **Full**
Location: **165 mi. SE of Portland** Pets: **No**
No. of Rooms: **5** Children: **Welcome, over 14**
No. of Private Baths: **5** Smoking: **Permitted**
Double/pb: **$55–$70** Social Drinking: **Permitted**
 Airport/Station Pickup: **Yes**

The Cedar Crest Inn is set on a tree-covered ridge overlooking the Cascade Mountains and the Deschutes River. The house is a sprawling Tudor, designed especially for bed-and-breakfasting. Hosts Dean and Kaye have decorated each bedroom in a different theme and color, created with wicker, brass, and Victorian and traditional furnishings. Early morning coffee is followed by a full country breakfast featuring freshly baked biscuits and a variety of other dishes prepared according to your preferences. The inn is located in an area known for its beautiful scenery and recreational activities, such as hunting, fishing, river rafting, and skiing at the Mt. Bachelor resort.

Mirror Pond House ✪
1054 N.W. HARMON, BEND, OREGON 97701

Tel: **(503) 389-1680** Suites: **$80**
Best Time to Call: **Mornings** Open: **All year**
Host(s): **Beryl Kellum** Breakfast: **Full**
No. of Rooms: **2** Pets: **No**
No. of Private Baths: **2** Children: **Welcome, over 12**
Double/pb: **$60** Smoking: **Permitted**
Single/pb: **$55** Social Drinking: **Permitted**

Mirror Pond House overlooks a wildlife sanctuary where wild ducks and geese glide ashore. A quiet residential area close to downtown and right at the water's edge, the location is both serene and convenient. Beryl Kellum's Cape Cod house has a high-ceilinged living room with mahogany moldings, flowered chintz chairs, and a curved sofa overlooking the pond. The upstairs suite has a view of the water and is furnished with a king-size bed, swivel rockers, and wood and polished brass accents. The downstairs bedroom has hardwood floors, Early American furnishings, and twin beds. Breakfast specialties such as champagne mimosas, creamy scrambled eggs, and breakfast steaks with mushrooms are served in a sunny dining room with cloth napkins and fine silver. Beryl will even cook fresh trout if you wake up early enough to catch it. Fish right off the bank or borrow the house canoe. Later, you can laze on the deck or just curl up by the living room fire with a complimentary glass of wine.

Sea Dreamer Inn ✪
P.O. BOX 1840, 15167 McVAY LANE, BROOKINGS, OREGON 97415

Tel: **(503) 469-6629**
Host(s): **Bob and Judy Blair**
Location: **On US Hwy. 101**
No. of Rooms: **4**
No. of Private Baths: **2**
Max. No. Sharing Bath: **4**
Double/pb: **$55–$60**
Single/pb: **$50–$55**
Double/sb: **$45–$50**

Single/sb: **$40–$45**
Open: **All year**
Breakfast: **Full**
Credit Cards: **MC, VISA**
Pets: **No**
Children: **No**
Smoking: **No**
Social Drinking: **Permitted**
Airport/Station Pickup: **Yes**

Situated midway between Portland and San Francisco, this vintage 1912 Colonial is set amid pine trees, fruit trees, and flowers that bloom all year long. It has a view of the famous lily fields that slope gently to the Pacific. Refreshments are served each evening to supplement the magnificent sunsets or by the cozy fire on chilly nights. Judy's breakfast specialties are apple pfannkuchen, French toast stuffed with ricotta cheese, and a variety of soufflés. Whale watching, sport fishing, jet-boat trips, and beachcombing are a few diversions. The climate is springlike in all seasons.

Wheeler's Bed & Breakfast ✪
BOX 8201, COBURG, OREGON 97401

Tel: **(503) 344-1366**
Host(s): **Joe and Isabel Wheeler**

Location: **7 mi. N of Eugene; ½ mi. from I-5, Exit 199**

No. of Rooms: **3**
Max. No. Sharing Bath: **4**
Double/sb: **$35**
Single/sb: **$30**
Open: **Mar. 1–Dec. 1**
Breakfast: **Full**

Pets: **Sometimes**
Children: **Welcome, over 10**
Smoking: **Permitted**
Social Drinking: **Permitted**
Airport/Station Pickup: **Yes**
Foreign Languages: **Spanish**

Joe and Isabel welcome you to their historic town, which offers a unique atmosphere of antiques shops and century-old homes. The guest quarters are separate from the rest of the house, offering complete privacy. Visit in the living room, use the washer-dryer, and make yourselves "at home." The University of Oregon and downtown Eugene are minutes away.

Captain's Quarters Bed & Breakfast ✪
P.O. BOX 3231, 265 SOUTH EMPIRE BOULEVARD, COOS BAY, OREGON 97420

Tel: **(503) 888-6895**
Best Time to Call: **8 AM–8 PM**
Host(s): **John and Jean Griswold**
Location: **3 mi. W of Coos Bay**
No. of Rooms: **2**
Max. No. Sharing Bath: **4**
Double/sb: **$45**

Open: **All year**
Breakfast: **Full**
Pets: **No**
Children: **Welcome, over 10**
Smoking: **No**
Social Drinking: **Permitted**
Airport/Station Pickup: **Yes**

Captain's Quarters is an 1890 Victorian painted gray with white trim. It was the home of Captain Thomas McGenn, chief of the steamship *Breakwater*. John and Jean have lovingly restored the house to its original beauty and created a homey atmosphere with antiques and even some of the old captain's memorabilia. Bedrooms face the beautiful bay and the North Spit, where you can watch the ships come in. Homemade hotcakes with berries, fresh-baked breads, and local cheeses are just some of the breakfast treats served in the dining room or sun parlor. Later, your hosts invite you to have a snack or a cup of coffee in the parlor. A vast selection of activities can be enjoyed nearby, including beachcombing, boat charters, crabbing, and clamming. You can take a trip to the botanical gardens, or just take a break at one of the restaurants tucked along the shores.

This Olde House B&B ✪
202 ALDER STREET, CORNER 2ND AVENUE, COOS BAY, OREGON 97420

Tel: **(503) 267-5224**
Host(s): **Ed and Jean Mosieur**

Location: **½ block from Hwy. 101**
No. of Rooms: **4**

No. of Private Baths: **1**
Max. No. Sharing Bath: **4**
Double/sb: **$40–$50**
Single/sb: **$35–$45**
Suite: **$65**
Open: **All year**
Reduced Rates: **10%, seniors**

Breakfast: **Full**
Pets: **No**
Children: **Welcome, over 12**
Smoking: **Permitted**
Social Drinking: **Permitted**
Airport/Station Pickup: **Yes**

Situated with a view of the bay, this stately Victorian beauty is located only one half block from Highway 101. Guests can catch a glimpse of ships on the bay just before they head downstairs to a breakfast of fresh fruit, eggs, muffins, coffee or tea, served in the dining room. Downtown Coos Bay is only two blocks away from the house, and after a short drive, guests will find a lovely state park, a small boat basin, beaches, South Slough Sanctuary, and the beautiful gardens of Shore Acres.

Huntington Manor
3555 N.W. HARRISON BOULEVARD, CORVALLIS, OREGON 97330

Tel: **(503) 753-3735**
Best Time to Call: **8 AM–8 PM**
Host(s): **Ann Sink**
Location: **84 mi. S of Portland**
No. of Rooms: **2**
No. of Private Baths: **2**
Double/pb: **$45**

Open: **All year**
Reduced Rates: **10%, weekly**
Breakfast: **Full**
Pets: **No**
Children: **Welcome, over 12**
Smoking: **Permitted**
Social Drinking: **Permitted**

Huntington Manor is a 64-year-old Williamsburg-style Colonial, set beneath towering trees and surrounded by gardens. The house has been completely refurbished and furnished with a mixture of American and European antiques. Guest rooms feature queen or double beds, color TV, down comforters, fine imported linens, and special touches such as a decanter of wine and fresh fruit. Your hostess has 20 years of experience in interior design, and she loves caring for her home and catering to guests. Breakfast specialties include ham-and-cheese-filled crêpes, egg strata, and homemade muffins; tea and scones are served in the afternoon. Huntington Manor is four blocks from Oregon State University and within walking distance of parks, churches, and the countryside.

McGillivray's Log Home and Bed and Breakfast ✪
88680 EVERS ROAD, ELMIRA, OREGON 97437

Tel: (503) 935-3564
Best Time to Call: 8 AM–8 PM
Host(s): Evelyn McGillivray
Location: 14 mi. W of Eugene
No. of Rooms: 2
No. of Private Baths: 2
Double/pb: $40–$50
Single/pb: $35–$45

Open: All year
Breakfast: Full
Credit Cards: MC, VISA
Pets: No
Children: Welcome
Smoking: No
Social Drinking: Permitted
Airport/Station Pickup: Yes

This massive home is situated on five acres covered with pines and firs. The structure is designed with six kinds of wood and features a split-log staircase, wooden door latches, and hollow log lamps, all handcrafted. Guests may choose from a spacious, wheelchair-accessible bedroom or an upstairs room that can accommodate a family. All are beautifully decorated in a classic Americana motif. Evelyn prepares buttermilk pancakes using an antique griddle her mother used to use. She also offers fresh-squeezed juice from farm-grown apples and grapes, fresh bread, eggs, and all the trimmings. It's just three miles to a local vineyard; country roads for bicycling and a reservoir for fishing and boating are close by.

The House in the Woods ✪
814 LORANE HIGHWAY, EUGENE, OREGON 97405

Tel: (503) 343-3234
Best Time to Call: Mornings; evenings
Host(s): Eunice and George Kjaer
Location: 3 mi. from I-5
No. of Rooms: 2
No. of Private Baths: 1
Max. No. Sharing Bath: 2
Double/pb: $55
Single/pb: $40
Double/sb: $50
Single/sb: $38

Open: All year
Reduced Rates: Available
Breakfast: Full
Pets: No
Children: Welcome, under 1 or over 14
Smoking: No
Social Drinking: Permitted
Airport/Station Pickup: Yes
Foreign Languages: German

This turn-of-the-century home is situated in a wooded glen surrounded by fir trees, rhododendrons, and azaleas. Inside, you'll find Oriental rugs on the original hardwood floors, a cozy fireplace, antiques, and a square grand piano. Guest rooms always have fresh flowers. Breakfast is served in the formal dining room or beside the warmth of the Franklin stove. Specialties of the house include homemade jams and breads, fruit soups, and a variety of egg dishes. The neighborhood is full of wildlife and bicycle and jogging trails, yet is close to shops, art galleries, museums, wineries, and restaurants.

Shelley's Guest House
1546 CHARNELTON STREET, EUGENE, OREGON 97401

Tel: (503) 683-2062
Host(s): **Bill and Lois Shelley**
Location: **100 mi. S of Portland**
No. of Rooms: **2**
No. of Private Baths: **1**
Max. No. Sharing Bath: **4**
Double/sb: **$40–$50**
Suite: **$65**
Single/sb: **$35–$45**

Open: **All year**
Reduced Rates: **Weekly**
Breakfast: **Full**
Pets: **No**
Children: **Sometimes**
Smoking: **No**
Social Drinking: **No**
Airport/Station Pickup: **Yes**

The Shelley's Guest House is a cottage-style retreat dating back to the 1920s. Traditional wallcoverings, restored brass accents, turn-of-the-century furnishings and antiques are in keeping with the architectural style of the house. Choose from the master bedroom with queen-size brass and iron bed, plush carpet and floral wallpaper, or the "Guest Room" with iron bed, homespun spread, and cozy rocker. Breakfast specialties like eggs Benedict and waffles with strawberries are served in an elegant dining room with oak parquet floors. After a day in Eugene or at the fairgrounds, enjoy fresh fruit and cheese or a cool lemonade, compliments of the Shelleys. You are welcome to soothe your weary bones in the gazebo's hot tub.

Endicott Gardens ✪
95768 JERRY'S FLAT ROAD, GOLD BEACH, OREGON 97444

Tel: (503) 247-6513
Best Time to Call: **10 AM–Noon**
Host(s): **Stewart and Mary Endicott**
No. of Rooms: **4**
No. of Private Baths: **4**
Double/pb: **$45**
Single/pb: **$35**

Open: **All year**
Breakfast: **Full**
Pets: **Sometimes**
Children: **Welcome**
Smoking: **Permitted**
Social Drinking: **Permitted**
Airport/Station Pickup: **Yes**

This classic contemporary B&B is across the road from Rogue River, famous for fishing and riverboat trips to white water. The guest rooms are located in a private wing of the house with decks overlooking the forest, mountains, and beautiful grounds. Homegrown strawberries, blueberries, apples, and plums are often featured in delicious breakfast treats served on the deck or in the dining room. In cool weather, the living room with its cozy fireplace is a favorite gathering spot. Mary and Stewart will be happy to share their collection of restaurant menus from nearby eating establishments with you.

Fair Winds Bed and Breakfast ✪
P.O. BOX 1274, GOLD BEACH, OREGON 97444

Tel: **(503) 247-6753**	Open: **All year**
Best Time to Call: **10 AM or 6 PM**	Reduced Rates: **20%, weekly**
Host(s): **Marion "Butch" Jarman**	Breakfast: **Full**
Location: **3 mi. S of Gold Beach**	Pets: **No**
No. of Rooms: **2**	Children: **Welcome**
Max. No. Sharing Bath: **3**	Smoking: **No**
Double/sb: **$40**	Social Drinking: **Permitted**
Single/sb: **$30**	Airport/Station Pickup: **Yes**

Fair Winds is a small, cedar-clad country home situated high in the foothills of the Siskiyou Mountains. Five acres of wooded, rolling hills create a parklike, private setting. Guests are invited to sun on the deck or stroll down the walkway to the gazebo, where a hot tub/Jacuzzi beckons in the shade of the myrtlewood trees. Marion enjoys gardening, reading, and making guests feel welcome. She has created a homespun look with a unique blend of Americana and finds from around the world. Her breakfast specialties include homemade breads, jams, cheeses, and a variety of hams. She will also be glad to offer a glass of sherry and nibbles or a light supper. This charming country retreat is in the middle of some of the most beautiful coastline anywhere. It is also five miles from the Rogue River, one of the first wilderness waterways in the country.

Ahlf House Bed & Breakfast ✪
762 N.W. 6TH STREET, GRANTS PASS, OREGON 97526

Tel: **(503) 474-1374**	Open: **All year**
Host(s): **Herbert and Betty Buskirk; Rosemary Althaus**	Breakfast: **Full**
	Pets: **No**
Location: **.6 mi. N of Grants Pass**	Children: **No**
No. of Rooms: **2**	Smoking: **No**
Max. No. Sharing Bath: **4**	Social Drinking: **Permitted**
Double/sb: **$60**	Airport/Station Pickup: **Yes**
Single/sb: **$50**	

Ahlf House is located on a main street on a hill overlooking the surrounding mountains. The house dates back to 1902 and is listed on the National Register of Historic Places. The rooms are beautifully appointed and furnished in fine antiques. Guest rooms feature fluffy comforters, down pillows, fresh flowers, and candles. Enjoy a cup of fresh coffee first thing in the morning in the quiet of your room or on the sunny front porch. Your coffee is followed by a full gourmet breakfast including fruit, fresh-baked muffins, and homemade jams and jellies. There is much to explore in Grants Pass, which is set on the Rogue River and is surrounded by the beautiful Cascade Mountains. Your hosts can direct you to guided fishing, raft trips, and jet boats. In the evening, return to this lovely Victorian for parlor music, complimentary wine, and a light snack.

The Handmaiden's Inn ✪
230 RED SPUR DRIVE, GRANTS PASS, OREGON 97527

Tel: **(503) 476-2932**
Host(s): **Bette and Jody Hammer**
Location: **3mi. S of Grants Pass**
No. of Rooms: **3**
No. of Private Baths: **1**
Max. No. Sharing Bath: **4**
Double/pb: **$65**
Double/sb: **$50**
Single/sb: **$45**
Open: **All year**

Reduced Rates: **15%, families**
Breakfast: **Full**
Other Meals: **Available**
Credit Cards: **MC, VISA**
Pets: **No**
Children: **Welcome, over 11**
Smoking: **No**
Social Drinking: **No**
Airport/Station Pickup: **Yes**

The Handmaiden's Inn is a newly built three-story cedar home. The house is surrounded by beautifully landscaped greenery and gardens. The inside is filled with elegant country oak furnishings. Guests are welcome to sun themselves on the spacious deck furnished with comfortable chairs and lounges or relax under the stars in the hot tub. Bette and Jody are professional cooks who used to have a catering business in Southern California. They lovingly prepare hearty breakfasts featuring sausage and egg dishes, homemade breads and jams, fresh fruit, and plenty of coffee. They also invite you to join them for complimentary wine and cheese. The inn is located 5 minutes from white-water rafting and salmon fishing, and is 45 minutes from the Ashland Shakespeare Festival.

Mt. Baldy Bed & Breakfast ✪
678 TROLL VIEW ROAD, GRANTS PASS, OREGON 97527

Tel: **(503) 479-7998**
Best Time to Call: **Before 10 AM; after 4 PM**

Host(s): **John and June Gustafson**
No. of Rooms: **2**
No. of Private Baths: **2**

Double/pb: **$50**
Open: **All year**
Breakfast: **Full**
Pets: **No**

Children: **Welcome, over 7**
Smoking: **No**
Social Drinking: **Permitted**

Relax and enjoy the fresh air and beautiful sunsets from high on the slope of Mt. Baldy overlooking Grants Pass and the Rogue River Valley. Each guest room has a queen-size bed and private entrance. John and June will spoil you with farm-fresh products at breakfast. Fishing, rafting, visiting caves, Crater Lake National Park, historic Jacksonville, and the Shakespeare Festival in Ashland are a few activities to keep you busy.

The Washington Inn Bed & Breakfast ✪
1002 N.W. WASHINGTON BOULEVARD, GRANTS PASS, OREGON 97526

Tel: **(503) 476-1131**
Host(s): **Maryan and Bill Thompson**
Location: **½ mi. from I-5**
No. of Rooms: **3**
No. of Private Baths: **2**
Max. No. Sharing Bath: **2**
Double/pb: **$50–$65**
Single/pb: **$40–$55**
Double/sb: **$40–$55**
Single/sb: **$30–$45**

Open: **All year**
Reduced Rates: **Available**
Breakfast: **Continental**
Credit Cards: **MC, VISA**
Pets: **No**
Children: **Welcome, over 14**
Smoking: **No**
Social Drinking: **Permitted**
Airport/Station Pickup: **Yes**

The Washington Inn is a charming Victorian listed on the National Register of Historic Places. Each guest room is named for one of the Thompsons' three children and offers individual charms. Linda's is a large suite with fireplace, queen-size bed, private bath, and balcony overlooking the mountains; Pattie's Parlor is a spacious red room with fireplace and large private bath with claw-footed tub; Sally's Sunny View overlooks the mountains, has a canopied bed, and is decorated in delicate pink. Your hosts offer bicycles for exploring the area, and many interesting shops and restaurants are within easy walking distance. Fishing, rafting, and jet-boat rides can be enjoyed on the Rogue River. If you prefer, spend the afternoon relaxing on the porch swing, taking in the view.

Country Lane Bed & Breakfast ✪
P.O. BOX Y, 777 COUNTRY LANE, LAKESIDE, OREGON 97449

Tel: **(503) 759-3869**
Best Time to Call: **8 AM–Noon**

Host(s): **Roy and Carolyn Sindell**
Location: **8 mi. from Hwy. 101**

No. of Rooms: **2**
Max. No. Sharing Bath: **4**
Double/sb: **$45**
Single/sb: **$40**
Open: **All year**
Breakfast: **Full**

Pets: **No**
Children: **Welcome, over 12**
Smoking: **No**
Social Drinking: **No**
Airport/Station Pickup: **Yes**

Nestled in a wooded cul-de-sac of Sunlake Park, this owner-built chalet is at the end of a scenic drive with picture postcard views. You are sure to feel right at home in the great room, which features exposed post-and-beam construction, oak floors, a fireplace, and a wood stove. Choose from the Garden View Room, with twin beds, or the Country Room, with queen-size bed. Both have electric blankets and comfortable furnishings. The Sindells invite you to explore the forest trails and country lanes, relax in a hammock near the creek, play badminton, or barbecue on the grill. Start your day off with a hearty breakfast of juice, homemade breads, honey, and special egg dishes, followed by homemade pie and lots of coffee.

Marjon Bed and Breakfast Inn ✪
44975 LEABURG DAM ROAD, LEABURG, OREGON 97489

Tel: **(503) 896-3145**
Host(s): **Marguerite Haas**
Location: **24 mi. E of Eugene**
No. of Rooms: **2**
No. of Private Baths: **2**
Double/pb: **$65**
Suites: **$80**

Open: **All year**
Breakfast: **Full**
Pets: **No**
Children: **No**
Smoking: **Permitted**
Social Drinking: **Permitted**
Airport/Station Pickup: **Yes**

This cedar chalet is located on the banks of the McKenzie River. The suite overlooks the river and a secluded Japanese garden, and features a sunken bath. The other has a fish bowl shower and a view of a 100-year-old apple tree. Relax in the living room with its wraparound seating and massive stone fireplace. One of the walls is made entirely of glass with sliding doors that lead to a terrace that faces the river. A multicourse breakfast is served there on balmy days. Waterfalls, trout fishing, white-water rafting, and skiing are all nearby.

The Owl's View B&B ✪
P.O. BOX 732, NEWBERG, OREGON 97132

Tel: **(503) 538-6498**
Best Time to Call: **8 AM–7 PM**

Host(s): **Chuck and Jean Carr**
Location: **25 mi. SW of Portland**

No. of Rooms: **2**
No. of Private Baths: **2**
Double/pb: **$55**
Single/pb: **$55**
Suites: **$85**
Open: **All year**

Breakfast: **Full**
Pets: **No**
Children: **No**
Smoking: **No**
Social Drinking: **Permitted**

Chuck and Jean welcome you to their large, contemporary home set on two and a half acres. The house overlooks the beautiful Willamette Valley and is surrounded by lush greenery and a flower garden with gazebo. The guest rooms share a mezzanine sitting room for relaxing. One room has a Jacuzzi and a small balcony. The other has a private bath and a view of the valley. In the morning, quiches and special egg dishes are served along with locally made honey, nut butter, and jams. The Owl's View is convenient to Yamhill County wineries and is 30 minutes from Portland.

The Highlands Bed and Breakfast ✪
608 RIDGE ROAD, NORTH BEND, OREGON 97459

Tel: **(503) 756-0300**
Host(s): **Jim and Marilyn Dow**
Location: **4 mi. from Hwy. 101**
No. of Rooms: **2**
No. of Private Baths: **2**
Double/pb: **$45–$55**
Single/pb: **$40–$50**

Open: **All year**
Breakfast: **Full**
Pets: **No**
Children: **Welcome, over 10**
Smoking: **No**
Social Drinking: **Permitted**
Airport/Station Pickup: **Yes**

This uniquely designed contemporary cedar home, with its wide expanses of glass and wraparound deck, has a spectacular view of the valley, inlet, and bay. From the floor-to-ceiling windows of the family room you'll be able to watch unforgettable sunrises and sunsets. Dark oak-pegged flooring, beamed vaulted ceilings, and cedar paneling make a perfect setting for the Dows' antiques. A separate entrance for guests assures privacy, and separate heat controls assure comfort. Breakfast includes fresh-squeezed juice, fruit compote with special sauce, baked eggs on rice with cheese, ham or bacon, and freshly baked muffins or popovers. A short drive away are Oregon's beaches, sand dunes, and many fine restaurants. The Dows are retired and like to fly, sail, and garden.

The Pringle House ✪
P.O. BOX 578, OAKLAND, OREGON 97462

Tel: **(503) 459-5038**	Single/sb: **$30**
Best Time to Call: **9 AM–10 PM**	Open: **All year**
Host(s): **Jim and Demay Pringle**	Breakfast: **Full**
Location: **1½ mi. from I-5, Exit 138**	Pets: **No**
No. of Rooms: **2**	Children: **Welcome, over 12**
Max. No. Sharing Bath: **4**	Smoking: **No**
Double/sb: **$40**	Social Drinking: **Permitted**

Built in 1893, Pringle House stands on a rise overlooking historic downtown Oakland. Returned to its original Victorian beauty by Jim and Demay, it is listed on the National Register of Historic Places. Breakfast of fresh juice, compote, cheese, freshly baked croissants, and often a house specialty is served in the dining room. You will enjoy seeing Demay's doll collection.

Corbett House B&B ✪
7533 SOUTH WEST CORBETT AVENUE, PORTLAND, OREGON 97219

Tel: **(503) 245-2580**	Open: **All year**
Host(s): **Sylvia Malagamba**	Reduced Rates: **Available**
Location: **3½ mi. S of Portland**	Breakfast: **Continental**
No. of Rooms: **3**	Credit Cards: **AMEX, DC, MC, VISA**
No. of Private Baths: **1**	Pets: **No**
Max. No. Sharing Bath: **3**	Children: **Welcome, over 10**
Double/pb: **$55–$65**	Smoking: **No**
Single/pb: **$50–$55**	Social Drinking: **Permitted**
Double/sb: **$50–$55**	Minimum Stay: **2 nights on summer holiday weekends**
Single/sb: **$45**	

This 1920s Art Deco residence is located in a gracious neighborhood, five minutes from downtown. The inn has views of Mount St. Helens, the Willamette River, and Mount Hood. Hardwood floors, artwork, antiques, and contemporary pieces create a look of casual elegance. King, queen, or twin beds are available. Your hosts provide robes and hair dryers for your convenience. Riverfront Park and interesting restaurants are minutes from the inn.

John Palmer House
4314 NORTH MISSISSIPPI AVENUE, PORTLAND, OREGON 97217

Tel: **(503) 284-5893**
Best Time to Call: **7 AM–8 PM**
Host(s): **Mary and Richard Sauter**
Location: **3½ mi. N of Portland**
No. of Rooms: **5**
No. of Private Baths: **1**
Max. No. Sharing Bath: **4**
Double/sb: **$40–$45**
Single/sb: **$30**
Guest Cottage: **$100, sleeps 5**
Suites: **$65 and $95**

Open: **All year**
Reduced Rates: **Weekly**
Breakfast: **Full**
Other Meals: **Available**
Credit Cards: **MC, VISA**
Pets: **No**
Children: **Welcome in cottage**
Smoking: **No**
Social Drinking: **Permitted**
Airport/Station Pickup: **Yes**

John Palmer built this ornate Victorian in 1890, and today it is a nationally registered landmark home. Hundred-year-old gaslight fixtures, gleaming woodwork, and hand-screened wallpapers have been beautifully preserved and are complemented by plush carpets, lace, and velvet accents. Your hosts cater to the romantic in everyone with afternoon tea, chilled champagne, and an occasional recital from the resident pianist. Guest quarters range from the main house's bridal suite with canopy bed and balcony to one of grandma's cottage rooms with its pretty wallpapers and brass beds. Breakfast choices such as blueberry crêpes and mushroom omelets are served in the formal dining room and enhanced by fresh roses and candlelight. This sprawling house has two parlors, a veranda, and a Jacuzzi on the porch. The Sauters will arrange a horse-and-carriage ride to your favorite restaurant or, if you like, can prepare a gourmet dinner at the house.

Home-by-the-Sea B&B Homestay ✪
444 JACKSON STREET, PORT ORFORD, OREGON 97465

Tel: **(503) 332-2855**
Host(s): **Brenda and Alan Mitchell**

Location: **54 mi. N of California border**

No. of Rooms: 2
No. of Private Baths: 2
Double/pb: $50
Single/pb: $45
Open: All year
Breakfast: Full

Credit Cards: **MC, VISA**
Pets: **No**
Children: **Sometimes**
Smoking: **No**
Social Drinking: **Permitted**
Airport/Station Pickup: **Yes**

This two-story contemporary was built by the Mitchells, longtime residents of Port Orford. The house offers a dramatic view of the ocean and is just a block from an extraordinary harbor, with easy access to miles of agate- and driftwood-festooned beaches. Each bedroom has a handcrafted myrtlewood queen-size bed, cable TV, and a telephone. Storm watchers love to observe the exciting winter storms; this part of the coast is also a favorite of scuba divers and surfers. Whale-watching season runs from October to May, and the Oregon National Wildlife Refuge is just offshore. Redwood National Park is nearby.

The Boarding House Bed & Breakfast
208 NORTH HOLLADAY DRIVE, SEASIDE, OREGON 97138

Tel: (503) 738-9055
Host(s): **Dick and Barb Edwards**
Location: ½ mi. from Rte. 101
No. of Rooms: 6
No. of Private Baths: 6
Double/pb: $45–$59
Single/pb: $40–$54
Separate Guest Cottage: $65;
  sleeps 4

Open: **All year**
Reduced Rates: **Available**
Breakfast: **Full**
Credit Cards: **MC, VISA**
Pets: **No**
Children: **Welcome**
Smoking: **No**
Social Drinking: **Permitted**
Airport/Station Pickup: **Yes**

Located on the banks of the Necanicum River, this rustic Victorian was built as a private residence in 1898. During World War I, the house became a boarding home. After an extensive renovation, the wood walls and beamed ceilings have been restored to their original charm. Guest rooms feature brass or white iron beds, down quilts, family heirlooms, wicker, and wood. Claw-footed tubs, window seats, antiques, and a picture of grandma make you feel as if this house is your own. A fire is often burning in the fir-paneled parlor, and an old melody sounds just right on the old-fashioned organ. A 100-year-old guest cottage with wood paneling, country furnishings, bedroom, loft, and lake view is also available. Breakfast specialties such as cheese-and-egg strata, oven-baked French toast, and caramel sticky buns are served in the dining room or outside on the wraparound porch. The house is just four blocks from the ocean and two blocks from downtown.

Horncroft ✪
42156 KINGSTON LYONS DRIVE, STAYTON, OREGON 97383

Tel: **(503) 769-6287**
Host(s): **Dorothea and Kenneth Horn**
Location: **17 mi. E of Salem**
No. of Rooms: **3**
No. of Private Baths: **1**
Max. No. Sharing Bath: **4**
Double/pb: **$35**
Single/pb: **$30**

Double/sb: **$30**
Single/sb: **$25**
Open: **All year**
Breakfast: **Full**
Pets: **No**
Children: **Sometimes**
Smoking: **No**
Social Drinking: **Permitted**

This lovely home is situated in the foothills of the Cascade Mountains on the edge of Willamette Valley. In summer, swim in the heated pool or hike on one of the scenic nature paths. The area is dotted with farms, and the valley is abundant in fruits, berries, and vegetables. Willamette and Oregon State universities are nearby. The Mount Jefferson Wilderness hiking area is an hour away. A guest comments, "The hospitality and breakfasts were topnotch!"

PENNSYLVANIA

Map of Pennsylvania showing regions: Alleghenies, Susquehanna County, Scranton/North Central Pennsylvania, Pocono Mountains, Allentown Area, Bucks County, Philadelphia Area, Pennsylvania Dutch Area, Gettysburg Area, Central Pennsylvania, Pittsburgh, Western Pennsylvania.

Bed & Breakfast in Pennsylvania ✪
P.O. BOX 169, PINE GROVE MILLS, PENNSYLVANIA 16868

Tel: **(814) 238-1484**
Best Time to Call: **1:30–5:30 PM (Mon.–Fri.)**
Coordinator: **Linda Feltman**

States/Regions Covered: **Statewide**
Rates (Single/Double):
 Average: **$20–$60 $25–$125**
Credit Cards: **Varies with each B&B**

Call Linda for the name and phone number of a B&B in the area you want to visit anywhere in the state. You can then call the host directly. Accommodations range from a clean, simple mountain lodge to a comfortable suburban split-level to a pre-Revolutionary manor house. There is no charge for this service. If you haven't decided where in the state you'd like to go, Linda sells a loose-leaf directory that includes all her inspected member homes for $10, post-paid.

PENNSYLVANIA • 483

ALLEGHENIES AREA

Allegheny Bed & Breakfast Association ✪
BOX 95, TURTLE POINT, PENNSYLVANIA 16750

Tel: **(814) 642-2334**
Coordinator: **Peter Meissner**
States/Regions Covered:
  Alleghenies—Potter County, McKean County, Warren County

Rates (Single/Double):
  Average: **$30–$35 $40–$50**
Credit Cards: **MC, VISA**

One can find peace and tranquillity at an unrushed pace in this rural pocket in the mountains. Horseback riding, hiking on mountain trails, cross-country skiing, the Kinzua Reservoir for boating and swimming, the Allegheny National Forest, summer fairs, and year-round antiquing are some of the local diversions. Truly off the beaten path, the area hosts genuinely appreciate the "excitement" of having visitors and go out of their way to please them.

BUCKS COUNTY

Maplewood Farm ✪
5090 DURHAM ROAD, P.O. BOX 239, GARDENVILLE, PENNSYLVANIA 18926

Tel: **(215) 766-0477**
Best Time to Call: **8 AM–10 PM**
Host(s): **Linda and Ray Psulkowski**
Location: **30 mi. NW of Philadelphia**
No. of Rooms: **5**
No. of Private Baths: **5**
Double/pb: **$75**
Single/pb: **$70**
Suites: **$100**
Open: **All year**

Reduced Rates: **Mon.–Thur.; 10%, weekly; 10%, seniors**
Breakfast: **Full**
Credit Cards: **AMEX**
Pets: **No**
Children: **Sometimes**
Smoking: **No**
Social Drinking: **Permitted**
Minimum Stay: **2 nights on weekends**
Airport/Station Pickup: **Yes**

Hundred-year-old maple trees shelter this fieldstone farmhouse built in 1826. The house is set on five acres, including a tranquil stream and a barn; you can gather your eggs fresh from the source each morning and have them turned into fluffy breakfast omelets. Fresh-baked breads, local fruits, and waffles or pancakes complete the meal, served in a romantic dining room with random-width wood floors and an exposed stone wall. Morning coffee can also be enjoyed at an intimate table for two on the sun porch. Guest rooms feature Linda's hand-stenciled walls, cozy comforters, or handmade quilts. Choose the

Homestead Room, with four-poster bed and ceiling fan, or the two-story loft suite, with exposed beams and sitting room. Linda and Ray invite you for afternoon and evening snacks in the antique summer kitchen, with its two walk-in fireplaces. They will direct you to nearby lakes, covered bridges, and the shops of New Hope.

Ash Mill Farm ✪
P.O. BOX 202, HOLICONG, PENNSYLVANIA 18928

Tel: **(215) 794-5373**
Host(s): **Caroline and Jeff Rawes**
Location: **30 mi. N of Philadelphia**
No. of Rooms: **4**
No. of Private Baths: **2**
Max. No. Sharing Bath: **4**
Double/pb: **$70**
Single/pb: **$65**
Double/sb: **$60–$70**
Single/sb: **$50–$60**

Open: **All year**
Reduced Rates: **Mon.–Thurs., all rooms $50–$60**
Breakfast: **Continental**
Credit Cards: **MC, VISA**
Pets: **No**
Children: **Sometimes**
Smoking: **Permitted**
Social Drinking: **Permitted**

This 18th-century farmhouse is set on ten wooded acres in the rolling hills of Bucks County. The Raweses' home has high ceilings, bright rooms, and a central stairway. The comfortably furnished bedrooms are accented with handcrafted quilts and family antiques. Mornings begin with homemade breads, fresh fruit with honey 'n yogurt dressing, or quiche, served before an open fire in winter, and on the stone porch in warm weather. The farm is located adjacent to Peddlers' Village and nearby state parks, the Bucks County Playhouse, the outlets of Flemington, New Jersey, and many fine restaurants. There is a two-night minimum on weekends from April through November.

Pineapple Hill ✪
1324 RIVER ROAD, NEW HOPE, PENNSYLVANIA 18938

Tel: **(215) 862-9608**
Host(s): **Suzie and Randy Leslie**
Location: **40 mi. N of Philadelphia**
No. of Rooms: **5**
No. of Private Baths: **3**
Max. No. Sharing Bath: **4**
Double/pb: **$60–$70**
Double/sb: **$50–$60**
Suites: **$70–$90**

Open: **All year**
Reduced Rates: **5 nights**
Breakfast: **Continental**
Credit Cards: **AMEX**
Pets: **No**
Children: **Sometimes**
Smoking: **No**
Social Drinking: **Permitted**
Minimum Stay: **2 nights weekends**

The 18-inch walls, fireplace, and traditional woodwork attest to the 18th-century origin of this charming farmhouse. Suzie and Randy have furnished it with spool and brass beds, antique furniture, folk art, Persian carpets, pewter, and stoneware. When you return from the dozens of activities the area offers, relax in front of the fire, read, play backgammon, and visit.

CENTRAL PENNSYLVANIA

Rest & Repast Bed & Breakfast Service ✪
P.O. BOX 126, PINE GROVE MILLS, PENNSYLVANIA 16868

Tel: **(814) 238-1484**
Coordinators: **Linda and Brent Peters**
States/Regions Covered: **State College, Bellefonte, Huntington, Lemont, Potters Mills, Spruce Creek, Tyrone**

Rates (Single/Double):
  Modest: **$25–$27** **$30–$34**
  Average: **$28–$30** **$35–$40**
  Luxury: **N/A** **$40–$75**
Credit Cards: **No**

You will enjoy touring historic mansions, Penns Cave, Woodward Cave, and several Civil War museums in this lovely area. A two-day minimum stay is required for the second week in July, the time of the annual Central Pennsylvania Festival of the Arts, and for the Penn State University Homecoming Football game in autumn. Rates are increased during peak weekends to a maximum of $75 per night double. (No single rates on football weekends.) Pennsylvania State University is close by.

The Garmanhaus ✪
BOX 307, BOILING SPRINGS, PENNSYLVANIA 17009

Tel: **(717) 258-3980**
Host(s): **John and Molly Garman**
Location: **5 mi. from Rtes. 76 & 81**
No. of Rooms: **4**
Max. No. Sharing Bath: **4**
Double/sb: **$49**

Open: **All year**
Breakfast: **Continental**
Pets: **No**
Children: **Welcome, over 12**
Smoking: **Permitted**
Social Drinking: **Permitted**

The Garmans' elegant Victorian is on Front Street, by the lake. John, an insurance agent, and Molly, a realtor, will help you feel at home. Snacks, beverages, wine, and beer are always on hand for your enjoyment. Feel free to use the grill, TV, and laundry facilities. Bicycles and a canoe may be rented. Dickinson College and Law School is nearby.

Yoders ✪
R.D. 1, BOX 312, HUNTINGDON, PENNSYLVANIA 16652

Tel: **(814) 643-3221**
Best Time to Call: **After 4 PM**
Host(s): **Randy and Peggy Yoder**
Location: **On Rte. 22**
No. of Rooms: **3**
No. of Private Baths: **2**
Double/pb: **$35**
Single/pb: **$28**
Open: **All year**

Reduced Rates: **10%, seniors**
Breakfast: **Continental**
Other Meals: **Available**
Pets: **Sometimes**
Children: **No**
Smoking: **No**
Social Drinking: **No**
Airport/Station Pickup: **Yes**

After you've visited the Swigart Museum of antique American automobiles, explored the caves of Lincoln Caverns, or taken advantage of Lake Raystown with its recreational diversions, come home to Randy and Peggy's. The house, fronted with a huge picture window and native stone, is located at the edge of a 200-acre forest where you may feel free to hike. Breakfast often features croissants, waffles, pancakes, or special omelets. Fresh fruit and cheese snacks are complimentary.

The White House B&B Inn ✪
861 WASHINGTON AVENUE, TYRONE, PENNSYLVANIA 16686

Tel: **(814) 684-5155**
Host(s): **Al and Beverly Bigelow**
Location: **120 mi. E of Pittsburgh**
No. of Rooms: **3**
No. of Private Baths: **1**
Max. No. Sharing Bath: **4**
Double/sb: **$45**
Suites: **$55**
Open: **All year**

Reduced Rates: **Families**
Breakfast: **Full**
Pets: **No**
Children: **Welcome, over 5**
Smoking: **Permitted**
Social Drinking: **No**
Minimum Stay: **2 nights, Penn State game weekends**
Airport/Station Pickup: **Yes**

This 92-year-old 18-room Federal-style mansion is a candidate for the National Register of Historic Places. Each guest room has elegantly draped windows, and beds with partial or full canopies. French doors lead out to a balcony or a sun porch. Borrow a book from the well-stocked library or relax in the living room, which is ornately decorated with period furnishings and enhanced by a wood-burning fireplace and a grand piano. Fresh flowers and seasonal fruits are just a few nice touches that spell welcome.

GETTYSBURG AREA

Historic Paul Sourss Plantation House ✪
P.O. BOX 238, BENDERSVILLE, PENNSYLVANIA 17306

Tel: **(717) 677-6688**	Open: **All year**
Best Time to Call: **After 6 PM**	Breakfast: **Full**
Host(s): **Mrs. Viola Earnst**	Pets: **No**
Location: **12 mi. N of Gettysburg**	Children: **No**
No. of Rooms: **3**	Smoking: **Permitted**
No. of Private Baths: **3**	Social Drinking: **Permitted**
Double/pb: **$55**	Airport/Station Pickup: **Yes**

This stone plantation house was built by G. C. Mason in 1802, and is located in a quiet orchard setting. The decor features antique furnishings, herbal showpieces, Oriental rugs, and handmade baskets. In warm weather, morning coffee is served on the veranda with a French country breakfast of homemade bread, fruit, and crêpes. In the evening, enjoy a snack of homegrown roasted chestnuts before dinner. Your hosts will gladly direct you to the many nearby antiques shops and markets. Hershey and Gettysburg National Park are also within an easy drive from the house.

The Leas-Bechtel Mansion Inn ✪
400 WEST KING STREET, EAST BERLIN, PENNSYLVANIA 17316

Tel: **(717) 259-7760**	Open: **All year**
Host(s): **Charles Bechtel**	Reduced Rates: **10%, seniors**
Location: **18 mi. E of Gettysburg**	Breakfast: **Continental**
No. of Rooms: **7**	Credit Cards: **AMEX, MC, VISA**
No. of Private Baths: **7**	Pets: **No**
Double/pb: **$75–$100**	Children: **Welcome**
Single/pb: **$45–$80**	Smoking: **No**
Suites: **$110–$125**	Social Drinking: **Permitted**

This sprawling mansion was designed for the William Leas family in 1897. It is listed on the National Register of Historic Places. The rooms have been beautifully restored and feature original brass chandeliers, stained glass, and oak sliding doors. Air-conditioned sleeping quarters are elegantly appointed with handmade quilts and antique furnishings. Choose from the Sara Leas Room, with its turret-shaped bay window, or the Downstairs Suite, with its handmade walnut furniture and folding oak interior shutters. Guests are welcome to relax in the living room with an oak-and-mahogany secretary and red Bokhara rug. Fresh muffins, juice, fruit ambrosia, coffee cake, and coffee are served in the dining room, which has a large window seat, etched-glass windows, and antique rug. There is a large front-and-side porch for sipping a glass of wine or just relaxing and watching the village activity.

The Herb Cottage
LINCOLN WAY EAST, RTE. 30, FAYETTEVILLE, PENNSYLVANIA 17222

Tel: **(717) 352-7733**
Best Time to Call: **8 AM–9 PM**
Host(s): **Jim and Lois Stewart**
Location: **14 mi. W of Gettysburg**
No. of Rooms: **6**
No. of Private Baths: **6**
Double/pb: **$65**
Separate Guest Cottage: **$85; sleeps 4**

Open: **All year**
Reduced Rates: **10%, Jan.–Mar.**
Breakfast: **Full**
Credit Cards: **MC, VISA**
Pets: **No**
Children: **No**
Smoking: **No**
Social Drinking: **No**
Airport/Station Pickup: **Yes**

Beautiful greenery and gardens surround this old-fashioned lodge, set on 20 acres. The inn is a rustic log retreat built with American chestnut wood and natural stone. Rooms are carefully decorated with primitive country antiques, handmade quilts, fresh flowers, and homespuns. Your hosts offer a country breakfast, including gourmet coffees, homemade breads, herb butters, and cheeses. They invite you to visit their gift shop, where you can find unusual handcrafts and collectibles. There are endless activities and attractions nearby, including Gettysburg Battlefield, ski resorts, Caledonia and Michaux State parks, fine dining, and brilliant fall foliage.

Goose Chase ✪
200 BLUEBERRY ROAD, GARDNERS, PENNSYLVANIA 17324

Tel: **(717) 528-8877**
Best Time to Call: **Weekdays**
Host(s): **Marsha and Rich Lucidi**
Location: **14 mi. N of Gettysburg**
No. of Rooms: **3**
No. of Private Baths: **1**
Max. No. Sharing Bath: **4**
Double/pb: **$65**
Double/sb: **$55**

Open: **All year**
Breakfast: **Full**
Credit Cards: **MC, VISA**
Pets: **In outbuilding only**
Children: **No**
Smoking: **No**
Social Drinking: **Permitted**
Airport/Station Pickup: **Yes**

This restored 18th-century stone house on a 25-acre farm is located in apple orchard country. It is handsomely furnished with handmade quilts, folk art, and carefully chosen American antiques. Wide-plank floors, Oriental rugs, stenciled walls, and deep-silled windows add to the charming atmosphere. Breakfast always features a delicious main dish and is served by Marsha in authentic Colonial garb. Fresh flowers and fruit, terry cloth robes, beds turned down with chocolate treats on the pillow are a few of the Lucidis' thoughtful touches. Wine or tea are graciously offered and, in winter, hot mulled cider is served by a crackling fire. Gettysburg, York, and Hershey are within easy reach. Winter skiing is a half hour away; summer swimming is available on the farm. Inquire about the package featuring a winery tour, wine tastings, and a seven-course gourmet dinner in a nearby historic home.

The Brafferton Inn ✪
44–46 YORK STREET, GETTYSBURG, PENNSYLVANIA 17325

Tel: **(717) 337-3423**
Host(s): **Mimi and Jim Agard**
Location: **90 mi. N of D.C.; 2 mi. from Rte. 15, York Exit**
No. of Rooms: **8**
No. of Private Baths: **4**
Max. No. Sharing Bath: **4**
Double/pb: **$65**
Double/sb: **$60**

Open: **All year**
Breakfast: **Full**
Credit Cards: **MC, VISA**
Pets: **No**
Children: **Welcome, over 7**
Smoking: **No**
Social Drinking: **Permitted**

This Early American stone structure is listed on the National Register of Historic Places. The clapboard addition dates back to pre–Civil War days. Four of the guest rooms, decorated with hand-painted stencils, are separated from the main house by an atrium where one may sit and enjoy the pretty plantings during the warm months. The sumptuous breakfast is served in the dining room on antique tables. There are hosts of activities to whet the appetite of the history buff, sportsman, antique collector, or nature lover.

Keystone Inn
231 HANOVER STREET, GETTYSBURG, PENNSYLVANIA 17325

Tel: **(717) 334-8273**
Best Time to Call: **7 AM–10 PM**
Host(s): **The Martin Family**
Location: **35 mi. S of Harrisburg**
No. of Rooms: **4**
No. of Private Baths: **2**
Max. No. Sharing Bath: **4**

Double/pb: **$65**
Double/sb: **$55**
Open: **All year**
Reduced Rates: **Available**
Breakfast: **Full**
Other Meals: **Available**
Credit Cards: **MC, VISA**

Pets: **No**
Children: **Welcome**

Smoking: **No**
Social Drinking: **No**

Keystone Inn is a large Victorian built in 1913 by Clayton Reaser, a local furniture maker. His talents as a craftsman are evident in the natural oak and chestnut found throughout the house. The beautiful woodwork is complemented with lace, ruffles, and floral designs favored by the Martin family. The guest rooms are decorated with brass or antique wood beds and soft pastel wallpapers, and each bedroom has a reading nook and windowside writing table overlooking historic Gettysburg. A full breakfast features such specialties as cinnamon-apple or blueberry pancakes, waffles, eggs, and fruits. Afternoon lemonade is served on the front porch in summer; in winter guests can enjoy a hot drink by the fireplace. The inn is close to historic sites and Civil War battlefields, antiques shops, state parks, and is nine miles from the Liberty ski area.

The Old Appleford Inn ✪
218 CARLISLE STREET, GETTYSBURG, PENNSYLVANIA 17325

Tel: (717) 337-1711
Host(s): **Del and Nancie Gudmestad**
No. of Rooms: **10**
No. of Private Baths: **2**
Max. No. Sharing Bath: **3**
Double/pb: **$72**
Double/sb: **$62**
Single/sb: **$55**
Suites: **$82**

Open: **All year**
Reduced Rates: **10% less weekdays Dec.–Mar.**
Breakfast: **Full**
Credit Cards: **MC, VISA**
Pets: **No**
Children: **Welcome, over 12**
Smoking: **Permitted**
Social Drinking: **Permitted**

This is a beautiful brick mansion built in 1867 and decorated with country antique furnishings dating back to the Civil War. After your tour of the battlefield, Del and Nancie invite you to enjoy the warmth of several fireplaces, sip a complimentary sherry, and bask in the mellifluous strains of the baby grand piano in the parlor. There are ski slopes nearby for winter sports enthusiasts, spring apple blossoms, and fall foliage to enjoy. All rooms are air-conditioned for summer comfort. You are certain to awaken each morning to the scent of homemade breads, muffins, or to the house specialty, Appleford French toast.

Twin Elms ✪
228 BUFORD AVENUE, GETTYSBURG, PENNSYLVANIA 17325

Tel: **(717) 334-4520**
Best Time to Call: **9 AM–9 PM**
Host(s): **Estella Williams**
No. of Rooms: **3**
Max. No. Sharing Bath: **6**
Double/sb: **$25**

Open: **All year**
Breakfast: **No**
Pets: **No**
Children: **Welcome, over 4**
Smoking: **Permitted**
Social Drinking: **No**

Estella's comfortable brick home is surrounded by the historic Gettysburg Battlefield. It is within walking distance of museums, the National Cemetery, swimming, golfing; the Eisenhower farm is close by, as well as diverse eating places. Your hostess is a former teacher and history buff who enjoys having guests.

The Doubleday Inn ✪
104 DOUBLEDAY AVENUE, GETTYSBURG BATTLEFIELD, PENNSYLVANIA 17325

Tel: **(717) 334-9119**
Host(s): **Joan and Sal Chandon, Olga Krossick**
Location: **3 mi. from US 15**
No. of Rooms: **11**
No. of Private Baths: **6**
Max. No. Sharing Bath: **4**
Double/pb: **$75–$90**

Double/sb: **$65**
Open: **All year**
Breakfast: **Full**
Credit Cards: **MC, VISA**
Pets: **No**
Children: **Welcome, over 7**
Smoking: **No**
Social Drinking: **Permitted**

Located on the battlefield above Oak Ridge, this beautifully restored Colonial recalls past-century charms with Civil War furnishings and antique accessories. Afternoon tea is served with country-style drinks and hors d'oeuvres on the outdoor patio, or by the fireplace in the main parlor. One of the largest known library collections devoted exclusively to the Battle of Gettysburg is available to you. On selected evenings, you are welcome to participate in a discussion with a Civil War historian who brings the battle alive with accurate accounts and displays of authentic memorabilia and weaponry.

Beechmont Inn ◐
315 BROADWAY, HANOVER, PENNSYLVANIA 17331

Tel: **(717) 632-3013**
Best Time to Call: **9 AM–9 PM**
Host(s): **The Hormel family**
Location: **13 mi. E of Gettysburg**
No. of Rooms: 7
No. of Private Baths: 3
Max. No. Sharing Bath: 4
Double/sb: **$55–$65**
Single/sb: **$49–$59**

Suites: **$70–$85**
Open: **All year**
Breakfast: **Full**
Credit Cards: **AMEX, MC, VISA**
Pets: **No**
Children: **Welcome, over 12**
Smoking: **Permitted**
Social Drinking: **Permitted**

This Georgian house, restored to its Federal-period elegance, offers the visitor a bridge across time. Climb the winding staircase to freshly decorated rooms named in honor of the gallant heroes of the Civil War. At breakfast time, enjoy homemade granola, baked goods, a hot entrée, and fruit. Join the other guests in the dining room, or take a tray to your room for breakfast in bed. Visit nearby Gettysburg, the Eisenhower Farm, Hanover Shoe Farms, Codorus State Park for boating and fishing, or go antique hunting in New Oxford. Upon your return, you may take tea in the quiet comfort of the parlor. The Hormels look forward to pampering you.

Country View Acres ✪
676 BEAVER CREEK ROAD, HANOVER, PENNSYLVANIA 17331

Tel: **(717) 637-8992**
Best Time to Call: **Evenings**
Host(s): **Alan and Teena Smith**
Location: **13 mi. E. of Gettysburg**
No. of Rooms: **1**
No. of Private Baths: **1**
Double/pb: **$39**

Single/pb: **$31**
Open: **All year**
Breakfast: **Full**
Pets: **Sometimes**
Children: **Welcome**
Smoking: **No**
Social Drinking: **Permitted**

This spacious Colonial-style home is on several acres within view of the mountains and valley. The interior features Early American furnishings and a player piano in the living room. Guests may stroll the grounds and use the outdoor whirlpool spa. Attractions such as the Hanover and Lana Lobell Standardbred horse farms and Gettysburg National Military Park are nearby. Boating and sailing are minutes away at Codorus State Park.

Red Lion B&B ✪
101 SOUTH FRANKLIN STREET, RED LION, PENNSYLVANIA 17356

Tel: **(717) 244-4739**
Best Time to Call: **After 4 PM**
Host(s): **Harry and Marilyn Brown**
Location: **9 mi. SE of York**
No. of Rooms: **2**
Max. No. Sharing Bath: **4**
Double/sb: **$50**

Open: **May 1–Oct. 31; weekends only May, Sept., Oct.**
Breakfast: **Full**
Pets: **No**
Children: **Welcome, over 5**
Smoking: **No**
Social Drinking: **No**

Sixty-foot pines surround this large, red-brick home dating back to the 1920s. Guests are welcomed with afternoon tea and shown to comfortable rooms decorated with an eclectic blend of attic treasures. Enjoy a country breakfast in the dining room or outside on the patio. Marilyn and Harry enjoy meeting new people and entertaining. They will gladly direct you to many fine shops, restaurants, and outlets. York was a meeting place of the Continental Congress and has many interesting and historic places to visit. It is a hub for York, Gettysburg, and the Pennsylvania Dutch area.

PENNSYLVANIA DUTCH AREA

Umble Rest ✪
R.D. #1, BOX 79, ATGLEN, PENNSYLVANIA 19310

Tel: **(215) 593-2274**
Host(s): **Ken and Marilyn Umble**
Location: **15 mi. E of Lancaster**
No. of Rooms: **2**
Max. No. Sharing Bath: **4**
Double/sb: **$20–$22**
Open: **May 15–Oct. 15**

Breakfast: **No**
Pets: **No**
Children: **Welcome**
Smoking: **No**
Social Drinking: **No**
Minimum Stay: **Holiday weekends**

Ken and Marilyn are busy Mennonite farmers with interests in crafts, quilting, and restoring their 1700 farmhouse. You are invited to watch the milking of their 50 cows, stroll a country lane to their pond, and to participate in the simple life-style. Bring your children to play with their boys, ages five and eight. All the popular tourist attractions are nearby.

Greystone Manor B&B ✪
2658 OLD PHILADELPHIA PIKE, P. O. BOX 270, BIRD-IN-HAND, PENNSYLVANIA 17505

Tel: **(717) 393-4233**
Host(s): **Sally and Ed Davis**
No. of Rooms: **12**
No. of Private Baths: **12**
Double/pb: **$52**
Single/pb: **$48**
Suites: **$66–$72**
Open: **All year**

Reduced Rates: **Available**
Breakfast: **Continental**
Credit Cards: **MC, VISA**
Pets: **No**
Children: **Welcome**
Smoking: **Permitted**
Social Drinking: **Permitted**

Situated on two acres of lush lawn and trees, the lodge was built in 1883. Back then, this French Victorian mansion and carriage house did not boast of air-conditioning, TV, and suites as it does today. Though a great deal of renovation has taken place, the antique features and charm of the mansion are intact. Good restaurants are nearby.

Winding Glen Farm Tourist Home
107 NOBLE ROAD, CHRISTIANA, PENNSYLVANIA 17509

Tel: **(215) 593-5535**
Host(s): **Minnie Metzler**
Location: **19 mi. E of Lancaster**

No. of Rooms: **5**
Max. No. Sharing Bath: **5**
Double/sb: **$35**

Single/sb: **$25**
Reduced Rates: **Families**
Breakfast: **Full**
Pets: **No**

Children: **Welcome**
Smoking: **No**
Social Drinking: **No**
Airport/Station Pickup: **Yes**

Watching 40 cows being milked on this dairy farm is a sight to behold, especially if your calcium usually comes from a container. You will also be impressed to learn that the walls in this 250-year-old stone farmhouse are 16 inches thick. It is air-conditioned for your summer comfort. Minnie's home cooking and baking are the focus of the family-style meals; breakfast and dinner are included in the rate. The Metzlers will be happy to share their slide show, "Our Way of Life," with you. If you're interested in taking home a handmade quilt or handcrafted souvenirs, there are many Amish shops nearby.

Red Door Studio B&B ✪
6485 LEMON STREET, EAST PETERSBURG, PENNSYLVANIA 17520

Tel: **(717) 569-2909**
Best Time to Call: **8–9 AM**
Host(s): **Mary Elizabeth Patton**
Location: **9 mi. N of Lancaster**
No. of Rooms: **3**
Max. No. Sharing Bath: **5**
Double/sb: **$30–$40**
Single/sb: **$20**

Open: **All year**
Reduced Rates: **10%, Mar., Apr., Nov.**
Breakfast: **Continental**
Pets: **Sometimes**
Children: **Welcome (crib)**
Smoking: **No**
Social Drinking: **Permitted**
Airport/Station Pickup: **Yes**

Open the red door and you instantly know you're in an artist's home. A former teacher of art history, Mary Elizabeth is now a full-time artist and portrait painter. Her B&B is warm, bright, and inviting, with many souvenirs and pictures of her world travels. Of special interest is her collection of Indian and African works. Breakfast is an inviting spread of fresh fruit, yogurt, granola, Danish pastry, coffee, or herb tea. You are welcome to relax in the backyard, use the barbecue, or watch TV. Watching tapes of Lancaster County on her VCR will prepare you to tour this interesting area.

Rocky-Side Farm
R.D. 1, ELVERSON, PENNSYLVANIA 19520

Tel: **(215) 286-5362**
Best Time to Call: **Before 5 PM**
Host(s): **Reba Yoder**
Location: **18 mi. S of Reading**
No. of Rooms: **2**

Max. No. Sharing Bath: **4**
Double/sb: **$30**
Single/sb: **$20**
Open: **All year**
Breakfast: **Full**

Other Meals: **Available**
Pets: **No**
Children: **Welcome (crib)**

Smoking: **No**
Social Drinking: **No**

You will be warmly welcomed by the Yoders to their farm, where they raise dairy cows, corn, wheat, soybeans, and hay. The stone-and-stucco farmhouse dates back to 1919 and has a wraparound columned porch for lazying away an afternoon. The rooms are furnished country style, complemented by handmade braided-wool rugs and pretty quilts. Bountiful breakfasts are Reba's style, so you're certain to be off your diet during your stay. Hopewell Village and the Amish countryside are pleasant destinations.

Covered Bridge Inn ✪
990 RETTEW MILL ROAD, EPHRATA, PENNSYLVANIA 17522

Tel: **(717) 733-1592**
Best Time to Call: **After 11 AM**
Host(s): **Betty Lee Maxey**
Location: **10 mi. from Lancaster**
No. of Rooms: **4**
Max. No. Sharing Bath: **4**
Double/sb: **$45–$50**
Single/sb: **$40**

Open: **All year**
Reduced Rates: **Available**
Breakfast: **Full**
Pets: **No**
Children: **Welcome, over 10**
Smoking: **No**
Social Drinking: **Permitted**
Airport/Station Pickup: **Yes**

Beautiful shade trees, an old stone mill, and a rustic covered bridge surround this limestone farmhouse. The inn was built 170 years ago on land purchased from William Penn's family. Guest rooms are large, sunny, and filled with fresh flower and herb bouquets from the garden. Air-conditioned, each is decorated with antiques, including the linens. One features a pencil-post bed with canopy and Laura Ashley linens. Another has a red-rope bed with an Amish star quilt. Breakfast specialties include hot breads, homemade jams, quiche, and cinnamon pancakes. Later, enjoy lemonade and cookies served on the porch or a cup of coffee by the living room hearth. Nearby sights include the Amish country, Ephrata Cloister, and antiques markets.

Gerhart House B&B
287 DUKE STREET, EPHRATA, PENNSYLVANIA 17522

Tel: **(717) 733-0263**
Best Time to Call: **9 AM–10 PM**
Host(s): **Shirley and Ray Smith**
Location: **13 mi. N of Lancaster**

No. of Rooms: **5**
No. of Private Baths: **3**
Max. No. Sharing Bath: **4**
Double/pb: **$55–$75**

Single/pb: **$45–$60**
Double/sb: **$45–$50**
Single/sb: **$40**
Open: **All year**
Reduced Rates: **10%, weekly**

Breakfast: **Full**
Pets: **No**
Children: **Sometimes**
Smoking: **Permitted**
Social Drinking: **Permitted**

Gerhart House was built in 1926 by one of Ephrata's most prominent designers. Alexander Gerhart saw to it that his spacious brick home reflected the rich woods and elegant fixtures of the period. The front parlor has oak flooring with walnut inlays, chestnut woodwork, and comfortable furnishing. Bedrooms are decorated in warm Williamsburg colors and have large, sunny windows, fresh flowers, and vintage carpets. In summer, enjoy a glass of lemonade on the porch or large veranda; in winter, afternoon tea is served. House specialties such as extra-thick French toast and quiche are served in a quiet breakfast room with small tables. Gerhart House is a short walk from the Ephrata Cloister, close to the Amish country, outlet shopping, and antiques markets.

Hershey Bed & Breakfast Reservation Service
P.O. BOX 208, HERSHEY, PENNSYLVANIA 17033

Tel: **(717) 533-2928**
Best Time to Call: **10 AM–4 PM**
Coordinator: **Renee Deutel**
States/Regions Covered: **Hanover, Harrisburg, Hershey, Lancaster, Palmyra**

Rates (Single/Double):
Modest: **$40** $45
Average: **$45** $55
Luxury: **$55** $60 and up
Credit Cards: **MC, VISA**

Renee has a small roster of lovely homes close to main thoroughfares. Hosts come from a variety of interesting backgrounds, and all share a common enthusiasm to share their homes and communities. You may choose a cozy farmhouse, a large older home with beautiful furnishings, or a country inn. Whatever your wishes, the town that chocolate made famous will welcome you.

Gibson's Bed & Breakfast ✪
141 WEST CARACAS AVENUE, HERSHEY, PENNSYLVANIA 17033

Tel: **(717) 534-1305**
Host(s): **Frances and Bob Gibson**
Location: **One block off Rte. 422**
No. of Rooms: **3**
Max. No. Sharing Bath: **3**

Double/sb: **$45**
Single/sb: **$35**
Open: **All year**
Breakfast: **Full**
Pets: **No**

Children: **Welcome, over 5**
Smoking: **Permitted**
Social Drinking: **Permitted**

Airport/Station Pickup: **Yes**
Foreign Languages: **Italian**

Bob and Frances Gibson have a 50-year-old Cape Cod, located in the center of Hershey, walking distance from many local attractions. The house has been recently renovated to enhance the charm of the hardwood floors, wood trim, and original windows. The atmosphere is friendly and informal, and your hosts are glad to offer complimentary nibbles such as wine and cheese. Gourmet specialties such as Scotch eggs, scones, homemade breads, jams, and cinnamon buns are served each morning in a cozy breakfast room. The Gibsons will gladly help you find local sights such as Hershey Park, Chocolate World, Founders Hall, and the Amish country.

Groff Tourist Farm Home O
766 BRACKBILL ROAD, KINZERS, PENNSYLVANIA 17535

Tel: **(717) 442-8223**
Best Time to Call: **7–8 AM, 5–7 PM**
Host(s): **Harold and Mary Ellen Groff**
Location: **12 mi. E of Lancaster**
No. of Rooms: **5**
No. of Private Baths: **1**
Max. No. Sharing Bath: **5**
Double/pb: **$45**
Double/sb: **$30**

Single/sb: **$28**
Reduced Rates: **Available**
Open: **All year**
Breakfast: **Continental**
Pets: **No**
Children: **Welcome**
Smoking: **No**
Social Drinking: **No**

This old-fashioned stone farmhouse, recently redecorated and air-conditioned, has a porch on which to relax; each comfortable bedroom is also cross-ventilated, so you can enjoy the crisp country air. In her spare time, hostess Mary enjoys visiting with her guests, while stitching the gorgeous quilts her grandmother taught her to make. Nearby restaurants serve good food. A two-night minimum stay is required.

White Rock Farm Guest House O
154 WHITE ROCK ROAD, KIRKWOOD, PENNSYLVANIA 17536

Tel: **(717) 529-6744**
Host(s): **Les and Lois Hershey**
Location: **18 mi. S of Lancaster**
No. of Rooms: **2**
Max. No. Sharing Bath: **4**
Double/sb: **$40–$45**
Single/sb: **$35–$40**

Open: **All year**
Breakfast: **Full**
Pets: **Sometimes**
Children: **Welcome (crib)**
Smoking: **No**
Social Drinking: **No**
Airport/Station Pickup: **Yes**

Experience the pleasure of country living on this 150-acre beef cattle farm bordered by scenic streams, nature trails, a historic covered bridge, and Amish farms. The large stone house, built in 1860, combines today's conveniences with yesterday's charm. The front porch, overlooking the spacious lawn and rolling countryside, is a perfect place for relaxing. Les and Lois have traveled extensively both in the States and abroad and know how to make a guest feel perfectly at home. Antiques and hardwood floors are a fine background for the lovely handicrafts and quilts, some of which are for sale.

Walkabout Inn ✪
837 VILLAGE ROAD, LAMPETER, PENNSYLVANIA 17537

Tel: **(717) 464-0707**	Suites: **$100**
Host(s): **Richard and Maggie Mason**	Open: **All year**
Location: **3 mi. S of Lancaster**	Reduced Rates: **Available**
No. of Rooms: **4**	Breakfast: **Full**
No. of Private Baths: **2**	Other Meals: **Available**
Max. No. Sharing Bath: **4**	Credit Cards: **AMEX, MC, VISA**
Double/pb: **$60**	Pets: **No**
Single/pb: **$50**	Children: **Welcome (crib)**
Double/sb: **$45**	Smoking: **No**
Single/sb: **$35**	Social Drinking: **Permitted**
Guest Cottage: **$125, sleeps 6**	Airport/Station Pickup: **Yes**

The Walkabout Inn takes its name from the Australian word, which means to go out and discover new places. Australian-born host Richard Mason and his wife, Maggie, will help you explore the Amish country that surrounds their brick Mennonite farmhouse. The 22-room house was built in 1925 and features wraparound porches, balconies, and chestnut woodwork. Guest rooms feature Maggie's hand stenciling and are decorated with antiques, Oriental rugs, and Pennsylvania Dutch quilts. When it's time to say "good-day," a candlelight gourmet breakfast is served on silver and crystal in the dining room. Homemade Australian bread, pastries, and tea imported from down under are always on the menu. Your hosts invite you to visit their country craft shop and can direct you to numerous other shops, restaurants, and historic sites.

The Dingeldein House ✪
1105 EAST KING STREET, LANCASTER, PENNSYLVANIA 17602

Tel: **(717) 293-1723**	Host(s): **Laurie and Keith Dingeldein**
Best Time to Call: **Weekends; after 6 PM weekdays**	No. of Rooms: **4**
	No. of Private Baths: **2**

Max. No. Sharing Bath: **4**
Double/pb: **$60**
Double/sb: **$50**
Open: **All year**
Reduced Rates: **Weekly**
Breakfast: **Full**

Credit Cards: **MC, VISA**
Pets: **Sometimes**
Children: **Welcome**
Smoking: **No**
Social Drinking: **No**
Airport/Station Pickup: **Yes**

This spanking-white Dutch Colonial home, surrounded by a large yard, offers freshly decorated candlelit rooms and friendly service. The delicious country breakfast features pastry and breads prepared by Keith, the pastry chef at the Hotel Hershey in nearby Hershey. The table is set with a variety of herb teas and fresh fruits of the season from local farms. A fine menu of egg dishes is graciously served. If she's not too busy, Laurie may favor you with a lovely piano sonata.

Hollinger House ✪
2336 HOLLINGER ROAD, LANCASTER, PENNSYLVANIA 17602

Tel: **(717) 464-3050**
Host(s): **Jean and Leon Thomas**
No. of Rooms: **4**
Max. No. Sharing Bath: **4**
Double/sb: **$45–$50**
Single/sb: **$35–$40**
Open: **All year**
Reduced Rates: **Dec.–Apr.**

Breakfast: **Full**
Pets: **No**
Children: **Welcome (crib)**
Smoking: **No**
Social Drinking: **Permitted**
Airport/Station Pickup: **Yes**
Foreign Languages: **German**

While this house, built in 1870, is undeniably grand in style, it is also homey. Leon and Jean invite you to relax on the wide porch, or stroll about the five acres of land crossed by a woodland stream. Although it is convenient to all the area's attractions, it is peacefully away from the tourist traffic. Jean has led tours throughout the Lancaster area and will be happy to answer your questions and give expert advice.

The King's Cottage
1049 EAST KING STREET, LANCASTER, PENNSYLVANIA 17602

Tel: **(717) 397-1017**
Best Time to Call: **9–11:30 AM**
Host(s): **Jim and Karen Owens**
Location: **2 mi. from Rte. 30, Exit Greenfield Rd.**
No. of Rooms: **5**
No. of Private Baths: **5**
Double/pb: **$79–$99**
Open: **All year**

Reduced Rates: **Nov. 1–Apr. 30, except holidays**
Breakfast: **Full**
Credit Cards: **MC, VISA**
Pets: **No**
Children: **Welcome over 12**
Smoking: **No**
Social Drinking: **Permitted**
Minimum Stay: **2 nights on weekends**

Airport/Station Pickup: **No** Foreign Languages: **Spanish**

Be prepared for the royal treatment at this Spanish-style mansion offering comfort and luxurious amenities. You'll start your day with a delicious breakfast consisting of freshly squeezed orange juice, just-ground coffee, and such specialties as peaches-and-cream French toast and Lancaster sausage purchased at the country's oldest continuously operated farmers' market. After touring, you are welcomed back with tea or lemonade and Karen's coconut-oatmeal pie, beautifully served in the lavishly decorated library. You can then relax in an oversized soaking tub, catch a quick nap in a queen- or king-size brass bed, and go off to dinner at one of the area's special restaurants. Calorie counters may find it hard to skip the traditional bedtime treat of chocolates and cordials.

Meadowview Guest House ✪
2169 NEW HOLLAND PIKE, LANCASTER, PENNSYLVANIA 17601

Tel: **(717) 299-4017**
Best Time to Call: **Before 10:30 PM**
Host(s): **Edward and Sheila Christie**
No. of Rooms: **3**
No. of Private Baths: **1**
Max. No. Sharing Bath: **4**
Double/pb: **$40**
Single/pb: **$40**
Double/sb: **$25–$30**

Reduced Rates: **$3 less on 3rd night; off-season**
Open: **Mar. 1–Nov. 30**
Breakfast: **Continental**
Pets: **No**
Children: **Welcome, over 7**
Smoking: **No**
Social Drinking: **Permitted**
Airport/Station Pickup: **Yes**

Situated in the heart of Pennsylvania Dutch country, the house has a pleasant blend of modern and traditional furnishings. Your hosts offer a fully equipped guest kitchen where you can store and prepare your own light meals. Ed and Sheila supply coffee and tea. The area is known for great farmers' markets, antique shops, craft shops, country auctions, and wonderful restaurants.

Wheatland Hills B&B ✪
36 WILSON DRIVE, LANCASTER, PENNSYLVANIA 17603

Tel: **(717) 393-7452**
Host(s): **Bonnie and Marlin Miller**
Location: **3 mi. from Rte. 30, Rohrerstown Exit**
No. of Rooms: **1**
No. of Private Baths: **1**
Double/pb: **$45**

Single/pb: **$35**
Open: **All year**
Breakfast: **Continental**
Pets: **No**
Children: **Sometimes**
Smoking: **No**
Social Drinking: **No**

Conveniently located in a pleasant, quiet neighborhood, this B&B is close to historical sites, Central Market, outlet shops, and is only a few blocks from Wheatland, home of President James Buchanan. Bonnie, a native Lancasterian, is a former tour guide and will gladly help you get the most out of your visit. The guest room is comfortably furnished in Early American decor accented with antiques. Breakfast features homemade jam, muffins, baked oatmeal, and fresh fruit in season.

The Loom Room
R.D. 1, BOX 1420, LEESPORT, PENNSYLVANIA 19533

Tel: **(215) 926-3217**
Host(s): **Mary and Gene Smith**
Location: **4 mi. N of Reading**
No. of Rooms: **3**
Max. No. Sharing Bath: **5**
Double/sb: **$40**
Single/sb: **$40**
Open: **All year**

Breakfast: **Full**
Reduced Rates: **Weekly**
Pets: **No**
Children: **Welcome (crib)**
Smoking: **Permitted**
Social Drinking: **Permitted**
Airport/Station Pickup: **Yes**

The Loom Room is a stucco-covered stone farmhouse dating back more than 175 years. It is located in the countryside surrounded by shade trees, flowers, and herb gardens. Inside, the spacious rooms feature country antiques, open beams, fireplaces, and handwoven accessories. Mary invites you to her studio, where her work is on display. Her talents also extend to the kitchen, where she helps Gene cook up eggnog French toast, homemade jams, muffins, and chipped beef. Breakfast may be served in the sunny kitchen or outside in the gazebo. This lovely farm is near Reading's outlet complexes, Blue Marsh Lake Recreation Area, Crystal Cave, and many historic sights.

The Sleepy Fir Bed & Breakfast ✪
RD2, BOX 2802, ZIEGLER NURSERY ROAD, LEESPORT, PENNSYLVANIA 19533

Tel: **(215) 926-1014**
Host(s): **Phil and Judy Whitmoyer**
Location: **7 mi. NW of Reading**
No. of Rooms: **2**
Max. No. Sharing Bath: **4**
Double/sb: **$40**
Single/sb: **$35**

Open: **All year**
Reduced Rates: **6%, families**
Breakfast: **Full**
Pets: **No**
Children: **Welcome, over 6**
Smoking: **No**
Social Drinking: **Permitted**

A brick Cape Cod with black shutters, this house offers rural privacy on three and a half acres of landscaped and wooded countryside. The guest rooms have double beds and share a luxury bath with a whirlpool and sauna. Your hosts, Phil and Judy Whitmoyer, are natives of the area, and they will be happy to direct you to outlet shopping, public golf courses, and the sights of Pennsylvania Dutch Country. The Whitmoyers have bicycles and a 17-foot canoe to lend for exploring the nearby Blue Marsh Lake Recreation Area. After a busy day they invite you to unwind with a game of pool or a stroll through the wooded property.

Dot's Bed & Breakfast ✪
525 WEST MARION STREET, LITITZ, PENNSYLVANIA 17543

Tel: **(717) 627-0483**
Best Time to Call: **7–9 AM; 6–11 PM**
Host(s): **Dorothy and Erwin Boettcher**
Location: **7 mi. N of Lancaster**
No. of Rooms: **1**
Max. No. Sharing Bath: **4**
Double/sb: **$35**
Single/sb: **$30**

Open: **All year**
Breakfast: **Continental**
Pets: **Sometimes**
Children: **Welcome (crib)**
Smoking: **No**
Social Drinking: **Permitted**
Foreign Languages: **German**

Dot's is located in a quiet, residential suburb of Lititz, home of the country's first pretzel bakery. Much of this quaint little town has stayed the way it was in 1756, the year it was founded. You are sure to enjoy an easy stroll past Lititz Springs Park, the historic buildings on Main Street, and the Linden Hall Girl's School. After a busy day, you'll be glad to return to Dot's, where you'll find a quiet guest room furnished with a cozy bed, lounge chair, rocker, and plenty of books. Awake to the birds singing and come downstairs for some of Dot's homemade muffins or shoofly pie. Your hosts will gladly direct you to the nearby sights, including the Wilbur Chocolate Factory.

Herr Farmhouse Inn
ROUTE 7, BOX 310, MANHEIM, PENNSYLVANIA 17545

Tel: **(717) 653-9852**
Best Time to Call: **After 4 PM**
Host(s): **Barry A. Herr**
Location: **9 mi. W of Lancaster; ¼ mi. from Rte. 283**
No. of Rooms: **4**
No. of Private Baths: **2**
Max. No. Sharing Bath: **4**
Double/pb: **$75**

Double/sb: **$65**
Suites: **$85**
Open: **All year**
Breakfast: **Continental**
Credit Cards: **MC, VISA**
Pets: **No**
Children: **Welcome, over 6**
Smoking: **Permitted**
Social Drinking: **Permitted**

Nestled on more than 11 acres of rolling farmland, this farmhouse, dating back to 1738, has been restored with the greatest of care and attention to detail. Fanlights adorn the main entrance, there are six working fireplaces, and it has the original pine floors. Whether spending a winter's night by a cozy fire, or a bright summer morning sipping tea in the sun room, it is the perfect retreat. It is less than 20 minutes to the sights, shops, and restaurants of Amish country.

Cedar Hill Farm ✪
305 LONGENECKER ROAD, MOUNT JOY, PENNSYLVANIA 17552

Tel: **(717) 653-4655**	Reduced Rates: **Weekly**
Host(s): **Russel and Gladys Swarr**	Breakfast: **Continental**
Location: **15 mi. W of Lancaster**	Credit Cards: **AMEX, MC, VISA**
No. of Rooms: **3**	Pets: **No**
No. of Private Baths: **3**	Children: **Welcome over 12**
Double/pb: **$45–$55**	Smoking: **No**
Single/pb: **$35–$45**	Social Drinking: **Permitted**
Open: **All year**	Airport/Station Pickup: **Yes**

Russel was born in this restored 1807 stone farmhouse and can tell you all about its history. It has an open, winding staircase, original pine floors, and an Indian door; breakfast is served beside a walk-in fireplace. Stroll the acreage or relax on the large porch overlooking a peaceful stream. Beautiful wallpapers and family heirlooms enhance the comfortable, air-conditioned bedrooms; the suite has a private balcony. Quilt auctions and other attractions for collectors are plentiful year-round. Every Tuesday a farmers' market and antiques auction take place just minutes away. Amish country, Hershey Park, and Chocolate World are nearby attractions.

Carriage House Manor ✪
143 WEST MAIN STREET, MOUNTVILLE, PENNSYLVANIA 17554

Tel: **(717) 285-5497**	Breakfast: **Full**
Host(s): **David and Patti Nace**	Pets: **No**
Location: **8 mi. W of Lancaster**	Children: **Welcome**
No. of Rooms: **3**	Smoking: **No**
Max. No. Sharing Bath: **4**	Social Drinking: **No**
Double/sb: **$50**	Minimum Stay: **2 nights on holidays**
Open: **All year**	Airport/Station Pickup: **Yes**
Reduced Rates: **20%, weekly; Dec.–Apr.**	

Built in 1914, this charming Victorian manor house was recently renovated. Decorated with country collectibles and antiques, its cheerful bedrooms have ceiling paddle fans as well as air conditioners for your summer comfort. Guests can sip tea on the shaded patio, relax on the front porch swing, or stroll around the well-kept grounds. The hearty country-style breakfast served in the dining room or on the patio will fortify you for explorations of the nearby country craft and antiques shops, farmers' markets, outlet stores, and amusement parks.

Maple Lane Guest House ✪
505 PARADISE LANE, PARADISE, PENNSYLVANIA 17562

Tel: **(717) 687-7479**
Host(s): **Marion and Edwin Rohrer**
Location: **10 mi. E of Lancaster**
No. of Rooms: **4**
No. of Private Baths: **1**
Max. No. Sharing Bath: **4**
Double/pb: **$35–$48**
Single/pb: **$32–$38**
Double/sb: **$35–$45**
Single/sb: **$35–$45**
Open: **All year**
Breakfast: **Continental**
Pets: **No**
Children: **Welcome (crib)**
Smoking: **No**
Social Drinking: **No**

From the hill nearby you can see for 40 miles. Stroll the 200 acres of this working farm, with its stream and woodland. Your hosts welcome you to rooms decorated with homemade quilts, needlework, and antiques. The sights of the Amish country, such as the farmers' market, antique shops, flea markets, and restaurants, are within easy reach. A two-night minimum stay is required on weekends.

The Rose and Crown ✪
44 FROGTOWN ROAD, PARADISE, PENNSYLVANIA 17562

Tel: **(717) 768-7684**
Host(s): **Allan and Linde Helmbrecht**
Location: **10 mi. E of Lancaster**
No. of Rooms: **4**
Max. No. Sharing Bath: **4**
Double/sb: **$45**
Single/sb: **$35**
Open: **All year**
Breakfast: **Full**
Pets: **No**
Children: **Welcome (crib, high chair)**
Smoking: **No**
Social Drinking: **Permitted**

Set amid the rolling pastures of the Pennsylvania Dutch farmlands, this was once the home of a country squire. The house was built circa 1850, and its large rooms have been fully restored and decorated with comfortable, informal furnishings. Each bedroom features a queen-size bed and can accommodate a family of four. Breakfast specialties such as French toast and Pennsylvania scrapple are served in your room or on the sun porch. The Rose and Crown is near canoeing and hiking at Pinnacle Point, Lake Eldred Recreational Area, and the attractions of the Pennsylvania Dutch countryside.

Lofty Acres ✪
R.D. 1, BOX 331, PEACH BOTTOM, PENNSYLVANIA 17563

Tel: **(717) 548-3052**
Host(s): **Gary Hufford**
Location: **20 mi. S of Lancaster; 1 mi. from Rte. 272**
No. of Rooms: **3**
No. of Private Baths: **1**
Max. No. Sharing Bath: **4**
Double/sb: **$65**
Suites: **$75**
Open: **All year**
Breakfast: **Full**
Pets: **Sometimes**
Children: **Welcome, over 12**
Smoking: **Permitted**
Social Drinking: **Permitted**
Airport/Station Pickup: **Yes**

This charming 200-year-old farmhouse is as rich in history as it is in charm. The quiet setting offers a relaxing environment. Take a stroll by the pond or watch the farmers at work from the porch. Inside, the antiques and collectibles are enhanced by a working fireplace in every room. The house is centrally located, and the nearby attractions of Strasburg and Paradise are yours to enjoy. It is also convenient to the lush country estates of Chester County where the local gentry still ride to the hunt. Longwood Gardens and Chadds Ford are close by. Gary is an excellent cook who enjoys serving a variety of Pennsylvania Dutch breakfast treats.

Kurr House ✪
BOX 144, GODFRY STREET, REHRERSBURG, PENNSYLVANIA 19550

Tel: **(717) 933-8219**
Host(s): **Richard and Sharon Kramer**
Location: **22 mi. NW of Reading**
No. of Private Baths: **1**
Guest Cottage: **$60, sleeps 3**
Open: **Mar. 1–Oct. 31**
Breakfast: **Continental**
Credit Cards: **MC, VISA**
Pets: **No**
Children: **Welcome, over 12**
Smoking: **No**
Social Drinking: **Permitted**
Airport/Station Pickup: **Yes**
Foreign Languages: **German**

Built in 1803 and fully restored after being vacant for over 40 years, this log house is listed on the Berks County Historic Register. You may choose from authentic rope beds, two of which are made up with feather ticking, just like the early Pennsylvania Germans used. The third double rope bed has been converted to modern standards. The house is entirely furnished in antiques; life-size mannequins dressed in authentic fashions of the 1800s are artfully placed throughout.

Photographs and accessories echo the feeling that you've somehow stepped back in time to a typical country home of the 19th century. A large yard and lovely English garden are yours to enjoy.

The Inn at Mundis Mills ☻
586 MUNDIS RACE ROAD, YORK, PENNSYLVANIA 17402

Tel: **(717) 755-2002**
Best Time to call: **Afternoons**
Host(s): **Joseph and Marilyn Korsak**
Location: **2½ mi. from Rte. 30**
No. of Rooms: **2**
No. of Private Baths: **2**
Double/pb: **$50**

Single/pb: **$40**
Open: **All year**
Breakfast: **Full**
Pets: **No**
Children: **Welcome**
Smoking: **No**
Social Drinking: **Permitted**

This quiet country inn is surrounded by York County farmland. The wide front porch welcomes guests to sit and spend some time listening to the chatter of the birds. The pre-Civil War Dutch farmhouse is restored and warmly furnished with antiques. Homemade muffins and jams, fruits, cereals, eggs, and meats will start your day. And, you can walk off the calories as you tour the nearby museums, battlegrounds, and wineries.

PHILADELPHIA AREA

Bed & Breakfast—The Manor ☻
P.O. BOX 656, HAVERTON, PENNSYLVANIA 19083

Tel: **(215) 464-9564**
Coordinators: **Jackie Curtis and Mary Lou Paolini**
States/Regions Covered: **Ardmore, Bryn Mawr, Havertown, Lancaster, Merion, Narberth, Philadelphia, Phoenixville, Springfield, Wynnewood**

Rates (Single/Double):
   Modest: **$30**   **$40**
   Average: **$35**   **$45**
   Luxury: **$45**   **$65**
Credit Cards: **MC, VISA**

Mary Lou and Jackie can place you in a variety of B&Bs in the Philadelphia area ranging from a cozy bedroom with a double bed, to a Main Line manor house where the guest room has a comfortable rocker from which you may watch TV, to a historic house built in 1790 that's furnished with antiques and has a canopy bed, afternoon tea, and a swimming pool as part of the package. Many are convenient to the University of Pennsylvania, Bryn Mawr, and Haverford and Villanova colleges. There's a $5 surcharge for one-night stays.

Bed & Breakfast of Chester County
P.O. BOX 825, KENNETT SQUARE, PENNSYLVANIA 19348

Tel: (215) 444-1367	Rates (Single/Double):	
Coordinator: **Doris Passante**	Modest: $35	$45–$50
States/Regions Covered: **Chester**	Average: $45	$55–$60
County, Chadds Ford, Valley Forge	Luxury: $50	$65 and up
	Credit Cards: **No**	

Doris has a wide selection of homes located in the beautiful and historic Brandywine Valley, which is known for the River Museum, Longwood Gardens, Winterthur, Brandywine Battlefield, and Valley Forge. The area is convenient to the Pennsylvania Dutch country. Send for her brochure, which fully describes each B&B. The University of Delaware, Lincoln University, and West Chester University are close by. There's a $5 surcharge for one-night stays.

Bed & Breakfast of Philadelphia
P.O. BOX 630, CHESTER SPRINGS, PENNSYLVANIA 19425

Tel: (215) 827-9650	Rates (Single/Double):	
Coordinator: **Betsy Augustine**	Modest: $40	$40
States/Regions Covered: **Philadelphia**	Average: $40	$55
and suburbs	Luxury: $60	$70 and up
	Credit Cards: **MC, VISA**	

Philadelphia is the "City of Brotherly Love" and you'll be made to feel like family in the B&Bs. Selections include luxury town houses in the heart of Society Hill, refurbished Victorians, suburban manor homes, country guest cottages, and places that are convenient to all the universities. There's a $5 surcharge for one night's lodging.

Bed & Breakfast of Valley Forge ✪
P.O. BOX 562, VALLEY FORGE, PENNSYLVANIA 19481-0562

Tel: (215) 783-7838	Rates (Single/Double):	
Best Time to Call: **9 AM–9 PM daily**	Average: $25–$50	$35–$75
Coordinator: **Carolyn J. Williams**	Credit Cards: **MC, VISA**	
States/Regions Covered: **Valley Forge,**		
Chester Springs, Collegeville, Devon,		
Gladwyne, King of Prussia, Radnor,		
Skippack		

George Washington would applaud the manner in which Carolyn has brought the British tradition of Bed and Breakfast to the area of his headquarters. Her roster includes town, country, historic, and ski locations convenient to major highways. Most are within 25 miles of such attractions as the Audubon Wildlife Sanctuary, Chadds Ford, the Devon Horse Show, King of Prussia, Longwood Gardens, Winterthur, Philadelphia, the Valley Forge Convention Center, and the Valley Forge Music Fair. The Valley Forge National Historic Park has wonderful hiking trails, bridle paths, and cross-country skiing within its 3,000 acres. There's a $5 surcharge for one-night lodging.

The Bed & Breakfast Connection O
P.O. BOX 21, DEVON, PENNSYLVANIA 19333

Tel: **(215) 687-3565**
Best Time to Call: **9 AM–9 PM daily; Noon–9 PM Sunday**
Coordinators: **Ann Goodman and Margaret Gregg**
States/Regions Covered: **Philadelphia and suburbs**

Rates (Single/Double):
Modest: **$25**   **$35**
Average: **$40**   **$50**
Luxury: **$60**   **$65**
Credit Cards: **AMEX, MC, VISA**

You may choose from a select group of B&Bs including a secluded, contemporary home with a ground-floor guest room. The adjoining den has a fireplace and TV just for you. There's a 1770 fieldstone farmhouse in the picturesque "hunt country" where your bedroom is appointed with antiques and a fireplace. Or luxuriate in a Tudor mansion with its billiard room, library, conservatory, and bedroom decorated in Dutch decor. Add a $5 surcharge for one-night stays plus a $5 handling fee for all reservations. A descriptive directory is free for the asking.

Guesthouses
BOX 2137, WEST CHESTER, PENNSYLVANIA 19380

Tel: **(215) 692-4575**
Best Time to Call: **Noon–4 PM**
Coordinator: **Joyce K. Archbold**
States/Regions Covered: **Main Line Philadelphia, Brandywine Valley, Chesapeake Bay; Delaware, Maryland, New Jersey**

Rates (Single/Double):
Modest: **$40–$45**
Average: **$50–$55**
Luxury: **$70**   **$75 and up**
Credit Cards: **AMEX, MC, VISA**

Most of the homes on Joyce's roster are architecturally or historically significant. Choose from an 18th-century home with a swimming pool and surrounded by gardens, or an authentic log house on a large estate adjacent to the Brandywine River. Some hosts are professional chefs, interior designers, or teachers who enjoy sharing cultural and scenic surroundings. Many homes are listed on the National Register of Historic Places. All are comfortable and friendly, serving the high-tech corridor, local prep schools and universities, and much more.

Buttonwood Farm ✪
231 PEMBERTON ROAD, KENNETT SQUARE, PENNSYLVANIA 19348

Tel: **(215) 444-0278**	Other Meals: **Available**
Host(s): **Loes and Ray Hutmacher**	Pets: **Sometimes**
Location: **45 mi. S of Philadelphia**	Children: **Welcome**
No. of Rooms: **3**	Smoking: **Permitted**
Max. No. Sharing Bath: **3**	Social Drinking: **Permitted**
Double/sb: **$60**	Airport/Station Pickup: **Yes**
Open: **All year**	Foreign Languages: **Dutch, French, German**
Breakfast: **Full**	

Ray and Loes Hutmacher have 20 years of experience as captain and chef aboard private luxury yachts throughout the world, and have recently dropped anchor in the rolling hills of Chester County. Their charming stone farmhouse is furnished in antiques and is situated on a lovely property with woods, pastures, a barn, and clay tennis courts. Relax with complimentary wine and cheese before dinner. The Hutmachers serve dinner by prior arrangement, and their own home-raised veal is the specialty of the house. There are also many fine restaurants in the area. Loes serves homemade French bread, blueberry muffins, jams, and fresh-squeezed orange juice as part of a hearty farm breakfast. This lovely home is within a 15-minute drive of Longwood Gardens and Brandywine River Museum, housing the Wyeth Family art collections. Trail riding, golf, canoeing, gliding, and Brandywine Polo can also be enjoyed nearby.

Meadow Spring Farm
201 EAST STREET ROAD, KENNETT SQUARE, PENNSYLVANIA 19348

Tel: **(215) 444-3903**	Open: **All year**
Host(s): **Anne and John Hicks**	Reduced Rates: **10%, families**
Location: **2 mi. from Rte. 1**	Breakfast: **Full**
No. of Rooms: **5**	Other Meals: **Available**
No. of Private Baths: **2**	Pets: **No**
Max. No. Sharing Bath: **3**	Children: **Welcome (crib)**
Double/pb: **$65**	Smoking: **Permitted**
Double/sb: **$45**	Social Drinking: **Permitted**
Single/sb: **$35**	Airport/Station Pickup: **Yes**

This large stone house dates back to the 1830s. A hot tub and screened-in porch are two of the recent additions. The rooms are decorated with family antiques and Victorian whimsy. Your hostess welcomes you with tea, wine, and goodies. In season, she serves corn fritters, mushroom omelets, and homemade breads on the porch. Local attractions include Longwood Gardens, Brandywine River Museum, Winterthur, and downtown Philadelphia. Anne's collection of dolls and teddy bears delights children of all ages.

Mrs. K's Bed & Breakfast O
404 RIDGE AVENUE, KENNETT SQUARE, PENNSYLVANIA 19348

Tel: **(215) 444-5559**
Best Time to Call: **7 AM–10 PM**
Host(s): **Charlotte Kanofsky**
Location: **30 mi. S of Philadelphia**
No. of Rooms: **3**
Max. No. Sharing Bath: **4**
Double/sb: **$45–$55**

Single/sb: **$35–$45**
Open: **All year**
Breakfast: **Full**
Pets: **No**
Children: **Welcome (crib)**
Smoking: **No**
Social Drinking: **Permitted**

Arriving guests are greeted with cheese, crackers, and appropriate beverages. Charlotte has made her guest-house business a labor of love. Her lovely air-conditioned home is on a quiet residential street but close to many attractions. This is Andrew Wyeth's territory (Chadds Ford). Longwood Gardens, Brandywine Battlefield, and Brandywine River Museum are all worthwhile stops to make. It's less than a half hour from Wilmington, Delaware, home of Winterthur, the Hagley and the Natural History museums. You are welcome to use the kitchen for snacks. West Chester University, the University of Delaware, and Delaware Art Museum are close by. Lancaster is an hour away.

The Waln House O
1242 BROWNSVILLE ROAD, LANGHORNE, PENNSYLVANIA 19047

Tel: **(215) 757-2921**
Best Time to Call: **9 AM–9 PM**
Host(s): **Terence and Virginia McGee**
Location: **25 mi. NE of Philadelphia**
No. of Rooms: **2**
Max. No. Sharing Bath: **4**
Double/sb: **$60**
Single/sb: **$55**
Open: **All year**

Reduced Rates: **10%, seniors; 3rd night**
Breakfast: **Full**
Pets: **No**
Children: **Welcome, over 12**
Smoking: **Permitted**
Social Drinking: **Permitted**
Airport/Station Pickup: **Yes**
Foreign Languages: **German**

At the end of a long driveway, bordered by ageless trees, is this fieldstone farmhouse built in 1682. Random-width pine floors and beamed ceilings are hallmarks of this historic home. Much of the furnishings have been handcrafted by Terence and Virginia and beautiful quilts grace the canopied beds. The 10-foot hearth of the walk-in fireplace is the setting for the bountiful breakfast. Breakfast features seasonal fruit such as raspberries, blueberries, or strawberries from the garden. Washington Crossing, New Hope, the shops of Peddlers' Village, the discount stores of Flemington, Sesame Place, and Princeton University are minutes away.

The Barn ✪
1131 GROVE ROAD, WEST CHESTER, PENNSYLVANIA 19380

Tel: **(215) 436-4544**
Host(s): **Susan Hager and son, Ted**
Location: **30 mi. SW of Philadelphia; 16 mi. from Penn. Turnpike**
No. of Rooms: **2**
No. of Private Baths: **1**
Max. No. Sharing Bath: **4**
Double/pb: **$55**
Double/sb: **$55**
Suites: **$90 (2 bedrooms)**

Open: **All year**
Reduced Rates: **$10 less after 1st night**
Breakfast: **Full**
Pets: **Welcome**
Children: **Welcome**
Smoking: **Permitted**
Social Drinking: **Permitted**
Airport/Station Pickup: **Train**

Dating back to the 1800s, the Barn has been beautifully restored without sacrificing its original identity. Old beams, random-width pine floors, and stone walls are enhanced by simple furnishings and special antiques. Susan's pewter collection, old earthenware, and dried flowers are artfully arranged to add a nice touch. Children love the third-floor "open room," with its double bed, cots, and TV. It's 15 minutes away from Longwood Gardens, Winterthur, and Brandywine Valley attractions. Breakfast often features scrambled eggs in crêpes with Hollandaise sauce, Philadelphia scrapple, popovers, and fresh fruit. Wine and cheese are graciously served in the evening.

POCONO MOUNTAINS

Beach Lake Hotel and Country Store ✪
MAIN STREET AND CHURCH ROAD, P.O. BOX 144, BEACH LAKE, PENNSYLVANIA 18404

Tel: **(717) 729-8239**
Host(s): **Erika and Roy Miller**
Location: **5 mi. E of Honesdale**

No. of Rooms: **6**
No. of Private Baths: **6**
Double/pb: **$75**

Open: **All year**
Breakfast: **Full**
Other Meals: **Available**
Credit Cards: **MC, VISA**
Pets: **No**

Children: **No**
Smoking: **Permitted**
Social Drinking: **Permitted**
Airport/Station Pickup: **Available**

The Beach Lake Hotel has been welcoming guests for well over 100 years. Today the rooms again reflect the Victorian elegance intended by the original owners back in the 1800s. Roy and Erika chose lace curtains, Oriental rugs, and floral wallpaper patterns to complement the antique furnishings and gleaming pine wood floors. Their love for antiques and collectibles is evident throughout the house and in the country store, where you'll find everything from brass lamps to folk art. In the formal dining room guests can enjoy gourmet selections such as apple pancakes with brandied grape sauce, eggs Benedict, or a simple bowl of hot oatmeal. In the evening, the Millers will tempt you back to this room for gourmet candlelight dinners served on antique china. The hotel is just a short walk from Beach Lake and four miles from the Delaware River. The area also offers hunting for antiques or for game, skiing, and spectacular foliage. After a busy day you can enjoy a cocktail in the parlor, curl up with one of the Millers' many books, or just relax on the porch.

Toby Valley Lodge ✪
P.O. BOX 431, ROUTE 940, BLAKESLEE, PENNSYLVANIA 18610

Tel: **(717) 646-4893**
Best Time to Call: **9 AM–9 PM**
Host(s): **Marion Whitner**
Location: **1½ mi. from Rte. 80**
No. of Rooms: **7**
No. of Private Baths: **7**
Double/pb: **$40–$50**
Open: **All year**

Reduced Rates: **Weekly**
Breakfast: **Continental**
Pets: **Sometimes**
Children: **Welcome**
Smoking: **Permitted**
Social Drinking: **Permitted**
Minimum Stay: **2 nights on weekends**

If you've ever longed for your own mountain retreat, you'll feel as if your dream came true at this B&B. It faces the woods and Tobyhanna Creek, an excellent trout stream. In chilly weather, the huge fireplace serves as a cheery backdrop to the breakfast area. The comfortable furnishings are accented with antiques, good prints, and western art. Marion provides a guest refrigerator, and you may stock it with drinks and snacks. Activities for the sportsminded abound in the area. Jack Frost Ski Area and Pocono International Raceway are nearby attractions.

Nearbrook ✪
ROUTE 447, CANADENSIS, PENNSYLVANIA 18325

Tel: **(717) 595-3152**
Best Time to Call: **Mornings; evenings**
Location: **15 mi. N of East Stroudsburg**
Host(s): **Barb and Dick Robinson**
No. of Rooms: **3**
No. of Private Baths: **1½**
Max. No. Sharing Bath: **4**
Double/pb: **$50**

Double/sb: **$40**
Single/sb: **$25**
Open: **All year**
Breakfast: **Full**
Pets: **Sometimes**
Children: **Welcome**
Smoking: **No**
Social Drinking: **Permitted**

Enjoy the Poconos while making Barb and Dick's charming, informal home your base. Meander through rock gardens and down a woodland path to a clear mountain stream. A hearty breakfast is served on the porch. You are welcome to use the piano and the puzzles and games. Barb offers lessons in sketching if you wish to try your hand.

La Anna Guest House ✪
R.D. 2, BOX 1051, CRESCO, PENNSYLVANIA 18326

Tel: **(717) 676-4225**
Host(s): **Kay Swingle and Julie Wilson**
Location: **9 mi. from I-80**
No. of Rooms: **4**
Max. No. Sharing Bath: **4**
Double/sb: **$25**
Single/sb: **$20**

Open: **All year**
Breakfast: **Continental**
Pets: **No**
Children: **Welcome (crib)**
Smoking: **Permitted**
Social Drinking: **Permitted**

This Victorian home has large rooms furnished with antiques; it is nestled on 25 acres of lush, wooded land, and has its own pond. Kay will happily direct you to fine dining spots that are kind to your wallet. Enjoy scenic walks, waterfalls, mountain vistas, Tobyhanna and Promised Land state parks; there's cross-country skiing right on the property. Lake Wallenpaupack is only 15 minutes away.

Hemlock Grove Bed and Breakfast ✪
R.D. 1, BOX 12-A, GREENTOWN, PENNSYLVANIA 18426

Tel: **(717) 676-4511**
Host(s): **Peggy and Mike Ackerman**
Location: **2 mi. from I-84**
No. of Rooms: **2**
Max. No. Sharing Bath: **4**
Double/pb: **$40**

Single/pb: **$35**
Double/sb: **$40**
Single/sb: **$35**
Open: **All year**
Breakfast: **Full**
Credit Cards: **MC, VISA**

Pets: **No**
Children: **Welcome, over 6**

Smoking: **Permitted**
Social Drinking: **Permitted**

This light and airy tri-level country home is surrounded by one and a half acres of groomed lawns, is edged by a stream, and is bordered by shade trees. It is attractively furnished in a comfortable mix of Laura Ashley and "Nana's treasures," and there's a pastoral view through every window. A wholesome breakfast with farm-fresh ingredients is served in the spacious, bright kitchen. Guests return in all seasons to this special area, unspoiled by the wheels of progress. Lake Wallenpaupack is only three miles away for boating, fishing, swimming, and snowmobiling. Golfing, riding, antiques shops, country fairs, restaurants, Bushkill Falls, and skiing are nearby. Best of all is returning "home," where Peggy and Mike will treat you to a snack, drinks, and a movie on the VCR. Justin and Travis, ages 7 and 14, will be happy to share their games and outdoor equipment with your children.

Academy Street Bed & Breakfast ✪
528 ACADEMY STREET, HAWLEY, PENNSYLVANIA 18428

Tel: **(717) 226-3430**
Host(s): **Judith and Sheldon Lazan**
Location: **100 mi. NW of New York City**
No. of Rooms: **7**
No. of Private Baths: **2**
Max. No. Sharing Bath: **4**
Double/pb: **$70**
Single/pb: **$40**
Double/sb: **$65**
Single/sb: **$35**
Open: **May–Oct.**
Breakfast: **Full**
Credit Cards: **MC, VISA**
Pets: **No**
Children: **Welcome, over 12**
Smoking: **Permitted**
Social Drinking: **Permitted**

This Italian-style Victorian (circa 1865) is situated on a rise near the Lackawaxen River. Judith and Sheldon have done a marvelous job of restoring the rare and beautiful woodwork, paneling, and inlay to make a fitting background for their lovely antiques and furnishings. You'd better diet before you arrive because you won't be able to resist the culinary delights at breakfast or the complimentary high tea. It's only minutes away from famed Lake Wallenpaupack.

The Harry Packer Mansion ✪
PACKER HILL, ROUTE 209, JIM THORPE, PENNSYLVANIA 18229

Tel: **(717) 325-8566**
Host(s): **Bob and Pat Handwerk**
Location: **On Rte. 209**
No. of Rooms: **14**
No. of Private Baths: **8**
Max. No. Sharing Bath: **4**
Double/pb: **$75**
Double/sb: **$65–$75**
Suites: **$110**
Open: **All year**
Breakfast: **Full**
Credit Cards: **MC, VISA**
Pets: **No**
Children: **Welcome, over 6**
Smoking: **Permitted**
Social Drinking: **Permitted**

The town, named for the Olympic legend, is a mecca of Victorian preservation and restoration. The mansion has been faithfully restored to recall an era of timeless ease featuring original Tiffany windows, English Minton tiles, exquisite chandeliers, and unique fireplace mantels. Pat and Bob have created fun themes including an Adventure Package for the sportsminded, a Romantic Getaway for a first or second honeymoon, and a Mystery Weekend with murder and mayhem to be solved. In addition, they plan guided tours, Victorian fetes, and fancy balls.

The Vines ✪
107 EAST ANN STREET, MILFORD, PENNSYLVANIA 18337

Tel: **(717) 296-6775**
Host(s): **Joan and Don Voce**
Location: **1 mi. from I-84**
No. of Rooms: **4**
Max. No. Sharing Bath: **3**
Double/sb: **$50–$60**
Single/sb: **$25–$30**
Open: **All year**
Reduced Rates: **20%, seniors**
Breakfast: **Full**
Pets: **No**
Children: **Welcome**
Smoking: **No**
Social Drinking: **Permitted**

The Vines is a Queen Anne Victorian, built in 1864, and has been completely restored. There are parks, flea markets, canoeing, antiquing, historical sites, skiing, fishing, and many charming restaurants within a short distance. Coffee and tea are available in the guest rooms; Saturday nights often have the added attraction of wine and cheese. It is a mile from Grey Towers, Apple Valley with its quaint little shops, and the Milford Theatre.

Bonny Bank ✪
P.O. BOX 481, MILLRIFT, PENNSYLVANIA 18340

Tel: **(717) 491-2250**
Best Time to Call: **9 AM–10 PM**
Host(s): **Doug and Linda Hay**
Location: **5 mi. from I-84**
No. of Rooms: **1**
No. of Private Baths: **1**
Double/sb: **$35**
Single/sb: **$25**

Open: **May 15–Oct. 15**
Reduced Rates: **15% weekly; seniors**
Breakfast: **Full**
Pets: **No**
Children: **No**
Smoking: **No**
Social Drinking: **Permitted**

Stay in a picture-book small town on a dead-end road. The sound of the rapids will lull you to sleep in this charming bungalow perched on the banks of the Delaware River. Doug and Linda invite you to use their private swimming area and will lend you inner-tubes for float trips. Nearby attractions include the Zane Grey house, Minisink Battlefield, Grey Towers Historical Site, the Victorian village of Milford, and all the sports and variety of restaurants the Poconos are known for.

Elvern Country Lodge ✪
P.O. BOX 177, STONE CHURCH–FIVE POINTS ROAD, MOUNT BETHEL, PENNSYLVANIA 18343

Tel: **(215) 588-7922**
Best Time to Call: **After 4 PM**
Host(s): **Dos and Herb Deen**
Location: **16 mi. N of Easton; 6 mi. from I-80**
No. of Rooms: **4**
No. of Private Baths: **2**
Max. No. Sharing Bath: **4**
Double/pb: **$60**
Single/pb: **$35**
Double/sb: **$50**
Single/sb: **$30**

Suite: **$70**
Open: **All year**
Reduced Rates: **10%, seniors; weekly; Former guests**
Breakfast: **Full**
Other Meals: **Available**
Pets: **Sometimes**
Children: **Welcome (crib)**
Smoking: **Permitted**
Social Drinking: **Permitted**
Airport/Station Pickup: **Yes**

This is a working farm in the foothills of the Pocono Mountains. The house dates back to the Victorian period and includes a sun deck and patio. Guest quarters have cool summer breezes, individual thermostats, and wall-to-wall carpeting. Your hosts raise their own beef, vegetables, and fruit. They prepare a breakfast of country bacon, fresh eggs, and homemade jams. Fishing, boating, and swimming can be enjoyed in the two-acre lake on the farm. The Delaware Water Gap Recreation Area, Appalachian Trail, and Pocono Recreation Area are nearby.

The Redwood House ✪
BOX 9B, EAST SIDE BORO, WHITE HAVEN, PENNSYLVANIA 18661

Tel: (717) 443-7186; (215) 355-1754	Suites: **$60**
Host(s): **John and Emma Moore**	Open: **All year**
No. of Rooms: **4**	Reduced Rates: **5%, seniors**
No. of Private Baths: **2**	Breakfast: **Continental**
Max. No. Sharing Bath: **4**	Pets: **No**
Double/pb: **$35**	Children: **Welcome**
Single/pb: **$25**	Smoking: **Permitted**
Double/sb: **$30**	Social Drinking: **Permitted**
Single/sb: **$20**	

This frame chalet is minutes from the slopes at Big Boulder and Jack Frost. In summer enjoy sunning and swimming at Hickory Run State Park. Nearby Lehigh River offers fishing and rafting. Your hosts recommend a visit to Eckley, where the movie *The Molly Maguires* was filmed—a true example of what life was like in a 19th-century mining community. After a day of touring, come and relax on the large, comfortable porch.

SCRANTON/NORTH-CENTRAL PENNSYLVANIA

Hill Top Haven ✪
RD #1, BOX 5C, LIBERTY, PENNSYLVANIA 16930

Tel: (717) 324-2608	Open: **All year**
Host(s): **Richard and Betty Landis**	Breakfast: **Full**
Location: **29 mi. N of Williamsport**	Pets: **No**
No. of Rooms: **2**	Children: **Welcome**
Max. No. Sharing Bath: **4**	Smoking: **No**
Double/sb: **$35**	Social Drinking: **No**
Single/sb: **$30**	

This sprawling ranch home is in a rural mountain area surrounded by fields, flower beds, and woods. The house is furnished with many antiques and offers beautiful views of the surrounding countryside. A 10-acre lake is available for fishing and snowmobiling, and biking trails abound. The kids will want to visit the ducks, geese, and dairy cows.

State parks and a ski resort are close by, but if all you desire is fresh air and quiet, you'll find plenty of both at Hill Top Haven.

The Carriage House at Stonegate ✪
RD #1, BOX 23, MONTOURSVILLE, PENNSYLVANIA 17754

Tel: **(717) 433-4340**	Open: **All year**
Best Time to Call: **5:30 PM–9:30 PM**	Breakfast: **Continental**
Host(s): **Harold and Dena Mesaris**	Pets: **Welcome**
Location: **6 mi. E of Williamsport**	Children: **Welcome**
No. of Rooms: **2**	Smoking: **Permitted**
No. of Private Baths: **1**	Social Drinking: **Permitted**
Guest Cottage: **$45 for 2; $55 for 4**	Airport/Station Pickup: **Yes**

This self-contained facility was converted from the original carriage house of an 1830 farmhouse. Perfect for a family, there are two bedrooms, a bathroom, a living room with cable television, a dining area, and a kitchen stocked with all your breakfast needs. Decorated in country fashion, with some antiques, it offers complete privacy just 30 yards from your host's home. You'll have access to a creek, a barn complete with a variety of animals, and 30 acres on which to roam. It's close to the Little League Museum and Loyalsock Creek for swimming, canoeing, tubing, and fishing. Bucknell University is less than an hour away.

The Bodine House ✪
307 SOUTH MAIN STREET, MUNCY, PENNSYLVANIA 17756

Tel: **(717) 546-8949**	Double/sb: **$40**
Best Time to Call: **Evenings**	Single/sb: **$25**
Host(s): **David and Marie Louise Smith**	Open: **All year**
Location: **15 mi. S of Williamsport; 10 mi. from I-80, Exit 31B**	Credit Cards: **AMEX, MC, VISA**
No. of Rooms: **4**	Breakfast: **Full**
No. of Private Baths: **2**	Pets: **No**
Max. No. Sharing Bath: **3**	Children: **Welcome, over 6**
Double/pb: **$40–$45**	Smoking: **No**
Single/pb: **$35–$40**	Social Drinking: **Permitted**

This restored town house dates back to 1805. A baby grand piano, four fireplaces, and a candlelit living room add to its old-fashioned appeal. A full country breakfast and wine and cheese are on the house. Local attractions include the Susquehanna River, the Endless Mountains, and the fall foliage.

SOUTHEASTERN PENNSYLVANIA

Brennans B&B ✪
3827 LINDEN STREET, ALLENTOWN, PENNSYLVANIA 18104

Tel: **(215) 395-0869**
Best Time to Call: **11:30AM–11:30 PM**
Host(s): **Lois and Edward Brennan**
Location: **1 mi. from 78 & 22**
No. of Rooms: **2**
No. of Private Baths: **1**
Max. No. Sharing Bath: **2**
Double/pb: **$40**
Single/pb: **$35**
Double/sb: **$30**
Single/sb: **$25**
Open: **Apr.–Dec.**
Breakfast: **Full**
Pets: **Sometimes**
Children: **Welcome**
Smoking: **Permitted**
Social Drinking: **Permitted**
Airport/Station Pickup: **Yes**

Furnished in Early American fashion, accented with lush plants and family treasures, this comfortable brick ranch-style house can be your home away from home. The Brennans are history buffs who, now that they're retired, enjoy traveling and entertaining travelers. Breakfast features bacon and eggs with home fries, or sausages and pancakes, or delicious muffins to go with the homemade jam. You can walk off the calories on your way to the Haines Mill, Dorney Park, or one of the area's many museums.

Longswamp Bed and Breakfast ✪
RD 2, BOX 26, MERTZTOWN, PENNSYLVANIA 19539

Tel: **(215) 682-6197**
Host(s): **Elsa Dimick and Dr. Dean Dimick**
Location: **12 mi. SW of Allenton**
No. of Rooms: **9**
No. of Private Baths: **5**
Max. No. Sharing Bath: **4**
Double/pb: **$60–$65**
Single/pb: **$50**
Double/sb: **$60–$65**
Single/sb: **$50**
Open: **All year**
Breakfast: **Full**
Credit Cards: **MC, VISA**
Pets: **No**
Children: **Welcome**
Smoking: **Permitted**
Social Drinking: **Permitted**
Airport/Station Pickup: **Yes**
Foreign Languages: **French**

This guest house was originally built around 1750 and served as the first post office in town. The main house, completed in 1863, was a stop on the underground railroad. Today, Longswamp is a comfortable place with high ceilings, antiques, large fireplaces, plants, and bookcases full of reading pleasure. Breakfast specialties include home-dried fruits, *pain perdu*, quiche, and homemade breads. Your hostess offers wine, cheese, and coffee anytime. She will gladly direct you to antiques shops, auction houses, Reading, and the Amish country.

WESTERN PENNSYLVANIA

Pittsburgh Bed & Breakfast ✪
2190 BEN FRANKLIN DRIVE, PITTSBURGH, PENNSYLVANIA 15237

Tel: **(412) 367-8080**	Rates (Single/Double):
Coordinator: **Judy Antico**	Modest: **$25** **$35**
States/Regions Covered: **Pittsburgh and western Pennsylvania**	Average: **$30** **$40**
	Luxury: **$45** **$65**
	Credit Cards: **MC, VISA**

Judy has many comfortable accommodations within a 60-mile radius as well as in Pittsburgh's metropolitan area. Many homes are convenient to Carnegie-Mellon University, Duquesne, the University of Pittsburgh, ski resorts, historic Bedford, and Lake Erie. This is a great place to stop off en route to Cleveland (80 miles), Chicago (400 miles), and West Virginia (60 miles).

Garrott's Bed & Breakfast ✪
RD 1, BOX 73, COWANSVILLE, PENNSYLVANIA 16218

Tel: **(412) 545-2432**	Open: **All year**
Host(s): **Denise Garrott**	Breakfast: **Full**
Location: **50 mi. NE of Pittsburgh**	Pets: **Sometimes**
No. of Rooms: **3**	Children: **Welcome, over 8**
Max. No. Sharing Bath: **3**	Smoking: **Permitted**
Double/sb: **$60**	Social Drinking: **Permitted**
Single/sb: **$50**	

Experience comfortable elegance in this 100-year-old restored farmhouse set on 40 acres. This is a nature lover's paradise, with rolling fields, groves of trees, and a fishing pond. Sled riding, ice skating, or cross-country skiing can be enjoyed on the grounds, followed by hot drinks around the wood stove. If you're an amateur astronomer, Garrott's is an ideal spot for serious star watching because of the altitude and absence of pollution. Denise offers comfortable rooms decorated in antiques, collectibles, and colorful rugs. A cozy TV room and a sunny sitting area are available for relaxing. Breakfast includes farm-fresh eggs, preserves, and freshly baked treats.

Mountain View Bed and Breakfast ✪
MOUNTAIN VIEW ROAD, DONEGAL, PENNSYLVANIA 15628

Tel: **(412) 593-6349**	Open: **All year**
Host(s): **Lesley and Jerry O'Leary**	Breakfast: **Continental**
Location: **1 mi. from Penn. Tpke.**	Pets: **Welcome**
No. of Rooms: **4**	Children: **Welcome**
Max. No. Sharing Bath: **4**	Smoking: **Permitted**
Double/sb: **$50**	Social Drinking: **Permitted**
Suites: **$60**	

Every window of this 1865 farmhouse has a beautiful view of the surrounding Laurel Mountains. The house is a county landmark set on six acres. Hosts Lesley and Jerry love antiques and have decorated the rooms with period furnishings from their shop, located in the adjacent barn. They offer fresh fruit and homemade bread and rolls for breakfast. Mountain View is near hiking, ski resorts, white-water rafting, and several historic sites. Your hosts will gladly guide you to recreational activities or invite you to simply relax on the porch and enjoy the view.

Blueberry Acres
3925 McCREARY ROAD, ERIE, PENNSYLVANIA 16506

Tel: **(814) 833-6833**	Open: **All year**
Host(s): **Nan and Don Fabian**	Breakfast: **Full**
Location: **100 mi. W of Buffalo**	Pets: **No**
No. of Rooms: **1 suite**	Children: **Welcome**
No. of Private Baths: **1**	Smoking: **Permitted**
Suites: **$25–$30**	Social Drinking: **Permitted**

This quaint red house is set on a country lane, surrounded by nine acres of wooded land and blueberry bushes. The house was originally built as a summer retreat and has been remodeled for year-round use. The Fabians offer a second-floor suite with private entrance and separate patio for guests. The suite includes a living room, small kitchen, and a bedroom decorated with maple furnishings and ruffled curtains. Breakfast is served in the downstairs dining room and features homemade blueberry muffins and blueberry pancakes served with plenty of bacon or sausage. In summer, when the bushes are bearing luscious fruit, the grounds are perfect for hiking and picnicking. Presque Isle State Park on the shores of Lake Erie offers year-round recreational activities and is located just two miles away.

Shady Elms Farm B&B ✪
P. O. BOX 188, RD #1, HICKORY, PENNSYLVANIA 15340

Tel: **(412) 356-7755**
Host(s): **Marjorie and Connie Curran**
Location: **7 mi. from I-70**
No. of Rooms: **3**
No. of Private Baths: **1**
Max. No. Sharing Bath: **4**
Double/pb: **$40**
Single/pb: **$35**
Double/sb: **$40**
Single/sb: **$35**

Suites: **$40**
Open: **All year**
Reduced Rates: **15%, weekly**
Breakfast: **Full**
Pets: **Sometimes**
Children: **Welcome**
Smoking: **Permitted**
Social Drinking: **Permitted**
Airport/Station Pickup: **Yes**

Built in 1840, this Colonial mansion is set on 140 acres in the rolling hills of Pennsylvania farm country. Sixteen rooms, many with fireplaces, have been refurbished and decorated with floral wallpapers, dark wood antiques, and an array of brass and canopy beds, quilts, plants, pictures, and curios. Marjorie and Connie Curran serve a hearty breakfast featuring egg dishes, home-baked rolls, muffins, and coffee cake. They invite you to get up early to watch the farm activities and visit with the horses and cattle. Swimming, fishing, and ice skating can be enjoyed right on the Currans' pond. For water sports of all kinds, Cross Creek Park is just three miles away. After a busy day, the Currans invite you to share a glass of wine and perhaps an impromptu concert in the music room.

Magoffin Guest House
129 SOUTH PITT STREET, MERCER, PENNSYLVANIA 16137

Tel: **(412) 662-4611**
Host(s): **Barbara Schmid**
Location: **60 mi. N of Pittsburgh; 2 mi. from I-80, Exit 2**
No. of Rooms: **7**
No. of Private Baths: **7**
Double/pb: **$60**
Single/pb: **$50**
Suites: **$65–$75**

Open: **All year**
Reduced Rates: **Available**
Breakfast: **Continental**
Credit Cards: **AMEX, MC, VISA**
Pets: **No**
Children: **Welcome**
Smoking: **Permitted**
Social Drinking: **Permitted**

The Magoffin Guest House is an elegant Victorian dating back to the turn of the century. It is situated on a tree-lined street next to a museum and opposite one of the country's most impressive courthouses. The rooms are furnished with antiques and handcrafted items from local dealers, including some from the Old Order Amish, who live in the countryside. If you like, items in the comfortable rooms and those in the "Spareroom" gift shop may be purchased. A public swimming pool, many lakes for boating and fishing, and the Amish country are all nearby.

The Stranahan House ✪
117 EAST MARKET STREET, MERCER, PENNSYLVANIA 16137

Tel: **(412) 662-4516**
Host(s): **Jim and Ann Stranahan**
Location: **60 mi. N of Pittsburgh**
No. of Rooms: **2**
Max. No. Sharing Bath: **4**
Double/sb: **$50**
Single/sb: **$45**

Open: **All year**
Reduced Rates: **15%, weekly**
Breakfast: **Full**
Pets: **No**
Children: **Welcome**
Smoking: **No**
Social Drinking: **Permitted**

Jim and Ann welcome you to share their 150-year-old Colonial Empire decorated with local antiques and cherished family heirlooms. After a delicious breakfast of quiche Lorraine, German apple pancakes, or ham and country eggs, Ann will be pleased to arrange a tour of the area based upon your interests. It may include Indian artifacts, a pioneer display, the historical museum, observing the Old Order Amish, visiting local artisans, with a stop at the corner drugstore with its old-fashioned soda fountain. Wine and snacks are offered while you sit around the fireplace or on the back porch.

Oakwood ✪
235 JOHNSTON ROAD, PITTSBURGH, PENNSYLVANIA 15241

Tel: **(412) 835-9565**
Best Time to Call: **8 AM–8 PM**
Host(s): **Cynthia Wagar**
Location: **5 mi. from Rte. 79, Bridgeville Exit**
No. of Rooms: **2**
No. of Private Baths: **2**

Double/pb: **$45**
Open: **All year**
Breakfast: **Full**
Pets: **No**
Children: **No**
Smoking: **Permitted**
Social Drinking: **Permitted**

Tea, complete with small sandwiches and sweets, is served at 4 PM at this Colonial home set on two acres of oaks, lawns, and gardens. You are welcome to enjoy the Scandinavian spa, pool, track, exercise equipment, and raquetball facility. Breakfast often features special omelets and home-baked banana bread. It is always served on fine Limoges or Spode china, with lovely silver, and linen napery. This is a charming home furnished with fine antiques of the 18th and 19th centuries. Area attractions include the Frick Museum, Trolley Museum, Buhl Planetarium, plus Carnegie-Mellon, Duquesne, and Pittsburgh universities.

Millstone Inn ✪
BOX 279, SCHELLSBURG, PENNSYLVANIA 15559

Tel: **(814) 733-4864**
Host(s): **Mike and Patti Murphy**
Location: **10 mi. from Penn. Tpk., Exit 11**
No. of Rooms: **4**
No. of Private Baths: **2**
Max. No. Sharing Bath: **4**
Double/pb: **$65**
Single/pb: **$60**
Double/sb: **$45–$60**
Single/sb: **$40-$55**
Open: **All year**
Breakfast: **Continental**
Pets: **No**
Children: **Welcome**
Smoking: **Permitted**
Social Drinking: **Permitted**

This Georgian-style stone house has porches off the first and second floors. In the evening, guests often roast marshmallows in the outdoor fireplace. A player piano keeps everyone entertained. Breakfast features home-baked breads and pastries, and occasionally, Patti's apple dumplings. Bedford County is noted for its gorgeous mountain scenery and 15 covered bridges. The Blue Knob Ski Resort is a short drive from the inn; in summer, swimming, boating, and fishing are within easy reach.

RHODE ISLAND

• Providence

Kingston •   • Newport
                • Narragansett
Westerly •   • Green Hill

Block Island

Bed & Breakfast of Rhode Island ✪
P. O. BOX 3291, NEWPORT, RHODE ISLAND 02840

Tel: **(401) 849-1298**
Best Time to Call: **9 AM–5:30 PM**
Coordinator: **Joy Meiser**
States/Regions Covered: **Rhode Island—statewide; Massachusetts; Connecticut—Mystic**

Rates (Single/Double)
  Modest: $40–$50 $45–$55
  Average: $50–$65 $65–$75
  Luxury: $65–$80 $75–$120
Credit Cards: **MC, VISA**
Minimum stay: **3 nights, holiday weekends; 2 nights, summer weekends**

Joy will share her interest in local history with you from the time she confirms your reservation. Many B&Bs are listed on the National Register of Historic Places; some are near the shore, and several are located in or near Newport. Send $2 for a descriptive host directory or phone with details of your needs and she will place you in a comfortable lodging that suits your taste and purse. There's a surcharge for one-night stays.

Fairfield-By-The-Sea ✪
527 GREEN HILL BEACH ROAD, GREEN HILL, RHODE ISLAND 02879

Tel: **(401) 789-4717**
Best Time to Call: **6 AM–10 AM**
Host(s): **Jeanne Ayers Lewis**
Location: **15 mi. from I-95**
No. of Rooms: **2**
Max. No. Sharing Bath: **4**
Double/sb: **$60**
Single/sb: **$55**

Open: **All year**
Reduced Rates: **Oct. 12–Apr. 1**
Breakfast: **Continental**
Pets: **No**
Children: **Welcome**
Smoking: **Permitted**
Social Drinking: **Permitted**

"Stress reduction is the order of the day here," says Jeanne. She's a home economist who has taught school and worked as a consultant for *McCall's*. Her house, designed and built by her artist-husband, is a contemporary gem graced with balconies, a sunning deck, and a spiral staircase that leads to the guest rooms. The walls are a gallery of art by her talented family. Seafood feasts are sometimes organized as a cooperative venture among guests, who may try their luck at catching blue crabs or harvesting mussels in the waters nearby. It is convenient to all sorts of sporting activities, the Mystic Seaport, and the University of Rhode Island.

Hedgerow Bed & Breakfast ✪
11 MOORESFIELD ROAD (RTE. 138), P.O. BOX 1586, KINGSTON, RHODE ISLAND 02881

Tel: **(401) 783-2671**
Host(s): **Ann and Jim Ross**
Location: **11 mi. from I-95, Exit 3A**
No. of Rooms: **2**
Max. No. Sharing Bath: **4**
Double/sb: **$55**
Single/sb: **$50**

Open: **All year**
Breakfast: **Full**
Pets: **No**
Children: **Welcome (crib)**
Smoking: **Permitted**
Social Drinking: **Permitted**
Airport/Station Pickup: **Yes**

Built in 1933, this white, shingled Colonial with its Wedgewood blue shutters is just half a mile from the University of Rhode Island. The grounds are maintained in accordance with the original horticultural blueprints and include hedgerows, gardens, a fish pond, and a gazebo. The tennis court in no way distracts from the landscaping. The dining room, with its pink marble fireplace and corner cabinets housing a lovely china collection, is the setting for a bountiful breakfast. Providence, Newport, and Block Island are nearby, but be sure to return at 5 PM for the wine-and-cheese hour.

The House of Snee ⊙
191 OCEAN ROAD, NARRAGANSETT, RHODE ISLAND 02882

Tel: **(401) 783-9494**
Best Time to Call: **After 6 PM**
Host(s): **Mildred Snee**
Location: **15 mi. SW of Newport**
No. of Rooms: **3**
Max. No. Sharing Bath: **4**
Double/sb: **$45–$50**
Single/sb: **$35**

Open: **All year**
Breakfast: **Full**
Pets: **No**
Children: **Welcome, over 2**
Smoking: **Permitted**
Social Drinking: **Permitted**
Airport/Station Pickup: **Yes**

This century-old Dutch Colonial overlooks the waters of Rhode Island Sound. It's just across the street from the fishing pier where you can buy tackle and everything you need to hook a big one. It's a mile to the beach and just minutes from the Block Island ferry. Mildred's kitchen is her kingdom and her breakfast often features delicious specialties such as crêpes, egg and meat combinations, homemade scones, and plenty of freshly brewed coffee. Winery tours are a fun diversion in the area. The University of Rhode Island is nearby.

Ilverthorpe Cottage ✪
41 ROBINSON STREET, NARRAGANSETT, RHODE ISLAND 02882

Tel: **(401) 789-2392**
Best Time to Call: **Before 10 AM; after 5 PM**
Host(s): **Chris and Jill Raggio**
Location: **15 mi. SW of Newport**
No. of Rooms: **4**
No. of Private Baths: **2**
Max. No. Sharing Bath: **4**
Double/pb: **$45–$65**

Double/sb: **$40–$60**
Open: **All year**
Reduced Rates: **Weekly**
Breakfast: **Full**
Pets: **No**
Children: **Welcome**
Smoking: **Permitted**
Social Drinking: **Permitted**
Airport/Station Pickup: **Yes**

Located in the heart of the historic district, three blocks from the town's pier beach, is this charming hip-roofed Victorian built in 1896. The rooms are tastefully decorated with family antiques, providing a perfect background for relaxing. The wicker rockers on the veranda are a favorite with the guests. Fine restaurants, shops, and the summer band concerts in town are close by, and Newport's mansions, the Block Island ferry, and the fishing village of Galilee are just a short drive. Breakfast often features Belgian waffles or soufflés. Complimentary wine, coffee, and tea are offered in the evening. Two-night minimum on weekends from June through September is requested.

Ellery Park House ✪
44 FAREWELL STREET, NEWPORT, RHODE ISLAND 02840

Tel: **(401) 847-6320**
Best Time to Call: **After 5 PM**
Host(s): **Margo Waite**
Location: **25 mi. from I-95**
No. of Rooms: **2**
Max. No. Sharing Bath: **4**
Double/sb: **$50**

Single/sb: **$50**
Open: **All year**
Breakfast: **Continental**
Pets: **No**
Children: **No**
Smoking: **Permitted**
Social Drinking: **Permitted**

Enjoy European hospitality in a turn-of-the-century home, just four blocks from the waterfront. Guest rooms are small and cozy, featuring fluffy towels and lots of reading material. Fresh juice, homemade jam, muffins, freshly ground coffee, and a variety of teas are served mornings. You may like a peek at the kitchen with its restaurant stove and array of copper cookware. Margo will gladly direct you to the beach, waterfront restaurants, and historic homes.

The Melville House ✪
39 CLARKE STREET, NEWPORT, RHODE ISLAND 02840

Tel: **(401) 847-0640**
Host(s): **Rita and Sam Rogers**
Location: **35 mi. from I-95**
No. of Rooms: **7**
No. of Private Baths: **5**
Max. No. Sharing Bath: **4**
Double/pb: **$75**
Double/sb: **$65**
Open: **Mar. 1–Jan. 1**

Reduced Rates: **Available**
Breakfast: **Continental**
Credit Cards: **MC, VISA**
Pets: **No**
Children: **Welcome, over 12**
Smoking: **Permitted**
Social Drinking: **Permitted**
Minimum Stay: **2 nights**

The Melville House is a 1750s shingled home set in Newport's historic hill section. This quiet street is just one block from the Brick Market and wharfs, and around the corner from Touro Synagogue and Trinity Church. Rita and Sam welcome you to guest rooms decorated with oak furnishings, braided rugs, and lace curtains, with special touches such as fresh flowers and a bowl of fruit. Rita will start your day off with homemade muffins and granola served at polished wood tables in her sunny kitchen. When you want to relax, the country parlor with its collection of old grinders and gadgets and comfortable wing chairs awaits. Rita will be glad to provide sightseeing advice, and when the day is at a close, enjoy a 5 o'clock sherry at the house.

The Pilgrim House ✪
123 SPRING STREET, NEWPORT, RHODE ISLAND 02846

Tel: **(401) 846-0040**
Best Time to Call: **Early mornings; evenings**
Host(s): **Bruce and Pam Bayuk**
Location: **10 mi. from I-95, Exit 3**
No. of Rooms: **10**
No. of Private Baths: **8**
Max. No. Sharing Bath: **4**
Double/pb: **$95**
Double/sb: **$85**
Open: **Feb. 14–Nov. 30**
Breakfast: **Continental**
Credit Cards: **MC, VISA**
Pets: **No**
Children: **Welcome, over 14**
Smoking: **No**
Social Drinking: **Permitted**

Centrally located, Pilgrim House (circa 1872) sits on a historic hill next to Trinity Church. It is an easy walk to shops, restaurants, the wharf area, the spectacular mansions, and the beaches. In summer, the third-floor deck is often the site for breakfast, when one may enjoy gourmet coffee and fresh fruit while watching the boats in the harbor. It is served fireside in cooler months. The rooms are immaculate, decorated with period furnishings and appropriate wallpapers.

Woody Hill Guest House ⊙
RR3, BOX 676E, WOODY HILL ROAD, WESTERLY, RHODE ISLAND 02891

Tel: **(401) 322-0452**	Single/sb: **$46**
Best Time to Call: **After 5 PM, during school year**	Open: **All year**
	Reduced Rates: **Off-season**
Host(s): **Ellen L. Madison**	Breakfast: **Full**
Location: **¾ mi. from Rte. 1**	Pets: **No**
No. of Rooms: **3**	Children: **Welcome**
Max. No. Sharing Bath: **4**	Smoking: **No**
Double/sb: **$56**	Social Drinking: **Permitted**

This Colonial reproduction is set on a hilltop among informal gardens and fields. Antiques, wide-board floors, and handmade quilts create an Early American atmosphere. Your hostess serves homemade jams, muffins, and fresh raspberries in the morning. She can direct you to Mystic Seaport, Block Island, and historic areas. Watch Hill and Westerly beaches are two miles away.

For key to listings, see inside front or back cover.

⊙ This star means that rates are guaranteed through December 31, 1989 to any guest making a reservation as a result of reading about the B&B in *BED & BREAKFAST U.S.A.*—1989 edition.

Please enclose a self-addressed, stamped, business-sized envelope when contacting reservation services.

For more details on what you can expect in a B&B, see Chapter 1.

Always mention *Bed & Breakfast U.S.A.* when making reservations!

If no B&B is listed in the area you'll be visiting, use the form on page 693 to order a copy of our "List of New B&Bs."

We want to hear from you! Use the form on page 691.

SOUTH CAROLINA

Old Point Inn ☉
212 NEW STREET, BEAUFORT, SOUTH CAROLINA 29902

Tel: **(803) 524-3177**
Best Time to Call: **After 5 PM**
Host(s): **Sandra and Charlie Williams**
Location: **69 mi. S of Charleston**
No. of Rooms: **3**
No. of Private Baths: **3**
Double/pb: **$55–$60**
Single/pb: **$50**

Open: **All year**
Breakfast: **Continental**
Credit Cards: **MC, VISA**
Pets: **No**
Children: **Welcome**
Smoking: **No**
Social Drinking: **Permitted**

Located in the historic district with views of the river, this Queen Anne Victorian was built in 1898 in the Beaufort style. The rooms are furnished in antiques, reproductions, and fine Southern crafts from your hosts' gift shop. Breakfast specialties include homemade cranberry and blueberry muffins, fresh fruit, yogurt, and granola. Guests are welcome to watch the boats go by on the Intracoastal Waterway from one of two porches. A comfortable hammock also awaits those who want to put up their feet. The inn is 1½ blocks from downtown shops, the marina, and Waterfront Park. Your hosts are happy to help you discover the delights of their town, which has been the backdrop for such films as *The Big Chill* and *The Great Santini*.

The Rhett House Inn
1009 CRAVEN STREET, BEAUFORT, SOUTH CAROLINA 29902

Tel: **(803) 524-9030**
Host(s): **Steve and Marianne Harrison**
Location: **69 mi. S of Charleston**
No. of Rooms: **8**
No. of Private Baths: **8**
Double/pb: **$60–$85**
Open: **All year**

Breakfast: **Continental**
Credit Cards: **MC, VISA**
Pets: **No**
Children: **Welcome, over 12**
Smoking: **Permitted**
Social Drinking: **Permitted**

If you ever wondered what the South was like before the Civil War, come visit this inn located in the historic district. Two of the bedrooms have fireplaces; all have homespun quilts and pretty touches such as freshly cut flowers. After breakfast, stroll in the lovely gardens or take a bicycle ride around town. The restored waterfront on the Intracoastal Waterway, with its shops and restaurants, is within walking distance. If you ask, your hosts will pack a picnic lunch and direct you to the beach. Hilton Head Island is 35 miles away.

The Cedars ✪
1325 WILLISTON ROAD, P.O. BOX 117, BEECH ISLAND, SOUTH CAROLINA 29841

Tel: **(803) 827-0248**
Host(s): **Ralph and Maggie Zieger**
Location: **6 mi. E of Augusta, Ga.**
No. of Rooms: **4**
No. of Private Baths: **3**
Double/pb: **$48**
Single/pb: **$42**
Suites: **$65 and up**
Open: **All year**
Reduced Rates: **10%, weekly; 10%, seniors**

Breakfast: **Continental**
Other Meals: **Available**
Credit Cards: **MC, VISA**
Pets: **No**
Children: **Welcome, over 12**
Smoking: **Permitted**
Social Drinking: **Permitted**
Airport/Station Pickup: **Yes**
Foreign Languages: **German**

Beautifully set in 12 parklike acres, surrounded by dogwood and wisteria, this elegant manor (circa 1835) has been completely renovated. The gracious guest rooms feature queen-size poster beds, ceiling fans, fireplaces, and traditional furniture with antique accents. It is easily accessible to the Masters Golf Tournament, fine restaurants, antique shops, and Aiken, South Carolina, famed for its Thoroughbred horse farms. Maggie and Ralph will be pleased to extend their country club privileges of golf, tennis, and swimming to you. A gift shop is on the premises.

The Carriage House ✪
1413 LYTTLETON STREET, CAMDEN, SOUTH CAROLINA 29020

Tel: **(803) 432-2430**
Best Time to Call: **After 10 AM**
Host(s): **Dr. and Mrs. Robert Watkins**
Location: **30 mi. N of Columbia**
No. of Rooms: **2**
No. of Private Baths: **1½**
Double/pb: **$50**

Open: **All year**
Breakfast: **Full**
Pets: **No**
Children: **Welcome, over 6**
Smoking: **Permitted**
Social Drinking: **Permitted**

The Carriage House is an antebellum cottage with window boxes and a picket fence. Located in the center of historic Camden, it is within walking distance of tennis, parks, and shops. The guest rooms have twin or double beds and are decorated with colorful fabrics and lovely antiques. Visitors are welcomed to their quarters with complimentary sherry, fruit, and cheese. Your hosts serve a Southern-style breakfast.

Charleston East Bed & Breakfast ✪
1031 TALL PINE ROAD, MOUNT PLEASANT, SOUTH CAROLINA 29464

Tel: **(803) 884-8208**
Best Time to Call: **4 PM–9 PM**
Coordinator: **Bobbie Auld**
States/Regions Covered: **East Cooper, Sullivans Island, Isle of Palms, Mt. Pleasant, McClellanville**

Rates (Single/Double):
Modest: **$20**   **$30**
Average: **$30**   **$45**
Luxury: **$35**   **$55**

Bobbie has lovely homes a short drive from downtown historic Charleston. Several are furnished in antiques; others are contemporary. One is a restored plantation on the inland waterway. One is accessible for the handicapped. The noncommercial beaches of Sullivans Island and the Isle of Palms are close by. There is a $5 surcharge for one night's lodging March 15 through May 1.

Historic Charleston Bed & Breakfast ✪
43 LEGARE STREET, CHARLESTON, SOUTH CAROLINA 29401

Tel: **(803) 722-6606**	Rates (Single/Double):
Best Time to Call: **1–6 PM**	Modest: **$50** **$60**
Coordinator: **Charlotte Fairey**	Average: **$65** **$75**
States/Regions Covered: **Charleston, Georgia—Savannah**	Luxury: **$80** **$100**
	Credit Cards: **AMEX, MC, VISA**

This port city is one of the most historic in the U.S. Through the auspices of Charlotte, you will enjoy your stay in a private home, carriage house, or mansion in a neighborhood of enchanting walled gardens, cobblestoned streets, and moss-draped oak trees. Each home is unique, yet each has a warm and friendly atmosphere provided by a host who sincerely enjoys making guests welcome. All are historic properties dating from 1720 to 1890, yet all are up to date with air conditioning, phones, and television. Reduced rates are available for weekly stays but there is a $5 surcharge for one-night visits.

Ann Harper's Bed & Breakfast
56 SMITH STREET, CHARLESTON, SOUTH CAROLINA 29401

Tel: **(803) 723-3947**	Single/sb: **$35**
Best Time to Call: **Before 10 AM; after 6 PM**	Open: **All year**
	Breakfast: **Full**
Host(s): **Ann D. Harper**	Pets: **No**
Location: **1 mi. from I-26**	Children: **Welcome, over 10**
No. of Rooms: **2**	Smoking: **Permitted**
Max. No. Sharing Bath: **3**	Social Drinking: **Permitted**
Double/sb: **$50**	

This attractive home (circa 1870) is located in Charleston's historic district. The rooms, ideally suited for two friends traveling together, are decorated with wicker pieces and family treasures. Take a moment to relax on the porch or in the intimate walled garden out back. Ann serves a hot, Southern-style breakfast each morning featuring homemade bread and hominy grits. She will gladly direct you to the interesting sights of this historic area. There is a $5 surcharge for one night's stay; no single rates March 15–June 15.

1837 Bed & Breakfast & Tea Room ✪
126 WENTWORTH STREET, CHARLESTON, SOUTH CAROLINA 29401

Tel: **(803) 723-7166**	Host(s): **Sherri and Richard Dunn**
Best Time to Call: **10 AM–8 PM**	Location: **60 mi. from I-95**

No. of Rooms: 7
No. of Private Baths: 7
Double/pb: $39–$69
Guest Cottage: $59–$89 for 2
Open: All year
Reduced Rates: Dec.–Feb.

Breakfast: Full
Pets: No
Children: Welcome
Smoking: Permitted
Social Drinking: Permitted

Located in the center of the historic district, this circa 1800 cotton planter's home is decorated in antiques and accented with artwork by Sherri and Richard, talented artists. Breakfast often features creamed eggs on puff pastry, ham frittata, and lemon bread. Each guest room has a private entrance. Most days in Charleston are fair, so rocking chairs on the three levels of porches provide excellent places to lounge. High tea is served, and during the high season the general public is invited to sip and snack, too.

Coosaw Plantation ✪
DALE, SOUTH CAROLINA 29914

Tel: (803) 846-8225; 846-6555
Best Time to Call: After 6 PM
Host(s): Peggy Sanford
Location: 50 mi. S of Charleston; 15 mi. from I-95
Guest Cottage: $45 (for 2); $55 (for 4)

Open: Mar.–Dec.
Breakfast: Continental
Pets: Welcome
Children: Welcome
Smoking: Permitted
Social Drinking: Permitted
Foreign Languages: French, Spanish

This sprawling plantation offers a relaxed setting on the Coosaw River. The guest cottage has a living room with fireplace, a full kitchen, and a bath. Your hosts will prepare a breakfast of muffins or casseroles, or will leave the fixings for you. Boating, fishing, or a visit to Beaufort and Savannah are just a few of the local possibilities. Or, stay "home" and use the pool and tennis court on-premises.

Shaw House ✪
8 CYPRESS COURT, GEORGETOWN, SOUTH CAROLINA 29440

Tel: (803) 546-9663
Best Time to Call: Early AM
Host(s): Mary Shaw
Location: 1 block off Hwy. 17
No. of Rooms: 3
No. of Private Baths: 3
Double/pb: $40
Single/pb: $40

Open: All year
Reduced Rates: 10% after 4 nights
Breakfast: Full
Pets: No
Children: Welcome
Smoking: Permitted
Social Drinking: Permitted
Airport/Station Pickup: Yes

Shaw House is a two-story Colonial with a beautiful view of the Willowbank Marsh. Your hostess is knowledgeable about antiques and has filled the rooms with them. The rocking chairs and cool breeze will tempt you to the porch. Each morning a pot of coffee and Southern-style casserole await you. Fresh fruit and homemade snacks are available all day. The house is within walking distance of the historic district and is near Myrtle Beach, Pawleys Island, golf, tennis, and restaurants.

Ambiance Bed & Breakfast ✪
8 WREN DRIVE, HILTON HEAD ISLAND, SOUTH CAROLINA 29928

Tel: **(803) 671-4981**	Single/pb: **$50–$60**
Best Time to Call: **Evenings**	Open: **All year**
Host(s): **Marny Kridel Daubenspeck**	Breakfast: **Continental**
Location: **40 mi. from I-95, Exit 28**	Pets: **No**
No. of Rooms: **2**	Children: **Welcome, over 12**
No. of Private Baths: **2**	Smoking: **Permitted**
Double/pb: **$55–$65**	Social Drinking: **Permitted**

This contemporary cypress home is located in the area of Sea Pines Plantation. Floor-length windows afford beautiful views of the subtropical surroundings. Marny runs an interior decorating firm, so it's no surprise that everything is in excellent taste. You are welcome to use the TV, laundry facilities, pool, and nearby tennis court.

Marsh Winds
2830 RESIDENTS CLUB WEST, HILTON HEAD ISLAND, SOUTH CAROLINA 29928

Tel: **(803) 671-9188**	Reduced Rates: **Available**
Best Time to Call: **After 5:30 PM; weekends**	Breakfast: **Continental**
	Pets: **Sometimes**
Host(s): **Donna McLean**	Children: **Welcome, over 12**
No. of Rooms: **1**	Smoking: **Permitted**
No. of Private Baths: **1**	Social Drinking: **Permitted**
Double/pb: **$65–$80**	Airport/Station Pickup: **Yes**
Open: **All year**	

Watch the herons wade in serene lagoons and the spectacular sunsets over the marsh while you relax on the screened porch of this private villa. This tranquil contemporary in prestigious Sea Pines Plantation is near ocean beaches, golf, tennis, and riding. The guest wing overlooks the garden courtyard, and consists of a sitting room, tropical bedroom, and private bath. Donna McLean goes out of her way to provide special touches such as fresh flowers, a complimentary fruit basket, and the morning paper. She invites you to go swimming on the premises and can direct you to nearby shops, restaurants, art galleries, and historical sites.

Serendipity, an Inn
407 71ST AVENUE NORTH, MYRTLE BEACH, SOUTH CAROLINA 29577

Tel: **(803) 449-5268**
Best Time to Call: **8 AM–11 PM**
Host(s): **Cos and Ellen Ficarra**
Location: **60 mi. from Rte. 95**
No. of Rooms: **15**
No. of Private Baths: **15**
Double/pb: **$42–$57**
Suites: **$60–$82**

Open: **Feb.–Nov.**
Breakfast: **Continental**
Credit Cards: **AMEX, MC, VISA**
Pets: **No**
Children: **Welcome**
Smoking: **Permitted**
Social Drinking: **Permitted**
Foreign Languages: **Italian, Spanish**

Serendipity is a Spanish Mission-style inn surrounded by lush tropical plants and flowers. The setting is peaceful, the street is quiet, and the ocean is less than 300 yards away. Bedrooms are highlighted with antiques drawing from Art Deco, Oriental, wicker, and pine motifs. The Garden Room is the place for a generous breakfast of homemade breads, fresh fruit, eggs, and cereal. Guests also gather here for afternoon drinks and conversation. Your hosts invite you to use the heated pool and spa, play shuffleboard, Ping-Pong, or just share a quiet moment beside the patio fountain. Myrtle Beach is known for its fine restaurants, but the Ficarras have a gas grill if you want to do your own cooking. Cos and Ellen have bikes to lend, and they will gladly direct you to nearby shops, fishing villages, golf courses, and miles of beaches.

Gadsden Manor Inn ✪
P.O. BOX 1710, OLD POSTERN ROAD, SUMMERVILLE, SOUTH CAROLINA 29483

Tel: **(803) 875-1710**
Best Time to Call: **8 AM–6 PM**
Host(s): **Antonio and Deborah Diz**
Location: **20 mi. NW of Charleston; 2 mi. from I-26, Exit 199**
No. of Rooms: **14**
No. of Private Baths: **14**
Double/pb: **$85**

Single/pb: **$75**
Suites: **$95**
Open: **All year**
Reduced Rates: **Available**
Breakfast: **Continental**
Credit Cards: **AMEX, DC, MC, VISA**
Pets: **No**
Children: **Welcome**

Smoking: **Permitted**
Social Drinking: **Permitted**

Airport/Station Pickup: **Yes**
Foreign Languages: **Spanish**

Gadsden Manor Inn is a Georgian Revival surrounded by lush foliage and gardens. The house dates back to 1906, and is furnished with four-poster beds and claw-footed tubs. Traditions such as live parlor music, bedtime turndown service, and leisurely afternoon refreshments also recall a more elegant past. Guests are given the royal treatment here with complimentary brandy and truffles, newspaper delivery, and even shoe shines. Breakfast specialties include blueberry muffins, currant scones, and croissants. Lunch is available Monday through Fridays for $4.

SOUTH DAKOTA

South Dakota Bed and Breakfast ✪
P.O. BOX 90137, SIOUX FALLS, SOUTH DAKOTA 57105

Tel: **(605) 528-6571 or 339-0759**
Best Time to Call: **After 6 PM**
Coordinators: **Kathy Hales and Karen Olson**
States/Regions Covered: **Buffalo, Canton, Deadwood, Hill City, Mitchell, Platte, Rapid City, Salem, Sioux Falls, Volga**

Rates (Single/Double):
   Average: **$20**   **$30**
   Luxury: **$45**   **$65**
Credit Cards: **No**

From the majestic Black Hills across rolling prairie to the city and to awesome Mt. Rushmore, you will be treated to midwestern hospitality at its best. Whether traveling through the state, skiing, hunting, or on business, you will enjoy staying in a private home of one of Kathy and Karen's hosts.

Skoglund Farm ☯
CANOVA, SOUTH DAKOTA 57321

Tel: **(605) 247-3445**
Best Time to Call: **Early AM, evenings**
Host(s): **Alden and Delores Skoglund**
Location: **12 miles from I-90**
No. of Rooms: **5**
Max. No. Sharing Bath: **3**
Double/sb: **$50**
Single/sb: **$25**
Open: **All year**

Reduced Rates: **Under 18**
Breakfast: **Full**
Other Meals: **Dinner included**
Pets: **Welcome**
Children: **Welcome (crib)**
Smoking: **Permitted**
Social Drinking: **Permitted**
Airport/Station Pickup: **Yes**

This is a working farm where the emphasis is on the simple, good life. It is a welcome escape from urban living. You may, if you wish, help with the farm chores, or just watch everyone else work; the family raises cattle, fowl, and peacocks. You may ride the horses over the wide, open spaces. You are welcome to use the laundry facilities or play the piano. The coffeepot is always on.

Adams House ☯
22 VAN BUREN, DEADWOOD, SOUTH DAKOTA 57732

Tel: **(605) 578-3877**
Host(s): **Bruce and Rebecca Crosswait**
Location: **40 mi. NW of Rapid City**
No. of Rooms: **4**
No. of Private Baths: **4**
Double/pb: **$75**
Single/pb: **$70**

Open: **May 30–Oct. 15; weekends Feb. 1–Mar. 30**
Breakfast: **Continental**
Credit Cards: **MC, VISA**
Pets: **No**
Children: **Welcome, over 12**
Smoking: **No**
Social Drinking: **Permitted**

Deadwood has retained the flavor of the Old West and the gold strikes of the 1870s. Listed on the National Register of Historic Places, this 1892 Queen Anne Victorian mansion was unoccupied for more than 50 years. Periodic, careful maintenance preserved the elegant furnishings, and they are today still in their original condition. Three presidents—Taft, Teddy Roosevelt, and Coolidge—were once houseguests here. You'll awaken to the fragrance of freshly ground coffee and home-baked breads and pastries. It's a short walk to Mt. Moriah, the burial place of Wild Bill Hickock and Calamity Jane. Back "home" you are welcome to play the parlor piano or play tennis not two blocks away. Bruce, a former college professor, and Rebecca, a registered nurse, invite you to join them for afternoon tea.

Cheyenne Crossing B&B ✪
HC 37, BOX 1220, LEAD, SOUTH DAKOTA 57754

Tel: **(605) 584-3510**	Reduced Rates: **Families; groups**
Host(s): **Jim and Bonnie LeMar**	Breakfast: **Continental**
Location: **Junction Hwys. 85 and 14A**	Other Meals: **Available**
No. of Rooms: **3**	Credit Cards: **MC, VISA**
Max. No. Sharing Bath: **4**	Pets: **No**
Double/sb: **$49**	Children: **Welcome, over 6**
Single/sb: **$45**	Smoking: **No**
Open: **All year**	Social Drinking: **No**

This two-story frame building with its facade of rough-sawed pine is situated in the heart of Spearfish Canyon. The main floor houses a typical country general store and café; the guest quarters are upstairs. From 1876 to 1885 the original building was a stop for the Deadwood–Cheyenne stagecoach. After it burned down in 1960, the present building was built to replace it. Jim and Bonnie will be delighted to map out special trips tailored to your interests. Spend the day visiting Mt. Rushmore and Crazy Horse Monument, pan for gold, hike, or fish for trout on Spearfish Creek, which flows behind the store. It's also close to the Black Hills Passion Play. Sourdough pancakes are a frequent breakfast treat.

Audrie's Cranbury Corner B&B ✪
RR 8, BOX 2400, RAPID CITY, SOUTH DAKOTA 57702

Tel: **(605) 342-7788**	Open: **All year**
Host(s): **Audrie Kuhnhauser**	Breakfast: **Full**
Location: **¼ mi. from Hwy. 44**	Pets: **No**
No. of Rooms: **2**	Children: **No**
No. of Private Baths: **2**	Smoking: **No**
Double/pb: **$65**	Social Drinking: **Permitted**
Single/pb: **$60**	Airport/Station Pickup: **Yes**

Located in the beautiful Black Hills, just 30 miles from Mt. Rushmore, Audrie's country home is the epitome of Old World hospitality. The fireplaced guest rooms have private entrances, private patios, hot tubs, and are furnished with lovely antiques. She will be happy to lend you a fishing pole so you can try your hand at trout fishing at nearby Rapid Creek. Complimentary wine, assorted beverages, and tempting appetizers are offered.

Bed and Breakfast Domivara ✪
KEYSTONE ROUTE, BOX 3004, RAPID CITY, SOUTH DAKOTA 57702

Tel: **(605) 574-4207**
Best Time to Call: **Mornings; 6–8 PM**
Host(s): **Betty Blount**
Location: **26 mi. SW of Rapid City**
No. of Rooms: **2**
No. of Private Baths: **2**
Double/pb: **$65**
Single/pb: **$45**
Open: **All year**

Breakfast: **Full**
Other Meals: **Available**
Pets: **Sometimes**
Children: **Welcome**
Smoking: **Permitted**
Social Drinking: **Permitted**
Airport/Station Pickup: **Yes**
Minimum Stay: **2 nights**

Enjoy Western hospitality in a unique log home located in the picturesque Black Hills of South Dakota. The homey wood interior is decorated with comfortable antiques and accents of stained glass. A large picture window overlooks the countryside where you may see an occasional wild turkey or deer. Betty Blount offers complimentary snacks served with wine or coffee. She prepares a variety of special breakfast dishes including sourdough pancakes, egg soufflés, fresh trout, and homemade blueberry muffins. There are good restaurants nearby, or if you prefer home cooking, your hostess will be glad to prepare dinner for you. Domivara is conveniently located just 20 minutes from Mt. Rushmore and the Crazy Horse Memorial.

Willow Springs Cabin ✪
SUBURBAN ROUTE, BOX 108, RAPID CITY, SOUTH DAKOTA 57702

Tel: **(605) 342-3665**
Host(s): **Joyce and Russell Payton**
Location: **15 mi. off I-90, Exit 57**
Guest Cottage: **$50, sleeps 4**
Open: **All year**

Breakfast: **Continental**
Pets: **Sometimes**
Children: **Welcome (crib)**
Smoking: **No**
Social Drinking: **Permitted**

Willow Springs is a one-room rustic log cabin nestled in the native pines just inside the Black Hills National Forest. The cabin is cozily decorated with family pieces. Guests begin each day with freshly ground coffee, seasonal fruits, and warm-from-the-oven breads. Afterward, diversions include hiking, swimming or fishing in a private mountain stream, or just relaxing on the front porch while admiring the breathtaking view. In winter, ice skating and cross-country skiing are popular. Centrally located in the Black Hills, it's just minutes away from the Mt. Rushmore National Monument.

Lakeside Farm ✪
RR 2, BOX 52, WEBSTER, SOUTH DAKOTA 57274

Tel: **(605) 486-4430**
Host(s): **Joy and Glenn Hagen**
Location: **60 mi. E of Aberdeen on Hwy. 12**
No. of Rooms: **2**
Double/sb: **$30**
Single/sb: **$20**

Open: **All year**
Breakfast: **Full**
Pets: **No**
Children: **Welcome**
Smoking: **No**
Social Drinking: **No**

This 750-acre farm where Joy and Glenn raise oats, corn, and a herd of 50 Holstein dairy cows, is located in the Lake Region where recreational activities abound. You are certain to be comfortable in their farmhouse, built in 1970 and furnished in a simple, informal style. You will awaken to the delicious aroma of Joy's heavenly cinnamon rolls or bread and enjoy breakfast served on the enclosed porch in view of the pretty garden. Nearby attractions include Fort Sisseton and the June festival that recounts Sam Browne's historic ride. You will also enjoy the Blue Dog fish hatchery, and the Game Reserve. Dakotah, Inc., manufacturers of linens and wall hangings, is located in Webster. They have an outlet shop where great buys may be found. Don't leave till you've watched the cows being milked and had a dish of home-churned ice cream!

The Mulberry Inn
512 MULBERRY STREET, YANKTON, SOUTH DAKOTA 57078

Tel: **(605) 665-7116**
Best Time to Call: **9 AM–9 PM**
Host(s): **Lisa M. Klug**
Location: **90 mi. SW of Sioux Falls**
No. of Rooms: **5**
No. of Private Baths: **1**
Max. No. Sharing Bath: **4**
Double/pb: **$57**
Single/pb: **$50**
Double/sb: **$45**

Single/sb: **$40**
Open: **All year**
Credit Cards: **MC, VISA**
Reduced Rates: **Available**
Breakfast: **Full**
Pets: **Sometimes**
Children: **Welcome**
Smoking: **Permitted**
Social Drinking: **Permitted**
Airport/Station Pickup: **Yes**

The Mulberry Inn is an 18-room red-brick house built in 1873. It is listed on the National Register of Historic Places, a distinction it shares with many of its neighbors. Open the massive hand-carved front door and enter a setting of parquet floors, high ceilings, and marble fireplaces. Guest rooms are beautifully decorated with pastel colors, pine antiques, and Laura Ashley prints. Breakfast is served in the beautiful country kitchen beside a wood-burning fireplace. Lisa prepares gourmet coffee, lemon bread, omelets, or quiches. She also invites you for an afternoon glass of wine in one of the parlors or out on the covered porch. This lovely inn is minutes away from the Missouri River for fishing and boating, and just as close to the Lewis and Clark Lake.

For key to listings, see inside front or back cover.

✪ This star means that rates are guaranteed through December 31, 1989 to any guest making a reservation as a result of reading about the B&B in *BED & BREAKFAST U.S.A.*—1989 edition.

Please enclose a self-addressed, stamped, business-sized envelope when contacting reservation services.

For more details on what you can expect in a B&B, see Chapter 1.

Always mention *Bed & Breakfast U.S.A.* when making reservations!

If no B&B is listed in the area you'll be visiting, use the form on page 693 to order a copy of our "List of New B&Bs."

We want to hear from you! Use the form on page 691.

TENNESSEE

Bed & Breakfast Host Homes of Tennessee ✪
P.O. BOX 110227, NASHVILLE, TENNESSEE 37222

Tel: (615) 331-5244 for information;
 (800) 458-2421 for reservations
Coordinator: Fredda Odom
States/Regions Covered:
 Chattanooga, Columbia, Franklin,
 Gatlinburg, Greeneville, Knoxville,
 Memphis, Nashville, Shelbyville

Rates (Single/Double):
 Modest: $28 $38
 Average: $30 $40
 Luxury: $80–$100 $80–$120
Credit Cards: AMEX, MC, VISA

From the Great Smoky Mountains to the Mississippi, here is a diversity of attractions that includes fabulous scenery, Tennessee's Grand Ole Opry and Opryland, universities, Civil War sites, horse farms, and much more. Fredda will arrange sightseeing tours, car rentals, tickets to events, and everything she can to assure you a pleasant stay. There is a $5 booking fee; $2 for the descriptive directory.

Big Spring Inn
315 NORTH MAIN STREET, GREENEVILLE, TENNESSEE 37743

Tel: (615) 638-2917
Host(s): Jeanne Driese and Cheryl Van Dyck
Location: 70 mi. NE of Knoxville
No. of Rooms: 5

No. of Private Baths: 4
Max. No. Sharing Bath: 2
Double/pb: $60–$70
Single/pb: $55–$65
Double/sb: $50

Single/sb: **$45**
Open: **All year**
Reduced Rates: **Available**
Breakfast: **Full**
Other Meals: **Available**
Credit Cards: **AMEX, MC, VISA**

Pets: **Sometimes**
Children: **Welcome, over 12**
Smoking: **Permitted**
Social Drinking: **Permitted**
Airport/Station Pickup: **Yes**

Big Spring Inn is a three-story manor house located in Greeneville's historic district, an area that includes Davy Crockett's birthplace. The inn has a grand entrance hall, leaded and stained-glass windows, and many fireplaces. The rooms are spacious, with high ceilings, and are decorated with a comfortable mix of antiques and reproductions. The bedrooms have special touches, such as fresh flowers, snacks, baskets of toiletries, and even terry cloth robes. Jeanne and Cheryl serve homemade breads and pastries, with a variety of egg dishes for breakfast; gourmet dinners are also available. Big Spring is within an hour of Smoky Mountain National Park and the Blue Ridge Parkway.

The Graustein Inn ✪
8300 NUBBIN RIDGE ROAD, KNOXVILLE, TENNESSEE 37923

Tel: **(615) 690-7007**
Best Time to Call: **8 AM–10 PM**
Host(s): **Darlene and Jim Lara**
Location: **10 mi. W of Knoxville**
No. of Rooms: **5**
No. of Private Baths: **3**
Max. No. Sharing Bath: **4**
Double/pb: **$65–$75**
Single/pb: **$59–$69**
Double/sb: **$55–$65**
Single/sb: **$49–$59**

Suites: **$84–$90**
Open: **All year**
Breakfast: **Full**
Other Meals: **Available**
Credit Cards: **MC, VISA**
Pets: **No**
Children: **No**
Smoking: **No**
Social Drinking: **Permitted**
Airport/Station Pickup: **Yes**

Constructed of cedar and limestone and set on 20 acres, the Graustein Inn resembles a European château. Hosts Darlene and Jim Lara have furnished the guest rooms with 17th- and 18th-century antiques, highlighted by Darlene's needlepoint, homemade candy, and fresh flowers. Some rooms have private balconies, and the suite features a canopy bed, fireplace, and marble bath. Breakfast is served on the porch or in the family kitchen. Among their specialties are homemade pastry, granola, and Austrian quark. The inn has a mile-long nature trail with dogwood and wildflowers, and you might even see an owl, quail, or fox.

Mountain Breeze Bed & Breakfast
501 MOUNTAIN BREEZE LANE, KNOXVILLE, TENNESSEE 37922

Tel: **(615) 966-3917**
Best Time to Call: **9 AM–9 PM**
Host(s): **Brad and Cindy Rogers**
Location: **2½ mi. from I-40, Exit 373**
No. of Rooms: **2**
No. of Private Baths: **2**
Double/pb: **$45**

Open: **All year**
Breakfast: **Full**
Pets: **No**
Children: **Welcome, over 12**
Smoking: **Permitted**
Social Drinking: **Permitted**

This two-story brick and clapboard Cape Cod is located on a quiet cul-de-sac in a wooded country setting. It is warmly furnished with antiques and country accents, and the den has a nautical theme and stained glass. Cindy loves to cook and serves a bountiful breakfast in the cozy nook or on the deck overlooking the wooded backyard. It is 15 minutes from the University of Tennessee; 20 minutes from the Blount Mansion, White Fort, and downtown Knoxville.

Windy Hill B&B ✪
1031 WEST PARK DRIVE, KNOXVILLE, TENNESSEE 37909

Tel: **(615) 690-1488**
Host(s): **Mary M. Mitchell**
Location: **1.6 mi. from I-75-40, Exit 380**
No. of Rooms: **1**
No. of Private Baths: **1**
Double/pb: **$40**
Single/pb: **$35**

Open: **All year**
Breakfast: **Continental**
Pets: **Sometimes**
Children: **Welcome**
Smoking: **Permitted**
Social Drinking: **Permitted**
Airport/Station Pickup: **Yes**

Located in a pleasant, quiet neighborhood with numerous shade trees, Mary's B&B is air-conditioned and has a private entrance with no steps to climb. There's a double bed and a rollaway is available. Breakfast features homemade muffins or cinnamon rolls with coffee. Windy Hill is convenient to the University of Tennessee; Oakridge is only a 15-minute drive while Smoky Mountain National Park is an hour away.

Snapp Inn B&B
ROUTE 3, BOX 102, LIMESTONE, TENNESSEE 37681

Tel: **(615) 257-2482**
Best Time to Call: **Before 10 AM; after 7 PM**
Host(s): **Dan and Ruth Dorgan**
Location: **4 mi. from Rte. 11 E**
No. of Rooms: **2**
Max. No. Sharing Bath: **4**
Double/sb: **$40**

Single/sb: **$35**
Open: **All year**
Breakfast: **Continental**
Pets: **Sometimes**
Children: **Welcome (one at a time)**
Smoking: **No**
Social Drinking: **Permitted**
Airport/Station Pickup: **Yes**

Built in 1815 and situated in farm country, this Federal brick home has lovely mountain views. The house is decorated with antiques, including a Victorian reed organ. Now retired, Ruth and Dan have the time to pursue their interests in antiques restoration, history, needlework, and bluegrass music. It is an easy walk to Davy Crockett Birthplace State Park, and 15 minutes to historic Jonesboro or the Andrew Johnson Home in Greeneville. A swimming pool, golf, and fishing are close by. You are welcome to use the laundry facilities, television and pool table.

River Road Inn ✪
ROUTE 1, BOX 372, RIVER ROAD, LOUDON, TENNESSEE 37774

Tel: **(615) 458-4861**
Best Time to Call: **Before 8 PM**
Host(s): **Dave, Dan, and Kaky Smith**
Location: **30 mi. SW of Knoxville; 1½ mi. from I-75, Exit 72**
No. of Rooms: **7**
No. of Private Baths: **5**
Max. No. Sharing Bath: **3**
Double/pb: **$50**
Double/sb: **$50**

Open: **All year**
Breakfast: **Full**
Other Meals: **Available**
Credit Cards: **MC, VISA**
Pets: **Sometimes**
Children: **Welcome**
Smoking: **Permitted**
Social Drinking: **Permitted**
Airport/Station Pickup: **Yes**

Nestled in the foothills of the Smoky Mountains stands the home, built in 1857, of the late Albert Lenoir. The inn is an antebellum mansion that was the site of General Sherman's encampment during the Civil War. It is newly restored and has earned a place on the National Register of Historic Places. Bedrooms are furnished with beautiful antiques and other period pieces. Five rooms have their own fireplaces and Oriental rugs on the hardwood floors. Three of the bedrooms have private half-baths, but share two full baths. Guests are invited to unwind in the parlor or relax by the pool. You will want to take the time to have an elegant dinner here, served in the formal dining room.

Lowenstein-Long House ✪
217 NORTH WALDRAN, MEMPHIS, TENNESSEE 38105

Tel: **(901) 527-7174 or 274-0509**
Host(s): **Martha and Charles Long**
No. of Rooms: **5**
No. of Private Baths: **5**
Double/pb: **$50**
Open: **All year**
Breakfast: **Continental**
Credit Cards: **AMEX, MC, VISA**
Pets: **No**
Children: **Welcome**
Smoking: **Permitted**
Social Drinking: **Permitted**

Listed on the National Register of Historic Places, Lowenstein-Long House has been fully restored to its original grandeur. It is located half a mile from a Victorian village, and close to Mud Island, the DeSoto Bridge, and Beale Street. Elvis fans will note that the route to Graceland is nearby.

Clardy's Guest House ✪
435 EAST MAIN STREET, MURFREESBORO, TENNESSEE 37130

Tel: **(615) 893-6030**
Best Time to Call: **After 4 PM**
Host(s): **Frank Clardy and Barbara Deaton**
Location: **2 mi. from I-24**
No. of Rooms: **6**
No. of Private Baths: **4**
Max. No. Sharing Bath: **4**
Double/pb: **$30**
Single/pb: **$20–$25**
Double/sb: **$25**
Single/sb: **$17.50–$20**
Open: **All year**
Breakfast: **Continental**
Pets: **Sometimes**
Children: **Welcome (crib)**
Smoking: **Permitted**
Social Drinking: **Permitted**

This Romanesque-style Victorian dates back to 1898. The 20 rooms are filled with antiques; with 40 antiques dealers in town, you can guess what Murfreesboro is best known for. The world championship horse show at Shelbyville is 30 minutes away. Your hosts will be glad to advise on local tours and can direct you to the home of Grand Ole Opry, one hour away in Nashville, and fine eating places. Middle Tennessee State University is close by.

Miss Anne's Bed & Breakfast ✪
3033 WINDEMERE CIRCLE, NASHVILLE, TENNESSEE 37214

Tel: **(615) 885-1899**
Best Time to Call: **After 4 PM**
Host(s): **Anne and Robin Cowell**
Location: **2 mi. from I-40**
No. of Rooms: **4**
No. of Private Baths: **1**
Max. No. Sharing Bath: **4**
Double/pb: **$30**
Single/pb: **$27**
Double/sb: **$27**
Single/sb: **$24**
Open: **All year**
Breakfast: **Full**
Pets: **No**
Children: **No**
Smoking: **No**
Social Drinking: **Permitted**
Airport/Station Pickup: **Yes**

Visiting Anne and Robin is easy and pleasant in their comfortable home furnished with a cozy blend of antiques and lots of wood and glass. Anne's collection of doll dishes is quite special. Breakfast features such delectables as French toast, German pancakes, and homemade raspberry preserves. Opryland, the Hermitage, and the Parthenon are all nearby, as is Vanderbilt University.

Parish Patch Farm and Inn
625 CORTNER ROAD, NORMANDY, TENNESSEE 37360

Tel: **(615) 857-3441**
Host(s): **Bill Hall, Marty Parish Ligon, and Michael Newton**
No. of Rooms: **9**
No. of Private Baths: **7**
Max. No. Sharing Bath: **3**
Double/pb: **$65**
Double/sb: **$60–$65**
Guest Cottage: **$110, sleeps 4–6**
Suites: **$95–$100**
Open: **All year**
Breakfast: **Full**
Other Meals: **Available**
Credit Cards: **MC, VISA**
Pets: **Welcome, in kennel**
Children: **Welcome**
Smoking: **Permitted**
Social Drinking: **Permitted**

Situated on the banks of the Duck River, this 150-acre working farm is convenient to Opryland USA, the Jack Daniels and George Dickel distilleries, and the Tennessee Walking Horse Farm. There are ample opportunities for hiking, fishing, and canoeing. The inn is a board-and-batten country house surrounded by cornfields and smoky blue hills. The rooms feature warm woods, bright prints, and are centrally heated and air-conditioned. Fireplaces and a beautiful swimming pool add to the appeal in all seasons. In addition to a huge Southern breakfast including fruit, eggs, sausage or bacon, grits, biscuits and gravy, and endless cups of coffee, the public dining room features delicious Southern cuisine.

The Oaks ✪
1001 MEMORIAL DRIVE, PARIS, TENNESSEE 38242

Tel: **(901) 642-4231**
Best Time to Call: **After 4 PM**
Host(s): **Mike and Joan Mills**
Location: **100 mi. NW of Nashville**
No. of Rooms: **1**
No. of Private Baths: **1**
Double/pb: **$30**
Single/pb: **$25**

Open: **All year**
Breakfast: **Full**
Other Meals: **Available**
Pets: **No**
Children: **Welcome**
Smoking: **Permitted**
Social Drinking: **Permitted**

This immaculate brick Colonial with its inviting front porch is furnished with country antiques. Paris Landing State Park, Land Between the Lakes, and the Tennessee River are just 10 miles away, with some of the best fishing in the nation. In fact, the World's Biggest Fishfry is held here in April every year. Your hosts are retired and interested in gardening and handicrafts. Breakfast is a hearty meal of your choosing.

The Homestead House Inn ✪
P.O. BOX 76, PICKWICK DAM, TENNESSEE 38365

Tel: **(901) 689-5500**
Best Time to Call: **9 AM–9 PM**
Host(s): **Gladys Youngblood**
Location: **100 mi. E of Memphis**
No. of Rooms: **5**
No. of Private Baths: **2**
Max. No. Sharing Bath: **4**
Double/pb: **$55**
Single/pb: **$40**
Double/sb: **$50**

Single/sb: **$45**
Suites: **$90, sleeps 4**
Open: **Mar. 1–Dec. 31**
Breakfast: **Continental**
Credit Cards: **AMEX, MC, VISA**
Pets: **No**
Children: **Welcome, over 12**
Smoking: **Permitted**
Social Drinking: **Permitted**

The Homestead House Inn was built in 1843 as the Red Sulphur Springs Hotel. In its glory days, people came to soak in the sulphur springs and attend annual fox hunts. Today the house sits on 14 wooded acres and offers beautifully restored rooms decorated with antiques. Your hostess loves catering to her guests and serves a selection of Danish pastries, seasonal fruit, and the house special strawberry bread for breakfast. You are sure to enjoy the colorful past of the inn, where it is said Jesse and Frank James hid out between raids. Your hosts will do all they can to ensure you a pleasant stay and will direct you to such historic sights as Shiloh National Park and Battlefield.

Hale Springs Inn ✪
ROGERSVILLE, TENNESSEE 37857

Tel: **(615) 272-5171**
Host(s): **Stan and Kim Pace**
Location: **60 mi. NE of Knoxville**
No. of Rooms: **10**
No. of Private Baths: **10**
Double/pb: **$40**
Single/pb: **$35**
Suites: **$55**

Open: **All year**
Breakfast: **Continental**
Other Meals: **Available**
Credit Cards: **AMEX, MC, VISA**
Pets: **Sometimes**
Children: **Welcome**
Smoking: **Permitted**
Social Drinking: **Permitted**

This three-story Federal inn dates from 1824. George Washington did not sleep here, but Andrew Jackson and James Polk did. Large, high-ceilinged rooms with fireplaces, antiques, and four-poster beds continue the hosting tradition. Guests will enjoy touring the rest of the historic district. Davy Crockett's home, Lake Cherokee, and the Smoky Mountains are nearby. Rogersville is one of Tennessee's oldest towns. Candlelight dinners are served in the lovely Colonial-style dining room.

Blue Mountain Mist Country Inn
ROUTE 3, BOX 490, SEVIERVILLE, TENNESSEE 37862

Tel: **(615) 428-2335**	Open: **All year**
Best Time to Call: **10 AM–4 PM**	Breakfast: **Full**
Host(s): **Norman and Sarah Ball**	Pets: **No**
Location: **4 mi. E of Pigeon Forge**	Children: **Welcome**
No. of Rooms: **12**	Smoking: **No**
No. of Private Baths: **12**	Social Drinking: **Permitted**
Double/pb: **$65**	Minimum Stay: **2–3 nights on holiday weekends**
Suites: **$90**	

This Victorian-style inn is remote from congestion and noise, yet has easy access to Pigeon Forge, Dollywood Theme Park, factory outlets, and the crafts community. A view of rolling meadows framed by the Great Smoky Mountains can be enjoyed from rocking chairs on the huge front porch or from the backyard hot tub and patio. Country antiques, claw-foot tubs, handmade quilts and accessories, all make for a homey atmosphere. Two suites have in-room Jacuzzis. The large, fireplaced living room is the gathering spot on cool evenings. The Southern breakfast often features fresh fruit, sausages and eggs, grits and gravy, and homemade biscuits.

TEXAS

The Bed & Breakfast Society of Texas O
8880-B2, BELLAIRE BOULEVARD, #296, HOUSTON, TEXAS 77036-4900

Tel: (713) 771-3919
Best Time to Call: **9 AM–5 PM**
Coordinator: **Pat Thomas**
States/Regions Covered: Texas—
   Statewide

Rates (Single/Double):
   Modest: $25 $35
   Average: $30 $40
   Luxury: $50 $75
Credit Cards: **MC, VISA**

Whether you're traveling for business or pleasure, Pat's hosts offer the kind of friendliness and individualized care that will make your stay pleasant. The area is known for the Astrodome, Galveston Bay, NASA, and the Texas Medical Center. There are wonderful restaurants, shops, museums, and historic sights, and Baylor, Rice, and the University of Houston are nearby. Many are conveniently located urban homes, serene country houses, historic inns, waterfront cottages, and one is a 42-foot yacht.

Bed & Breakfast Texas Style ✪
4224 W. RED BIRD LANE, DALLAS, TEXAS 75237

Tel: **(214) 298-8586**
Best Time to Call: **9 AM–5 PM**
Coordinator: **Ruth Wilson**
States/Regions Covered: **Arlington, Austin, Dallas, El Paso, Fort Worth, Houston**

Rates (Single/Double):
  Modest: **$25**   **$39**
  Average: **$30**   **$45**
  Luxury: **$40**   **$70**
Credit Cards: **MC, VISA**

The above cities are only a small sample of the locations of hosts waiting to give you plenty of warm hospitality. Ruth's register includes comfortable accommodations in condos, restored Victorians, lakeside cottages, and ranches. To make your choice, please send $3 for her descriptive directory. Texas University, Southern Methodist University, Baylor University, Rice University, and Texas Christian University are convenient to many B&Bs.

Parkview House ✪
1311 SOUTH JEFFERSON, AMARILLO, TEXAS 79101

Tel: **(806) 373-9464**
Best Time to Call: **Before 10 am; after 5 PM**
Host(s): **Nabil and Carol Dia**
Location: **5/10 mi. from I-40**
No. of Rooms: **4**
No. of Private Baths: **1**
Max. No. Sharing Bath: **4**
Double/pb: **$55**
Double/sb: **$45**
Single/sb: **$40**

Suite: **$70**
Open: **All year**
Breakfast: **Continental**
Credit Cards: **MC, VISA**
Pets: **No**
Children: **No**
Smoking: **No**
Social Drinking: **Permitted**
Foreign Languages: **Arabic**
Airport/Station Pickup: **Yes**

Carol is a full-time hostess; Nabil a civil engineer. Both share interests in restoration and stained glass, which is evident in their charming Victorian located in the historic district. The guest rooms are furnished with selected antiques, lace, and luxurious linens. The large columned porch is a fine place to start the day with breakfast or to relax. Carol will lend you a bike and be glad to prepare a picnic basket to take to nearby Palo Duro Canyon State Park or Lake Meredith. West Texas State University is nearby. They enjoy having guests join them for a "social hour" before dinner.

The McCallum House ✪
613 WEST 32ND, AUSTIN, TEXAS 78705

Tel: **(512) 451-6744**
Host(s): **Roger and Nancy Danly**
Location: **2 mi. from I-35**
No. of Rooms: **3**
No. of Private Baths: **3**
Double/pb: **$50**
Single/pb: **$40**
Suites: **$50**

Open: **All year**
Reduced Rates: **10%, weekly**
Breakfast: **Full**
Credit Cards: **MC, VISA**
Pets: **No**
Children: **Welcome, over 8**
Smoking: **No**
Social Drinking: **Permitted**

This late Victorian home is just 10 blocks north of the University of Texas and 20 blocks from the capitol and downtown. Air-conditioned and furnished with antiques, the house has one guest room with a large screened-in porch with wicker furniture; the other guest rooms have kitchen facilities ideal for longer stays. Roger and Nancy will be happy to share the interesting history of their house, built by a former Texas secretary of state and her husband. Fruit cups, quiches, and muffins are breakfast delights.

Southard House ✪
908 BLANCO, AUSTIN, TEXAS 78703

Tel: **(512) 474-4731**
Host(s): **Jerry, Rejina, Kara Southard**
No. of Rooms: **5**
No. of Private Baths: **5**
Double/pb: **$45**
Single/pb: **$35**
Suites: **$100**
Open: **All year**

Reduced Rates: **15%, after 2 nights**
Breakfast: **Continental (weekdays)**
Credit Cards: **AMEX, MC, VISA**
Pets: **No**
Children: **Welcome, over 12**
Smoking: **Permitted**
Social Drinking: **Permitted**
Airport/Station Pickup: **Yes**

Conveniently located in downtown Austin, this 1900 manor house is furnished with antiques and original art. White cutwork lace coverlets are on the queen-size beds, and breakfast is served on a 19th-century English refectory table. On weekends, the breakfast is expanded to include such delicious fare as apple pancakes, eggs-and-cheese casserole, and a variety of meats and berries. Complimentary drinks and snacks are always offered. You are welcome to use their extensive library and to relax on the deck, porch, or in the gazebo.

Hudspeth House ✪
1905 4TH AVENUE, CANYON, TEXAS 79015

Tel: **(806) 655-9800**
Host(s): **Sally and David Haynie**
Location: **14 mi. S of Amarillo**
No. of Rooms: **6**
No. of Private Baths: **3**
Max. No. Sharing Bath: **4**
Double/pb: **$65–$75**
Double/sb: **$40–$45**
Suites: **$90**
Open: **All year**

Reduced Rates: **15%, Jan. 1–Apr. 30; 20%, weekly**
Breakfast: **Full**
Other Meals: **Available**
Credit Cards: **MC, VISA**
Pets: **No**
Children: **Welcome (crib)**
Smoking: **Permitted**
Social Drinking: **Permitted**
Airport/Station Pickup: **Yes**

Named for Mary E. Hudspeth, a leading Texas educator, this landmark home is rich in local history. Restored several times, the house was bought by Sally and Dave in 1987, and they have again refurbished it while retaining much of the original stained glass and chandeliers. In keeping with the elegant tone, breakfast features such delights as eggs Benedict. Sally, a former manager of the chic Zodiac Dining Room at Neiman-Marcus in Dallas, knows all about elegance with comfort. Within walking distance are Canyon Square, West Texas State University, and the Panhandle Plains Museum.

Lain's Bed and Breakfast ✪
1118 PRAIRIE STREET, COLUMBUS, TEXAS 78934

Tel: **(409) 732-8373**
Host(s): **Earnest and Dorothy Lain**
Location: **60 mi. W of Houston**
No. of Rooms: **2**
No. of Private Baths: **1**
Max. No. Sharing Bath: **4**
Double/pb: **$45**
Double/sb: **$35**
Open: **All year**

Reduced Rates: **10%, seniors**
Breakfast: **Full**
Pets: **No**
Children: **Welcome**
Smoking: **No**
Social Drinking: **Permitted**
Airport/Station Pickup: **Yes**
Foreign Languages: **Spanish**

Earnest and Dorothy Lain have a Southern-style home decorated with antiques and family pieces. The rooms are large, with high ceilings and plenty of windows. The Lains love entertaining and making new friends. Breakfast features homemade bread and jam and wraparounds, sausages in flour tortillas. Columbus has all the advantages of a small town, yet is only one hour from Houston. Guests will want to tour the historic domed courthouse and the many old, elegant homes. There are also plenty of recreational activities to be enjoyed on the Colorado River, which borders the northern and eastern parts of town.

Be My Guest ✪
125 EAST MAIN, FREDERICKSBURG, TEXAS 78624

Tel: **(512) 997-7227**
Best Time to Call: **8 AM–8 PM**
Coordinator: **Helen K. Taylor**
States/Regions Covered:
  Fredericksburg

Rates (Double):
  Modest: **$48**
  Average: **$55**
  Luxury: **$76**
Credit Cards: **MC, VISA**

Helen's hosts pride themselves on providing more than just lodging. They extend a warm "Willkommen," for many of them speak fluent German. You may choose an 1848 pioneer home in the historic district, a newly decorated Victorian close to downtown, a farmhouse backed by the Pedernales River, or a restored log cabin on 10 acres. Discounts are offered on two-night stays or longer.

Lone Star Inn ✪
ROUTE 3, BOX 1895, GEORGETOWN, TEXAS 78664

Tel: **(512) 863-7527**
Best Time to Call: **Mornings**
Host(s): **Patty Thomas and Carol Gafford**
Location: **30 mi. N of Austin**
No. of Rooms: **4**
No. of Private Baths: **2**
Max. No. Sharing Bath: **4**
Double/pb: **$68**

Double/sb: **$52**
Open: **All year**
Breakfast: **Full**
Pets: **No**
Children: **Welcome, over 12**
Smoking: **No**
Social Drinking: **Permitted**
Airport/Station Pickup: **Yes**

Surrounded by three acres of trees, the inn is located in historic Georgetown, just east of Southwestern University. It's a restored 1910 farmhouse complete with a wraparound porch and a porch swing. The extraordinary Texas breakfasts include orange muffins and ham with red-eye gravy. An outstanding collection of antiques furnishes each room, creating an ambience that preserves a time now past. The LBJ Library and Highland Lakes are nearby. Patty and Carol will be pleased to recommend good dinner spots, but be sure to save room for their complimentary evening dessert buffet.

Sara's Bed & Breakfast Inn ✪
941 HEIGHTS BOULEVARD, HOUSTON, TEXAS 77008

Tel: **(713) 868-1130**
Best Time to Call: **After 11 AM**
Host(s): **Donna and Tillman Arledge**
Location: **6 blocks from I-10**
No. of Rooms: **12**
No. of Private Baths: **3**
Max. No. Sharing Bath: **4**
Double/pb: **$50**
Double/sb: **$46–$58**

Suites: **$96 for 4**
Open: **All year**
Breakfast: **Continental**
Credit Cards: **AMEX, CB, DC, MC, VISA**
Pets: **No**
Children: **Welcome, over 10**
Smoking: **No**
Social Drinking: **Permitted**

This Queen Anne Victorian, with its turret and widow's walk, is located in Houston Heights, a neighborhood of 90 historic homes, many of which are on the National Historic Register. Each bedroom is uniquely furnished, having either single, double, queen-size or king-size beds. The Balcony Suite consists of two bedrooms, two baths, full kitchen, living area, and a fine view overlooking the deck and spa. Cool drinks or hot coffee are graciously offered in the afternoon. The sights and sounds of downtown Houston are four miles away.

Woodlake House
2100 TANGLEWILDE, #371, HOUSTON, TEXAS 77063

Tel: **(713) 972-1979**
Best Time to Call: **After 6 PM**
Host(s): **Marilynn Wrigley**
Location: **3 mi. from Hwy. 10**
No. of Rooms: **2**
No. of Private Baths: **1**
Max. No. Sharing Bath: **3**
Double/pb: **$40**
Single/pb: **$35**
Double/sb: **$35**

Single/sb: **$30**
Open: **All year**
Reduced Rates: **5% seniors**
Breakfast: **Continental**
Pets: **No**
Children: **Welcome**
Smoking: **Permitted**
Social Drinking: **Permitted**
Airport/Station Pickup: **Yes**

This charming town house, part of a condominium complex, is set in a lovely wooded area complete with a park, walking trails, tennis and racquetball courts, swimming pools, and a health club. It is beautifully furnished in lovely pastels with antique accents. A full English breakfast is offered on weekends, and includes eggs, meats, grilled mushrooms and tomatoes, and, of course, English muffins. Marilynn used to run a B&B in England, so she is an expert in such matters. The AstroDome, AstroWorld, NASA, and Galleria are within easy reach.

McKay House ✪
306 EAST DELTA, JEFFERSON, TEXAS 75657

Tel: **(214) 665-7322**
Host(s): **Peggy Taylor and Nobie West**
Location: **150 mi. E of Dallas**
No. of Rooms: **6**
No. of Private Baths: **4**
Max. No. Sharing Bath: **4**
Double/pb: **$70–$80**
Single/pb: **$65**
Double/sb: **$60**
Single/sb: **$55**
Separate Cottage: **$70**
Open: **All year**
Breakfast: **Full**
Credit Cards: **MC, VISA**
Pets: **No**
Children: **Welcome**
Smoking: **No**
Social Drinking: **Permitted**

The McKay House is listed on the National Register of Historic Places. It dates back to 1851 and is within walking distance of more than 200 homes and commercial buildings in the historic district. This Greek Revival house has 14-foot ceilings and 9-foot windows. Each room has been restored and features a fireplace and antique furnishings. Your hostess wears a long period dress when she serves breakfast. Enjoy country ham and biscuits with the sun streaming through the lace curtains of the morning room. After you've had a gentleman's breakfast, you're ready to explore the delights of this riverboat town.

Three Oaks ✪
609 NORTH WASHINGTON AVENUE, MARSHALL, TEXAS 75670

Tel: **(214) 938-6123**
Host(s): **Sandra and Bob McCoy**
Location: **30 mi. W of Shreveport, La.**
No. of Rooms: **1 suite**
No. of Private Baths: **1½**
Suites: **$65–$115 (2–4)**
Open: **All year**
Reduced Rates: **Weekdays**
Breakfast: **Full**
Pets: **No**
Children: **Welcome, over 9**
Smoking: **No**
Social Drinking: **Permitted**
Airport/Station Pickup: **Yes**

Towering oak trees shelter this lovely 1893 Victorian home, located in a National Historic District. Original leaded-glass transoms, seven hand-carved fireplaces, beamed ceilings, and polished oak floors will take you back to an earlier era. If you like, breakfast is wheeled into your bedroom on a tea cart adorned with antique linens, silver, and fine china. Your hosts invite you to browse through their vintage newspaper collection or watch a video movie. They will gladly direct you to the many interesting sights nearby.

The White House
217 MITTMAN CIRCLE, NEW BRAUNFELS, TEXAS 78130

Tel: **(512) 629-9354**
Best Time to Call: **9 AM–9 PM**
Host(s): **Beverly and Jerry White**
Location: **25 mi. N of San Antonio**
No. of Rooms: **3**
Max. No. Sharing Bath: **4**
Double/sb: **$30–$35**
Single/sb: **$25–$30**

Open: **All year**
Breakfast: **Full**
Other Meals: **Available**
Pets: **Sometimes**
Children: **Welcome (crib)**
Smoking: **No**
Social Drinking: **Permitted**
Airport/Station Pickup: **Yes**

This Spanish-style white-brick ranch home is nestled among the cedar and oaks in the Texas hill country. Guests are welcomed here with tea and pastries and shown to comfortable rooms with antique iron beds and cozy quilts. A large fishing pond is located on the premises, and a few miles away you may enjoy a refreshing tube or raft ride down the Guadalupe River. Your hosts have giant inner tubes to lend. In the fall, visitors flock to the New Braunfels famous Wurstfest, the largest held outside Germany. Other attractions include the Alamo, the River Walk, and the many old missions located in nearby San Antonio.

Bed & Breakfast Hosts of San Antonio ✪
166 ROCKHILL, SAN ANTONIO, TEXAS 78209

Tel: **(512) 824-8036**
Best Time to Call: **9 AM–5 PM**
Coordinator: **Lavern Campbell**
States/Regions Covered: **San Antonio**

Rates (Single/Double):
Modest: **$29** $42.50
Average: **$40.50** $59
Luxury: **$51.70** $85
Credit Cards: **MC, VISA**

You'll find hospitable hosts waiting to welcome you and to suggest how best to enjoy this beautiful and historic city. Don't miss the Paseo del Rio (a bustling river walk), the Alamo, the Arneson River Theatre showplace, El Mercado (which is a restored Mexican and Farmers Market), the Southwest Craft Center, wonderful restaurants, marvelous shops, and delightful, friendly folks. The University of Texas,

Trinity University, and St. Mary's University are nearby. There is a booking fee of $7.50 per person; the descriptive directory is free.

The Belle of Monte Vista
505 BELKNAP PLACE, SAN ANTONIO, TEXAS 78212

Tel: **(512) 732-4006**
Host(s): **Mary Lou and Jim Davis**
Location: **1 mi. from San Antonio**
No. of Rooms: **5**
No. of Private Baths: **1**
Max. No. Sharing Bath: **4**
Double/pb: **$50**
Single/pb: **$40**
Double/sb: **$50**

Single/sb: **$40**
Open: **All year**
Breakfast: **Full**
Pets: **No**
Children: **Welcome**
Smoking: **No**
Social Drinking: **Permitted**
Airport/Station Pickup: **Yes**

J. Riely Gordon designed this Queen Anne Victorian as a model house for a local developer. Built in 1890 with limestone that was quarried less than half a mile away, the house has been beautifully restored and is located in the elegant Monte Vista historic district. Inside, you'll find eight fireplaces, stained-glass windows, a hand-carved oak staircase, and Victorian furnishings. Mary Lou and Jim serve a Southern breakfast with homemade muffins and jellies each morning. They are happy to help you plan your day and will direct you to nearby attractions such as Alamo Plaza, the River Walk, and El Mercado Market Place.

Cardinal Cliff ✪
3806 HIGHCLIFF, SAN ANTONIO, TEXAS 78218

Tel: **(512) 655-2939**
Host(s): **Roger and Alice Sackett**
No. of Rooms: **3**
Max. No. Sharing Bath: **4**
Double/sb: **$30**
Single/sb: **$23**

Open: **All year**
Breakfast: **Full**
Pets: **No**
Children: **Welcome (crib)**
Smoking: **No**
Social Drinking: **Permitted**

Roger and Alice offer warm hospitality in their comfortable home in a quiet residential area. It overlooks a wooded river valley that is home to a variety of birds. Homemade bread and preserves are a breakfast feature, served on the porch overlooking the valley, weather permitting. The downtown attractions of historic San Antonio, with its delightful mix of the old and new, are only 20 minutes away.

International House ☉
4910 NEWCOME DRIVE, SAN ANTONIO, TEXAS 78229

Tel: **(512) 647-3547**
Best Time to Call: **7 PM–9 PM**
Host(s): **Virginia Y. Wong**
No. of Rooms: **2**
No. of Private Baths: **2**
Double/pb: **$45**
Single/pb: **$30**
Open: **All year**

Reduced Rates: **10%, seniors**
Breakfast: **Continental**
Other Meals: **Available**
Pets: **No**
Children: **No**
Smoking: **Permitted**
Social Drinking: **Permitted**
Airport/Station Pickup: **Yes**

Here is your chance to experience both Eastern and Western Cultures in the south of Texas. This split-level home is beautifully decorated with Oriental art and furniture. Your hostess, a global education consultant, welcomes you to her eclectic home with Chinese tea and cookies. She offers a choice of Continental or Oriental-style breakfast in the morning. Dinners are prepared on request, featuring Oriental, Mexican, or downhome Texas cooking. Ginny is a native of this exciting city and will gladly make suggestions to enhance your visit. The Alamo, Paseo del Rio, South Texas Medical Center, and Convention Center are all nearby.

Rosevine Inn ☉
415 SOUTH VINE AVENUE, TYLER, TEXAS 75702

Tel: **(214) 592-2221**
Host(s): **Bert and Rebecca Powell**
Location: **10 mi. from I-20**
No. of Rooms: **5**
No. of Private Baths: **5**
Double/pb: **$55–$65**
Open: **All year**

Breakfast: **Full**
Pets: **No**
Children: **Welcome, over 12**
Smoking: **No**
Social Drinking: **Permitted**
Airport/Station Pickup: **Yes**

Dr. Irwin Pope, Jr., made his home here on a quaint brick street back in the 1930s. Years later a devastating fire burned all but the foundation and beautiful grounds. Your hosts bought the property in 1986 and built the Rosevine Inn, a Federal-style red-brick home. They have furnished the house with antiques and country collectibles. In the morning, wake-up coffee is provided in the central hallway. When you come downstairs, hot muffins, baked breads, fresh fruit, and quiches are served. Your hosts will help you discover the charms of Tyler, known as the "Rose Capital of the World." Antique shops are nearby, and the Rosevine makes an excellent base for discovering the many parks and lakes in the area. After a busy day, return to the inn, where you can sip a hot chocolate by the fire or relax in a quiet courtyard.

Bellsen Bed & Breakfast ✪
401 N. CRAIG, VICTORIA, TEXAS 77901

Tel: **(512) 573-4980**	Reduced Rates: **10%, seniors**
Best Time to Call: **Evenings**	Breakfast: **Continental**
Host(s): **Lynette and Amy Dugat**	Pets: **No**
Location: **125 mi. SW of Houston**	Children: **Welcome, over 12**
No. of Rooms: **1 suite**	Smoking: **No**
No. of Private Baths: **1**	Social Drinking: **Permitted**
Suites: **$35–$45**	Airport/Station Pickup: **Yes**
Open: **All year**	

Built nearly 90 years ago, this two-story white Victorian home with dark green shutters is located in a beautiful, tree-shaded neighborhood in the old section of the city. The guest suite is furnished with family treasures and antiques. The suite leads onto a large private wraparound porch with antique rockers, perfect for relaxing among the treetops. You are also welcome to swim in the pool or to enjoy the player piano. Victoria has several festivals throughout the year, as well as a variety of cultural choices.

UTAH

Bed 'n' Breakfast Homestay of Utah ✪
P.O. BOX 355, SALT LAKE CITY, UTAH 84110-0355

Tel: **(801) 532-7076**
Best Time to Call: **9 AM–5 PM**
Coordinators: **Barbara Baker, Nadine Smith**
States/Regions Covered: **Statewide**

Rates (Single/Double):
  Average: **$35–$50**   **$45–$65**
  Luxury: **$55 and up**   **$65–$125**
Credit Cards: **No**
Minimum Stay: **2 nights in Salt Lake City**

Utah has something for everyone, and Barbara and Nadine have a roster of hosts who delight in making you feel at home. A full breakfast is included with most of the accommodations. Location and season are taken into consideration in the rate, and discounts are offered to families, and for extended stays. Brigham Young University, University of Utah, Southern Utah State College (site of the Utah Shakespeare Festival in summer) are near many B&Bs.

Bed and Breakfast Rocky Mountains—Utah ✪
P.O. BOX 804, COLORADO SPRINGS, COLORADO 80901

Tel: (719) 630-3433
Best Time to Call: 9 AM–5 PM, May–
   Sept.; in winter, 12–5 PM
Coordinator: Kate Peterson Winters
States/Regions Covered: Statewide

Rates (Single/Double):
  Modest: $25 $35
  Average: $30 $45
  Luxury: $65 $95–$140
Credit Cards: MC, VISA

Don't miss Salt Lake City and the Mormon Tabernacle, especially the Sunday morning Free Mormon Tabernacle Choir Broadcast. The B&Bs range from a modest inn to an elegant mansion. In winter, ski Park City, Alta, Snowbird, Brighton, or Solitude! Reservations for any other cities or areas are two-night minimum. There is a $4.50 charge for Kate's directory.

Bluff Bed and Breakfast ✪
BOX 158, BLUFF, UTAH 84512

Tel: (801) 672-2220
Host(s): Rosalie Goldman
Location: On Rtes. 163 and 191
No. of Rooms: 2
No. of Private Baths: 2
Double/pb: $50
Single/pb: $45
Open: All year
Reduced Rates: 10%, after 3 nights

Breakfast: Full
Other Meals: Available
Pets: Sometimes
Children: Welcome
Smoking: No
Social Drinking: Permitted
Airport/Station Pickup: Yes
Foreign Languages: Dutch, French

Close to the Four Corners (the junction of Colorado, New Mexico, Arizona, and Utah), this air-conditioned Frank Lloyd Wright–style home is nestled among huge boulders at the foot of redrock cliffs. On the main highway between Grand Canyon and Mesa Verde, it is secluded in its 17 desert acres. Bluff is next door to the Navaho Reservation, and prehistoric ruins have been discovered by archaeologists on Rosalie's property. Simply furnished, it is bright, clean, and tidy. Large picture windows frame four different spectacular views. The nearby San Juan is a favorite run with wild-river buffs.

Center Street Bed and Breakfast Inn ✪
169 EAST CENTER STREET, LOGAN, UTAH 84321

Tel: (801) 752-3443
Best Time to Call: 8 AM–10 PM

Host(s): Clyne and Ann Long
Location: 84 mi. N of Salt Lake City

No. of Rooms: **10**
No. of Private Baths: **8**
Max. No. Sharing Bath: **4**
Double/pb: **$25–$35**
Single/pb: **$20**
Double/sb: **$20–$25**
Suites: **$50–$70**

Open: **All year**
Breakfast: **Continental**
Pets: **No**
Children: **Welcome, over 12**
Smoking: **No**
Social Drinking: **Permitted**

Relax in a spacious Victorian in the center of Logan's historic district. Nineteenth-century charm fills the house, and each room offers something special. The Blue Room has a king-size, four-poster canopy bed and large bathroom with antique fixtures. The Garden Suite has a canopied water bed, marble Jacuzzi, and a crystal chandelier hanging from a vaulted ceiling. Your hosts will gladly direct you to a nearby Mormon temple, the ski slopes, and Utah State University.

Peterson's Bed and Breakfast
95 NORTH 300 WEST, MONROE, UTAH 84754

Tel: **(801) 527-4830**
Host(s): **Mary Ann Peterson**
Location: **8 mi. SW of Richfield**
No. of Rooms: **3**
No. of Private Baths: **2**
Double/pb: **$35**
Single/pb: **$25**
Suite: **$35**

Open: **Mar.–Nov.**
Reduced Rates: **5%, families**
Breakfast: **Full**
Other Meals: **Available**
Pets: **No**
Children: **Welcome**
Smoking: **No**
Social Drinking: **No**

Halfway between Los Angeles and Denver, this immaculate farmhouse, casual and comfortable, is surrounded by 10,000-foot mountains in the heart of hunting and fishing country. Mary Ann has written a marvelous cookbook called *Country Cooking*, containing rural Mormon recipes. Hot Springs is seven blocks away. It's a 2½-hour drive to Provo, Salt Lake City, or St. George. A swimming pool, tennis, golf, and historic sites are nearby.

The Pullman Bed and Breakfast ✪
415 SOUTH UNIVERSITY AVENUE, PROVO, UTAH 84601

Tel: **(801) 374-8141**
Best Time to Call: **After 8 AM**
Host(s): **The Morganson Family**
Location: **1 mi. from I-15**
No. of Rooms: **6**
No. of Private Baths: **4**

Max. No. Sharing Bath: **4**
Double/pb: **$47.50–$49.50**
Single/pb: **$40–$42**
Double/sb: **$35.50–$39.50**
Single/sb: **$28–$32**
Open: **All year**

Reduced Rates: **10%, families; 3 nights or more**
Breakfast: **Full**
Other Meals: **Available**
Credit Cards: **AMEX, MC, VISA**

Pets: **No**
Children: **Welcome**
Smoking: **No**
Social Drinking: **Permitted**

The Pullman is a magnificent Victorian built in 1898 by a railroad magnate. It has been beautifully restored and is listed on the National Register of Historic Places. The house has an old-fashioned character with its winding staircase, handcarved woodwork, stained glass, and wide porch. In the guest rooms you'll find a hand-stitched quilt on the bed, and a tray of hand-dipped chocolates on the bed table. In the morning, enjoy homemade breads, jams, and fluffy omelets in the sunny dining room. The house is within walking distance of the sights of Provo, including the historic town square. Your hosts also specialize in luncheons, receptions, and meetings.

Seven Wives Inn ✪
217 NORTH 100 WEST, ST. GEORGE, UTAH 84770

Tel: **(801) 628-3737**
Best Time to Call: **After 9 AM**
Host(s): **Jay and Donna Curtis and Alison and Jon Bowcutt**
Location: **125 mi. NE of Las Vegas**
No. of Rooms: **9**
No. of Private Baths: **9**
Double/pb: **$25–$65**

Open: **All year**
Breakfast: **Full**
Credit Cards: **MC, VISA**
Pets: **Welcome**
Children: **Welcome (crib)**
Smoking: **No**
Social Drinking: **Permitted**
Airport/Station Pickup: **Yes**

This delightful inn is featured on the walking tour of St. George; it is just across from the Brigham Young home and two blocks from the historic Washington County Court House. Your hosts offer traditional Western hospitality. Their home is decorated with antiques collected in America and Europe. Each bedroom is named after one of the seven wives of Donna's polygamous great-grandfather. A gourmet breakfast is served in the elegant dining room that will give you a hint of the past. St. George is located near Zion and Bryce National Parks, boasts six golf courses, and is noted for its mild winters. Dixie College is nearby. There's a swimming pool and hot tub for your pleasure.

Anton Boxrud House ✪
57 SOUTH 600 EAST, SALT LAKE CITY, UTAH, 84102

Tel: **(801) 531-8575**
Best Time to Call: **9 AM–9 PM**
Host(s): **Joy and Tom Stechschulte**
Location: **5 blocks from downtown**
No. of Rooms: **4**
No. of Private Baths: **2**
Max. No. Sharing Bath: **4**
Double/pb: **$55**
Single/pb: **$45**
Double/sb: **$50**

Single/sb: **$40**
Open: **All year**
Reduced Rates: **10% weekly, families**
Breakfast: **Full**
Credit Cards: **MC, VISA**
Pets: **No**
Children: **Welcome (crib)**
Smoking: **Permitted**
Social Drinking: **Permitted**
Airport/Station Pickup: **Yes**

Located in the downtown historic district, the Anton Boxrud House is one of Salt Lake City's grand old homes. The beveled-glass windows and beautiful woodwork have been carefully restored according to the original 1899 plans. Rooms are furnished with antiques, including a handcarved German dining room table where breakfast is served. Guests are invited to meet one another at 5 o'clock, when wine and cheese are served to the tunes of the old player piano. This Victorian inn is close to the governor's mansion, Temple Square, and two major shopping malls. Tom and Joy can guide you to the sights and can arrange to have a horse-drawn carriage take you on a tour.

The National Historic Bed & Breakfast ✪
936 EAST 1700 SOUTH, SALT LAKE CITY, UTAH 84105

Tel: **(801) 485-3535**
Best Time to Call: **7 AM–11 PM**
Host(s): **Katie and Mike Bartholome**
Location: **6 blocks from I-80**

No. of Rooms: **5**
No. of Private Baths: **3**
Max. No. Sharing Bath: **4**
Double/pb: **$67**

Single/pb: **$57**
Double/sb: **$47**
Single/sb: **$47**
Suites: **$77**
Open: **All year**
Reduced Rates: **Weekly**

Breakfast: **Full**
Credit Cards: **AMEX, MC, VISA**
Pets: **No**
Children: **Welcome, over 3**
Smoking: **No**
Social Drinking: **Permitted**

The ornate facade of this house combines brick, wood, and stained glass to achieve its handsome Victorian style. Located in the historic Sugarhouse section, its 19th-century pieces meld attractively with Art Deco and contemporary furnishings. The pretty floral designs created by Katie enhance the decor. Mike is justifiably proud of their antique radios, a Victrola, and a jukebox. Conveniently located, it's just 2 blocks from Westminster College, 5 minutes to the Mormon Temple and downtown, and only 20 minutes away from the famed ski slopes of Snowbird, Alta, and Solitude.

Quail Hills Country Guesthouse ✪
3744 E. NORTH LITTLE COTTONWOOD ROAD, SANDY, UTAH 84092

Tel: **(801) 942-2858**
Host(s): **Jean Smith**
Location: **15 mi. SE of Salt Lake City**
No. of Rooms: **3**
No. of Private Baths: **1**
Max. No. Sharing Bath: **4**
Double/pb: **$52**
Single/pb: **$48**
Double/sb: **$45**

Single/sb: **$40**
Open: **All year**
Reduced Rates: **20%, seniors**
Breakfast: **Continental**
Pets: **No**
Children: **Welcome, over 12**
Smoking: **No**
Social Drinking: **Permitted**
Airport/Station Pickup: **Yes**

Located on five acres of secluded land at the mouth of Little Cottonwood Canyon, this guest house offers year-round enjoyment. In winter, the "greatest snow on earth" is just ten minutes away at Alta and Snowbird. Summer brings relaxing days at the pool and spa surrounded by the beautiful Wasatch Mountains. Choose from a spacious bedroom with a king-size brass bed, lilac floral quilt, and traditional furnishings, or from two rooms with double beds, Laura Ashley–style country quilts, and coordinated curtains. Fresh seasonal fruit and assorted muffins and breads are served at a glass dining room table overlooking the yard. Later, Jean invites you for a glass of wine beside the living room fire.

Under the Eaves Guest House ✪
P.O. BOX 29, 980 ZION PARK BOULEVARD, SPRINGDALE, UTAH 84767

Tel: **(801) 772-3457**
Host(s): **Kathleen Brown and John O'Shea**
Location: **45 mi. E of St. George**
No. of Rooms: **3**
No. of Private Baths: **2**
Max. No. Sharing Bath: **4**
Double/pb: **$65**
Single/pb: **$55**
Double/sb: **$45**
Single/sb: **$35**
Suites: **$65**
Open: **All year**
Reduced Rates: **Available**
Breakfast: **Full**
Other Meals: **Available**
Credit Cards: **MC, VISA**
Pets: **Sometimes**
Children: **Welcome**
Smoking: **No**
Social Drinking: **Permitted**

Under the Eaves is a historic stone-and-stucco cottage located at the gate of Zion National Park. Constructed of massive sandstone blocks from the canyon, the guest house has served as a landmark for visitors to Zion for more than 50 years. Choose from two antique-filled bedrooms or a luxurious suite. Your hosts provide turndown service at night.

VERMONT

Locations shown on map: North Troy, North Hero, West Charleston, Jericho, East Burke, Craftsbury Common, Waterbury, Stowe, Plainfield, Warren, Barre, Middlebury, Brookfield, Chelsea, Bethel, South Strafford, Gaysville, Cuttingsville, Rutland, Reading, Danby, Belmont, Dorset, Weston, Manchester, Chester, Manchester Center, Townshend, West Dover, East Dorset

Woodruff House ✪
13 EAST STREET, BARRE, VERMONT 05641

Tel: **(802) 476-7745**
Best Time to Call: **Evenings**
Host(s): **Robert and Terry Somaini**
Location: **60 mi. S of Montreal**
No. of Rooms: **2**
Max. No. Sharing Bath: **4**
Double/sb: **$55**
Single/sb: **$45**

Reduced Rates: **Weekly**
Open: **All year**
Breakfast: **Full**
Pets: **No**
Children: **Welcome**
Smoking: **No**
Social Drinking: **No**

Woodruff House is located in a quiet park in the heart of town. Guest rooms are furnished in antiques and decorated with flair. Guests are welcome to relax in the two living rooms and use the TV and piano. Breakfast specialties include homemade breads and eggs prepared with Vermont cheddar. Your host will point the way to the state capital, five ski areas, museums, and some of the greatest fall foliage in the state.

The Parmenter House ✪
BOX 106, BELMONT, VERMONT 05730

Tel: **(802) 259-2009**	Open: **May 27–Apr. 3**
Best Time to Call: **8–10 AM; evenings**	Reduced Rates: **Available**
Host(s): **Lester and Cynthia Firschein**	Breakfast: **Continental**
Location: **25 mi. SE of Rutland; 2 mi. from Rte. 155**	Credit Cards: **MC, VISA**
	Pets: **No**
No. of Rooms: **5**	Children: **Welcome, over 7**
No. of Private Baths: **5**	Smoking: **No**
Double/pb: **$65–$90**	Social Drinking: **Permitted**
Single/pb: **$55**	Airport/Station Pickup: **Yes**

You are certain to benefit from the clear mountain air of this idyllic lakeside village. In summer, swim or canoe on Star Lake by day, stargaze from the large deck by night. Explore a country lane on a crisp autumn morning or rent an all-terrain bike for an excursion. In winter, follow cross-country skiing with mulled cider by the wood stove. Cynthia and Lester invite you to relax in the serene atmosphere of their parlor. Retire to your bedroom furnished with Victorian antiques, handmade quilts, and herbal wreaths. The bountiful breakfast buffet of fruit, local cheeses, homemade granola, and freshly baked breads is a gastronomic treat.

Greenhurst Inn
RIVER STREET, BETHEL, VERMONT 05032

Tel: **(802) 234-9474**	Single/sb: **$30–$35**
Host(s): **Lyle and Barbara Wolf**	Open: **All year**
Location: **30 mi. E of Rutland**	Breakfast: **Continental**
No. of Rooms: **13**	Credit Cards: **MC, VISA**
No. of Private Baths: **7**	Pets: **Welcome (no cats)**
Max. No. Sharing Bath: **5**	Children: **Welcome (crib)**
Double/pb: **$60–$80**	Smoking: **Permitted**
Single/pb: **$50–$70**	Social Drinking: **Permitted**
Double/sb: **$40–$45**	

Located 100 yards from the White River, this elegant Queen Anne mansion is listed on the National Register of Historic Places. Built in 1890, the heavy brass hinges, embossed floral brass doorknobs, and etched windows at the entry have withstood the test of time. The cut-crystal collection is magnificent, and the stereoscope and old Victrola add to the old-fashioned atmosphere. It's close to many points of historic interest, and seasonal recreational activities are abundant. There's tennis and croquet on the premises. Vermont Law School is close by.

Poplar Manor ✪
RD 2, ROUTES 12 & 107, BETHEL, VERMONT 05032

Tel: **(802) 234-5426**
Host(s): **Carmen and Bob Jaynes**
Location: **16 mi. N of Woodstock**
No. of Rooms: **4**
Max. No. Sharing Bath: **4**
Double/sb: **$31**
Single/sb: **$23**
Suites: **$33**

Open: **All year**
Reduced Rates: **10%, weekly**
Breakfast: **Continental**
Pets: **Sometimes**
Children: **Welcome**
Smoking: **Permitted**
Social Drinking: **Permitted**
Foreign Languages: **Spanish**

This early 19th-century Colonial is surrounded by green meadows and cornfields. The rooms are large and bright, with exposed-beam ceilings, collectibles, and plants. Your hosts offer wine and mulled cider, served "spiked," if you wish. The fields back up to the White River and a swimming hole. Other area attractions include the National Fish Hatchery, Silver Lake, seasonal sports and the shops of Woodstock. Vermont Law School is nearby. There's a two-night minimum stay during foliage and holiday weekends.

Green Trails Country Inn
POND VILLAGE, BROOKFIELD, VERMONT 05036

Tel: **(802) 276-3412**
Host(s): **Peter and Pat Simpson**
Location: **8 mi. from I-89, Exit 4**
No. of Rooms: **15**
No. of Private Baths: **9**
Max. No. Sharing Bath: **4**
Double/pb: **$68.50**
Single/pb: **$49.50**
Double/sb: **$61**
Single/sb: **$44.50**

Open: **May–Mar.**
Reduced Rates: **Groups**
Breakfast: **Full**
Other Meals: **Available**
Pets: **No**
Children: **Welcome (crib)**
Smoking: **No**
Social Drinking: **Permitted**
Airport/Station Pickup: **Yes**

The inn consists of two buildings. One is an 1840 farmhouse; the other was built in the late 1700s and has pumpkin pine floorboards. They are located across from the famous Floating Bridge and Sunset Lake. Furnished in antiques and "early nostalgia," the rooms have stenciling (circa 1800), handmade quilts, and fresh flowers. The historic village is a perfect base for seasonal excursions to the Shelburne Museum or

Woodstock. Cross-country skiers can start at the doorstep, while downhill enthusiasts can try Sugarbush and Killington.

Shire Inn ✪
MAIN STREET, CHELSEA, VERMONT 05038

Tel: **(802) 685-3031**	Breakfast: **Full**
Host(s): **James and Mary Lee Papa**	Other Meals: **Available**
Location: **20 mi. from I-87**	Credit Cards: **MC, VISA**
No. of Rooms: **6**	Pets: **No**
No. of Private Baths: **6**	Children: **Welcome, over 6**
Double/pb: **$65–$95**	Smoking: **No**
Open: **All year**	Social Drinking: **Permitted**

In 1832 a successful Chelsea businessman built this stately home entirely of Vermont brick. The Federal-style house was made to last, from the unusually high ceilings above to the pine floors below, now carefully restored and gleaming under coats of varnish. Enter through the granite front archway and step into the parlor, where a crackling fire and a warm welcome awaits. Jim and Mary are transplanted New York professionals who have left the city life for a white picket fence and a river flowing out back. They invite you to antique-filled bedrooms, several with fireplaces, and modern baths with fluffy, oversized towels and English soaps. A typical Shire breakfast features German pancakes served with apricot sauce. Home cooking can also be enjoyed in the evening, when a six-course meal is served in the dining room. The inn is set on 17 acres in a quiet country village that is said to have the state's oldest general store.

Stone Hearth Inn ✪
ROUTE 11, CHESTER, VERMONT 05143

Tel: **(802) 875-2525**	Reduced Rates: **Available**
Host(s): **Janet and Don Strohmeyer**	Breakfast: **Full**
Location: **10 mi. from I-91, Exit 6**	Pets: **Sometimes**
No. of Rooms: **10**	Children: **Welcome (crib)**
No. of Private Baths: **8**	Smoking: **Permitted**
Max. No. Sharing Bath: **4**	Social Drinking: **Licensed pub**
Double/pb: **$56–$80**	Airport/Station Pickup: **Yes**
Single/pb: **$36–$60**	Foreign Languages: **Dutch, French, German**
Double/sb: **$48–$70**	
Open: **All year**	

This white 19th-century Colonial is set on seven acres of fields and wooded land. The rooms have been lovingly restored and feature wide-board pine floors and open beams, floral wallpapers, antiques, quilts, and a player piano. A fire-warmed living room and library are available. After a busy day, relax in the licensed pub and recreation room, or enjoy the whirlpool spa. Horseback riding, downhill and cross-country skiing, and swimming in the river across the road are but a handful of the local pleasures. Your hosts offer fresh-baked breads, pancakes, and French toast for breakfast. The dining room is open to the public for lunch and dinner.

Craftsbury Bed & Breakfast on Wylie Hill ✪
CRAFTSBURY COMMON, VERMONT 05827

Tel: **(802) 586-2206**
Best Time to Call: **Morning or evening**
Host(s): **Margaret Ramsdell**
Location: **40 mi. N of Montpelier**
No. of Rooms: **4**
Max. No. Sharing Bath: **4**
Double/sb: **$45–$55**
Single/sb: **$30–$40**

Open: **All year**
Breakfast: **Full**
Other Meals: **Available**
Pets: **No**
Children: **Welcome (crib)**
Smoking: **No**
Social Drinking: **Permitted**
Foreign Languages: **French**

This 1860 Georgian hilltop farmhouse has beautiful views. The homey guest rooms adjoin the living room with its wood stove, where you are welcome to relax and visit. You may use Margaret's kitchen, barbecue, and picnic table should the crisp mountain air stoke your appetite. You're sure to enjoy the bountiful breakfast that often features apple pancakes with fresh maple syrup. Other meals are served only by prior arrangement. The ski slopes of Stowe are 30 miles away, and lakes and rivers are within a two-mile radius. Cross-country skiing starts at the door.

Buckmaster Inn ✪
LINCOLN HILL ROAD, CUTTINGSVILLE, VERMONT 05738

Tel: **(802) 492-3485**
Best Time to Call: **8 AM–8 PM**
Host(s): **Sam and Grace Husselman**
Location: **8 mi. SE of Rutland**
No. of Rooms: **4**
No. of Private Baths: **1**
Max. No. Sharing Bath: **4**
Double/pb: **$50–$65**
Single/pb: **$50–$65**
Double/sb: **$40–$50**

Single/sb: **$35–$50**
Open: **All year**
Reduced Rates: **Weekly**
Breakfast: **Full**
Pets: **No**
Children: **Welcome, over 8**
Smoking: **No**
Social Drinking: **Permitted**
Airport/Station Pickup: **Yes**
Foreign Languages: **Dutch**

The Buckmaster Inn, located near Cuttingsville in the Green Mountains, is a Federal clapboard Colonial overlooking a picturesque valley. Its center hall, grand staircase, and wide pine floors are typical of 19th-century style. This is New England relaxation at its best: fireplaces, wood-burning stove, library, and two porches. Homemade muffins, casseroles, and jams are among the specialties served in the country kitchen each morning. A pond for skating and fishing is within walking distance, and ski slopes, hiking trails, and craft shops are nearby.

The Quail's Nest Bed and Breakfast O
P.O. BOX 221, MAIN STREET, DANBY, VERMONT 05739

Tel: **(802) 293-5099**
Host(s): **Chip and Anharad Edson**
Location: **13 mi. N of Manchester**
No. of Rooms: **5**
No. of Private Baths: **1**
Max. No. Sharing Bath: **4**
Double/pb: **$50–$55**
Single/pb: **$40–$45**
Double/sb: **$45–$50**

Single/sb: **$35–$40**
Open: **All year**
Breakfast: **Full**
Credit Cards: **MC, VISA**
Pets: **No**
Children: **Welcome, over 10**
Smoking: **Permitted**
Social Drinking: **Permitted**

The Quail's Nest is a Federal-style inn circa 1835. The guest rooms are furnished with antiques and handmade country quilts. Your hostess loves entertaining and offers such homemade breakfast specialties as apple-puff pancakes, muffins, and quiches. Danby is a quiet village close to five major ski areas. The Green Mountains are just east of here, offering some of the finest swimming, fishing, hiking, and downhill and cross-country skiing in the state.

The Little Lodge at Dorset O
ROUTE 30, BOX 673, DORSET, VERMONT 05251

Tel: **(802) 867-4040**
Host(s): **Allan and Nancy Norris**
Location: **6 mi. N of Manchester**
No. of Rooms: **5**
No. of Private Baths: **5**
Double/pb: **$80–$95**
Single/pb: **$70–$85**

Open: **All year**
Breakfast: **Continental**
Credit Cards: **AMEX**
Pets: **No**
Children: **Welcome (crib)**
Smoking: **Permitted**
Social Drinking: **Permitted**

Situated in one of the prettiest little towns in Vermont, this delightful 1820 Colonial house, on the Historic Register, is perched on a hillside overlooking the mountains and its own trout pond that's used for skating in winter or canoeing in summer. The original paneling and wide floorboards set off the splendid antiques. After skiing at nearby Stratton or Bromley, toast your feet by the fireplace while sipping hot chocolate. If you prefer, bring your own liquor, and Nancy and Allan will provide Vermont cheese and crackers.

Maplewood Colonial House ✪
BOX 1019, ROUTE 30, DORSET, VERMONT 05251

Tel: **(802) 867-4470**	Double/sb: **$60**
Best Time to Call: **After 5 PM**	Single/sb: **$50**
Host(s): **Marge and Leon Edgerton**	Open: **All year**
No. of Rooms: **5**	Breakfast: **Continental**
No. of Private Baths: **3**	Pets: **Sometimes**
Max. No. Sharing Bath: **4**	Children: **Welcome**
Double/pb: **$70**	Smoking: **No**
Single/pb: **$55**	Social Drinking: **Permitted**

This large, 20-room white Colonial with green shutters is in a lovely setting. The five corner bedrooms are airy, comfortably furnished with antiques; the dining table is pre-Civil War vintage. You are welcome to wander the acreage, canoe on the pond, bicycle, or browse in Marge and Leon's library. In winter, skiing at Bromley or Stratton is convenient. The fall foliage is fabulous. Credit cards may be used to secure a reservation. A three-night minimum is required on holiday weekends.

The Kiln Guest House
BENEDICT ROAD, EAST DORSET, VERMONT 05253

Tel: **(802) 362-4889**	Open: **All year**
Host(s): **Dennis and Catherine Conroy**	Breakfast: **Full**
Location: **4.5 mi. N of Manchester**	Pets: **Sometimes**
No. of Rooms: **4**	Children: **Welcome**
Max. No. Sharing Bath: **4**	Smoking: **No**
Double/sb: **$43**	Social Drinking: **Permitted**
Single/sb: **$22**	

Dennis and Catherine invite you to share their contemporary wood-paneled home where you are welcome to relax on the deck or in front of the wood stove, depending upon the season. There's a pond and a stream for fishing, and it is located close to Emerald Lake State Park. It is 15 minutes from the slopes at Bromley; 30 minutes to Stratton. The coffeepot is always on, and pretzels and chips are complimentary.

Cobble House Inn ◐
P.O. BOX 49, GAYSVILLE, VERMONT 05746

Tel: **(802) 234-5458**	Open: **All year**
Best Time to Call: **8 AM–9 PM**	Breakfast: **Full**
Host(s): **Philip and Beau Benson**	Other Meals: **Available**
Location: **Off Rte. 107**	Credit Cards: **MC, VISA**
No. of Rooms: **6**	Pets: **No**
No. of Private Baths: **6**	Children: **Welcome, over 5**
Double/pb: **$84.70–$97**	Smoking: **No**
Single/pb: **$72.60–$84**	Social Drinking: **Permitted**

A grand 1860s mansion awaits you on a hilltop overlooking the beautiful Green Mountains. Each guest room is decorated with antiques and accented with country furnishings. Ornate carved beds, colorful quilts, and flannel sheets are sure to offer a peaceful night's rest. Breakfast specialties such as French apple pancakes, homemade coffee cakes, peach fritters, or eggs Benedict are served each morning. Just outside the door is the White River, with its clear waters for fishing, canoeing, tubing, and swimming. Skiing, golf, tennis, and horseback riding are all within easy reach. In the evening, the inn offers Italian and French cuisine served in the country dining room.

Milliken's ◐
R.D. 2, BOX 397, JERICHO, VERMONT 05465

Tel: **(802) 899-3993**	Suites: **$57**
Best Time to Call: **Mornings; evenings**	Open: **All Year**
Host(s): **Rick and Jean Milliken**	Breakfast: **Full**
Location: **12 mi. E of Burlington**	Pets: **No**
No. of Rooms: **3**	Children: **Welcome**
Max. No. Sharing Bath: **4**	Smoking: **No**
Double/sb: **$37**	Social Drinking: **Permitted**
Single/sb: **$25**	Airport/Station Pickup: **Yes**

This Second Empire early Victorian was built in 1867 by a lumber magnate. The house has a graceful mansard roof, original woodwork, and floors of alternating cherry and white maple. The spaciousness of the rooms is enhanced by high ceilings, large windows, and gracious decor. Rick is a hotel manager and Jean is a choreographer and hostess. She prepares such breakfast specialties as French toast with maple syrup and hot mulled cider. In the evening, a good-night brandy and snack is offered. Your family is sure to enjoy its stay with the Millikens, their two children, and a friendly dog named Bailey. Nearby attractions are hiking trails on Mt. Mansfield, skiing, and fabulous fall foliage.

Brook 'n' Hearth
STATE ROAD 11/30, BOX 508, MANCHESTER CENTER, VERMONT 05255

Tel: (802) 362-3604	Open: **June 1–Oct. 28; Nov. 24–Apr. 30**
Best Time to Call: **2 PM–10 PM**	Reduced Rates: **Available**
Host(s): **Larry and Terry Greene**	Breakfast: **Full**
Location: **1 mi. E of US 7**	Credit Cards: **AMEX, MC, VISA**
No. of Rooms: **3**	Pets: **No**
No. of Private Baths: **3**	Children: **Welcome (crib)**
Max. No. Sharing Bath: **4**	Smoking: **Permitted**
Double/pb: **$60**	Social Drinking: **Permitted**
Single/pb: **$40**	
Suites: **$70 for 2**	

True to its name, a brook runs through the property and a fire warms the living room of this country home. Terry and Larry offer setups and happy-hour snacks for your self-supplied cocktails. You're within five miles of the ski slopes at Bromley and Stratton; it is also convenient to art centers, summer theater, restaurants, and a score of sports that include hiking on the Long Trail. In summer, enjoy the heated pool, lawn games, and barbecue. The game room, with its VCR, pocket billiards, and Ping-Pong, is always available.

Brookside Meadows ✪
RD 3, BOX 2460, MIDDLEBURY, VERMONT 05753-8751

Tel: (802) 388-6429	Open: **All year**
Location: **2½ mi. from Rte. 7**	Breakfast: **Full**
Host(s): **Linda and Roger Cole**	Pets: **No**
No. of Rooms: **4**	Children: **Welcome, over 5**
No. of Private Baths: **4**	Smoking: **Permitted**
Double/pb: **$55–$65**	Social Drinking: **Permitted**
Suites: **$85–$125**	Airport/Station Pickup: **Yes**

This attractive farmhouse was built in 1979, based on a 19th-century design. The house is on a country road, on 20 acres of meadowland. The property borders on a brook. It is also home to geese and two dogs. The two-bedroom suite has a wood stove in the living room as well as a private entrance. Relax on cedar lawn chairs and enjoy a view of the Green Mountains. Area attractions include excellent downhill and cross-country skiing, hiking, maple syrup operations, Middlebury College, and the University of Vermont Morgan Horse Farm. Two-night stays are required at peak times.

Charlie's Northland Lodge ✪
BOX 88, NORTH HERO, VERMONT 05474

Tel: **(802) 372-8822**
Best Time to Call: **Before 8 PM**
Host(s): **Charles and Dorice Clark**
Location: **60 mi. S of Montreal, Canada**
No. of Rooms: **3**
Max. No. Sharing Bath: **5**
Double/sb: **$40**
Single/sb: **$38**

Guest Cottage: **$425 weekly; sleeps 6**
Open: **All year**
Reduced Rates: **Sept. 2–Oct. 15**
Breakfast: **Continental**
Pets: **No**
Children: **Welcome, over 5**
Smoking: **Permitted**
Social Drinking: **Permitted**

The lodge is a restored Colonial (circa 1850) located on Lake Champlain, where bass and walleye abound. A sport and tackle shop is on the premises. Fall and winter fishing should appeal to all anglers. In summer, tennis, hiking, or relaxing in the reading room are pleasant activities.

Rose Apple Acres Farm ✪
RFD 1, BOX 300, EAST HILL ROAD, NORTH TROY, VERMONT 05859

Tel: **(802) 988-4300**
Best Time to Call: **Evenings**
Host(s): **Jay and Camilla Mead**
Location: **60 mi. N of St. Johnsbury**
No. of Rooms: **3**
No. of Private Baths: **1**
Max. No. Sharing Bath: **4**
Double/pb: **$44**
Double/sb: **$36**

Single/sb: **$24**
Open: **All year**
Breakfast: **Full**
Pets: **No**
Children: **Welcome, over 6**
Smoking: **No**
Social Drinking: **Permitted**
Airport/Station Pickup: **Yes**

Located two miles from the Canadian border and 2 hours from Montreal or Burlington, the farm is situated on 52 acres of fields, woods, and streams. The farmhouse has a bright and friendly atmosphere, enhanced by panoramic mountain views. Hiking, cross-country skiing, snowshoeing, and horseback riding may be enjoyed on-premises. It is only 10 miles to Jay Peak for skiing. Camilla and Jay are interested in classical music, gardening, and horses.

Yankees' Northview Bed & Breakfast ✪
R.D. #2, PLAINFIELD, VERMONT 05667

Tel: **(802) 454-7191**
Best Time to Call: **Evenings**

Host(s): **Joani and Glenn Yankee**
Location: **9 mi. NE of Montpelier**

No. of Rooms: **3**
Max. No. Sharing Bath: **6**
Double/sb: **$35**
Single/sb: **$30–$35**
Open: **All year**
Reduced Rates: **Available**

Breakfast: **Full**
Pets: **Sometimes**
Children: **Welcome**
Smoking: **No**
Social Drinking: **Permitted**

Although it has a Plainfield mailing address, this roomy Colonial is located on a quiet country lane in the picturesque town of Calais. The house is surrounded by stone walls and white fences. Fresh flowers and after-dinner mints are just a few of the special touches you will find in your antique-filled bedroom. A delightful breakfast is served on the garden patio overlooking the mountains and the meadows. In cold weather, specialties such as homemade Swedish coffee ring, French toast, pancakes, and eggs are offered in the stenciled dining room or beside the pot-belly stove in the country kitchen. Your hosts invite you to relax with a cup of coffee by the fire, or stroll down to the unique quaking bog, just a five-minute walk from the house. Yankees' Northview is minutes from swimming, boating, horseback riding, and historic Kent's Corner.

The Peeping Cow Bed & Breakfast
P.O. BOX 47, ROUTE 106, READING, VERMONT 05062

Tel: **(802) 484-5036**
Best Time to Call: **7:30–9:45 AM; 5:30–7 PM**
Host(s): **Nancy and Frank Lynch**
Location: **14 mi. from I-91, Exit 9**
No. of Rooms: **2**
No. of Private Baths: **1**
Max. No. Sharing Bath: **4**
Double/pb: **$50**
Double/sb: **$40**

Single/sb: **$20**
Open: **All year**
Breakfast: **Continental**
Pets: **No**
Children: **Welcome, over 16**
Smoking: **No**
Social Drinking: **Permitted**
Airport/Station Pickup: **Yes**
Foreign Languages: **French, Spanish**
Minimum Stay: **2 nights during fall foliage**

The "peeping bovines" are 50 Jerseys in the meadows surrounding Nancy and Frank's circa-1800 white farmhouse. It is attractively furnished with fine English antiques and family heirlooms. Outdoor mountain recreation abounds in all seasons. Mt. Ascutney is five minutes away, convenient to many downhill ski areas, and cross-country skiing starts outside the door. Fishing, horseback riding, tennis, golf, bicycling, swimming, fun summer festivals, hot-air ballooning, steamboat rides on Lake Sunapee are just a few things to do. Dartmouth College is a short drive. There's a two-night minimum during fall foliage.

Hillcrest Guest House ⊙
RR 1, BOX 4459, RUTLAND, VERMONT 05701

Tel: **(802) 775-1670**	Open: **All year**
Host(s): **Bob and Peg Dombro**	Breakfast: **Continental**
Location: **³⁄₁₀ mi. from Rte. 7**	Pets: **No**
No. of Rooms: **3**	Children: **Welcome (crib)**
Max. No. Sharing Bath: **5**	Smoking: **No**
Double/sb: **$35**	Social Drinking: **Permitted**
Single/sb: **$25**	Airport/Station Pickup: **Yes**

This 150-year-old farmhouse, with a comfortable screened porch for warm-weather relaxing, is furnished with country antiques. Pico and Killington ski areas are 7 and 16 miles away. Summer brings the opportunity to explore charming villages, covered bridges, and antiques and craft centers. Country auctions, marble quarries, trout streams, and Sunday-evening band concerts are pleasant pastimes. Bob and Peg always offer something in the way of between-meal refreshments.

Watercourse Way ⊙
ROUTE 132, SOUTH STRAFFORD, VERMONT 05070

Tel: **(802) 765-4314**	Open: **All year**
Host(s): **Lincoln and Anna Alden**	Breakfast: **Full**
Location: **10 mi. from I-91**	Pets: **Sometimes**
No. of Rooms: **3**	Children: **Welcome**
Max. No. Sharing Bath: **3**	Smoking: **Permitted**
Double/sb: **$50**	Social Drinking: **Permitted**
Single/sb: **$25**	

Watercourse Way is situated on the Ompompanoosuc River, surrounded by towering evergreens and fragrant herb gardens. It is an 1850 farmhouse cape with wide pine floors and original Shaker-style doors. Guests will find all the small touches to make them feel at home, such as fresh flowers, cozy quilts, braided rugs, and interesting pictures on the walls. There's a place for everyone beside the giant fieldstone fireplace, and plenty of books to borrow. Freshly ground gourmet coffee and herbal teas from the garden are part of a large country breakfast. Specialties include home-baked muffins, jellies and jams, and French toast or pancakes with fresh local syrup. Skiing, biking, museums, and Lake Fairlee are nearby, and fishing, kayaking, and wading can be enjoyed a few steps from the front door. Dartmouth College in Hanover, New Hampshire, is close by.

Bittersweet Inn
RR #2, BOX 2900, ROUTE 100, STOWE, VERMONT 05672

Tel: **(802) 253-7787**
Best Time to Call: **7 AM–11 PM**
Host(s): **Barbara and Paul Hansel**
Location: **36 mi. W of Burlington**
No. of Rooms: **8**
No. of Private Baths: **5**
Max. No. Sharing Bath: **2**
Double/pb: **$55**
Double/sb: **$51**
Suites: **$112**

Open: **All year**
Reduced Rates: **5-day stays**
Breakfast: **Continental**
Credit Cards: **AMEX, MC, VISA**
Pets: **Yes, small ones**
Children: **Welcome (play area)**
Smoking: **Permitted**
Social Drinking: **Permitted**
Airport/Station Pickup: **Yes**
Foreign Languages: **German**

Bittersweet Inn is a brick cape with converted clapboard carriage house, dating back to 1835. The house is set on nine and a half acres, overlooking Camel's Hump Mountain. Inside you'll find comfortable rooms decorated with a combination of antiques and family pieces. It's just a half mile to the center of town and minutes to ski lifts and a cross-country touring center. A good-sized swimming pool is located out back with plenty of room for laps or just taking it easy. In the winter season, hot soup will be waiting after your last ski run. Your hosts, Barbara and Paul, invite you to relax in the game room with BYOB bar and will help you plan your evening.

Ski Inn ✪
ROUTE 108, STOWE, VERMONT 05672

Tel: **(802) 253-4050**
Best Time to Call: **9–11 AM; evenings**
Host(s): **Larry and Harriet Heyer**
Location: **47 mi. NE of Burlington**
No. of Rooms: **10**
No. of Private Baths: **5**
Max. No. Sharing Bath: **5**
Double/pb: **$35–$80**
Double/sb: **$27.50–$60**

Single/sb: **$25–$45**
Open: **All year**
Reduced Rates: **Off-season**
Breakfast: **Continental**
Other Meals: **Included in winter**
Pets: **Sometimes**
Children: **Welcome**
Smoking: **Permitted**
Social Drinking: **Permitted**

This traditional New England inn, set back from the highway among evergreens on a gentle sloping hillside, is a quiet place to relax and sleep soundly. In winter, it's a skier's delight, close to Mt. Mansfield's downhill and cross-country trails. A full breakfast and delicious dinner are included in winter rates of $45 to $80. In summer, the rates drop and include just Continental breakfast. Larry and Harriet offer warm hospitality in all seasons.

Boardman House ✪
P.O. BOX 112, TOWNSHEND, VERMONT 05353

Tel: (802) 365-4086
Host(s): **Sara Messenger and Paul Weber**
Location: **125 mi. NW of Boston**
No. of Rooms: **5**
No. of Private Baths: **5**
Double/pb: **$75**
Single/pb: **$65**
Open: **All year**

Reduced Rates: **10%, Nov. & Apr.; 15%, weekly; 10%, seniors**
Breakfast: **Full**
Pets: **Welcome**
Children: **No**
Smoking: **Permitted**
Social Drinking: **Permitted**
Airport/Station Pickup: **Yes**
Foreign Languages: **Sign Language**

The Boardman House is a white clapboard farmhouse set on the village green. The house has a large lawn, lovely gardens, and is next door to one of the most photographed churches in Vermont. Choose from queen or twin beds in bright airy rooms with white walls, brass fixtures, and colorful quilts. The breakfast room has natural pine tables and wooden chairs painted Colonial blue. Here guests enjoy homemade muffins, fruit compotes, and individual cheese soufflés. The inn is minutes from prime foliage areas, antique shops, and is at the crossroads of the state's southern and central ski areas. Your hosts have 39 years of experience in Vermont and can assist in planning daytrips and cross-country and downhill skiing lessons.

South Hollow Farm ✪
RR#1, BOX 287, WARREN, VERMONT 05674

Tel: (802) 496-5627
Best Time to Call: **Early AM; evenings**
Host(s): **Pat and Bob Dockendorf**
Location: **25 mi. SW of Montpelier**
No. of Rooms: **4**
No. of Private Baths: **2**
Max. No. Sharing Bath: **4**
Double/pb: **$55–$65**
Single/pb: **$45–$55**
Double/sb: **$50**
Single/sb: **$45**

Open: **All year**
Reduced Rates: **10%, seniors; $5 less, Apr. 1–June 15, Oct. 15–Dec. 15**
Breakfast: **Full**
Credit Cards: **MC, VISA**
Pets: **No**
Children: **Welcome, over 6**
Smoking: **No**
Social Drinking: **Permitted**
Minimum Stay: **2 nights, Dec. 16–Mar. 31**

Built in 1837, South Hollow has been completely restored. Furnished with many antiques, it offers a comfortable and homey atmosphere. The hearty breakfast often includes homemade breads, jams, blueberry pancakes, or French toast with Vermont maple syrup. It is less than three miles to the slopes of Sugarbush for winter skiing and not far to the Mad River for summer swimming and fishing. Covered bridges, quaint villages, hiking, antiquing, or just sitting and gazing at the spectacular views are enough to make this a very special spot. A Robert Trent Jones golf course and glider rides are nearby attractions.

Inn at Blush Hill House ✪
BOX 1266, BLUSH HILL ROAD, WATERBURY, VERMONT 05676

Tel: **(802) 244-7529**
Host(s): **Gary and Pam Gosselin**
Location: **22 mi. E. of Burlington**
No. of Rooms: **6**
No. of Private Baths: **4**
Max. No. Sharing Bath: **4**
Double/pb: **$65**
Double/sb: **$55**
Open: **All year**

Reduced Rates: **Available**
Breakfast: **Full**
Credit Cards: **MC, VISA**
Pets: **Sometimes**
Children: **Welcome**
Smoking: **Permitted**
Social Drinking: **Permitted**
Airport/Station Pickup: **Yes**

This 170-year-old brick farmhouse is located halfway between the Stowe and Sugarbush ski areas. The atmosphere is warm and homey, with antiques, old-time rockers, books, and lots of fireplaces. Your hostess is a gourmet cook and enjoys making her own bread and muffins each morning. Cheese, crackers, and setups are offered in the evening to go along with cocktails. A huge lake with boating, swimming, and fishing is located just one and a half miles from the house, and a nine-hole golf course is located directly across the street. At the end of the day, sit back and enjoy the surroundings, relaxing on the large, old-fashioned porch.

Hunt's Hideaway ✪
RR1, BOX 570, MORGAN, WEST CHARLESTON, VERMONT 05872

Tel: **(802) 895-4432 or 334-8322**
Best Time to Call: **7 AM–11 PM**
Host(s): **Pat Hunt**
Location: **6 mi. from I-91**
No. of Rooms: **3**
Max. No. Sharing Bath: **4**
Double/sb: **$30**
Single/sb: **$20**

Open: **All year**
Reduced Rates: **Available**
Breakfast: **Full**
Pets: **Sometimes**
Children: **Welcome**
Smoking: **Permitted**
Social Drinking: **Permitted**

This modern, split-level home is located on 100 acres of woods and fields, with a brook, pond, and large swimming pool. Pancakes with Vermont maple syrup are featured at breakfast. Ski Jay Peak and Burke, or fish and boat on Lake Seymour, two miles away. Visiting antique shops or taking a trip to nearby Canada are other local possibilities.

The Weathervane ✪
DORR FITCH ROAD, BOX 57, WEST DOVER, VERMONT 05356

Tel: **(802) 464-5426**
Host(s): **Liz and Ernie Chabot**
Location: **1 mi. from Rte. 100**
No. of Rooms: **10**
No. of Private Baths: **2**
Max. No. Sharing Bath: **5**
Double/pb: **$64–$72**
Double/sb: **$42–$56**
Single/sb: **$39–$42**

Suites: **$88**
Open: **All year**
Reduced Rates: **Ski weeks; off-season**
Breakfast: **Full**
Pets: **No**
Children: **Welcome (crib)**
Smoking: **Permitted**
Social Drinking: **Permitted**

Only four miles from Haystack, Mount Snow, and Corinthia, this Tyrolean-style ski lodge is decorated with authentic antiques and Colonial charm. The lounge and recreation room have fireplaces and a bring-your-own bar. Winter rates include cross-country ski equipment, sleds, and snowshoes, so that you may explore the lovely marked trails. Summer brings lakeshore swimming, boating, fishing, tennis, riding, museums, and the Marlboro Music Festival.

VIRGINIA

Bed & Breakfast of Tidewater Virginia ○
P.O. BOX 3343, NORFOLK, VIRGINIA 23514

Tel: **(804) 627-1983 or 627-9409**
Coordinators: **Ashby Willcox and Susan Hubbard**
States/Regions Covered: **Chesapeake, Chincoteague, Eastern Shore of Virginia, Norfolk, Northern Neck, Virginia Beach**

Rates (Single/Double):
Modest:	$30	$35
Average:	$35	$45
Luxury:	$55	$75

Credit Cards: **No**

The world's largest naval base is in Norfolk, as are the famed Chrysler Museum and MacArthur Memorial. It is also a cultural hub in which top-rated opera, symphony, and stage productions abound. There are miles of scenic beaches to explore on Chesapeake Bay and the Atlantic Ocean. Old Dominion University, Eastern Virginia Medical School, and Virginia Wesleyan College are conveniently located.

Blue Ridge Bed & Breakfast ✪
ROUTE 2, ROCKS & RILLS, BOX 3895, BERRYVILLE, VIRGINIA 22611

Tel: (703) 955-2410
Best Time to Call: 9 AM–2 PM
Coordinator: **Rita Z. Duncan**
States/Regions Covered: **Virginia—Amissville, Berryville, Flint Hill, Hamilton, Luray, Winchester; West Virginia—Charlestown, Middleway**

Rates (Double):
 Modest: $40
 Average: $50
 Luxury: $135
Credit Cards: **MC, VISA**

Rita's hosts are within 50 to 200 miles of the Capitol, perfect for those wishing to visit rural areas near Washington, D.C. The variety includes houses on the Historic Register, mountain retreats, quaint inns, and traditional private homes in small towns. This beautiful area is known for its part in American history, horses, and farming.

Shenandoah Valley Bed & Breakfast Reservations ✪
P.O. BOX 634, WOODSTOCK, VIRGINIA 22664

Tel: (703) 459-8241
Best Time to Call: 9 AM–9 PM
Coordinators: **Patricia Lee Kollar**
States/Regions Covered: **I-81, Exit 66; Amissville, Front Royal, Harrisonburg, Maurertown, McGaheysville, Rawley Springs, Woodstock**

Rates (Single/Double):
 Modest: $40 $45
 Average: $50 $55
 Luxury: $60 $125
Credit Cards: **MC, VISA (for deposit only)**

Since the 1700s, travelers have raved about the magnificent scenery of the Shenandoah Valley. Patricia has a roster of historic homes, farmhouses, and contemporary residences that share the rolling hills between the Alleghenies and Blue Ridge Mountains. The valley is alive with artists, theater, heritage days, fairs, golf courses, ski resorts, and colleges. You are bound to be warmly welcomed and advised on the best restaurants and activities by an interested host. Please send $1 for the descriptive directory.

Summerfield Inn ✪
101 WEST VALLEY STREET, ABINGDON, VIRGINIA 24210

Tel: (703) 628-5905
Best Time to Call: **Mornings; after 3 PM**
Host(s): **Champe and Don Hyatt**

Location: **15 mi. NE of Bristol**
No. of Rooms: **4**
No. of Private Baths: **4**
Double/pb: **$60**

Single/pb: **$50**
Suites: **$100**
Open: **Apr. 1–Nov. 1**
Reduced Rates: **15%, 3-night stays; off-season**
Breakfast: **Continental**

Credit Cards: **MC, VISA**
Pets: **No**
Children: **Welcome, over 12**
Smoking: **Permitted**
Social Drinking: **Permitted**
Airport/Station Pickup: **Yes**

A large covered porch with comfortable rockers graces the front and side of this meticulously restored Victorian residence. Guests are welcome to share the large living room, handsomely appointed morning room, and a sunroom. Your hosts will gladly pack picnic lunches for trips to the mountain trails or for a fishing trip to one of the nearby lakes or rivers. A guests' pantry is also available for preparing light snacks. Summerfield Inn is a short walk from Barter Theatre, Old Abingdon, and fine dining. Set at 2,300 feet and surrounded by mountains, this was one of the first communities formed in western Virginia.

The Old Mansion ✪
BOX 845, BOWLING GREEN, VIRGINIA 22427

Tel: **(804) 633-5781**
Host(s): **Peter Larson**
Location: **40 mi. N of Richmond**
No. of Rooms: **3**
Max. No. Sharing Bath: **2**
Single/sb: **$55**
Suites: **$75 (family of 4)**

Open: **All year**
Reduced Rates: **Available**
Breakfast: **Full**
Pets: **Sometimes**
Children: **Welcome (crib)**
Smoking: **No**
Social Drinking: **Permitted**

The Old Mansion was built in 1669 by Thomas Hoomes. Although George Washington never slept inside the house, the general and his troops did camp on the grounds on their way to Yorktown in 1781. Today, guests play croquet on the same grassy lawn surrounded by 126 acres of ancient cedars, boxwood, and gardens. Inside, every room is furnished with antiques of all kinds, some as old as the house. Breakfast specialties include fresh eggs, country sausages, and homemade breads and pastries. Your host will gladly direct you to such attractions as Stratford Hall, Washington's Birthplace, Fredericksburg Historic District, and much more.

Nottingham Ridge
P.O. BOX 97-B, CAPE CHARLES, VIRGINIA 23310

Tel: **(804) 331-1010**
Best Time to Call: **Evenings**
Host(s): **Bonnie Nottingham**
Location: **20 mi. N of Norfolk**
No. of Rooms: **3**
No. of Private Baths: **1**
Max. No. Sharing Bath: **4**
Double/pb: **$60**
Double/sb: **$60**

Single/sb: **$50**
Open: **All year**
Breakfast: **Full**
Other Meals: **Available**
Pets: **No**
Children: **Welcome, over 10**
Smoking: **Permitted**
Social Drinking: **Permitted**
Airport/Station Pickup: **Available**

Nottingham Ridge is a picturesque country retreat high atop the sand dunes of Virginia's eastern shore. Guests can spend hours on a private beach, or charter a fishing boat for the day. Bonnie offers comfortable rooms furnished with antiques and reproductions. She loves entertaining and offers homemade biscuits, Virginia ham, and quiche for breakfast. Later in the day, enjoy wine, cheese, and a breathtaking view of the sun setting over the water. This lovely home is just three and a half miles north of the Chesapeake Bay Bridge Tunnel, and 25 minutes from the Norfolk and Virginia Beach areas. Bonnie will gladly direct you to historic sights, the Nature Conservancy, and the U.S. Fish and Wildlife Refuge.

Picketts Harbor
CAPE CHARLES, VIRGINIA 23310

Tel: **(804) 331-2212**
Best Time to Call: **After 5 PM**
Host(s): **Sara and Cooke Goffigon**
Location: **21 mi. N of Norfolk**
No. of Rooms: **6**
Max. No. Sharing Bath: **4**
Double/sb: **$50**
Single/sb: **$40**

Open: **All year**
Breakfast: **Full**
Other Meals: **Available**
Pets: **No**
Children: **Welcome**
Smoking: **No**
Social Drinking: **Permitted**
Airport/Station Pickup: **Yes**

Picketts Harbor is set in a rural, wooded section of Virginia's Eastern Shore. The house is decorated "country-style," with antiques, reproductions, plants, and collectibles. Outside, the property spans 17 acres including a large private beach. Breakfast is served overlooking Chesapeake Bay. There are many local opportunities for fishermen and hunters, and your hosts will gladly provide a picnic lunch. Williamsburg, Yorktown, and many historic sights are within an hour's drive.

Sandy Hill Farm B&B ✪
ROUTE 1, BOX 55, CAPRON, VIRGINIA 23829

Tel: (804) 658-4381
Host(s): **Anne Kitchen**
Location: **11 mi. from I-95**
No. of Rooms: 2
Max. No. Sharing Bath: 4
Double/sb: $27
Single/sb: $22
Open: **Mar. 20–Dec.**

Reduced Rates: **Families; 5 nights**
Breakfast: **Continental**
Other Meals: **Available**
Pets: **Welcome**
Children: **Welcome**
Smoking: **Permitted**
Social Drinking: **Permitted**

Experience the pleasures of an unspoiled rural setting at this ranch-style farmhouse. There are animals to visit, quiet places to stroll, and a lighted tennis court on the grounds. This is an ideal hub from which to tour southeastern and central Virginia . . . day trips to Williamsburg, Norfolk, or Richmond. Fresh fruits and homemade breads are served at breakfast.

Guesthouses Reservation Service ✪
P.O. BOX 5737, CHARLOTTESVILLE, VIRGINIA 22905

Tel: (804) 979-7264
Best Time to Call: **12–5, Mon.–Fri.**
Coordinator: **Mary Hill Caperton**
States/Regions Covered:
  Charlottesville, Luray, Albemarle County

Rates (Single/Double):
  Modest: $36 $48
  Average: $56 $60
  Luxury: $68 $160
  Estate Cottages: $72 and up
Credit Cards: **AMEX, MC, VISA**

Charlottesville is a gracious town. The hosts in Mary's hospitality file offer you a genuine taste of Southern hospitality. All places are close to Thomas Jefferson's Monticello and James Madison's Ash Lawn, as well as the University of Virginia. Unusual local activities include ballooning, steeplechasing, and wine festivals. Please note that the office is closed from Christmas through New Year's Day. Reduced rates are available for extended stays, and most hosts offer a full breakfast. Please send $1 for her directory.

Fountain Hall ✪
609 SOUTH EAST STREET, CULPEPER, VIRGINIA 22701-3222

Tel: (703) 825-8200
Best Time to Call: **8 AM–8 PM**
Host(s): **Steve and Kathi Walker**

Location: **1 mi. from Va. Rte. 29/522**
No. of Rooms: 6
No. of Private Baths: 4

Max. No. Sharing Bath: **4**
Double/pb: **$70**
Single/pb: **$60**
Single/sb: **$45**
Suites: **$85**
Open: **All year**
Reduced Rates: **Dec.–Mar.; 10%, seniors; after 3 nights; business travelers**

Breakfast: **Continental**
Credit Cards: **AMEX, MC, VISA**
Pets: **No**
Children: **Welcome (crib)**
Smoking: **Permitted**
Social Drinking: **Permitted**
Airport/Station Pickup: **Yes**

The first county surveyor of Culpeper was a teenaged George Washington, who called it "a high and pleasant situation." Indeed it still is, with many unspoiled historic and natural treasures for you to enjoy. Fountain Hall is furnished with antiques, comfortable beds, and an old-fashioned flavor. It is a fine home base from which to explore north-central Virginia. Some local points of interest include the Cavalry Museum, the Civil War reenactment of the Battle of Cedar Mountain, Little Fork Church, Commonwealth Park horse shows, wineries, antiquing, and some fine restaurants. Steve and Kathi serve tea, coffee, or lemonade upon your return from touring.

Caledonia Farm ✪
ROUTE 1, BOX 2080, FLINT HILL, VIRGINIA 22627

Tel: **(703) 675-3693**
Host(s): **Phil Irwin**
Location: **68 mi. SW of Washington, D.C.; 4 mi. N of Washington, Va.**
No. of Rooms: **3**
Max. No. Sharing Bath: **4**
Suite: **$100**
Double/sb: **$70**

Open: **All year**
Breakfast: **Full**
Credit Cards: **MC, VISA**
Pets: **No**
Children: **Welcome, over 12**
Smoking: **No**
Social Drinking: **Permitted**

This charming 1812 stone manor house and its companion "summer kitchen" are located on a working beef cattle farm adjacent to Shenandoah National Park. Each accommodation has a fireplace, period furnishings, individual temperature controls for heat or air-conditioning, and spectacular views of the Blue Ridge Mountains. A candlelight breakfast is served from a menu that offers a choice of omelet, smoked salmon, or eggs Benedict. The Skyline Drive, fine dining, caves, wineries, hayrides, antiquing, historic sites, and sporting activities are a few of the possible diversions. Afterward, join Phil for the evening social hour.

Brookfield Inn
P.O. BOX 341, FLOYD, VIRGINIA 24091

Tel: **(703) 763-3363**
Best Time to Call: **Before 8 AM; after 5 PM**
Host(s): **Gaynell Thompson**
Location: **12 mi. S of I-81**
No. of Rooms: **2**
Max. No. Sharing Bath: **4**
Double/sb: **$30 and up**
Single/sb: **$25**
Open: **All year**
Breakfast: **Full**
Credit Cards: **MC, VISA**
Pets: **No**
Children: **No**
Smoking: **No**
Social Drinking: **Permitted**

A private road lined with native plants and wildflowers leads to this spacious country home, located on a mountaintop in the heart of the Blue Ridge. The relaxing setting includes several acres of greenery and native woods, a trout pond, and nature trails. Inside, you'll find beautifully furnished bedrooms and a comfortable living area for reading or conversation. The Southern-style breakfast of ham, eggs, and biscuits is served on the patio in warm weather. Your hosts will gladly help you discover the pleasures of rural Floyd County and the beautiful Blue Ridge Mountains.

La Vista Plantation ✪
ROUTE 3, BOX 1255, FREDERICKSBURG, VIRGINIA 22401

Tel: **(703) 898-8444**
Host(s): **Michele and Edward Schiesser**
Location: **60 mi. S of D.C.; 4.5 mi. from I-95**
No. of Rooms: **1 Suite**
No. of Private Baths: **1**
Double/pb: **$65**
Single/pb: **$50**
Suites: **$65, can sleep 6**
Open: **All year**
Reduced Rates: **7th night free; families**
Breakfast: **Full**
Credit Cards: **MC, VISA**
Pets: **Sometimes**
Children: **Welcome**
Smoking: **Permitted**
Social Drinking: **Permitted**
Airport/Station Pickup: **Yes**

Guest lodgings at La Vista are located in an English basement blessed with a sunny exposure and featuring a private entrance. The spacious, air-conditioned suite has a large living room with fireplace, full kitchen, sitting room, and bath. Ten acres surround the manor house (circa 1838), and you are welcome to stroll, bird-watch, or fish in a pond stocked with bass and sunfish.

The McGrath House ✪
225 PRINCESS ANNE STREET, FREDERICKSBURG, VIRGINIA 22401

Tel: **(703) 371-4363**
Best Time to Call: **Mornings**
Host(s): **Sylvia McGrath**
Location: **50 mi. S of Washington, D.C.**
No. of Rooms: **3**
Max. No. Sharing Bath: **6**
Double/sb: **$35**

Single/sb: **$30**
Open: **All year**
Reduced Rates: **Weekly**
Breakfast: **Continental**
Pets: **No**
Children: **Welcome**
Smoking: **No**
Social Drinking: **Permitted**

This carefully restored house, featured on walking tours, dates back to the early 19th century and is located in the oldest part of Fredericksburg on a quiet, tree-lined street. You'll enjoy breakfast in the country kitchen that overlooks a small Colonial herb garden. In the evening, you are welcome to a drink and snacks with Sylvia before retiring. Don't miss seeing the President James Monroe Law Offices, Rising Sun Tavern, the Battlefield, and Kenmore. Mary Washington College is nearby.

Rainbow's End B&B
ROUTE 1, BOX 335, GORE, VIRGINIA 22637

Tel: **(703) 858-2808**
Best Time to Call: **10 AM–8 PM**
Host(s): **Eleanor and Thom McKay**
Location: **20 mi. W of Winchester**
No. of Rooms: **2**
Max. No. Sharing Bath: **3**
Double/sb: **$40**

Single/sb: **$35**
Open: **All year**
Breakfast: **Continental**
Pets: **No**
Children: **No**
Smoking: **No**
Social Drinking: **Permitted**

Rainbow's End is a brick and wood ranch situated on Timber Ridge in the Blue Ridge Mountains. The McKays offer cozy rooms filled with comfortable family furnishings. Eleanor serves a tasty breakfast of homemade breads, muffins, cakes, and coffee. Later in the day, join your hosts for wine and cheese. Guests can experience rural life in the heart of apple country. You may see a deer, a fox, or any one of a number of colorful birds that frequent the pond nestled among the pines. Nearby attractions include George Washington's Office, Ole Towne Winchester with its quaint stores, several famous caverns, and Civil War battlefields.

Fassifern Bed & Breakfast ✪
ROUTE 5, BOX 87, LEXINGTON, VIRGINIA 24450

Tel: **(703) 463-1013**
Best Time to Call: **1 PM–10 PM**
Host(s): **Pat and Jim Tichenor**
Location: **50 mi. N of Roanoke**
No. of Rooms: **6**
No. of Private Baths: **4**
Max. No. Sharing Bath: **4**
Double/pb: **$50–$65**
Single/pb: **$45–$60**
Double/sb: **$40–$45**
Single/sb: **$35–$40**
Suites: **$80**
Open: **All year**
Breakfast: **Continental**
Credit Cards: **MC, VISA**
Pets: **No**
Children: **Welcome, over 16**
Smoking: **No**
Social Drinking: **Permitted**
Airport/Station Pickup: **Yes**

Fassifern is a 19th-century manor home, located on three and a half acres with a pond and stately trees. Over the years, the house has been rebuilt and authentically restored. Rooms are furnished with antiques and souvenirs collected during 26 years of worldwide military service. When you relax on the porch, patio, or in the conservatory, your hosts will gladly supply reading or writing materials. They offer such breakfast specialties as homemade breads and pastries, seasonal fruit, freshly ground coffee, and gourmet teas; evening snacks are also offered. Fassifern is adjacent to the Virginia Horse Center, near Lexington, and 20 minutes away from the Blue Ridge Parkway and the Natural Bridge.

Llewellyn Lodge at Lexington ✪
603 SOUTH MAIN STREET, LEXINGTON, VIRGINIA 24445

Tel: (703) 463-3235
Best Time to Call: 8 AM–1 PM
Host(s): Ellen Thornber and John Roberts
Location: 50 mi. N of Roanoke
No. of Rooms: 5
No. of Private Baths: 5
Double/pb: $55
Single/pb: $45
Suite: $65

Open: All year
Breakfast: Full
Other Meals: Available
Credit Cards: AMEX, MC, VISA
Pets: No
Children: Welcome, over 5
Smoking: Permitted
Social Drinking: Permitted
Airport/Station Pickup: Yes

Guests are welcomed to this lovely brick Colonial with seasonal refreshments. Your hostess has 20 years of experience in the travel and hospitality business, and guarantees to make you feel at home. The decor combines traditional and antique furnishings. Homemade coffee cake, biscuits, and omelets are favorites at the breakfast table. Llewellyn is close to local attractions such as the homes of Robert E. Lee, Stonewall Jackson, and the Natural Bridge.

Shenandoah Countryside ✪
ROUTE 2, BOX 377, LURAY, VIRGINIA 22835

Tel: (703) 743-6434
Best Time to Call: 9 AM–9 PM
Host(s): Phel and Bob Jacobsen
No. of Rooms: 3
No. of Private Baths: 1
Max. No. Sharing Bath: 4
Double/pb: $55
Single/pb: $45
Double/sb: $55

Single/sb: $45
Open: All year
Breakfast: Full
Pets: Sometimes
Children: Welcome, over 10 on weekdays
Smoking: No
Social Drinking: Permitted
Airport/Station Pickup: Yes

Shenandoah Countryside is a new, custom brick farmhouse overlooking magnificent pastoral and mountain scenes. The house is set on 45 acres, including a Christmas tree farm, and is surrounded by gardens. One guest room features a brass bed and private balcony; another has walnut twin beds and a small dressing room. Guests are welcome to unwind in the Finnish sauna or outside on one of the three porches overlooking the Shenandoah Valley. Breakfast is served outdoors in season, and at the harvest table in winter. The Jacobsens offer homemade breads and jams, eggs Benedict, goldenrod toast, pancakes, and more. Later, they invite you for tea and cookies. Enjoy sightseeing in

Shenandoah National Park, canoeing on the Shenandoah River, and touring Luray Caverns, or borrow a bicycle and explore the country roads.

Riverfront House ✪
ROUTE 14 EAST, P.O. BOX 310, MATHEWS, VIRGINIA 23109

Tel: **(804) 725-9975**
Host(s): **Annette Goldreyer**
Location: **18 mi. from US 17**
No. of Rooms: **7**
Max. No. Sharing Bath: **4**
Double/sb: **$50–$75**
Open: **Apr.–Dec.**

Reduced Rates: **Available**
Breakfast: **Full**
Pets: **No**
Children: **Welcome, over 4**
Smoking: **Permitted**
Social Drinking: **Permitted**

This clapboard farmhouse is set on seven acres near the mouth of the East River, which feeds into Chesapeake Bay. The 19th-century design features a gracious front hall and mahogany mantelpieces. The bedrooms blend contemporary with antique furnishings. A buffet of fruit, cheese, and muffins is offered each morning. Breakfast can be enjoyed inside or on the wraparound porch. Sunbathe right on the dock, or drop a crab line and try your luck. Your host invites you to share a glass of wine in late afternoon. It is within an hour of Williamsburg. There are excellent flat roads for hiking and biking that lead to Chesapeake Bay. Day cruises on the bay or river are popular.

Greenvale Manor ✪
P.O. BOX 174, MOLLUSK, VIRGINIA 22517

Tel: **(804) 462-5995**
Host(s): **Pam and Walt Smith**
Location: **70 mi. NE of Richmond**
No. of Rooms: **9**
No. of Private Baths: **5**
Max. No. Sharing Bath: **4**
Double/pb: **$60**
Single/pb: **$55**
Double/sb: **$55**
Single/sb: **$40**
Guest Cottage: **$110 for 4; $170 for 6**

Suites: **$75**
Open: **All year**
Breakfast: **Full**
Other Meals: **Available**
Pets: **Sometimes**
Children: **Welcome, over 12**
Smoking: **Permitted**
Social Drinking: **Permitted**
Minimum Stay: **Holiday weekends**
Airport/Station Pickup: **Yes**

Greenvale Manor is an 1840 Colonial set on the Rappahannock River and Greenvale Creek. It is located in an area known for its historic waterfront homes. The house has been owned by several prominent Virginia families and has been beautifully restored and maintained.

The 13-acre estate includes a sandy beach, pool, and private dock. The house is furnished in period antiques and reproductions and its large windows make the most of its best feature . . . the waterfront. Breakfast is served on a large screened veranda in summer, and in winter the day begins beside a crackling fire in the Federal Room. The manor offers many diversions, such as croquet, badminton, boating with a licensed captain, fishing, and crabbing right off the dock. Pam and Walt invite you to share a glass of wine and will gladly suggest nearby restaurants and historic sites.

The Inn at Montross ✪
COURTHOUSE SQUARE, MONTROSS, VIRGINIA 22520

Tel: **(804) 493-9097**
Host(s): **Eileen and Michael Longman**
Location: **46 mi. E of Fredericksburg**
No. of Rooms: **6**
No. of Private Baths: **6**
Double/pb: **$65**
Single/pb: **$55**
Open: **All year**
Reduced Rates: **10%, seniors; corporations**

Breakfast: **Continental**
Other Meals: **Available**
Credit Cards: **AMEX, DINERS, MC, VISA**
Pets: **Sometimes**
Children: **Welcome**
Smoking: **Permitted**
Social Drinking: **Permitted**

The original sections of the Inn at Montross date back over 300 years. Your hosts have decorated the rooms with a mixture of primitive and modern art, porcelains, antiques, and reproductions. Each guest room is furnished with four-poster beds, with extras such as bedside brandy and chocolates. The main floor boasts a magnificent grand piano, which guests are welcome to use. A small lounge with television and a spacious living room are available for relaxing. Your hosts serve home-baked croissants, fresh fruit, muffins, or Danish for breakfast. Bountiful meals at affordable prices are served in the Colonial dining rooms, which are open to the public. The Longmans will be glad to direct you to Stratford Hall, Ingleside Winery, and Westmoreland State Park. Golf and fishing can be enjoyed nearby, and there are tennis courts on the grounds.

The Widow Kip's ✪
ROUTE 1, BOX 117, MT. JACKSON, VIRGINIA 22842

Tel: **(703) 477-2400**
Best Time to Call: **Before Noon; after 3 PM**

Host(s): **Rosemary Kip**
Location: **1 mi. from I-81, Exit 69**
No. of Rooms: **7**

No. of Private Baths: **5**
Max. No. Sharing Bath: **4**
Double/pb: **$60**
Single/pb: **$45**
Double/sb: **$55**
Single/sb: **$40**
Suites: **$70**
Open: **All year**

Reduced Rates: **10%, seniors**
Breakfast: **Full**
Other Meals: **Available**
Pets: **Sometimes**
Children: **Welcome**
Smoking: **Permitted**
Social Drinking: **Permitted**

This Colonial homestead, built in 1830, is nestled on seven acres in the Shenandoah Valley. After a breakfast of sausage patties, biscuits with homemade apple butter, and plum gumbo (or other specialties), you may hike, canoe, play tennis, fish, or visit a cavern. Bikes are provided and Rosemary will pack a picnic lunch for your day's jaunt. If you'd rather "stay home," you may enjoy a dip in the 32-foot pool on warm days, sip sherry or tea in front of your bedroom's fireplace in cool weather, or wander through the rooms where all the furnishings are priced for sale. A gift shop is on the premises.

The Newport House ✪
ROUTE 2, BOX 10, NEWPORT, VIRGINIA 24128

Tel: **(703) 961-2480**
Host(s): **Harold and Pamela Kurstedt**
Location: **15 mi. from I-81**
No. of Rooms: **3**
No. of Private Baths: **3**
Double/pb: **$65**
Open: **All year**
Breakfast: **Full**

Other Meals: **Available**
Credit Cards: **MC, VISA**
Pets: **No**
Children: **Welcome, over 12**
Smoking: **No**
Social Drinking: **Permitted**
Airport/Station Pickup: **Yes**

Built in 1840, the farmhouse has been enlarged and enhanced by a two-story addition, a sun porch, and commodious bathrooms, including one equipped for the handicapped. Decorated with family furnishings, the beds are covered with Amish quilts; Harold's mother created the needlepoint wall hangings. The cook prepares such delights as fluffy ham biscuits, stewed apples, sausage gravy, and a variety of omelets. Complimentary coffee, tea, and cake are served each afternoon. The well-tended grounds, patios, and porches are perfect for relaxing. Virginia Tech, New River canoeing, the Appalachian Trail, and several covered bridges are nearby.

Erika's Bed & Breakfast ✪
232 EAST BAYVIEW BOULEVARD, NORFOLK, VIRGINIA 23503

Tel: **(804) 583-5725**	Reduced Rates: **10%, seniors**
Best Time to Call: **8 AM–Noon**	Breakfast: **Continental**
Host(s): **Erika Straddeck**	Pets: **No**
No. of Rooms: **2**	Children: **No**
Max. No. Sharing Bath: **4**	Smoking: **Permitted**
Double/sb: **$35**	Social Drinking: **Permitted**
Single/sb: **$30**	Foreign Languages: **German**
Open: **All year**	

Less than a five-minute drive from the naval base and Interstate 64, this charming Cape Cod house is not far from Virginia Beach, Old Dominion University, Colonial Williamsburg, and Busch Gardens. The house is attractively furnished in Bavarian style, and cleanliness and comfort are evident in each room. You are welcome to use the swimming pool, hot tub, laundry facilities, and the kitchen for light snacks.

Mayhurst Inn ✪
ROUTE 15 SOUTH, P.O. BOX 707, ORANGE, VIRGINIA 22960

Tel: **(703) 672-5597**	Open: **All year**
Best Time to Call: **9 AM–9 PM**	Reduced Rates: **Available**
Host(s): **Stephen and Shirley Ramsey**	Breakfast: **Full**
Location: **27 mi. N of Charlottesville**	Pets: **No**
No. of Rooms: **7**	Children: **Welcome, over 12**
No. of Private Baths: **7**	Smoking: **No**
Double/pb: **$85–$105**	Social Drinking: **Permitted**
Guest Cottage: **$105**	

The Mayhurst is an early Victorian mansion noted for its fanciful architecture and oval spiral staircase ascending four stories to the rooftop gazebo. The rooms are large and sunny, with original floor-to-ceiling windows made of handblown glass. Bedrooms are elegantly furnished with 18th- and 19th-century beds, chests, and tables. Each room is named for someone who spent the night at the inn or is associated with it in some way. The Stonewall Jackson Room was offered to the Confederate general the night before the Battle of Cedar Mountain. Four rooms in the main house have working fireplaces, and the guest cottage features a fireplace, exposed beams, and pine floors. Guests are welcome to congregate in the main hall for afternoon tea or port. In the dining room, the full country breakfast includes Virginia ham or sausage, eggs, baked apples, pumpkin muffins, and homemade marmalade. The Mayhurst is situated on 36 acres with a swimming pond, fields, and magnolias, and is listed on the National Register of Historic Places.

Bensonhouse ✪
2036 MONUMENT AVENUE, RICHMOND, VIRGINIA 23220

Tel: **(804) 648-7560**	Rates (Single/Double):
Best Time to Call: **10 AM-6 PM**	Modest: **$45** **$52**
Coordinator: **Lyn Benson**	Average: **$46-$55** **$55-$66**
States/Regions Covered: **Bowling Green, Fredericksburg, Northern Neck, Petersburg, Richmond, Williamsburg**	Luxury: **$60-$94** **$68-$100**
	Credit Cards: **MC, VISA**

Houses on Lyn's list are of architectural or historic interest, offering charm in the relaxed comfort of a home. The hosts delight in guiding you to the best sights, and advising you on how to get the most out of your visit.

Hanover Hosts
P.O. BOX 25145, RICHMOND, VIRGINIA 23260

Tel: **(804) 355-5855**	Single/sb: **$50**
Best Time to Call: **9 AM-8 PM**	Suites: **$155**
Host(s): **Barbara and Bill Fleming**	Open: **All year**
Location: **2½ mi. from I-95**	Reduced Rates: **Weekly**
No. of Rooms: **3**	Breakfast: **Full (weekends)**
No. of Private Baths: **2**	Pets: **No**
Max. No. Sharing Bath: **3**	Children: **Welcome, over 12**
Double/pb: **$65**	Smoking: **Permitted**
Single/pb: **$55**	Social Drinking: **Permitted**
Double/sb: **$60**	Airport/Station Pickup: **Yes**

This Colonial Revival town house is located in a historic residential district close to museums, restaurants, and galleries. The house features a sunny deck secluded from the street. The rooms are decorated with many antiques, quilts, handcrafts, and stenciling. Nearby sights include Virginia's Capitol Building and St. John's Church. Homemade jams and special muffins are served for breakfast.

The Leonine Experience ✪
P.O. BOX 4772, RICHMOND, VIRGINIA 23220

Tel: **(804) 359-1952**	Host(s): **J. P. Blankenship**
Best Time to Call: **Before 9 AM; after 5 PM**	Location: 2½ mi. from I-95
	Suite: **$50 for 2; $40 for**

Open: **All year**
Breakfast: **Continental**
Pets: **No**
Children: **Welcome, over 12**

Smoking: **Permitted**
Social Drinking: **Permitted**
Airport/Station Pickup: **Yes**

Complete privacy awaits you on the lower level of a restored Greek Revival town house located in Richmond's historic Fan District. Guest quarters feature an entrance foyer, living room with sleeper sofa, bedroom with TV, and a complete kitchenette and refreshment bar. The suite has its own garden gate entrance and opens onto a charming New Orleans–style brick courtyard. Choose from a light breakfast of fresh muffins, cereal, homemade jellies, and hot coffee, or enjoy a heartier meal served in the formal dining room. Your host invites you to relax on the patio or have a picnic lunch in the rear garden. This is the ideal location for exploring Richmond, and is within walking distance of the Virginia Museum, Monument Boulevard, Virginia Commonwealth University, and the delightful shops of Carytown.

The Mary Bladon House ✪
381 WASHINGTON AVENUE SOUTH WEST, ROANOKE, VIRGINIA 24016

Tel: **(703) 344-5361**
Host(s): **Sally D. Pfister**
Location: **220 mi. S of Washington, D.C.**
No. of Rooms: **4**
No. of Private Baths: **4**
Double/pb: **$55–$65**
Single/pb: **$45–$52**
Suites: **$65**
Open: **All year**

Reduced Rates: **Available**
Breakfast: **Full**
Credit Cards: **MC, VISA**
Pets: **No**
Children: **Welcome, over 12**
Smoking: **Permitted**
Social Drinking: **Permitted**
Airport/Station Pickup: **Yes**
Foreign Languages: **Spanish**

The Mary Bladon House is located in the old southwest neighborhood, just five minutes away from the Blue Ridge Parkway. This Victorian dates back to the late 1800s and has four porches. Although the original brass light fixtures are still in place, the decor in the public rooms is constantly changing, with works by local artists and craftsmen. All the rooms are elegantly appointed with antiques, and guest rooms feature fresh flowers in season. Breakfast is served by candlelight in the dining room or on the porch in summer months.

High Meadows—Virginia's Vineyard Inn ✪
ROUTE 4, BOX 6, ROUTE 20 SOUTH, SCOTTSVILLE, VIRGINIA 24590

Tel: **(804) 286-2218**
Host(s): **Peter and Jae Abbitt Sushka**
Location: **17 mi. S of Charlottesville**
No. of Rooms: **5**
No. of Private Baths: **5**
Double/pb: **$75**
Single/pb: **$65**
Suites: **$125**
Open: **All year**

Reduced Rates: **10% after 3 nights**
Breakfast: **Full**
Other Meals: **Available**
Pets: **Sometimes**
Children: **Welcome, over 8**
Smoking: **No**
Social Drinking: **Permitted**
Foreign Languages: **French**
Minimum Stay: **Weekends Apr., May, Sept., Oct.**

This Virginia Historic Landmark is situated on 23 acres, and comprises dwellings built in 1832 and 1882 that are joined by a longitudinal "grand" hall. Recently restored, it is furnished with carefully chosen period antiques. You will enjoy the many fireplaces and whirlpool baths, the lovely flower gardens, the Pinot Noir vineyard, the ponds, and the gazebo. Bicycles are available for local touring. Jefferson's Monticello, Monroe's Ash Lawn, the University of Virginia, and James River tubing, fishing, and canoeing are nearby. Peter is a retired naval submariner; Jae's a financial analyst with the Securities Exchange Commission; son Peter plays classical guitar. Afternoon tea and Virginia wine with hors d'oeuvres are daily traditions.

Isle of Wight Inn
1607 SOUTH CHURCH STREET, SMITHFIELD, VIRGINIA 23430

Tel: **(804) 357-3176**
Best Time to Call: **9 AM–5 PM**
Host(s): **Bob, Sam, and Marcella Earl**
Location: **27 mi. N of Norfolk**
No. of Rooms: **10**
No. of Private Baths: **10**
Double/pb: **$59**
Single/pb: **$49**

Suites: **$78**
Open: **All year**
Breakfast: **Continental**
Credit Cards: **AMEX, MC, VISA**
Pets: **No**
Children: **Welcome**
Smoking: **Permitted**
Social Drinking: **Permitted**

The Isle of Wight Inn is a sprawling brick Colonial, one mile from downtown Smithfield. Inside you will find antiques, reproductions, motifs of glass, wood, and wicker, and an old player piano. Wake up to fresh coffee and Smithfield's own ham rolls. This riverport town has numerous historic homes that will surely delight you. Williamsburg, Norfolk, and Virginia Beach are less than an hour's drive from the house.

The Manor at Taylor's Store ✪
ROUTE 1, BOX 533, SMITH MOUNTAIN LAKE, VIRGINIA 24184

Tel: **(703) 721-3951**
Host(s): **Lee and Mary Lynn Tucker**
Location: **20 mi. E of Roanoke**
No. of Rooms: **4**
No. of Private Baths: **4**
Double/pb: **$50–$70**
Guest Cottage: **$100, sleeps 8**
Open: **All year**
Reduced Rates: **$400 week for cottage; 10%, seniors**
Breakfast: **Full**
Other Meals: **Available**
Credit Cards: **MC, VISA**
Pets: **No**
Children: **Welcome, over 12**
Smoking: **No**
Social Drinking: **Permitted**
Airport/Station Pickup: **Yes**

Situated on 90 acres in the foothills of the Blue Ridge Mountains, this original manor house (c. 1800) was the focus of a prosperous tobacco plantation. It has been restored and refurbished, and you'll experience the elegance of the past combined with the comfort of tasteful modernization. The estate invites hiking, picnicking, and fishing. The sun room, parlor, and hot tub are special spots for relaxing. Smith Mountain Lake, with its seasonal sporting activity, is five miles away. Breakfast, designed for the health-conscious, features a variety of fresh gourmet selections.

Thornrose House at Gypsy Hill ✪
531 THORNROSE AVENUE, STAUNTON, VIRGINIA 24401

Tel: **(703) 885-7026**
Best Time to Call: **8 AM–10 PM**
Host(s): **Carolyn and Ray Hoaster**
Location: **I-81 Shenandoah Valley, Exit 57**
No. of Rooms: **3**
No. of Private Baths: **3**
Double/pb: **$45–$50**
Single/pb: **$35**
Open: **All year**
Breakfast: **Full**
Pets: **No**
Children: **Welcome**
Smoking: **No**
Social Drinking: **Permitted**
Airport/Station Pickup: **Yes**

A wraparound veranda and Greek colonnades distinguish the entrance of this turn-of-the-century Georgian residence. Inside, family antiques, a grand piano, and fireplaces create a formal but comfortable atmosphere. An unusual winding staircase leads to restful, attractive rooms. The house specialty, "Birchermuesli," A Swiss concoction made from oats, fresh fruits, nuts, and whipped cream, is just part of the hearty breakfast. Your hosts also offer afternoon tea and evening sherry. They are located adjacent to a 300-acre city park with tennis, golf, walks, and ponds. Other nearby attractions include Blue Ridge

National Park, Natural Chimneys, Skyline Drive, the birthplace of Woodrow Wilson, and the Museum of American Frontier Culture.

Lambsgate Bed and Breakfast ✪
ROUTE 1, BOX 63, SWOOPE, VIRGINIA 24479

Tel: **(703) 337-6929**
Host(s): **Daniel and Elizabeth Fannon**
Location: **6 mi. W of Staunton; 10 mi. from I-81**
No. of Rooms: **3**
Max. No. Sharing Bath: **6**
Double/sb: **$35**
Single/sb: **$30**

Open: **All year**
Reduced Rates: **10%, weekly**
Breakfast: **Full**
Pets: **No**
Children: **Welcome**
Smoking: **No**
Social Drinking: **Permitted**

Lambsgate is a restored vernacular farmhouse on seven acres in the Shenandoah Valley. The house dates back to 1816 and though it has been added to and modernized, the bedrooms have retained their original woodwork and floors. The Fannons offer a breakfast of homemade muffins, bacon, eggs, grits, and jellies each morning. They will provide information on such local sights as George Washington National Forest, Shenandoah National Park, and Luray Caverns. There is also plenty to see on the farm. Guests are invited to visit the lambs or relax and enjoy the view from the wraparound veranda.

At-the-Beach
4501 OCEANFRONT AVENUE, VIRGINIA BEACH, VIRGINIA 23451

Tel: **(804) 425-7666**
Host(s): **Carol and Gary Matuck**
No. of Rooms: **3**
Max. No. Sharing Bath: **4**
Double/pb: **$75**
Single/pb: **$60**
Double/sb: **$75**
Single/sb: **$60**

Open: **All year**
Reduced Rates: **20%, Oct.–Apr.**
Breakfast: **Full**
Pets: **No**
Children: **Welcome (crib)**
Smoking: **Permitted**
Social Drinking: **Permitted**

This cedar-shingled home was originally built as an elegant beach manor. The 1920s design features leaded glass windows, a curving staircase, and spacious common rooms with elegant moldings and 12-foot ceilings. The double parlor has a reading area at one end and, at the other, a conversation area surrounding the Italian marble fireplace. Homemade breads, omelets, pancakes, and crêpes are served on china and crystal in the dining room. Guests may choose from two rooms overlooking the water or the one with twin beds and private bath. All rooms have freshly cut flowers and a welcome basket of fruit and cheese with crackers. Your hosts invite you to relax in the wicker-furnished sun room or outside on the brick terrace surrounded by holly trees. They have beach towels, umbrellas, and chairs to take to the beach, which is just 100 yards away. At-the-Beach is located in a residential neighborhood three blocks from restaurants and shops.

The Picket Fence ✪
209 43RD STREET, VIRGINIA BEACH, VIRGINIA 23451

Tel: **(804) 428-8861**	Reduced Rates: **Weekly**
Host(s): **Kathleen Hall**	Breakfast: **Full**
Location: **20 mi. E of Norfolk**	Pets: **No**
No. of Rooms: **2**	Children: **No**
No. of Private Baths: **2**	Smoking: **No**
Double/pb: **$50–$65**	Social Drinking: **Permitted**
Single/pb: **$50–$65**	Airport/Station Pickup: **Yes**
Guest Cottage: **$75**	Minimum Stay: **2 nights**
Open: **All year**	

The furnishings in Kathy's comfortable Colonial home glow with the patina of loving care. She thoroughly enjoys her hobbies of fishing and cooking and often incorporates the two into special breakfasts for her guests. The beach is just a block away and beach chairs and umbrellas are provided for your comfort. Complimentary wine and cheese are graciously served before you go out to dinner. Don't leave the area without visiting the new Marine Science Museum.

The Foster-Harris House
P.O. BOX 333, WASHINGTON, VIRGINIA 22747

Tel: **(703) 675-3757**	Single/sb: **$50**
Host(s): **Patrick Foster and Camille Harris**	Suites: **$75–$85**
	Open: **All year**
Location: **65 mi. W of Washington, D.C.**	Reduced Rates: **3 nights or more**
	Breakfast: **Continental**
No. of Rooms: **3**	Pets: **Sometimes**
No. of Private Baths: **1**	Children: **Welcome**
Max. No. Sharing Bath: **4**	Smoking: **Permitted**
Double/sb: **$60**	Social Drinking: **Permitted**

This pastoral Victorian is surrounded by the Blue Ridge Mountains. The rooms are furnished with many antiques and the guest quarters are newly renovated. There is much to see in this historic village, which was surveyed by George Washington and was the first place in the country to be named for him. Your hosts serve freshly baked treats each morning and offer wine and cheese or coffee and cookies in the afternoon. They recommend five-star dining at a nearby inn and will gladly direct you to Skyline Drive, antique shops, horseback riding, and hiking trails.

The Pink House ✪
WATERFORD, VIRGINIA 22190

Tel: **(703) 882-3453**
Host(s): **Charles and Marie Anderson**
Location: **38 mi. W of D.C.**
No. of Rooms: **2 three-room suites**
No. of Private Baths: **2**
Suites: **$90**
Open: **All year**

Reduced Rates: **$10 less after 2 nights**
Breakfast: **Full**
Pets: **Sometimes**
Children: **Welcome, over 12**
Smoking: **Permitted**
Social Drinking: **Permitted**

Pink House is in the center of Waterford, one of the few villages entirely designated as a national landmark. Through the years, the house has been a Civil War officers' billet and an apothecary shop. Today, two three-room suites overlook a formal garden, with private entrance, terrace, color TV, and whirlpool among the luxurious features. A breakfast of homemade breads, grits, and sausage is served each morning. Nearby sights include plantations, museums, and the equestrian center at Morvan Park.

The Travel Tree ✪
P.O. BOX 838, WILLIAMSBURG, VIRGINIA 23187

Tel: **(804) 253-1571**
Best Time to Call: **6–9 PM, Mon.– Thurs.**
Coordinator(s): **Joann Proper and Sheila Zubkoff**
States/Regions Covered:
  Williamsburg, Jamestown, Yorktown

Rates (Single/Double):
  Average: **$44**   **$55**
  Luxury: **$60**   **$75**
Credit Cards: **No**
Minimum Stay: **2 nights**

You will thoroughly enjoy Colonial Williamsburg, historic Jamestown and Yorktown, Busch Gardens, and Carter's Grove Plantation. Your bedroom might be furnished with four-poster beds and antiques, or be tucked under the eaves in a wooded setting, or be a two-room suite with a private entrance.

Bluebird Haven ✪
8691 BARHAMSVILLE ROAD, TOANO, WILLIAMSBURG, VIRGINIA 23168

Tel: **(804) 566-0177**
Best Time to Call: **Mornings**
Host(s): **June and Ed Cottle**
Location: **10 mi. N of Williamsburg**
No. of Rooms: **3**
No. of Private Baths: **1**
Max. No. Sharing Bath: **4**
Double/pb: **$48**
Single/pb: **$48**
Double/sb: **$38**
Single/sb: **$38**
Open: **All year**
Breakfast: **Full**
Other Meals: **Available**
Pets: **Sometimes**
Children: **Welcome**
Smoking: **Permitted**
Social Drinking: **Permitted**
Airport/Station Pickup: **Yes**

June and Ed Cottle welcome you to their ranch-style home, located 20 minutes from Colonial Williamsburg. June is interested in many kinds of handcrafts and has decorated the rooms with handmade quilts, spreads, and pictures. Guest rooms are located in a private wing of the house and feature comfortable furnishings and handmade linens. Breakfast includes a Southern-style assortment of homemade breads, jams, country ham, red-eye gravy, and omelets. June also offers gourmet hors d'oeuvres to accompany your evening cocktail. Bluebird Haven is convenient to Busch Gardens and 35 miles outside of Richmond.

For Cant Hill Guest Home
4 CANTERBURY LANE, WILLIAMSBURG, VIRGINIA 23185

Tel: **(804) 229-6623**
Host(s): **Martha and Hugh Easler**
No. of Rooms: **2**
No. of Private Baths: **2**
Double/pb: **$49.50**
Open: **All year**
Breakfast: **Continental**
Pets: **No**
Children: **Welcome, over 8**
Smoking: **No**
Social Drinking: **Permitted**
Airport/Station Pickup: **Yes**

Martha and Hugh's home is set in a secluded, wooded area overlooking a lake, which is part of the campus of William and Mary. It is a short walk to the historic district. The guest rooms are comfortably decorated, accented with antiques and pretty glass pieces. Homemade quilts adorn the beds. Restaurants to suit every budget are nearby.

Fox Grape of Williamsburg ✪
701 MONUMENTAL AVENUE, WILLIAMSBURG, VIRGINIA 23185

Tel: (804) 229-6914
Host(s): **Pat and Bob Orendorff**
Location: **2 mi. from I-64, Exit 56**
No. of Rooms: **4**
No. of Private Baths: **1**
Max. No. Sharing Bath: **4**
Double/pb: **$50**
Single/pb: **$45**
Double/sb: **$45**

Single/sb: **$40**
Open: **All year**
Reduced Rates: **10%, seniors**
Breakfast: **Continental**
Pets: **No**
Children: **Welcome**
Smoking: **Permitted**
Social Drinking: **Permitted**
Airport/Station Pickup: **Yes**

This brick Cape Cod is within walking distance of the restored area. The rooms have a Colonial decor, with poster beds, stenciled walls, needlepoint, antiques, and folk art. The Orendorffs offer fresh muffins, fruit, and cereal in the morning, served in the dining room, which is attractively decorated with decoy ducks. They will advise on nearby tourist attractions and restaurants. William and Mary College is nearby.

Himmelbed Inn ✪
706 RICHMOND ROAD, WILLIAMSBURG, VIRGINIA 23185

Tel: (804) 229-6421
Host(s): **Phil and Barbara Craig**
Location: **45 mi. E of Richmond**
No. of Rooms: **2**
No. of Private Baths: **2**
Double/pb: **$70**
Single/pb: **$55**

Open: **All year**
Breakfast: **Full**
Pets: **No**
Children: **Welcome, over 6**
Smoking: **No**
Social Drinking: **Permitted**
Airport/Station Pickup: **Yes**

This air-conditioned, Cape Cod–style house is attractively furnished in country antiques. It is within walking distance of the historic area and William and Mary College. You are welcome to borrow a bicycle.

War Hill ✪
4560 LONG HILL ROAD, WILLIAMSBURG, VIRGINIA 23185

Tel: (804) 565-0248
Best Time to Call: **Mornings; evenings**
Host(s): **Shirley and Bill Lee**
Location: **2 mi. from Rte. 60**
No. of Rooms: **5**

No. of Private Baths: **5**
Double/pb: **$45–$55**
Suite: **$75**
Open: **All year**
Breakfast: **Continental**

Credit Cards: **AMEX, MC, VISA**
Pets: **No**
Children: **Welcome**
Smoking: **No**
Social Drinking: **Permitted**

War Hill is situated in the center of a 32-acre working farm, just three miles from the tourist attractions. Built in 1968, this Colonial replica couples the charm of yesteryear with today's contemporary conveniences. The suite is comprised of two bedrooms and a bath. The wide heart-pine floors came from an old school, the stairs from a church, the overhead beams from a barn; the oak mantel is over 200 years old. Fruits from a variety of trees in the orchard are yours to pick in season. In autumn, Shirley and Bill serve delicious homemade applesauce and cider. Angus show cattle graze in the pasture, and the sounds you'll hear are crickets, frogs, owls, and the morning crowing of the rooster.

The Williamsburg Legacy ✪
930 JAMESTOWN ROAD, WILLIAMSBURG, VIRGINIA 23185

Tel: **(804) 220-0524**
Host(s): **Ed and Mary Lucas**
Location: **2 mi. from Rte. 64, Exit 59**
No. of Rooms: **3**
No. of Private Baths: **1**
Max. No. Sharing Bath: **4**
Double/pb: **$65**
Double/sb: **$65**
Suites: **$100**

Open: **All year**
Breakfast: **Full**
Credit Cards: **AMEX, MC, VISA**
Pets: **No**
Children: **No**
Smoking: **No**
Social Drinking: **Permitted**
Airport/Station Pickup: **Yes**

Ed and Mary have furnished their 18th-century-style home with lovely antiques from that era. The suite is the ultimate in privacy, and features a four-poster bed in the bedroom and a comfortable sofa facing a fireplace in the living room. Flowers, fruit, wine, and candy will make you feel welcome. You'll awaken to the aroma of freshly baked breads, just the beginning of a hearty breakfast. Afterward, stroll across the street to the campus of William and Mary College, walk to the restored area, or drive to Busch Gardens nearby.

The Country Fare ✪
402 NORTH MAIN STREET, WOODSTOCK, VIRGINIA 22664

Tel: **(703) 459-4828**
Best Time to Call: **7–11 AM; 6–10 PM**
Host(s): **Bette Hallgren**
Location: **35 mi. S of Winchester**

No. of Rooms: **3**
No. of Private Baths: **1**
Max. No. Sharing Bath: **3**
Double/pb: **$55**

Double/sb: **$45**
Single/sb: **$40**
Open: **All year**
Breakfast: **Continental**

Pets: **No**
Children: **Welcome, by arrangement**
Smoking: **No**
Social Drinking: **Permitted**

This is a small cozy inn, circa 1772, within walking distance of the village. The rooms are decorated with hand stenciling and a mixture of grandmother's antiques and country collectibles. Choose from the master bedroom with private shower, an ample guest room with twin beds, and a single room with a fireplace all its own. Guests may enjoy homemade breads and biscuits on the enclosed sun porch, or by the dining room wood stove when the air turns colder. An inviting brick patio overlooks the grounds, and the den includes a television. Your hostess will gladly help you get to know this historic Shenandoah Valley town, and can suggest many restaurants, shops, and interesting sights.

Schlisselsmith ✪
ROUTE 1, BOX 217A1, WOODSTOCK, VIRGINIA 22664

Tel: **(703) 459-5369**
Best Time to Call: **9 AM–9 PM**
Host(s): **Pat and Steve Kollar**
Location: **10 mi. from I-81, Exit 73**
No. of Rooms: **8**
No. of Private Baths: **7**
Max. No. Sharing Bath: **4**
Double/pb: **$60**
Single/pb: **$60**
Double/sb: **$60**
Single/sb: **$55**

Suites: **$85**
Open: **All year**
Breakfast: **Full**
Other Meals: **Available**
Credit Cards: **MC, VISA**
Pets: **No**
Children: **Welcome (crib)**
Smoking: **Permitted**
Social Drinking: **Permitted**
Foreign Languages: **German, Hungarian**

The Kollars have translated the elegance of a small European hotel to their stately Victorian mansion set at the base of Massanutten Mountain and furnished with fine antiques and lace curtains. Steve, a professional chef, glories in presenting unusual fare served on silver by a maid or butler. You are apt to be spoiled by drawn baths, tea served in your room, and turndown service before tucking yourself into one of the romantic bedrooms. Several have fireplaces for winter coziness, while a lovely swimming pool is a summer attraction. If you can tear yourself away from all this luxury, it's only 20 minutes to the Skyline Drive, the New Market Battlefield, and the famed caverns.

For key to listings, see inside front or back cover.

✪ This star means that rates are guaranteed through December 31, 1989 to any guest making a reservation as a result of reading about the B&B in *BED & BREAKFAST U.S.A.*—1989 edition.

Please enclose a self-addressed, stamped, business-sized envelope when contacting reservation services.

For more details on what you can expect in a B&B, see Chapter 1.

Always mention *Bed & Breakfast U.S.A.* when making reservations!

If no B&B is listed in the area you'll be visiting, use the form on page 693 to order a copy of our "List of New B&Bs."

We want to hear from you! Use the form on page 691.

WASHINGTON

Map of Washington showing locations: Lummi Island, Eastsound, Orcas, Ferndale, Deer Harbor, Anacortes, Bellevue, Langley, Pateros, Port Angeles, Edmonds, Port Orchard, Redmond, Gig Harbor, Seattle, Spokane, Tacoma, Maple Valley, Olympia, Seabeck, Ashford, Little Cape Horn, Cathlamet, White Salmon.

Pacific Bed & Breakfast Agency ✪
701 N.W. 60TH STREET, SEATTLE, WASHINGTON 98107

Tel: **(206) 784-0539**	Rates (Single/Double):
Best Time to Call: **9 AM–5 PM**	Modest: **$35** **$45**
TELEX: **329473 ATT PBB 580**	Average: **$40** **$55**
Coordinator: **Irmgard Castleberry**	Luxury: **$70** **$145**
States/Regions Covered: **Statewide;**	Credit Cards: **AMEX, MC, VISA**
Canada—Vancouver, Victoria,	
British Columbia	

Victorians, contemporaries, island cottages, waterfront houses, and private suites with full kitchens are available. Most are close to downtown areas, near bus lines, in fine residential neighborhoods, or within walking distance of a beach. Many extras are included, such as pickup service, free use of laundry facilities, guided tours and more.

The University of Washington and the University of Puget Sound are nearby. There is a $5 surcharge for one-night stays in Seattle. Send $2 for her descriptive directory.

Burrow's Bay B&B ✪
4911 MACBETH DRIVE, ANACORTES, WASHINGTON 98221

Tel: **(206) 293-4792**	Credit Cards: **MC, VISA**
Host(s): **Beverly and Winfred Stocker**	Pets: **Sometimes**
Location: **92 mi. N of Seattle**	Children: **Welcome**
Suites: **$55; sleeps 2–6**	Smoking: **No**
Open: **All year**	Social Drinking: **Permitted**
Breakfast: **Full**	Airport/Station Pickup: **Yes**

Enjoy sweeping views of the San Juan Islands from this lovely contemporary Northwest home. The guest suite consists of a large sitting room with a view and a comfortable bedroom with a blue-and-tan motif and wall-to-wall carpeting. You are sure to enjoy the privacy and relaxation of having your own private deck, fireplace, TV, and a separate entrance. Beverly and Winfred Stocker offer an extensive menu from which you may select breakfast. They are located within walking distance of Washington Park, restaurants, and ferry rides to the nearby islands. Your hosts will be glad to provide touring advice for day trips to Victoria, B.C., Deception Pass, and Port Townsend.

The Channel House ✪
2902 OAKES AVENUE, ANACORTES, WASHINGTON 98221

Tel: **(206) 293-9382**	Reduced Rates: **$10 less Oct. 1–Apr. 30**
Host(s): **Dennis and Patricia McIntyre**	Breakfast: **Full**
Location: **65 mi. N of Seattle; 18 mi. W of I-5, Exit 230**	Credit Cards: **MC, VISA**
No. of Rooms: **4**	Pets: **No**
Max. No. Sharing Bath: **4**	Children: **Welcome, over 12**
Double/sb: **$55–$65**	Smoking: **No**
Single/sb: **$45**	Social Drinking: **Permitted**
Open: **All year**	Airport/Station Pickup: **Yes**

Built in 1902 by an Italian count, this three-story Victorian house has stained-glass windows, rare antiques, gracious ambience, and is in mint condition. The guest rooms have beautiful views of Puget Sound and the San Juan Islands. It's an ideal getaway for relaxing in the "cleanest corner of the country." Your hosts serve gourmet breakfasts in front of the fireplace. The communal hot tub is a treat after salmon fishing, tennis, or golf. And it's only minutes from the ferry for visiting Victoria, British Columbia.

Dutch Treat House ✪
1220 31ST STREET, ANACORTES, WASHINGTON 98221

Tel: **(206) 293-8154**
Best Time to Call: **10 AM–1 PM**
Host(s): **Bill and Mary O'Connor**
Location: **8 mi. from I-5, Exit 230**
No. of Rooms: **3**
Max. No. Sharing Bath: **3**
Double/sb: **$50**

Open: **Feb. 1–Dec. 31**
Breakfast: **Full**
Credit Cards: **MC, VISA**
Pets: **No**
Children: **Welcome, over 8**
Smoking: **No**
Social Drinking: **Permitted**

The large, comfortable rooms have views of Mt. Baker and the marina and are decorated in a casual, country theme, enhanced by calico cats, pretty pillows, and other items crafted by Bill and Mary. Breakfast is tastefully prepared with fresh fruits in season, homemade biscuits, eggs, hotcakes, or waffles. In the evening, enjoy the never-empty coffeepot while using the library to read, play cards, or exchange travel experiences with your hosts, who are world travelers. Visit the tidal rapids at Deception Pass, the Naval Air Station, and in spring, the tulip fields at Skagit Valley.

Mountain Meadows Inn ✪
28912 STATE ROUTE 706 E, ASHFORD, WASHINGTON 98304

Tel: **(206) 569-2788**
Best Time to Call: **Before 6 PM**
Host(s): **Tanna Barney**
Location: **6 mi. from Hwy. 7, Mt. Ranier Exit**
No. of Rooms: **3**
No. of Private Baths: **1**
Max. No. Sharing Bath: **4**
Double/pb: **$70**
Single/pb: **$60**
Double/sb: **$65**
Single/sb: **$55**
Suites: **$70**
Open: **All year**
Reduced Rates: **$10 less, weekdays Nov.–Apr.; seniors**
Breakfast: **Full**
Credit Cards: **MC, VISA**
Pets: **No**
Children: **Welcome, over 12**
Smoking: **Permitted**
Social Drinking: **Permitted**
Minimum Stay: **Holidays—2-night minimum**

Tanna Barney welcomes you to her historic home, set on a picture-perfect pond. The water attracts a wide variety of wildlife, and you'll find it a fine spot for fishing and evening campfires. Inside, gracious, comfortable rooms are decorated in Early American antique furnishings. French omelets, pancakes, and homemade muffins are lovingly prepared each morning. Guests are invited to relax on the expansive veranda overlooking the pond or visit with the pet llama. Tanna is a Northwest tour specialist well-versed in the area's recreational activities. She can direct you to nearby Mt. Ranier Park, beautiful scenic spots, waterfalls, skiing, and much more.

Bellevue Bed and Breakfast ✪
830-100TH AVENUE S.E., BELLEVUE, WASHINGTON 98004

Tel: **(206) 453-1048**
Host(s): **Cy and Carol Garnett**
Location: **2 mi. E of Seattle**
No. of Rooms: **2**
No. of Private Baths: **1**
Max. No. Sharing Bath: **4**
Double/sb: **$45**
Single/sb: **$35**
Suites: **$100**
Open: **All year**
Breakfast: **Full**
Credit Cards: **MC, VISA**
Pets: **No**
Children: **Welcome, over 10**
Smoking: **No**
Social Drinking: **Permitted**
Airport/Station Pickup: **Yes**

Enjoy spectacular views of the city and mountains from this contemporary hilltop home. Guest quarters are on the first floor and consist of two bedrooms and a large living room. Family or friends traveling together can use the accommodations as a suite, and all can take advantage of the microwave, washer and dryer, and privacy of a separate entrance. Early risers will enjoy the view from the deck as the sun comes up over the Cascade Mountains. Others will wake up to the smell of hot coffee made from freshly ground beans. The Garnetts are half a mile from downtown and within walking distance of Lake Washington.

The Gallery Bed & Breakfast ✪
4 LITTLE CAPE HORN, CATHLAMET, WASHINGTON 98612

Tel: **(206) 425-7395**
Host(s): **Carolyn and Eric Feasey**
Location: **15 mi. W of Longview**
No. of Rooms: **2**
No. of Private Baths: **2 half-baths**
Max. No. Sharing Bath: **4**
Double/pb: **$60**
Open: **All year**

Reduced Rates: **$10 less for Continental breakfast; weekly**
Breakfast: **Full**
Credit Cards: **MC, VISA**
Pets: **Sometimes**
Children: **Welcome, over 10**
Smoking: **No**
Social Drinking: **Permitted**

Surrounded by tall trees, a waterfall, and flowers, this contemporary home is situated on the bank of the lower Columbia River between Portland, Oregon, and the Long Beach Peninsula. Carolyn, a former art teacher, has deftly combined select antiques with an eclectic art collection to create a warm and comfortable atmosphere. The beds are covered with lovely linens and down comforters. Breakfast is beautifully served on fine china with crystal and silver accessories. Stroll the beach or watch the ships and boats from the deck or hot tub. Browse in the Gallery's shop for a special memento of your visit. If you are arriving by boat, Eric will arrange for you to be met at the local marina.

Palmer's Chart House ✪
P.O. BOX 51, ORCAS ISLAND, DEER HARBOR, WASHINGTON 98243

Tel: **(206) 376-4231**
Host(s): **Majean and Don Palmer**
Location: **50 mi. N of Seattle**
No. of Rooms: **2**
No. of Private Baths: **2**
Double/pb: **$60–$70**
Single/pb: **$45**
Open: **All year**

Breakfast: **Continental**
Other Meals: **Dinner: $7.50**
Pets: **No**
Children: **Welcome, over 10**
Smoking: **No**
Social Drinking: **Permitted**
Foreign Languages: **Spanish**

It's just an hour's ride on the Washington State ferry from Anacortes to Orcas Island. Seasoned travelers, Majean and Don know how to make your stay special. Each guest room has a private deck from which you may survey the harbor scene. Local seafood often provides the basis for Majean's special dinners. *Amante,* the 33-foot sloop, is available for sailing when Don, the skipper, is free.

Turtleback Farm Inn ✪
ROUTE 1, BOX 650, EASTSOUND, WASHINGTON 98245

Tel: **(206) 376-4914**	Reduced Rates: **Available off-season**
Best Time to Call: **9 AM–9 PM**	Breakfast: **Full**
Host(s): **William and Susan Fletcher**	Other Meals: **Available**
Location: **60 mi. NW of Seattle**	Credit Cards: **MC, VISA**
No. of Rooms: **7**	Pets: **No**
No. of Private Baths: **7**	Children: **Welcome, over 8**
Double/pb: **$55–$95**	Smoking: **No**
Single/pb: **$45–$95**	Social Drinking: **Permitted**
Open: **All year**	Airport/Station Pickup: **Yes**

This peaceful retreat is situated on 80 acres of meadow, pasture, ponds, and woods overlooking lovely Crow Valley. The farmhouse dates back to the early 1900s. Each bedroom is furnished with antiques and each bed boasts an unusual cotton-covered wool comforter. Breakfast might consist of strawberry crêpes, corn waffles, or a delectable quiche, served on Aynsley china with pretty crystal. Guests enjoy leisurely walks, bird-watching, the music of Mozart, relaxing on the expansive deck, and the pleasant peace of being pampered.

The Harrison House ✪
210 SUNSET AVENUE, EDMONDS, WASHINGTON 98020

Tel: **(206) 776-4748**	Open: **All year**
Host(s): **Jody and Harve Harrison**	Breakfast: **Full**
Location: **15 mi. N of Seattle**	Pets: **No**
No. of Rooms: **1**	Children: **No**
No. of Private Baths: **1**	Smoking: **No**
Double/pb: **$35–$45**	Social Drinking: **Permitted**
Single/pb: **$25–$35**	

This new, informal, waterfront home has a sweeping view of Puget Sound and the Olympic Mountains. It is a block north of the ferry dock and two blocks from the center of this historic town. Many fine restaurants are within walking distance. Your spacious room has a private deck, TV, wet bar, telephone, and king-size bed. The University of Washington is nearby.

Heather House ✪
1011 "B" AVENUE, EDMONDS, WASHINGTON 98020

Tel: **(206) 778-7233**
Best Time to Call: **5–6:30 PM**
Host(s): **Harry and Joy Whitcutt**
Location: **15 mi. N of Seattle**
No. of Rooms: **1**
No. of Private Baths: **1**
Double/pb: **$35–$41**

Single/pb: **$30–$33**
Open: **All year**
Breakfast: **Continental**
Pets: **No**
Children: **No**
Smoking: **Permitted**
Social Drinking: **No**

This contemporary home has a spectacular view of Puget Sound and the Olympic Mountains. The guest room has a comfortable king-size bed and opens onto a private deck. Joy and Harry are world travelers and enjoy their guests. The homemade jams, jellies, and marmalades are delicious. You can work off breakfast by walking a mile to the shops, beaches, and fishing pier.

Hudgens Haven ✪
9313 190 SOUTH WEST, EDMONDS, WASHINGTON 98020

Tel: **(206) 776-2202**
Best Time to Call: **4–8 PM**
Host(s): **Lorna and Edward Hudgens**
No. of Rooms: **1**
No. of Private Baths: **1**
Double/pb: **$35**
Single/pb: **$30**

Open: **Mar. 1–Nov. 30**
Breakfast: **Continental**
Pets: **No**
Children: **Welcome, over 10**
Smoking: **No**
Social Drinking: **Permitted**

Hudgens Haven is located in a picture postcard town on the shores of Puget Sound. The house overlooks the water as well as the Olympic Mountain Range. The rooms are decorated with antiques and the guest room has a queen-size bed, a desk, an easy chair, and plenty of drawer space. Your hostess offers a full breakfast at a reasonable cost. She will gladly help plan daytrips and can suggest waterfront restaurants, fine shopping, and a score of recreational activities.

The Maple Tree ✪
18313 OLYMPIC VIEW DRIVE, EDMONDS, WASHINGTON 98020

Tel: **(206) 774-8420**
Host(s): **Marion and Hellon Wilkerson**
Location: **15 mi. N of Seattle**
No. of Rooms: **1**
No. of Private Baths: **1**

Double/pb: **$35**
Single/pb: **$30**
Open: **All year**
Breakfast: **Continental**
Pets: **No**

Children: **Welcome, over 5** Social Drinking: **Permitted**
Smoking: **No**

The Maple Tree is a beautifully restored older home with landscaped grounds. Located across the street from Puget Sound, it commands a stunning view of the Olympic Mountains. You're welcome to watch the activity on Puget Sound through the telescope in the solarium. Lounge on the brick patio or watch the sun set over the snowcapped mountains as you sip a glass of Washington State wine. Hellon and Marion enjoy having guests and exchanging travel experiences with them. Hellon loves to cook; both like to work in their rose garden.

Anderson House ✪
P.O. BOX 1547, 2140 MAIN STREET, FERNDALE, WASHINGTON 98248

Tel: **(206) 384-3450**
Host(s): **Dave and Kelly Anderson**
Location: **8 mi. N of Bellingham**
No. of Rooms: **5**
No. of Private Baths: **2**
Max. No. Sharing Bath: **4**
Double/pb: **$45**
Double/sb: **$35–$40**
Suites: **$65**

Open: **All year**
Breakfast: **Full**
Credit Cards: **MC, VISA**
Pets: **No**
Children: **Welcome, over 8**
Smoking: **No**
Social Drinking: **Permitted**
Minimum Stay: **2 nights on holiday weekends**

Anderson House is a slice of America as it was a hundred years ago. The authenticity of the period is evident in the carefully selected furnishings; the Bavarian crystal swan chandelier is frequently photographed by guests. It hangs over the dining room table, where freshly baked scones and muffins are served with homemade jams, fruit, and freshly ground Kona coffee. It is minutes away from the Strait of Georgia waterfront, 16 miles to Canada, and a one-hour drive to Mt. Baker.

Hill Top Bed and Breakfast ✪
5832 CHURCH STREET, FERNDALE, WASHINGTON 98248

Tel: **(206) 384-3619**
Best Time to Call: **Mornings; evenings**
Host(s): **Paul and Doris Matz**
Location: **100 mi. N of Seattle**
No. of Rooms: **2**
No. of Private Baths: **2**
Double/pb: **$34**
Single/pb: **$29**
Suites: **$39**

Open: **All year**
Reduced Rates: **Available**
Breakfast: **Continental**
Pets: **No**
Children: **Welcome (crib)**
Smoking: **No**
Social Drinking: **Permitted**
Airport/Station Pickup: **Yes**

Hill Top Bed and Breakfast is located in the Puget Sound area close to several beautiful state and local parks. The house overlooks Mt. Baker and the Cascade Mountain Range, and the view is especially nice from the patio. The house is decorated with Early American charm and the rooms have four-poster beds and homemade quilts to snuggle up in. The suite has a fireplace. Homemade breakfast specialties include coffee cakes, muffins, jams, and applesauce. This is a perfect spot for families and is convenient to Birch Bay, local islands, and Vancouver, Canada.

No Cabbages B&B ☉
7712 GOODMAN DRIVE NW, GIG HARBOR, WASHINGTON 98335

Tel: **(206) 858-7797**
Host(s): **Jamee and Dale Holder**
Location: **10 mi. from I-5**
No. of Rooms: **2**
Max. No. Sharing Bath: **4**
Double/sb: **$35**
Open: **All year**
Breakfast: **Full**
Pets: **Sometimes**
Children: **Welcome**
Smoking: **Permitted**
Social Drinking: **Permitted**
Airport/Station Pickup: **Yes**

Dwarfed by huge evergreens on the shore of the harbor, this remodeled knotty pine beach house is a peaceful place with easy access to windsurfing, boating, and fishing. It is built into a hill, with windows and a porch facing the water. Jamee, a former restaurant owner, and Dale, an avid fisherman, will direct you to local art galleries, beaches, and the University of Puget Sound.

The Parsonage ☉
4107 BURNHAM DRIVE, GIG HARBOR, WASHINGTON 98335

Tel: **(206) 851-8654**
Best Time to Call: **10 AM–10 PM**
Host(s): **Edward and Sheila Koscik**
Location: **9 mi. W of Tacoma**
No. of Rooms: **2**
Max. No. Sharing Bath: **4**
Double/sb: **$45**
Single/sb: **$35**
Open: **All year**
Breakfast: **Full**
Pets: **Sometimes**
Children: **Sometimes**
Smoking: **Permitted**
Social Drinking: **Permitted**

The Parsonage is a 1901 Victorian surrounded by towering pines and strawberry fields. This was Gig Harbor's first Methodist parsonage, until 1984 when the Kosciks purchased the house. They added modern touches, such as a new guest bath, but were careful to retain the old-fashioned charm of the rooms. Breakfast features fresh seasonal berries, homemade muffins, and applesauce. The Parsonage is just a short walk from the picturesque harbor, with a variety of restaurants, shops, galleries, and marinas. Rental bicycles are available, and sightseeing and charter boats offer hours of fun and relaxation.

Log Castle Bed & Breakfast ✪
3273 EAST SARATOGA ROAD, LANGLEY, WASHINGTON 98260

Tel: **(206) 321-5483**
Best Time to Call: **8 AM–9 PM**
Host(s): **Jack and Norma Metcalf**
Location: **40 mi. N of Seattle**
No. of Rooms: **3**
No. of Private Baths: **3**
Double/pb: **$60–$75**
Open: **All year**

Breakfast: **Full**
Credit Cards: **MC, VISA**
Pets: **No**
Children: **Welcome, over 11**
Smoking: **No**
Social Drinking: **No**
Airport/Station Pickup: **Yes**

You don't have to build your castle on the sand on Whidbey Island, because one already awaits you. The imaginative design of this log lodge includes an eight-sided tower where any modern-day princess would feel at home. Taredo wood stairways, leaded and stained-glass motifs, and comfortable furnishings create a rustic yet sophisticated atmosphere. The three guest rooms all offer beautiful views of the surrounding mountains and water. Relax beside a large stone fireplace, take a rowboat ride, or a long walk on the beach. Your hostess offers breads and cinnamon rolls right from the oven as part of a hearty breakfast served on a big, round, log table. Host Jack Metcalf is a state senator and also loves to entertain when he is not working at the legislature.

West Shore Farm B&B ✪
2781 WEST SHORE DRIVE, LUMMI ISLAND, WASHINGTON 98262

Tel: **(206) 758-2600**
Best Time to Call: **8 AM–9 PM**
Host(s): **Polly and Carl Hanson**
Location: **10 mi. from I-5, Exit 260**
No. of Rooms: **2**
Max. No. Sharing Bath: **2**
Double/pb: **$45**
Single/pb: **$35**
Open: **All year**

Breakfast: **Full**
Other Meals: **Available**
Credit Cards: **MC, VISA**
Pets: **No**
Children: **Welcome (crib)**
Smoking: **No**
Social Drinking: **Permitted**
Airport/Station Pickup: **Yes**

Architects are intrigued by the Hansons' self-built home, marveling at the design and innovative solution to common storage problems. Large windows overlook the Puget Sound islands and Canadian mountains. Sunsets are stunning. You can sit on the beach and watch bald eagles fly by, seals sunning on the offshore rocks, and boats on course to Alaska and Canada. Polly is a librarian and Carl is an aeronautical engineer who built and flies his own plane. They both enjoy having guests and often treat them to homemade ice cream topped with just-picked local fruit.

Maple Valley Bed & Breakfast ✪
20020 SE 228, MAPLE VALLEY, WASHINGTON 98038

Tel: **(206) 432-1409**
Host(s): **Clarke and Jayne Hurlbut**
Location: **26 mi. SE of Seattle**
No. of Rooms: **2**
Max. No. Sharing Bath: **4**
Double/sb: **$45**
Single/sb: **$35**

Open: **All year**
Breakfast: **Full**
Pets: **No**
Children: **Welcome**
Smoking: **No**
Social Drinking: **Permitted**
Airport/Station Pickup: **Yes**

After a good night's sleep in either of the B&B's guest rooms—one with a four-poster log bed and the other complete with a pink rosebud tea set, you'll come down to breakfast at a table that overlooks the lawn, the Hurlbuts' resident peacocks, and a wildlife pond teeming with a variety of northwestern birds. If the morning is cool, you'll be warmed by a stone fireplace and you won't go away hungry after orange juice, lemon-blueberry muffins, a plate-sized hootenany pancake (served with whipped cream, strawberries, slivered almonds, and syrup), ham, sausage or bacon, fresh-ground coffee, tea, or hot chocolate.

Puget View Guesthouse ✪
7924 61ST NORTHEAST, OLYMPIA, WASHINGTON 98506

Tel: **(206) 459-1676**
Best Time to Call: **Evenings**
Host(s): **Dick and Barbara Yunker**
Location: **4½ mi. from I-5, Exit 111**
No. of Rooms: **1 cottage**
No. of Private Baths: **1**
Guest Cottage: **$49–$90; sleeps 2–4**
Open: **All year**

Reduced Rates: **10%, seniors; families**
Breakfast: **Continental**
Credit Cards: **MC, VISA**
Pets: **Sometimes**
Children: **Welcome**
Smoking: **Permitted**
Social Drinking: **Permitted**

This charming waterfront guest cottage is located next to Tolmie State Park and adjacent to Dick and Barbara's log home. The panoramic Puget Sound setting makes it a popular, romantic getaway. You are apt to discover simple pleasures such as beachcombing or bird-watching and activities such as kayaking or scuba diving. Barbara and Dick are likely to invite you on a boat picnic or an oystering excursion. Your breakfast tray, a lavish and elegant repast, is brought to the cottage. You are welcome to use the beachside campfire for an evening cookout or to barbecue on your deck.

Sylvester House B&B
1803 CAPITOL WAY, OLYMPIA, WASHINGTON 98501

Tel: **(206) 786-8582**
Best Time to Call: **9 AM–9 PM**
Host(s): **Art and Jane Van Allen**
Location: **½ mi. from I-5**
No. of Rooms: **3**
Max. No. Sharing Bath: **3**
Double/sb: **$45**
Single/sb: **$39**

Open: **All year**
Breakfast: **Full**
Credit Cards: **MC, VISA**
Pets: **No**
Children: **Welcome**
Smoking: **No**
Social Drinking: **Permitted**
Airport/Station Pickup: **Yes**

Listed on the Olympia Historical Register, the house is within walking distance of the State Capitol Campus with its rotunda, gardens, lawns, legislative offices, and governor's mansion. Art and Jane provide thoughtful touches such as fresh flowers in the bedrooms or a candlelit bath for romantics. If you're in town on business, use of their copy machine, personal computer, and phone services can be arranged.

Orcas Hotel
P.O. BOX 155, ORCAS, WASHINGTON 98280

Tel: **(206) 376-4300**
Host(s): **Barbara and John Jamieson**
Location: **90 mi. NW of Seattle**
No. of Rooms: **12**
No. of Private Baths: **3**
Max. No. Sharing Bath: **4**
Double/pb: **$75**
Single/pb: **$65**
Double/sb: **$48–$62**
Single/sb: **$38–$52**
Open: **All year**

Reduced Rates: **Available**
Breakfast: **Continental**
Other Meals: **Available**
Credit Cards: **AMEX, MC, VISA**
Pets: **No**
Children: **Welcome**
Smoking: **Permitted**
Social Drinking: **Permitted**
Airport/Station Pickup: **Yes**
Foreign Languages: **French, Spanish**

The Orcas Hotel is a Victorian seaside inn overlooking Harney Channel and the ferry landing. The hotel has been lovingly restored and is listed on the National Register of Historic Places. The rooms feature antiques and modern, queen-size beds, with quilts custom stitched by island quilters. A fully stocked cocktail lounge with a bar menu and fine wine list is available for your relaxing pleasure. A wide range of homemade pastries, fruit-filled pancakes, sticky buns, omelets, and meats are served for breakfast. Your hosts will gladly direct you to Moran State Park, Cascade Lake, hiking and mo-ped trails, and a score of other activities in the San Juan Islands.

French House at Lake Pateros ✪
206 WEST WARREN, BOX 595, PATEROS, WASHINGTON 98846

Tel: **(509) 923-2626**
Host(s): **Bob and Charlene Knoop**
Location: **19 mi. N of Chelan**
No. of Rooms: **2**
Max. No. Sharing Bath: **4**
Double/sb: **$45**
Single/sb: **$32**
Open: **All year**

Reduced Rates: **20% off-season; seniors**
Breakfast: **Full**
Pets: **No**
Children: **Welcome**
Smoking: **No**
Social Drinking: **Permitted**

This white Dutch Colonial has a red roof, red shutters, and is furnished with oak, wicker, and plants. The beds have handmade quilts and fluffy down pillows. It is located in the north-central part of the state, the heart of Apple Country. Columbia River provides fabulous year-round fishing and water sports. Bob and Charlene invite you to use the kitchen for light snacks. They will arrange river-raft trips, horseback riding, and llama pack trips if you are enthusiastic outdoorsmen, as they are.

Ogle's Bed and Breakfast ✪
1307 DOGWOOD HILL SOUTH WEST, PORT ORCHARD, WASHINGTON 98366

Tel: **(206) 876-9170**
Host(s): **Quentin and Louise Ogle**
Location: **25 mi. N of Tacoma**
No. of Rooms: **2**
Max. No. Sharing Bath: **3**
Double/sb: **$40**
Single/sb: **$35**

Open: **All year**
Breakfast: **Full**
Pets: **No**
Children: **Welcome, over 10**
Smoking: **No**
Social Drinking: **Permitted**

This single-level contemporary is located on a quiet private road in the hills of Port Orchard. The house is surrounded by fruit trees and blackberry bushes, and overlooks Puget Sound. The rooms are comfortably furnished with special touches like hand-braided wool rugs, Korean brass-bound chests, and nautical memorabilia. Guest rooms have beautiful views of the surrounding hills. Each morning an elegant breakfast may be enjoyed on the sun deck or in front of picture windows. Port Orchard is known for its marinas, marquee-covered sidewalks, specialty shops, and restaurants. It's a good jumping-off point for exploring Seattle and the historic towns of the Olympic Peninsula.

Cedarym—A Colonial Bed & Breakfast ✪
1011 240TH AVENUE NORTHEAST, REDMOND, WASHINGTON 98053

Tel: **(206) 868-4159**
Host(s): **Mary Ellen and Walt Brown**
Location: **15 mi. E of Seattle**
No. of Rooms: **2**
Max. No. Sharing Bath: **4**
Double/sb: **$40**
Open: **All year**

Breakfast: **Full**
Credit Cards: **MC, VISA**
Pets: **No**
Children: **No**
Smoking: **No**
Social Drinking: **Permitted**

Cedarym is a spacious Colonial reproduction located on the Sammamish Plateau. The house has Cape Cod-style pine floors, wrought-iron door latches, and a large cooking-style fireplace in the keeping room.

Guest rooms feature antique brass beds and comfortable sitting areas for reading or watching television, and each has old-fashioned wall stenciling. The breakfast table glows with hand-dipped candles and is covered with specialties such as Dutch Babies, muffins, and a variety of egg dishes. Guests are welcome to stroll the spacious grounds and visit the rose garden and the cottage garden, with its flowers and herbs. A gazebo-sheltered spa is guaranteed to relax you. This lovely Colonial is a short drive from the sights of Seattle. Cedarym is featured on our cover.

Summer Song B&B ○
P.O. BOX 82, SEABECK, WASHINGTON 98380

Tel: **(206) 830-5089**	Breakfast: **Continental**
Host(s): **Ron and Sharon Barney**	Credit Cards: **MC, VISA**
Location: **9 mi. SW of Silverdale**	Pets: **Sometimes**
No. of Rooms: **1**	Children: **Sometimes**
No. of Private Baths: **1**	Smoking: **Permitted**
Double/pb: **$50**	Social Drinking: **Permitted**
Open: **All year**	

Enjoy your own private cottage on the shores of Hood Canal when you visit Summer Song. The cabin sleeps four, and features a bedroom, living and dining room, full kitchen, and bath. A cozy fireplace, old-fashioned wainscoting, and private decks with fire pit, barbecue, and mountain view complete this cozy retreat. Your hosts serve breakfast at the cottage or on the beach. Huckleberry muffins made from freshly picked fruit are the house specialty. Ron and Sharon provide all the comforts of home, such as beach towels and robes. Their beach is perfect for swimming and a public boat launch is just one mile away. Beautiful nature trails at Scenic Beach State Park are just a short walk away.

Beech Tree Manor ○
1405 QUEEN ANNE AVENUE NORTH, SEATTLE, WASHINGTON 98109

Tel: **(206) 281-7037**	Open: **All year**
Best Time to Call: **After 10 AM**	Reduced Rates: **Weekly, Jan.–Apr.**
Host(s): **Virginia Lucero**	Breakfast: **Continental**
Location: **2 mi. from I-5, Exit 166**	Credit Cards: **MC, VISA**
No. of Rooms: **4**	Pets: **Sometimes**
Max. No. Sharing Bath: **4**	Children: **Welcome**
Double/sb: **$55–$60**	Smoking: **No**
Single/sb: **$50–$55**	Social Drinking: **Permitted**

The manor's name is derived from the massive copper beech tree in the front yard. The English-style interior, accented by open-beam ceilings and antiques, has been artistically decorated by Virginia. Special touches, such as pure cotton bed linens, oversized, plush bath towels, a shady porch with wicker rockers, and a pleasant parlor reading room, add to your comfort. Breakfast often features Dutch Babies with blackberries, freshly baked scones or popovers, and fresh fruits of the season. Electric trolleys link the manor to downtown Seattle.

Chambered Nautilus Bed and Breakfast Inn ✪
5005 22ND AVENUE NORTH EAST, SEATTLE, WASHINGTON 98105

Tel: **(206) 522-2536**
Host(s): **Kate McDill and Deborah Sweet**
Location: **4 mi. NE of downtown**
No. of Rooms: **6**
No. of Private Baths: **2**
Max. No. Sharing Bath: **4**
Double/pb: **$60–$85**
Single/pb: **$55–$80**
Double/sb: **$50–$76**
Single/sb: **$48–$72**
Open: **All year**
Reduced Rates: **10% on 5th night**
Breakfast: **Continental**
Credit Cards: **AMEX, DC, MC, VISA**
Pets: **No**
Children: **Welcome, over 12**
Smoking: **No**
Social Drinking: **Permitted**

This 1915 Georgian mansion faces the Cascade Mountains and Lake Washington. One bedroom is romantic, with lots of oak; another is sunny, with inlaid mahogany pieces; several have balconies. Breakfast is served in the fireplaced dining room. Your hosts will be happy to direct you to local theaters, restaurants, and sports activities. The University of Washington is nearby.

Galer Place B&B Guest House ✪
318 WEST GALER, SEATTLE, WASHINGTON 98119

Tel: **(206) 282-5339**
Host(s): **Chris Chamberlain**
Location: **2 mi. from I-5, Mercer St. Exit**
No. of Rooms: **4**
No. of Private Baths: **2**
Max. No. Sharing Bath: **4**
Double/pb: **$75**
Single/pb: **$70**
Double/sb: **$65**
Single/sb: **$60**
Open: **All year**
Breakfast: **Full**
Credit Cards: **AMEX, DC, MC, VISA**
Pets: **Welcome**
Children: **Welcome, over 12**
Smoking: **Permitted**
Social Drinking: **Permitted**

A south Queen Anne Hill location sets this early-1900s home within walking distance of Seattle Center. A trolley line provides front-door service to the downtown area. The hallmarks of the generous breakfast are its fresh-baked breads, homemade preserves, and just-ground coffee. Several parks and scenic viewpoints are within strolling distance, as are an indoor swimming pool and running track. A hot tub, on the backyard deck, is a delightful place to unwind. You are invited to join your British hostess for tea and homemade cookies.

Hainsworth House ✪
2657 37TH SOUTH WEST, P.O. BOX 16438, SEATTLE, WASHINGTON 98126

Tel: **(206) 938-1020 or 932-0654**
Host(s): **Carl and Charlotte Muia**
Location: **3 mi. W of Seattle**
No. of Rooms: **2**
No. of Private Baths: **2**
Double/pb: **$65–$75**
Open: **All year**

Reduced Rates: **Weekly**
Breakfast: **Full**
Pets: **No**
Children: **No**
Smoking: **No**
Social Drinking: **Permitted**

The Hainsworth House is an English Tudor mansion overlooking Seattle. It is surrounded by beautiful lawns and is across the street from a park donated to the city by the Hainsworth family. The present owners, Carl and Charlotte Muia, have done extensive restoration work to the interior, following the original drawings down to the last ceiling beam. Guests will find the antique-filled rooms and gourmet breakfasts in keeping with the elegant traditions of the house. Eggs Benedict, salmon strata, German pancakes, and omelets are a few of the favorites.

Hanson House B&B
1526 PALM AVENUE SW, SEATTLE, WASHINGTON 98116

Tel: **(206) 937-4157**
Host(s): **Jody and F. Ken Weaver**
Location: **3 mi. from I-5**
No. of Rooms: **2**
No. of Private Baths: **2**
Double/pb: **$70**
Single/pb: **$60**
Open: **All year**

Breakfast: **Continental**
Pets: **Welcome**
Children: **No**
Smoking: **No**
Social Drinking: **Permitted**
Airport/Station Pickup: **Yes**
Foreign Languages: **Spanish**

Hanson House guests are always awed by the spectacular view of Elliott Bay and the Seattle skyline, from Mt. Rainier to Mt. Baker. Ferries slide by every 20 to 30 minutes, the *Princess Marguerite* leaves her berth every day during the summer, and the *Victoria Clipper* makes its round-trips from Seattle to Victoria and Vancouver and back. Originally built as a summer home, Hanson House was extensively remodeled in 1984. Breakfasts feature the specialty of the house, Dutch Babies pancakes.

Marit's Bed and Breakfast ✪
6208 PALATINE AVENUE, SEATTLE, WASHINGTON 98103

Tel: **(206) 782-7900**
Best Time to Call: **Mornings; evenings**
Host(s): **Marit Nelson**
Location: **5 mi. N of City Center**
No. of Rooms: **2**
Max. No. Sharing Bath: **4**
Double/sb: **$45**
Single/sb: **$35**
Open: **All year**

Reduced Rates: **10%, weekly; seniors**
Breakfast: **Full**
Pets: **No**
Children: **Welcome (crib)**
Smoking: **No**
Social Drinking: **Permitted**
Airport/Station Pickup: **Yes**
Foreign Languages: **Norwegian**

This brick, ivy-covered Tudor home is just ten minutes from downtown Seattle. Guests can enjoy the convenience of being close to the city while staying in comfortable rooms overlooking the mountains and the water. Marit Nelson specializes in Scandinavian hospitality. She prepares Norwegian specialties for breakfast along with homemade bread and jam, juice, fruit, freshly ground coffee, and assorted teas. The house is close to the University of Washington and is within walking distance of the Woodland Park Zoo and Green Lake.

Roberta's Bed and Breakfast
1147 SIXTEENTH AVENUE EAST, SEATTLE, WASHINGTON 98112

Tel: **(206) 329-3326**
Host(s): **Roberta Barry**
No. of Rooms: **4**
No. of Private Baths: **1**
Max. No. Sharing Bath: **3**
Double/pb: **$65–$75**
Single/pb: **$57–$67**
Double/sb: **$57–$67**

Single/sb: **$47–$57**
Open: **All year**
Breakfast: **Full**
Credit Cards: **AMEX, DC, MC, VISA**
Pets: **No**
Children: **Sometimes**
Smoking: **No**
Social Drinking: **Permitted**

Roberta's is a 1904 frame Victorian with a large, old-fashioned front porch. The house is located in a quiet, historic neighborhood near the heart of the city. Cheerful rooms filled with antiques await you: the Peach Room has a brass bed, bay windows, and grandma's fancy desk; the Plum Room has twin beds and a loft that can sleep an extra person. In the morning you'll smell a pot of coffee right beside your door. That's just a warmup for the large breakfast to come. The specialty of the house is Dutch Babies, a local dish, served with powdered sugar or fresh berries. Guests are welcome to relax in the living room and join Roberta for a glass of sherry.

Salisbury House
750 16TH AVENUE EAST, SEATTLE, WASHINGTON 98112

Tel: **(206) 328-8682**
Best Time to Call: **10 AM–1 PM; 5 PM–8 PM**
Host(s): **Mary and Catherine Wiese**
Location: **1 mi. from I-5**
No. of Rooms: **4**
Max. No. Sharing Bath: **4**
Double/sb: **$48–$58**
Single/sb: **$43–$53**

Open: **All year**
Reduced Rates: **10%, weekly**
Breakfast: **Continental**
Credit Cards: **AMEX, MC, VISA**
Pets: **No**
Children: **Welcome, over 12**
Smoking: **No**
Social Drinking: **Permitted**
Foreign Languages: **Spanish**

This elegant family home, built in 1904, has been lovingly restored by your hostesses, a mother-daughter team. It is located in a quiet neighborhood within walking distance of parks, restaurants, shops, and the Seattle Art Museum. Two of the guest rooms are small and cozy; the other two face the front of the house with window seats providing an attractive accent. A renovated Victorian-style bathroom features a six-foot clawfoot tub. You are invited to enjoy your morning coffee on the sun porch and an evening glass of sherry in the library.

Seattle Bed & Breakfast ✪
2442 N.W. MARKET # 300, SEATTLE, WASHINGTON 98107

Tel: **(206) 783-2169**
Host(s): **Inge Pokrandt**
Location: **1 mi. from I-5**
No. of Rooms: **4**
No. of Private Baths: **2**
Suites: **$35–$45**
Guest Cottage: **$55 for 2**
Open: **All year**

Breakfast: **Continental**
Credit Cards: **AMEX, MC, VISA**
Pets: **No**
Children: **Welcome, over 8**
Smoking: **No**
Social Drinking: **Permitted**
Foreign Languages: **German**

The charming two-bedroom cottage is close to downtown, the University of Washington, the zoo, and all sightseeing. Enjoy the privacy, the fine oak furniture, the fireplace, and all the little touches that make you feel welcome. The private suite in Inge's home has a full kitchen, and breakfast food is provided. Fresh flowers, fruits, and candy all spell out a warm welcome.

William House Bed & Breakfast ✪
1505 FOURTH AVENUE NORTH, SEATTLE, WASHINGTON 98109

Tel: **(206) 285-0810**
Best Time to Call: **Mornings**
Host(s): **Susan, Danielle, and Doug Williams**
Location: **½ mi. from I-5**
No. of Rooms: **5**
No. of Private Baths: **1½**
Max. No. Sharing Bath: **4**
Double/pb: **$70**
Single/pb: **$60**

Double/sb: **$49–$60**
Single/sb: **$45–$50**
Open: **All year**
Reduced Rates: **Available**
Breakfast: **Full**
Credit Cards: **AMEX, DC, MC, VISA**
Pets: **No**
Children: **Welcome (crib)**
Smoking: **Permitted**
Social Drinking: **Permitted**

This large family home is located in a quiet neighborhood on top of Queen Anne Hill. It combines easy city access with commanding views of the Cascade Mountains, Mount Rainier, the downtown skyline and Puget Sound. Built in 1900, the original woodwork and sculptured tin wallcovering give warmth, charm and character to the living room and dining area. Your hosts feel their primary job is to make your stay the right mix of personal contact and personal privacy.

Luckey's Residence
WEST 828 28TH AVENUE, SPOKANE, WASHINGTON 99203

Tel: **(509) 624-3627**
Host(s): **Robert, Patricia, and Royden Luckey**
Location: **2 mi. from I-90**
No. of Rooms: **4**
No. of Private Baths: **2**
Max. No. Sharing Bath: **4**
Double/sb: **$35**
Single/sb: **$25**
Open: **All year**
Breakfast: **Continental**
Pets: **No**
Children: **Welcome**
Smoking: **No**
Social Drinking: **No**

Luckey's has been described as a "Hansel and Gretel" house. It was built in the 1930s to look like an English cottage. The house is set in the South Hill section, a neighborhood set on a hillside covered with pine trees and volcanic rock. Your hosts offer a choice of twin- or queen-size beds. They serve a breakfast of homemade breads, cheeses, fruits, assorted juices, and plenty of coffee or tea. Luckey's is two blocks from High Drive, a scenic parkway along the hillside overlooking the canyon. A park with a large public swimming pool, children's wading pool, tennis court, and play area is a short walk from the house.

Inge's Place ✪
6809 LAKE GROVE S.W., TACOMA, WASHINGTON 98499

Tel: **(206) 584-4514**
Host(s): **Ingeborg Deatherage**
Location: **3 mi. from I-5**
No. of Rooms: **3**
No. of Private Baths: **1**
Max. No. Sharing Bath: **4**
Double/pb: **$40**
Single/pb: **$30**
Double/sb: **$40**
Single/sb: **$30**
Suites: **$60**
Open: **All year**
Reduced Rates: **Available**
Breakfast: **Full**
Pets: **No**
Children: **Welcome**
Smoking: **Permitted**
Social Drinking: **Permitted**
Airport/Station Pickup: **Yes**
Foreign Languages: **German**

This spic-and-span home is in a lovely Tacoma suburb called Lakewood. Feel welcome to use the hot tub, large backyard, and patio. There are many restaurants and shopping centers within walking distance, and several nearby lakes where fishing is excellent. Tacoma is the gateway to Mount Rainier. Inge is a world traveler, teacher, and enthusiast about B&Bs.

Keenan House ✪
2610 NORTH WARNER, TACOMA, WASHINGTON 98407

Tel: **(206) 752-0702**
Host(s): **Lenore Keenan**
Location: **2½ mi. from I-5**
No. of Rooms: **8**
No. of Private Baths: **1**
Max. No. Sharing Bath: **4**
Double/pb: **$45**
Single/pb: **$40**
Double/sb: **$40**

Single/sb: **$30**
Open: **June 1–Dec. 31**
Reduced Rates: **Weekly; 15%, families**
Breakfast: **Full**
Pets: **No**
Children: **Welcome**
Smoking: **No**
Social Drinking: **Permitted**

This spacious Victorian house is located in the historic district near Puget Sound. It is furnished in antiques and period pieces. Afternoon tea is served, and ice is available for cocktails; fruit and croissants are served with breakfast. Local possibilities include Puget Sound, Vashon Island, the state park, zoo, and ferry. It's only five blocks to the University of Puget Sound.

Llama Ranch Bed & Breakfast ✪
1980 HIGHWAY 141, WHITE SALMON, WASHINGTON 98672

Tel: **(509) 395-2786**
Host(s): **Jerry and Rebeka Stone**
Location: **50 mi. E of Portland, Ore.**
No. of Rooms: **5**
Max. No. Sharing Bath: **4**
Double/sb: **$45**
Single/sb: **$35**
Open: **All year**

Reduced Rates: **$5 less, Dec.–Mar.; 15%, weekly**
Breakfast: **Continental**
Credit Cards: **Discover, MC, VISA**
Pets: **Sometimes**
Children: **Welcome**
Smoking: **No**
Social Drinking: **Permitted**

Jerry and Rebeka enjoy sharing their love of llamas with their guests, and it is a rare person who can resist a llama's charm. Their B&B commands stunning views of Mt. Adams and Mt. Hood. The guest rooms are unpretentious and comfortable. Llama Ranch is located on 97 acres at the base of the Mt. Adams Wilderness Area. Nearby activities include horseback riding, white-water rafting, plane trips over Mount Saint Helens, water sports, and cave exploration. The less adventurous are certain to enjoy learning about the ranch's serene animals.

WEST VIRGINIA

- Wheeling
- Morgantown
- Shepherdstown
- Gerrardstown
- Summit Point
- Moorefield
- Mathias
- Marlinton

Prospect Hill
BOX 135, GERRARDSTOWN, WEST VIRGINIA 25420

Tel: **(304) 229-3346**
Best Time to Call: **Evenings**
Host(s): **Hazel and Charles Hudock**
Location: **4 mi. from Rte. 81**
No. of Rooms: **3**
No. of Private Baths: **3**
Double/pb: **$75–85**
Single/pb: **$65–$75**
Separate Guest Cottage: **$85 for 2; $125 for 4**

Open: **All year**
Reduced Rates: **Weekdays**
Breakfast: **Full**
Pets: **No**
Children: **Welcome (in cottage)**
Smoking: **Permitted**
Social Drinking: **Permitted**

Prospect Hill is a Georgian mansion set on 225 acres. The house dates back to the 1790s and is listed on the National Register of Historic

Places. One can see that this was a well-to-do gentleman's home, with permanent Franklin fireplaces, antiques, and a hall mural depicting life in the days of the early Republic. Guests may choose one of the beautifully appointed rooms in the main house or the former servants' quarters, complete with country kitchen and a fireplace in the living room. There is much to do on this working farm, including visiting the antebellum outbuildings, fishing, biking, and exploring the vast grounds. Near historic Harpers Ferry, Martinsburg, and Winchester, the area offers fine sightseeing and splendid restaurants.

The Carriage House Inn ✪
STAR ROUTE 1, BOX 56, MARLINTON, WEST VIRGINIA 24954

Tel: **(304) 799-7356**
Best Time to Call: **9 AM–8 PM**
Host(s): **Shari and Dave Gonyea**
Location: **65 mi. W of Staunton, Virginia**
No. of Rooms: **5**
No. of Private Baths: **3**
Max. No. Sharing Bath: **4**
Double/pb: **$45**
Single/pb: **$35**
Double/sb: **$35**
Single/sb: **$25**

Suites: **$65–$85**
Open: **All year**
Reduced Rates: **Available**
Breakfast: **Full**
Other Meals: **Available**
Credit Cards: **AMEX, MC, VISA**
Pets: **Welcome**
Children: **Welcome**
Smoking: **No**
Social Drinking: **No**
Airport/Station Pickup: **Yes**

Dave and Shari dreamed of opening a bed and breakfast for many years before they found this Greek Revival home. Built in 1852 by Amos Barlow, it is sure to satisfy many other dreamers and romantics. The house is painted Williamsburg blue with white trim and barn-red doors. Inside, you'll be surrounded by scents of potpourri, by fresh flowers, folk art, and brass. Select one of the antique-filled rooms or a carriage house suite, all furnished with designer linens, quilts, antiques, and stenciling. On cool mornings, homemade breads, waffles, and omelets are served beside the dining room wood stove; breakfast is served on the deck in summer, or in your room if you prefer. Your hosts will direct you to the best local hiking, fishing, golf, and skiing. When you want to take a break, home-baked goodies, a library full of books, and a relaxing hot tub await at the inn.

Valley View Farm ✪
RTE. 1, BOX 467, MATHIAS, WEST VIRGINIA 26812

Tel: **(304) 897-5229**
Best Time to Call: **Evenings after 7 PM**

Host(s): **Ernest and Edna Shipe**
Location: **130 mi. SW of D.C.**

No. of Rooms: **4**
Max. No. Sharing Bath: **6**
Double/sb: **$30**
Single/sb: **$15**
Open: **All year**
Reduced Rates: **Weekly**
Breakfast: **Full**

Other Meals: **Available**
Pets: **Welcome**
Children: **Welcome (crib)**
Smoking: **Permitted**
Social Drinking: **Permitted**
Airport/Station Pickup: **Yes**

Edna and Ernest raise cattle and sheep on their 250-acre farm. The 1920s farmhouse is decorated with comfortable Early American-style furniture and family mementos, and there's a nice porch for relaxed visiting. This is no place to diet because Edna is a good cook. Seasonal recreational activities are available in nearby Lost River State Park and on Rock Cliff Lake. You are certain to enjoy the local festivals, house tours, and interesting craft shops.

McMechen House Inn ✪
109 N. MAIN STREET, MOOREFIELD, WEST VIRGINIA 26836

Tel: **(304) 538-2417**
Host(s): **Art and Evelyn Valotto**
Location: **At junction of Rtes. 55 and 220**
No. of Rooms: **11**
No. of Private Baths: **6**
Double/pb: **$45**
Single/pb: **$30**

Suites: **$45 for 2**
Open: **Jan. 16–Dec. 24**
Breakfast: **Full**
Credit Cards: **AMEX, MC, VISA**
Pets: **No**
Children: **Welcome**
Smoking: **Permitted**
Social Drinking: **Permitted**

Cradled in the historic South Branch Valley and surrounded by the majestic mountains of the Potomac Highlands, the inn, built in 1853, is a three-story brick Federal-style house. During the Civil War it served as headquarters for both North and South as the region changed hands. It is furnished in antiques of the period. Breakfast is served family-style in the dining room. When calling, please allow 10 rings.

Thomas Shepherd Inn ✪
300 WEST GERMAN STREET, P.O. BOX 1162, SHEPHERDSTOWN, WEST VIRGINIA 25443

Tel: **(304) 876-3715**
Host(s): **Ed and Carol Ringoot**
Location: **70 mi. W of Baltimore, Md.**
No. of Rooms: **6**
No. of Private Baths: **4**
Max. No. Sharing Bath: **4**

Double/pb: **$65–$75**
Double/sb: **$60–$70**
Open: **All year**
Reduced Rates: **Available**
Breakfast: **Full**
Credit Cards: **MC, VISA**

Pets: **No**
Children: **Welcome, over 12**
Smoking: **No**
Social Drinking: **Permitted**
Foreign Languages: **Flemish, French**

Located in the beautiful Eastern Panhandle, this brick Federal-style house, built in 1868, is furnished with period antiques, with an emphasis on comfort and quality. All the guest rooms have antique beds, wing chairs, and Oriental rugs. It is within minutes of the Potomac River and the C&O Canal for hiking and biking (bikes are available), the Shenandoah River for white-water rafting, and an excellent selection of restaurants and shops. Breakfast favorites of puffed apple pancakes, Belgian waffles, or ham-and-cheese soufflé are often featured. Complimentary beverages are always generously offered. Washington, D.C., is 65 miles away.

Countryside ✪
BOX 57, SUMMIT POINT, WEST VIRGINIA 25446

Tel: **(304) 725-2614**
Best Time to Call: **8–10 AM; 4–10 PM**
Host(s): **Lisa and Daniel Hileman**
Location: **6 mi. from Rtes. 7, 340**
No. of Rooms: **2**
No. of Private Baths: **2**
Double/pb: **$40–$50**
Single/pb: **$40–$50**

Open: **All year**
Breakfast: **Continental**
Pets: **No**
Children: **No**
Smoking: **No**
Social Drinking: **Permitted**
Airport/Station Pickup: **Yes**

In the Shenandoah Valley of the Eastern Panhandle, only 20 minutes from Harpers Ferry, this country home with white shutters, large yard, and patio is on a quiet street in a charming old village. It is furnished with country oak furniture, antique quilts, and original art. Lisa and Daniel offer hospitable touches of fruit and candy, placed in each guest room. Afternoon tea is served; snacks and beverages are always available.

Yesterdays Ltd. Bed and Breakfast ○
MAIN HOUSE, 651 MAIN STREET, WHEELING, WEST VIRGINIA 26003

Tel: **(304) 232-0864**
Best Time to Call: **Afternoons; evenings**
Host(s): **Julie and David Sapper**
Location: **55 mi. S of Pittsburgh**
No. of Rooms: **4**
No. of Private Baths: **2**
Max. No. Sharing Bath: **4**
Double/pb: **$60**
Double/sb: **$60**
Suites: **$70**
Open: **All year**
Reduced Rates: **Available**
Breakfast: **Full**
Credit Cards: **MC, VISA**
Pets: **No**
Children: **Welcome (crib)**
Smoking: **Permitted**
Social Drinking: **Permitted**
Airport/Station Pickup: **Yes**

David and Julie Sapper left Chicago to be part of the Victorian restoration of Wheeling. The town fits in with their appreciation for old things and a desire to make new friends. They invite you to a four-story red brick town house dating back to 1895. The house is filled with fine architectural detail, from the ruby-red window to the ornately hand-carved woodwork. Bedrooms have brass or walnut beds with eyelet comforters, hardwood floors, Oriental rugs, and special touches such as fresh flowers and mints on the pillows. Julie's special French toast recipe is served in a rose-and-oak breakfast room overlooking the Ohio River. Guests are welcome to browse through the old hats, soldiers' letters, and antique journals in the parlor, or you may be inspired to find your own Victoriana in the town's many shops. After a day of browsing, join the Sappers for wine and cheese on the porch overlooking the water.

WISCONSIN

Bed & Breakfast Guest-Homes
ROUTE 2, ALGOMA, WISCONSIN 54201

Tel: **(414) 743-9742**
Best Time to Call: **7 AM–9 PM**
Coordinator: **Eileen Wood**
States/Regions Covered: **Statewide**

Rates (Single/Double):
  Modest: $28–$35 $35–$40
  Average: $35–$45 $40–$55
  Luxury: $45–$70 $55–$75
Credit Cards: **MC, VISA**

This reservation service offers you local color and relaxing surroundings with many accommodations in popular Door County. Eileen carefully selects the accommodations to assure each guest of a hospitable host in clean, comfortable homes. Most serve full breakfasts.

Homes on the waterfront are slightly more expensive from July to early September. There is a 10% discount for week-long stays.

Bed & Breakfast Information Service—Wisconsin
458 GLENWAY STREET, MADISON, WISCONSIN 53711

Tel: **(608) 238-6776**
Best Time to Call: **8–12 AM**
Coordinator: **Carol Jean Buelow**
States/Regions Covered: **Statewide**

Rates (Single/Double):
  Modest: **$20–$30** **$25–$45**
  Average: **$30–$40** **$45–$60**
  Luxury: **N/A** **$60–$120**
Credit Cards: **Some hosts do**

Many of Wisconsin's bed and breakfasts are in historic homes or in areas listed on the National Register of Historic Places, some are near ski hills or popular canoeing spots, and some are in Door County, a midwestern Cape Cod. Send $4.80 for a descriptive brochure, and make your reservation directly with the host of your choice.

The Parkside ✪
402 E NORTH STREET, APPLETON, WISCONSIN 54911

Tel: **(414) 733-0200**
Best Time to Call: **After 6 PM**
Host(s): **Bonnie Riley**
Location: **100 mi. NNW of Milwaukee**
No. of Rooms: **1 suite**
No. of Private Baths: **1**
Suites: **$50–$60**

Open: **All year**
Breakfast: **Full**
Pets: **No**
Children: **Welcome, over 8**
Smoking: **Permitted**
Social Drinking: **Permitted**
Airport/Station Pickup: **Yes**

Appleton's historic City Park area, once the neighborhood of magician Harry Houdini and author Edna Ferber, is the setting for this 1906

Richardson Romanesque-style home. It's located a short walk from the campus of Lawrence University and downtown shops and restaurants. Decorative leaded glass is prominent throughout the home. You are invited to enjoy breakfast featuring seasonal fruits, warm breads, and Wisconsin cheese beside the dining room's curved glass window. The bright and airy third-floor suite has a treetop view of City Park.

The Barrister's House ✪
226 9TH AVENUE, BOX 166, BARABOO, WISCONSIN 53913

Tel: **(608) 356-3344**	Open: **Daily June–Aug.; Weekends only Sept.–May**
Host(s): **Glen and Mary Schulz**	
Location: **45 mi. NW of Madison**	Breakfast: **Continental**
No. of Rooms: **4**	Pets: **No**
No. of Private Baths: **4**	Children: **Welcome, over 6**
Double/pb: **$45–$55**	Smoking: **No**
Single/pb: **$40–$50**	Social Drinking: **Permitted**

This elegant Colonial is named for the prominent town attorney who once lived here. Guests are welcome to settle down with a book in the library or relax around the fireplace in the living room. In summer, enjoy a glass of lemonade on the screened porch, veranda, or terrace. Sleeping quarters include the Garden Room, furnished in wicker and wrought iron, and the Colonial Room, appointed in 18th-century pieces. The Barrister's Room is a favorite for special occasions, because of its canopy bed, natural cherry wood, and cranberry-glass appointments. Juice, sweet rolls, fresh fruit, and cheese are served beside the black marble fireplace in the dining room, or outside, if you prefer. Glen and Mary will gladly direct you to such nearby sights as Devil's Lake State Park and the Wisconsin Dells.

Frantiques Showplace ✪
704 ASH STREET, BARABOO, WISCONSIN 53913

Tel: **(608) 356-5273**	Breakfast: **Full**
Host(s): **Fran and Bud Kelly**	Pets: **No**
Location: **13 mi. from I-90**	Children: **Welcome**
No. of Rooms: **1 suite**	Smoking: **No**
No. of Private Baths: **1**	Social Drinking: **Permitted**
Suites: **$50**	Airport/Station Pickup: **Yes**
Open: **All year**	

Fran Kelly has turned her three-story 125-year-old house into a Baraboo tourist attraction. She conducts tours through her house, showing off her antique dishes, children's toys, turn-of-the-century clothing, cameras, 1918 fireless cook stove, and more. The Cinema Suite has movie posters on the walls and comes with an antique brass bed, a refrigerator, stove, microwave oven, private bath, and private entrance. Baraboo is the "Circus City of the World," and Fran seems to have more than just a bit of the showman in her, too. Nearby you'll find the Circus World Museum, the Al Ringling Theater, Devil's Lake State Park, the International Crane Foundation, and, 10 miles away, Wisconsin Dells.

The House of Seven Gables ✪
215 6TH STREET, BARABOO, WISCONSIN 53913

Tel: **(608) 356-8387**
Best Time to Call: **8 AM–10 PM**
Host(s): **Ralph and Pamela W. Krainik**
Location: **13 mi. from I-90**
No. of Rooms: **2**
No. of Private Baths: **2**
Double/pb: **$55**
Single/pb: **$50**

Open: **All year**
Breakfast: **Full**
Credit Cards: **MC, VISA**
Pets: **No**
Children: **Welcome, over 5**
Smoking: **No**
Social Drinking: **Permitted**

Seven Gables is a restored 1860 Gothic Revival home. It is on the National Register of Historic Places as one of the best examples of this architecture. The 17 rooms are furnished entirely in the Civil War period. Circus World Museum, Wisconsin Dells, and Devils Head and Cascade ski resorts are close by.

Abendruh Bed and Breakfast Swiss Style
7019 GEHIN ROAD, BELLEVILLE, WISCONSIN 53508

Tel: **(608) 424-3808**
Best Time to Call: **7 AM–9 PM**
Host(s): **Mathilde and Franz Jaggi**
Location: **18 mi. SW of Madison**
No. of Rooms: **2**
No. of Private Baths: **1**
Max. No. Sharing Bath: **4**
Double/pb: **$50**
Single/pb: **$40**
Double/sb: **$45**

Single/sb: **$35**
Open: **All year**
Reduced Rates: **Available**
Breakfast: **Full**
Pets: **No**
Children: **No**
Smoking: **No**
Social Drinking: **Permitted**
Foreign Languages: **French, German, Swiss**

Abendruh is a stucco-and-stone ranch designed and built by the Jaggi family. The house is filled with homemade items ranging from the furniture to the afghans. Your host, Franz, is a master brick-and-stone mason. Mathilde is certified as a French chef, and in hotel and restaurant management. Together they provide a Swiss atmosphere and the utmost in international service. The breakfast menu changes daily according to guest preference. Specialties include homemade muffins, croissants, and a variety of egg dishes. Guests are welcome to explore the spacious grounds or relax in front of a crackling fire at one of the four fireplaces. Abendruh is 30 minutes from downtown Madison and is close to such attractions as New Glarus, America's Little Switzerland, Mt. Horeb, Cave of the Mounds, skiing, and biking.

Hillcrest ✪
540 STORLE AVENUE, BURLINGTON, WISCONSIN 53105

Tel: **(414) 763-4706**
Best Time to Call: **After 3 PM weekdays; weekends**
Host(s): **Dick and Karen Granholm**
Location: **30 mi. SW of Milwaukee**
No. of Rooms: **3**
No. of Private Baths: **1**
Max. No. Sharing Bath: **4**
Double/pb: **$55**
Double/sb: **$45**
Open: **All year**
Breakfast: **Full**
Credit Cards: **MC, VISA**
Pets: **No**
Children: **Welcome, over 12**
Smoking: **No**
Social Drinking: **Permitted**

The Granholms welcome you to their 100-year-old home with a snack of locally prepared cheese and sausage. Hillcrest is a historic estate set on four wooded acres, just a short walk from downtown. The house is peaceful and quiet, with a spectacular view of Echo Lake. It has several leaded and beveled-glass windows and doors, mahogany

WISCONSIN • 647

woodwork, beamed ceilings, and a huge staircase dominating the first and second floors. Each guest room is decorated with antiques, lace curtains, and brass accents. Two large porches furnished with wicker chairs, love seats, and rockers will tempt you to doze away the afternoon. Breakfast dishes include fresh fruit and homemade muffins, served with omelets and plenty of hot coffee. Your hosts will gladly direct you to nearby craft and antique shops, golf courses, and lakes.

Stagecoach Inn Bed & Breakfast ✪
W61 N520 WASHINGTON AVENUE, CEDARBURG, WISCONSIN 53012

Tel: **(414) 375-0208**
Host(s): **Brook and Liz Brown**
Location: **17 mi. N of Milwaukee**
No. of Rooms: **12**
No. of Private Baths: **12**
Double/pb: **$55**
Single/pb: **$45**
Suites: **$85**

Open: **All year**
Breakfast: **Continental**
Credit Cards: **AMEX, Discover, MC, VISA**
Pets: **No**
Children: **Welcome**
Smoking: **No**
Social Drinking: **Permitted**

The inn, listed on the National Register of Historic Places, is housed in a completely restored 1853 stone building in downtown, historic Cedarburg. The rooms, air-conditioned for summer comfort, combine antique charm with modern conveniences. Each bedroom is decorated with Laura Ashley linens and trimmed with wall stenciling. A bookstore, candy shop, and a pub that is a popular gathering place for guests, occupy the first floor. Specialty stores, antique shops, a winery, a woolen mill, and a variety of fine restaurants are within walking distance.

The Allyn House ✪
511 E. WALWORTH, DELAVAN, WISCONSIN 53115

Tel: **(414) 728-9090**
Best Time to Call: **Weekends**
Host(s): **Joe Johnson and Ron Markwell**
Location: **2 mi. from Rte. 15**
No. of Rooms: **4**
Max. No. Sharing Bath: **4**
Double/sb: **$60**
Single/sb: **$50**

Open: **All year**
Breakfast: **Full**
Pets: **No**
Children: **Welcome, over 12**
Smoking: **No**
Social Drinking: **Permitted**
Airport/Station Pickup: **Yes**
Foreign Languages: **French**

This 22-room Victorian mansion will transport you to an era of elegant marble fireplaces, gleaming chandeliers, stained glass, and parquet floors. The rooms are furnished with Oriental rugs, antiques, and period pieces, some of which are for sale. Enjoy wine and Wisconsin cheese in front of the parlor fireplace. The hearty breakfast includes home-baked breads, rolls, and preserves in the oak-paneled dining room. In the 19th century, Delavan was home to many circus shows, and many of the past entertainers are buried in nearby Spring Grove Cemetery. Only five minutes away is Delavan Lake, where you may go horseback riding, play golf, or enjoy many water sports. Some of the best skiing in the state is just ten miles from the house.

Westlin Winds ✪
3508 HALSEY STREET, EAU CLAIRE, WISCONSIN 54701

Tel: **(715) 832-1110**
Best Time to Call: **After 5 PM**
Host(s): **Mary B. Marcus**
Location: **85 mi. E of St. Paul, Minn.**
No. of Rooms: **3**
Max. No. Sharing Bath: **5**
Double/sb: **$35**
Single/sb: **$25**

Open: **All year**
Reduced Rates: **10%, seniors**
Breakfast: **Continental**
Pets: **No**
Children: **Welcome, over 8**
Smoking: **No**
Social Drinking: **Permitted**

This rambling ranch-style home is comfortably decorated in a blend of contemporary furniture and heirloom antiques. Enjoy the cozy fireplace in the winter or the screened porch overlooking the flower and herb gardens in summer. The guest rooms have either queen-size or twin beds, each covered with a handmade quilt. Breakfast, served at your convenience, may be enjoyed on the porch or in the dining room. Evening snacks may include a hot or cold beverage, popcorn, and fresh fruit. Nearby attractions and activities include the University of Wisconsin at Eau Claire, Chippewa Valley Museum, Wise Nature Center, and biking, hiking, and skiing.

La Baye House ✪
803 OREGON, GREEN BAY, WISCONSIN 54303

Tel: **(414) 437-5081**
Best Time to Call: **Mornings; evenings**
Host(s): **Kate Helms**
Location: **1 mi. from I-43**
No. of Rooms: **2**
Max. No. Sharing Bath: **3**

Double/sb: **$50**
Single/sb: **$45**
Open: **All year**
Breakfast: **Continental**
Pets: **No**
Children: **Welcome**

Smoking: **No**
Social Drinking: **Permitted**

Airport/Station Pickup: **Yes**
Foreign Languages: **French**

For a taste of Paris without leaving the States, visit this turn-of-the-century Victorian located in the historic Old Fort Settlement. Your host has worked and lived in Europe and is eager to share experiences. Guest rooms are decorated with many antiques, plants, and special touches such as oak paneling and beveled-glass windows. Afternoon beverages and cheese are served by the fire, or when the weather permits, outside on the wraparound porch. Kate hopes you will have the time to take a walking tour that highlights the early French history of this area. La Baye House is near the Fox River and five blocks from the Neville Public Museum.

Jackson Street Inn ✪
210 SOUTH JACKSON STREET, JANESVILLE, WISCONSIN 53545

Tel: **(608) 754-7250**
Host(s): **Ilah and Bob Sessler**
Location: **1.9 mi. from I-90, Exit 11**
No. of Rooms: **4**
No. of Private Baths: **2**
Max. No. Sharing Bath: **4**
Double/pb: **$55**
Single/pb: **$45**
Double/sb: **$45**
Single/sb: **$30**

Suites: **$55**
Open: **All year**
Reduced Rates: **Available**
Breakfast: **Full**
Credit Cards: **MC, VISA**
Pets: **No**
Children: **Welcome**
Smoking: **Permitted**
Social Drinking: **Permitted**
Airport/Station Pickup: **Yes**

This turn-of-the-century home is finely appointed, with brass fixtures, leaded beveled-glass windows, and Italian fireplace mantels. The air-conditioned rooms are in soft colors with Colonial-period English wallpaper, fancy pillows, dust ruffles, and cozy quilts. The guest sitting room has books and a refrigerator with ice. Your hosts serve breakfast on the screened-in porch or in the fireplaced dining room overlooking the grounds. A four-hole putting green, shuffleboard, and a horseshoe court are part of their landscaping. Local attractions include the beach, Old Town restorations, hiking trails, golf, and museums.

Ty Bach B&B ✪
3104 SIMPSON LANE, LAC DU FLAMBEAU, WISCONSIN 54538

Tel: **(715) 588-7851**
Best Time to Call: **8 AM–10 PM**

Host(s): **Janet and Kermit Bekkum**
Location: **70 mi. N of Wausau**

650 • WISCONSIN

No. of Rooms: **2**
Max. No. Sharing Bath: **4**
Double/sb: **$40**
Single/sb: **$35**
Open: **All year**

Breakfast: **Full**
Pets: **Welcome**
Children: **No**
Smoking: **No**
Social Drinking: **Permitted**

In Welsh, *ty-bach* means "little house." Located on an Indian reservation in Lac Du Flambeau, this modern little house overlooks a small, picturesque Northwoods lake. Sit back on the deck and enjoy the beautiful fall colors, the call of the loons, and the tranquillity of this out-of-the-way spot. Choose from two comfortable rooms, each furnished with antique brass beds. Your hosts offer oven-fresh coffee cakes, homemade jams, and plenty of fresh coffee along with hearty main entrées.

Trillium ✪
ROUTE 2, BOX 121, LA FARGE, WISCONSIN 54639

Tel: **(608) 625-4492**
Best Time to Call: **Mornings; evenings**
Host(s): **Joe Swanson and Rosanne Boyett**
Location: **40 mi. SE of LaCrosse**
Guest Cottage: **$63 for 2**
Open: **All year**

Breakfast: **Full**
Pets: **No**
Children: **Welcome (crib)**
Smoking: **Permitted**
Social Drinking: **Permitted**
Airport/Station Pickup: **Yes**

This private cottage is on a working farm located in the heart of a thriving Amish community. It is surrounded by an orchard, garden, and a lovely tree-shaded yard. There's a path beside the stream that winds through woods and fields. The cottage is light and airy, with comfortable wicker furniture. Rosanne and Joe stock your kitchen with homemade breads, jams, cheese, farm-fresh eggs, coffee, tea, and even goat's milk if you wish.

O. J.'s Victorian Village Guest House ✪
P.O. BOX 98, LAKE DELTON, WISCONSIN 53940

Tel: **(608) 254-6568**
Best Time to Call: **Evenings**
Host(s): **O.J. and Lois Thompto**
Location: **50 mi. N of Madison; 1 mi. from I-94, Exit 92**
No. of Rooms: **4**
No. of Private Baths: **4**
Double/pb: **$40–$55**
Single/pb: **$30**

Guest Cottage: **$65 for 4**
Open: **All year**
Reduced Rates: **10% Nov. 1–May 31**
Breakfast: **Continental**
Pets: **Sometimes**
Children: **Sometimes**
Smoking: **No**
Social Drinking: **Permitted**
Airport/Station Pickup: **Yes**

Located at Wisconsin Dells, midway between Chicago and the Twin Cities, this brand-new house was built especially for B&B. It is situated on a major waterway; there's access to an enchanting creek and lake for fishing, swimming, and boating. It's five miles from the International Crane Foundation, where you can watch cranes from Africa, Asia, and America. O.J. and Lois look forward to greeting you, and will arrange for discounts in many restaurants and shops. The University of Wisconsin at Baraboo is nearby.

Hill House Bed & Breakfast ✪
2117 SHERIDAN DRIVE, MADISON, WISCONSIN 53704

Tel: **(608) 244-2224**
Host(s): **Anne and Lar Stuart**
No. of Rooms: **3**
No. of Private Baths: **1**
Max. No. Sharing Bath: **4**
Double/pb: **$70**
Double/sb: **$55**
Single/sb: **$45**
Suite: **$85**

Open: **All year**
Reduced Rates: **Weekdays, Nov.–Mar.**
Breakfast: **Full**
Pets: **Sometimes**
Children: **Welcome, over 8**
Smoking: **Permitted**
Social Drinking: **Permitted**
Airport/Station Pickup: **Yes**

This hand-cut cedar shake and stucco home overlooks a large park and is half a block from Lake Mendota's eastern shore. It's 10 minutes from the Capitol and the university campus, and one minute from a lovely natural setting of prairie meadows, wetland lagoons, and oak woods. Tennis courts and an exercise course, swimming beach, and boat launch are available nearby for summer fun; cross-country skiing, skating, and a sledding hill will add to your winter enjoyment. Anne and Lar are longtime Madison residents who look forward to sharing their knowledge with you.

The Plough Inn Bed & Breakfast
3402 MONROE STREET, MADISON, WISCONSIN 53711

Tel: **(608) 238-2981**
Best Time to Call: **After 6 PM**
Host(s): **Roger Ganser and Katherine Naherny**
No. of Rooms: **3**
No. of Private Baths: **3**
Double/pb: **$49–$64**
Suites: **$69–$79**
Open: **All year**

Reduced Rates: **10% less per night, Sun.–Thurs.**
Breakfast: **Continental**
Credit Cards: **MC, VISA**
Pets: **No**
Children: **No**
Smoking: **No**
Social Drinking: **Permitted**

Originally built as a tavern on the edge of town, the Plough Inn has been a Madison landmark since the mid 1800s. Today this handsome Greek Revival nestled among the trees is listed on the National Register of Historic Places. The Parkside Room on the first floor is a sunny place with pine floors and furnishings. The Tap Room, where travelers once quenched their thirsts, is now decorated in a nautical theme with plaids and brass accents. The Arborview Room is a spacious second-floor suite with original fireplace, whirlpool bath, and wet bar. All have queen-size brass beds, down quilts, and comfortable reading chairs. Hot coffee, freshly squeezed juice, and baked goods are brought to your room or served on the terrace. On weekend mornings, Katherine prepares custard French toast or apple pancakes along with fresh fruit and cheeses. In the afternoon, relax on the porch with a glass of sherry. The inn is conveniently located within walking distance of Lake Wingra, and is near shopping, golf, and the University of Wisconsin.

Bed & Breakfast of Milwaukee, Inc. O
320 EAST BUFFALO STREET, MILWAUKEE, WISCONSIN 53202

Tel: **(414) 271-2337**
Best Time to Call: **9 AM–6 PM**
Coordinator: **Barbara Gardner**
States/Regions Covered: **Milwaukee and southeastern Wisconsin**

Rates (Single/Double):
Modest: **$25–$30** **$30–$35**
Average: **$35–$40** **$35–$50**
Luxury: **$55–$70** **$75–$90**
Credit Cards: **MC, VISA**

Choose from a variety of homes in the city, suburbs, or countryside, all with easy reach of Milwaukee. A city of great ethnic diversity, Milwaukee is the site of many festivals and cultural celebrations. There is no shortage of fine restaurants; your host will be happy to make suitable recommendations to suit your taste and purse. There is a fine zoo, museums, and renowned cultural attractions. Major league sports and miles of Lake Michigan offer diversion and fun. The University of Wisconsin and Marquette University are convenient to many B&Bs.

Ogden House O
2237 NORTH LAKE DRIVE, MILWAUKEE, WISCONSIN 53202

Tel: **(414) 272-2740**
Host(s): **Mary Jane and John Moss**
No. of Rooms: **2**
No. of Private Baths: **2**
Double/pb: **$65**
Single/pb: **$65**
Suites: **$75**

Open: **All year**
Breakfast: **Continental**
Pets: **No**
Children: **Welcome**
Smoking: **Permitted**
Social Drinking: **Permitted**

The Ogden House is a white-brick Federal-style home listed on the National Register of Historic Places. It is located in the North Point-South district, a neighborhood shared by historic mansions overlooking Lake Michigan. Miss Ogden herself would feel at home here having homemade butterhorns for breakfast in the sun room overlooking the garden. You are sure to feel at home, too, whether you're relaxing on the sun deck, sitting by the fire, or retiring to your four-poster bed. Ogden House is convenient to theaters, the botanical garden, the Brewers' Stadium, the breweries, and many fine restaurants.

The Wilson House Inn ✪
110 DODGE STREET, MINERAL POINT, WISCONSIN 53565

Tel: **(608) 987-3600**
Best Time to Call: **Mornings**
Host(s): **Bev and Jim Harris**
Location: **50 mi. SW of Madison**
No. of Rooms: **4**
No. of Private Baths: **2**
Max. No. Sharing Bath: **4**
Double/pb: **$45**
Single/pb: **$40**
Double/sb: **$40**
Single/sb: **$35**
Open: **All year**
Breakfast: **Full**
Credit Cards: **MC, VISA**
Pets: **Welcome**
Children: **Welcome (crib)**
Smoking: **Permitted**
Social Drinking: **Permitted**

The Wilson House Inn is located in the heart of the beautiful uplands area. This red-brick Federal mansion was built in 1853 by Alexander Wilson, who became one of the state's first attorneys general. A veranda was added later, and it is where guests are welcomed with lemonade. The rooms are airy, comfortable, and furnished in antiques. Mineral Point was a mining and political center in the 1880s, and it is filled with many historic sites. Fishing, golfing, swimming, skiing, and the House on the Rock are all nearby.

Rambling Hills Tree Farm ✪
8825 WILLEVER LANE, NEWTON, WISCONSIN 53063

Tel: **(414) 726-4388**
Best Time to Call: **Evenings**
Host(s): **Pete and Judie Stuntz**
Location: **18 mi. N of Sheboygan**
No. of Rooms: **3**
No. of Private Baths: **2**
Max. No. Sharing Bath: **5**
Double/pb: **$35**
Single/pb: **$25**
Double/sb: **$35**
Single/sb: **$25**
Open: **All year**
Breakfast: **Full**
Pets: **Sometimes**
Children: **Welcome**
Smoking: **Permitted**
Social Drinking: **Permitted**
Airport/Station Pickup: **Yes**

Enjoy the serenity of country living in a comfortable new home, set on 50 acres. The house overlooks the beautiful hills and a private lake. Guests are welcome to make themselves at home, enjoy the whirlpool spa on the screened-in porch, or curl up with a book before the fire. Outside there are hiking trails, boats, swimming, and a play area for the children. When the snow falls, the trails are suitable for cross-country skiing and the lake freezes for skating. Your hosts recommend several nearby supper clubs, and can direct you to the attractions of Lake Michigan and the city of Manitowoc.

The Limberlost Inn
HIGHWAY 17, #2483, PHELPS, WISCONSIN 54554

Tel: **(715) 545-2685**
Host(s): **Bill and Phoebe McElroy**
No. of Rooms: **3**
Max. No. Sharing Bath: **4**
Double/sb: **$42**
Single/sb: **$32**
Open: **All year**
Reduced Rates: **10%, weekly**

Breakfast: **Continental**
Other Meals: **Available**
Pets: **No**
Children: **Welcome, over 10**
Smoking: **No**
Social Drinking: **Permitted**
Airport/Station Pickup: **Yes**

The inn was designed and constructed by Bill and Phoebe McElroy. They picked a fine spot for their log home, just a minute from one of the best fishing lakes and largest national forests in the state. Each guest room is decorated with antiques, and the beds all have cozy down pillows and hand-stitched coverlets. Breakfast is served on the screened porch, by the fieldstone fireplace, in the dining room, or in your room. Stroll through the garden, rock on the porch swing, or take a picnic lunch and explore the streams and hiking trails. When you return, a Finnish sauna and a glass of wine or a mug of beer awaits.

Breese Waye Bed & Breakfast ✪
816 MacFARLANE ROAD, PORTAGE, WISCONSIN 53901

Tel: **(608) 742-5281**
Host(s): **Keith and Gretchen Sprecher**
Location: **35 mi. N of Madison**
No. of Rooms: **3**
No. of Private Baths: **3**
Double/pb: **$55**
Single/pb: **$45**

Open: **All year**
Breakfast: **Full**
Pets: **Welcome**
Children: **Welcome (crib)**
Smoking: **Permitted**
Social Drinking: **Permitted**
Airport/Station Pickup: **Yes**

This century-old Victorian mansion has three original fireplaces. It is comfortably furnished in "early attic" with lovely wood, glass, and antique accents. Portage is a historic city, so don't miss the Old Indian Agency House and the famed Portage Canal. Bikes are available for leisurely touring. Wisconsin Dells is 16 miles away.

Country Aire ✪
ROUTE 2, BOX 175, PORTAGE, WISCONSIN 53901

Tel: **(608) 742-5716**
Best Time to Call: **Evenings**
Host(s): **Bob and Rita Reif**
Location: **37 mi. N of Madison**
No. of Rooms: **3**
No. of Private Baths: **2**
Double/pb: **$40**
Single/pb: **$30**

Suites: **$55**
Open: **All year**
Breakfast: **Continental**
Pets: **No**
Children: **Welcome**
Smoking: **No**
Social Drinking: **Permitted**

Forty acres of woods and meadows surround this spacious country home, built into a hillside overlooking the Wisconsin River. The house has open cathedral ceilings and a beautiful view from every room. Choose from comfortable bedrooms with queen-size or twin beds; the kids will enjoy the room with bunk beds. Guests are welcome to use the tennis court or go canoeing in the river. In the winter, great skating can be enjoyed on the pond, and the area is perfect for cross-country skiing. Devil's Head and Cascade Mountain are close by for downhill skiing. Bob and Rita are minutes away from the Wisconsin Dells, Baraboo, and Devil's Lake State Park. At the end of the day, relax with wine and cheese, and enjoy a beautiful sunset.

Inn at Cedar Crossing ✪
336 LOUISIANA STREET, STURGEON BAY, WISCONSIN 54235

Tel: **(414) 743-4200**
Host(s): **Terry Wulf**
Location: **45 mi. N of Green Bay**
No. of Rooms: **9**
No. of Private Baths: **9**
Double/pb: **$58–$86**
Single/pb: **$49–$79**
Suites: **$76–$86**
Open: **All year**
Reduced Rates: **Available**

Breakfast: **Continental—summer;**
    Full—winter
Other Meals: **Lunch available**
Credit Cards: **Discover, MC, VISA**
Pets: **No**
Children: **Welcome, over 5**
Smoking: **Permitted**
Social Drinking: **Permitted**
Airport/Station Pickup: **Yes**

The inn, located in Door County, was built in 1884 as a two-story hotel and enjoys a place on the National Register of Historic Places. The interior features the original 13-foot tin ceilings and a sweeping banistered staircase. The rooms are decorated in country antiques and primitives, with handwoven rag rugs, fine wallpapers, and beautiful knotty pine woodwork. Double whirlpools are featured in three. Enjoy a restful night in a canopy bed and wake up to homemade muffins, coffee cakes, juice, and coffee. Moravian Sugar Cake, a traditional breakfast bread handed down by the area's original settlers, is the house specialty. Terry invites you for evening popcorn by the fire, or you may retire to the privacy of your room, where hand-dipped chocolates are left on the pillow. The inn is within walking distance of fine restaurants, shops, and the waterfront.

White Lace Inn—A Victorian Guest House
16 NORTH FIFTH AVENUE, STURGEON BAY, WISCONSIN 54235

Tel: **(414) 743-1105**
Host(s): **Dennis and Bonnie Statz**
Location: **150 mi. N of Milwaukee**
No. of Rooms: **15**
No. of Private Baths: **15**
Double/pb: **$65–$95**
Single/pb: **$48–$88**
Suites: **$125**
Open: **All year**

Reduced Rates: **Nov.–May**
Breakfast: **Continental**
Credit Cards: **MC, VISA**
Pets: **No**
Children: **Welcome, over 6**
Smoking: **Permitted**
Social Drinking: **Permitted**
Airport/Station Pickup: **Yes**

This elegant Victorian guest house is beautifully furnished with quality antiques, down pillows, cozy comforters, brass canopy beds, lace curtains, and fine rugs. Six rooms have fireplaces. Located in a residential area close to the bay, it is near shops and historic sites. Winter features great cross-country skiing, snow sports, and hot chocolate in front of the fireplace. Summer offers boating, tennis, and swimming, with iced tea served on the front porch.

WYOMING

Spahn's Big Horn Mountain Bed and Breakfast
P.O. BOX 579, BIG HORN, WYOMING 82833

Tel: (307) 674-8150
Host(s): **Ron and Bobbie Spahn**
Location: **15 mi. SW of Sheridan**
No. of Rooms: **3**
No. of Private Baths: **3**
Double/pb: **$45**
Single/pb: **$35**
Open: **All year**

Reduced Rates: **Families**
Breakfast: **Continental**
Pets: **Sometimes**
Children: **Welcome (baby-sitting)**
Smoking: **No**
Social Drinking: **Permitted**
Airport/Station Pickup: **Yes**

Ron and Bobbie Spahn and their two children built their home and this authentic log cabin. The house is set on 40 acres of whispering pines and borders the Big Horn Mountain forestland, which stretches for over a million acres. The main house has two guest bedrooms with private baths, a three-story living room, and an outside deck. The cabin is secluded from the main house and features a bedroom, large sleeping loft, bath, kitchen facilities, and front porch. You are invited to relax in the hot tub, sip a drink beside the wood stove, or take in the 100-mile view from an old porch rocker. Ron Spahn is a geologist and former Yellowstone Ranger. He can direct you to nearby fishing and hunting and can also tell you where to find the best walking and cross-country skiing trails.

Fall River Ranch (formerly Spring Creek Ranch)
P.O. BOX 33, BONDURANT, WYOMING 82922

Tel: **(307) 733-1184**
Best Time to Call: **Evenings**
Host(s): **Brad and Denise Warburton**
Location: **41 mi. S of Jackson Hole**
No. of Rooms: **4**
Max. No. Sharing Bath: **4**
Double/pb: **$35**
Single/pb: **$25**
Suites: **$60**
Open: **All year**
Reduced Rates: **10%, weekly**
Breakfast: **Full**
Other Meals: **Available**
Pets: **No**
Children: **Welcome**
Smoking: **Permitted**
Social Drinking: **Permitted**
Airport/Station Pickup: **Yes**

This is a working horse ranch in what is primarily a cattle ranch community. The ranch is quiet, and is surrounded by the beautiful Bridger-Teton National Forest and the Hoback River. It is a serene and uncrowded area in which trout fishing is excellent. The cabins are built of native log in keeping with the style of the Old West. Jackson Hole and Yellowstone Park are nearby.

The Lockhart Inn ✪
109 WEST YELLOWSTONE AVENUE, CODY, WYOMING 82414

Tel: **(307) 587-6074**
Best Time to Call: **After Noon**
Host(s): **Mark and Cindy Baldwin**
No. of Rooms: **6**
No. of Private Baths: **6**
Double/pb: **$35–$60**
Open: **All year**
Breakfast: **Full**
Other Meals: **Available**
Credit Cards: **AMEX, CB, Discover, MC, VISA**
Pets: **No**
Children: **Welcome, over 4**
Smoking: **Permitted**
Social Drinking: **Permitted**
Airport/Station Pickup: **Yes**

Once the home of Cody's famous turn-of-the-century novelist, Caroline Lockhart, Mark and Cindy's historic frontier home has been beautifully restored while retaining the flavor of the Old West. The old-fashioned decor is combined with such modern amenities as cable TV, phones, and individually controlled heat. Breakfast is graciously served on fine china in the dining room. Located 50 miles from the eastern entrance to Yellowstone National Park, there's plenty to do in addition to relaxing on the front porch. The Trail Town Museum, Buffalo Bill Historical Center, and the Cody Nightly Rodeo are just some of the attractions.

Pine Gables Bed and Breakfast Inn ✪
1049 CENTER STREET, EVANSTON, WYOMING 82930

Tel: **(307) 789-2069**	Open: **All year**
Best Time to Call: **7 AM–10 PM**	Reduced Rates: **15%, seniors**
Host(s): **Jessie and Arthur Monroe**	Breakfast: **Continental**
Location: **83 mi. E of Salt Lake City; ½ mi. from I-80**	Credit Cards: **AMEX, DC, MC, VISA**
	Pets: **Sometimes**
No. of Rooms: **5**	Children: **Welcome (crib)**
No. of Private Baths: **5**	Smoking: **Permitted**
Double/pb: **$34.50**	Social Drinking: **Permitted**
Single/pb: **$28.50**	Airport/Station Pickup: **Yes**
Suites: **$65**	

This antiques-filled inn is a site on the tour of Evanston's historic district. Each bedroom is furnished with collectibles and decorated using different woods—oak, cherry, mahogany, and walnut. Your hosts operate an antiques shop on-premises. They prepare a breakfast of homemade breads and pastries. Hiking, fishing, skiing, and hunting are nearby.

Hotel Higgins ✪
416 WEST BIRCH, GLENROCK, WYOMING 82637

Tel: **(307) 436-9212**	Single/sb: **$29**
Best Time to Call: **3 PM**	Open: **All year**
Host(s): **Jack and Margaret Doll**	Breakfast: **Full**
Location: **18 mi. E of Casper**	Other Meals: **Available**
No. of Rooms: **10**	Credit Cards: **AMEX, MC, VISA**
No. of Private Baths: **7**	Pets: **No**
Max. No. Sharing Bath: **3**	Children: **Welcome**
Double/pb: **$49**	Smoking: **Permitted**
Single/pb: **$34**	Social Drinking: **Permitted**
Double/sb: **$42**	

This fascinating hotel was built in the early 1900s and is today a Designated Historic Site. Filled with many of the original furnishings, beveled-glass doors, and terrazzo tile floors, it currently boasts the award-winning Paisley Shawl restaurant. Located on the historic Oregon Trail, it is minutes from Deer Creek, the home station of the Pony Express. An exquisite variety of quiches or omelets, champagne and orange juice, fresh fruits, and breakfast meats are offered at breakfast. Complimentary hors d'oeuvres are served in the lounge from 4 to 6 PM.

Black Mountain Ranch ✪
ROUTE 63, 548 NORTH FORK ROAD, LANDER, WYOMING 82520

Tel: **(307) 332-6442**
Host(s): **Dan Ratigan and Rosie Booke**
Location: **5.3 mi. from Hwy. 287**
No. of Rooms: **3**
No. of Private Baths: **3**
Double/pb: **$50**
Single/pb: **$30**
Suites: **$50–$100 (sleeps 2–4)**
Open: **May 1–Nov. 1**

Reduced Rates: **Available**
Breakfast: **Full**
Other Meals: **Available**
Credit Cards: **MC, VISA**
Pets: **No**
Children: **Welcome (crib)**
Smoking: **No**
Social Drinking: **Permitted**

The ranch is nestled among the foothills of the Wind River Mountain Range on the way to Yellowstone National Park, which is only 2½ hours away. It offers all the peace and quiet you can handle and all the outdoor activities you can imagine. The rooms are decorated with a country flair and offer homey comfort. The tasty breakfast features whole wheat blueberry pancakes with choke cherry syrup as well as homemade granola. Trout fishing, hiking, hayrides, and bird-watching are just a few of the on-premises recreations. Within an hour's drive are a restored 1870 gold mining town and the Wind River Indian Reservation, where powwows are scheduled throughout the summer.

Cottonwood Ranch
951 MISSOURI VALLEY ROAD, RIVERTON, WYOMING 82501

Tel: **(307) 856-3064**
Best Time to Call: **After 7 PM**
Host(s): **Earl and Judie Anglen**
Location: **13 mi. N of Riverton**
No. of Rooms: **3**
Max. No. Sharing Bath: **6**
Double/sb: **$35**
Single/sb: **$30**
Open: **All year**

Reduced Rates: **10%, seniors; $5 less, Oct. –May**
Breakfast: **Full**
Other Meals: **Available**
Pets: **Sometimes**
Children: **Welcome**
Smoking: **Permitted**
Social Drinking: **Permitted**
Airport/Station Pickup: **Yes**

Cottonwood is a working farm where you can observe firsthand the cattle being rounded up by men on horseback and getting branded in the old corral. Earl and Judie offer warm western hospitality, home cooking with homegrown produce and beef, and wide open spaces to enjoy and explore. Judie's "ranch" breakfast includes homemade breads, jams and salsa, biscuits and gravy, eggs, and "whatever you like." The guest quarters include a family room with a pool table and TV set. This is the West made familiar by old John Wayne movies, with spectacular mountain scenery, horseback riding, a historic gold mine, buffalo herds, a nearby Indian reservation, and friendly folks to show you around.

Teton Tree House ✪
P.O. BOX 550, WILSON, WYOMING 83014

Tel: **(307) 733-3233**	Reduced Rates: **Available**
Host(s): **Chris and Denny Becker**	Breakfast: **Full**
Location: **8 mi. W of Jackson**	Credit Cards: **MC, VISA**
No. of Rooms: **5**	Pets: **No**
No. of Private Baths: **5**	Children: **Welcome**
Double/pb: **$55–$75**	Smoking: **No**
Single/pb: **$50–$70**	Social Drinking: **Permitted**
Open: **All year**	

This is an impressive house of rustic open-beam construction, where guests are entertained in the large living room. The bedroom windows and decks overlook a private, forested mountainside. Wildflowers and berry bushes cover the land in summer; in winter it's a pristine, snowy wonderland. Breakfast is a low-cholesterol feast featuring huckleberry pancakes, zucchini breads, and other homemade treats. It is only eight miles from Grand Teton National Park, ski areas, a mountain climbing school, and a rodeo.

6

CANADA

ALBERTA

Note: All prices listed in this section are quoted in Canadian dollars.

Alberta Bed & Breakfast ✪
P.O. BOX 15477, M.P.O., VANCOUVER, BRITISH COLUMBIA, CANADA V7L 4L2

Tel: **(604) 682-4610**
Best Time to Call: **8 AM–2 PM**
Coordinator: **June Brown**
States/Regions Covered: Alberta—
  Banff, Calgary, Canmore, Hinton, Jasper; British Columbia—Ft. Steele, Kamloos, North Vancouver

Rates (Single/Double):
  Modest: **$30** $40
  Average: **$35** $45
  Luxury: **$45–$90** $50–$95
Credit Cards: **No**

Try a bit of Canadian western hospitality by choosing from June's variety of lovely homes in Alberta and British Columbia. Make a circle tour of Calgary, Banff, Lake Louise, the Columbia Icefields, Jasper, and Edmonton, and stay in B&Bs all the way. Send one dollar for a descriptive list of the cordial hosts on her roster, make your selections, and June will do the rest. The agency is closed on Canadian holidays and October through December.

BRITISH COLUMBIA

Note: *All prices listed in this section are quoted in Canadian dollars.*

Canada-West Accommodations ✪
P.O. BOX 86607, NORTH VANCOUVER, BRITISH COLUMBIA, CANADA V7K 1V5

Tel: **(604) 987-9338**
Best Time to Call: **Evenings; weekends**
Coordinator: **Ellison Massey**
States/Regions Covered: **Greater Vancouver**

Rates (Single/Double):
 Average: **$35** **$45–$60**
Credit Cards: **MC, VISA**

This registry has over 30 homes, offering suites, or simple bed-and-breakfast rooms in a comfortable host home. All serve a full breakfast, and most accommodations have a private bath for guests use. Some are near the international airport; all are near fast, efficient public transportation. Canada-West features friendly host families eager to share their knowledge of cultural and scenic attractions.

Charterre B&B House ✪
45360 HODGINS AVENUE, CHILLIWACK, BRITISH COLUMBIA, CANADA V2P 1P5

Tel: **(604) 792-1455**
Best Time to Call: **After 4 PM**
Host(s): **Sharon and Terry Coffin**
Location: **60 mi. E of Vancouver**
No. of Rooms: **4**
Max. No. Sharing Bath: **6**
Double/sb: **$35**
Single/sb: **$25**

Open: **All year**
Breakfast: **Continental**
Pets: **No**
Children: **Welcome**
Smoking: **Permitted**
Social Drinking: **Permitted**
Airport/Station Pickup: **Yes**
Foreign Languages: **French**

Isaac Kipp, one of the Fraser Valley's first settlers and the owner of much of what became the town of Chilliwack, built this farmhouse in 1873. Kipp came from Ontario via the California gold fields. His wife, Mary Ann, was Chilliwack's first white woman settler. Sharon and

Terry Coffin have restored the house, retaining its 10-foot ceilings, plate rails, and the original locks and doorknobs. Among the breakfast specialties are fresh fruit compote, stewed rhubarb, cinnamon rolls, and homemade jams and jellies. You can enjoy your meal in the dining room beside a 100-year-old cast iron fireplace. In the summer iced tea and lemonade are served on the large veranda. The Cultus Lake resort area has horseback riding, swimming, and boating seven miles away, and it is a short drive to both the Vedder and Fraser rivers.

Weston Lake Inn ✪
813 BEAVER POINT ROAD RR1, FULFORD HARBOUR, BRITISH COLUMBIA, CANADA V0S 1C0

Tel: **(604) 653-4311**
Host(s): **Susan Evans and Ted Harrison**
Location: **30 mi. N of Victoria**
No. of Rooms: **3**
No. of Private Baths: **1**
Max. No. Sharing Bath: **4**
Double/pb: **$60**
Single/pb: **$50**
Double/sb: **$48**
Single/sb: **$38**

Open: **All year**
Reduced Rates: **10%, weekly; $5 less, Oct. –May**
Breakfast: **Full**
Credit Cards: **MC, VISA**
Pets: **Sometimes**
Children: **Welcome, over 14**
Smoking: **No**
Social Drinking: **Permitted**
Foreign Languages: **French**

Nestled on a knoll of flowering trees and shrubs overlooking Weston Lake, the Inn offers Old World charm in a comfortable new home. The house is on a 10-acre farm on Salt Spring Island, the largest of British Columbia's Gulf Islands. Each guest room overlooks the countryside and has a down comforter. The rooms all have different finishing touches such as a brass bed, Chilean folk art, or Eskimo prints. Throughout the house there are a number of original Canadian art pieces and intricate petitpoint needlework crafted by your host, Ted. Breakfast is a full-course meal served to the sounds of classical music in the antique-filled dining room. Eggs Benedict, quiche, homemade muffins, and jams are specialties of the house. Guests can relax on the garden terrace or enjoy a book in the lounge beside a wood-burning stove. It's just a few steps to swimming, boating, and fishing. You can also follow forest trails or take to a bicycle and explore this quaint country village with its miles of country roads and pastoral beauty.

Grouse Mountain Bed and Breakfast ✪
900 CLEMENTS AVENUE, NORTH VANCOUVER, BRITISH COLUMBIA, CANADA V7R 2K7

Tel: **(604) 986-9630**	Double/pb: **$60**
Best Time to Call: **Early morning; evening**	Double/sb: **$60**
	Open: **All year**
Host(s): **Lyne and John Armstrong**	Breakfast: **Full**
Location: **10 min. from city core**	Pets: **Welcome**
No. of Rooms: **2**	Children: **Welcome (crib)**
No. of Private Baths: **1**	Smoking: **No**
Max. No. Sharing Bath: **2**	Social Drinking: **Permitted**

Your hosts welcome you to a comfortable, modern home in the foothills of Grouse Mountain. Enjoy views of Vancouver Island from two sun decks overlooking the secluded grounds, with close proximity to Stanley Park, the beaches, and downtown. Large rooms await you, one with cedar-paneled bath, the other with flagstone fireplace. Both have ample sitting room. Breakfast features something different each day, such as French toast or omelets with homemade jam. Skiing is only five minutes away.

Laburnum Cottage B&B ✪
1388 TERRACE AVENUE, NORTH VANCOUVER, BRITISH COLUMBIA, CANADA V7R 1B4

Tel: **(604) 988-4877**	Open: **All year**
Host(s): **Alex and Delphine Masterton**	Reduced Rates: **Weekly; 15%, seniors; 20%, families**
Location: **3 blocks from Trans-Canada Hwy.**	Breakfast: **Full**
No. of Rooms: **4**	Credit Cards: **MC, VISA**
No. of Private Baths: **3**	Pets: **Sometimes**
Max. No. Sharing Bath: **4**	Children: **Welcome**
Double/pb: **$68**	Smoking: **No**
Single/pb: **$39**	Social Drinking: **Permitted**
Double/sb: **$56**	Foreign Languages: **German**
Single/sb: **$37**	
Guest Cottage: **$74**	

This charming home with a Victorian air and antiques is set in a half acre of an award-winning English garden surrounded by virgin forest, yet only minutes from downtown Vancouver, Horseshoe Bay, and Grouse Mountain. Delphine and Alex invite you to share the den with its fireplace and TV set, or relax on the patio or in the garden. Homemade preserves, berry pancakes, omelets, and French toast are breakfast delights.

Kenya Court Guest House At-the-Beach ☉
2230 CORNWALL AVENUE, VANCOUVER, BRITISH COLUMBIA, CANADA V6K 1B5

Tel: **(604) 738-7085**
Host(s): **Dorothy-Mae Williams**
Location: **20 mi. from the U.S. border**
No. of Rooms: **4**
No. of Private Baths: **4**
Double/pb: **$65**
Single/pb: **$55**
Suites: **$80**

Open: **All year**
Breakfast: **Full**
Pets: **No**
Children: **Welcome, over 8**
Smoking: **No**
Social Drinking: **Permitted**
Foreign Languages: **French, German, Italian**

There is an unobstructed view of the park, ocean, mountains, and downtown Vancouver from this heritage building on the waterfront. Across the street are tennis courts, a large heated outdoor saltwater pool, and walking and jogging paths along the water's edge. Just minutes from downtown, it's an easy walk to Granville Market, the Planetarium, and interesting shops and restaurants. All the rooms are large and tastefully furnished. Breakfast is served in a glass solarium with a spectacular view of English Bay.

Sunnymeade House Inn
1002 FENN AVENUE, VICTORIA, BRITISH COLUMBIA, CANADA V8Y 1P3

Tel: **(604) 658-1414**
Best Time to Call: **Mid-morning; evenings**
Host(s): **Jack and Nancy Thompson**
Location: **1½ mi. from Rte. 17**
No. of Rooms: **4**
Max. No. Sharing Bath: **4**
Double/sb: **$55–$57**
Single/sb: **$40**
Suites: **$75–$85 (3–4)**

Open: **All year**
Reduced Rates: **25%, Nov. 15–Apr. 15**
Breakfast: **Full**
Other Meals: **Available**
Pets: **No**
Children: **Welcome (crib)**
Smoking: **No**
Social Drinking: **Permitted**
Airport/Station Pickup: **Yes**

Take the scenic route into Victoria and discover this inn on a winding country road by the sea. The Thompsons designed, built, decorated, and custom furnished the English-style house. Nancy, a former professional cook, will prepare your choice of breakfast from a choice of seven. You'll be steps away from the beach and within walking distance of tennis courts. All bedrooms have vanity sinks.

V.I.P. Bed and Breakfast ✪
1786 TEAKWOOD ROAD, VICTORIA, BRITISH COLUMBIA, CANADA V8N 1E2

Tel: **(604) 477-5604**
Best Time to Call: **7 AM–10 PM**
Coordinator: **Helen J. Ridley**
States/Regions Covered: **Victoria, Sidney**

Rates (Single/Double):
Average: **$30**   **$40**
Luxury: **$40**   **$60**
Credit Cards: **No**

You have a wide choice of B&Bs on Helen's roster, including traditional older homes close to the city center, a contemporary home near the University of Victoria, a country home near Butchart's Gardens, or waterfront homes near the ferry terminals. Family and weekly rates are often available, and some homes welcome children and your well-behaved pet. Beacon Hill Park, Butchart's Gardens, Craigdarroch Castle, Maritime Museum, and Provincial Museum are some of the major attractions.

Beachside Bed and Breakfast ✪
4208 EVERGREEN AVENUE, WEST VANCOUVER, BRITISH COLUMBIA, CANADA V7V 1H1

Tel: **(604) 922-7773**
Host(s): **Gordon and Joan Gibbs**
Location: **4 mi. W of Vancouver**
No. of Rooms: **3**
No. of Private Baths: **2**
Max. No. Sharing Bath: **3**
Double/pb: **$85–$95**
Double/sb: **$75**
Single/sb: **$55**

Open: **All year**
Breakfast: **Full**
Credit Cards: **AMEX, MC, VISA**
Pets: **Sometimes**
Children: **Welcome**
Smoking: **No**
Social Drinking: **Permitted**
Airport/Station Pickup: **Yes**
Foreign Languages: **French**

Guests are welcomed to this beautiful waterfront home with a fruit basket and fresh flowers. The house is a Spanish-style structure, with stained-glass windows, located at the end of a quiet cul-de-sac. Its southern exposure affords a panoramic view of Vancouver. A sandy beach is just steps from the door. You can watch the waves from the patio or spend the afternoon fishing or sailing. The hearty breakfast features homemade muffins, French toast, and Canadian maple syrup. Gordon and Joan are knowledgeable about local history, and can gladly direct you to Stanley Park, the site of Expo 86, hiking, skiing, and much more.

NEW BRUNSWICK

Note: All prices listed in this section are quoted in Canadian dollars.

Oakley House ✪
LOWER JEMSEG, NEW BRUNSWICK, CANADA E0E 1S0

Tel: **(506) 488-3113**
Host(s): **Max and Willi Evans Wolfe**
Location: **33 mi. E of Fredericton; 3 mi. from Trans-Can. Hwy.**
No. of Rooms: **3**
Max. No. Sharing Bath: **6**
Double/sb: **$45**
Single/sb: **$27**
Open: **All year**
Breakfast: **Full**

Other Meals: **Available**
Credit Cards: **VISA**
Pets: **Sometimes**
Children: **Sometimes**
Smoking: **No**
Social Drinking: **Permitted**
Airport/Station Pickup: **Yes**
Foreign Languages: **French, Russian, Spanish**

Max and Willi's home is set right in the heart of strawberry country; their 20-acre property borders the Jemseg River, the waterway that connects Saint John River and Grand Lake. The 150-year-old house is surrounded by lilacs, acacias, and old apple trees. Whatever the season, there's plenty to do nearby—swimming and sailing in summer, and cross-country skiing and ice skating in winter. Bird-watching is excellent, especially in migratory season—loons, osprey, and eagles nest nearby. Thanks to a Jersey cow and a large organic garden, your hosts produce most of their own food. Breakfasts are bountiful—buckwheat pancakes with maple syrup, hot muffins, eggs and sausages, and more. Gagetown—just a short ferry ride away—is a favorite, with its craft shops, restaurants, marina, and historic sites.

NOVA SCOTIA

Note: All prices listed in this section are quoted in Canadian dollars.

National Bed 'n Breakfast™ ✪
RR #1, BELMONT, COLCHESTER COUNTY, NOVA SCOTIA, CANADA B0M 1C0

Tel: **(902) 662-3733**
Best Time to Call: **After 5 PM**
Coordinator: **Carol Robertson**
States/Regions Covered: **Nova Scotia—Belmont, Masstown, Tatamagouche, Wallace**

Rates (Single/Double):
  Modest: **$25**   **$35**
  Average: **$34**   **$42**
  Luxury: N/A   N/A
Credit Cards: **MC, VISA**

In Nova Scotia visitors discover breathtaking clifftop vistas, storybook fishing villages, and unpopulated beaches begging to be explored. Carol's hosts are sincere in their motto: "We'll make you feel at home." They are all carefully selected individuals who take pride in their accommodations, the quality of service, and the full breakfast they offer. Ranging from a 150-year-old farmland estate to a refurbished turn-of-the-century train station, charming amenities and gracious hospitality abound.

ONTARIO

Note: All prices listed in this section are quoted in Canadian dollars.

Bed & Breakfast—Kingston ✪
10 WESTVIEW ROAD, KINGSTON, ONTARIO, CANADA K7M 2C3

Tel: **(613) 542-0214**
Coordinator: **Ruth MacLachlan**
Best Time to Call: **8 AM–10 PM, Mon.–Sat.**
States/Regions Covered: **Ontario— Bath, Gananoque, Harrowsmith, Kingston, Morrisburg, Prescott, Seeley's Bay, Sydenham, Westport**

Rates (Single/Double):
  Average: **$35** **$42–$45**
  Luxury: **$40** **$47–$60**
Credit Cards: **No**

Situated at the eastern end of Lake Ontario, at the head of the St. Lawrence River, Kingston has much to offer besides gorgeous scenery. There's Old Fort Henry, boat cruises through the Thousand Islands, historic sites, museums, and sports activities of every sort. Send $1 for the detailed directory.

The Webster House ✪
37 JAMES STREET E., BROCKVILLE, ONTARIO, CANADA K6V 1K3

Tel: **(613) 345-4707**
Host(s): **Doli and Peter Darrach**
Location: **68 mi. S of Ottawa**
No. of Rooms: **3**
Max. No. Sharing Bath: **3**
Double/sb: **$40–$50**
Single/sb: **$35–$45**
Open: **All year**

Breakfast: **Full**
Pets: **No**
Children: **No**
Smoking: **No**
Social Drinking: **Permitted**
Airport/Station Pickup: **Yes**
Foreign Languages: **Spanish**

The Webster House has been painstakingly preserved—the formal parlor has ten-foot windows and an original ceiling medallion; the less-formal second parlor is the perfect spot to work on the jigsaw puzzles or read any of the books and magazines available to guests. The outdoors is as beautiful as the indoors, with its terraced garden shaded by an ancient tree, and a Victorian porch where guests may "take tea" surrounded by wicker and chintz. Convenient to a parklike waterfront, excellent shopping, and many fine restaurants, the Webster House is a perfect stopping point for anyone visiting the Thousand Islands.

Knechtel's Guest House ✪
7 PARK AVENUE WEST, ELMIRA, ONTARIO, CANADA N3B 1K9

Tel: **(519) 669-2066**
Best Time to Call: **Evenings**
Host(s): **Marguarite and Ross Knechtel**
Location: **10 mi. NE of Waterloo, ½ mi. from Hwy. 86, Elmira Exit**
No. of Rooms: **3**
Max. No. Sharing Bath: **3**
Double/sb: **$40**

Single/sb: **$35**
Open: **All year**
Breakfast: **Full**
Pets: **Sometimes**
Children: **Welcome (crib)**
Smoking: **Permitted**
Social Drinking: **Permitted**
Foreign Languages: **French**

You may sit on the porch and watch the Mennonites' horse-drawn buggies pass by on the tree-lined street. Guests at this 75-year-old Queen Anne home, with its stained-glass windows and spiral staircase, enjoy strolling in the garden or through town and visiting the horse-racing track at the end of the street. Ross and Marguarite and their teenage son and daughter enjoy having guests. Tea and cookies are served in the evening.

Windmere Bed & Breakfast ✪
SELWYN, RR3, LAKEFIELD, ONTARIO, CANADA K0L 2H0

Tel: **(705) 652-6290**
Host(s): **Joan and Wally Wilkins**
Location: **12 mi. NE of Peterborough**
No. of Rooms: **3**
No. of Private Baths: **1**
Max. No. Sharing Bath: **4**
Double/pb: **$40**
Double/sb: **$35**
Single/sb: **$28**
Guest Cottage: **$50, sleeps 2–4**

Open: **All year**
Reduced Rates: **Available**
Breakfast: **Full**
Pets: **No**
Children: **Welcome**
Smoking: **No**
Social Drinking: **Permitted**
Airport/Station Pickup: **Yes**
Foreign Languages: **French**

Windmere is located in the heart of the Kawartha Lakes, a waterskiers' and fishermen's paradise. Joan and Wally have an 1839 stone farmhouse, set amid shaded lawns and a large spring-fed swimming pond. The older part of the house has high-ceilinged rooms decorated with fine art and Victorian antiques. In the new wing, the accent is on wood, warmth, and informality. Freshly baked bran muffins and homemade jams are served each morning; in the evening, tea and a snack are offered in the family room. Your hosts can direct you to walking trails, art galleries, golf courses, and Petroglyphs Provincial Park, known for its Indian rock carvings.

Hiebert's Guest House ✪
BOX 1371, 275 JOHN STREET, NIAGARA-ON-THE-LAKE, ONTARIO, CANADA L0S 1J0

Tel: **(416) 468-3687**
Host(s): **Otto and Marlene Hiebert**
Location: **10 mi. N of Niagara Falls**
No. of Rooms: **3**
Max. No. Sharing Bath: **3**
Double/sb: **$50**
Single/sb: **$45**

Open: **All year**
Reduced Rates: **$5 less Jan.–Apr.**
Breakfast: **Full**
Pets: **No**
Children: **Welcome**
Smoking: **No**
Social Drinking: **No**

We wish we could share with you the many letters of reference attesting to "the cleanliness," "the warm Mennonite hospitality," "the delicious food," "the friendliness of the Hieberts." Their air-conditioned home is 10 miles from Niagara Falls, Ontario, and the U.S. border. The Shaw Festival Theatre and all of the area's points of interest are within walking distance. The breakfast muffins, served with homemade jams, are a special treat.

Ottawa Area Bed & Breakfast ✪
P.O. BOX 4848, STATION E, OTTAWA, ONTARIO, CANADA K1S 5J1

Tel: **(613) 563-0161**
Best Time to Call: **10 AM–10 PM**
Coordinators: **Robert Rivoire and R. G. Simmens**
States/Regions Covered: **Ontario— Kanata, Nepean, Gloucester, Ottawa; Quebec—Hull**

Rates (Single/Double):
   Average: **$30**   **$40**
Credit Cards: **No**

If you are seeking an interesting but inexpensive holiday, then Canada's capital, Ottawa, is the place for you. The city is packed with free activities including museums, the House of Parliament, art galleries, and historic sites. You can skate on the Rideau Canal or bike on miles of parkways and trails.

Toronto Bed & Breakfast ✪
P.O. BOX 74, STATION M, TORONTO, ONTARIO, CANADA M6S 4T2

Tel: **(416) 233-3887 or 233-4041**
Best Time to Call: **Evenings; weekends**
Coordinator: **Randy Lee**
States/Regions Covered: **Toronto**

Rates (Single/Double):
   Modest: $35 $45
   Average: $40 $50
   Luxury: $45 $55
Credit Cards: **No**
Minimum Stay: **2 nights**

Toronto, located on Lake Ontario, is a sophisticated city, but the hosts in Randy's network of homes are warm, friendly, and helpful. Accommodations vary from a bedroom in a British Colonial to a terraced penthouse suite in a luxury condo; full breakfast is included. All homes are convenient to public transportation, so that you can easily visit the CN Tower, the Ontario Science Centre, Fort York, and the exciting Harbourfront with its craft galleries and ethnic restaurants. Send $3 for the descriptive directory and make your reservations directly with the host of your choice.

PRINCE EDWARD ISLAND

Note: All prices listed in this section are quoted in Canadian dollars.

Woodington's Country Inn ✪
RR 2, KENSINGTON, PRINCE EDWARD ISLAND, CANADA C0B 1M0

Tel: **(902) 836-5518**
Best Time to Call: **Noon**
Host(s): **Marion and Claude "Woody" Woodington**
No. of Rooms: **5**
Max. No. Sharing Bath: **4**
Double/sb: **$44**
Single/sb: **$22**

Open: **All year**
Reduced Rates: **10%, after Sept. 15**
Breakfast: **Full**
Other Meals: **Available**
Pets: **Welcome**
Children: **Welcome**
Smoking: **Permitted**
Social Drinking: **Permitted**

Relax on the spacious lawns surrounding this immaculate Victorian farmhouse or stroll to the private beach. You'll feel at home immediately. Marion is a fabulous cook and her table reflects all that is fresh and wholesome. Woody hand-carves the most realistic duck decoys you've ever seen. Marion's spare time is spent making gorgeous quilts. A wood carving or quilt would make a memorable souvenir to take home.

Smallman's Bed and Breakfast
KNUTSFORD, O'LEARY, RR 1, PRINCE EDWARD ISLAND, CANADA C0B 1V0

Tel: **(902) 859-3469**
Best Time to Call: **10 AM–Noon; 6–10 PM**
Host(s): **Arnold and Eileen Smallman**
Location: **7½ mi. from Rte. 2**
No. of Rooms: **4**
Max. No. Sharing Bath: **6**
Double/sb: **$25–$30**
Single/sb: **$15–$20**

Suites: **$30**
Open: **All year**
Breakfast: **Full**
Other Meals: **Available**
Pets: **Sometimes**
Children: **Welcome**
Smoking: **Permitted**
Social Drinking: **No**
Airport/Station Pickup: **Yes**

This comfortable, split-level home is just 10 minutes from the beach. The kids will enjoy the backyard sandbox as well as a private track where the family racehorses train. Your hostess is a dedicated baker, always ready with coffee and a homemade snack. Breakfast specialties include homemade biscuits and cereals. Many local restaurants serve fresh lobster, clams, and oysters in season. Your hosts can direct you to the better buys in town, as well as the Gulf of St. Lawrence, golf courses, mills, and museums.

Dyment Bed & Breakfast ✪
RR 3, WILMOT VALLEY, SUMMERSIDE, PRINCE EDWARD ISLAND, CANADA C1N 4J9

Tel: **(902) 436-9893**
Best Time to Call: **Before noon; after 6 PM**
Host(s): **Earle and Wanda Dyment**
Location: **On Rte. 107**
No. of Rooms: **3**
Max. No. Sharing Bath: **6**
Double/sb: **$28**

Single/sb: **$20**
Open: **May 20–Oct. 31**
Breakfast: **Full**
Pets: **Sometimes**
Children: **Welcome (crib)**
Smoking: **No**
Social Drinking: **Permitted**

This spanking-clean house is set in a picturesque farming area overlooking the Wilmot River. Wanda delights in having people stay, and allows you to use her kitchen for light snacks. There is much to do and see, including swimming, golf, deep-sea fishing, and going to the racetrack.

QUEBEC

Note: All prices listed in this section are quoted in Canadian dollars.

Bed & Breakfast à Montréal ○
4912 VICTORIA, MONTREAL, QUEBEC, CANADA H3W 2N1

Tel: **(514) 738-9410 or 738-3859**
Coordinator: **Marian Kahn**
States/Regions Covered: **Montreal, Ste. Adele (Laurentian Mountains), Sutton**

Rates (Single/Double):
  Average: **$40–$60**
Credit Cards: **MC, VISA (deposits only)**

Marian has a list of lovely homes in Montreal and surrounding countryside. Many hosts are French Canadian and the full breakfasts included in the rate often reflect a gourmet's touch. Visit Old Montreal and The Harbor for a glimpse of history, the Museum of Fine Arts, Place Des Arts for a touch of culture. McGill University, Mount Royal Park, St. Helen's Island, and the Laurentian Mountains are all worth a visit too. There are marvelous restaurants, wonderful shops, and the people are warm and friendly.

Montrealers at Home, a Downtown B&B Network ○
3458 LAVAL AVE., MONTREAL, QUEBEC, CANADA H2X 3C8

Tel: **(514) 289-9749**
Best Time to Call: **3–7 PM**
Coordinator: **Robert Finkelstein**
States/Regions Covered: **Montreal, Westmount, Outremont, Quebec City**

Rates (Single/Double):
  Modest: **$25**   **$35**
  Average: **$30–$40** **$45–$55**
  Luxury: **$55–$65** **$65–$75**
Credit Cards: **MC, VISA**

Bob specializes in downtown accommodations with hosts ready to introduce you to good shopping, diverse restaurants, and places of special interest with an experienced eye on good value. After a day of hectic activity that might include a *calèche* ride through the cobbled streets of the Old Quarter, or a visit to the futuristic high-fashion urban area, and samples of excellent cuisine from all over the world, your hosts look forward to having you return to relax in their homes.

Bed & Breakfast Bonjour Québec ✪
3765 BD MONACO, QUEBEC, CANADA G1P 3J3

Tel: **(418) 527-1465**
Best Time to Call: **7:30–11:30 AM; 7–8:30 PM**
Coordinators: **Denise and Raymond Blanchet**
States/Regions Covered: **Quebec City**

Rates (Single/Double):
  Modest: **$30** $40
  Average: **$40** $60
  Luxury: **$85** $95
Credit Cards: **No**

Denise and Raymond's accommodations are in the two districts that border Old Quebec. Their carefully selected hosts delight in making your visit a genuine French experience. The boulevard Grand-Allée is reminiscent of the Champs Elysée in Paris. Historic sites, the St. Lawrence River, charming restaurants, and shops are within easy reach of every B&B.

Appendix: UNITED STATES AND CANADIAN TOURIST OFFICES

Listed here are the addresses and telephone numbers for the tourist offices of every U.S. state and Canadian province. When you write or call one of these offices, be sure to request a map of the state and a calender of events. If you will be visiting a particular city or region, or if you have any special interests, be sure to specify them as well.

State Tourist Office

Alabama Bureau of Tourism and Travel
532 South Perry Street
Montgomery, Alabama 36104-4614
(205) 261-4169 or (800) 252-2262
 (out of state) or (800) 392-8096
 (within Alabama)

Alaska Division of Tourism
P.O. Box E, TIA
Juneau, Alaska 99811
(907) 465-2010

Arizona Office of Tourism
1100 W. Washington Avenue
Suite 1100A
Phoenix, Arizona 85007
(602) 255-4764

Arkansas Tourism Office
Dept. 7701
1 Capitol Mall
Little Rock, Arkansas 72201
(501) 682-7777 or (800) 643-8383
 (out of state) or (800) 482-8999
 (within Arkansas)

California Office of Tourism
1121 L Street, Suite 103
Sacramento, California 95814
(916) 322-2881
(800) TOCALIF

Colorado Office of Tourism
1625 Broadway
Suite 1700
Denver, Colorado 80202
(303) 592-5410 or (800) 433-2656

Connecticut Department of Economic Development
210 Washington Street, Room 900
Hartford, Connecticut 06106
(203) 566-3948 or (800) 243-1685
 (out of state) or (800) 842-7492
 (within Connecticut)

Delaware Tourism Office
99 Kings Highway, P.O. Box 1401
Dover, Delaware 19903
(302) 736-4271 or (800) 441-8846
 (out of state) or (800) 282-8667
 (in Delaware)

APPENDIX • 679

Washington, D.C. Convention and
  Visitors' Association
Suite 250
1575 I Street, N.W., 88STD
Washington, D.C. 20005
(202) 789-7000

Florida Division of Tourism
126 Van Buren Street, FLDA
Tallahassee, Florida 32399-2000
(904) 487-1462

Georgia Department of Industry and
  Trade
Tourist Division
P.O. Box 1776
Atlanta, Georgia 30301
(404) 656-3590

Hawaii Visitors Bureau
P.O. Box 8527, HVB
Honolulu, Hawaii 96815
(808) 923-1811

Idaho Travel Council
Statehouse Mail, Dept. C
Boise, Idaho 83720
(208) 334-2470 or (800) 635-7820

Illinois Office of Tourism
310 South Michigan Avenue, Dept.
  10T
Suite 108
Chicago, Illinois 60604
(312) 793-2094 or (800) 223-0121

Indiana Tourism Development
  Division
1 North Capitol, Suite 700
Indianapolis, Indiana 46204-2288
(317) 232-8860 or (800) 2 WANDER

Iowa Department of Economic
  Development
Bureau of Tourism and Visitors
200 East Grand, Box 6127
Des Moines, Iowa 50309-2882
(515) 281-3100 or (800) 345-IOWA

Kansas Department of Economic
  Development—Travel and Tourism
  Division
400 West 8th Street
Fifth Floor
Topeka, Kansas 66603
(913) 296-2009

Kentucky Department of Travel
  Development
2200 Capitol Plaza Tower, Dept. DA
Frankfort, Kentucky 40601
(502) 564-4930 or (800) 225-TRIP

Louisiana Office of Tourism
Inquiry Department
P.O. Box 94291
Baton Rouge, Louisiana 70804-9291
(504) 925-3860 or (800) 334-8626

Maine Publicity Bureau
97 Winthrop St., Dept. DA
Hallwell, Maine 04347-2300
(207) 289-2423 or (800) 533-9595
  (Sept–Apr. East Coast)

Maryland Office of Tourist
  Development
45 Calvert Street, Dept. A
Annapolis, Maryland 21401
(301) 974-3519 or (800) 331-1750,
  Operator 250

Massachusetts Office of Travel and
  Tourism
100 Cambridge Street—13th Floor
Boston, Massachusetts 02202
(617) 727-3201 or (800) 942-MASS;
  (800) 624-MASS

Michigan Travel Bureau
P.O. Box 30226
Lansing, Michigan 48909
(517) 373-0670 or (800) 543-2 YES

Minnesota Tourist Information
375 Jackson Street
Dept. 21, 250 Skyway Level
St. Paul, Minnesota 55101
(612) 296-5029 or (800) 328-1461
  (out of state) or (800) 652-9747
  (in Minnesota)

Mississippi Division of Tourism
P.O. Box 22825, Dept. T
Jackson, Mississippi 39205
(601) 359-3426 or (800) 647-2290

Missouri Division of Tourism
P.O. Box 1055
Jefferson City, Missouri 65102
(314) 751-4133

680 • APPENDIX

Travel Montana
Room 835
Deerlodge, Montana 59722
(406) 444-2654 or (800) 541-1447

Nebraska Division of Travel and Tourism
P.O. Box 94666, Room 88937
Lincoln, Nebraska 68509-4666
(402) 471-3794 or (800) 742-7595
(in state); (800) 228-4307 (out of state)

Nevada Commission on Tourism
Capitol Complex
Carson City, Nevada 89710
(702) 885-3636 or (800) NEVADA 8

New Hampshire Office of Vacation Travel
P.O. Box 856, 105 Loudon Road
Concord, New Hampshire 03301
(603) 271-2665

New Jersey Division of Travel and Tourism
C.N. 826, 20 West State Street
Trenton, New Jersey 08625
(609) 292-2470 or (800) JERSEY 7

New Mexico Travel Division
Joseph Montoya Building
1100 St. Francis Drive
Santa Fe, New Mexico 87503
(505) 827-0291 or (800) 545-2040

New York State Division of Tourism
1 Commerce Plaza
Albany, New York 12245
(518) 474-4116 or (800) CALL NYS

North Carolina Travel and Tourism Division
430 North Salisbury Street, Dept. 867
Raleigh, North Carolina 27611
(919) 733-4171 or (800) VISIT NC

North Dakota Tourism Promotion
Room 250, Liberty Memorial Building
State Capitol Grounds
Bismarck, North Dakota 58505
(701) 224-2525 or (800) 472-2100
(within North Dakota) or (800) 437-2077 (out of state); (800) 537-8879 (in Canada)

Ohio Office of Tourism
P.O. Box 1001
Columbus, Ohio 43266-0101
(614) 466-8844 or (800) BUCKEYE (out of state)

Oklahoma Division of Tourism
Marketing Services Division
500 Will Rogers Building
Oklahoma City, Oklahoma 73105
(405) 521-2406 or (800) 652-6552
(in neighboring states)

Oregon Economic Development
Tourism Division
595 Cottage Street, N.E.
Salem, Oregon 97310
(503) 378-3451 or (800) 547-7842
(out of state) or (800) 233-3306 (within Oregon)

Pennsylvania Bureau of Travel Development
416 Forum Building, Dept. PR 901
Harrisburg, Pennsylvania 17120
(717) 787-5453 or (800) VISIT PA, Ext. 275

Rhode Island Department of Economic Development
Tourism and Promotion Division
7 Jackson Walkway
Providence, Rhode Island 02903
(401) 277-2601 or (800) 556-2484
(East Coast from Maine to Virginia, also northern Ohio)

South Carolina Division of Tourism
Box 71, Room 902
Columbia, South Carolina 29202
(803) 734-0122

South Dakota Division of Tourism
Capitol Lake Plaza
711 Wells Avenue
Pierre, South Dakota 57501
(605) 773-3301 or (800) 843-8000
(out of state); (800) 952-3625 (in state)

Tennessee Tourist Development
P.O. Box 23170
Nashville, Tennessee 37202
(615) 741-2158

Texas Tourist Development
P.O. Box 12008
Austin, Texas 78711
(512) 462-9191

Utah Travel Council
Council Hall
Capitol Hill
Salt Lake City, Utah 84114
(801) 533-5681

Vermont Travel Division
134 State Street
Montpelier, Vermont 05602
(802) 828-3236

Virginia Division of Tourism
202 North 9th Street
Suite 500, Dept. Va.
Richmond, Virginia 23219
(804) 786-2051 or (800) VISIT VA

Washington State Tourism
  Development Division
101 General Administration Building,
  MS AX-13, WASH
Olympia, Washington 98504-0613
(206) 753-5600 or (800) 544-1800
  (out of state) or (800) 562-4570
  (within Washington)

West Virginia Department of
  Commerce
2101 Washington Street E., Dept. TIA
Charleston, West Virginia 25305
(304) 348-2286 or (800) CALL WVA

Wisconsin Division of Tourism
P.O. Box 7606
Madison, Wisconsin 53707
(608) 266-2161 or (800) 432-TRIP
  (except Nebraska, Hawaii, Alaska)

Wyoming Travel Commission
I-25 and College Drive, Dept. WY
Cheyenne, Wyoming 82002-0660
(307) 777-7777 or (800) 225-5996

Canadian Province Tourist Office

Travel Alberta
15th Floor
10025 Jasper Avenue
Edmonton, Alberta, Canada T5J 3Z3
(403) 427-4321 (from Edmonton area)
  or 800-222-6501 (from Alberta) or
  800-661-8888 (from the U.S. and
  Canada)

Tourism British Columbia
  Parliament Buildings
Victoria, British Columbia, Canada
  V8V 1X4
(604) 387-1642

Travel Manitoba
Dept. 6020
7th Floor
155 Carlton Street
Winnipeg, Manitoba, Canada R3C
  3H8
800-665-0040 (from mainland U.S. and
  Canada)

Tourism New Brunswick
P.O. Box 12345
Fredericton, New Brunswick, Canada
  E3B 5C3
800-442-4442 (from New Brunswick)
  or 800-561-0123 (from mainland
  U.S. and Canada)

Tourism Branch
Department of Development
P.O. Box 2016
St. John's, Newfoundland, Canada
  A1C 5R8
(709) 576-2830 (from St. John's area)
  or 800-563-6353 (from mainland
  U.S. and Canada)

TravelArctic
Yellowknife
Northwest Territories, Canada X1A
  2L9
(403) 873-7200

Department of Tourism
P.O. Box 130
Halifax, Nova Scotia, Canada B3J 2M7

Nova Scotia Tourist Information Office
136 Commercial Street
Portland, Maine 04101
U.S.A.
800-341-6096 (from mainland U.S. except Maine) or 800-492-0643 (from Maine)

Ontario Travel
Queen's Park
Toronto, Ontario, Canada M7A 2E5
800-268-3735 (from mainland U.S. and Canada—except Yukon and the Northwest Territories)

Department of Finance and Tourism
Visitor Services Division
P.O. Box 940
Charlottetown, Prince Edward Island, Canada C1A 7M5
(902) 892-2457 or 800-565-7421 (from New Brunswick and Nova Scotia—May 15 to October 31)

Tourisme Québec
C.P. 20 000
Québec (Québec), Canada G1K 7X2
800-443-7000 (from 26 Eastern States) or (514) 873-2015 Collect from all other U.S. locations

Tourism Saskatchewan
2103—11th Avenue
Regina, Saskatchewan, Canada S4P 3V7
(306) 787-2300 or 800-667-7191 (from mainland U.S. except Alaska)

Tourism Yukon
P.O. Box 2703
Whitehorse, Yukon, Canada Y1A 2C6
(403) 667-5340

BED AND BREAKFAST RESERVATION REQUEST FORM

Dear _____
     Host's Name

I read about your home in *Bed & Breakfast U.S.A. 1989*, and would be interested in making reservations to stay with you.

My name: _____

Address: _____
    street

_____ _____ _____
  city   state   zip

Telephone: _____
     area code

Business address/telephone: _____

_____

Number of adult guests: _____

Number and ages of children: _____

Desired date and time of arrival: _____

Desired length of stay: _____

Mode of transportation: _____
(car, bus, train, plane)

Additional information/special requests/allergies: __

_____

_____

_____

_____

_____

I look forward to hearing from you soon.

                                                Sincerely,

APPLICATION FOR MEMBERSHIP
(Please type or print)
(Please refer to Preface, pages xxxiii–xxxiv for our membership criteria.)

Name of Bed & Breakfast: _____

Address: _____

City: _____ State: _____ Zip: _____ Phone: (___) _____

Best Time to Call: _____

Host(s): _____

Located: No. of miles _____ compass direction _____ of Major City _____ Geographic region _____

No. of miles _____ from major route _____ Exit: _____

No. of guest bedrooms with private bath: _____
No. of guest bedrooms that share a bath: _____
How many people (including *your* family) must use the shared bath? _____
How many bedrooms, if any, have a sink in them? _____

Room Rates:
$ _____ Double—private bath $ _____ Double—shared bath
$ _____ Single—private bath $ _____ Single—shared bath
$ _____ Suites
Separate Guest Cottage $ _____ Sleeps _____

Are you open year-round? ☐ Yes   ☐ No
If "No," specify when you are open: _____

Do you require a minimum stay? _____

Do you discount rates at any time? ☐ No ☐ Yes If "Yes," specify (i.e., 10% less during March, April, November; 15% less than daily rate if guests stay a week; $10 less per night Sunday through Thursday). _____

Do you offer a discount to senior citizens? ☐ No   ☐ Yes: ___ %

Do you offer a discount for families? ☐ No   ☐ Yes: ___ %

Breakfast: Type of breakfast included in rate:
☐ Full ☐ Continental

Describe breakfast specialties: _____
_____

Are any other meals provided? ☐ No ☐ Yes
Lunch ☐ cost: $ _____ Dinner ☐ cost: $ _____

Do you accept credit cards? ☐ No ☐ Yes:
☐ AMEX ☐ DINERS ☐ DISCOVER ☐ MASTERCARD ☐ VISA

Will you GUARANTEE your rates from January through December 1990? ☐ Yes ☐ No

Note: This Guarantee applies only to those guests making reservations having read about you in *Bed & Breakfast U.S.A., 1990.*

If you have household pets, specify how many:
☐ Dog(s) ☐ Cat(s) ☐ Other

Can you accommodate a guest's pet?
☐ No ☐ Yes ☐ Sometimes

Are children welcome? ☐ No ☐ Yes If "Yes," specify age restriction _____

Do you permit smoking anywhere inside your house?
☐ No ☐ Yes

Do you permit social drinking? ☐ No ☐ Yes

Guests can be met at ☐ Airport ____ ☐ Train ____ ☐ Bus ____

Can you speak a foreign language fluently? ☐ No ☐ Yes
Describe: _____

GENERAL AREA OF YOUR B&B (i.e., Boston historic district; 20 minutes from Chicago Loop):

GENERAL DESCRIPTION OF YOUR B&B (i.e., brick Colonial with white shutters; Victorian mansion with stained-glass windows):

AMBIENCE OF YOUR B&B (i.e., furnished with rare antiques; lots of wood and glass):

THE QUALITIES THAT MAKE YOUR B&B SPECIAL ARE:

THINGS OF HISTORIC, SCENIC, CULTURAL, OR GENERAL INTEREST NEARBY (i.e, one mile from the San Diego Zoo; walking distance to the Lincoln Memorial):

YOUR OCCUPATION and SPECIAL INTERESTS (i.e., a retired teacher of Latin interested in woodworking; full-time hostess interested in quilting):

If you do welcome children, are there any special provisions for them (i.e., crib, playpen, high chair, play area, baby-sitter)?

Do you offer snacks (i.e., complimentary wine and cheese; pretzels and chips but BYOB)?

Can guests use your kitchen for light snacks? ☐ No ☐ Yes

Do you offer the following amenities? ☐ Guest refrigerator
☐ Air-conditioning ☐ TV ☐ Piano ☐ Washing machine
☐ Dryer ☐ Hot tub ☐ Pool ☐ Tennis court
Other _____

What major college or university is within 10 miles?
_____

Please supply the name, address, and phone number of three personal references from people not related to you (please use a separate sheet).

Please enclose a copy of your brochure, if possible, along with color photos including exterior, guest bedrooms, baths, and breakfast area. Use a label to identify the name of your B&B on each. If you have a black-and-white line drawing, send it along. If you have an original breakfast recipe that you'd like to share, send it along, too. (Of course, credit will be given to your B&B.) **Nobody can describe your B&B better than you, so please do. Limit your description to 100 words and submit it typed, double spaced, on a separate sheet of paper. We will of course reserve the right to edit.** As a member of the Tourist House Association of America, your B&B will be described in the next edition of our book, *Bed & Breakfast U.S.A.*, published by E. P. Dutton and distributed to bookstores and libraries throughout the U.S. The book is also used as a reference for B&Bs in our country by major offices of tourism throughout the world.

Note: If the publisher or authors receive negative reports from your guests regarding a deficiency in our standards of CLEANLINESS, COMFORT, and CORDIALITY, and/or failure to honor the rate guarantee, we reserve the right to cancel your membership.

This membership application has been prepared by:

_____
(Signature)
Please enclose your $25 membership dues.   Date: _____

Yes! ☐ I'm interested in Group Liability Insurance.
No ☐ I am insured by _____ .

Return to:
Tourist House Association of America
R.D. 2, Box 355A
Greentown, Pennsylvania 18426

To assure that your listing will be considered for the 1990 edition of *Bed & Breakfast U.S.A.*, we MUST receive your completed application by March 31, 1989. Thereafter, listings will be considered only for the semiannual supplement. (See page 693.)

APPLICATION FOR MEMBERSHIP FOR A
BED & BREAKFAST RESERVATION SERVICE

NAME OF BED & BREAKFAST SERVICE: _____

ADDRESS: _____

CITY: _____ STATE: ____ ZIP: ____ PHONE:(   ) ____

COORDINATOR: _____

BEST TIME TO CALL: _____

Do you have a telephone answering ☐ machine? ☐ service?

Names of state(s), cities, and towns where you have Hosts (in alphabetical order, please, and limit to 10):

Number of Hosts on your roster: _____

THINGS OF HISTORIC, SCENIC, CULTURAL, OR GENERAL INTEREST IN THE AREA(S) YOU SERVE:

Range of Rates:
  Modest: Single $ _____   Double $ _____
  Average: Single $ _____   Double $ _____
  Luxury: Single $ _____   Double $ _____

Will you GUARANTEE your rates through December 1990?
☐ Yes ☐ No

How often do you re-inspect listings? _____
Do you require a minimum stay? _____
Surcharges for one-night stay? _____
Do you accept credit cards? ☐ No ☐ Yes:
☐ AMEX ☐ DINERS ☐ DISCOVER ☐ MASTERCARD
☐ VISA

Is the guest required to pay a fee to use your service?
☐ No ☐ Yes—The fee is $ _____

Do you publish a directory of your B&B listings?
☐ No ☐ Yes—The fee is $ _____

Are any of your B&Bs within 10 miles of a university? Which? ___

Briefly describe a sample Host Home in each of the above categories: e.g., A cozy farmhouse where the host weaves rugs; a restored 1800 Victorian where the host is a retired general; a contemporary mansion with a sauna and swimming pool.

Please supply the name, address, and phone number of three personal references from people not related to you (please use a separate sheet of paper). Please enclose a copy of your brochure.

This membership application has been prepared by:

_____
(Signature)

Please enclose your $25 membership dues.   Date: _____

If you have a special breakfast recipe that you'd like to share, send it along. (Of course, credit will be given to your B&B agency.) As a member of the Tourist House Association of America, your B&B agency will be described in the next edition of our book, *Bed & Breakfast U.S.A.*, published by E. P. Dutton. Return to: Tourist House Association, RD 2, Box 355A, Greentown, PA 18426.

To assure that your listing will be considered for the 1990 edition, we must receive your completed application by March 31, 1989. Thereafter, listings will be considered only for the semiannual supplement. (See page 693.)

WE WANT TO HEAR FROM YOU!

Name: _____

Address: _____
        street

_____
city   state   zip

Please contact the following B&Bs; I think that they would be great additions to the next edition of *Bed & Breakfast U.S.A.*

Name of B&B: _____

Address: _____
        street

_____
city   state   zip

Comments: _____

Name of B&B: _____

Address: _____
        street

_____
city   state   zip

Comments: _____

_____

The following is our report on our visit to the home of:

Name of B&B: _____ Date of visit: _____

Address: _____ I was pleased. ☐

_____ I was disappointed. ☐

Comments: _____

Just tear out this page and mail it to us. It won't ruin your book!

Return to:
Tourist House Association of America
R.D. 2, Box 355A
Greentown, Pennsylvania 18426

INFORMATION ORDER FORM

We are constantly expanding our roster to include new members in the Tourist House Association of America. Their facilities will be fully described in the next edition of *Bed & Breakfast U.S.A.* In the meantime, we will be happy to send you a list including the name, address, telephone number, etc.

For those of you who would like to order additional copies of the book or perhaps send one to a friend as a gift, we will be happy to fill mail orders. If it is a gift, let us know and we'll enclose a special gift card from you.

ORDER FORM

To:
Tourist House
Association—
Book Dept.
R.D. 1, Box 12A
Greentown, PA
18426

From: _____
(Print your name)
Address: _____

_____
City   State   Zip

Date: _____

Please send:
☐ List of new B&Bs ($2.00); available July to December.
☐ _____ copies of *Bed & Breakfast U.S.A.* @ $12 each (includes 4th class mail)

Send to: _____

Address: _____

_____
City   State   Zip

☐ Enclose a gift card from:

Please make check or money order payable to Tourist House Association.